New Contexts of Canadian Criticism

New Contexts of Canadian Criticism

edited by Ajay Heble, Donna Palmateer Pennee,
and J.R. (Tim) Struthers

broadview press

Canadian Cataloguing in Publication Data

Main entry under title:
New contexts of Canadian criticism

Includes bibliographical references.
ISBN 1-55111-106-3

1. Canadian Literature – History and criticism.
2. Criticism – Canada.   I. Heble, Ajay, 1961–   .
II. Pennee, Donna Palmateer, 1959–   .
III. Struthers, J.R. Tim, 1950–   .

PS8045.N48 1996   801'.95'0971   C96-932119-8
PR9184.3.N48 1996

Broadview Press
Post Office Box 1243, Peterborough, Ontario, Canada K9J 7H5

in the United States of America:
3576 California Road, Orchard Park, NY 14127

in the United Kingdom:
B.R.A.D. Book Representation & Distribution Ltd.,
244A, London Road, Hadleigh, Essex SS7 2DE

Broadview Press gratefully acknowledges the support of the Canada Council, the Ontario Arts Council, and the Ministry of Canadian Heritage.

PRINTED IN CANADA

In Memory of Eli Mandel

Contents

Preface

Who's Listening? Artists, Audiences, and Language
M. Nourbese Philip • 1

National Theatre / National Obsession
Alan Filewod • 15

Cultural Diversity and Canadian Literature: A Pluralistic Approach
to Majority and Minority Writing in Canada
Enoch Padolsky • 24

Le Postmodernisme québécois: tendances actuelles
Janet M. Paterson • 43

Women in the Shadows: Reclaiming a Métis Heritage
Christine Welsh • 56

The New Social Gospel in Canada
Gregory Baum • 67

New Contexts of Canadian Criticism:
Democracy, Counterpoint, Responsibility
Ajay Heble • 78

The Politics of Recognition
Charles Taylor • 98

Beyond Disputation: Anglophone-Canadian Artists
and the Free Trade Debate
Frank Davey • 132

Anthologies and the Canon of Early Canadian Women Writers
Carole Gerson • 146

One More Woman Talking
Bronwen Wallace • 168

The Good Red Road: Journeys of Homecoming
in Native Women's Writing
Beth Brant • 175

Me voici, c'est moi, la femme qui pleure
François Paré • 188

"Après Frye, rien"? Pas du tout! From *Contexts* to *New Contexts*
Donna Palmateer Pennee • 202

Ideology in the Classroom: A Case Study in the Teaching
of English Literature in Canadian Universities
Arun Mukherjee • 220

Unsettling the Empire: Resistance Theory for the Second World
Stephen Slemon • 228

Godzilla vs. Post-Colonial
Thomas King • 241

Back to the Future: The Short Story in Canada
and the Writing of Literary History
W.H. New • 249

On the Rungs of the Double Helix: Theorizing the Canadian Literatures
Cynthia Sugars • 265

Culture, Intellect, and Context: Recent Writing
on the Cultural and Intellectual History of Ontario
A.B. McKillop • 288

Once More to the Lake: Towards a Poetics of Receptivity
J.R. (Tim) Struthers • 319

Is That All There Is? Tribal Literature
Basil H. Johnston • 346

Disunity as Unity: A Canadian Strategy
Robert Kroetsch • 355

The End(s) of Irony: The Politics of Appropriateness
Linda Hutcheon • 366

Acknowledgements

Preface

Times change, lives change, and the terms we need to describe our literature or society or condition – what Raymond Williams calls "keywords" – change with them. Perhaps the most significant development in the quarter-century since Eli Mandel edited his anthology *Contexts of Canadian Criticism* has been the growing recognition that not only do different people need different terms, but the same terms have different meanings for different people and in different contexts. Nation, history, culture, art, identity – the positions we take discussing these and other issues can lead to conflict, but also hold the promise of a new sort of community. Speaking of First Nations people and their literature, Beth Brant observes that "Our connections ... are like the threads of a weaving. ... While the colour and beauty of each thread is unique and important, together they make a communal material of strength and durability." *New Contexts of Canadian Criticism* is designed to be read, to work, in much the same manner.

To prepare a sequel to Eli Mandel's book was not a project to be attempted by a single individual, however enthusiastic and responsive. Nor was it a project that could pretend to be, or that would wish to be, definitive and conclusive. *New Contexts of Canadian Criticism*, like the culture that we collectively envision and work towards, had to be a product of tough coalitional thinking and negotiation. It had to present, for scholars and students alike, an opportunity – or, rather, opportunities – to begin anew.

In the unending process of our own education as critics, we, the editors of *New Contexts of Canadian Criticism*, have enjoyed, and have benefitted profoundly from, the perceptions and the support of our teachers and advisors, of our colleagues and friends, and, equally, of our students. In the course of this particular project we have received cheerful and scrupulous assistance at the University of Guelph from Gerry Manning, Gail McGinnis, Pearl Milne, Stephen Burke, and David Sage – and through Broadview Press from the book's several academic assessors as well as designer George Kirkpatrick, production editor Barbara Conolly, and publisher Don LePan. Finally, we would like to extend special thanks to the various contributors to *New Contexts of Canadian Criticism* for stimulating our own thinking and for making this collection all that it is.

Who's Listening? Artists, Audiences, and Language

M. Nourbese Philip

> If no one listens and cries
> is it still poetry
> if no one sings the note between the silences
> if the voice doesn't founder on the edge of the air
> is it still music
> if there is no one to hear
> is it love
> or does the sea always roar
> in the shell at the ear?[1]

Male, white, and Oxford-educated, he stands over my right shoulder; she is old, Black, and wise and stands over my left shoulder – two archetypal figures symbolizing the two traditions that permeate my work. He – we shall call him John-from-Sussex – represents the white colonial tradition, the substance of any colonial education. Abiswa, as we shall call the other figure, represents the African-Caribbean context which, as typical of any colonial education, was ignored. She is also representative of a certain collective race memory of the African.

Neither of these archetypes individually represents what I would call my ideal listener or audience. John-from-Sussex has always represented his standards as universal, but they all – with the exception of excellence which knows no race, class, or gender – bore the trademark "Made in Britain." Abiswa, through an artificially imposed ignorance which I have tried to correct, I know too little of. To partake in her wisdom requires a different process from the one learnt from John-from-Sussex, demanding that one trust the body which, together with the mind, forms one intelligence. This was not what John-from-Sussex was about.

There has been a recent shift – since the completion of two manuscripts of poetry[2] – in my positioning of this audience of two: John-from-Sussex has become less substantial, more of an apparition; Abiswa has emerged even more clearly from the shadows. Bridging the split that these two archetypes represent is a difficult process: each represents what the other is not – each is, so to speak, the other's Other. A dialogue between the two is essential.

All of this may seem an unusual introduction to the issue of audience, but since I believe that each artist (*artist* here and throughout this piece is used inclusively to refer to all disciplines) has an ideal audience – made up of one or several individuals – lurking somewhere in her psyche, it seemed appropriate. These "ideal" audiences have some bearing on the real audience the artist and/or her work seeks or finds.

If we take the example given above, for instance, both John-from-Sussex and Abiswa have some rooting in a certain reality which faces me whenever I write – the need to make choices around language and place, both of which inevitably impact on audience. If I use John-from-Sussex's language, will Abiswa and her audience understand and vice versa? Which is the more important audience? Which do I value most and from what perspective? Will Abiswa even care to understand a piece such as this? One audience may have more economic clout than others, and one, certainly in my case, offers me a more profound emotional and psychic satisfaction. And some may ask: why choose at all – why the need to have to choose any audience?

Unless the writer creates only for herself, there comes a time when she must become aware, however vaguely, that there exists such an animal as an audience. It may only be an awareness that operates at a very basic level of trying to determine who will come out to a poetry reading, installation, or display, or who will buy books, but it begins to make itself felt. And often the artist may only be aware of who her audience is not – often more predictable than who it is.

Audience is a complex and difficult issue for any artist, particularly in today's world where any sense of continuity and community seems so difficult to develop. It becomes even more complex for the artist in exile – working in a country not her own, developing an audience among people who are essentially strangers to all the traditions and continuities that helped produce her. Scourges such as racism and sexism can also create a profound sense of alienation, resulting in what can best be described as psychic exile, even among those artists who are not in physical exile. The Canadian-born Black artist, artist of colour, or the white lesbian artist, for example, all face dilemmas over audience similar to that of the artist who has more recently – relatively speaking – arrived in this country.

It is as well to note that legal citizenship in no way affects the profound and persistent alienation within a society at best indifferent, if not hostile, to the artist's origins, her work, and her being. Many of us, no matter how old our citizenship, remain immigrants in a profoundly psychic sense. Some of us, recognizing this, choose to emphasize that alienation – it appearing a more positive position. This choice, however, results in all sorts of contradictions when it comes to funding and meeting funding requirements. Where the immigrant worker is required to have Canadian experience, the immigrant artist must show the Canadian component in her work to qualify for funding.

Even for those who have managed to adapt to Canada, there still remains the fact that much of their work will continue to draw on the imagery, rhythms, the emotional resources developed in their countries of origin. This was how an Australian painter described the issue for her: "As an artist you use certain reference points which have a bearing in a different geographic location – unless the viewer knows what these reference points are, there is no comprehension beyond organization of the work in terms of shape, form, and colour." A more blatant example of this problem lies in the different sense of colour that countries have. A Jamaican artist described to me how her colours became more muted and sombre when she painted here in Canada.

Which Canada do I speak of – the West or the East? Urban or rural Canada? These are important questions since most immigrants come to the large metropolitan areas which is where many artists attempt to carve out a niche, however uncomfortable, for themselves. My experience is with the urban East – Toronto, to be more specific – and is that of a Black, female writer. I do not pretend to speak for all of Canada, and only the audience of this piece will be able to judge whether my experience may be easily transferable.

I cannot and do not intend to provide any definitive answers on the issue of audience for those in exile (by exile I mean not only those of us who have physically come to this country, but the many, many others who count themselves in exile for any number of reasons, in this society). I don't think there are any definitive answers, and I am not even sure whether the questions I pose are the right ones for anyone else but myself. What I want to do, however, is raise the issues and questions, reveal the contradictions as they have affected me and others like myself, and see where, if anywhere, they take us. More than anything else, what follows is a meditation on the issues of audience.

Reception, Response, Completion

One of the most important impulses in all art is, I believe, the impulse to communicate; this in turn depends on reception and response for completion of the work in question. The late Raymond Williams, the Marxist critic, wrote as follows: "... in the case of art, where simple consumption is not in question, no work is in any full practical sense produced until it is also received." How, then, is work from communities that appear marginal to the mainstream, with what Williams so aptly describes as their "emergent energies," completed – that is, received and responded to, both by audiences of the more dominant culture, as well as audiences that comprise the artist's natural community? A few examples will best highlight this dilemma.

The Rez Sisters. I saw this play several months ago among a predominantly, if not completely, white audience. Everyone appeared to enjoy the play tremendously, yet I was uncomfortable. Uncomfortable because, although I was convinced that what I was watching was an authentic and successful attempt to portray one aspect of Native life on the reservation, I felt that the audience, which was, in fact, a settler audience, was being let off too easily. I felt that they could – I am sure they did – leave the theatre feeling that "reservation life wasn't so bad after all." Those who were feminist could comfort themselves with the remarkable strength of the women. I was equally convinced that a Native audience would complete that play in a very different way – they could and would be able to contextualize much more completely the events that played themselves out on the stage. They would not leave the theatre as comfortably, or as comforted, as did the white audience.

So too with *The Coloured Museum*, which also played to full houses of predominantly white people. Here was a powerful, painful, and at times funny collage of Black American life over the centuries. There were many scenes that were "funny" which I laughed at, my laughter always tinged with the pain represented in those opening scenes on the slave plane – a pain that circumscribes my history. Why were *they* laughing though? Were they laughing at the *same* things I was laughing at, and if their laughter lacked the same admixture of pain, was it laughter which, having been bought too cheaply, came too easily? Were they, therefore, laughing at me and not with me?

These are but two examples. There are several others that elaborate the same issue; they raise complex issues around marketing and audience. *The Coloured Museum*, for instance, was never advertised in the Black newspapers, which is where many Black people get their information about activities of interest and relevance to them. Tarragon Theatre, however, did not need to advertise in the Black press to fill its house. Do they, indeed, have an onus to do so when they are staging Black works or works that relate specifically to a particular group in society? *The Rez Sisters* played first at the Native Centre on Spadina, then returned for a run at a more mainstream theatre.

These examples raise issues applicable to all disciplines of art – even music, which appears to be the discipline that most easily crosses cultural barriers. The lyrics and music of the late Bob Marley were wrought and wrested out of the unrelenting poverty and grimness of the Trenchtown ghetto; he sang of better times for Black people, when "Babylon" would be no more. How many North Americans who "grooved" on his music cared to understand this or even cared?

It is a truism that we each complete a novel, play, poem, or painting differently, depending on factors as diverse as age, gender, class, and cul-

M. NOURBESE PHILIP

ture. What concerns me is the ever-present danger that a white main-stream audience in Toronto is likely to come away from a play like *The Rez Sisters* or *The Coloured Museum* with none of their stereotypes shaken or disturbed, which is not necessarily the fault of the playwright. He or she may have written the play in question with a Native or Black audience in mind.

Can you ever have a valid completion of a work by an audience that is a stranger to the traditions that underpin the work? This question leads us back to that dichotomy between dominant and sub-dominant cultures – the old "mainstream versus margin" argument. The significance of this dichotomy lies in the fact that those of us who belong to those sub-dominant groups – women, Africans, peoples of the formerly colonized world – have been rigorously schooled in the traditions of the dominant cultures – European and patriarchal. This experience along with the fact that we are constantly immersed in the dominant culture of the world – still patriarchal and now American – makes it much more possible for us to receive and respond to work from these cultures than it is or ever has been in the reverse. We are, at times, even better able to understand and respond more positively to works from the dominant culture than we do to work coming out of our own traditions – such is the pernicious effect of racism, sexism, and colonialism. Could we, however, argue that education offers one solution to this problem? Possibly, but we would do well to remember that the education of colonized peoples – I include women in this group – has traditionally been closer to brainwashing than to education.

Exotica/Nostalgia

Those of us from hot, moist parts of the world (sex-positive cultures as I have recently seen them described), who work in traditions originating in our countries of origin, face the ever-present danger that our work may be considered and categorized as "different" or "exotic." Not understanding the tradition and standards, the audience, including critics and reviewers, suspends the practice of criticism, replacing it with meaningless adjectives like "great" or "wonderful."

Another kind of reception and response is best illuminated by the following excerpt from a review of an anthology, *Other Voices: Writings by Blacks in Canada*, edited by Lorris Elliott:

> European literature has benefited from black writers such as Aesop, Pushkin, and Dumas. American culture has incorporated the voices of Langston Hughes, Gwendolyn Brooks, Alice Walker, Marge Piercy, or Imamu Amiri Baraka (Leroi Jones). But Canadian blacks, like Canadian whites, still do not know if they are coming or going with

their identity problems. *Other Voices: Writings by Blacks in Canada*, edited by Lorris Elliott, is a collection of poetry, prose, and drama without any direction beyond herd instinct.

The very word "other" in the title is a dim bulb in regard to visible minorities. It cues the reader (black, white, or other) to expect stereotypes. That is exactly what follows. "Nigger," "fight," "pain," "passion," "cause," "rage," "tears": the language falls predictably flat – though the suffering motivating the outpourings is very real. A few entries break through the barrier of boredom to move a heart and mind willing to open this anthology, which could have been an important book.[3]

Apart from revealing a profound ignorance – writers like Pushkin and Dumas did not write as Black men, but as Europeans, and to parallel their experiences with that of American Black writers serves neither experience well – the quotation reveals the latent racism always at work in Canada. By attempting to parallel the experience of Canadian whites and Blacks, the reviewer seeks to dissemble his racism: "Canadian blacks, like Canadian whites, still do not know if they are coming or going with their identity problems." He exculpates, under the guise of "objective criticism," the white Canadian audience, including critics and reviewers like himself, for their massive failure to understand the history and traditions of racism that would give rise to the use of words like "Nigger," "fight," and "pain."

What is, however, even more instructive of the issues I raise in this section is the imagery the reviewer approved of and selected to quote as examples of the better work appearing in the anthology: from "Market in the Tropics," "Mangoes / Tamarinds / ... wild meat on hooks," and from "The Profile of Africa," which "expresses the sensuous beauty of blackness" (sic), "the beautiful, strong, exotic in profile / flowering lips / silhouette obsidian planes...." These poems may very well have been the better ones (not having read them I make no comment on them here), but it is, in my opinion, no accident that these are the poems and the imagery that the reviewer believes "saves the volume from being another boohoo job." The sensuous beauty of Blackness – I could write volumes on this subject – is a far more appealing image for most whites than an angry Black man or woman. While I acknowledge writing about one's anger and pain without appearing to descend into rhetoric, polemic, and cant is difficult, to dismiss the work of writers attempting to bring a long tradition of struggle against racism into literature as another "boohoo job" is racist in the extreme.

Ignorance and laziness. These are the qualities at the heart of both kinds of responses described above – the over-eager response reserved for anything in the slightest bit different or appearing exotic, or dismissal. The welcome change in the picture comes from the attempts now being made by feminist critics, some of whom have finally begun to assess critically the works of women from other traditions.

The nostalgia factor presents another conundrum for the artist in exile – particularly those, like immigrants, in physical exile. The "natural" audience for such an artist is the audience from "back home." So starved, however, is this audience for anything remotely evocative of "home," that it accepts uncritically whatever is reminiscent of it. This is what I mean by the nostalgia factor.

The need to maintain continuity and traditions is a powerful one with all groups; it is a need which is assuaged in the articulation of many mainstream art forms – the ballet, opera, Shakespearean drama. The more newly arrived (relatively speaking) are not the only ones who indulge in nostalgia.

There is, however, a danger for the artist – the danger of falling into complacency. In my case, for instance, coming from the Caribbean where the use of demotic variants of English (dialect) is widespread, use of dialect is an immediate entry into the hearts and minds of a Caribbean audience. In such a context the audience is less concerned with what the artist is doing with his or her discipline, provided the need to be reminded of "how it stay" back home is met. If the artist is content with this response, then a sort of stasis results which is fatal to any growth on her part. But audience response in this context is powerful, seductive, *and* difficult to turn one's back on for the less tangible, less certain rewards of "growth" or "practising one's art seriously." I do not suggest that the last two goals are incompatible with a strong audience response – they should not be – but they often mean the audience has to do some work as well, and nostalgia appears far more compatible with entertainment rather than with art.

Audience and Language

The choice facing a writer from Eastern Europe or Italy or Latin America is a stark one: work in your mother tongue and – at least in Canada – be restricted to an audience sharing a similar linguistic heritage, or work in English with the potential of a much wider audience – minus your natural audience.

For the writer from the English or French Caribbean, the two official languages of Canada are also their languages. English is "theoretically" as much my mother tongue as it is for a writer from London, Ontario. But we know differently, and my experience with English encompasses a very different experience from that of the English-speaking Canadian. Like the writer from Eastern Europe, we too have a nation language (dialect) which is, however, a variant of English.

The choice of language for the Caribbean writer can, therefore, be as stark as that outlined in the first paragraph in this section. If you work entirely in nation language or the Caribbean demotic of English, you do, to a large degree, restrict your audience to those familiar enough with it; if you move to standard English, you lose much of that audience and, along with that loss, an understanding of many of the traditions, history, and culture which contextualize your work.

Language has been and remains – as the South African example shows – a significant and essential part of the colonization process; the choice between Caribbean demotic and standard English becomes, therefore, more than choice of audience. It is a choice which often affects the choice of subject matter, the rhythms of thought patterns, and the tension within the work. It is also a choice resonant with historical and political realities *and* possibilities.

In writing correct sentences, ending words with "ing" instead of "in'," making my verbs agree with their subjects, I am choosing a certain tradition – that of John-from-Sussex. My audience, for the most part, is going to be a white audience, and possibly an educated Black Caribbean audience. However, in order to keep faith with Abiswa, I must, within my writing self, constantly subvert the tradition of John-from-Sussex. This doesn't necessarily enlarge my audience to include the less formally educated speakers of nation language – on the contrary it probably reduces that segment of the audience since the work becomes more "difficult." It does, however, I hope, leave whatever audience there is less complacent and less comfortable with things as they appear to be.

Community, Audience, Market

Raymond Williams writes that

> [o]ur way of seeing things is literally our way of living, the process of communication is in fact the process of community: the sharing of common meanings, and thence common activities and purposes; the offering, reception, and comparison of new meanings, leading to the tensions and achievements of growth and change.

Toronto is a city of many communities which individually meet the above description; these communities do not, however, make up a larger community – particularly in the arts where there is undeniably a dominant culture – a "central system of practices, meanings, and values" (Williams).

The artist has always been sustained by community even if it was a community he or she rebelled against. Within traditional societies there was, and is, a constant dialogue between audience and artist. When, for instance, the African "commissioned" a piece of sculpture from a village sculptor (usually for spiritual reasons), he or she had a very clear idea as to what satisfied them and what was a good piece of sculpture: they exercised aesthetic judgements. So too in European cultures where the artist was in dialogue with the community in terms of its traditions, they shared or understood values, even if the understanding was but the first step to rejection.

Within the larger grouping of community, then, the artist may find her audience where she could find a "hearing" and with which she might be in some form of dialogue.

"Market" on the other hand suggests a role for art as a commodity, with all the trappings of that representation we have come to expect: manipulation of the market; selling the product – art – as investment and/or fashion.

There is a certain connectedness between these three apparently disparate groupings – audience, community, market – at the centre of which is the artist. Bringing them together raises certain contradictions. Is, for instance, audience synonymous with market? Can you have an audience but lack a market? To answer that last question: as a Black writer I may have an audience for a novel about Black people – that audience being those Black people who are eager to read about themselves, as well as a growing number of whites who have begun to come to the understanding that other worlds apart from theirs exist. It is, however, clearly the opinion of publishers in Canada that there is no market for books about Black people: they believe that whites are not interested and that Blacks either do not, or are unable to, buy books. Therefore, there is no market for books about Black people. Despite the audience I may have, the perceived market forces, interpreted with a sizeable dollop of racist arguments, supersede.

That a popular art form – dub poetry – has been able to widen the audience for its poetry is, I believe, because of the welding of the Black oral and musical traditions. The strongest African art form to survive outside Africa among its scattered peoples has been its music; it has been the most pervasive and persistent. In the case of the dub poets like Linton Kwesi Johnson, one of the first proponents of this style, the poetry was written in the Jamaican demotic – patois or creole – and underscored with reggae rhythms. Canadian dub poets, also using a demotic variant of English, have not restricted themselves to these rhythms, but use a variety of others. They are essentially protest poets working in the powerful oral and musical traditions of Abiswa.

The crossover mechanism between Black and white audiences, in dub, has been the music. As the earlier example of Leonard Cohen showed, music serves the function of drawing those audiences who would rather be dead than caught at a high art gathering – the poetry reading. And whether white audiences "get" the same message Blacks do from dub is not known. (In some instances the language *must* present a barrier to complete understanding.)

That white audiences "get" something from dub is clear – one only has to look at the audiences that attend various events to know that, which may mean that the question is irrelevant. But not necessarily so, since the artist's audience does provide some challenge to the artist, if only in terms of expectations. That audiences often have a tendency to want only more of what pleased them before cannot be denied. The dub poet *may*, therefore, have to make decisions as to which traditions to emphasize – the one more familiar to Black audiences, or those with which white audiences are more comfortable. Not having discussed this particular issue with any dub poets, it may all be irrelevant to them – as an observer and writer, however, the issues present a challenge.

To say that the average size of the traditional poetry audience is small – I have counted as many as ten bodies at some readings of mine – is an understatement. The audience for dub poetry, however, has increased this average substantially. It is still, however, not a mass audience here in Canada – in that respect, rock and rap still reign supreme.

An artist with a market has little need for community. The reverse, however, is not as assured – the artist with both community and audience but no market will, undoubtedly, starve, unless someone supports her. The market, with its forces, can be a positive factor provided it underpins the forces created by audience and community. The market becomes a negative force when it replaces or obliterates audience and community or, even more dangerously, determines "our way of seeing things" and replaces the "process of community: the sharing of common meanings, and thence common activities and purposes" with the process of commodification.

The Audience on the Margin

As mentioned above, Toronto is a city of communities alongside the dominant Anglo-Saxon culture. Many of these communities share very little with each other except residence in the same city. Many would describe these communities as marginal to the dominant one. I have great difficulty with the concept of marginality as it is ordinarily articulated: it suggests a relationship with the dominant culture in which the marginal is considered inferior, and implies that the marginal wishes to lose its quality of marginality and be eventually absorbed by the more dominant culture.

Margin, however, has another meaning, which I prefer to hold uppermost in my mind when I work as a member of two groups – Blacks and women – traditionally described as marginal. That meaning is "frontier." Surely this meaning is encapsulated in Williams' phrase "emergent energies and experiences which stubbornly resist" the dominant culture. The concept of frontier changes our perception of ourselves and the so-called mainstream. All of which is not to deny that there is a dominant culture, with a "central system of practices, meanings, and values." And this culture receives by far the lion's share of funding and government support. However, exploiting the other meaning of margin offers another perspective, one which challenges the old, lazy ways of thinking by which we have colluded in our own management. To twist the aphorism somewhat – marginality is in the eye of the beholder.

Many of these communities on the frontier are communities under stress. In the case of the Black community, for instance, there is always the issue of racism, as well as issues flowing from economic depression within the community. Artists with audiences within such communities often become spokespersons for the community – this is an activity very much in keeping with the role of the poet in African cultures where he (traditionally) was the voice of the community. In our more contemporary situation, the issues are many and complex: should the artist take the audience as she finds it and reflect its views and demands, or is there an obligation on the artist's part to change the audience? Is the artist sharing with or challenging the audience, or both? And what of the Canadian audience – does the artist from the community on the margin/frontier have an obligation to teach such an audience that their practices may be negatively affecting other communities? Does culture change political realities any?

In South Africa, events have rendered many of these questions irrelevant; there the African dramatist, poet, novelist, painter have all been drafted into the struggle – willingly or otherwise. Njabulo S. Ndebele, the South African writer, in an issue of *Staffrider* writes:

> The matter is simple: there is a difference between art that "sells" ideas to people, and art whose ideas are embraced by the people, because they have been made to understand them through the evocation of lived experience in all its complexities. In the former case, the readers are anonymous buyers; in the latter they are equals in the quest for truth.

These opinions offer one way of approaching the issues raised in the previous paragraph.

Cut off from his natural audience, Argueta has to imagine a public for himself, and is unsure how much he can take for granted at either the linguistic or the cultural level.

The pitfall is obvious: that of becoming over-simple or over-didactic, as the writer strives to inform a foreign audience how things are in his country, rather than being able *to share with them feelings about experiences that have a common base.*[4] (emphasis added)

In many respects this quotation encapsulates the issues I have attempted to explore in this piece. I stress the last phrase both because it harked back to the opinions expressed by Williams and Ndebele, and because it provides me with an entry into the issue of feminism and audience.

There is much that I find to criticize in the articulation of Western liberal feminism: the movement has become racist and classist in its practices, although there have been some tiny tremors and even some cracks along fault lines. This is not to suggest that the movement is monolithic – quite the contrary; but its diversity and variety may be its weakness as well as its strength. It is, however, a movement which has the potential, often unrealized, to bridge some of those gaps – race and class for instance – isolating communities and audiences. It could, in some instances, promote that "common base" through which experiences might be shared.

The common base for women is a shared history of oppression in all its varieties and forms, as well as, I hope, a shared commitment to establishing communities organized along non-patriarchal, woman-centred, non-racist principles. While wishing to avoid reductionist arguments, as well as those body-centred theories which become at times tiresome, we must acknowledge that a basic common denominator of female experience – in all cultures and in all classes – has been the fact that our bodies have achieved a universal negative significance; bodies which have become palimpsests upon which men have inscribed and reinscribed their texts.

Feminism alone, however, is not the answer: we can hardly afford to jettison theories of class analysis. With modification and development in the face of change, they continue to offer indispensable insight into the arrangements of society; we need to continue to hone our arguments and analysis of the powerful workings of racism. While it is not *the* answer, feminism could make important and significant contributions to helping to resolve some of these issues – Black and white men, for instance, are certainly not talking to each other about race and class – or anything for that matter.

Feminist communities are in many cases ad hoc, but there *is* a feminist audience and market. Thoughts of the recent Montreal Book Fair come to mind. It is a market which differs in some degree from the traditional mainstream market. It is not, in the words of Ndebele, a market selling ideas to the people but one trying to evoke the lived experiences of women. It is a market which is still plagued by racism and classism, but it is a market which has grown out of a need on the part of women to know about their selves, their histories, and their futures; a need to communicate about feelings and experiences that have a *common* vis-à-vis the *same* base; as well as the need to find out about other women.

We are a long way from a true feminist community, and even further away from a true feminist culture – one that would not, as it has tended to do, emphasize one aspect (the white and middle class) of that culture, but a culture in which the word feminist is enlarged to include those groups which have, to date, been excluded. When that is accomplished – the establishment of a true feminist culture – we shall be a long way towards having audiences who are able to complete, in more authentic ways, the works of artists *whatever* their background.

Working in Canada as an "Afrosporic" writer, I am very aware of the absence of a tradition of Black writing as it exists in England or the U.S. The great Canadian void either swallows you whole, or you come out the other side the stronger for it. The Black writers here are, in fact, creating a tradition which will be different from both the English and American traditions of writing and literature by Black writers. Being the trail blazer for other writers to follow has been overwhelmingly difficult and daunting, for it has often appeared that there is nothing out there. Which was an accurate observation – for a long time there *was* nothing out there. As one dub poet described it, he felt responsible for everything – not only did he create the work, but he published *and* marketed it, as well as developing an audience for it.

All artists working in the tradition of Abiswa have felt this burden – even those Black artists working more closely within the tradition of John-from-Sussex have felt it. But there are changes – the audience for newer genres like dub and hip hop are growing not only among Black people, but also among whites. These are two forms in which Abiswa's heritage can be most clearly seen and strongly felt. Subversion of the old order – which, in fact, was not order but chaos masquerading as order – and of the new old order is alive and well in Abiswa's hands – in our art, writing, and music. And there *is* an audience for it.

In keeping faith with Abiswa we find that many from John-from-Sussex's audiences are deserting in droves to seek the wisdom and vitality of the former. If revenge is what is called for, this may be the best revenge; it is also a way of reconciliation between these two traditions. It is the audience which helps to mediate this process.

Notes

1   M. Nourbese Philip, "Anonymous," *Salmon Courage* (Toronto: Williams-Wallace, 1983) 3.

2   *She Tries Her Tongue, Her Silence Softly Breaks* (Charlottetown: Ragweed, 1989); and *Looking for Livingstone: An Odyssey of Silence* (Stratford, ON: Mercury, 1991).

3   Ray Filip, "Skin Deep," rev. of *Other Voices: Writings by Blacks in Canada*, ed. Lorris Elliott, *Books in Canada* Oct. 1987: 28.

4   Nick Caistor, "Too Much To Bear," rev. of *Cuzcatlan*, by Manlio Argueta, trans. Clark Hansen, *New Statesman* 11 Dec. 1987: 33.

National Theatre / National Obsession

Alan Filewod

Why have Canadian theatre critics been so obsessed with the absence of a national theatre? The question of what kind of national theatre might be most appropriate to this country has worried cultural pundits for a century, and occupies most of the deliberations on theatre in the Massey Report, the seminal document presented to Parliament in 1951 that shaped the development of the arts in Canada over the subsequent four decades. The Massey Report didn't invent that obsession. Since the 1890s theatre critics in Canada have wrestled with what appeared to be a simple problem: if we have a Canadian nation, then a Canadian drama must be one of its proofs; therefore we must have a national theatre to advance the national drama.

This logic is not as self-evident as it might appear, because there are many countries that do very well without a national theatre. Certainly, Great Britain has a nominal one, and a case can be made that the Comédie Française is the national theatre of France (although many would argue against it). But the United States does not have one; nor does the USSR; nor do either of the Germanies. In fact it can be argued that the idea of a national theatre is a rhetorical construct that predates the concept of the modern state which redefines the idea of nation. If this is the case, the reason that we have never succeeded in establishing a national theatre in Canada is that the very idea is a historical anachronism inapplicable to this country. But then, if that is the case, why does the subject keep coming up? The answer, I suggest, lies in Canada's complex experience of colonialism, in which the theatre has been identified throughout our history as a site for a debate on the nature of nationhood. What makes this complex is that the evolution of the theatre as an expression of post-colonialism coincides with the historical transformation of the theatre as a cultural industry.

Throughout this century critics around the world have bewailed the displacement of the theatre as a mass art by the cinema. That was certainly true of the first decades of the twentieth century, when the movies destroyed the centralized theatre touring industry. Ironically, however, the marginalization of the theatre has also coincided with the greatest burst of theatrical activity – and, in the commercial theatre sector, the greatest profits – this country has ever known. Fifty years ago Vincent Massey could see only a slim sign of hope in the (erroneous) fact that "Canadian drama ... at present represents no more than twelve or fifteen produced plays" (197); today we know that thousands of Canadian plays have been produced, most of them never published and irretrievably lost. Yet, from these relatively few which have been published, some critics are attempting to establish a canon; others are questioning not only the concept of one but also questioning the ideological function of anthologies and university courses that canonize particular playwrights and modes of theatrical production. The sheer volume of plays written in this country would amaze the critics of five decades ago; it surpasses their wildest hopes. What would amaze them more is that our present theatrical culture has evolved without a consensual recognition of a national drama, and without the one thing that most critics of the past identified as necessary to the evolution of the drama: a specifically defined national theatre.

The idea of a national theatre was initially proposed as a means of recuperating Canadian theatre from American cultural expansion. It was an idea predicated on a model of national culture that few would subscribe to today. It can be argued that our theatrical culture evolved to its present vigorous, if financially tenuous, state precisely because it didn't fall into the trap of working towards a centralized National Theatre dedicated to the performance of a National Drama.

The obsession with a Canadian identity is not a modern phenomenon; it can be traced to the early years of the last century, and it fuelled the movement of romantic poetic drama that produced the ponderous pseudo-Shakespearean tragedies which plague today's students of CanLit. When Charles Mair wrote his epic *Tecumseh* in 1886, he called for a national drama "tasting of the wood" (77). The nineteenth century anthropomorphized culture according to the ideas of "racialism" so prevalent at the time. If Canada is a unique nation, this argument went, then it must reflect a national character. As Carl Berger points out in his landmark study of the Canada First movement, *The Sense of Power*, this character was originally proposed as rugged, Nordic, pure, and Anglo-Saxon to the bone. The notion of the Canadian character was revised, and is still revised, according to the ideological fashions of the day. (Few outside Quebec considered the French factor in this equation. In *Tecumseh* Mair wrote the Québécois out of the history of the War of 1812 to prove that the war was one between American "mobocracy" and British constitutional liberty.) For all of Vincent Massey's snobbery and his allegiance to British cultural models, as an essayist and a cultural politician he did more than perhaps any other individual to create the conditions in which Canadian theatre could flourish.

Before looking at Massey's effect on the idea of a national theatre, we have to retrace our steps to examine how that idea became inextricably entwined with the idea of a national drama. For that we must look at the

ALAN FILEWOD

turn of the century, when the stage in Canada was a branch-plant extension of the novel American discovery that if theatre was business, then it
could be big business; in fact it could be organized as a monopoly trust.
By 1910 almost every playhouse in Canada was owned directly by or con-
tractually locked into the American theatrical syndicates, a condition that
alarmed nationalistic critics only after it was well entrenched. This early
experiment in theatrical free trade created a situation in which Canadian
playwrights were effectively denied access to the theatre – a situation with
uncomfortable parallels to the problems of Canadian film distribution
today. The first alarms sounded against this colonizing monopoly were not
raised in objection to the American lock-out of Canadian theatre artists,
but rather questioned the cultural effects of subjecting Canadian audiences
to a steady diet of what amounted to American propaganda. In 1897, the
young Hector Charlesworth, taking his cue from the growing agitation for
public theatres in Britain, suggested that perhaps the only alternative to the
deleterious diet of banal American sit-coms on the stage was some form
of "Government subsidies" (Charlesworth). This radical suggestion was of
course unheeded at the time, but it grew in the minds of the more per-
ceptive critics of the day.

In the first decade of this century, B.K. Sandwell, who like
Charlesworth rose to become editor of *Saturday Night*, wrote a slew of
articles and speeches in which he decried "the annexation of our stage."[1]
The problem was clear: even as Canada was stumbling towards
autonomous nationhood, it was in danger of cultural absorption by the
vast commercial power of the United States. How to preserve Canadian
identity? What in fact *was* Canadian identity? These were the questions
that our dramatists could answer, if only they could be found.
Charlesworth and Sandwell were among the first to recognize the relationship between cultural identity and the economic conditions of the
stage.

The first proposed solutions to this American influence may seem in
retrospect to be regressive but they were inevitable. Canadians – English
Canadians – saw themselves as citizens of a "Vaster Britain," in the phrase
coined by the arch-Imperialist poet Wilfred Campbell. The antidote to
Americanism was plainly Imperialism, a renewed emphasis on the "British
Connexion." When theatre critics sought alternatives to the American
monopoly control, they naturally turned to the British example, at a time
when writers like Granville-Barker, William Archer, and Bernard Shaw
were advocating a public National Theatre for Britain. If such a scheme
could work in the Mother Country, then it was a natural for provincial
Canada. There were of course dissenters, like Frederic Robson, who in
1908 advised readers of *The Canadian Magazine* that it would be "impossible for many years to have a Canadian 'stage' or a Canadian drama" (60).

Popular mythology of the first half of this century advanced the thesis that Canadian nationhood was won on the battlefield, not on Queenston Heights, as Mair and his contemporaries would have it, but in the trenches of Flanders and Vimy Ridge. Perhaps Canadians were envious of the forged-in-battle myths of Agincourt and Valley Forge that justified the expansionist ideology of our big cousins. Canadian critics leapt upon the Canadian victories of the Great War as proof of nationhood, with a typically colonial twist. In 1915, when the first self-declared National Theatre in Canada emerged out of the amateur Drama League of Ottawa, its advent was greeted with hysterical rapture by *Maclean's*, which screamed, "In the agony of the present conflict, Canada has given birth to a national consciousness.... *'By the living God, we're British!'* ... Canada had found herself" (Baxter 27). The writer, Arthur Beverly Baxter, saw the formation of the Canadian National Theatre (which incidently proved still-born) as a decisive indication of cultural maturity; he wanted to see a Canadian nation that held up its end of the Empire, martially and culturally. He concluded that "Canada must seek artistic expression. It is the law of nations, and the law of individuals, and the law of Nature" (29).

For Baxter, as with many in his day, Canadian drama must necessarily be a celebration of Canadian nationhood; Canadian culture was an extension of British culture. In this he differed little from the writers of the previous generation. Mair's *Tecumseh* is predicated on the seemingly rational assumption that an Indian warrior speaking blank verse is no more ludicrous than Shakespeare's Romans and Celts. Tecumseh would take his stand beside Caesar and Lear.

The idea that Canadian national drama was an appropriation of British cultural models gathered strength in the years after the Great War, and led directly to the model of public regional theatres advocated by the Canada Council in the 1960s. The key figure in this was the man who most successfully combined Canadian nationalism and arch anglomania, Vincent Massey. His nationalism was not the same as the nationalism that inspired the post-war generation; it was not predicated on the post-colonial sense of difference that identified the Canadian experience as unique, but rather on a concept of civilization. To Massey, a flourishing Canadian drama was a mark of cultural maturity, but his understanding of culture maintained the British axis of the generations that preceded him. His was a concept of culture that expressed the ideals of the proprietary class schooled at Oxford and infused with the genteel British attitudes of power, privilege, and cultural purity. This brought with it a polite anti-semitism; one of Massey's disparagements of the New York-based theatre syndicates noted that the producers had "Old Testament names" (197). Any foreign influence other than British was to him alien to the natural tendencies of Canadian cultural evolution. And even so he doubted the value of British imports unless they were "the best" (198).

Massey used his social privilege to advance the cause of Canadian drama materially, by his founding of Hart House Theatre in 1919, his anthologies of Canadian plays produced there, and his numerous articles advocating the Canadian dramatist. Ironically, the first important playwright to emerge out of the Hart House experiment argued an antithetical nationalism. Merrill Denison's 1928 article, "Nationalism and the Drama" went against the main current to propose that Canadian drama was an essentially regional American drama. (Denison doesn't mention in the article that he himself had dual citizenship; is this why he could assert that "Life in Cleveland and Toronto is identical" [68]?) But Denison's was a dissenting voice, barely heard amidst the clamour for a national theatre, an ideal to which Massey still aspired. His belief that an institutional theatre was a necessary precondition of a national drama shaped public policy in the theatre thereafter.

The 1930s and 40s saw repeated attempts to raise the national theatre idea to the level of action rather than rhetoric. By the end of the 40s, when Massey and his Royal Commission heard the briefs of arts organizations across the country, the idea of government intervention was not just acceptable, but inevitable. This was in large part a consequence of the Depression and the Second World War, struggles that were won because of massive government intervention in what was soon to be known as the "private sector." The legitimization of a "public sector" in social policy made the idea of government funding for the arts feasible. In fact the Massey Report equates cultural funding with national defence; in ponderous cold war logic the report introduces its recommendations with the admonition that "we must strengthen those permanent instruments which give meaning to our unity and make us conscious of the best in our national life.... Our military defences must be made secure; but our cultural defences equally demand national attention; the two cannot be separated" (274-75). In other words, a national arts policy is a necessary defence against un-Canadian communism. Small wonder that the Massey Report's survey of Canadian theatrical achievements omits any mention of the workers' theatres of the preceding decade.

The Massey Report's remarks on theatre are a masterful example of fence-sitting. The report implies the necessity of a national theatre, and even proposes the founding of a national theatre school as an adjunct of such a company. It questions the idea of a single centralized national theatre, but finds merit in the idea of a touring company. The report seems to favour the construction of playhouses as a means of bringing professional theatre to cities across the country, but also notes that "whether this would mean a renaissance of the theatre in Canada has been sharply questioned" (197). On one issue the Commission was clear: a national theatre could "give counsel to local dramatic societies," and would uplift "gifted amateur actors" (197). In a passage of brilliant ambivalence, the report notes that "It would, of course, be disastrous to conceive of the National Theatre merely as a playhouse erected in the capital or in one of the larger centres; but it seems apparent that the national company of players would require a base for their operations..." (198).

Massey was inspired in large part by the example of the Dominion Drama Festival, which the report endorses enthusiastically, and which had in the years immediately preceding the Commission's inquiry moved to establish just such a company. In fact, in the years immediately preceding the Massey Commission it seemed that the DDF would successfully initiate a National Theatre plan. Under the leadership of Earle Grey (not to be confused with the earlier, titled, Earl Grey, the Governor General who left such an indelible mark on Canadian football) and the Arts and Letters Club of Toronto, this scheme, initiated in 1945, proposed a national organization of regional affiliates. Despite the endorsement of names such as John Coulter, Brian Doherty (who later founded the Shaw Festival), Lister Sinclair, and Father Legault, the scheme floundered for several years before collapsing under the weight of divergent interests. Some, like Coulter, called for a national touring company; others argued for a National Theatre Association comprised of professional, amateur, and university theatres. Again the problem of location proved insuperable. But in good committee procedure the DDF planned and generated numerous reports, articles in *Saturday Night*, and bylaws. As early as 1945 the committee had circulated a proposal that outlined the structure of a national council and even suggested a title for a national theatre newsletter (to be called, not surprisingly for a committee decision, *The National Theatre News*).

The DDF plan was unable to surmount the paradoxes that informed it from the beginning; much like the Meech Lake Accord (and, for that matter, Confederation) it was an attempt to reconcile the irreconcilable. What is of particular interest in retrospect is that the plan completely ignored the material conditions that gave evidence of a national theatre movement in the making. The proposal proceeded from an imposed model of what a national theatre meant; and because it emanated from the amateur theatre it found its evidence in the Little Theatres that made up the DDF. It was the product of a particular class that could not accommodate opposing models. But the closest that Canadians came to a true national theatre was the workers' theatre movement of the preceding decade. The workers' theatres were themselves oriented towards a foreign model, but they were an authentic populist movement generating plays out of the experience of the community. The workers' theatre was not just a left-wing mirror of the DDF; it differed in that it generated a dramatic literature out of its own experience, even though that literature (the classic example being *Eight*

Men Speak) was marginalized by contemporary critics. The workers' theatre movement anticipated later developments in that its plays repudiated traditional notions of literary drama in favour of a textuality of performance. The very negation of the workers' theatre movement and its successors, such as Toronto Workshop Productions and today's popular theatres, as marginal, as outside the "mainstream" of Canadian theatrical development, proved its fundamental assertion that theatre in Canada was an expression of class interests.

The social orientation of the national theatre idea was nowhere more evident than in its next manifestation following the implosion of the DDF plan. With the founding of the Stratford Festival in 1953 and the Canada Council in 1957, the Massey Commission's implied concept of a national theatre acquired a material basis and a political structure. The Stratford Festival presented the country with just the classic repertory company the Commission envisioned as the basis of a national theatre. On the one hand, Stratford's offshoot, the Canadian Players, fulfilled the model of a touring national company; on the other, the Festival itself aspired to National Theatre status. This aspiration grew even as it was challenged by the alternative theatres of the 1970s that rejected Stratford as the ultimate expression of a colonized theatre. In the midst of the debate over nationalism in the arts in the 70s, the Festival briefly renamed itself the Stratford National Theatre of Canada when on tour, prompting critics abroad to ask why Canada's national theatre was devoted to the canon of a foreign country.

Stratford's claim to national theatre status was in effect a minor historical trope. What was more important during the post-war decades was the *de facto* realization of the Massey Commission's alternative suggestion of a decentralized national theatre. This is in effect the situation we are left with today. With the founding of the regional theatres during the 1950s and 60s, the dream of a professional theatre movement emerging out of the amateur theatres was fulfilled, and by the 1970s, there seemed to be a network of regional civic theatres that could in effect be called a national theatre. It fulfilled all the expectations of the earlier generation: these companies were generously subsidized, and they brought professional standards and the international repertoire to cities across the country. What they didn't bring was a vision of Canadian theatre; they accepted the nineteenth-century premise that a national drama would emerge out of the nurturing influence of international "mature" repertoires. An exposure to Ibsen, the logic went, would eventually result in a Canadian Ibsen. This was the logic that John Palmer so brilliantly parodied with his 1976 monodrama, *Henrik Ibsen on the Necessity of Producing Norwegian Theatre*.

In retrospect it seems easy to point out that the authentic English-language national theatre developed in the alternative theatre movement, in the plays of groups like Theatre Passe Muraille, The Mummers Troupe, and 25th Street House. The historic success of these companies in validating the voice of the Canadian playwright (who was often the Canadian actor equipped with a tape recorder) may have proved the case that a national theatre emerges from the engagement of the theatre with the living culture of its audience, but it also attenuated the idea of a National Theatre to the point where it became a tautology: the theatre is a national expression, therefore it is a national theatre. By this point the term effectively disallows itself. This was a point made but unheard as early as 1933 when Archibald Key wrote in the pages of *The Canadian Forum*, "I visualize Canada's National Theatre in the form of a little red schoolhouse, a Ford sedan with trailer, a few drapes, props, and an elementary lighting set" (462).

Key's voice was prophetic but his point was made too soon. In fact, it still hasn't sunk in: the hegemonic idea of a monumental National Theatre continues to recur. It surfaced in 1968 with the original aspirations of the National Arts Centre, whose dream of a central showcase fell apart with the disbanding of its English-language theatre company after the 1983-84 season. And it surfaced again in 1987 when Toronto Free Theatre and CentreStage merged to form the Canadian Stage Company. When the merger was announced CentreStage's artistic director, Bill Glassco, proudly informed *The Globe and Mail* that the new theatre could be the seed of a "national theatre company" (Alaton and Conlogue C6). Once again the point of reference was British, even though Canadian Stage subsequently moved its sights from the National Theatre of Great Britain to the more recent identification with the English Stage Company of the Royal Court Theatre (Wilson).

A century after it was first proposed, the recurring obsession of a national theatre remains with us. But it is an obsession that may be impossible to gratify because its primary term of reference, the idea of a nation itself, is taken entirely from the cultural experience of another country. "National theatre" is a rhetorical idea that expresses particular values of nationhood and the theatre's place as a nation's "shining glory." Inscribed in it is an idea of national culture that can be rendered topographically as a pyramid: the national drama is the summit of the national culture, which takes its vertical structure of "low" popular culture and "high" educated culture from the historical arrangement of wealth and power. When critics of past decades spoke of raising the level of Canadian culture, they meant it literally: they meant raising the artistic consciousness of the bottom levels of the social pyramid to meet that of the educated élite at the top. The very idea of a national theatre rests upon the hegemonic idea of a nation that can be expressed in simple cultural codes. Vincent Massey's idea of Canadian nationhood was very different from mine today; and mine is very different from Brian Mulroney's. The rhetorical proposal of a national theatre in effect means the canonization of a theatre and drama that reflects the national ideals of the governing élite.

Note

1   B.K. Sandwell, "The Annexation of Our Stage." See also his "Our Adjunct Theatre."

Works Cited

Alaton, Salem, and Ray Conlogue. "TFT, CentreStage Merger Is Announced." *The Globe and Mail* [Toronto] 16 Apr. 1986: C6.

Baxter, Arthur Beverly. "The Birth of the National Theatre." *Maclean's Magazine* Feb. 1916: 27-29.

Berger, Carl. *The Sense of Power: Studies in the Ideas of Canadian Imperialism 1867-1914*. Toronto: U of Toronto P, 1970.

Charlesworth, Hector. ["Touchstone."] "Modern Instances." *The Evening News* [Toronto] 5 June 1897: 4.

Denison, Merrill. "Nationalism and Drama." *Dramatists in Canada*. Ed. W.H. New. Vancouver: U of British Columbia P, 1972. 65-69.

Key, Archibald. "The Theatre on Wheels." *The Canadian Forum* Sept. 1933: 462-63.

Mair, Charles. *Tecumseh, a Drama*. 1886. *Tecumseh, a Drama and Canadian Poems*. Toronto: Radisson Society of Canada, 1926. 75-219.

Massey, Vincent. "The Prospects of a Canadian Drama." *Queen's Quarterly* 30 (1922-23): 194-212.

Robson, Frederic. "The Drama in Canada." *The Canadian Magazine* 31 (1908): 58-61.

Royal Commission on National Development in the Arts, Letters and Sciences 1949-1951. *Report*. Ottawa: Edmond Cloutier, 1951.

Sandwell, B.K. "The Annexation of Our Stage." *The Canadian Magazine* 38 (1911-12): 22-26.

—. "Our Adjunct Theatre." *Addresses Delivered before The Canadian Club of Montreal: Season 1913-1914*. Montreal: The Canadian Club of Montreal, [1914]. 95-104.

Wilson, Ann. "The English Stage Company Visits the Canadian Stage Company." *Queen's Quarterly* 97 (1990): 140-53.

Cultural Diversity and Canadian Literature:
A Pluralistic Approach
to Majority and Minority Writing in Canada

Enoch Padolsky

If the Canadian government's policy of multiculturalism and the Quebec government's policies toward the "communautés culturelles" have not solved all the problems of Canadian ethnic minority groups, they have nevertheless helped to foster public awareness of the increasing role of minority writers within Canadian and Quebec literatures and cultures in general. With the help of this official recognition and support, Canadian minority writing is being published at an unprecedented rate along with a growing body of accompanying scholarly materials, including translations, editions, anthologies, bibliographies, collections of critical articles, and even whole journals.

The growing corpus of minority writing, however, has not yet had a corresponding impact on the critical conceptualization of Canadian and Quebec literatures. This is particularly true in English Canada, even if some signs of change are apparent. A few more minority writers have been added to the canon of literary histories or university courses. Writers such as Skvorecky and Ricci have won Governor General's Awards, and established journals such as *Canadian Literature* have devoted special issues to Italian-Canadian, Caribbean, or Native writing. In spite of this evidence of an accommodation of Canadian cultural diversity, Canadian criticism has not yet made an equal adjustment to the larger critical framework comprised by the social and cultural terms of reference that have long dominated the conceptualization of literature in Canada. Though it is difficult to summarize these traditional critical assumptions, they characteristically address so-called "national questions": the struggle to establish Canadian and Quebec literatures as valid areas of academic study, the struggle on the English side to establish a national identity and to accommodate the "French fact" in Canada, the struggle in Quebec on the question of independence. Thus, as Joseph Pivato has noted (20-26), critics in English Canada have traditionally attempted to establish a Canadian "mainstream" and have looked for national unifying theses, whether thematic, mythopoeic, or environmental, while writers and critics within Quebec have looked at Quebec literature from the perspective of French "survivance" on a continent of "Anglais." Within these critical frameworks – and older literary histories such as those of Klinck, Tougas, or Bessette may be cited as evidence of these traditional concerns – minority writing has tended to be ignored or, if included, treated within the "mainstream" areas of concern. Minority writers who reflect minority rather than "mainstream" concerns have been relegated to critically peripheral sub-categories: "ethnic," "immigrant," "multicultural," or "non-official language" writing in English Canada; the writing of "Néo-Québécois," "allophones," "immigrants," or "ethniques" in Quebec. The persistence of these critical perspectives in many quarters is evident in the continuing critical influence of Atwood and Frye, in new literary histories such as that of Keith, or in the format and coverage of large scale Quebec projects such as that of Lemire.

The growing diversity of Canadian and Quebec literatures, however, makes these traditional approaches less and less adequate in providing a general literary critical framework. But how can Canadian literature be approached in a way that more fully takes account of the fact that it exists in a multi-ethnic society in which the various ethnic groups tend to be "inter-dependent" (Barth 18), and, yet, reflect culturally-specific concerns. How, in other words, can a more pluralistic and cross-cultural framework be developed, for as John Berry has argued in the field of psychology (424 ff.), cross-cultural study has a number of advantages, is less culture-bound, and is more likely to recognize what is unique in individual cases as well as in the literature as a whole.

The question that needs to be addressed, therefore, is what such a cross-cultural and pluralistic approach to Canadian literature would entail. What new elements need to be examined and what impact would there be on the traditional view of Canadian literature? In short, what are the conceptual issues and critical implications of a culturally pluralistic approach to Canadian literature?

1

There are a great many ways of approaching literature and of defining "culture," but the two elements which seem most central to a cross-cultural and pluralistic approach are ethnicity and social status. Cultural pluralism implies ethnicity, and ethnicity in Canada implies such things as immigration history and policy, social stratification, attitudinal and prestige differences, and a host of other issues deriving from the historical and social realities of ethnic group experience in Canadian society.

From a pluralistic approach, therefore, the first task (see Padolsky 1986-87: 148-49; 1990: 26-27) is to replace the current terminology – "mainstream" and "ethnic" writers/writing – by the terms "ethnic majority" and "ethnic minority." The "mainstream-ethnic" distinction implies a "we-they" unicultural perspective in which, as is often the case, ethnicity is attributed by the dominant social group(s) only to others (Royce 3; Gordon 5). The "ethnic majority-minority" distinction, on the other hand, represents a more objective cross-cultural frame of reference. Canadians, regardless of origin, share the common characteristic of ethnicity, but differ in whether the ethnicity is of majority or minority status in Canadian society. The advantage of this terminology and the critical perspective it implies is two-fold. First, majority writers are no longer treated as if ethnic issues were not applicable to them, and new emphasis is put on the fact that, socially, they are in a majority position. Second, minority writers are no longer marginalized into categorical "ghettos," but are fully comparable on the basis of ethnicity and status to majority writers.

Putting ethnicity into the critical centre does, however, introduce new problems for literary criticism. "'Ethnicity,'" as Diana Brydon noted (94), "is a minefield." Yet, literary critics can look to work already done in other areas of ethnic studies to understand the issues involved in the study of ethnicity. These issues can perhaps be summarized in a series of questions. Is ethnicity "objective" or "subjective," that is, is it merely a manifestation of structural, institutional, or other measurable features such as common descent, religion, language, customs, and so on, or is it also a question of self-definition and attribution by others, or is it both (Isajiw; Kallen)? Is ethnicity a question of maintaining boundaries between ethnic groups or is it what is enclosed by those boundaries (Barth)? Is ethnicity behaviourly "real" or is it only "symbolic" (Gans) or "affective" (Weinfeld)? Then, there are a number of related questions: the difference between group and category; theoretical and descriptive aspects of ethnic change, acculturation, and assimilation; the relation between cultural and socio-economic aspects of ethnicity; and so on.[1] In sum, a pluralistic approach to Canadian literature raises for Canadian literary criticism all the same problems about the concept of ethnicity which historians, sociologists, social psychologists, and others have had to deal with for many years. At the same time, it is worth noting that the critical analysis of these issues in Canadian literature has a unique contribution to make to the general discussion of ethnicity. This is because the literary text often has a special cultural status. It not only reflects the issues of ethnicity mentioned above, but it is, itself, a primary vehicle of ethnic culture and, as such, provides evidence for a discussion of the concept.[2]

A similar set of problems arises in the area of social status. The terms "minority" and "majority" are also problematic in the Canadian context since they refer more often to status (economic, political, institutional, prestige-related, etc.) than to numbers. Furthermore, from a historical and social perspective, they are relative and context-related concepts. Thus, depending on such things as time (pre- or post-Conquest; pre- or post-

World War II), place (region, city), structure (political, economic), or aspect (language, religion), French-Canadians and British-Canadians could, in different contexts, be considered as having majority *or* minority status. For French-Canadians in particular, this ambiguity has always been an important consideration since their internal perspective of themselves has been that of a North American (francophone) minority and of a subordinated or dominated group nationally. Yet, even for British-Canadians, as Darroch has reminded us (175-76), majority membership does not always equate with majority status in all socially stratified situations. Nevertheless, it does seem to me that the situation of the dominant Canadian groups, regardless of the complexities, can be meaningfully differentiated on historical and social bases from that of the Canadian ethnic minority groups. Ongoing references of "founding nations or peoples," "charter groups," "official and non-official languages," and structural and institutional manifestations of these terms of reference argue not only for the persistence of ethnicity and its diachronic and synchronic relevance to social status in Canada, but also for a fundamental and underlying division of Canadian society into majority and minority groupings.[3] And again, from a literary perspective, and particularly where language and other cultural features are involved, literature itself forms part of the basis for the discussion of these questions of status. The very fact that a case has to be made to include minority writing in the Canadian and Quebec literary critical frameworks is evidence of the relevance of this analysis of status.

Turning to the area of literary criticism as such, a number of other issues arise. What, for example, constitutes minority or majority ethnicity in the literary text? This is an important question since the writer's membership in a minority or majority ethnic group is clearly not enough. As has often been noted, ethnicity is a dependent variable, and its salience, centrality, and valence, to use Kallen's terms (81), vary with the context.[4] Writers do not like to be labelled; and if they sometimes address and reflect the concerns of their individual and group ethnicity and status, at other times they do not. This is as true for minority writers, who are generally perceived as having "ethnicity," as for majority writers, who are often perceived as lacking it. The onus, thus, rests with the critic to establish the degree to which and the ways in which ethnicity and status are reflected in the work, writer, or group of writers being investigated. It is hardly possible, here, to specify all the ways in which these elements manifest themselves in literature since they may appear not only thematically (ethnic identity, family relationships, language, religion, inter-group relations, discrimination, and so on), but structurally, formally, or in the writer's or reader's perspective. Indeed, there are already a number of studies of ethnic minority writers and texts that have adopted a variety of such non-thematic approaches.[5] Note also that the writer being studied need not agree with the critic's analysis. Balan's study of the importance of Ukrainian ethnicity in George Ryga's works stands on its own, in spite of Ryga's own denial of its importance (Balan 142). It is even possible to argue, as Arun Mukherjee does with reference to Michael Ondaatje, that the lack of concern for ethnicity and status may itself be a response by a writer to his or her ethnic minority status.

2

The issues discussed to this point might be termed mainly theoretical or conceptual. But what are the *practical* implications of a pluralistic approach to Canadian majority and minority writing? How does new attention to ethnicity and status affect the general view of Canadian literature and past criticism of it? In the case of British-Canadian majority writing what is most striking is that the important element of majority ethnicity has attracted relatively little conscious or overt discussion. If, as Milton Gordon once quipped, "the fish never discovers water" (5), then critics of British-Canadian writing, swimming in the same water, have hardly noticed that the element in which they all move is a sea of ethnicity. This does not mean that they have been unable to describe the fish. But a pluralistic approach may provide a useful reinterpretation or a different perspective on many of the critical analyses that have been made. Two aspects of majority ethnicity seem most salient in this regard: first, the development of British-Canadian ethnicity with related questions of intra-group relations and Old World connections; and, second, a focus on inter-group relations from the perspective of majority status.

Seen from this perspective, early British-Canadian literature could be described as reflecting an ongoing process in the development of a new ethnic group and ethnic identity. Indeed, many of the descriptive categories in literary histories or other "mainstream" overviews of this period – the transplantation of cultural traditions from Old to New World, the growth of Canadian nationalism (e.g. the Confederation poets), the constant preoccupation with the North Atlantic triangle – may all be better described as participating in this process of ethnogenesis. The works of early writers such as Thomas Haliburton, Susanna Moodie, Stephen Leacock, Sara Jeannette Duncan, Ralph Connor, and Charles G.D. Roberts, to name just a few, can thus be seen as reflecting a struggle to redefine individual and group ethnic identity, and to adjust group values and boundaries in light of the changing environment which developed in the New World. Loyalty to a British heritage, adjustment of cultural perceptions in a new situation, and differentiation from a non-loyal British group to the south, features that marked the changing boundaries and ethnic characteristics of the developing British-Canadian ethnicity, are centrally treated by all these writers.

At the same time, early British-Canadian writing is highly aware of both the intra-group and inter-group context in which the British-Canadian ethnicity developed. The treatment of British sub-groups in the literature is particularly interesting and certainly deserves more study. My own hypothesis is that, over time, a shift occurs from a strong awareness of sub-group differences (Moodie on the English, Irish, and Yankees; Connor on the Scots; etc.) to a growing sense of nested, macro-group ethnicity vis-à-vis non-British ethnic groups in Canadian society. Ralph Connor assimilates his Slavic hero Kalman, in *The Foreigner* (1909), into a "Canadian" (i.e. British-Canadian) rather than "Scottish-Canadian" identity, and Stephen Leacock, in *Sunshine Sketches* (1912), includes the culture of all those of British stock, even Americans, into the warmth of his sunny town. This last point may be surprising in the light of Leacock's well-known anti-American views, but his attitude toward Americans seems to have had a political rather than an ethnic basis. On ethnic grounds, he apparently hoped for the ultimate reunification of the "Anglo-Saxon peoples" (Bowker xx-xxi), and held strongly negative views on (non-British) European immigrants to Canada (see Palmer 46-51) and on non-Europeans generally (Bowker xxi).

Early inter-group relations with the two largest non-British ethnic groups – aboriginals and French-Canadians – also figure prominently in early British-Canadian literature, and both relationships clearly reflect British-Canadian majority concerns. Critical studies such as that by Monkman may be interpreted as showing that the depiction of aboriginals in British-Canadian writing reflects an image which serves the developing British-Canadian ethnic identity ("white man's Indian") as well as the lines of power between the two groups. A great deal undoubtedly needs to be done with this relationship, as seen not only in the recognized "Indian" works of writers such as John Richardson and Duncan Campbell Scott, but in the works of a great many other writers (Monkman 2), and even, as Parker Duchemin has shown, in quasi-literary sources such as the journals of the early explorers.

The treatment of French Canada in British-Canadian writing, another major element which has drawn considerable critical attention, also needs to be reexamined as a feature of British-Canadian ethnicity *per se*. That this relationship, too, reveals issues of ethnic identity and of majority dominance is clearly evident, for example, in the case of Charles G.D. Roberts, whose interest in French Canada is well known and who championed it as part of the new Canadian nationalism of the post-Confederation period (Roberts 248-49). On close examination, however, what is striking about Roberts' nationalism is the degree to which it reflects his unmistakably British-Canadian outlook. His patriotic poem, "Canada," for instance, makes a point of lauding the equal valour of "Montcalm and Wolfe! Wolfe and Montcalm!" (Note the balance in the line.) But in the end, Roberts finds his unified Canadian glory in an unquestioning allegiance to British Imperial interests: the Canadian expedition to the Sudan of 1885. An even more striking example is again the enormously popular and socially progressive Ralph Connor (Charles Gordon), who helps define the "men of Glengarry" by off-setting them against French-Canadian characters and values. The mastery and "conversion" of LeNoir in *The Man from Glengarry* thus parallels the "Canadianization" of Slavic hero Kalman in *The Foreigner*, and reveals Gordon's ideological pattern of British-Canadian nation building, a pattern which clearly reflects his British-Canadian ethnic perspective.

The study of majority ethnicity should not, of course, be limited to early writers. The same two aspects – ethnicity and majority status – continue to be salient in modern British-Canadian writing as well. In the study of other periods, however, one has to take account of the changing demographic make-up of Canada and the changed context of British-Canadian ethnicity. As Linda Deutschmann has argued, the relative "decline of the WASP" in Canada has had important implications for the understanding of both Canadian society and of modern British-Canadian ethnicity. If she is right, then, the fixation with roots and "Canadian" identity of British-Canadian writers in the 1960s, for example, should perhaps be attributed to an ethnic identity crisis among British-Canadians as they became more aware of themselves as "merely" another ethnic group in Canada (*cf.* the flag debate, resistance to the metric system, the appearance of British pubs and clubs, the advent of groups to "defend" the English language in Canada, changing attitudes toward French Canada, etc.). In any case, it is within the bounds of this kind of discussion that the works of modern British-Canadian writers need to be considered. To treat major writers such as Munro, Davies, Findley, MacLennan, Mitchell, Laurence, and Atwood, to name just a few, as if they were merely "Canadian" and not "British-Canadian," is to neglect the implications of modern British-Canadian ethnicity and status in Canada.

The Manawaka series by Margaret Laurence may be cited as a prime example of a modern British-Canadian writer openly exploring both her ethnic heritage and related questions of identity and status in the Canadian context. From Hagar Shipley to Morag Gunn, Laurence can be seen tracing through the generations the psychology, values, identity, and social place of her Scottish-Canadian characters. But Laurence's exploration of British-Canadian ethnicity is not a simple one. Embedded in her novels is an awareness of both the nested nature of her own ethnicity (consider Morag's English husband, Brooke) and the importance of majority (or minority) status in Canadian society. Writing out of the Canadian West,

and with her African experience behind her, Laurence, unlike many earlier British-Canadian writers, is particularly conscious of Canadian pluralism and of the historically privileged role of her own group. Her analysis
of class issues in Manawaka not only points to differences between being
the daughter of a merchant (Hagar) or the daughter of a garbage collector (Morag), but notices that the wrong side of the tracks only starts with
the poor British-Canadian characters and works its way down the hill past
German and Ukrainian railroad workers to the Métis at the bottom. It is
thus very significant (and generally unnoticed I might add) that one of the
crucial "free" acts of Hagar in *The Stone Angel*, acts by which she over-
comes her fierce "Scottish" pride, involves Sandra Wong, a young Chinese-
Canadian girl who is associated, in Hagar's mind, with an early version of
Canadian "boat people." "Maybe," Hagar speculates, "I owe my house to
her grandmother's passage money" (Laurence 1964: 286-87). Laurence's
point is both humanistic and pluralistic: the social and cultural differences
of the pioneering generation, including those of majority and minority,
are being levelled in succeeding generations. Not only do the Curries and
Shipleys share the same tombstone, but Sandra reminds Hagar of her own
granddaughter.

In similar terms, Stacey Cameron in *The Fire-Dwellers* is forced to
reevaluate the identity crisis and social situation she is in when she meets
Piquette, a Métis girl from Manawaka, on the street in Vancouver. In *The
Diviners*, as Monkman has pointed out (61-64), Morag, too, gains, a perspective on her own situation and on the possibility of alternative values
by comparing herself to the Métis characters. Morag's search for identity
entails not only a "return journey" to ancestral Britain, but a long-term
relationship with Jules Tonnerre and a complex parallel of the Piper Gunn
mythology and the Métis mythology of Rider Tonnerre. Yet, the Métis
perspective is not the only alternative in the novel. When Morag leaves
Manawaka, her perspective is also broadened in the culturally different
(Jewish-Canadian) environment of her friend Ella's house, where she first
learns to cry and "first truly realizes that English is not the only literature"
(Laurence 1974: 151). Similarly, Morag's use of Jules as a vehicle of "eth-
nic" freeing has its counterpart in the situation of Rachel Cameron in *A
Jest of God* who is able to escape from the constricting values of her own
ethnic environment through an affair with the Ukrainian-Canadian Nick
Kazlik. In all these relationships, male-female and majority-minority,
Laurence shows sympathy and understanding for the situation of minority
figures, but her focus is nevertheless solidly fixed on the majority figures.
What she knows and what she is investigating is the nature and status of
her own (Scottish) British-Canadian ethnicity. Her perspective on Canada
is pluralistic, but she is conscious that her point of view is a majority one
in Canadian society. This gives Laurence's presentation of inter-cultural

relations a great deal of subtlety and tact. If Morag is aghast at racial discrimination toward the Métis in *The Diviners*, she does not know what to say, and feels that she has no right to say it, even when her own (half-Métis) daughter is involved, because she has never experienced racial discrimination herself.

Laurence cannot be used as an example to suggest that all modern British-Canadian writers approach their majority ethnicity in the same way or to the same degree. Yet, returning to the main point of this section, the usefulness of a pluralistic perspective on these writers is that it opens a discussion of the importance of ethnicity and status and focusses on the role of modern British-Canadian writers in the continuing development of British-Canadian identity and culture.

3

What has been said about the lack of critical attention to ethnicity and status in British-Canadian writing is somewhat less true about French-Canadian and Quebec writing since French-Canadian writers and critics have tended to focus much more consciously and frequently on their group concerns. In part, no doubt, because of their previously mentioned view of themselves as a North American minority, and the historical, social, and psychological implications of the Conquest and of British-Canadian socio-economic dominance over the years. "La survivance," the necessity to struggle to maintain language, religion, and culture in the Canadian social structure, has always meant a strong and self-conscious emphasis on ethnic and status concerns in French-Canadian literature, from *Jean Rivard* and *Maria Chapdelaine* to the present.

It could be argued, however, that the French-Canadian literary critical approach to issues of ethnicity and status has traditionally been too unicultural, particularly in the larger Canadian context. The perception of Quebec as a kind of beseiged French cultural "garrison," the language difference, and other social factors have tended to produce a literary critical perspective which has historically been internal, Quebec-oriented, and limited to the perspective of French "minority" status in the dynamic of English-French group relations in Canada. The result has been the tendency to neglect the comparative context of English-Canadian writing (even within Quebec) and of Canadian and Quebec minority writing generally. (Consider the relatively small number, until recently, of translations of English-Canadian or other language works into French.) As a result, the social, psychological, and cultural complexities to be found in the rest of Canada (or in other groups in Quebec) have rarely entered into the discussion of Quebec literature.

The case for a more cross-cultural and pluralistic perspective on

ENOCH PADOLSKY

French-Canadian and Quebec literature can, thus, also be made. As part of this perspective, the image of the "Anglais" in Quebec writing would need to be examined much more systematically, for it might be expected to reveal as much about French-Canadian ethnicity as the image of French-Canadians in British-Canadian writing does about British-Canadian ethnicity. Another key area is the study of *majority* aspects of French-Canadian ethnicity in a Canadian and Quebec context. Thus, for example, the depiction of ethnic minorities – immigrants, aboriginal peoples, and other long-established minority groups – in Quebec literature and in French-Canadian literature set outside Quebec (Gabrielle Roy on aboriginal peoples and other ethnic minorities in the West, for example) deserves close attention.[6]

A good example would be the literary treatment of the historically large Jewish minority in Quebec. Ronald Sutherland (50), Naïm Kattan, Ben Shek (1984), and others have already noted the large number of Jewish characters in Quebec fiction. And the study of how a non-Catholic, even non-Christian, and primarily English-speaking minority is treated in Quebec literature should reveal a great deal about French-Canadian writing as ethnic majority writing. A sense of ethnic boundaries, questions of social discrimination, given Quebec's historical undercurrent of anti-Semitism,[7] and the perception of Jewish-Canadians (and other minorities) as part of "les Anglais" are all involved. And yet, in spite of a very large body of studies on the Canadian Jewish experience, Pierre Anctil and Gary Caldwell are forced to note in their recent ground-breaking work on the Jews of Quebec that, from a French-Canadian perspective, "Les recherches portant sur tous les aspects d'une présence juive au Québec viennent à peine d'être entreprises de façon sérieuse" and that major studies on the Jewish experience in Quebec, such as those of David Rome, "ne recurent pas d'écho dans le milieu universitaire" (10). The same point is made by Ben Shek (in the same volume) regarding the literary treatment of Jews "dans la littérature québécoise de langue française." With one exception, he writes: "Il s'agit d'un sujet vaste auquel n'a été consacrée, jusqu'à ce jour, aucune thèse de doctorat ni aucune recherche d'envergure ..." (1984: 257). Good examples of what needs to be done are not hard to find. It has always struck me as significant, for example, that three of the major works in the 1960s that focussed on the FLQ crisis used non-British characters to represent the "power" structure of English Canada at that time of extreme crisis (Jasmin; Aquin; Godbout). Two of these were Jewish or partly Jewish women, Jasmin's Ethel and Godbout's Patricia; the third character, used by Aquin, was the unspecific but clearly non-British H. de Heutz. What are the implications of this in the larger context of French-Canadian majority ethnicity? Similar points could be made about the perception of other minority groups in Quebec literature. What, for example, is the relationship between the expressed empathy of many nationalist writers of the 1960s for Third World countries, the idea of "négritude," the presence or absence of Latin American, Asian, Black, or Haitian characters in modern Quebec writing, and the reception in Quebec of works by Haitian writers such as Dany Laferrière?

Critical interest in Quebec in questions such as these and, indeed, in minority writers generally, seems to be increasing. Paradoxically, this interest can partly be attributed to the continuing self-image of French-Canadians as a "minority"[8] (i.e. a perception of shared experience) and in part to the assertion of "majority" power within the Quebec context. One result of the "success" (surely a sign of majority status) of Bill 101 and other measures (including immigration policy) to enhance the status of French within Quebec has been the arrival on Quebec's literary scene of unprecedented numbers of minority *French* language writers (Haitian, Italian, Arab, Jewish, etc.). This linguistic factor, together with the near consensus among writers and critics in Quebec on the question of sovereignty, has begun to provoke critical responses to Quebec minority writing far more than was the case in the past. It remains to be seen whether this trend will carry over to English (or other) language Quebec minority writers. Yet, recent articles on "la culture immigrée," a special "dossier comparatiste: Québec-Amérique Latine" in *Voix et images*, the success of "transcultural" journals such as *Vice versa*, the increasing pace of translation of English-Canadian and English language minority writing (for example, Kogawa and Klein) into French, growing interest in the sociology, history, and politics of Quebec minority groups (*cf.* the impact of the Oka crisis), and a new awareness of the "femmes minoritaires et immigrantes" in feminist literary circles are all signs that minority writing in Quebec is being conceptualized more inclusively within a Québécois framework, and that a more pluralistic view of Quebec literature is in fact emerging.[9]

4

One of the main advantages of a pluralistic approach to Canadian literature, as noted earlier, is that it provides not only a new perspective on British-Canadian and French-Canadian writing, but also a coherent and balanced framework for the consideration of Canadian minority writing. Putting the critical emphasis on issues of ethnicity and status in a comprehensive Canadian context brings minority writing out of an "ethnic" periphery and into a common "Canadian" centre. Just as majority writing can be studied for the ways it reflects ethnicity in a majority Canadian context, so Canadian minority writing can be studied not just for its "ethnic" characteristics *per se*, but also for how it manifests this ethnicity in minority Canadian situations. The implication of this statement is that the study of minority writing must encompass the full range of historical, social, and cultural realities which have an impact on issues of individual (and group) ethnicity and on the interplay of these issues in the culturally pluralistic situation of Canadian society. The issues that need to be examined, the perspectives that need to be delineated, even the very ways we understand the conceptual categories may vary depending on whether we are considering the works of Mordecai Richler, Tomson Highway, Joy Kogawa, W.D. Valgardson, Austin Clarke, Bharati Mukherjee, Vera Lysenko, Armin Wiebe, Maria Campbell, Josef Skvorecky, Naïm Kattan, Marco Micone, Dany Laferrière, and so on. For each of these writers, issues of ethnic and minority status are, to varying degrees, salient in the literary works; at the same time, the works reflect particular parts of Canadian historical, social, and cultural reality. Taken together, of course, they provide a composite view of how minority ethnicity is manifested in Canadian and Quebec literatures.

Although the complexity of Canadian minority writing may be daunting, once recognized, it highlights the futility (and distortion) of previous "mainstream" attempts to assimilate such a diverse body of literature into a fixed and preconceived "Canadian" critical frame. As Frederick Philip Grove argued as early as 1928 (see Padolsky 1987), the value of the immigrant to Canada is lost if he or she merely assimilates to a "Canadian" norm. In similar terms, one could argue that an assimilative critical approach ignores the special value that a diverse perspective offers. Thus, to say, for example, that minority writers are all part of the Canadian "survival" psychology (Atwood) is far less interesting than to study the differences and variations implied by the diversity of situations to be found in the Canadian context.

As Pivato has already argued (29-30), a second consequence of considering Canadian minority writing in this way will certainly be the broadening of Canadian literature into an international arena. Some immigrant writers in Canada already have international reputations (Sam Selvon, Josef Skvorecky, etc.). Many set their works in other countries as well as in Canada (Rohinton Mistry, Bharati Mukherjee, Austin Clarke, etc.), while others maintain close contact with literary trends in other countries (Latin American-Canadian writers, for example). In addition to this international intertextuality, the linguistic implications also broaden. From a pluralistic perspective, on what basis can Canadian literature be restricted to merely English and French language writing? Indeed, the writings of some groups and even some individual writers exist in four or more languages (or dialects). Do we simply ignore the other linguistic works? "Mainstream" critical frameworks have only been possible in the past because of the total neglect of this considerable body of "non-official" language writing in

Canada (Ukrainian, Yiddish, Polish, Italian, Urdu, etc.). To push this argument to its extreme, there is even a case for connecting the international, extra-territorial, and multilingual dimensions. Thus, for example, as Riedel has argued (10), there are German-language writers writing in Canada who publish in Germany for a German audience, but who reflect a very clear Canadian perspective in their works. This may seem an extreme case, but it illustrates the potential scope of a serious pluralism in Canadian literature. And in what way is the case raised by Riedel different from the list of majority writers who, in a variety of ways, have also raised such international and intertextual issues (Richardson, Duncan, Gallant, etc.)? At the same time, it points to the need for multilingual criticism in Canadian literature and, for the critical institution, of the special value and importance of critical evaluations (in English or French) of Canadian minority writing in other languages.

Coming to terms with the phenomenon of Canadian minority writing will, thus, entail a solid respect for diversity. Generalizations about minority writers or about particular aspects of Canadian experience with relation to specific groups of writers will need to be contextualized by a broader, pluralistic awareness. Thus, Arun Mukherjee, writing on Sri Lankan Canadian poets, suggests that they raise questions that "their 'Canadian' contemporaries" do not, "questions about ideology, about domination, about race, and about class" (44). The difficulty here is not in Mukherjee's assessment of Sri Lankan Canadian poets or in her statement that "mainstream critics and academics" have ignored these issues "for too long." Her article is exactly the sort of study that needs to be done in a great many areas of Canadian minority writing. However, from a broader, more comparative view of Canadian minority writing, the same ideological issues are raised by other minority writers. At the same time, there are notable cases of majority writers (Frank Scott, Dorothy Livesay, etc.) who, it could be argued, also raise these questions directly, and a great many other majority writers who raise them *indirectly* by their (unconscious) perspectives on Canadian minority groups. From a pluralistic perspective, then, the issue is not whether certain questions are raised by different groups of writers, but rather what the differences (and similarities) are, and what significance we can give to the difference between majority and minority perspectives on ideological and social issues of this kind. Ethnicity and social status do matter. They are reflected in the literature of Canadian experience, and the challenge will be how to interpret the literature, in all its diversity, from a common perspective which tries to take them into account.

By way of conclusion, I would like to point out two general corollaries which follow from the kind of approach to Canadian literature outlined in this paper. Although a pluralistic perspective provides a common framework for discussing majority and minority Canadian writing, it does not in itself reduce the differences. Particular minority writers reflect issues of ethnicity and status, but they do not necessarily do so in the same way as majority writers or, indeed, as other minority writers. Immigrant writers, aboriginal writers, third-generation minority writers, and so on, all see the world from different vantage points, have different attitudes toward dominant Canadian groups, and different histories within Canadian society. John Marlyn's perspective on the dynamics of group ethnicity and status in Canadian society is not that of Mary di Michele or of Tomson Highway. And all three differ from that of Laurence or Atwood. The same could be said about Marco Micone's view of Quebec compared to that of Mordecai Richler, Régine Robin, or Jacques Godbout. Coming to terms with this diversity of situations as they are reflected in ethnic majority and ethnic minority writing in Canada will, thus, give a new importance to the multidisciplinary contexts of Canadian literary criticism. It will not be enough to study a work or a writer from a broadly "majority" or "minority" basis. A host of specific factors also enter into the discussion: regional, historical, or political aspects of the majority experience, immigrant or aboriginal experience, period of immigration, reasons for immigration, immigrant status relative to Canadian immigration policy, generations since immigration, acceptance by other groups in Canadian society, visible or invisible minority status, socio-economic status, degree of salience of ethnicity, regional distribution of status, cultural characteristics and categories, acculturation attitudes, etc.

Secondly, the contingent nature of ethnic and majority/minority awareness and the relativity implied in the concepts of ethnicity and majority/minority (Kallen 110) both give added importance to the cross-cultural nature of a pluralistic approach to Canadian literature. This implies that a pluralistic approach is, in effect, fundamentally comparative and it is probably in this comparative area that such an approach has the most to offer. The richness inherent in this kind of comparative analysis could undoubtedly form the basis of another whole paper but perhaps even a few examples here can convey some idea of the potential in comparative Canadian criticism from a pluralistic perspective. Such examples might include comparative treatments of Canadian feminist writers (e.g. Margaret Atwood, Nicole Brossard, and Mary di Michele); the analysis of class issues in Canadian literature (e.g. Austin Clarke, Marco Micone, and Dorothy Livesay); the depiction of aboriginal-white relations (e.g. Yves

Thériault, Tomson Highway, Rudy Wiebe, and W.O. Mitchell); comparative treatment of the immigrant experience (e.g. Susanna Moodie, Adele Wiseman, Else Seel, and Bharati Mukherjee); comparative perspectives on the literary treatment of inter-group dynamics (e.g. Joy Kogawa, Mordecai Richler, Roch Carrier, and Margaret Laurence); a comparative analysis of identity issues in various majority and minority Canadian writers; and so on. The list could easily be extended.

A pluralistic approach to majority and minority writing in Canada thus offers a much needed and highly promising perspective on Canadian literature. It brings majority ethnicity into focus and minority writing into an equitable, common framework. It also encourages new kinds of analyses and some very suggestive cross-cultural comparisons. In its multidisciplinary aspects, it offers a strengthened connection to work being done in other areas of Canadian studies. Finally, it is simply more complete, offering a more comprehensive view of how the diversity and complexity of Canadian society and culture are reflected in Canadian literature.

Notes

1   These kinds of issues are much more substantial than the historical ambiguities of the term "ethnicity" noted by Sollors 20 ff. His distinction between a particularist ("us-them") and a universalist ("we are all ethnic") sense can be seen as mainly a definitional dispute. Any pluralistic view of ethnicity has to imply a universalist definition.

2   For a discussion of the differences in approach to ethnicity by the humanities as opposed to the "sciences," see Novak 27-29.

3   *Cf.* the discussion in Dahlie and Fernando 1-5. For a recent Quebec expression of the traditional view of "la dualité fondamentale du pays," see Bernier.

4   For other treatments of ethnic salience in Canada, see Mackie and Brinkerhoff; Edwards and Doucette.

5   Examples include Mandel; Blodgett; Amprimoz and Viselli; Gürttler; Kroetsch; Simon, "Language." *Cf.* also Deleuze and Guattari. For an argument for the centrality of signature and against formalist approaches to ethnicity, see Loriggio.

6   See, for example, Sirois; Shek 1986. Also relevant to this point are the articles by André Dommergues and Pádraig Ó Gormghaile.

7   For discussions of anti-Semitism in Quebec, see Betcherman; Anctil and Caldwell; Langlais and Rome.

8   *Cf.* Anctil and Caldwell's description of both Jews and French-Canadians as "peuples minoritaires" (10) without any attempt to distinguish their status situations.

9   Micone; *Voix et images* 34 (1986): 10-66; *cf.* also the ongoing translation series
    by Québec-Amérique; reviews such as the one by Sherry Simon of *Histoires
    d'immigrées* in *Spirale*; the appearance of magazines and journals such as *La
    parole métèque, Humanitas, Vice versa*; the chapter on "Écritures migrantes" in
    Nepveu; recent books by Simon Harel, Gina Stoiciu and Odette Brosseau; etc.
    Of particular interest is the work being done by the "Montréal imaginaire"
    research project at the Université de Montréal. See, for example, their bibliog-
    raphy of Montreal minority writing (Melançon).

Works Cited

Amprimoz, Alexandre L., and Sante E. Viselli. "Death Between Two Cultures:
    Italian-Canadian Poetry." *Contrasts: Comparative Essays on Italian-Canadian
    Writing*. Ed. Joseph Pivato. Montreal: Guernica, 1985. 101-20.
Anctil, Pierre, and Gary Caldwell, eds. *Juifs et réalités juives au Québec*. Montreal:
    IQRC, 1984.
Aquin, Hubert. *Prochain épisode*. Montreal: Le cercle du livre de France, 1965.
Atwood, Margaret. *Survival: A Thematic Guide to Canadian Literature*. Toronto:
    Anansi, 1972.
Balan, Jars. "Ukrainian Influences in George Ryga's Work." *Identifications: Ethnicity
    and the Writer in Canada*. Ed. Jars Balan. Edmonton, AB: The Canadian Institute
    of Ukrainian Studies, 1982. 36-52.
Barth, Fredrik. *Ethnic Groups and Boundaries*. Boston: Little, Brown, 1969.
Bernier, Jacques. "Les minorités ethno-culturelles et l'État au Canada." *Études cana-
    diennes* 21.2 (1986): 177-83.
Berry, John W. "Research in Multicultural Societies: Implications of Cross-Cultural
    Methods." *Journal of Cross-Cultural Psychology* 10 (1979): 415-34.
Bessette, G., L. Geslin, and C. Parent. *Histoire de la littérature canadienne-française*.
    Montreal: Centre éducatif et culturel, 1968.
Betcherman, Lita-Rose. *The Swastika and the Maple Leaf*. Toronto: Fitzhenry and
    Whiteside, 1975.
Blodgett, E.D. *Configuration: Essays in the Canadian Literatures*. Downsview, ON:
    ECW, 1982.
Bowker, Alan, ed. *The Social Criticism of Stephen Leacock*. Toronto: U of Toronto P,
    1973.
Brydon, Diana. "Discovering 'Ethnicity': Joy Kogawa's *Obasan* and Mena Abdullah's
    Time of the Peacock." *Australian/Canadian Literatures in English: Comparative
    Perspectives*. Ed. Russell McDougall and Gillian Whitlock. Melbourne:
    Methuen, 1987. 94-110.
Connor, Ralph. *The Foreigner*. New York: Hodder and Stoughton, 1909.
—. *The Man from Glengarry*. New York: Grosset and Dunlap, 1901.
Dahlie, Jorgen, and Tissa Fernando. *Ethnicity, Power and Politics in Canada*. Toronto:
    Methuen, 1981.

Darroch, A. Gordon. "Another Look at Ethnicity, Stratification, and Social Mobility in Canada." 1979. Rpt. in *Ethnicity and Ethnic Relations in Canada*. 2nd ed. Ed. Rita M. Bienvenue and Jay E. Goldstein. Toronto: Butterworths, 1985. 153-79.

Deleuze, Gilles, and Felix Guattari. *Kafka: pour une littérature mineure*. Paris: Minuit, 1975.

Deutschmann, Linda Bell. "Decline of the WASP? Dominant Group Identity in the Ethnic Plural Society." *Ethnic Canadians: Culture and Education*. Ed. Martin L. Kovacs. Regina: Canadian Plains Research Center, 1978. 411-18.

Dommergues, André. "Le discours du père Pierre Biard sur les Amérindiens dans *La relation de la Nouvelle-France (1616)*." *Études canadiennes* 21.1 (1986): 245-55.

Duchemin, Parker. "'A Parcel of Whelps': Alexander Mackenzie among the Indians." *Canadian Literature* 124-25 (1990): 49-74.

Edwards, John, and Lori Doucette. "Ethnic Salience, Identity and Symbolic Ethnicity." *Canadian Ethnic Studies* 19.1 (1987): 52-62.

Frye, Northrop. *The Bush Garden: Essays on the Canadian Imagination*. Toronto: Anansi, 1971.

Gans, Herbert J. "Symbolic Ethnicity: The Future of Ethnic Groups and Cultures in America." *Ethnic and Racial Studies* 2 (1979): 1-20.

Godbout, Jacques. *Le couteau sur la table*. Paris: Seuil, 1965.

Gordon, Milton M. *Assimilation in American Life*. New York: Oxford UP, 1964.

Gürttler, Karin. "Henry Kreisel: A Canadian Exile Writer?" *Another Country: Writings by and about Henry Kreisel*. Ed. Shirley Neuman. Edmonton, AB: NeWest, 1985. 293-303.

Harel, Simon. *Le voleur de parcours: identité et cosmopolitisme dans la littérature québécoise contemporaine*. Montreal: Préambule, 1989.

Isajiw, Wsevolod. "Definitions of Ethnicity." *Ethnicity* 1 (1974): 111-24.

Jasmin, Claude. *Ethel et le terroriste*. Montreal: Déom, 1964.

Kallen, Evelyn. *Ethnicity and Human Rights in Canada*. Toronto: Gage, 1982.

Kattan, Naïm. "Jews and French Canadians." *One Church, Two Nations?* Ed. Philip LeBlanc and Arnold Edinborough. Don Mills, ON: Longmans, 1968. 104-15.

Keith, W.J. *Canadian Literature in English*. London: Longman, 1985.

Klinck, Carl F., gen. ed. *Literary History of Canada: Canadian Literature in English*. 2nd ed. 3 vols. Toronto: U of Toronto P, 1976.

Kroetsch, Robert. "The Grammar of Silence: Narrative Patterns in Ethnic Writing." *Canadian Literature* 106 (1985): 65-74.

Langlais, Jacques, and David Rome. *Juifs et Québécois français: 200 ans d'histoire commune*. Montreal: Fides, 1986.

Laurence, Margaret. *The Diviners*. Toronto: McClelland and Stewart, 1974.

—. *The Fire-Dwellers*. Toronto: McClelland and Stewart, 1969.

—. *A Jest of God*. Toronto: McClelland and Stewart, 1966.

—. *The Stone Angel*. Toronto: McClelland and Stewart, 1964.

Leacock, Stephen. *Sunshine Sketches of a Little Town*. 1912. New Canadian Library. Toronto: McClelland and Stewart, 1960.

Lemire, Maurice. *Dictionnaire des œuvres littéraires du Québec.* Montreal: Fides, 1980.

Loriggio, Francesco. "The Question of the Corpus: Ethnicity and Canadian Literature." *Future Indicative: Literary Theory and Canadian Literature.* Ed. John Moss. Ottawa: U of Ottawa P, 1987. 53-69.

Mackie, Marlene, and Merlin B. Brinkerhoff. "Measuring Ethnic Salience." *Canadian Ethnic Studies* 16.1 (1984): 114-31.

Mandel, Eli. "The Ethnic Voice in Canadian Writing." *Identities: The Impact of Ethnicity on Canadian Society.* Ed. Wsevolod Isajiw. Toronto: Peter Martin, 1977. 57-68.

Melançon, Benoît. "La littérature montréalaise des communautés culturelles: prolégomènes et bibliographie." Montreal: Université de Montréal, 1990.

Micone, Marco. "Écrire la culture immigrée." *Écrits du Canada français* 55 (1984): 114-19.

Monkman, Leslie. *A Native Heritage: Images of the Indian in English-Canadian Literature.* Toronto: U of Toronto P, 1981.

Mukherjee, Arun. "The Sri Lankan Poets in Canada: An Alternative View." *The Toronto South Asian Review* 3.2 (1984): 32-45.

Nepveu, Pierre. "Écritures migrantes." *L'écologie du réel: mort et naissance de la littérature québécoise contemporaine.* Montreal: Boréal, 1988. 197-210, 233-35.

Novak, Michael. "Pluralism in Humanistic Perspective." *Concepts of Ethnicity.* By William Petersen, Michael Novak, and Philip Gleason. Cambridge, MA: Belknap, 1982. 27-56.

Ó Gormghaile, Pádraig. "Une minorité ambiguë: les Irlandais du Québec vus par J. Ferron." *Études canadiennes* 21.1 (1986): 277-84.

Padolsky, Enoch. "Establishing the Two-Way Street: Literary Criticism and Ethnic Studies." *Canadian Ethnic Studies* 22.1 (1990): 22-37.

—. "Grove's 'Nationhood' and the European Immigrant." *Journal of Canadian Studies* 22.1 (1987): 32-50.

—. "The Place of Italian-Canadian Writing." *Journal of Canadian Studies* 21.4 (1986-87): 138-52.

Palmer, Howard, ed. *Immigration and the Rise of Multiculturalism.* Toronto: Copp Clark, 1975.

Pivato, Joseph. "Ethnic Writing and Comparative Canadian Literature." *Contrasts: Comparative Essays on Italian-Canadian Writing.* Ed. Joseph Pivato. Montreal: Guernica, 1985. 15-34.

Riedel, Walter, ed. *The Old World and the New: Literary Perspectives of German-Speaking Canadians.* Toronto: U of Toronto P, 1984.

Roberts, Charles G.D. *Selected Poetry and Critical Prose.* Ed. W.J. Keith. Toronto: U of Toronto P, 1974.

Rome, David. *Clouds in the Thirties: On Anti-Semitism in Canada, 1929-1939.* 13 vols. Montreal: Canadian Jewish Congress, 1979-81.

Royce, Anya Peterson. *Ethnic Identity: Strategies of Diversity.* Bloomington: Indiana UP, 1982.

Shek, Ben-Zion. "'La généreuse disparité humaine' dans l'oeuvre de Gabrielle Roy, de *Bonheur d'occasion* à *La détresse et l'enchantement.*" *Études canadiennes* 21.1 (1986): 235-44.

—. "L'image des Juifs dans le roman québécois." *Juifs et réalités juives au Québec.* Ed. Pierre Anctil and Gary Caldwell. Montreal: IQRC, 1984. 255-88.

Simon, Sherry. "The Language of Difference: Minority Writers in Quebec." *A/Part: Papers from the 1984 Ottawa Conference on Language, Culture and Literary Identity in Canada.* Ed. J.M. Bumsted. *Canadian Literature* Supp. No. 1 (1987): 119-28.

—. "Du travail et des femmes." Rev. of *Histoires d'immigrées: itinéraires d'ouvrières colombiennes, grecques, haïtiennes et portugaises de Montréal,* by Micheline Labelle et al. *Spirale* été 1987: 6.

Sirois, Antoine. "L'étranger de race et d'ethnie dans le roman québécois." *Imaginaire social et représentations collectives: mélanges offerts à Jean-Charles Falardeau.* Quebec: Les presses de l'Université Laval, 1982. 187-204.

Sollors, Werner. *Beyond Ethnicity: Consent and Descent in American Culture.* New York: Oxford UP, 1986.

Stoiciu, Gina, and Odette Brosseau. *La différence: Comment l'écrire? Comment la vivre? Communication internationale et communication interculturelle.* Montreal: Humanitas, 1989.

Sutherland, Ronald. *Second Image: Comparative Studies in Quebec/Canadian Literature.* Don Mills, ON: New, 1971.

Tougas, Gérard. *Histoire de la littérature canadienne-française.* Paris: Presses universitaires de France, 1964.

Weinfeld, Morton. "Myth and Reality in the Canadian Mosaic: 'Affective Ethnicity.'" 1981. Rpt. in *Ethnicity and Ethnic Relations in Canada.* 2nd ed. Ed. Rita M. Bienvenue and Jay E. Goldstein. Toronto: Butterworths, 1985. 65-86.

Le Postmodernisme québécois: tendances actuelles

Janet M. Paterson

Au départ fort riche et stimulant, le sujet du «postmodernisme québécois» pose d'incontournables questions d'ordre méthodologique, et a de quoi laisser perplexe. À partir de quels critères peut-on décrire ce phénomène? En dégageant les caractéristiques de certaines pratiques narratives? En interrogeant les enjeux des discours critiques? En examinant les cadres théoriques qui définissent, tant bien que mal, les problématiques postmodernes? Comment, en d'autres termes, cerner la spécificité du postmodernisme québécois?

Certes, une réponse partielle est possible. Une lecture, même rapide, de nombreux romans postmodernes québécois montre les liens étroits entre les textes et leur contexte socio-culturel. À l'encontre de la plupart des romans postmodernes français et américains, qui privilégient l'écriture du signifiant aux dépens de la représentation du réel, le roman postmoderne québécois inscrit toujours le sujet et le social dans ses stratégies discursives. Tout se passe en fait comme si les jeux des formes, des signes et des genres ne pouvaient se réaliser qu'en se greffant à une donnée référentielle qui est, d'ailleurs, souvent problématisée. Les nombreux détours des sujets énonciatifs dans les textes de Aquin, de Godbout et de Bessette, par exemple, renvoient toujours, au bout du compte, à un sujet, singulier ou collectif, qui prend son sens dans un contexte politique, culturel ou social.

Il faut aussi signaler que le discours féministe joue un rôle capital dans le postmodernisme québécois. Ce facteur est très important, car dans de nombreux autres contextes culturels, comme l'a noté Craig Owens, le postmodernisme semble exclure le féminin de ses textes littéraires, critiques et théoriques. Fécond, varié et inventif, le discours féministe québécois enrichit la facture du postmodernisme d'une forte dimension éthique. Tout en déployant les multiples stratégies de l'écriture postmoderne, de l'éclatement du langage jusqu'au mélange des genres, de la jouissance de la parole jusqu'à celle du sujet, le discours féminin remet en cause le métarécit patriarcal. Aussi la quête de nouvelles formes se conjugue-t-elle étroitement à une visée téléologique qui inscrit dans le texte même la reconnaissance de l'altérité de la femme. Ceci n'est pas sans conséquence: le discours féministe élargit ainsi considérablement la portée signifiante du postmodernisme québécois.

Pourtant, le postmodernisme québécois ne se limite pas aux seules pratiques narratives. En effet, le postmodernisme ne peut se concevoir en dehors des théories qui lui confèrent une valeur conceptuelle. L'intelligibilité de ses discours narratifs, en termes de «postmodernité,» dépend des interprétants théoriques. Par ailleurs, comme Frances Fortier l'a pertinemment signalé, la postmodernité doit également s'envisager comme une «régularité discursive qui traverse tout autant les pratiques esthétiques que le discours critique qui les examine» («Liminaire» 5). Dans le contexte québécois, il est en fait impossible de faire l'économie des discours critiques qui, en privilégiant certaines problématiques et en écartant d'autres, contribuent à définir les paramètres du postmodernisme littéraire.

C'est ainsi non pas dans un seul discours – si puissant soit-il – mais dans l'articulation réciproque des pratiques théoriques, critiques et narratives, que se dessinent les contours du postmodernisme québécois.

Théories et critiques postmodernes

Tout chercheur intéressé par le postmodernisme fait face à un champ très large de discours théoriques. Quelles théories servent de cadre de référence dans le contexte québécois? Celles de Lyotard (philosophe français), Scarpetta (critique d'art français), Baudrillard (sociologue français), Vattimo (philosophe italien), Habermas (philosophe allemand), Fokkema (critique néerlandais), Jameson (théoricien marxiste américain), Rorty (philosophe américain), Hutcheon (théoricienne anglophone) ou Kroker et Cook (critiques montréalais et torontois), pour citer les plus connus? Un cadre théorique aussi vaste entraîne inévitablement des choix et des prises de position.

Un regard sur les études consacrées au postmodernisme québécois révèle qu'elles s'inspirent de façon magistrale des théories de Lyotard (en particulier de *La Condition postmoderne*) et de Scarpetta (notamment de *L'Impureté* et de l'*Éloge du cosmopolitisme*). En effet, presque tous les articles et ouvrages critiques qui s'intéressent au sujet renvoient à ces écrits. On mentionne, ici et là, Baudrillard et Vattimo, quelquefois Hutcheon, mais rarement les théoriciens américains Jameson et Hassan dont les propos ont pourtant fait couler beaucoup d'encre dans le domaine anglo-américain. Inversement, les travaux de Scarpetta, souvent cités au Québec, sont presque inconnus aux États-Unis et au Canada anglais.

Plusieurs concepts sont utilisés pour interroger l'écriture postmoderne. À Lyotard, on emprunte surtout la notion d'incrédulité à l'égard des grands discours – on cite presque toujours sa définition: «En simplifiant à l'extrême, on tient pour "postmoderne" l'incrédulité à l'égard des métarécits» (1979: 7). On sait que, pour Lyotard, le postmodernisme représente une crise de légitimation dans laquelle les grands discours philosophiques et politiques ont perdu leur valeur d'unification. La critique utilise également la notion lyotardienne d'hétérogénéité, qui s'oppose aux notions de centre, d'homogénéité et d'unité que la société postmoderne remet en cause. Selon Lyotard, le postmoderne est essentiellement un savoir hétérogène lié à une nouvelle légitimation qui est fondée sur la reconnaissance des jeux de langage: «Le savoir postmoderne n'est pas seulement l'instrument des pouvoirs. Il raffine notre sensibilité aux différences et renforce notre capacité de supporter l'incommensurable» (1979: 8-9).

Quant à Scarpetta, il donne de précieux outils d'analyse aux chercheurs intéressés par des questions esthétiques et formelles en situant le postmodernisme dans l'impureté des formes et des contenus et dans les manifestations d'art et de pensée hybrides:

> «l'impureté» [n'est] pas seulement une dimension formelle ou stylistique, pas seulement une façon de répondre aux mythologies de «l'art pur» par le mélange des genres, ou d'assumer qu'aucun code ne soit jamais naturel [...], l'impureté, si l'on veut, c'est aussi quelque chose qui touche à la façon de penser, à l'idéologie. (Scarpetta 1985: 307)

Enfin, on se reporte également à Scarpetta pour étudier le phénomène très actuel du cosmopolitisme: «On définira volontiers "l'écriture" comme une traversée des frontières, comme migration et exil» (Scarpetta 1981: 183).

Le discours postmoderne québécois est ainsi marqué par un lien étroit avec la pensée française, à la différence des postmodernismes américain et canadien-anglais, fortement influencés par les écrits de Jameson, Hassan et Hutcheon. En plus, il fait montre d'une attitude critique sensiblement différente de celle qui se manifeste, depuis trente ans, au Canada anglais et aux États-Unis.

Sans entreprendre une comparaison très poussée, signalons tout d'abord que l'inflation qui caractérise le discours critique anglo-américain est absente du domaine québécois. En comparaison des centaines de textes publiés par les Anglo-Américains,[1] les études consacrées au postmodernisme au Québec demeurent à ce jour assez peu nombreuses. Qui plus est, la manière de penser le postmodernisme et le rapport de la critique à cette notion ne sont pas du tout les mêmes.

Pour nous en convaincre, remarquons que les polémiques, les conflits et les querelles qui ne cessent de se manifester chez les théoriciens et les critiques anglophones sont rares dans le contexte québécois. Chez les anglophones, on peut dailleurs s'étonner de la virulence de certains débats: on accuse le postmodernisme de tous les excès, le disant tour à tour frivole, insensé, dénué d'idées, bourgeois, capitaliste, narcissique, prétentieux, excessif, peu rentable, anti–humaniste, anti-historique, élitiste, schizo-phrénique.[2] «Everything testifies to the insanity of postmodernism,» dira John O'Neill, sociologue torontois (72).

Dans la critique québécoise, le concept n'a pas suscité de telles polémiques et n'a pas donné lieu, jusqu'ici, à de véritables conflits intel-lectuels. L'orientation des discussions est, à vrai dire, fort différente. La cri-tique québécoise s'intéresse très peu, par exemple, à la question de périodisation étudiée par les Anglo-Américains qui, pour leur part, se penchent souvent sur la différence entre le «modernism» et le «postmod-ernism» et sur la relation qu'entretiennent les deux mouvements.[3] Mais il n'est pas surprenant que ce débat soit absent du domaine québécois où les termes «moderne» et «modernité» semblent échapper à toute tentative de définition. D'autre part, le concept même de postmodernisme ne représente pas un enjeu philosophique et idéologique majeur pour la cri-tique québécoise. Sont également écartées du contexte québécois les dis-cussions, en grande partie suscitées par Jameson, sur l'aspect capitaliste du postmodernisme. Enfin, on ne trouvera pas non plus d'étude dont la finalité serait de savoir si les romans d'un auteur particulier sont, ou ne sont pas, postmodernes (ce genre de questionnement vise surtout les ouvrages de Beckett, Robbe-Grillet et Joyce[4]).

Si les débats consacrés aux postmodernismes québécois et anglo-améri-cain se distinguent au niveau de leur intensité, s'ils se démarquent par leur contenu, cela tient, sans doute, aux relations qu'entretiennent les critiques avec la notion de postmodernisme. À l'encontre des Anglo-Américains, la critique québécoise utilise le mot «postmodernisme» avec une certaine distance qui n'est pas sans rappeler l'attitude de Scarpetta: «Il ne [s']agit] pas [...] d'adhérer au terme, mais de s'en servir légèrement, à distance, presque allusivement» (1985: 18). Par ailleurs, peu intéressée par les querelles sur le sens philosophique et la valeur idéologique du terme (à moins que celle-ci ne soit contextuelle), cette critique s'oriente plutôt vers l'étude des textes littéraires. Utilisant le mot comme tremplin ou comme catalyseur, elle veut surtout interroger des pratiques textuelles ou aborder des pro-blématiques inédites. C'est sans doute dans cette démarche que s'affirme le plus visiblement la différence: à une herméneutique du concept, souvent pratiquée par les anglophones, la critique québécoise préfère une her-méneutique des textes.

Aussi assiste-t-on, de toutes parts, à des analyses qui témoignent d'un désir de lire et de relire certains romans à la lumière du phénomène post-moderne. S'inspirant de Lyotard et de Scarpetta – tout en juxtaposant librement leurs idées à celles d'autres penseurs – les chercheurs ouvrent de nouvelles voies d'interrogation en examinant des pratiques narratives dans un vaste contexte culturel, social et littéraire. Point de grands discours au sujet du postmodernisme, point de querelles sur les positions idéologiques, mais plutôt une recherche orientée vers l'interprétation des textes et des «moments» postmodernes.

Il se peut d'ailleurs que ce soit l'absence même de polémique autour du concept de postmodernisme – absence comblée, d'un autre côté, par la richesse des pratiques narratives – qui ait permis, comme nous le verrons maintenant, un développement critique très fécond.

Les axes d'interrogation

La critique littéraire mène un travail de reconnaissance et de définition du fait postmoderne en privilégiant certains axes d'interrogation. Comme Fortier l'a souligné, ce travail se caractérise par trois lieux argumentatifs:

> un consensus sur l'existence d'une pratique postmoderne sur la foi de critères formels, un rapport à la réalité qui tend à une appréhension globale du phénomène et, enfin, une position énonciative complice qui participe activement à la création d'un espace d'interprétation. («Archéologie d'une postmodernité» 30)

Par le biais d'une participation effectivement complice, la critique québécoise propose des lectures et des relectures de textes postmodernes selon six axes principaux.

1) L'aspect formel du postmodernisme littéraire représente un champ d'analyse très fertile. L'intertextualité, le mélange des genres, les mutations au niveau de l'énonciation (l'affirmation du «je» mais en même temps sa fragmentation), l'autoreprésentation et les jeux de langage – toutes ces stratégies ont fait l'objet d'analyses fines et détaillées. Cet intérêt n'est pas surprenant, car les théories structuralistes et post-structuralistes qui ont nourri la critique depuis plus de vingt ans se prêtent facilement à la mise au jour des mécanismes complexes de l'écriture postmoderne.

Par ailleurs, dotée d'une fonction conceptuelle, la notion de postmo-dernisme permet de situer l'analyse des instances textuelles dans un cadre qui s'ouvre à de multiples problématisations. Dans ce contexte, on peut citer les articles qu'Amaryll Chanady, Marie-Claire Ropars-Wuilleumier et Sylvia Söderlind (1984) consacrent aux romans de Aquin, l'analyse de l'écriture poulinienne entreprise par Ginette Michaud, celle de Max Roy portant sur les stratégies de lecture dans la fiction et mon examen de différentes pratiques discursives dans plusieurs romans québécois (1993). Récemment, André Lamontagne a élargi, de façon importante, le cadre des analyses formelles en examinant la poétique intertextuelle dans les romans de Aquin à la lumière du postmodernisme.

On perçoit aisément un croisement théorique, critique et romanesque dans ces études: la notion lyotardienne de remise en question des grands récits et les notions scarpétiennes d'hybride et d'impureté des formes s'allient facilement, tout naturellement même, aux intérêts des critiques formalistes. Et comme si le postmodernisme était à même de nous dire «l'air du temps» littéraire, un grand nombre de romans écrits au Québec depuis le début des années soixante se caractérisent par une expérimentation formelle très poussée, par exemple, les romans de Aquin et de Godbout, *Le Désert mauve* de Brossard, *L'Avalée des avalés* de Ducharme, *Les Anthropoïdes* de Bessette, *Le Nombril* de La Rocque, *La Vie en prose* de Villemaire et *L'Euguélionne* de Bersianik.

2) Depuis quelques années, plusieurs discours postmodernes évoquent la notion paradoxale de la «fin de l'Histoire.» Loin de faire l'objet d'un consensus, cette notion se prête à des interprétations différentes. Certains théoriciens, comme Baudrillard, perçoivent la fin de l'Histoire en fonction d'une amnésie qui est en train d'effacer la conscience collective:

> C'est que nous sommes en train, dans une sorte de travail de deuil enthousiaste, de ravaler tous les événements marquants de ce siècle, de le *blanchir*, comme si tout ce qui s'était passé là (les révolutions, la partition du monde, l'extermination, la trans-nationalité violente des États, le suspense nucléaire) bref l'Histoire dans sa phase moderne n'était qu'un imbroglio sans issue. (Baudrillard 103-04)

Par contre, pour Barthes, Lyotard et Paul Veyne, c'est la question non pas de la fin, mais de la *légitimation* de l'Histoire comme récit véridique, objectif et scientifique, qui fait l'objet de sérieuses interrogations. Le statut cognitif du discours historique est remis en question de même que la spécificité de son écriture. Ces théoriciens démontrent que le discours de l'Histoire est non pas hégémonique et totalisant, mais subjectif, limité et soumis aux contraintes de la narration.

Dans un mouvement parallèle, de nombreux romans québécois problématisent le grand discours de l'Histoire pour en montrer les lacunes et les failles. Mentionnons pour mémoire *La Maison Trestler* (Ouellette-Michalska), *Les Têtes à Papineau* et *Une histoire américaine* (Godbout), *Volkswagen Blues* (Poulin), *La Tribu* (Barcelo), *Monsieur Melville: dans les aveilles de Moby Dick* (Victor-Lévy Beaulieu) et *Christophe Colomb: naufrage sur les côtes du Paradis* (Georges-Hébert Germain). En contestant un de nos grands savoirs, ces romans ajoutent une perspective importante à la dimension épistémologique de la fiction postmoderne.

Quant aux discours critiques, ils s'attachent soit à souligner les stratégies textuelles de la mise en procès de l'Histoire − par exemple, l'essai de Caroline Bayard, mon étude (1993: 53-66) et celle de Jane Moss consacrées à *La Maison Trestler* − ou bien à ouvrir les champs d'interrogation en reliant

JANET M. PATERSON

l'historiographie postmoderne au postcolonialisme – notamment dans les articles d'Eva-Marie Kröller et de Marie Vautier et dans l'ouvrage de Sylvia Söderlind (1991).

3) Si, comme nous l'avons vu plus haut, les écrivaines féministes jouent un rôle capital dans le postmodernisme québécois, il n'est pas étonnant que plusieurs études critiques interrogent, explicitement ou implicitement, la relation du postmodernisme au féminisme. Ces deux champs partagent-ils la même vision philosophique? Les traits d'écriture sont-ils les mêmes dans l'un comme dans l'autre? Est-ce vrai comme l'a soutenu récemment, Kate Taylor, journaliste torontoise, que le féminisme représente un des piliers du postmodernisme?

Depuis plusieurs années, ces questions – et beaucoup d'autres – ont fait l'objet d'études stimulantes de la part de Dupré, Godard, Gould Potvin et Smart. Récemment, toutefois, est paru un volume entier consacré à ce sujet: *Les Discours féminins dans la littérature postmoderne au Québec*, édité par Raïja Koski, Kathleen Kells et Louise Forsyth. Issu d'un colloque qui a eu lieu à l'Université de Western Ontario en novembre 1989, ce volume ouvre des débats passionnants sur différents aspects du féminisme postmoderne. On y trouve des points de vue variés, voire opposés, sur la question des rapports entre le postmodernisme et le féminisme. Ne pouvant entrer ici dans les détails, je signale tout simplement que certains critiques voient des jonctions et des intersections alors que d'autres perçoivent surtout les différences incontournables.

Par ailleurs, plusieurs articles élargissent de façon significative le corpus postmoderne québécois en examinant différents genres, en particulier le journal intime, le théâtre et la traduction. D'autres intègrent à ce courant des textes rarement considérés postmodernes, comme les oeuvres de Line McMurray et de Jovette Marchessault. Enfin, plusieurs articles étudient les stratégies subversives de l'écriture féminine postmoderne. Par la pluralité de leurs points de vue, les études critiques font écho aux multiples interrogations mises en place dans les textes de fiction tels *Le Désert mauve*, *La Vie en prose*, *La Maison Trestler*, *Le Pique-nique sur l'Acropole*, *La Main tranchante du symbole* et *Copies conformes*. Mais souvent les frontières entre les textes fictifs, critiques et théoriques s'estompent pour créer l'espace d'un nouveau discours – hétérogène, indéterminé, exploratoire.

4) Pour d'aucuns, la postmodernité se rattache moins à une esthétique plurielle et à une revendication des «petits récits,» historiques ou féministes, qu'à des images et des thématiques de décadence, de ruine et de mort. Influencés par la pensée nihiliste de Nietzsche, plusieurs théoriciens et critiques littéraires – tels Baudrillard, Kroker et Cook et Pierre Nepveu – mettent de l'avant une conception essentiellement apocalyptique du postmodernisme. Baudrillard, par exemple, souligne les apories et les échecs de la libération des systèmes contemporains – l'art, la politique, la

sexualité et la communication:

> Aujourd'hui, tout est libéré, les jeux sont faits, et nous nous retrouvons collectivement devant la question cruciale: QUE FAIRE APRÈS L'ORGIE?
> Nous ne pouvons plus que simuler l'orgie et la libération, faire semblant d'aller dans le même sens en accélérant, mais en réalité nous accélérons dans le vide.... (11)

Dans le même ordre d'idées, en ayant recours aux notions de catastrophe, d'étrangeté et d'exil, Nepveu demande: y a-t-il une fin de la littérature québécoise (14)? En d'autres termes: le postmodernisme artistique représente-t-il le crépuscule de l'art et de l'humanité? L'enjeu de cette interrogation est énorme: dépassant le cadre des remises en question des métarécits et des expérimentations formelles, il atteint le coeur même de la réflexion philosophique sur la postmodernité.

Jusqu'à ce jour, peu d'études se sont penchées sur cette question, à part celle, d'envergure, de Nepveu et mon analyse du *Désert mauve* (1993). Par contre, à l'instar de Christian Mistral, plusieurs romanciers s'attachent à décrire «une civilisation qui s'écroule dans la poussière et l'indifférence» (Mistral, *Vamp* 158), comme Brossard dans *Le Désert mauve*, Ducharme dans *Dévadé* et Baillie dans *La Nuit de la Saint-Basile*.

5) La science-fiction peut-elle être postmoderne? Voilà la question que pose Jean-Pierre April (1992) en examinant trois anthologies de nouvelles représentatives des années 1980.[5] Il montre, de façon très convaincante, que la science-fiction contemporaine se caractérise pas son postmodernisme. On y trouve les thèmes analogues à ceux des romans postmodernes, soit la réécriture de l'Histoire et la contestation du pouvoir. Quant aux stratégies discursives, April révèle qu'elles sont les mêmes que dans les romans, à savoir, discontinuité, citation, multiplication des voix narratives, fragmentation et ironie.

Pour conclure, April, qui est lui-même auteur de récits postmodernes,[6] soutient que, loin de s'inscrire tout simplement dans le cadre de l'esthétique postmoderne, la science-fiction y apporte une dimension nouvelle:

> il m'apparaît évident que la SF, avec ses artefacts, ses carnavals, ses simulacres et ses oxymorons, avec ses gadgets composites [...], avec ses êtres bio-cybernétiques et ses nombreux paradigmes hétérogènes, donne un élan vigoureux et une dimension nouvelle à l'hybridation typique du postmodernisme. («Post-SF» 109-10)

6) Depuis peu, un nouveau domaine se développe dans le territoire postmoderne québécois, celui de l'hétérogène, du métissage et de l'altérité.

Ce domaine correspond à une nouvelle réalité sociale (comme le démontre, entre autres, Sherry Simon), qui se caractérise par la mutation d'une identité collective homogène à une conception plus problématique et hétérogène de la culture. Or, à partir des notions d'hétérogénéité, de multiplicité, de valorisation de la marge et de revendication des petits ré-cits, le postmodernisme offre un cadre à la fois riche et souple pour interroger l'inscription de cette diversité culturelle dans la littérature. Les études critiques dans ce domaine sont stimulantes, originales et variées: de l'extra-territorialité examinée par Simon Harel à l'identitaire pluriel étudié par Sherry Simon en passant par l'hétérogène romanesque mis au jour par Pierre L'Hérault. Plusieurs romans postmodernes explorent différentes formes d'hétérogénéité (identitaire, raciale et sexuelle), par exemple, *Trou de mémoire, Une histoire américaine, Le Désert mauve* et *Volkswagen Blues*.

Conclusion

Au terme de ce rapide parcours, quelques observations s'imposent. Polysémique, le concept de postmoderne, dont on peut facilement déceler les failles et les pièges, s'avère un outil de travail extrêmement fécond, sans doute, parce qu'il relève, à la fois, des champs esthétique et philosophique. Perçu comme une pratique discursive, le postmoderne pose de passionnants problèmes d'analyse et d'interprétation au niveau des stratégies textuelles, en particulier, l'énonciation fragmentée, l'intertextualité hétéroclite, la discontinuité narrative et le mélange des genres. Nourri par des théories philosophiques, il ouvre la lecture à la problématisation du sens dans de vastes contextes socio-culturels en s'attachant, entre autres, aux questions du sujet féminin, de l'identitaire, de la légitimation et du savoir.

Par ailleurs, il est intéressant de noter que la critique québécoise du postmodernisme n'est pas, à vrai dire, postmoderne. Se réclamant de certaines théories structuralistes et adoptant des méthodologies cohérentes, elle est, pour reprendre l'expression de Robert Dion, «moderne.» En effet, comme le signale Dion, elle demeure «attachée à une rigueur ennemie de tout éclectisme (trop) apparent» (98). En d'autres termes, si la critique québécoise accepte allégrement l'aspect hétérogène et éclaté de l'écriture postmoderne, elle n'en mime pas pour autant la pratique discursive. Pour être véritablement postmoderne, il faudrait qu'elle s'inscrive dans le courant de la déconstruction inspirée par Derrida et De Man. Or ce mouvement, pratiqué surtout aux États-Unis et au Canada anglais, a très peu influencé la critique québécoise.

Enfin, pour qui s'intéresse aux connexions du postmodernisme québécois, le moment est sans doute venu de détourner les regards des discours américains et français pour examiner de nouveaux horizons. Ils s'en dessinent actuellement en Chine, en Slovaquie et en Hongrie[7] où, à l'instar du phénomène québécois, le postmodernisme représente moins une nouvelle *doxa* qu'un espace multiple et ouvert de réflexion et d'interprétation.

Notes

1   Voir la bibliographie d'Hélène Volat-Shapiro.
2   Voir, par exemple, les articles de Donald Kuspit et John O'Neill.
3   Voir, par exemple, David Antin et Harry R. Garvin. Dans le domaine québécois, Pierre Milot a examiné le postmodernisme en fonction des textes de la *Nouvelle Barre du jour* et des *Herbes rouges*.
4   Voir, par exemple, l'article de Breon Mitchell.
5   *Dix nouvelles de science-fiction québécoise, SF: dix années de science-fiction québécoise* et *Anthologie de la science-fiction québécoise contemporaine*.
6   Voir surtout «Coma-123, automatexte» dans *Chocs baroques* 305-33.
7   Voir l'article de Wang Ning, la revue *Slovenska Literatura* et le livre de Petho Bertalan.

Références

Études critiques et théoriques

Antin, David. «Modernism and Postmodernism.» *Boundary 2* 1 (1972): 98-133.
April, Jean-Pierre. «Post-SF: du post-modernisme dans la science-fiction québécoise des années 80.» *Imagine* 61 (1992): 75-118.
Barthes, Roland. «Le Discours de l'histoire.» *Le Bruissement de la langue*. Paris: Seuil, 1984. 61-67.
Baudrillard, Jean. *La Transparence du Mal: essai sur les phénomènes extrêmes*. Paris: Galilée, 1990.
Bayard, Caroline. *The New Poetics in Canada and Quebec: From Concretism to Post-Modernism*. Toronto: U of Toronto P, 1989.
Bertalan, Petho. *A Posztmodern*. Budapest: Gondolat, 1992.
Chanady, Amaryll. «Autoreprésentation, autoréférence et spécularité: le narcissisme libérateur de *Trou de mémoire*.» *Revue de l'Université d'Ottawa* 57.2 (1987): 55-67.
—. «Entre la quête et la métalittérature: Aquin et Cortázar comme représentants du postmoderne excentrique.» *Voix et images* 12 (1986-87): 42-53.
Dion, Robert. «Une critique du postmoderne.» *Tangence* 39 (1993): 89-101.
Dupré, Louise. *Stratégies du vertige*. Montréal: Remue-ménage, 1989.
Fokkema, Douwe W. *Literary History, Modernism, and Postmodernism*. Amsterdam et Philadelphia: John Benjamins, 1984.
Fortier, Frances. «Archéologie d'une postmodernité.» *Tangence* 39 (1993): 21-36.
—. «Liminaire.» *Tangence* 39 (1993): 5-6.

Garvin, Harry R., éd. *Romanticism, Modernism, Postmodernism*. Lewisburg, PA: Bucknell UP, 1980.

Godard, Barbara. «Re: post.» *Québec Studies* 9 (1989-90): 131-43.

Gould, Karen. «Féminisme, postmodernité, esthétique de lecture: *Le Désert mauve* de Nicole Brossard.» *Le Roman québécois depuis 1960*. Éd. Louise Milot et Jaap Lintvelt. Sainte-Foy, PQ: Les Presses de l'Université Laval, 1992. 195-213.

Habermas, Jürgen. «La Modernité: un projet inachevé.» *Critique* 37 (1981): 950-67.

Harel, Simon. *Le Voleur de parcours: identité et cosmopolitisme dans la littérature québécoise contemporaine*. Montréal: Préambule, 1989.

Hassan, Ihab. *The Dismemberment of Orpheus: Toward a Postmodern Literature*. 2e éd. Madison: U of Wisconsin P, 1982.

—. *The Postmodern Turn: Essays in Postmodern Theory and Culture*. Columbus: Ohio State UP, 1987.

Hutcheon, Linda. *The Canadian Postmodern: A Study of Contemporary English-Canadian Fiction*. Toronto: Oxford UP, 1988.

—. *A Poetics of Postmodernism: History, Theory, Fiction*. London et New York: Routledge, 1988.

—. *The Politics of Postmodernism*. London et New York: Routledge, 1989.

Jameson, Fredric. «Postmodernism, or the Cultural Logic of Late Capitalism.» *New Left Review* 146 (1984): 53-92.

Koski, Raïja, Kathleen Kells et Louise Forsyth, éds. *Les Discours féminins dans la littérature postmoderne au Québec*. San Francisco: Mellen Research UP, 1993.

Kroker, Arthur et David Cook. *The Postmodern Scene: Excremental Culture and Hyper-Aesthetics*. Montréal: New World Perspectives, 1986.

Kröller, Eva-Marie. «Postmodernism, Colony, Nation: The Melvillean Texts of Bowering and Beaulieu.» *Revue de l'Université d'Ottawa* 54.2 (1984): 53-61.

Kuspit, Donald. «The Contradictory Character of Postmodernism.» *Postmodernism: Philosophy and the Arts*. Éd. Hugh J. Silverman. London et New York: Routledge, 1990. 53-68.

Lamontagne, André. *Les Mots des autres*. Sainte-Foy, PQ: Les Presses de l'Université Laval, 1992.

L'Hérault, Pierre. «Pour une cartographie de l'hétérogène: dérives identitaires des années 1980.» *Fictions de l'identitaire au Québec*. Par Sherry Simon, Pierre L'Hérault, Robert Schwartzwald et Alexis Nouss. Montréal: XYZ, 1991. 53-114.

Lyotard, Jean-François. *La Condition postmoderne: rapport sur le savoir*. Paris: Minuit, 1979.

—. *Le Postmoderne expliqué aux enfants*. Paris: Galilée, 1986.

Michaud, Ginette. «Récits postmodernes?» *Études françaises* 21.3 (1985-86): 67-88.

Milot, Pierre. *La Camera obscura du postmodernisme*. Montréal: L'Hexagone, 1988.

Mitchell, Breon. «Samuel Beckett and the Postmodernism Controversy.» *Exploring Postmodernism*. Éd. Matei Calinescu et Douwe Fokkema. Amsterdam et Philadelphia: John Benjamins, 1987. 109-21.

Moss, Jane. «A House Divided: Power Relations in Madeleine Ouellette-Michalska's *La Maison Trestler*.» *Québec Studies* 12 (1991): 59-65.

Nepveu, Pierre. *L'Écologie du réel: mort et naissance de la littérature québécoise contemporaine*. Montréal: Boréal, 1988.

O'Neill, John. «Postmodernism and (Post)Marxism.» *Postmodernism: Philosophy and the Arts*. Éd. Hugh J. Silverman. London et New York: Routledge, 1990. 69-79.

Owens, Craig. «The Discourse of Others: Feminists and Postmodernism.» *The Anti-Aesthetic: Essays on Postmodern Culture*. Éd. Hal Foster. Port Townsend, WA: Bay, 1983. 57-82.

Paterson, Janet M. *Moments postmodernes dans le roman québécois*. 2e éd. Ottawa: Les Presses de l'Université d'Ottawa, 1993.

—. «Postmodernisme et féminisme: où sont les jonctions?» *Les Discours féminins dans la littérature postmoderne au Québec*. Éd. Raïja Koski, Kathleen Kells et Louise Forsyth. San Francisco: Mellen Research UP, 1993. 27-44.

Potvin, Claudine. «Féminisme et postmodernisme: *La Main tranchante du symbole*.» *Voix et images* 49 (1991): 66-74.

Ropars-Wuilleumier, Marie-Claire. «Le Spectateur masqué: étude sur le simulacre filmique dans l'écriture d'Hubert Aquin.» *Revue de l'Université d'Ottawa* 57.2 (1987): 79-95.

Rorty, Richard. «Habermas, Lyotard et la postmodernité.» *Critique* 40 (1984): 181-97.

Roy, Max. «Stratégies de lecture dans le roman contemporain.» *Tangence* 39 (1993): 76-88.

Scarpetta, Guy. *Éloge du cosmopolitisme*. Paris: Grasset, 1981.

—. *L'Impureté*. Paris: Grasset, 1985.

Simon, Sherry. «Espaces incertains de la culture.» *Fictions de l'identitaire au Québec*. Par Sherry Simon, Pierre L'Hérault, Robert Schwartzwald et Alexis Nouss. Montréal: XYZ, 1991. 3-52.

Slovenska Literatura 37.6 (1990).

Smart, Patricia. «Postmodern Male Narratives.» *Québec Studies* 9 (1989-90): 146-50.

Söderlind, Sylvia. «Hubert Aquin et le mystère de l'anamorphose.» *Voix et images* 9.3 (1984): 103-11.

—. *Margin/Alias: Language and Colonization in Canadian and Québécois Fiction*. Toronto: U of Toronto P, 1991.

Taylor, Kate. «A Pillar of Postmodernism.» *The Globe and Mail* [Toronto] 24 déc. 1992: C1.

Vautier, Marie. «Le Mythe postmoderne dans quelques romans historiographiques québécois.» *Québec Studies* 12 (1991): 49-57.

—. «La Révision postcoloniale de l'Histoire et l'exemple réaliste magique de François Barcelo.» *Studies in Canadian Literature* 16.2 (1992): 39-53. ·

Vattimo, Gianni. *La Fin de la modernité*. Trad. Charles Alunni. Paris: Seuil, 1987.

Veyne, Paul. *Comment on écrit l'histoire*. Texte abrégé. Paris: Seuil, 1979.

Volat-Shapiro, Hélène. «Bibliography.» *Postmodernism: Philosophy and the Arts*. Éd.

Hugh J. Silverman. London et New York: Routledge, 1990. 300-14.

Wang Ning. «Reception and Metamorphosis: Post-Modernity in Contemporary Avant-Garde Fiction.» *Social Sciences in China* 19.1 (1993): 5-13.

Romans et nouvelles

April, Jean-Pierre. *Chocs baroques*. Montréal: Fides, 1991.

Aquin, Hubert. *Trou de mémoire*. Montréal: Le Cercle du livre de France, 1968.

Baille, Robert. *La Nuit de la Saint-Basile*. Montréal: L'Hexagone, 1991.

Barcelo, François. *La Tribu*. Montréal: Libre Expression, 1981.

Beaulieu, Victor-Lévy. *Monsieur Melville: dans les aveilles de Moby Dick*. Montréal: VLB Éditeur, 1978.

Bersianik, Louky. *L'Euguélionne*. Montréal: La Presse, 1976.

—. *La Main tranchante du symbole: textes et essais féministes*. Montréal: Remue-ménage, 1990.

—. *Le Pique-nique sur l'Acropole: cahiers d'Ancyl*. Montréal: VLB Éditeur, 1979.

Bessette, Gérard. *Les Anthropoïdes*. Montréal: La Presse, 1977.

—. *Le Semestre*. Montréal: Québec-Amérique, 1979.

Brossard, Nicole. *Le Désert mauve*. Montréal: L'Hexagone, 1987.

Carpentier, André, éd. *Dix nouvelles de science-fiction québécoise*. Montréal: Quinze, 1985.

Ducharme, Réjean. *L'Avalée des avalés*. Paris: Gallimard, 1966.

—. *Dévadé*. Paris/Montréal: Gallimard/Lacombe, 1990.

Germain, Georges-Hébert. *Christophe Colomb: naufrage sur les côtes du Paradis*. Montréal: Québec-Amérique, 1991.

Godbout, Jacques. *D'Amour, P.Q.* Montréal/Paris: Hurtubise-HMH/Seuil, 1972.

—. *Les Têtes à Papineau*. Paris, Seuil, 1981.

—. *Une histoire américaine*. Paris: Seuil, 1986.

Gouavic, Jean-Marc, éd. *SF: dix années de science-fiction québécoise*. Montréal: Logiques, 1988.

La Rocque, Gilbert. *Le Nombril*. Montréal: Éditions du Jour, 1970.

Larue, Monique. *Copies conformes*. Montréal: Lacombe, 1989.

Lord, Michel, éd. *Anthologie de la science-fiction québécoise contemporaine*. Montréal: Fides, 1988.

Mistral, Christian. *Vamp*. Montréal: Québec-Amérique, 1988.

Ouellette-Michalska, Madeleine. *La Maison Trestler ou le 8e jour d'Amérique*. Montréal: Québec-Amérique, 1984.

Poulin, Jacques. *Volkswagen Blues*. Montréal: Québec-Amérique, 1984.

Villemaire, Yolande. *La Vie en prose*. Montréal: Les Herbes rouges, 1980.

Women in the Shadows:
Reclaiming a Métis Heritage

Christine Welsh

> As with any generation
> the oral tradition depends upon each person
> listening and remembering a portion
> and it is together –
> all of us remembering what we have heard together –
> that creates the whole story
> the long story of the people.
>
> I remember only a small part.
> But this is what I remember.[1]

From the air, the Qu'Appelle Valley of southern Saskatchewan is an aberration, a great green gash that slices crookedly across a precise geometric patchwork of yellow wheat fields and brown summer fallow. The muddy stream that snakes across its flat bottom widens here and there to form broad shallow lakes, creating an oasis of cool greenery in an arid and treeless plain. Before the coming of the Europeans, the valley provided a welcome haven for aboriginal people and the wildlife upon which they depended, and at the height of the fur trade it formed an important link in the system of waterways and cart-trails that began at the forks of the Red and Assiniboine Rivers and ran west and north to Fort Edmonton and south to the Cypress Hills and Montana. It was here, in the late 1860s, that Métis[2] buffalo hunters from Red River, in pursuit of the great herds that were being pushed farther and farther west, established temporary winter camps that would eventually become the permanent settlement of Lebret.

My great-grandparents were among those first Métis families from Red River who set up camp down on the flats beside Mission Lake where the village of Lebret now stands. As long as the buffalo were plentiful they continued to live from the hunt, wintering in the Cypress Hills and returning to Lebret each summer to sell their buffalo robes, meat, and pemmican at the Hudson's Bay Company post at Fort Qu'Appelle. With the disappearance of the buffalo they no longer wintered out on the plains, choosing to remain at Lebret and earn their living by trading, freighting, farming, and ranching. They are buried there beside the lake

among their kinfolk, and the names on the headstones in that little cemetery – Blondeau, Delorme, Desjarlais, LaRocque, Ouellette, Pelletier, and
many more – bear silent witness to the diaspora of the Red River Métis.

Of course the word Métis meant nothing to me when, as a child, I
accompanied my parents and grandparents and brother and sisters on our
annual mid-summer pilgrimage to Lebret. We all piled into my father's car
and made the trip out to the valley in a state of great excitement. The
saskatoons would be ripe, and there were always plenty of berries to pick
in the deep gullies of the valley – not to mention the milkshakes we'd have
at the Valley Café in Fort Qu'Appelle before we started back to the city.
But first there was the obligatory climb to the little white chapel that
perched high above Lebret, a hot dusty trek up a narrow trail cut straight
into the side of the hill and marked at intervals by towering white crosses
signifying the Stations of the Cross that could be seen for miles up and
down the valley. The chapel was invariably locked in a futile attempt to
discourage vandals, so after catching our breath we made our descent, slid-
ing and scrambling, grabbing tufts of sagebrush to break our fall. After that
there was a visit to the big stone church down on the flats beside the lake,
and then a tour of the graveyard during which my grandmother prayed
for all our relatives, both living and dead. I can still remember the taste of
the berries and the milkshakes, and the smell of dust, sagebrush, and
incense. And I still remember those headstones with all the strange-sound-
ing names. "French," my grandmother said. "French." That was all.

I don't know when I first realized that amongst those ghostly relatives
there was Indian blood. It was something that just seemed to seep into my
consciousness through my pores. I remember my bewilderment when the
other children in my mostly white, working-class school began to call me
"neechi" on the playground. I had never heard the word before and was
blissfully ignorant of its meaning; it was only later that I came to understand that to them it meant "dirty Indian." Snippets of family mythology
reinforced my growing sense that this was something to be ashamed of –
especially the story of how my other, eastern grandmother had not wanted
my mother to marry my father because he was Native.

By the time I was in high school I had invented an exotic ethnicity to
explain my black hair and brown skin and I successfully masqueraded as
French or even Hawaiian, depending on who asked. But I lived in mortal
terror that the truth would get out. Then, in 1969, Prime Minister Pierre
Trudeau came to Regina to dedicate a monument to Louis Riel. All the
other girls in my grade ten class took advantage of a perfect autumn day
and skipped classes to attend the ceremonies. I decided not to go with
them and afterward, much to my horror, was commended by the teacher
in front of the whole class for behaviour which he deemed to be exem-

plary – given the fact, he said, that I was the only one who could claim a legitimate right to attend such an observance by virtue of my ancestry. This oblique reference went right over the heads of most of my classmates, but my cheeks still burned with the knowledge that I had been found out. It was no use; no matter how hard I tried to hide it, my Native background seemed to be written all over me.

The 1960s gave rise to a new pride in Native identity among Native people across Canada, and even though I had no contact with other Native people I was swept up by the spirit of the times and began to feel that it was no longer necessary to try to hide who I was. But the question remained: who was I? By the time I reached university in the early 1970s, denial of my Native ancestry had given way to a burning need to know. My curiosity was fuelled by the discovery of a much-worn volume entitled *The Last Buffalo Hunter*, a biography of my great-grandfather, Norbert Welsh, which had been written in the 1930s and rescued by my mother from a second-hand bookshop. I revelled in the references to Norbert's Indian mother and his part-Indian wife, but they were shadowy figures – half-formed, incomplete – who seemed to inhabit only the margins of Norbert's story. And though I was clearly interested in tearing away the shroud of mystery that seemed to surround them, my attempts were largely futile. Whenever I tried to raise the subject, strenuous attempts were made, especially by my grandmother, to diminish and deny any connection we might have to Native people. She actively discouraged my burgeoning interest in things Indian; we were very different from them, she implied, and such associations would only bring me grief.

Despite my grandmother's dire predictions, I was increasingly drawn to Indian people by my desperate need to find out who I was and where I belonged. I spent much of the next fifteen years travelling to Indian communities across Canada, making documentary films on issues of concern to Native people. The work was enormously satisfying and rewarding, but my personal goal remained elusive. Even though I made every effort to fit into Indian society I was continually made aware that here, too, I was an outsider – this time because I was too "white." I learned the hard way that one who swims between cultures can get stranded, cut off from either shore; I found myself adrift in a treacherous current of confusion, self-loathing, and despair, and I began to wonder if perhaps my grandmother had been right after all.

I saw very little of my grandmother during those years. I was living in Toronto, she was in Regina, and our contact consisted of occasional letters and brief visits once or twice a year. But the passage of time and my own lonely struggle to try to understand and come to terms with my

Native heritage gradually led me to see her in a whole new light. Whereas in my youth I had felt nothing but contempt for the values that had led her to deny her Native heritage, I now began to feel a genuine bond of compassion and respect for this formidable old woman who seemed to shrink and grow more fragile with each passing season. I was acutely aware that just as we were getting to know each other we would soon be separated for good. She was my only living connection with my past, my only hope of finding out who I really was, and so despite her reluctance to talk about the past I kept asking my questions. While she continued to steadfastly maintain the distinctions between our family and other Native people, she must have had some sense of how important these questions were to me for she began to try to give me some answers. We spent hours poring over old family photographs, putting names and faces to those ghostly ancestors who had haunted my childhood. And then, quite suddenly, she died.

I was uncomfortably pregnant with my first child and was unable to undertake the journey from Toronto to Regina for my grandmother's funeral, but I was there in spirit as she made the trip out to the Qu'Appelle Valley for the last time and was laid to rest in the little cemetery on the flats down by the lake. She never saw my son, Daniel; he was born a few months after she died. Somehow those two events marked a turning point for me. I was determined that my child was not going to grow up as I had, cut off from his past. But how could I give him a sense of who he was and where he came from if I didn't know myself? And with my grandmother gone, how would I ever find out? The only thing she left me was a child's sampler, mounted in a faded quilt frame, which had been embroidered by my great-grandmother and bore her name: *Maggie Hogue*.

I put my great-grandmother's sampler up on the wall in my kitchen, but with the demands of being a new mother I scarcely gave it a moment's thought during the months that followed. I had returned to university and was pursuing my deepening interest in Native history by studying the recent work that had been done on the role of Native women in the North American fur trade. For almost 200 years, beginning with the founding of the Hudson's Bay Company in 1670, the fur trade dominated the history of what is now eastern Canada. I learned that, initially, very few white women were permitted to brave the perils of the "Indian Country" so most fur traders took Indian (and later mixed-blood) women as "country wives." These marriages *à la façon du pays* were socially sanctioned unions, even though they were not formalized according to the laws of church or state. But with the establishment of the Red River Settlement in the early 1800s white women began to go west, and it soon became fashionable for the traders to legally marry white women and to try to sever their ties with their Native country wives.

In the forefront of this trend was Sir George Simpson, Governor of Rupert's Land[3] and, by all accounts, the most important personage in the Canadian fur trade, who had taken as his country wife a mixed-blood woman named Margaret Taylor. Though she bore him two sons, Margaret Taylor was abandoned by Simpson when he married his English cousin, a move which signalled the widespread rejection of Native women as marriage partners by "men of station" in fur-trade society and reflected the increasing racial and social prejudice against Native women in pre-Confederation Canada. Clearly, Margaret Taylor's story epitomized a crucial chapter in the history of Native women in Canada, but I was equally intrigued by its epilogue – her hastily arranged marriage to a Métis employee of the Hudson's Bay Company whose name was startlingly familiar: *Amable Hogue.*

On the basis of my great-grandmother's sampler and that rather incidental footnote in a history book, I began a search that eventually verified my connection to my great-great-great-grandmother, Margaret Taylor – a search that culminated in the making of my documentary film, *Women in the Shadows*. For me, finding Margaret was the beginning of a journey of self-discovery – of unravelling the thick web of denial, shame, bitterness, and silence that had obscured my past and picking up the fragile threads that extend back across time, connecting me to the grandmothers I never knew and to a larger collective experience that is uniquely and undeniably Métis.

My search for my Native grandmothers was hampered both by the inadequacies of traditional historical sources with respect to women and by the code of silence that existed in my own family with respect to our Native heritage. But after venturing down a couple of blind alleys I finally called my great-aunt Jeanne, my grandmother's youngest sister and the oldest surviving female relative on that side of my family. When I called Grandma Jeanne I hadn't seen or spoken to her in more than twenty years, yet she was surprised and touched that I remembered her and seemed eager to help me in any way she could. Grandma Jeanne knew about Margaret Taylor, and knew that she had some connection to George Simpson, but said that this had never been discussed because, in the words of Jeanne's mother, it had brought shame on the family. Nevertheless, Grandma Jeanne was able to tell me the names of Margaret Taylor's granddaughters and daughters – right back to Margaret Taylor.

Like most Native women of her time, Margaret Taylor left no diaries, no letters, no wills – no written record that might have helped me reconstruct her life as she perceived it. Her voice is not heard in the historical record, and so I was forced to rely on the logs, journals, letters, and account books that form the written history of the fur trade for the few maddening snippets of factual information to be found about her life. For it was the men of the fur trade – our European forefathers – who wrote the story of the historic encounter between First Nations and Europeans on this continent. And because they wrote it, the history that has been passed down to their descendants – the history that has been taught to generations of Métis children, including me – is their story, from their point of view. In the absence of any other version of the story, we have identified with them – with their struggle, their courage, their triumph. But what about our Indian foremothers? What about their struggle and their courage? The fur traders wrote almost nothing about the Indian women who shared their lives. And so the voices of our grandmothers remain silent, leaving us to wonder about the story they would have told if they'd been able to write it down.

The existing records show that my great-great-great-grandmother, Margaret Taylor, was born on Hudson Bay in 1810. Her mother was an Indian woman who was known only as Jane. Jane is almost nameless, certainly faceless, but I can make some reasonably well-informed assumptions about what her life might have been like. She was probably one of the Homeguard Cree – the "Great House people" who, by the late 1700s, had forged close ties with the traders who lived in the isolated trading posts on the shores of Hudson Bay. It was incomprehensible to these people that the fur traders had brought no women with them for women were the strength, the backbone of aboriginal society – those with power to give life and the wisdom to sustain it. In offering their women as wives for the newcomers, the Cree were making a remarkable gesture of friendship and goodwill – one that drew the white men into the heart of aboriginal society in a way that nothing else could and established bonds of kinship, understanding, and trust that formed the very foundation of the fur trade. For it was the women who taught their new husbands the skills needed to survive in what the Europeans regarded as a wilderness, and it was their comfort and companionship that made life bearable for the traders in a strange new land. As guides, teachers, helpmates, and wives they occupied an important and privileged position as "women in between" two worlds, and it was they who bridged the gulf between the old ways and the new.[4]

Margaret Taylor's mother, Jane, was one of these women. I don't know when or where she was born, but I know that sometime in the late 1790s she became the country wife of one George Taylor, the Hudson Bay Company's sloopmaster at York Factory on Hudson's Bay. I'll never know whether Jane approached her marriage to a white man with enthusiasm, indifference, or dread. But I do know that their union produced at least eight children, including Margaret, and that when George Taylor retired from service with Hudson's Bay Company in 1815 he returned to

England, leaving Jane and the children behind.[5]

It seems that Jane remained at York Factory, at least for a time, for the post journal indicates that she continued to receive provisions during the following winter – some damaged salt beef, a little flour, a few biscuits. But after that, nothing – no record of where she went or how she managed. Most likely she returned to live with her own people, taking her children with her. There they would have learned to live according to her ways, to know the animals and birds, and to recognize the voices of their ancestors. Yet they carried within them the spirit of two peoples; they remembered other voices, other ways, and they must have known that they were different. Not Cree like their mother, though they spoke her language. Not English like their father, though they bore his name. But something else, something unique: a new people.

It must have been Jane who taught her children to make the best of who and what they were – to take from two cultures the things they would need to make their way in a world that was shifting and changing before their very eyes. No longer could her daughters rely on those skills that had made her so indispensable to her husband, those things that had been passed from mother to daughter among her people for as long as anyone could remember. The fur traders no longer needed Indian wives to help them survive; they now looked with pleasure on the light-skinned, mixed-blood daughters of their own kind for the womanly qualities they sought in a wife. With no father to look to their future and pave the way for a suitable marriage, it must have been Jane who groomed her daughters to survive in the only way that seemed possible – by becoming shining examples of all that the traders most desired. And in time her diligence paid off, for it was her daughter who eventually caught the eye of the Governor himself, George Simpson.

Margaret Taylor was just sixteen years old when she became the country wife of the Governor of Rupert's Land. Her brother Thomas was George Simpson's personal servant, and it was probably through him that Margaret first came to the Governor's attention. Though young Simpson was notorious for indulging in short-lived liaisons with young native women whom he referred to as "bits of brown," his relationship with Margaret Taylor appeared to be different. He referred to Thomas Taylor as his brother-in-law, provided financial support to her mother, and gave Margaret and the rest of fur-trade society every reason to believe that their relationship constituted a legitimate country marriage.

But Simpson's public regard for his country wife was not matched by evidence of similar devotion in his private correspondence. In the fall of 1826, before departing on a long tour of the Company's inland posts, Simpson made arrangements for Margaret to stay at York Factory in the

CHRISTINE WELSH

care of Chief Factor McTavish. Though Margaret was pregnant with their first child, Simpson's instructions to McTavish betrayed a singular lack of sentiment: "Pray keep an Eye on the commodity," he wrote, "If she bring forth anything in proper time & of the right colour let them be taken care of but if anything be amiss let the whole be bundled about their business."[6] A few months later Margaret gave birth to their first child, George Stewart Simpson, and thereafter Simpson assumed responsibility for their support.

Simpson seems to have relied on Margaret's companionship to an unusual degree for he insisted that she accompany him on his historic cross-continental canoe journey to the Pacific in 1828. Their route through the Rocky Mountains by-passed the familiar Columbia River in favour of the Fraser, a treacherous passage of awesome canyons and terrifying rapids that Simon Fraser himself had pronounced unnavigable only twenty years before. The Governor set a killing pace, and they made the trip in a record sixty-five days. Margaret became so exhausted that Simpson considered leaving her at a post in the Athabasca country, but she must have drawn on some remarkable reserves of strength for she was eventually able to continue. Simpson clearly valued her presence for he wrote to McTavish: "The commodity has been a great consolation to me."[7]

During their stay at Fort Vancouver Margaret became pregnant with their second child. Still, she accompanied Simpson on his return trip to Fort Garry, making the arduous trek across the snow-covered Rockies on snowshoes. Simpson himself was so exhausted by the journey that he decided to go to England to try to regain his health and vigour, leaving Margaret at Fort Alexander at the mouth of the Winnipeg River to be cared for by Chief Factor John Stuart whose country wife was her sister, Mary. There, in August 1829, Margaret gave birth to her second son, John McKenzie Simpson. Six months later, while still in England, Simpson married his English cousin, Frances Simpson.

It is not hard to imagine Margaret's shock when she learned that the Governor was returning with a new wife. No doubt she and her children were kept well out of sight when Simpson and his new bride stopped at Fort Alexander during their triumphant journey from Montreal to Red River. Once the Simpsons were installed at Red River, the Governor lost no time in arranging for Margaret's "disposal" and a few months later she was married to Amable Hogue, an event which drew this comment from one contemporary observer: "The Govrs little tit bit Peggy Taylor is ... Married to Amable Hogue ... what a downfall is here ... from a Governess to Sow."[8]

Amable Hogue, who had been among Simpson's élite crew of voyageurs, was hired as a stonemason on the construction of Simpson's new headquarters at lower Fort Garry. From her vantage point in the Métis labourers' camp just outside the walls, Margaret would have been able to watch the Governor and his bride take up residence in their magnificent new home. For his service, the Hudson's Bay Company gave Hogue a riverfront lot on the Assiniboine River just west of the Forks, and it was there on the banks of the Assiniboine River that Margaret Taylor spent the rest of her life, raising her family, working beside her husband on their riverfront farm, and joining with her neighbours in the buffalo hunts that were the lifeblood of the Red River Métis.

My great-great-great-grandmother's life spanned the rise and fall of the first Métis nation. By the time she died in December 1885, just a few weeks after the hanging of Louis Riel, the world that she and other Métis women had known had changed irrevocably. Rupert's Land had become part of the emerging Canadian nation and immigrants from eastern Canada and Europe were pouring into the old Northwest to lay claim to homesteads on land that had been the home of the Indian and Métis people for generations. The buffalo were gone, the fur trade was no more, the Indians were confined to reserves, and the Métis had lost their land and their way of life. The Métis resistance that had begun at Red River in 1870 and ended at Batoche in 1885 resulted in the dispossession of the Métis people, and they found themselves relegated to the road allowances and the margins of Canadian society. In the dark years that followed, very few Métis people spoke about being Métis and there was widespread denial of Métis identity among generations of Métis who survived that troubled time and who grew up in its aftermath. While most Métis people were not subjected to the brutal suppression of language and identity that the Indian people experienced in the residential school system, they were nonetheless made to feel ashamed of their heritage and many Métis came to see assimilation to the "white ideal" as the only way to escape desperate lives of oppression and grinding poverty.

It is impossible to know when the process of denial and assimilation began in my own family, but I feel in my heart that it goes right back to what happened to Margaret Taylor. Here, I believe, are the roots of our denial – denial of that fact of blood that was the cause of so much pain and suffering and uncertainty about the future. Is it such a surprise that, many years later, Margaret's own son would choose to describe his mother as "a sturdy Scotswoman" rather than the halfbreed that she really was? Perhaps Margaret herself perpetuated this myth – if not for her sons' sake, then certainly for her daughters' – to try to spare them a fate similar to her own and that of her mother. I'll never know. But I do know that the denial of our Native heritage which has been passed on from generation to generation of my family is explicable in light of those events that took place so long ago, and I am finally able to see it not as a betrayal but as the survival mechanism that it most certainly was. For we did survive – even though, for a time, we were cut off from our past and our people – and we did so largely because of the resourcefulness, adaptability, and courage of my grandmothers.

Unlike those whose search for roots is prompted by obscure snatches of stories passed from one generation to the next, my search for my grand-mothers was prompted by silence – the silence that is the legacy of assim-ilation. When I began I assumed that no fragments, no messages from the past, had survived in my family. Yet in Grandma Jeanne I found surprising evidence that this was not the case. For Grandma Jeanne, the answer to the question "Do you remember?" was like coming up from very deep water, giving voice to things which had not been forgotten but which had been deliberately submerged in a process of alienation from her Native heritage and assimilation into the dominant society which had become more firmly entrenched with each new generation. So for me, for Grandma Jeanne, and for all the other Native women who helped me in my search and who participated in the making of *Women in the Shadows*, the act of remembering – of reclaiming that which had been lost – was a process of affirmation: affirmation of the importance of Native women's experience; affirmation of the strength, courage, and resilience of our foremothers; affirmation of our ability to speak both our past and our present and to make our voices heard.

Women in the Shadows is about one woman's struggle to come to terms with loss – with the price that has been paid for assimilation by countless numbers of indigenous people in Canada and indeed throughout the world. But it is also a celebration of survival. And as Métis poet and his-torian Emma LaRocque pointed out to me during the making of the film, our survival carries certain responsibilities:

> You and I are survivors. We're here because the generations that came before us survived, and maybe generations a hundred years from now will be there because we survived. We have to go on, and part of going on is that we are creating and recreating and freshly creating. That's our role right now. But unlike Margaret and your grandmoth-ers and my grandmothers, the challenge for us today is to survive – to be who we are – without paying the price of hating ourselves and rejecting a part of ourselves. That's the big issue – not just that we sur-vive, but that we survive well and healthily and without having to abandon anything that is of us.[9]

Métis women are responding to that challenge. Our stories, poems, songs, and films have a recurring theme – that of survival, continuance. It is a theme born of what Emma LaRocque describes as a haunting and hounding sense of loss that is unique to a people dispossessed and that compels us to keep saying over and over again: "I remember."[10] For our words and music and images are testaments to the remarkable fact that we are still here – that we have survived near-annihilation and that we continue to resist – and though they necessarily give voice to our pain, they also express our vision for the future, and in so doing they become tools for healing, for empowerment, and for change.

Notes

1   Leslie Marmon Silko, *Storyteller* (New York: Seaver, 1981) 6-7.

2   Métis: In Canada, the name given to the mixed-blood population that resulted from the intermingling and intermarriage between aboriginal people and Europeans that followed the European invasion and colonization of the Americas. With a small "m," métis is a racial term for anyone of mixed aboriginal and European ancestry. With a capital "M," Métis is a term for those originally of mixed ancestry who evolved into a distinct indigenous people during a certain historical period in western Canada, including those to whom this paper refers.

3   Rupert's Land: The vast drainage basin of Hudson Bay, given by royal charter to the Hudson's Bay Company in 1670.

4   For a thorough discussion of the role of Native women in the Canadian fur trade, see Sylvia Van Kirk, *"Many Tender Ties": Women in Fur-Trade Society in Western Canada, 1670-1870* (Winnipeg: Watson & Dwyer, [1980]).

5   For information on the family of George Taylor, see Hudson's Bay Company Archives (HBCA) biographical file on George Taylor; see also HBCA D4/113, fo. 146-d.

6   See HBCA B239/c/1, fo. 283.

7   See HBCA B239/c/1, fo. 365-66.

8   W. Sinclair to Ermatinger, 15 Aug. 1831, qtd. in John S. Galbraith, *The Little Emperor: Governor Simpson of the Hudson's Bay Company* (Toronto: Macmillan of Canada, 1976) 109.

9   Emma LaRocque, transcript of interview for *Women in the Shadows*.

10 Emma LaRocque, "Preface; or, Here Are Our Voices – Who Will Hear?" *Writing the Circle: Native Women of Western Canada*, ed. Jeanne Perreault and Sylvia Vance (Edmonton, AB: NeWest, 1990) xxviii.

The New Social Gospel in Canada

Gregory Baum

Almost every day we read in the newspapers that the churches have made a critical statement in regard to an important social issue. Earlier this year, along with the synagogues, they called for a more generous legislation in regard to refugees. The churches have expressed their solidarity with the Native Peoples and supported their land claims. And they have published statements on unemployment, Northern development, world hunger, the farm crisis, immigration, arms production, and free trade. Canadians have been puzzled by this new concern.

At the same time, the newspapers report almost every day that the churches in other countries, especially the Third World countries, also exercise their social responsibility. They stand in solidarity with the victims of society. What has happened?

In Canada this new faith-and-justice movement took off at the end of the sixties, occurring in an ecumenical context. The churches were ready to work together. They created several interchurch committees with the mandate to study what social justice meant in various sectors of Canadian life. The churches did this as a response to the aspirations of a network of socially concerned Christians all over Canada. Some of these groups represented people suffering injustice in this country, for instance Native Peoples or the unemployed. Other groups were in solidarity with struggles in the Third World and tried to influence Canadian public policy. The new movement, therefore, began at the grass roots. It has received the support of the church leaders. Still, it represents a minority in the churches.

For the Protestant and Anglican churches, this recent development represents the return of the Social Gospel. The Social Gospel was a faith-and-justice movement that began in the late nineteenth century. It offered a wider interpretation of the Christian message: God demanded justice in society. In Canada the Social Gospel exerted political influence in the twenties and in the thirties during the dark years of the Depression. It was involved in the creation of the radical political party, the Cooperative Commonwealth Federation (CCF). Not surprisingly, the faith-and-justice movement at that time did not receive the blessing of the church leaders. The return of the Social Gospel in our day is based on a sounder theology and a better grasp of the social sciences. And this time around it is endorsed by the ecclesiastical leadership. It is, moreover, part of a world-wide movement.

As for the Roman Catholic Church, the recent development represents a startling evolution of its traditional social teaching. The Canadian bishops were willing to listen to the victims of society, to learn from the prophetic tradition of the Bible, and to enter into dialogue with Canadian political scientists who analyzed the ills of society. The bishops were accompanied in this by the other Canadian churches. They were inspired by the radical position adopted by many Third World churches and supported by John Paul II's recent encyclicals.

The Canadian Catholic bishops published many pastoral messages and statements that tried to clarify what the radical commitment to social justice means in Canadian society. Since the early seventies they have produced a body of literature that contains the beginning of a Canadian critical social theory. In this lecture I shall present some of the dominant themes of this new teaching.

Let me start with the Labour Day message of 1976. Here the Canadian bishops offer a brief statement of what the new Social Gospel means in Canada. The pastoral document is a gem. It is in my opinion the best expression we have of a Canadian liberation theology.

It begins by recognizing the historical situation: "We live in a world that oppresses at least half of the human race and this scandal threatens to get worse." This is a strong statement by the bishops. While we in Canada have our own suffering, we belong nonetheless to the small sector of the world that claims the larger part of available resources. "The present social and economic order fails to meet the human needs of the majority of people." It widens the gap between the rich and the poor and leaves the control of resources in the hands of an élite. The peoples of the Third World in particular clamour for the creation of a new economic order, based on a more just distribution of wealth and power.

What is the summons of the Gospel in this situation? As disciples of Christ we must act out of dedication to justice. One sentence in particular reveals how deeply the bishops feel the urgency of their faith in God: "We stand in the biblical tradition of the prophets of Israel where to know God is to seek justice for the disinherited, the poor, and the oppressed. The same Spirit of God that came upon the prophets filled Jesus of Nazareth. With the power of that Spirit he announced that he was the message of the prophets come true – 'the good news to the poor' and 'liberty to the oppressed' [Luke 4: 18-19]."

The Labour Day message continues: "For Christians the struggle for justice is not an optional activity. It is integral to bringing the gospel to the world."

I have quoted the bishops verbatim to reveal the spiritual foundation of their radical social teaching. In their eyes, the commitment to social justice is not purely secular; it has profound religious meaning. In compassion and solidarity, people find God.

It is the Church's task to evaluate society in accordance with the values revealed in the Gospel. The bishops realize that this is new and radical. It is a call for conversion, addressed to all members of the Church. "Unfortunately," they admit, "those who are committed to this Christian way of life are presently a minority in the life of the Catholic community." They call this minority "significant" because it summons the whole Church to greater fidelity. The bishops actually defend this minority against the criticism levelled against them – "particularly," as they say, "by the affluent and powerful sectors of the community."

What does the bishops' call to conversion mean in practical terms? How should Christians think and act in a society such as ours? The Labour Day message proposes several guidelines.

The guidelines call upon us to reread the Bible, to hear in it God's call to justice. In the past, we tended to hear in the Gospel only the call to love our neighbours individually, to be generous and to help them as much as possible. A rereading of the Bible in our day has revealed a new definition of neighbour: "We want to build a society in which all members are treated as neighbours, as people deserving respect." Today, almsgiving is no longer enough. Love of neighbour calls for social justice, for a transformation of society, so that the victims will be delivered from their crushing burdens. In our day the love of neighbour generates a passion for justice.

The guidelines ask us to listen to the victims of society. We cannot come to know Canadian society if we only talk to our friends. Even our newspapers tend to see social issues from the perspective of the middle class. Mainstream culture tries to make invisible the sins of society and allow the victims to disappear from our consciousness. Many of us never meet the poor, the unemployed, and the people who live in daily fear of insecurity. The dominant culture tries to give the middle class a good conscience. What the bishops dare to tell us is that to arrive at an honest evaluation of our society, we must first listen to the people who suffer injustice, we must look at history from below. And then we can speak out against injustice.

Many people find this difficult. A certain modesty and a desire to be kind and well-behaved often makes it difficult for church-oriented Christians to participate in public demonstrations. To be seen on protest marches is embarrassing to them. Respectable people don't do this. The bishops ask us to reconsider our feelings here. Faith and solidarity call for public protest.

Yet it is also necessary to analyze the causes of social injustice. Why are the Native Peoples oppressed? Why is there massive unemployment? The bishops claim that the causes of these fateful historical developments can

be analyzed scientifically. At one time, before the advent of modern medicine, people thought that illnesses happened out of the blue: they did not
know then that the cause of disease could be analyzed scientifically.
Similarly, many people believe that poverty and other collective misfortunes just happen. However, dialogue with social science is convincing
ever-wider sectors of the population that the causes of unjust social conditions can be analyzed scientifically. The Canadian bishops, following here
a famous remark of Pope Paul VI, urge Catholics to engage in social analysis. And then we must act.

Christians are asked to participate with other citizens in political action
to remove the causes of oppression from society and transform the social
order.

Clearly, the Canadian bishops fully endorse what the Latin American
bishops have called the preferential option for the poor. This option comprises a double commitment: to look at society from the perspective of its
victims and to express solidarity with them in public action.

Allow me to mention here that this bold option for the poor has been
endorsed by Pope John Paul II, in his 1981 encyclical on labour. Applying
this option to the developed nations of East and West, communist and capitalist, the Pope provocatively called for "the solidarity of labour supported
by the solidarity with labour."

In the guidelines of the Canadian Labour Day message, Christians are
also asked to help the poor and needy. The new, politically responsible
understanding of Christian discipleship must not make us forget the continuing need for almsgiving and acts of compassion. They remain essential.
While foodbanks, for instance, do not deal with the causes of unemployment and hunger, they are nonetheless necessary in the present situation.
Christians should support both the struggle to transform society and the
effort to offer temporary assistance to its victims. The struggle for justice
must always be accompanied by compassion.

In my opinion, the brief Labour Day message of 1976 is a cogent statement of a Canadian liberation theology. The statement affirms that the
redemption brought by Jesus Christ and preached by the Church includes
the liberation of people from the conditions of oppression. The statement
unfolds the meaning of this Christian message in the concrete conditions
of Canadian society.

In subsequent pastoral messages – especially in the famous statement of
1983, called "Ethical Reflections on the Economic Crisis" – the bishops
have applied their own critical principles to come to a better understanding of the contradictions of Canadian society. They worked together with
the other churches and were attentive to the debate among Canadian
social and political scientists, and from this produced elements of a critical
social analysis. They laid the foundation for an original social theory.

In the second part of this lecture I wish to present the critical analysis of Canadian society found in the pastoral messages of the Catholic bishops. I must warn listeners that the social analysis and the recommendations are quite radical. To put their cards on the table, the bishops revealed the methodology they employed in preparing their pastoral messages. The pertinent text is so important that I shall quote from it, in a slightly abbreviated form.

"Our pastoral methodology involves a number of steps: (a) to be present with and listen to the experiences of the poor, the marginalized, the oppressed in our society, (b) to develop a critical analysis of the economic, political, and social structures that cause human suffering, (c) to make judgements in the light of the Gospel principles concerning social values and priorities, (d) to stimulate creative thought and action regarding alternative models for social and economic development, and (e) to act in solidarity with popular groups in their struggles to transform society."

Let me jump right into the social analysis offered by the bishops. They focus on the injustice and inequality produced by the economic institutions. They present what is called a structural analysis. They look at the changing face of capitalism in Canada and relate it to the wider crisis of the world economy.

This approach is new in Catholic social teaching. In the past, Church teaching tended to put primary emphasis on the moral dimension. The Church denounced hard-heartedness, greed, and selfishness. It called for an ethical conversion on the part of all, and it held out the hope that love of justice and greater generosity could reform the existing economic institutions.

More recently, especially since the Pope's encyclical on labour, church documents begin their analysis of social evil by focussing first on the economic infrastructure. Only after that do they call for new values. Economic analysis here precedes value analysis.

Some people might ask what do theologians know about economics. In the last two decades or so, theologians have been studying economic developments from an ethical point of view. Nowadays church seminaries hire faculty in this area to instruct the students.

To begin with a structural analysis is important, the Canadian bishops say: otherwise we are tempted to blame innocent people for unemployment and economic decline. Some may claim, for instance, that workers are lazy and do bad work. Others suggest that immigrants or women take away their jobs. Society has an unfortunate tendency to blame the victims.

We cannot understand the social deterioration taking place in Canada and in the world unless we analyze the changes in the structure of capital. The bishops outline five trends: the concentration of capital, its centralization, its internationalization, the increasing foreign ownership of the industries, and the switch to computer technology. I want to look at these five trends.

By the concentration of capital the bishops refer to the trend to move financial and commercial institutions into the metropolitan areas. This is done to increase efficiency and profits. Yet this trend leads to regional disparity. Visible examples of this concentration are the new head-office banking towers in Toronto, the giant structures built like temples, gold-tinted and decorated, that shape the city's skyline and symbolize the new economic gods. Many regions in Canada now find themselves deserted by companies and offices that had brought economic life to their communities.

By the centralization of capital the bishops refer to the trend of large corporations to increase their profitability by buying out and taking over smaller and medium-sized companies. Because these takeovers are regularly reported in the newspapers, they are perhaps the most visible sign of where the economy is going. Concentration of capital means concentration of power. An ever-shrinking élite is involved in making the important decisions in regard to Canada's economic life. So great can the power of these giant corporations become that they are able to force government to serve their interests.

By the internationalization of capital the bishops mean the recent trend to increase the profits of industries by relocating them in parts of the world where labour is cheap, where safety regulations are minimal, and where governments forbid the unionization of workers. This trend has led to the deindustrialization of many regions in Canada. Companies that have for a generation or two drawn upon the labour and the cooperation of entire communities suddenly decide to leave them.

By increasing foreign ownership the bishops refer to the trend of foreign – especially American – companies to increase their holdings of certain industries in Canada. Several of our industries have become branch plants of American companies, and the decisions regarding their operation and development are made by directors in a foreign country who have no reason to be concerned about Canadian workers. It is not surprising that in a recent Church document the bishops express their fear that the free trade agreement with the United States will make Canadian workers even more vulnerable.

And finally the bishops point to the social impact of the new technology. Industries are becoming more capital-intensive. This means that more money will be spent on the technological equipment and less on wages. And fewer people will be employed.

It is this changing structure of capital, the bishops conclude, that is responsible for growing unemployment and the widening of the gap between the rich and the poor in Canada. This trend is universal. Capitalism is entering a new phase, one that will lead to the suffering of the masses. The bishops offer an interpretation of what is happening that is identical to the analysis proposed by the Pope.

After World War Two, forty-three years ago, capitalism entered a relatively benign phase. Capitalists realized that they needed the support of society. Under the pressure of labour unions and progressive political parties, they entered into an unwritten contract with society to provide full employment, support welfare legislation, and respect labour unions. But this unwritten contract is now coming apart at the seams. Unemployment has become massive, welfare legislation is under attack, and efforts are being made to discredit and even destroy labour organizations. In the opinion of John Paul II, the new phase of capitalism, unless stopped by political forces, will create enormous suffering in world society.

This analysis of society is unsettling. Most commentators on the Pope's teaching pretend that he did not say such things. But the Canadian bishops have been severely criticized for it. They have been called idealists, Marxists, or woolly socialists. One argument repeated many times is that the bishops are against profit. For them, it is said, profit is a dirty word. But this argument misinterprets their teaching. Everyone knows that a business or a company must pay for itself and make some profit. An economic system that does not make a profit cannot serve the needs of the people. What the bishops criticize is the maximization of profit. They argue that if an industry maximizes profit and technical efficiency, workers will be looked upon simply as material factors in the productive process, along with the raw materials and the machinery. Workers will become "objects" of the productive process, while they ought to be and are destined to be "subjects," that is, responsible agents, of production.

The bishops evaluate the present economic situation in ethical terms. They have produced an ethical critique of capitalism. Ethics is the Church's concern. The principal moral argument used in this context is the dignity of human beings. Because of their dignity, people are meant to be subjects or responsible agents of their society. Workers are meant to be subjects of the productive process. The dignity of workers is such that they are entitled to share in the ownership of what they produce and in the decisions regarding the organization of labour.

According to John Paul II, if workers are excluded from this coresponsibility, they live in a state of alienation. They feel pushed to the margin. Many of us know what this means. Workers are thus alienated in the two antagonistic systems, in communism and in capitalism. In communism the power over the product of labour is in the hands of the state bureaucracy. In capitalism this power is in the hands of the owners, or the directors plus managers. The social imagination which the Christian tradition brings to the great economic debate calls for increased participation of workers in the industries and greater democratic control of the economic institutions.

It is impossible to do justice to the emerging Catholic social theory in a single lecture. The bishops' teaching raises many questions that deserve careful answers. The reason that this teaching sounds so radical to us is that we are surrounded by cultural symbols that legitimate the existing order. To question capitalism seems daring in our culture, almost dangerous. While the dominant culture encourages us to raise critical questions in regard to many values, including religion, it regards it as improper to challenge the existing economic system. It is almost as if capitalism were something sacred. One of the great services the bishops have performed for us through their teaching is that they have demythologized the taboos of the dominant culture and invited us to engage fearlessly in ethical reflection on the economic trends of our times.

The bishops have looked at Canada from the perspective of the disadvantaged. Some people have objected to such a negative approach to Canadian society. Don't the bishops love their country? Does not the love of country demand that we adopt a more positive perspective and show gratitude for the benefits we receive? I reply to this objection by recalling a sentence, uttered under quite different circumstances, by Paul Tillich, the great German-born Protestant theologian. He, too, was criticized for being too negative. He replied that to love your country well means to long for it to be just.

Exactly what policies do the bishops recommend? And who is to be the agent, the motive force, to introduce these changes in society? We have time only for brief answers to these important questions.

According to their pastoral methodology, the bishops make proposals to stretch people's imagination and give rise to a public debate open to alternative models of economic and social developments. They feel that we are caught in a cultural trap. Our imagination has been so impoverished that we think the only choice available to society is between capitalism and communism. What we need are alternative models.

What the bishops propose is based both on old Catholic teaching and on more recent developments. They recommend two policy orientations in tension with one another. On the one hand, we need more democratically controlled economic planning around the supply of the essential human needs. This includes planning around the production of food, housing, and jobs. This involves policies that protect our farmers and policies in regard to Third World countries that take into consideration their needs as well. This centralizing trend in public policy is to be balanced by a decentralizing trend. The bishops propose a greater decentralization of capital. Is the existence of the giant corporations, which control a substantial sector of the economy, good for society? What would a decentralization of capital look like? It would involve a diversification of ownership. Anti-trust legislation could break up the giant concerns, and new forms of public and cooperative ownership could be encouraged. One can easily imagine a society in which privately owned companies represent one sector of the economy, the other being made up of community-owned and worker-owned industrial and commercial enterprises. The bishops' proposals here follow the labour encyclical of John Paul II.

At this time, the only countries that increase productivity – Japan, Sweden, and some other European countries – are societies where workers are admitted to responsible participation and where it has therefore become possible for management, workers, and government to cooperate.

The new social imagination proposed by the bishops is made of two contrasting trends, one centralizing – more democratic overall planning – and the other decentralizing – more democratic forms of ownership. The tension between these two trends is to guarantee the freedom of persons in society. The emphasis on more central planning recalls the socialist tradition, while the emphasis on the diversification of ownership balances this and invokes the cooperative movement. These are home-grown Canadian ideas: the wheat pools of the prairies, the credit unions of Quebec, the farmers' and fishermen's cooperatives in the Maritimes. While the bishops base this social imagination on Catholic values, they are keenly aware that the same sort of imagination is generated by other Christians, and by secular groups in society.

The bishops' proposals are controversial. Are they practical and will they steer the country toward greater social justice? Or will they lead to economic decline, as some of their adversaries insist? The bishops join here the great economic debate that engages the Western world at this time. Economists themselves are in disagreement. Economics departments at universities are communities in conflict. Some economists defend the more recent monetary trend as the solution; others advocate a return to Keynesian principles; and a third group, while by no means unanimous, advocates somewhat more radical surgery for the present economic order. It is my impression that it is with this third group, or at least with some of its members, that the Catholic bishops have the greatest affinity.

Why do economists disagree among themselves? Do they not all regard economics as an empirical science? They all follow the scientific method. They all try to demonstrate their economic theories with empirical evidence. How then can we explain this profound disagreement among them? The cause for the difference among economists lies in the value assumptions implicit in their approach to economic science. What is the aim of an economic system? What primary issue attracts an economist's attention? How do economists conceive of the human being in their investigations? What role do they assign to cultural values in the process of production? While economics – like medicine – is indeed an empirical science, it is a scientific enterprise divided by a conflict over values.

In 1982 the MacDonald Commission, presenting itself as non-partisan, invited groups and agencies in this country to submit briefs that would analyze the economic ills and recommend policies that could overcome them. Among these submissions were those of the Christian churches. Once published, the MacDonald Report turned out to reflect only the recommendations of the economically powerful groups. Whereupon two political economists, Daniel Drache and Duncan Cameron, decided to publish a book, called *The Other MacDonald Report*, that made available to the public the submissions of "the popular sector" to which no attention had been paid. This popular sector included trade unions, women's groups, social agencies, and organizations representing Native Peoples, farmers, and the disadvantaged. It also included the churches. What is remarkable is the unanimity among these various groups.

This is how Drache and Cameron describe the consensus: "The popular sector groups contradict the urgings of business that government reduce its role in the economy and give free reign to 'market forces.' The economy must serve human well-being rather than corporate balance sheets, the popular sector says, and for this end a fundamental break with the conventional value system of policy-making is the only means available. They reject a view of economics that separates ends from means and that is based on having people adjust, accommodate, and lower their expectations to the short-term profit considerations of business."

Many Canadian political economists have come forward and declared that the bishops' proposals make good economic sense. What these scholars have in common, and what they share with the bishops, is that they analyze Canadian society from the perspective of the people at the bottom and in the margin.

This remark leads us to the next question: Who is to introduce these changes in Canadian society? Who is to be the agent of social transformation? The older Catholic social teaching made proposals for the reform of society that depended on the good will and generosity of all concerned. All citizens, poor, rich, and in between, were called to an ethical conversion. The more recent Catholic social teaching rejects this idealistic approach. Society will only change if those who are disfavoured in it get organized and exert political pressure. John Paul II called this principle "the solidarity of the workers and with the workers."

In line with this new orientation, the Canadian bishops recommend the creation of a solidarity movement made up of the various groups and sectors which suffer under the present economic order, and supported by all citizens who love justice. The Church itself, according to them, should be in solidarity with such a movement.

This recommendation differs from what Marxists call "class struggle." In ideological Marxism, "class" is defined in purely economic terms. Each class is here seen as following its own collective economic self-interest. By contrast, the solidarity movement of which the bishops speak – and to which *The Other MacDonald Report* alludes – is an ethical achievement. Each group is obviously concerned with improving its material situation, whether the group is made up of workers, of women, of Native Peoples, of the unemployed, or the handicapped. Yet to create a joint movement each group must respect and make room for the aims of the others. To create a coalition that can exercise pressure in society and become an agent of social change, each group must be willing to modify and adjust its own aim. A solidarity movement of this kind is an ethical achievement. It serves the material betterment of all in a context defined by principles of justice. That is why people in more favoured circumstances who love justice are called upon to support the movement.

This is the bold teaching of the Canadian bishops. This is the Social Gospel in Canada.

New Contexts of Canadian Criticism:
Democracy, Counterpoint, Responsibility

Ajay Heble

I want to begin by invoking a context not signalled by my title, but one which, I think, is central for the kinds of arguments I would like to rehearse regarding both the social function and responsibility of criticism, and the cultural, political, and institutional consequences of the kind of interpretive activity that engages scholars in the humanities. That context, postmodernism, is undoubtedly the dominant model of intellectual inquiry in our era. It has monumentally transformed, by problematizing, our understanding of knowledge, truth, history, and power, and has thus facilitated an important process of denaturalization. More precisely, it has been tremendously valuable for oppositional critics because it exposes the constructed and ideological nature of hegemonic positions which have traditionally been naturalized as objective, true, or universal. As the dominant "new" context for Canadian criticism, it has contributed in important ways to our rethinking of time-honoured questions of identity formation and national consciousness. Indeed, as it has been theorized in a Canadian context by Linda Hutcheon and others, postmodernism, despite its axiomatic and canonical status within the academy, is largely an oppositional discourse. In Hutcheon's words, "Canada's own particular moment of cultural history does seem to make it ripe for the paradoxes of postmodernism, by which I mean those contradictory acts of establishing and then undercutting prevailing values and conventions in order to provoke a questioning, a challenging of 'what goes without saying' in our culture" (*Canadian Postmodern* 3).[1] How precisely are we to understand the oppositional valence of a dominant model of inquiry? In part, what concerns me here is the extent to which the very institutionalization and academicization of postmodernism has functioned to prevent us – as teachers, scholars, students, and citizens – from attending to struggles and inequalities in the social and political world *outside* the academy. Does postmodernism, perhaps even in spite of itself, lead us in some way to think that it is only by reading and writing about *texts* within the context of the academy that effective social change can take place?[2]

I'm obviously stumbling across some other large and important contexts here – pedagogy, the public sphere, social justice, the question of why we read – and I'm realizing, as I write this, that none of these is, at least in any easily definable way, Canadian. What, then, is a *Canadian* context?

How precisely do we determine what counts as *Canadian* criticism? Eli Mandel, in his introduction to *Contexts of Canadian Criticism*, suggests that "as soon as we add the word *Canadian* to criticism, we move the object of our concern into a particular space and time, a geographical and historical context, where what might normally remain simply an element of the background – the sociology of literature – becomes the foreground" (3). What Mandel is probing is the question of how we negotiate between text and context, or, put another way, between literary criticism *per se* (that is, criticism that concerns itself with formal, structural, and generic considerations and/or traditional literary patterns) and the specificities of a national context. I certainly want to hold onto those specificities – and indeed to argue that even literary criticism *per se* is rooted in and largely determined by specific histories and particular cultural formations – but I also wonder precisely what it means to speak of *Canadian* criticism in an era which seems to be engaged in the process of articulating what Frank Davey calls "post-national arguments," an era which, as Marshall McLuhan predicted some time ago, may well be moving toward the end of distinct nation-states. How do we reconcile our emphasis on *Canadian* criticism with this global framework of knowledge?

Though I cannot pretend to have any easy answers, it does seem to me that recent developments in Canadian cultural and literary history have made clear the need to move beyond a nationalist critical methodology – where "the desire to come to terms with oneself in place and time and in relation to others" is, as David Tarras suggests, "a national instinct" (10) – into a sustained consideration of what Edward Said, writing in "The Future of Criticism," calls "the traffic between [and I would add *within*] cultures, discourses and disciplines" (956). If, with Mary Louise Pratt, we agree (as I do) that the "three historical processes ... transforming the way literature and culture are conceived and studied in the academy" are "globalization, democratization, and decolonization" (59), then we need, in light of these transformations, to attend much more rigorously to our own "sense of purpose" (Pratt 62) as scholars and teachers, and to the institutional consequences of these three processes. One such consequence, as Pratt outlines it, is "a broadening of subject matter which calls for shifts, among other things, in priorities and modes of accountability" (61). Part of what seems to be involved here is a recognition of the value of using theories and methodologies from elsewhere to rethink the national, to expand the contexts of Canadian criticism. At issue, then, is what Bruce Robbins calls "a new framing of the whole which revalues both unfamiliar and long-accepted genres, produces new concepts and criteria of judgment, and affects even those critics who never 'do' world literature or colonial discourse at all – affects all critics, that is, by shifting criticism's whole sense of intellectual enterprise" ("Comparative" 170). Canadian criticism, without losing sight of its cultural specificities, needs, in short, to see itself as part of a broader discourse of social, cultural, pedagogical, and institutional transformation.[3]

Gregory Baum's essay on the emergence of – and indeed the urgency for – a Canadian critical social theory is particularly relevant here for it asks what may well be the most pressing question for Canadians at this particular moment in our cultural history: what does a radical commitment to social justice and forms of democratization mean in Canadian society? (53) And, to ask the question in relation to the context with which I began, a context which, as Fredric Jameson has so convincingly shown, occupies the dominant position in contemporary critical thought,[4] what would such a radical commitment mean in the face of postmodernism's critique of empirical verifiability, its skepticism about truth and knowledge? If, as Linda Hutcheon concludes in her remarkable essay on the ethical implications of irony, "there are times when a reflexive, ironic [and postmodern] challenge is either not appropriate or simply not strong enough" ("End(s)" 202), then what kinds of strategies *are* appropriate, what kinds of critical and intellectual effort would it take to clarify our sense of purpose?

My purpose, in this essay, is to reintroduce ethics into the discourse of Canadian criticism, to make the case that as scholars, critics, teachers, and citizens we are responsible for negotiating and making requisite moral choices. And it seems to be imperative that we do so precisely because of our particular cultural and social moment. While, as one critic has recently put it, "virtually all the leading voices of the Theoretical Era ... organized their critiques of humanism as *exposés* of ethics, revelations of the transgressive, rebellious, or subversive energies that ethics had effectively masked and suppressed" (Harpham 388; emphasis added), I want to argue that a commitment to the ethical value of our reading and teaching practices and to our responsibilities as critics needs to be seen as a vital part of our struggle for what Henry Giroux calls "the democratization, pluralization, and reconstruction of public life" (52).

Various factors necessitate such a commitment. As Baum puts it, "Unemployment has become massive, welfare legislation is under attack, and efforts are being made to discredit and even destroy labour organizations" (61-62). Cornel West, in *Keeping Faith*, makes a similar point when he reminds us that "most of the [world's] resources, wealth and power are centered in huge corporations and supportive political élites" (31). He asks, "Can a civilization that evolves more and more around market activity, more and more around the buying and selling of commodities, expand the scope of freedom and democracy?" (31) Baum and West are both concerned with the ways in which unequal social relations of power and privilege continue to perpetuate "enormous suffering in world society" (Baum

62). Their concerns strike me as being particularly resonant today here in Ontario, where I live and teach, and where citizens of the province in 1995 elected a Progressive Conservative government, led by Mike Harris, whose campaign promises expressed a strong determination to destroy existing labour laws, welfare programmes, and employment equity legislation, to work, in short, *against* the processes of democratization that we need urgently to maintain and deepen. It's also, we ought to note, a government whose current Education Minister, John Snobelen, a high-school dropout and millionaire businessman, met in session with senior bureaucrats shortly after his appointment to make clear, as Richard Brennan pointed out in a story which exposed Snobelen's remarks, his "intention to speak of Ontario's schools as being in worse shape than he actually believed to be the case" (Brennan A1). In Snobelen's own words, "Creating a useful crisis is part of what this will be about" (quoted in Brennan A1).

The Education Minister's comments reveal his government's plan to "invent a crisis" (Snobelen quoted in Brennan A1) in education in order to set the terms of reference for its attempt to undermine the school system and thus restructure it according to its own corporate agenda. Snobelen, in fact, has explicitly used the language of business to indicate just how he thinks the school system should be restructured. He also, during that same session, appeared to brag about how businessmen like himself have for years dodged taxes – this coming, as Brennan suggests, from a Minister whose government is busy cracking down on alleged welfare cheats: "You know the goal of a private business, a privately owned business? To break even higher and higher each year. I can tell you I did that for a while.... I've been fighting taxes for years" (quoted in Brennan A2). As Earl Manners, President of the Ontario Secondary School Teachers' Federation, stated in a news release calling for Snobelen's resignation, "Never before in the history of Ontario education has the Minister responsible for education attempted to undermine the system from within so he could impose his agenda on it.... He has betrayed his responsibility to act as an advocate for the students, parents, and educators committed to the education system under his jurisdiction." Needless to say, as teachers and scholars (and as students and citizens) we ought to be troubled by the government's appointment of such a Minister because it emphasizes the degree to which a delegitimation of the academy is grounded in institutional practices that shape the social organization and codification of knowledge. Capitalizing on, and indeed fostering, the crisis of delegitimation that has resulted from an increasing privatization of and specialization within the academy (see Lecker, and Graff 347), the Harris government is not only signalling to us that education will not be a high or serious priority on its agenda, but also institutionalizing its devaluation of the intellectual enterprise by providing (and, in fact, inventing) the very terms of reference and consensus.

One of the consequences of such a devaluation, of course, is that intellectuals have to work even harder to clarify their role in the public sphere. For, in Gerald Graff's words, "as long as academic humanists are unable or unwilling to make their debates accessible in the public sphere, it will continue to be their detractors who speak for them" (355). If, as Jim Merod argues in his important book, *The Political Responsibility of the Critic*, "critical activity is (or might be) the one human force most committed to clarifying the world's structure in order to change it" (1), then the Harris government's contribution to the delegitimation of the academy will threaten our democratic processes by impeding the transformative possibilities of human agency. I want to argue, along with Merod, and with Paulo Freire, bell hooks, Henry Giroux, Cornel West, and others, that our teaching and criticism have to be connected to the world outside the academy, that our work, as teachers and critics, *has* to involve a radical intervention into the processes and the politics both of the academic institutions in which we work and of everyday life. Critical activity, that is, needs to be mobilized into an effort to transform power relations in institutional practices, and to participate, in Freire's words, in the "construction of new social formations dependent upon divergent cultural and gendered practices, discourses, and identities" (xi). In short, we must, as teachers, critics, and citizens, actively work to interrogate and alter the forces that shape the production, maintenance, and distribution of knowledge.

This is, of course, no easy task. West, for instance, discusses the ways in which, in the United States, "recent cutbacks of social service programs, business takebacks at the negotiation tables of workers and management, speedups at the workplace and buildups of military budgets reinforce the perception" that "the new cultural politics of difference may be solely visionary, utopian and fanciful" (31).[5] Similar kinds of perception are continually, and in various ways, generated by the media and reinforced by the fact that, as Raymond Williams put it in 1961, "under the system of an open market in communications we have seen an actual *shrinking* of independent organs of communication and a *diminution* in the number of hands which control communications. We have seen in fact a *concentration* of power over communications, and we have not yet seen the end of this" (26; emphasis added). If, as Williams argues, "the basis of a democratic system is that ordinary people should have control in their own hands" (29), then it is imperative for us "to think of ways which would truly disperse the control of communications, and truly open the channels of participation" (30). In a Canadian context, of course, Harold Innis has written widely on the way in which dominant forms of media facilitate a "monopoly or an oligopoly of knowledge" which reflects prevailing institutional structures of power (4). More recently, Noam Chomsky's ground-breaking work has thoroughly demonstrated the media's role in fixing the very premises of discourse (*Manufacturing* xi) and in shaping and controlling the production of knowledge in the interests of the corporate and political elite. Chomsky may well be the most important and powerful oppositional critic of our time, and his work makes it very clear just what is at stake in the media's hegemonic control over the production, maintenance, and distribution of knowledge. His work gives a special kind of urgency to our teaching and scholarship and makes Jim Merod's question – "What kind of intellectual solidarity in what form of political affiliation could penetrate the tightly held control of the concepts and political analyses that dominate televised news and most public discussions of major issues?" (159) – particularly resonant.

Indeed, the issues opened up by Chomsky's work on the media and its corporate links, I want to argue, have become strikingly relevant for teachers, students, and scholars because of "the immense pressure on the educational system in so many countries to make the goals of business and industry into the primary if not the only goals of schooling" (Apple vii). I find myself thinking about the kind of restructuring that is currently going on in academic institutions throughout the country, and about the extent to which, especially in light of John Snobelen's plans, that process may, in the main, be serving the needs, interests, and priorities of corporations. As John Calvert suggests in *Pandora's Box: Corporate Power, Free Trade and Canadian Education*, post-secondary education is currently being reshaped not simply, or even primarily, to promote educational objectives, but rather "to conform to the commercial, investment and labour force development requirements of transnational corporations" (131). What does it mean for university administrators and others to be operating under the "unquestioned assumption that Canadian universities should overcome their recent misfortunes by building links with the corporate sector" (Newson 9)? What are the implications (for scholars in the humanities, for curriculum development, for learning) of formalizing and institutionalizing linkages between universities and corporations through the creation of a Corporate-Higher Education Forum which "brought together the presidents of 32 Canadian universities with the chief executive officers of 38 major corporations" (Calvert 127)? Whose interests are being served by such linkages? As education itself is increasingly seen and treated as a commodity which needs to be opened up to the competitive pressures of the marketplace (Calvert 5), we can begin to see more precisely how the institutional conditions of our work can impede the kind of democratizing of knowledge that I'm suggesting needs to emerge from the academy.

And, again, I find myself thinking about Ontario's 1995 election, and, in particular, the coverage of that election by *The Globe and Mail*, "Canada's National Newspaper." In the editorial of June 1 – one week

before the election – *The Globe* explicitly endorsed the Conservative platform: "we believe the Conservatives under Mike Harris are the party of
choice" (A14). "The Conservative platform," the editorial continues, "is
the only one ... that grasps the nettle on the big issues facing Ontario –
its financial health, its tax levels, its employment markets, and the status of
individual rights in a multicultural society" (A14). For whom, though, is
the Conservative platform the *only* choice? Whose interests are being
served by the Conservative government's agenda, or by this editorial statement? While such an endorsement should hardly, given *The Globe*'s ownership and business interests, come as a surprise, the effect such a
pronouncement would have on varying constituencies of readers is profoundly troubling, especially when combined with the accommodation
and naturalization of business priorities and interests within educational
practices and processes. What we're seeing – to borrow Cornel West's way
of putting it – is "a public sphere regulated by and for well-to-do, white
males in the name of freedom and democracy" (30).[6] It is perhaps no surprise that one of the slogans used during the 1995 provincial election campaign was "White Males Have Rights Too." One of the most important
tasks for Canadian criticism, I would argue, is to interrogate the assumptions governing the distribution and legitimation of knowledge in both
the academy and the public sphere. As critics and teachers, we need to
expose the interests determining "the pursuit of truth and knowledge"
within academies and the interests governing the media-sanctioned view
of reality, both of which, under the guise of "objectivity," have the function of limiting what can be known or discussed (see McKenna 111).

Now, clearly, Canadian criticism need not lend itself to the kind of critical pedagogy and research that I'm proposing: there are many people currently *doing* Canadian criticism – or some version of it – who would not
feel comfortable with the directions I've been trying to map out. But I
want to suggest that if we are to take seriously our responsibilities as critics and educators, especially at a moment in our cultural history where the
academy is increasingly subject to a process of delegitimation and where
our very frames of reference are massively determined by corporate political interests, then we need to raise some hard pedagogical and methodological issues. What *is* the function of Canadian criticism at the present
time? Just how *should* we teach and practise Canadian criticism? How do
we reaffirm the value of ethics in a postmodern age? How do we define
the politics of Canadian criticism, of the university? Or, in David Noble's
words, "who rules the universities and in whose interests" (quoted in
Calvert 110)? "And do we," as Michael Keefer asks in his compelling
account of "political correctness" debates, "wish to retain some measure of
public control over the contributions our universities make to the reproduction of our social order and to the production and dissemination of

knowledge, or are we willing to allow these functions to pass ever more completely into the power of corporate interests" (37)? How best can we, as academics, begin to initiate politically responsible and accountable work given the hegemonic controls within the academy which shape our production of knowledge and influence our relations with the non-academic world? And what are the implications of staking out such specific methodological and pedagogical imperatives in a conflicting and heterogeneous field of inquiry? What does it mean to suggest that democracy is a "new context of Canadian criticism"?

There is a moment in "Radio as Music: Glenn Gould in Conversation with John Jessop" which, I'd like to argue, offers a valuable point of entry into both the history and the future of Canadian criticism. Gould is telling the story of how, in creating his radio documentary *The Idea of North*, he invented what he would later call "contrapuntal radio":

> I had laid out the program in terms of material that was appropriate to a certain number of scenes. Well, it turned out that if we really wanted all of those scenes to be heard, we were going to need about one hour and twenty-five minutes airtime. We had, of course, one hour at our disposal. So I thought, "Well, obviously one scene has got to go." We had a scene on the Eskimo – couldn't lose that; we had a scene on isolation and its effects – that had to stay, obviously; we had our closing soliloquy, we had our opening trio and other indispensables – and I couldn't part with any of them. We had a scene on the media which somehow had seemed terribly relevant when I got going on it ... but it now seemed that was the one scene that was not wholly communicative and which could be cut. That brought the time down to about one hour, twelve minutes – at least fourteen minutes too long, allowing for Harry Manni's closing credits – and I thought to myself, "Look, we really could hear some of these people speaking simultaneously – there's no particular reason why not." (375-76)

Gould's description of the way in which he evolved for himself a series of techniques and strategies for *The Idea of North* might seem to have little to do with either of the other two topics – democracy, responsibility – signalled in my title. But if the complex, and sometimes conflicting, forces that reveal and determine Canada's discursive self-representation(s) need to be confronted (as I think they do), then Gould's comments have a special, if unsuspected, resonance. In what follows, then, I'd like to consider the extent to which Gould's sensitivity to the importance, indeed the cultural significance, of counterpoint, his predilection for having people in his radio documentary speak "simultaneously," can contribute to the democratization of Canadian criticism.

Gould's "contrapuntal radio" is, in part, a response to the tendency in documentaries to "show respect for the human voice ... such that one shuts down all other patterns to an appropriately reverential level" (380). Critical of this respect, of the fact that "the moment any character ... happens to open his mouth, all other activity has to grind to a halt" (380), Gould sees the art of combining voices, like the art of combining melodies, as a way of encouraging "a type of listener who will not think in terms of precedence, in terms of priority" (380). The de-hierarchization process that Gould wants to set into motion through contrapuntal activity is, I think, akin to the process of *cultural* listening that I'm arguing for in this paper. Indeed, if, as I've already suggested, the most compelling "new contexts" of Canadian criticism are telling us that we need to move beyond a nationalist framework into genuinely democratic forms of cross-cultural work, then cultural listening is predicated on our ability to recognize and understand the role that multiple voices ("speaking simultaneously") have played in the construction of Canada.

Canada, as many critics are fond of reminding us, has long been obsessed with both the thematics and the problematics of its national character. "The search for a Canadian identity, and for a definition of Canadian nationalism," argues Herschel Hardin in *A Nation Unaware*, "has gone on for so long, and is so gloriously rich in idiosyncrasy, that it constitutes one of the wonders of the world" (2). Hardin's claim is that Canadians, far from asserting their nationalism by looking for it, assert nationalism by *not* finding it (26). Implicit in such an assertion is the sense that Canadians have not *found* their national character because they have been too busy defining themselves through comparative acts: as Hutcheon puts it, Canada's "history is one of defining itself against centres" (*Canadian Postmodern* 4). Yet for all its rhetoric of "ex-centricity," its insistence, for example, on distinguishing itself from the cultural agenda of the United States (mosaic vs. melting pot), Canada, as the authors of *The Empire Writes Back* argue, has failed to translate its "internal perception of [itself as] a mosaic ... into corresponding theories of literary hybridity to replace the nationalist approach" (36). Gould's contrapuntal model, I'd like to argue, offers the potential of enabling Canadians to generate such theories, to engage in critical (and self-representational) acts which permit the kind of "traffic between cultures" that Edward Said speaks of and has indeed helped to foster.

The cultural significance of counterpoint is, of course, something that both Paulo Freire and Said, himself a long-time admirer of Gould (see *World* 31-35), have, in their own ways, urged us to take note of in our

teaching and research. In *Culture and Imperialism*, for example, Said explicitly calls for a "contrapuntal" approach to reading: "a simultaneous awareness both of the metropolitan history that is narrated and of those other
histories against which (and together with which) the dominating discourse acts" (51). Said, however, is not directly concerned with Canada,
and his importance for Canadian cultural criticism has not yet been as
profoundly registered as I think it ought to be.[7] What would it mean, then,
to have this "simultaneous awareness" in a settler-invader society such as
Canada? What are the implications of "contrapuntal reading" for our
understanding of Canadian social, cultural, and intellectual history? What
can counterpoint teach us about the politics of Canadian self-representation?

That self-representation is a *political* act is a fact that hardly needs
rehearsing here. Work by Said, Michel Foucault, Hayden White, and, in a
Canadian context, Frank Davey and Linda Hutcheon, has made the point
much more thoroughly and provocatively than I can pretend to do in this
paper. But if, with White, we acknowledge that "narrative is not merely a
neutral discursive form that may or may not be used to represent real
events," but rather a form which "entails ontological and epistemic choices
with distinct ideological and even specifically political implications" (ix),
then we need also to recognize, in Michael Shapiro's words, that "the construction of *national* stories that legitimate the state's boundaries of inclusion and exclusion [constitutes] a primary normalizing strategy" (485). For
self-representational acts are indeed narrative acts; they seek to construct a
story of subjectivity and belonging, and, in doing so, they have the power
to shape the production, maintenance, and transmission of knowledge
"about" both self and other.

Canada's story, as Hardin points out, has emerged out of a series of contradictions: French Canada against English Canada, the regions against the
federal centre, and, of course, Canada against the United States: "It is
across these contradictions that Canada has defined itself" (Hardin 12).
Important recent developments in critical and cultural theory, in Canada
and elsewhere, have, however, invited a radical reassessment of received
models of inquiry and necessitated an altered set of strategies for reading
and responding to Canada's self-representational acts. In effect, many of
the new contexts of Canadian criticism have forced Canadians to expand
their repertoire of contradictory experiences to include, for example, a
consideration of the tensions between some of the following: race, class,
ethnicity, and gender; nationalism and globalism; postmodernism and post-
colonialism (see Hutcheon, "End(s)"); Canadian Studies and postcolonial
theory (see Slemon and Mukherjee); Canadian, Native, and Postcolonial
contexts (see King); subaltern or oppositional voices and hegemonic or
media-constructed narratives (see McKenna). More generally, most of

these contemporary theoretical accounts of Canadian literary and cultural history are part of a larger debate focussing on what Charles Taylor identifies as "the need, sometimes the demand, for recognition" (25), a need which Amy Gutmann, in an introduction to Taylor's essay, calls one of the "most salient and vexing [items] on the political agenda of many democratic and democratizing societies today" (5). "Due recognition," says Taylor, "is not just a courtesy we owe people. It is a vital human need" (26). This need, or demand, is, of course, the result of complex levels of engagement between, on the one hand, institutionally-sanctioned and media-generated accounts of Canada and, on the other, the roles that ethnicity, race, gender, sexual orientation, and class have played in the cultural construction of Canada.

Ethnicity (to focus for a moment on just one factor in this complex set of overlapping experiences) remained, especially in the 1950s and 1960s, "a non-existent and discredited topic." It was seen, according to Francesco Loriggio in "The Question of the Corpus: Ethnicity and Canadian Literature," as "a residue of more primitive, non-modern phases, soon to be expelled by progress" (64). During this time of widespread nationalist activity in Canada (which culminated in the Centennial celebrations of 1967), it is hardly surprising that, again as Loriggio remarks, "Canada's intelligentsia [he's thinking here primarily of Frye, McLuhan, and Grant] sought above all to protect, to reinforce the durability of the large, the whole" (64). And, insofar as "the maintenance of territorial [and national] legitimacy requires narratives which construct the state as a continuous, homogenous subject" (Shapiro 485), Canada sought, at that time, to locate its own (national) subjectivity in its wholeness rather than in its constituent parts.

This emphasis on wholeness, on Canada as a kind of homogenous national community, manifests itself in a variety of ways in Canadian criticism, and, indeed, in Canadian literary and cultural history. It's there, for example, in E.J. Pratt's epic poem, *Towards the Last Spike* (1952), where Canada's very status as a nation is presented as depending so heavily on the rhetorical power of Macdonald's unifying ("from sea to sea") vision. F.R. Scott's famous response to Pratt, in "All the Spikes but the Last" (1957), correctly points out that Pratt's poem, despite its epic reach, effectively silences and thus writes out of history the Chinese labourers who built the railway, and, if we accept the poem's central metaphor, who indeed built the nation. While it might be argued that Pratt was justified in leaving the Chinese labourers out of the poem because he was concerned to present Canada as a unified and autonomous entity, Scott's comments seem to me very convincingly to point to the unsustainability of such a construction.

Pratt, of course, was not alone in promoting representational acts which sought to define Canada as a unified whole. Historian Arthur Lower, for example, published in the 1930s a series of articles which argued that immigration is detrimental to "the emergence of a national point of view and a national culture" ("Can Canada Do Without the Immigrant?" 70). "Even were all our immigrants successful and readily assimilable," Lower writes, "there would still be a grave objection to populating the country in that way *rather than by the way of Nature*" (70; emphasis added). He argues that "a people must be slowly molded *by the forces of Nature*, by the soil and the climate before they are true children of the fatherland" (70; emphasis added). As these comments make clear, Lower's construction of Canada as a homogenous, racially pure nation presents itself as a *natural*, filiative relation between parent (in this case, father) and offspring.

If these comments, with their unmistakable racialist assumptions, seem outdated, I'd like to turn my attention once again to *The Globe and Mail*, "Canada's National Newspaper," and, in particular, to two articles published in 1994 by columnist Michael Valpy. In these articles, Valpy is taking issue with the Ontario Ministry of Education's Common Curriculum, and with how the Ministry has opted to teach Canadian history. In Valpy's words, "it proposes that historical content – where it is taught at all – should portray the country as little more than the aggregate sum of its multiple ethnic and cultural parts." What worries Valpy is that the Ministry, in its attempt to "implant the recognition in children's minds that Canada is a multicultural society and that children from all its constituent groups must feel proud of their respective heritages," is encouraging "to an intolerable degree the disintegration of what can be called the sociological anglophone-Canadian nation – the society that functions with an agreed-upon set of rules and values." Arguing that the "Common Curriculum ... gives short shrift to the need for maintaining a transcendent Canadianness in our society," Valpy insists that schools have a responsibility to teach "the importance and the values of the greater Canadian society" ("Openness" A2).

In another column, published a few days earlier, Valpy tells us that the Common Curriculum is, in fact, "an attempt to eliminate the collective identity" ("Sailing" A2). While he is perhaps more willing than Lower to recognize that Canada *is* an ethnically diverse nation (he is writing, after all, in 1994), he still wants to define history and to represent Canadian values (values which we *all*, supposedly, share) in terms that are not all that different from Lower's. Instead of Canada's connection with Britain being natural and filiative, as it was for Lower, it now, for Valpy, becomes "transcendent." Valpy, in other words, is invoking another structure of authority to justify a familiar argument, to secure what Shapiro calls "the privileging of abstract rights within a historical narrative of state legitimation" (499). Like Lower, Valpy insists that a pure and homogenous society is a necessary prerequisite for Canadian nationalism.

Counterpoint (to return to Gould) works to unsettle such processes of identity formation, and to encourage us to reconceive the relationship between the whole and its parts. Indeed, if identity, as Gould's contrapuntal method invites us to see, is multiple, dialogic, and ever-evolving, then what is at issue is, in large part, an attack on forms and structures of authority, on constructions and representations which authoritatively claim to be able to have access to some pure, definitive, or whole truth about, say, the identity of Canada. In bell hooks' words, "Arguing, as many feminist scholars do, against the notion of a definitive work or the very idea of 'authority' can help to create a climate where scholarship from diverse groups could flourish and we would be better able to appreciate the significance of scholarship that emerges from a particular race, sex, and class perspective" (45). While Gould's contrapuntal radio techniques have been criticized for the "absence of a coherent series of statements" (see Friedrich 198), his abandonment of authoritarian structures of meaning and his emphasis on multiple voices speaking simultaneously have the potential to encourage the kind of critical climate which hooks sees as being conducive to the production of responsible scholarship. Gould himself has justified his technique in his response to Roy Vogt – one of the people he interviewed in his documentary on the Mennonites, *The Quiet in the Land*: "counterpoint is not a dry academic exercise … but rather a method of composition in which, if all goes well, each individual voice leads a life of its own" (*Selected Letters* 150). "Quite frankly," Gould continues, "I would do less than justice to my role as a producer if I were to deliberately sacrifice the 'contrapuntal' integrity of one value-system in order to enhance another" (*Selected Letters* 150). Refusing to privilege one voice or meaning at the expense of others, Gould, in effect, invites us to recognize that the combination of simultaneous voices (each significant in itself) results in a complex, but nevertheless coherent, structure.

As Robert Kroetsch argues in "Disunity as Unity: A Canadian Strategy," this kind of emphasis on multiplicity, this "willingness to refuse privilege to a restricted or restrictive cluster of meta-narratives [has become] a Canadian strategy for survival" (23). Following Jean-François Lyotard in *The Postmodern Condition*, Kroetsch argues that Canadians, far from defining themselves through homogenizing or unifying narratives, "insist on staying multiple, and by that strategy we accommodate to our climate, our economic situation, and our neighbours" (28). Like Kroetsch, Hutcheon sees this valorization of the multiple as one of the salient features of postmodernism: "There has been a general (and perhaps healthy) turning from the expectation of sure and single meaning to a recognition of the value of difference and multiplicity" (Hutcheon, *Canadian Postmodern* 23). How, though, do we adjudicate the competing claims that emerge out of such multiplicity?

There is a moment in Joy Kogawa's extraordinary novel *Obasan* which invites us to ask precisely this question. Aunt Emily, the character most committed to speaking out against the internment of Japanese Canadians during the Second World War, tells us

> Some people ... are so busy seeing all sides of every issue that they neutralize concern and prevent necessary action. There's no strength in seeing all sides unless you can act where real measurable injustice exists. A lot of academic talk just immobilizes the oppressed and maintains oppressors in their positions of power. (35)

What sorts of allowances does postmodernism, with its commitment to a relativist position, to a position which argues that truth and knowledge are functions of discourse and that meaning is never unproblematically fixed or stable, make for our understanding of the possibilities for genuine social change? Does its celebration of multiplicity run the risk of immobilizing the oppressed? Has postmodernism become, as Aijaz Ahmad suggests, "a marketplace of ideas, with massive supplies of theory as usable commodity" (70), a site of continuing critical conversation which militates against our ability to "*conclude* a conversation or to advocate strict partisanship in the politics of theory" (70)? Or, in W.H. New's words, "is the willingness to accept all answers as valid preferable to the willingness to accept only one, or only the easy ones, or only the familiar ones, or only the institutionally approved ones? Safety-from-judgement is not the only option there is to safety-of-judgement. To accept it as though it were is to ... turn relativism into a new absolute, to deny both the subtlety and effect of choice and to reject even the possibility of a culture being a shared experience" (26). And "doesn't it seem funny," asks Kenyan feminist Debra Amory, "that at the very point when women and people of color are ready to sit down at the bargaining table with the white boys, that the table disappears? That is, suddenly there are no grounds for claims to truth and knowledge anymore and here we are, standing in the conference room making all sorts of claims to knowledge and truth but suddenly without a table upon which to put our papers and coffee cups, let alone to bang our fists" (quoted in Shohat 174). Does Gould's method, then, end up valorizing a kind of postmodern skepticism of *all* systems of value, end up, that is, preventing us from making requisite moral choices and ethical decisions, from attending in any meaningful way to struggles for democracy and social justice?

These are, it seems to me, among the most pressing kinds of questions confronting scholars in the humanities. More and more in my own teaching and research on texts and contexts, on literary and cultural histories, I find myself struggling to articulate the relevance of what I do, as a teacher and a scholar, in terms of my work's relation to the world outside the academy. Though trained primarily as a postmodernist, I remain uncertain about the viability of continuing to engage in theoretical assaults on our understanding of truth and knowledge when, for example, Canada, as David Matas documents, "is now or in recent years has been in violation of international human rights standards in a number of different respects" (146). What does it mean to affirm, with postmodernism, the radical inadequacy of all accounts which purport to deal with facts, all knowledge-claims made on behalf of human history, in the face of suffering, injustice, and human rights violations both here in Canada and throughout the world? Bruce Robbins has argued that "the common assumption for all of us who begin, in the study of colonial and postcolonial culture, with the intolerable facts of global suffering and injustice ought surely to be ... that progress is an absolute necessity" ("Secularism" 33). If, as Chomsky writes, "intellectuals are in a position to expose the lies of governments, to analyze actions according to their causes and motives and often hidden intentions" ("Responsibility" 324), then is it utopian of me to suggest that Canadian critics and teachers have a responsibility, however modest, to initiate and nurture forms of solidarity which will help bring about progress, help facilitate change both in the current distribution of social relations and in the popular understanding? I agree with Jim Merod when he suggests that "criticism currently and traditionally is an almost solely élitist academic effort without social or political commitment to people who stand outside the circle of institutional authority and political power. The way critics of a radical inclination assert themselves professionally, as morally and politically adept people," he tells us, "will thus determine what kind of involvement literary scholarship and critical theory can have, directly or indirectly, with oppressed and unrepresented people" (156). Academic humanists thus need to take responsibility not only, as Gerald Graff remarks, "for controlling the way their ideas and projects are represented to a wider public" (354), but also, in Diana Brydon's words, for committing themselves to working "for change in order to create a more inclusive environment and a more varied repertoire of valued knowledges" (106).

Clearly, then, there is much to be gained by adapting Gould's contrapuntal strategies in the classroom and in scholarly research, but these strategies (and the kinds of postmodern openings they permit) need to be tempered with a careful admixture of other sorts of commitment to and solidarity with what Merod calls "nonspecialized, global human interests" (165). For, in Baum's words, "to arrive at an honest evaluation of our society, we must first listen to the people who suffer injustice, we must look at history from below. And then we can speak out against injustice" (55). This sense of solidarity with marginalized and oppressed peoples is, as

Baum notes (and as Chomsky has documented), particularly urgent given the interests which shape and determine the production of knowledge in our newspapers, in academies, and in mainstream culture. In this context, then, counterpoint needs to be reconfigured as part of what Brydon calls our continuing "search for non-repressive alternatives to the present organization of knowledge and its limiting representations of otherness" (110). As a model for cultural listening, counterpoint remains useful because it forces us to acknowledge the unsustainability of notions of cultural purity, and, to borrow Aimé Cesaire's words, because it invites us to recognize that it is "a good thing to place different civilizations in contact with each other; it is an excellent thing to blend different worlds" (quoted in Shapiro 497). By, in Said's words, creating a space for subaltern cultural traditions to "assert their own identity and the existence of their own history" (*Culture* xii) while concomitantly attending to the intricate overlap between and within dominant and subaltern traditions, identities, and histories, Canadian criticism can foster forms of intellectual solidarity which invite us to recognize and to value the role of cultural differences in representations of Canada.[8] If counterpoint succeeds in encouraging us to ask, "How can diverse communities speak in concert? How might we interweave our voices, whether in chorus, in antiphony, in call and response, or in polyphony? What are the modes of collective speech?" (Shohat 177), then it will also succeed in opening up space for a more rigorous consideration of our responsibilities not only as Canadians but, perhaps more suggestively, as cultural citizens in a global community. In place of the pure, homogenous, and whole Canada that Valpy, Lower, and – if somewhat differently – E.J. Pratt sought authoritatively to construct and legitimize, we can thus move toward an alternative vision, a vision articulated by Baum, Kogawa, and, perhaps, Gould, a vision which recognizes that authoritative constructions can, in themselves, be a source of impoverishment because they corrode such realities as imagination, hope, and genuine human possibility.

Notes

I would like to thank Christine Bold, Diana Brydon, Michael Keefer, Ric Knowles, Sheila O'Reilly, Erika Shaker, Jill Siddall, Donna Pennee, and Tim Struthers for their comments on and help with this paper.

1   Janet Paterson, similarly, speaks of the way in which postmodernism, after the manner of its specific Québécois variant, has called into question received notions of knowledge: "il [le postmoderne] ouvre la lecture à la problématisation du sens dans de vastes contextes socioculturels en s'attachant, entre autres, aux questions du sujet féminin, de l'identitaire, de la légitimation et du savoir" (84).

2   See also Lennard Davis, who argues that "novel reading as a social behavior helps prevent change. ... reading novels is an activity that prevents or inhibits social action as do many leisure activities in a consumer society" (17-18).

3   The question of how Canadian critics negotiate between, on the one hand, the specificities of a national context and, on the other, a commitment to the kind of broader discourse I have in mind here is, of course, a highly complex one. A potential danger in trying to work my way through these sets of negotiations is, I suppose, a certain kind of inaccuracy, what Edward Said, in his introduction to *Orientalism*, describes as "the kind of inaccuracy produced by too dogmatic a generality and too positivistic a localized focus" (8).

4   Jameson, indeed, argues that "this whole global, yet American, postmodern culture is the internal and superstructural expression of a whole new wave of American military and economic domination throughout the world: in this sense, as throughout class history, the underside of culture is blood, torture, death, and terror" (9).

5   "The new cultural politics of difference" is West's term for new forms of intellectual consciousness which aim "to preserve people's agency, increase the scope of their freedom and expand the operations of democracy" (30). These new forms of intellectual consciousness, clearly, are among the most important and powerful of the new contexts of Canadian criticism.

6   Michael Apple refers to this strategy of regulation as an "authoritarian populism": "The results have been a partial dismantling of social democratic policies that largely benefited working people, people of colour, and women (these groups are obviously not mutually exclusive), the building of a closer relationship between government and the capitalist economy, a radical decline in the institutions and power of political democracy, and attempts to curtail liberties that had been gained in the past. And all this has been very cleverly connected to the needs, fears, and hopes of many groups of people who feel threatened during a time of perceived crisis in the economy, in authority relations, in the family, and elsewhere" (xii).

7   A notable exception can be found in Peter Dale Scott: "in his combination of a capacious, locative cultural critique with a defense of criticism as an independent, antidogmatic activity, Said is more easily comparable to his Canadian colleagues than to many of his American ones. His writings also constitute the challenge for Canadian literary studies at the present time of whether these critical concerns will sustain a vision of social empowerment or merely lapse into a new separatism or guild mentality" (27).

8   See also François Paré: "il nous faut réorienter l'historiographie des littératures, ouvrir ses structures d'accueil, tenir compte ainsi des marginalités" (10).

Works Cited

Ahmad, Aijaz. *In Theory: Classes, Nations, Literatures.* London: Verso, 1992.

Apple, Michael W. *Ideology and Curriculum.* 2nd ed. New York: Routledge, 1990.

Ashcroft, Bill, Gareth Griffiths, and Helen Tiffin. *The Empire Writes Back: Theory and Practice in Post-Colonial Literatures.* New York: Routledge, 1989.

Baum, Gregory. *Compassion and Solidarity: The Church for Others.* CBC Massey Lectures. Toronto: CBC Enterprises, 1987.

Brennan, Richard. "Minister Called Dishonest." *The Spectator* [Hamilton] 13 Sept. 1995: A1-A2.

Brydon, Diana. "Response to Hart." *Arachne* 1.1 (1994): 100-11.

Calvert, John, with Larry Kuehn. *Pandora's Box: Corporate Power, Free Trade and Canadian Education.* Toronto: Our Schools/Our Selves, 1993.

Chomsky, Noam. "The Responsibility of Intellectuals." *American Power and the New Mandarins.* New York: Pantheon, 1969. 323-66.

Chomsky, Noam, and Edward S. Herman. *Manufacturing Consent: The Political Economy of the Mass Media.* New York: Pantheon, 1988.

Davey, Frank. *Post-National Arguments: The Politics of the Anglophone-Canadian Novel since 1967.* Toronto: U of Toronto P, 1993.

Davis, Lennard J. *Resisting Novels: Ideology and Fiction.* New York: Methuen, 1987.

"For the Conservatives in Ontario." Editorial. *The Globe and Mail* [Toronto] 1 June 1995: A14.

Freire, Paulo. Foreword. Trans. Donald Macedo. *Paulo Freire: A Critical Encounter.* Ed. Peter McLaren and Peter Leonard. New York: Routledge, 1993. ix-xii.

Friedrich, Otto. *Glenn Gould: A Life and Variations.* Toronto: Lester & Orpen Dennys, 1989.

Giroux, Henry. *Living Dangerously: Multiculturalism and the Politics of Difference.* New York: Peter Lang, 1993.

Gould, Glenn. "Radio as Music: Glenn Gould in Conversation with John Jessop." *The Glenn Gould Reader.* Ed. Tim Page. Toronto: Lester & Orpen Dennys, 1984. 374-88.

—. *Selected Letters.* Ed. John P.L. Roberts and Ghyslaine Guertin. Toronto: Oxford UP, 1992.

Graff, Gerald. "The Scholar in Society." *Introduction to Scholarship in Modern Languages and Literatures.* Ed. Joseph Gibaldi. New York: MLA, 1992. 343-62.

Gutmann, Amy. Introduction. *Multiculturalism: Examining the Politics of Recognition.* Ed. Amy Gutmann. Princeton, NJ: Princeton UP, 1994. 3-24.

Hardin, Herschel. *A Nation Unaware: The Canadian Economic Culture.* Vancouver: J.J. Douglas, 1974.

Harpham, Geoffrey Galt. "Ethics." *Critical Terms for Literary Study.* 2nd ed. Ed. Frank Lentricchia and Thomas McLaughlin. Chicago: U of Chicago P, 1995. 387-405.

hooks, bell. "Feminist Scholarship: Ethical Issues." *Talking Back: Thinking Feminist, Thinking Black.* Toronto: Between the Lines, 1988. 42-48.

Hutcheon, Linda. *The Canadian Postmodern: A Study of Contemporary English-Canadian Fiction.* Toronto: Oxford UP, 1988.

—. "The End(s) of Irony: The Politics of Appropriateness." *Irony's Edge: The Theory and Politics of Irony.* New York: Routledge, 1994. 176-204.

Innis, Harold. *The Bias of Communication.* Toronto: U of Toronto P, 1951.

Jameson, Fredric. "The Cultural Logic of Late Capitalism." *Postmodernism, or, The Cultural Logic of Late Capitalism.* Durham, NC: Duke UP, 1991. 1-54.

Keefer, Michael. *Lunar Perspectives: Field Notes from the Culture Wars.* Toronto: Anansi, 1996.

King, Thomas. "Godzilla vs. Post-Colonial." *World Literature Written in English* 30.2 (1990): 10-16.

Kogawa, Joy. *Obasan.* 1981. Markham, ON: Penguin, 1983.

Kroetsch, Robert. "Disunity as Unity: A Canadian Strategy." *The Lovely Treachery of Words: Essays Selected and New.* Toronto: Oxford UP, 1989. 21-33.

Lecker, Robert. "Privacy, Publicity, and the Discourse of Canadian Criticism." *Essays on Canadian Writing* 51-52 (1993-94): 32-82.

Loriggio, Francesco. "The Question of the Corpus: Ethnicity and Canadian Literature." *Future Indicative: Literary Theory and Canadian Literature.* Ed. John Moss. Ottawa: U of Ottawa P, 1987. 53-69.

Lower, A.R.M. "Can Canada Do Without the Immigrant?" *Maclean's* 1 June 1930: 3-4, 70-71.

Mandel, Eli. Introduction. *Contexts of Canadian Criticism.* Ed. Eli Mandel. Chicago: U of Chicago P, 1971. 3-25.

Manners, Earl. "Credibility Destroyed, Minister of Education Must Resign." Ontario Secondary School Teachers' Federation News Release. 13 Sept. 1995.

Matas, David. *No More: The Battle Against Human Rights Violations.* Toronto: Dundurn, 1994.

McKenna, Kate. "Subjects of Discourse: Learning the Language That Counts." *Unsettling Relations: The University as a Site of Feminist Struggles.* By Himani Bannerji, Linda Carty, Kari Dehli, Susan Heald, Kate McKenna. Toronto: Women's, 1991. 109-28.

Merod, Jim. *The Political Responsibility of the Critic.* Ithaca, NY: Cornell UP, 1987.

Mukherjee, Arun. "Whose Post-Colonialism and Whose Postmodernism?" *World Literature Written in English* 30.2 (1990): 1-9.

New, W.H. "Back to the Future: The Short Story in Canada and the Writing of Literary History." *Australian-Canadian Studies* 4 (1986): 15-27.

Newson, Janice, and Howard Buchbinder. *The University Means Business: Universities, Corporations, and Academic Work.* Toronto: Garamond, 1988.

Paré, François. *Les littératures de l'exiguïté.* Hearst, ON: Nordir, 1994.

Paterson, Janet M. "Le Postmodernisme québécois: tendances actuelles." *Études littéraires* 27.1 (1994): 77-88.

Pratt, E.J. *Towards the Last Spike. An Anthology of Canadian Literature in English*. Rev. and abridged ed. Ed. Russell Brown, Donna Bennett, and Nathalie Cooke. Toronto: Oxford UP, 1990. 216-56.

Pratt, Mary Louise. "Comparative Literature and Global Citizenship." *Comparative Literature in the Age of Multiculturalism*. Ed. Charles Bernheimer. Baltimore: Johns Hopkins UP, 1995. 58-65.

Robbins, Bruce. "Comparative Cosmopolitanism." *Social Text* 31-32 (1992): 169-86.

—. "Secularism, Élitism, Progress, and Other Transgressions: On Edward Said's 'Voyage In.'" *Social Text* 40 (1994): 25-37.

Said, Edward W. *Culture and Imperialism*. New York: Alfred A. Knopf, 1993.

—. "The Future of Criticism." *Modern Language Notes* 99 (1984): 951-58.

—. *Orientalism*. 1978. New York: Vintage, 1979.

—. *The World, the Text, and the Critic*. Cambridge, MA: Harvard UP, 1983.

Scott, F.R. "All the Spikes but the Last." *An Anthology of Canadian Literature in English*. Rev. and abridged ed. Ed. Russell Brown, Donna Bennett, and Nathalie Cooke. Toronto: Oxford UP, 1990. 277.

Scott, Peter Dale. "The Difference Perspective Makes: Literary Studies in Canada and the United States." *Essays on Canadian Writing* 44 (1991): 1-60.

Shapiro, Michael J. "Moral Geographies and the Ethics of Post-Sovereignty." *Public Culture* 6 (1994): 479-502.

Shohat, Ella. "The Struggle Over Representation: Casting, Coalitions, and the Politics of Identification." *Late Imperial Culture*. Ed. Román de la Campa, E. Ann Kaplan, and Michael Sprinker. London: Verso, 1995. 166-78.

Slemon, Stephen. "Unsettling the Empire: Resistance Theory for the Second World." *World Literature Written in English* 30.2 (1990): 30-41.

Tarras, David. Introduction. *A Passion for Identity: An Introduction to Canadian Studies*. Ed. David Tarras and Eli Mandel. Toronto: Methuen, 1987. 10-16.

Taylor, Charles. "The Politics of Recognition." *Multiculturalism: Examining the Politics of Recognition*. Ed. Amy Gutmann. Princeton, NJ: Princeton UP, 1994. 25-73.

Valpy, Michael. "An Openness to Change, but Not a Blank Slate." *The Globe and Mail* [Toronto] 5 Apr. 1994: A2.

—. "Sailing through History in Different Boats." *The Globe and Mail* [Toronto] 1 Apr. 1994: A2.

West, Cornel. *Keeping Faith: Philosophy and Race in America*. New York: Routledge, 1993.

White, Hayden. *The Content of the Form: Narrative Discourse and Historical Representation*. Baltimore: Johns Hopkins UP, 1987.

Williams, Raymond. "Communications and Community." *Resources of Hope: Culture, Democracy, Socialism*. London: Verso, 1989. 19-31.

The Politics of Recognition

Charles Taylor

A number of strands in contemporary politics turn on the need, sometimes the demand, for recognition. The need, it can be argued, is one of
the driving forces behind nationalist movements in politics. And the
demand comes to the fore in a number of ways in today's politics, on
behalf of minority or "subaltern" groups, in some forms of feminism, and
in what is called the politics of multiculturalism.

The demand for recognition in these cases is given urgency by the supposed links between recognition and identity, where "identity" designates
something like an understanding of who we are, of our fundamental
defining characteristics as human beings. The thesis is that our identity is
partly shaped by recognition or its absence, often by the *mis*recognition of
others, and so a person or group of people can suffer real damage, real distortion, if the people or society around them mirror back a confining or
demeaning or contemptible picture of themselves. Nonrecognition or
misrecognition can inflict harm, can be a form of oppression, imprisoning
someone in a false, distorted, and reduced mode of being.

Thus some feminists have argued that women in patriarchal societies
have been induced to adopt a depreciatory image of themselves. They have
internalized a picture of their own inferiority, so that even when some of
the objective obstacles to their advancement fall away, they may be incapable of taking advantage of the new opportunities. And beyond this, they
are condemned to suffer the pain of low self-esteem. An analogous point
has been made in relation to blacks: that white society has for generations
projected a demeaning image which some blacks have been unable to
resist adopting. Their own self-depreciation, on this view, becomes one of
the most potent instruments of their oppression. Their first task ought to
be to purge themselves of this imposed and destructive identity. A similar
point has been made in relation to indigenous and colonized people in
general. It is held that since 1492 Europeans have projected an image of
such people as somehow inferior, "uncivilized," and through the force of
conquest have often been able to impose this image on the conquered.
The figure of Caliban has been held to epitomize this crushing portrait of
contempt for New World aboriginals.

Within these perspectives, misrecognition shows not just a lack of due
respect. It can inflict a grievous wound, saddling its victims with a crip-

pling self-hatred. Due recognition is not just a courtesy we owe people. It is a vital human need.

In order to examine some of these issues, I'd like to take a step back, achieve a little distance, and look first at how this discourse of recognition and identity came to seem familiar, or at least readily understandable, to us. For it was not always so, and our ancestors of more than a few centuries ago would have stared at us uncomprehendingly if we had used these terms in their current sense. How did we get started on this?

Hegel comes to mind right off, with his famous dialectic of master and slave. This is an important stage, but we need to go a little farther back to see how this passage came to have the sense it did. What changed to make this kind of talk have sense for us?

We can distinguish two changes that together have made the modern preoccupation with identity and recognition inevitable. The first is the collapse of social hierarchies, which used to be the basis for honour. I'm using *honour* in the ancien régime sense in which it is intrinsically linked to inequalities. For some to have honour in this sense, it is essential that not everyone have it. This is how Montesquieu uses it in his description of monarchy. Honour is intrinsically a matter of preferences.[1] It is also the sense in which we use the term when we speak of honouring someone by giving her a public award, for instance, the Order of Canada. Clearly, this award would be without worth if tomorrow we decided to give it to every adult Canadian.

As against this notion of honour, we have the modern notion of dignity, now used in a universalist and egalitarian sense, where we talk of the inherent "dignity of human beings" or of citizen dignity. The underlying premise here is that everyone shares in it.[2] It is obvious that this concept of dignity is the only one compatible with a democratic society, and that it was inevitable that the old concept of honour was superseded. But it has also meant that the forms of equal recognition have been essential to democratic culture. For instance, calling everyone "Mr.," "Mrs.," or "Miss," rather than calling some people "Lord" or "Lady" and others simply by their surnames – or, even more demeaning, by their first names – has been thought essential in some democratic societies, such as the United States. More recently, for similar reasons, "Mrs." and "Miss" have been collapsed into "Ms." Democracy has ushered in a politics of equal recognition, which has taken various forms over the years, and has now returned in the form of demands for the equal status of cultures and of genders.

But the importance of recognition has been modified and intensified by the new understanding of individual identity that emerged at the end of the eighteenth century. We might speak of an *individualized* identity, one that is particular to me and that I discover in myself. This notion arises along with an ideal, that of being true to myself and my own particular way of being. Following Lionel Trilling's usage in his brilliant study, I will speak of this as the ideal of "authenticity."[3] It will help to describe in what it consists and how it came about.

One way of describing its development is to see its starting point in the eighteenth-century notion that human beings are endowed with a moral sense, an intuitive feeling for what is right and wrong. The original point of this doctrine was to combat a rival view, that knowing right and wrong was a matter of calculating consequences, in particular, those concerned with divine reward and punishment. The idea was that understanding right and wrong was not a matter of dry calculation, but was anchored in our feelings.[4] Morality has, in a sense, a voice within.

The notion of authenticity develops out of a displacement of the moral accent in this idea. On the original view, the inner voice was important because it tells us the right thing to do. Being in touch with our moral feelings matters here, as a means to the end of acting rightly. What I'm calling the displacement of the moral accent comes about when being in touch with our feelings takes on independent and crucial moral significance. It comes to be something we have to attain if we are to be true and full human beings.

To see what is new here, we have to see the analogy to earlier moral views, where being in touch with some source – for example, God or the Idea of the Good – was considered essential to full being. But now the source we have to connect with is deep within us. This is part of the massive subjective turn of modern culture, a new form of inwardness, in which we come to think of ourselves as beings with inner depths. At first, this idea that the source is within may not exclude our being related to God or the Idea; it can be considered our proper way of relating to them. In a sense, it can be seen as just a continuation and intensification of the development inaugurated by Augustine, who saw the road to God as passing through our own self-awareness. The first variants of this new view were theistic, or at least pantheistic.

The most important philosophical writer who helped to bring about this change was Jean-Jacques Rousseau. Rousseau is important not because he inaugurated the change; rather, I would argue that his great popularity comes in part from his articulating something that was in a sense already occurring in the culture. Rousseau frequently presents the issue of morality as that of our following the voice of nature within us. This voice is often drowned out by the passions that are induced by our dependence on others, the main one being *amour propre*, or pride. Our moral salvation comes from recovering authentic moral contact with ourselves. Rousseau even gives a name to the intimate contact with oneself, more fundamental than any moral view, that is a source of such joy and contentment: "le sentiment de l'existence."[5]

The ideal of authenticity becomes crucial owing to a development that occurs after Rousseau, which I associate with the name of Herder – once again, as its major early articulator rather than its originator. Herder put forward the idea that each of us has an original way of being human: each person has his or her own "measure."[6] This idea has burrowed very deep into modern consciousness. It is a new idea. Before the late eighteenth century, no one thought that the differences between human beings carried this kind of moral significance. There is a certain way of being human that is *my* way. I am called upon to live my life in this way, and not in imitation of anyone else's life. But this notion gives a new importance to being true to myself. If I am not, I miss the point of my life; I miss what being human is for *me*.

This is the powerful moral ideal that has come down to us. It accords moral importance to a kind of contact with myself, with my own inner nature, which it sees as in danger of being lost, partly through the pressures toward outward conformity, but also because in taking an instrumental stance toward myself, I may have lost the capacity to listen to this inner voice. It greatly increases the importance of this self-contact by introducing the principle of originality: each of our voices has something unique to say. Not only should I not mold my life to the demands of external conformity; I can't even find the model by which to live outside myself. I can only find it within.[7]

Being true to myself means being true to my own originality, which is something only I can articulate and discover. In articulating it, I'm also defining myself. I'm realizing a potentiality that is properly my own. This is the background understanding to the modern ideal of authenticity, and to the goals of self-fulfilment and self-realization in which the ideal is usually couched. I should note here that Herder applied his concept of originality at two levels, not only to the individual person among other persons, but also to the culture-bearing people among other peoples. Just like individuals, a *Volk* should be true to itself, that is, to its own culture. Germans shouldn't try to be derivative and (inevitably) second-rate Frenchmen, as Frederick the Great's patronage seemed to be encouraging them to do. The Slavic peoples had to find their own path. And European colonialism ought to be rolled back to give the peoples of what we now call the third world their chance to be themselves unimpeded. We can recognize here the seminal idea of modern nationalism, in both benign and malignant forms.

This new ideal of authenticity was, like the idea of dignity, also in part an offshoot of the decline of hierarchical society. In those earlier societies, what we would now call identity was largely fixed by one's social position. The background that explained what people recognized as important to themselves was to a great extent determined by their place in society, and whatever roles or activities attached to this position. The birth of demo-cratic society doesn't by itself do away with this phenomenon, because people can still define themselves by their social roles. What does decisively undermine this socially derived identification, however, is the ideal of authenticity itself. As this emerges, for instance with Herder, it calls on me to discover my own original way of being. By definition, this way of being cannot be socially derived, but must be inwardly generated.

But in the nature of the case, there is no such thing as inward genera-tion, monologically understood. In order to understand the close connec-tion between identity and recognition, we have to take into account a crucial feature of the human condition that has been rendered almost invisible by the overwhelmingly monological bent of mainstream modern philosophy.

This crucial feature of human life is its fundamentally dialogical char-acter. We become full human agents, capable of understanding ourselves, and hence of defining our identity, through our acquisition of rich human languages of expression. For my purposes here, I want to take language in a broad sense, covering not only the words we speak, but also other modes of expression whereby we define ourselves, including the "languages" of art, of gesture, of love, and the like. But we learn these modes of expres-sion though exchanges with others. People do not acquire the languages needed for self-definition on their own. Rather, we are introduced to them through interaction with others who matter to us – what George H. Mead called "significant others."[8] The genesis of the human mind is in this sense not monological, not something each person accomplishes on his or her own, but dialogical.

Moreover, this is not just a fact about *genesis*, which can be ignored later on. We don't just learn the languages in dialogue and then go on to use them for our own purposes. We are of course expected to develop our own opinions, outlook, stances toward things, and to a considerable degree through solitary reflection. But this isn't how things work with such important issues as the definition of our identity. We define our identity always in dialogue with, sometimes in struggle against, the things our significant others want to see in us. Even after we outgrow some of these others – our parents, for instance – and they disappear from our lives, the conversation with them continues within us as long as we live.[9]

Thus the contribution of significant others, even when it is provided at the beginning of our lives, continues indefinitely. Some people may still want to hold on to some form of the monological ideal. It is true that we can never liberate ourselves completely from those whose love and care shaped us early in life, but we should strive to define ourselves on our own to the fullest extent possible, coming as best we can to understand and thus get some control over the influence of our parents, and not fall into any more such dependent relationships. We need relationships to fulfil, but not to define, ourselves.

The monological ideal seriously underestimates the place of the dialogical in human life. It wants to confine it as much as possible to genesis. It forgets how our understandings of the good things in life can be transformed by our enjoying them in common with people we love; how some goods become accessible to us only through such common enjoyment. Because of this, it would take a great deal of effort, and probably many wrenching breakups, to *prevent* our identity's being formed by the people we love. Consider what we mean by identity. It is who we are, "where we're coming from." As such it is the background against which our tastes and desires and opinions and aspirations make sense. If some of the things I value most are accessible to me only in relation to the person I love, then she becomes part of my identity.

To some people this might seem a limitation, from which they might aspire to free themselves. This is one way of understanding the impulse behind the life of the hermit or, to take a case more familiar to our culture, the solitary artist. But from another perspective, we might see even these lives as aspiring to a certain kind of dialogicality. In the case of the hermit, the interlocutor is God. In the case of the solitary artist, the work itself is addressed to a future audience, perhaps still to be created by the work. The very form of a work of art shows its character as *addressed*.[10] But however one feels about it, the making and sustaining of our identity, in the absence of a heroic effort to break out of ordinary existence, remains dialogical throughout our lives.

Thus my discovering my own identity doesn't mean that I work it out in isolation, but that I negotiate it through dialogue, partly overt, partly internal, with others. That is why the development of an ideal of inwardly generated identity gives a new importance to recognition. My own identity crucially depends on my dialogical relations with others.

Of course, the point is not that this dependence on others arose with the age of authenticity. A form of dependence was always there. The socially derived identity was by its very nature dependent on society. But in the earlier age recognition never arose as a problem. General recognition was built into the socially derived identity by virtue of the very fact that it was based on social categories that everyone took for granted. Yet inwardly derived, personal, original identity doesn't enjoy this recognition a priori. It has to win it through exchange, and the attempt can fail. What has come about with the modern age is not the need for recognition but the conditions in which the attempt to be recognized can fail. That is why the need is now acknowledged for the first time. In premodern times, people didn't speak of "identity" and "recognition" – not because people didn't have what we call identities, or because these didn't depend on recognition, but rather because these were then too unproblematic to be thematized as such.

It is not surprising that we can find some of the seminal ideas about citizen dignity and universal recognition, even if not in these specific terms, in Rousseau, who is one of the points of origin of the modern discourse of authenticity. Rousseau is a sharp critic of hierarchical honour, of preferences. In a significant passage of the *Discourse on Inequality*, he pinpoints a fateful moment when society takes a turn toward corruption and injustice, when people begin to desire preferential esteem.[11] By contrast, in republican society, where all can share equally in the light of public attention, he sees the source of health.[12] But the topic of recognition is given its most influential early treatment in Hegel.[13]

The importance of recognition is now universally acknowledged in one form or another; on an intimate plane, we are all aware of how identity can be formed or malformed through the course of our contact with significant others. On the social plane, we have a continuing politics of equal recognition. Both planes have been shaped by the growing ideal of authenticity, and recognition plays an essential role in the culture that has arisen around this ideal.

On the intimate level, we can see how much an original identity needs and is vulnerable to the recognition given or withheld by significant others. It is not surprising that in the culture of authenticity, relationships are seen as the key loci of self-discovery and self-affirmation. Love relationships are not just important because of the general emphasis in modern culture on the fulfilments of ordinary needs. They are also crucial because they are the crucibles of inwardly generated identity.

On the social plane, the understanding that identities are formed in open dialogue, unshaped by a predefined social script, has made the politics of equal recognition more central and stressful. It has, in fact, considerably raised the stakes. Equal recognition is not just the appropriate mode for a healthy democratic society. Its refusal can inflict damage on those who are denied it, according to a widespread modern view, as I indicated at the outset. The projection of an inferior or demeaning image on another can actually distort and oppress, to the extent that the image is internalized. Not only contemporary feminism but also race relations and discussions of multiculturalism are undergirded by the premise that the withholding of recognition can be a form of oppression. We may debate whether this factor has been exaggerated, but it is clear that the understanding of identity and authenticity has introduced a new dimension into the politics of equal recognition, which now operates with something like its own notion of authenticity, at least so far as the denunciation of other-induced distortions is concerned.

And so the discourse of recognition has become familiar to us, on two levels. First, in the intimate sphere, where we understand the formation of identity and the self as taking place in a continuing dialogue and struggle with significant others. And then in the public sphere, where a politics of equal recognition has come to play a bigger and bigger role. Certain feminist theories have tried to show the links between the two spheres.[14] I want to concentrate here on the public sphere and try to work out what a politics of equal recognition has meant and could mean.

In fact, it has come to mean two rather different things, connected, respectively, with the two major changes I've been describing. With the move from honour to dignity has come a politics of universalism, emphasizing the equal dignity of all citizens, and the content of this politics has been the equalization of rights and entitlements. What is to be avoided at all costs is the existence of first-class and second-class citizens. Naturally, the actual detailed measures justified by this principle have varied greatly, and have often been controversial. For some, equalization has affected only civil rights and voting rights; for others, it has extended into the socioeconomic sphere. People who are systematically handicapped by poverty from making the most of their citizenship rights are deemed on this view to have been relegated to second-class status, necessitating remedial action through equalization. But through all the differences of interpretation, the principle of equal citizenship has come to be universally accepted. Every position, no matter how reactionary, is now defended under the colours of this principle. Its greatest, most recent victory was won by the U.S. civil-rights movement of the 1960s. It is worth noting that even the adversaries of extending voting rights to blacks in the southern states found some pretext consistent with universalism, such as tests to be administered to would-be voters at the time of registration.

By contrast, the second change, the development of the modern notion of identity, has given rise to a politics of difference. There is, of course, a universalist basis to this as well, making for the overlap and confusion between the two. *Everyone* should be recognized for his or her unique identity. But recognition here means something else. With the politics of equal dignity, what is established is meant to be universally the same, an identical basket of rights and immunities; with the politics of difference, what we are asked to recognize is the unique identity of this individual or group, its distinctness from everyone else. The idea is that it is precisely this distinctness that has been ignored, glossed over, assimilated to a dominant or majority identity. And this assimilation is the cardinal sin against the ideal authenticity.[15]

Now underlying the demand is a principle of universal equality. The politics of difference is full of denunciations of discrimination and refusals of second-class citizenship. This gives the principle of universal equality a point of entry within the politics of dignity. But once inside, as it were, its demands are hard to assimilate to that politics. For it asks that we give acknowledgement and status to something that is not universally shared. Or, otherwise put, we give due acknowledgement only to what is universally present – everyone has an identity – through recognizing what is peculiar to each. The universal demand powers an acknowledgement of specificity.

The politics of difference grows organically out of the politics of universal dignity through one of those shifts with which we are long familiar, where a new understanding of the human social condition imparts a radically new meaning to an old principle. Just as a view of human beings as conditioned by their socioeconomic plight changed the understanding of second-class citizenship, so that this category came to include, for example, people in inherited poverty traps, so here the understanding of identity as formed in interchange, and as possibly so malformed, introduces a new form of second-class status into our purview. As in the present case, the socioeconomic redefinition justified social programs that were highly controversial. For those who had not gone along with this changed definition of equal status, the various redistributive programs and special opportunities offered to certain populations seemed a form of undue favouritism.

Similar conflicts arise today around the politics of difference. Where the politics of universal dignity fought for forms of nondiscrimination that were quite "blind" to the ways in which citizens differ, the politics of difference often redefines nondiscrimination as requiring that we make these distinctions the basis of differential treatment. So members of aboriginal bands will get certain rights and powers not enjoyed by other Canadians, if the demands for native self-government are finally agreed on, and certain minorities will get the right to exclude others in order to preserve their cultural integrity, and so on.

To proponents of the original politics of dignity, this can seem like a reversal, a betrayal, a simple negation of their cherished principle. Attempts are therefore made to mediate, to show how some of these measures meant to accommodate minorities can after all be justified on the original basis of dignity. These arguments can be successful up to a point. For instance, some of the (apparently) most flagrant departures from "difference-blindness" are reverse discrimination measures, affording people from previously unfavoured groups a competitive advantage for jobs or places in universities. This practice has been justified on the grounds that historical discrimination has created a pattern within which the unfavoured struggle at a disadvantage. Reverse discrimination is defended as a temporary measure that will eventually level the playing field and allow the old "blind" rules to come back into force in a way that doesn't disadvantage anyone. This argument seems cogent enough – wherever its factual basis is sound. But it won't justify some of the measures now urged on the grounds of difference, the goal of which is not to bring us back to an eventual "difference-blind" social space but, on the contrary, to maintain and cherish distinctness, not just now but forever. After all, if we're concerned with identity, then what's more legitimate than our aspiration that it never be lost?[16]

So even though one politics springs from the other, by one of those shifts in the definition of key terms with which we're familiar, the two diverge quite seriously from each other. One basis for the divergence comes out even more clearly when we go beyond what each requires that we acknowledge – certain universal rights in one case, a particular identity on the other – and look at the underlying intuitions of value.

The politics of equal dignity is based on the idea that all humans are equally worthy of respect. It is underpinned by a notion of what in human beings commands respect, however we may try to shy away from this "metaphysical" background. For Kant, whose use of the term *dignity* was one of the earliest influential evocations of this idea, what commanded respect in us was our status as rational agents, capable of directing our lives through principles.[17] Something like this has been the basis for our intuitions of equal dignity ever since, though the detailed definition of it may have changed.

Thus what is picked out as of worth is a *universal human potential*, a capacity that all humans share. This potential, rather than anything a person may have made of it, is what ensures that each person deserves respect. Indeed, our sense of the importance of potentiality reaches so far that we extend this protection even to people who through some circumstance that has befallen them are incapable of realizing their potential in the normal way – handicapped people or those in a coma, for instance.

In the case of the politics of difference, we might also say that a universal potential is at its basis, namely, the potential for forming and defining one's own identity, as an individual and also as a culture. This potentiality must be respected equally in everyone. But at least in the intercultural context, a stronger demand has recently arisen: that we accord equal respect to actually evolved cultures. Critiques of European or white domination, to the effect that they have not only suppressed but failed to appreciate other cultures, consider these depreciatory judgements not only factually mistaken but somehow morally wrong. When the novelist Saul Bellow is quoted as saying something like, "When the Zulus produce a Tolstoy we will read him,"[18] this is taken as a quintessential statement of European arrogance, not just because Bellow is allegedly being insensitive to the value of Zulu culture, but frequently also because it is seen to reflect a denial in principle of human equality. The possibility that the Zulus, while having the same potential for culture formation as anyone else, might nevertheless have come up with a culture that is less valuable than others is ruled out from the start. Even to entertain this possibility is to deny human equality. Bellow's error here, then, would not be a (possibly insensitive) particular mistake in evaluation, but a denial of a fundamental principle.

To the extent that this stronger reproach is in play, the demand for equal recognition extends beyond an acknowledgement of the equal value of all humans potentially, and comes to include the equal value of what they have made of this potential in fact. This creates a serious problem, as we shall see below.

These two modes of politics, then, both based on the notion of equal respect, come into conflict. For one, the principle of equal respect requires that we treat people in a difference-blind fashion. The fundamental intuition that humans command this respect focuses on what is the same in all. For the other, we have to recognize and even foster particularity. The reproach the first makes to the second is just that it violates the principle of nondiscrimination. The reproach the second makes to the first is that it negates identity by forcing people into a homogeneous mold that is untrue to them. This would be bad enough if the mold were itself neutral – nobody's mold in particular. But the complaint generally goes further. The claim is that the supposedly neutral set of difference-blind principles is in fact a reflection of one hegemonic culture. As it turns out, then, only the minority or suppressed cultures are being forced to take alien form. So the supposedly fair and difference-blind society is not only inhuman (because suppressing identities) but also, in a subtle and unconscious way, itself highly discriminatory.[19]

This last attack is the cruellest and most upsetting of all. The liberalism of equal dignity seems to have to assume that there are some universal, difference-blind principles. Even though we may not have defined them yet, the project of defining them remains alive and essential. Different theories may be put forward and contested – and a number have been proposed in our day[20] – but the shared assumption of all of them is that one is right.

The charge levelled by the most radical forms of the politics of difference is that blind liberalisms are themselves the reflection of particular cultures. And the worrying thought is that this bias might not just be a contingent weakness of all hitherto proposed theories, that the very idea of such a liberalism may be a kind of pragmatic contradiction, a particularism masquerading as the universal.

I want now to move, gently and gingerly, into this nest of issues, glancing at some of the important stages in the emergence of these two kinds of politics in western societies. First let's look at the politics of equal dignity.

CHARLES TAYLOR

The politics of equal dignity has emerged in western civilization in two ways, which we could associate with the names of two standard bearers, Rousseau and Kant. This doesn't mean that all instances of each have been influenced by those masters (though that is arguably true for the Rousseauean branch), just that Rousseau and Kant are prominent early exponents of the two models. Looking at the models should enable us to gauge to what extent they are guilty of the charge of imposing a false homogeneity.

I stated earlier that Rousseau can be seen as one of the originators of the discourse of recognition. I say this not because he uses the term, but because he begins to think out the importance of equal respect and, indeed, deems it indispensable for freedom. Rousseau, as is well known, tends to oppose a condition of freedom-in-equality to one characterized by hierarchy and other-dependence. In this state, you are dependent on others not just because they wield political power, or because you need them for survival or success in your cherished projects, but above all because you crave their esteem. The other-dependent person is a slave to "opinion."

This idea is one of the keys to the connection that Rousseau assumes between other-dependence and hierarchy. Logically, these two things are separable. Why can't there be other-dependence in conditions of equality? It seems that for Rousseau this can't be, because he associates other-dependence with the need for others' good opinion, which in turn is understood in the framework of the traditional conception of honour, that is, as intrinsically bound up with preferences. The esteem we seek in this condition is intrinsically differential. It is a positional good.

It is because of this crucial place of honour that the depraved condition of mankind has a paradoxical combination of properties such that we are unequal in power, and yet *all* dependent on others – not just the slave on the master, but also the master on the slave. This point is frequently made. The second sentence of *The Social Contract*, after the famous first line about men born free and yet everywhere in chains, runs: "Tel se croit le maître des autres, qui ne laisse pas d'être plus esclave qu'eux" (One thinks himself the master of others, and still remains a greater slave than they).[21] And in *Émile* Rousseau tells us that in this condition of dependence, "le maître et l'esclave se dépravent mutuellement" (master and slave corrupt each other).[22] If it were simply a question of brute power, one might think the master free at the expense of the slave. But in a system of hierarchical honour, the deference of the lower orders is essential.

Rousseau often sounds like the stoics, who undoubtedly influenced him. He identifies pride as one of the great sources of evil. But he doesn't end up where the stoics do. There is a long-standing discourse on pride, both stoic and Christian, which recommends that we completely overcome our concern for the good opinion of others. We are asked to step outside this dimension of human life, in which reputations are sought, gained, and unmade. How you appear in public space should be of no concern to you. Rousseau sometimes sounds as if he endorses this line. In particular, it is part of his own self-dramatization that he could maintain his integrity in the face of undeserved hostility and calumny from the world. But when we look at his accounts of a potentially good society, we can see that esteem does still play a role in them, that people live very much in the public gaze. In a functioning republic, the citizens do care very much what others think. In a passage of "Considerations on the Government of Poland," Rousseau describes how ancient legislators took care to attach citizens to their fatherland. One of the means used to achieve this connection was public games. Rousseau speaks of the prizes with which,

> aux acclamations de toute la Grèce, on couronnoit les vainqueurs dans leurs jeux qui, les embrasant continuellement d'émulation et de gloire, portèrent leur courage et leurs vertus à ce degré d'énergie dont rien aujourd'hui ne nous donne l'idée, et qu'il n'appartient pas même aux modernes de croire.

> successful contestants in Greek games were crowned amidst applause from all their fellow-citizens – these are the things that, by constantly re-kindling the spirit of emulation and the love of glory, raised Greek courage and Greek virtues to a level of strenuousness of which nothing existing today can give us even a remote idea – which, indeed, strikes modern men as beyond belief.[23]

Glory, public recognition, mattered very much here. Moreover, the effect of their mattering was highly beneficent. Why is this so, if modern honour is such a negative force?

The answer seems to be equality or, more exactly, the balanced reciprocity that underpins equality. One might say (Rousseau didn't) that in these ideal republican contexts, though everyone did depend on everyone else, all did so equally. Rousseau is arguing that the key feature of these events, games, festivals, and recitations, which made them sources of patriotism and virtue, was the total lack of differentiation or distinction between different classes of citizen. They took place in the open air, and they involved everyone. People were both spectator and show. The contrast drawn in this passage is with modern religious services in enclosed churches, and above all with modern theatre, which operates in closed halls, which you have to pay to get into, and consists of a special class of professionals making presentations to others.

This theme is central to the "Letter to M. D'Alembert," where again Rousseau contrasts modern theatre and the public festivals of a true republic, which take place in the open air. Here he makes it clear that the identity of spectator and performer is the key to these virtuous assemblies.

Mais quels seront enfin les objets de ces spectacles? qu'y montrera-t-on? Rien, si l'on veut. Avec la liberté, partout où règne l'affluence, le bien-être y règne aussi. Plantez au milieu d'une place un piquet couronné de fleurs, rassemblez-y le peuple, et vous aurez une fête. Faites mieux encore: donnez les spectateurs en spectacle; rendez-les acteurs eux-mêmes; faites que chacun se voie et s'aime dans les autres, afin que tous en soient mieux unis.

But what then will be the objects of these entertainments? What will be shown in them? Nothing, if you please. With liberty, wherever abundance reigns, well-being also reigns. Plant a stake crowned with flowers in the middle of a square; gather the people together there, and you will have a festival. Do better yet; let the spectators become an entertainment to themselves; make them actors themselves; do it so that each sees and loves himself in the others so that all will be better united.[24]

Rousseau's unstated argument would seem to be this: a perfectly balanced reciprocity takes the sting out of our dependence on opinion, and makes it compatible with liberty. Complete reciprocity, along with the unity of purpose that it makes possible, ensures that in following opinion I am not in any way pulled outside myself. I am still "obeying myself" as a member of this common project or general will. Caring about esteem in this context is compatible with freedom and social unity, because the society is one in which all the virtuous will be esteemed equally and for the same (right) reasons. In contrast, in a system of hierarchical honour, we are in competition; one person's glory must be another's shame, or at least obscurity. Our unity of purpose is shattered, and in this context attempting to win the favour of another, who by hypothesis has goals distinct from mine, must be alienating. Paradoxically, the bad other-dependence goes along with separation and isolation;[25] the good kind, which Rousseau doesn't call other-dependence at all, involves the unity of a common project, even a "common self."[26]

Thus Rousseau is at the origin of a new discourse about honour and dignity. To the two traditional ways of thinking about honour and pride he adds a third, which is quite different. There was a discourse denouncing pride, as I mentioned above, which called on us to remove ourselves from this whole dimension of human life and to be utterly unconcerned with esteem. And then there was an ethic of honour, frankly nonuniversalist and inegalitarian, which saw the concern with honour as the first mark of the honourable man. Someone unconcerned with reputation, unwilling to defend it, had to be a coward, and therefore contemptible.

Rousseau borrows the denunciatory language of the first discourse, but he doesn't end up calling for a renunciation of all concern with esteem. On the contrary, in his portrait of the republican model, caring about esteem is central. What is wrong with pride or honour is its striving after preferences, hence division, hence real other-dependence, and therefore loss of the voice of nature; consequently corruption, the forgetting of boundaries, and effeminacy. The remedy is not rejecting the importance of esteem, but entering into a quite different system, characterized by equality, reciprocity, and unity of purpose. This unity makes possible the equality of esteem, but the fact that esteem is in principle equal in this system is essential to the unity of purpose itself. Under the aegis of the general will, all virtuous citizens are to be equally honoured. The age of dignity is born.

This new critique of pride, leading not to solitary mortification but to a politics of equal dignity, is what Hegel took up and made famous in his dialectic of master and slave. Against the old discourse on the evil of pride, he takes it as fundamental that we can flourish only to the extent that we are recognized. Each consciousness seeks recognition in another, and this is not a sign of a lack of virtue. But the ordinary conception of honour as hierarchical is crucially flawed, because it doesn't answer the need that sends people after recognition in the first place. Those who fail to win out in the honour stakes remain unrecognized. But even those who do win are more subtly frustrated, because they win recognition from the losers, whose acknowledgement is by hypothesis not really valuable, since they are no longer free, self-supporting subjects on the same level with the winners. The struggle for recognition can find only one satisfactory solution, and that is a regime of reciprocal recognition among equals. Hegel follows Rousseau in finding this regime in a society with a common purpose, one in which there is a "'we' that is an 'I,' and an 'I' that is a 'we.'"[27]

But if we think of Rousseau as inaugurating the new politics of equal dignity, we can argue that his solution is crucially flawed. In terms of the question posed at the beginning of this section, equality of esteem requires a tight unity of purpose that seems to be incompatible with any differentiation. The key to a free polity for Rousseau seems to be a rigorous exclusion of any differentiation of roles. Rousseau's principle seems to be that for any two-place relation R involving power, the condition of a free society is that the two terms joined by the relation be identical: xRy is compatible with a free society only when x equals y. This is true when the relation involves the x's presenting themselves in public space to the y's, and it is of course famously true when the relation is "exercises sover-

eignty over." In the social-contract state, the people must be both sover-
eign and subject.

In Rousseau three things seem to be inseparable: freedom (nondomi-
nation), the absence of differentiated roles, and a very tight common purpose. We must all be dependent on the general will, lest there arise bilateral
forms of dependence.[28] This has been the formula for the most terrible
forms of homogenizing tyranny, starting with the Jacobins and extending
to the totalitarian regimes of our century. But even where the third element of the trinity is set aside, the aligning of equal freedom with the
absence of differentiation has remained a tempting mode of thought.
Wherever it reigns, be it in modes of feminist thought or liberal politics,
the margin to recognize difference is very small.

We might well agree with this analysis and want to gain some distance
from the Rousseauean model of citizen dignity. Yet still we might want to
know whether any politics of equal dignity, based on the recognition of
universal capacities, is bound to be equally homogenizing. Is this true of
those models – which I inscribed above, perhaps arbitrarily, under the ban-
ner of Kant – that separate equal freedom from the two other elements of
the Rousseauean trinity? These models not only have nothing to do with
a general will, but abstract from any issue of the differentiation of roles.
They simply look to an equality of rights accorded to citizens. Yet this
form of liberalism has come under attack by radical proponents of the politics of difference as in some way unable to give due acknowledgement to
distinctness. Are the critics correct?

The fact is that there are forms of this liberalism that in the minds of
their own proponents can give only a very restricted acknowledgement of
distinct cultural identities. The notion that any of the standard schedules
of rights might apply differently in one cultural context than they do in
another, that their application might have to take account of different collective goals, is considered quite unacceptable. The issue, then, is whether
this restrictive view of equal rights is the only possible interpretation. If it
is, then it would seem that the accusation of homogenization is well
founded. But perhaps it isn't. I think it isn't, and perhaps the best way to
lay out the issue is to see it in the context of the Canadian case, where this
question has played a role in the impending breakup of the country. In
fact, two conceptions of rights liberalism have confronted each other,
albeit in confused fashion, throughout the long and inconclusive constitutional debates of recent years.

The issue came to the fore because of the adoption in 1982 of the
Canadian Charter of Rights, which aligned Canada's political system in
this regard with the American system in having a schedule of rights to
serve as a basis for the judicial review of legislation at all levels of govern-

ment. The question had to arise how to relate this schedule to the claims for distinctness put forward by French Canadians, particularly Quebeckers, on the one hand, and aboriginal peoples on the other. Here what was at stake was the desire of these peoples for survival, and their consequent demand for certain forms of autonomy in their self-government, as well as the ability to adopt certain kinds of legislation deemed necessary for survival.

For instance, Quebec has passed a number of laws in the area of language. One regulates who can send their children to English-language schools (not francophones or immigrants); another requires that businesses with more than fifty employees be run in French; a third outlaws commercial signs in any language other than French. In other words, restrictions have been placed on Quebeckers by their government, in the name of their collective goal of survival, which in other Canadian communities might easily be disallowed by virtue of the Charter.[29] The fundamental question was: is this variation acceptable or not?

The issue was addressed by a proposed constitutional amendment, named after the site of the conference where it was first drafted, Meech Lake. The Meech amendment proposed to recognize Quebec as a "distinct society," and wanted to make this recognition one of the bases for judicial interpretation of the rest of the constitution, including the Charter. This seemed to open up the possibility for variation in its interpretation in different parts of the country. For many, such variation was fundamentally unacceptable. Examining why brings us to the heart of the question of how rights liberalism is related to diversity.

The Canadian Charter follows the trend of the last half of the twentieth century, and gives a basis for judicial review on two scores. First, it defines a set of individual rights that are similar to those protected in other charters and bills of rights in western democracies. Second, it guarantees equal treatment of citizens in a variety of respects, or, alternatively put, it protects against discriminatory treatment on a number of irrelevant grounds, such as race or sex. There is a lot more in the Charter, including provisions for linguistic rights and aboriginal rights, which could be understood as according powers to collectivities, but the two themes I singled out dominate in the public consciousness.

This is no accident. The two kinds of provisions are now quite common in entrenched schedules of rights that provide the basis for judicial review. In this sense, the western world, perhaps the world as a whole, is following U.S. precedent. The Americans were the first to write out and entrench a bill of rights, which they did during the ratification of their constitution and as a condition of its successful outcome. One might argue that they weren't entirely clear on judicial review as a method of securing those rights, but this rapidly became the practice. The early amendments protected individuals, and sometimes state governments,[30] against encroachment by the new federal government. It was after the Civil War, in the period of triumphant reconstruction, and particularly with the Fourteenth Amendment, which called for "equal protection" for all citizens under the law, that the theme of nondiscrimination became central to judicial review. But this theme is now on a par with the older norm of the defense of individual rights, and in public consciousness perhaps even ahead.

For a number of people in "English Canada," a political society's espousing certain collective goals threatens to run against both of these basic provisions of the Charter, or indeed any acceptable bill of rights. First, the collective goals may require restrictions on the behaviour of individuals that violate their rights. For many nonfrancophone Canadians, both inside and outside Quebec, this feared outcome had already materialized with Quebec's language legislation. Quebec legislation prescribes, as already mentioned, the type of school to which parents can send their children; and in the most famous instance, it forbids certain kinds of commercial signage. The latter provision was struck down by the Supreme Court as contrary to Quebec's bill of rights, as well as the Charter, and only reenacted through the invocation of a clause in the Charter that permits legislatures in certain cases to override decisions of the courts relative to the Charter for a limited period of time (the so-called notwithstanding clause).

But second, even if overriding individual rights were not possible, espousing collective goals on behalf of a national group can be thought to be inherently discriminatory. In the modern world it will always be the case that not all those living as citizens under a certain jurisdiction will belong to the national group thus favoured. This in itself could be thought to provoke discrimination. But beyond this, the pursuit of the collective end will probably involve treating insiders and outsiders differently. Thus the schooling provisions of Law 101 forbid (roughly speaking) francophones and immigrants to send their children to English-language schools, but allow Canadian anglophones to do so.

This sense that the Charter clashes with basic Quebec policy was one of the grounds of opposition in the rest of Canada to the Meech Lake accord. The cause for concern was the distinct-society clause, and the common demand for amendment was that the Charter be "protected" against this clause, or take precedence over it. There was undoubtedly in this opposition a certain amount of old-style anti-Quebec prejudice, but there was also a serious philosophical point.

Those who take the view that individual rights must always come first, and, along with nondiscrimination provisions, must take precedence over collective goals, are often speaking from a liberal perspective that has become more and more widespread in the Anglo-American world. Its source is of course the United States, and it has recently been elaborated and defended by some of the nation's best philosophical and legal minds, including John Rawls, Ronald Dworkin, and Bruce Ackerman.[31] There are various formulations of the main idea, but perhaps the one that encapsulates most clearly the relevant point is expressed by Dworkin in his short paper on "Liberalism."

Dworkin makes a distinction between two kinds of moral commitment. We all have views about the ends of life, about what constitutes a good life, which we and others ought to strive for. But we also acknowledge a commitment to deal fairly and equally with each other, regardless of how we conceive our ends. We might call this latter commitment "procedural," while commitments concerning the ends of life are "substantive." Dworkin claims that a liberal society is one that adopts no particular substantive view about the ends of life. The society is, rather, united around a strong procedural commitment to treat people with equal respect. The reason that the polity as such can espouse no substantive view – say that one of the goals of legislation should be to make people virtuous – is that this would involve a violation of its procedural norm. For, given the diversity of modern societies, it would unfailingly be the case that some people and not others would be committed to the favoured conception of virtue. They might be in a majority; indeed, it's likely that they would be, for otherwise a democratic society probably wouldn't espouse their view. Yet this view would not be everyone's view, and in espousing this substantive outlook the society would not be treating the dissident minority with equal respect. It would be saying to them, in effect, "your view is not as valuable, in the eyes of this polity, as that of your more numerous compatriots."

There are profound philosophical assumptions underlying this view of liberalism, which is rooted in the thought of Kant. Among other features, this view understands human dignity to consist largely in autonomy, that is, in the ability of each person to determine for himself or herself a view of the good life. Dignity is associated less with any particular understanding of the good life, such that one's departure from this would detract from one's own dignity, than with the power to consider and espouse for oneself some view or other. We don't respect this power equally in all subjects, it is claimed, if we raise the outcome of some people's deliberations officially over that of others. A liberal society must remain neutral on the good life and restrict itself to ensuring that, however they see things, citizens deal fairly with one another and the state deals equally with all.

The popularity of this view of the human agent as primarily a subject of self-determining or self-expressive choice helps to explain why this model of liberalism is so strong. But we must also consider that it has been urged with great force and intelligence by liberal thinkers in the United States, and precisely in the context of constitutional doctrines of judicial review.[32] Thus it is not surprising that the idea has become widespread, well beyond those who might subscribe to a Kantian philosophy, that a liberal society can't accommodate publicly espoused notions of the good. This is the conception, as Michael Sandel has noted, of the procedural republic, which has a strong hold on the political agenda in the United States, and which has helped to place increasing emphasis on judicial review at the expense of the ordinary political process of building majorities with a view to legislative action.[33]

But a society with collective goals like Quebec's violates this model. It is axiomatic for Quebec governments that the survival and flourishing of French culture in Quebec is a good. Political society is not neutral between those who value remaining true to the culture of our ancestors and those who might want to cut loose in the name of some individual goal of self-development. It might be argued that you could after all capture a goal like *survivance* for a proceduralist liberal society. You could consider the French language, for instance, as a collective resource that individuals might want to make use of, and act for its preservation just as you do for clean air or green spaces. But this can't capture the full thrust of policies designed for cultural survival. It is not just a matter of having the French language available for those who might choose it. This might be seen to be the goal of some of the measures of federal bilingualism over the last twenty years. But it also involves making sure that there is a community of people in the future that will want to avail itself of the opportunity to use the French language. Policies aimed at survival actively seek to *create* members of the community, for instance, in their assuring that future generations continue to identify as French speakers. There is no way that these policies could be seen as just providing a facility to already existing people.

So Quebeckers, and those who give similar importance to this kind of collective goal, tend to opt for a rather different model of liberal society. On their view, a society can be organized around a definition of the good life, without this being seen as a depreciation of those who do not personally share this definition. Where the nature of the good requires that it be sought in common, this is the reason for its being a matter of public policy. According to this conception, a liberal society singles itself out as such by the way in which it treats minorities, including those who do not share public definitions of the good, and above all by the rights it accords to its members. But now the rights in question are conceived to be the fundamental and crucial ones that have been recognized as such from the very beginning of the liberal tradition: rights to life, liberty, due process, free speech, free practice of religion, and so on. On this model, there is a dangerous overlooking of an essential boundary in speaking of fundamental rights to things like commercial signs in the language of one's choice. One has to distinguish the fundamental liberties, those that should never be infringed and therefore ought to be unassailably entrenched, from privileges and immunities that are important but can be revoked or restricted for reasons of public policy – although one would need a strong reason to do this.

A society with strong collective goals can be liberal, on this view, provided it is also capable of respecting diversity, especially when dealing with those who don't share its common goals; and provided it can offer adequate safeguards for fundamental rights. There will undoubtedly be tensions and difficulties in pursuing these objectives together, but such a pursuit is not impossible, and the problems are not in principle greater than those encountered by any liberal society that has to combine, for example, liberty and equality, or prosperity and justice.

Here are two incompatible views of liberal society. One of the great sources of our current disharmony is that the sides have squared off against each other over the last decade. The resistance to the "distinct society" that called for precedence to be given to the Charter came in part from a spreading procedural outlook in English Canada. From this point of view, attributing the goal of promoting Quebec's distinct society to a government is to acknowledge a collective goal, and this move had to be neutralized by being subordinated to the existing Charter. From the standpoint of Quebec, this attempt to impose a procedural model of liberalism not only would deprive the distinct-society clause of some of its force as a rule of interpretation, but would bespeak a rejection of the model of liberalism on which this society was founded. Each society misperceived the other throughout the Meech Lake debate. But here both perceived each other accurately – and didn't like what they saw. The rest of Canada saw that the distinct-society clause legitimated collective goals. And Quebec saw that the move to give the Charter precedence imposed a form of liberal society that was alien, and to which Quebec could never accommodate itself without surrendering its identity.[34]

I have delved into this case because it seems to illustrate the fundamental questions. There is a form of the politics of equal respect, as enshrined in a liberalism of rights, that is inhospitable to difference, because (a) it insists on uniform application of the rules defining these rights, without exception, and (b) it is suspicious of collective goals. Of course, this doesn't mean that the model seeks to abolish cultural differences. That would be an absurd accusation. But I call it inhospitable to difference because it can't accommodate what the members of distinct societies really aspire to, which is survival. This is (b) a collective goal, which (a) almost inevitably will call for some variations in the kinds of law

CHARLES TAYLOR

we deem permissible from one cultural context to another, as the Quebec case clearly shows.

I think this form of liberalism is guilty as charged by the proponents of a politics of difference. Fortunately, however, there are other models of liberal society that take a different line on (a) and (b). These forms do call for the invariant defense of certain rights, of course. There would be no question of cultural differences determining the application of *habeas corpus*, for example. But they distinguish these fundamental rights from the broad range of immunities and presumptions of uniform treatment that have sprung up in modern cultures of judicial review. They are willing to weigh the importance of certain forms of uniform treatment against the importance of cultural survival, and opt sometimes in favor of the latter. They are thus in the end not procedural models of liberalism, but are grounded very much on judgements about what makes a good life – judgements in which the integrity of cultures has an important place.

Although I can't argue it here, obviously I would endorse this kind of model. Indisputably, though, more and more societies today are turning out to be multicultural, in the sense of including more than one cultural community that wants to survive. The rigidities of procedural liberalism may rapidly become impractical in tomorrow's world.

The politics of equal respect, then, at least in this more hospitable variant, can be cleared of the charge of homogenizing difference. But there is another way of formulating the charge that is harder to rebut. In this form, however, it perhaps ought not to be rebutted, or so I want to argue.

The charge I'm thinking of is provoked by the claim sometimes made on behalf of difference-blind liberalism that it can offer a neutral ground on which people of all cultures can meet and coexist. On this view, it is necessary to make a certain number of distinctions – between what is public and what is private, for instance, or between politics and religion – and only then can one relegate the contentious differences to a sphere that doesn't impinge on the political.

But a controversy like that over Salman Rushdie's *Satanic Verses* shows how wrong this view is. For mainstream Islam, there is no question of separating politics and religion as we have come to expect in western liberal society. Liberalism is not a possible meeting ground for all cultures; it is the political expression of one range of cultures, and quite incompatible with other ranges. Moreover, as many Muslims are well aware, western liberalism is not so much an expression of the secular, postreligious outlook that happens to be popular among liberal *intellectuals* as it is a more organic outgrowth of Christianity – at least as seen from the alternative vantage of Islam. The division of church and state goes back to the earliest days of Christian civilization. The early forms of the separation were very different from ours, but the basis was laid for modern developments. The very term *secular* was originally part of the Christian vocabulary.[35]

All this is to say that liberalism can't and shouldn't claim complete cultural neutrality. Liberalism is also a fighting creed. The hospitable variant I espouse, as well as the most rigid forms, has to draw the line. There will be variations when it comes to applying the schedule of rights, but not where incitement to assassination is concerned. This shouldn't be seen as a contradiction. Substantive distinctions of this kind are inescapable in politics, and at least the nonprocedural liberalism I was describing is fully ready to accept this.

But the controversy is still disturbing, for the reason mentioned above: all societies are becoming increasingly multicultural while, at the same time, becoming more porous. The two developments go together. Their porousness means that they are more open to multinational migration; more of their members live the life of diaspora, whose centre is elsewhere. In these circumstances there is something awkward about replying simply, "This is how we do things here." This reply must be made in cases like the Rushdie controversy, where "how we do things" covers issues such as the right to life and freedom of speech. The awkwardness arises from the face that there are substantial numbers of citizens who also belong to the culture that calls into question our philosophical boundaries. The challenge is to deal with their sense of marginalization without compromising our basis political principles.

This brings us to the issue of multiculturalism as it is often debated today, which has a lot to do with the imposition of some cultures on others, and with the assumed superiority that powers this imposition. Western liberal societies are thought to be supremely guilty in this regard, partly because of their colonial past, and partly because of their marginalization of segments of their populations that stem from other cultures. It is in this context that "This is how we do things here" can seem crude and insensitive. Even if, in the nature of things, compromise is close to impossible – one either forbids murder or allows it – the attitude presumed by the reply is seen as one of contempt. Often, in fact, this presumption is correct. So we arrive again at the issue of recognition.

Recognition of equal value was not what was at stake – at least in a strong sense – in my earlier discussion. There it was a question of whether cultural survival will be acknowledged as a legitimate goal, whether collective ends will be allowed as legitimate considerations in judicial review, or for other purposes of major social policy. The demand there was that we let cultures defend themselves, within reasonable bounds. But the further demand we're looking at here is that we all recognize the equal value of different cultures; that we not only let them survive, but acknowledge their *worth*.

CHARLES TAYLOR

What sense can be made of this demand? In a way it has been opera-
tive in an unformulated state for some time. The politics of nationalism has
been powered for well over a century partly by the sense that people have
had of being despised or respected by others around them. Multinational
societies can break up because of a lack of perceived recognition of the
equal worth of one group by another. This is, I believe, the case in Canada
– though my diagnosis will certainly be challenged by some. On the international scene, the tremendous sensitivity of certain supposedly closed
societies to world opinion – as shown in their reactions to findings of, say,
Amnesty International, or in their attempts through UNESCO to build a
new world information order – attests to the importance of external
recognition.

But all this is still *an sich*, not *für sich*, in the Hegelian jargon. The actors
themselves are often the first to deny that they are moved by such considerations, and plead other factors, say inequality, exploitation, and injustice, as their motives. Very few Quebec independentists, for instance, can
accept that what's winning them their fight is the lack of recognition from
English Canada.

What is new, therefore, is that the demand for recognition is now
explicit. And it has been made explicit, in the way I indicated above, by
the spread of the idea that we are formed by recognition. We could say
that, thanks to this idea, misrecognition has now graduated to the rank of
a harm that can be hardheadedly enumerated along with those mentioned
in the previous paragraph.

One of the key authors in this transition is undoubtedly Frantz Fanon,
who in his influential *Les damnés de la terre* (1961) argued that the major
weapon of the colonizers was the imposition of their image of the colonized on the subjugated people. The colonized, in order to be free, must
first of all purge themselves of these demeaning self-images. Fanon recommended violence as the way to this freedom, matching the original
violence of the alien imposition. Not all those who have drawn from
Fanon have followed him in this, but the notion that there is a struggle for
a changed self-image, which takes place both with the subjugated and
against the dominator, has been very widely applied. The idea has become
crucial to certain strands of feminism, and is also an important element in
the contemporary debate on multiculturalism.

The main locus of this debate is the world of education (in a broad
sense). One focus is on university humanities departments, where demands
are made to alter, enlarge, or scrap the canon of accredited authors on the
grounds that the one currently favoured consists almost entirely of "dead
white males." A greater place ought to be made for women and for people of non-European races and cultures. A second focus is on the secondary schools, where an attempt is being made, for instance, to develop

Afrocentric curricula for pupils in mainly black schools.

The reason for these proposed changes is not, or not mainly, that all students may be missing something important through the exclusion of a certain gender or certain races or cultures, but rather that women and students from the excluded groups are given, either directly or by omission, a demeaning picture of themselves, as though all creativity and worth inhered in men of European provenance. Enlarging and changing the curriculum is essential not so much in the name of a broader culture for everyone as in order to give due recognition to the hitherto excluded. The background premise of these demands is that recognition forges identity, particularly in its Fanonist application: dominant groups tend to entrench their hegemony by inculcating an image of inferiority in the subjugated. The struggle for freedom and equality must therefore pass through a revision of these images. Multicultural curricula are meant to help in this process of revision.

Although it is not often stated clearly, the logic behind some of these demands seems to depend on a premise that we owe equal respect to all cultures. This emerges from the nature of the reproach made to the designers of traditional curricula. The claim is that the judgements of worth on which these curricula were based were in fact corrupt, marred by narrowness or insensitivity or, even worse, a desire to downgrade the excluded. The implication seems to be that, without these distorting factors, true judgements of value of different works would place all cultures more or less on the same footing. Of course the attack could come from a more radical, neo-Nietzschean standpoint, which questions the very status of judgements of worth as such, but short of this extreme step (whose coherence I doubt), the presumption seems to be one of equal worth.

I'd like to maintain that there is something valid in this presumption, but that it is by no means unproblematic and involves something like an act of faith. As a presumption, the claim is that all human cultures that have animated whole societies over some considerable stretch of time have something important to say to all human beings. I word it this way to exclude partial cultural milieux within a society, as well as short phases in a major culture. There is no reason to believe that, for instance, the different art forms of a given culture should all be of equal, or even of considerable, value; and every culture can go through phases of decadence.

But when I call this claim a presumption, I mean that it is a starting hypothesis with which we ought to approach the study of any other culture. The validity of the claim has to be demonstrated concretely in the actual study of the culture. Indeed, for a culture sufficiently different from our own, we may have only the foggiest idea *ex ante* of what its valuable contribution might be. Because, for a sufficiently different culture, the very understanding of what it means to be of worth will be strange and unfa-

CHARLES TAYLOR

miliar to us. To approach, say, a raga with the presumptions of value implicit in the well-tempered clavier would be forever to miss the point. What has to happen is what Gadamer calls a "fusion of horizons."[36] We learn to move in a broader horizon, where what we once took for granted as the background to valuation can be situated as one possibility alongside the different background of the unfamiliar culture. The fusion of horizons operates through our developing new vocabularies of comparison, for articulating these new contrasts.[37] So that if and when we ultimately find substantive support for our initial presumption, it is on the basis of an assessment of worth that we couldn't possibly have had at the beginning. We have reached the judgement partly through transforming our standards.

We might want to argue that we owe all cultures a presumption of this kind. From this point of view, withholding the presumption might be seen as the fruit of prejudice or ill will. It might even be tantamount to a denial of equal status. Something like this might lie behind the accusation levelled by supporters of multiculturalism against defenders of the traditional canon. Supposing that the reluctance to enlarge the canon comes from a mixture of prejudice and ill will, the multiculturalists charge them with the arrogance of assuming their superiority over formerly subjugated peoples.

This presumption would help to explain why the demands of multiculturalism build on established principles of equal respect. If withholding the presumption is tantamount to a denial of equality, and if important consequences flow for people's identity from the absence of recognition, then a case can be made for insisting on the universalization of the presumption as a logical extension of the politics of dignity. Just as all must have equal civil rights, and equal voting rights, regardless of race or culture, so all should enjoy the presumption that their traditional culture has value. This extension, however logically it may seem to flow from the accepted norms of equal dignity, fits uneasily within them because it challenges the difference-blindness that was central to them. Yet it does indeed seem to flow from them, albeit uneasily.

I'm not sure about the validity of demanding this presumption as a right. But we can leave this issue aside, because the demand being made seems much stronger. The claim is that a proper respect for equality requires more than a presumption that further study will make us see things this way; there have to be actual judgements of equal worth applied to the customs and creations of these different cultures. Such judgements seem to be implicit in the demand that certain works be included in the canon, and in the implication that these works were not included earlier only because of prejudice or ill will or the desire to dominate. (Of course the demand for inclusion is *logically* separable from a claim of equal worth.

The demand could be: "Include these because they're ours, even though they may be inferior." But this isn't how the people making the demand talk.)

Still there's something very wrong with the demand in this form. It makes sense to insist as a matter of right that we approach the study of certain cultures with a presumption of their value. But it can't make sense to insist as a matter of right that we come up with a final concluding judgement that their value is great, or equal to others'. That is, if the judgement of value is to register something independent of our own wills and desires, it can't be dictated by a principle of ethics. On examination, either we'll find something of great value in culture C, or we won't. But it makes no more sense to demand that we do so than it does to demand that we find the earth round or flat, the temperature of the air hot or cold.

I have stated this rather flatly when, as everyone knows, there is a vigorous controversy over the "objectivity" of judgements in this field, and whether there is a "truth of the matter" here, as there seems to be in natural science or, indeed, whether even in natural science objectivity is a mirage.[38] I don't have much sympathy for these forms of subjectivism, which I find shot through with confusion. But there seems to be some special confusion in invoking them in this context. The moral and political thrust of the complaint concerns unjustified judgements of inferior status allegedly made of nonhegemonic cultures. But if those judgements are ultimately a question of the human will, then the issue of justification falls away. One doesn't, properly speaking, make judgements that can be right or wrong; one expresses liking or dislike, one endorses or rejects another culture. But then the complaint must shift to address the refusal to endorse, and the validity or invalidity of judgements has nothing to do with it.

Then, however, the act of declaring another culture's creations to be of worth and the act of declaring yourself on their side, even if their creations aren't all that impressive, become indistinguishable. The difference is only in the packaging. Yet the first is normally understood as a genuine expression of respect, the second as insufferable patronizing. The supposed beneficiaries of the politics of recognition, the people who might actually benefit from acknowledgement, make a crucial distinction between the two acts. They know they want respect, not condescension. Any theory that wipes out the distinction seems at least prima facie to be distorting crucial facets of the reality it purports to deal with.

In fact, subjectivist, half-baked, neo-Nietzschean theories are quite often invoked in this debate. Deriving frequently from Foucault or Derrida, they claim that all judgements of worth are based on standards that are ultimately imposed by and further entrench structures of power. It should be clear why these theories proliferate. A favorable judgement on demand is nonsense, unless some such theories are valid. Moreover, the giving of a judgement on demand is an act of breathtaking condescension. No one can really mean it as a genuine act of respect. It is more in the nature of a pretended act of respect given at the insistence of its supposed beneficiary. Objectively, such an act involves contempt for the latter's intelligence; to be an object of such an act demeans. The proponents of neo-Nietzschean theories hope to escape this nexus of hypocrisy by turning the entire issue into one of power and counterpower. Then the question is no longer one of respect, but of taking sides, of solidarity. This is hardly a satisfactory solution, because in taking sides they miss the driving force of this kind of politics, which is precisely the search for recognition and respect.

Moreover, even if we could demand it of them, the last thing we want at this stage from Eurocentred intellectuals is positive judgements of the worth of cultures they have not studied intensively. For real judgements of worth suppose a fused horizon of standards, where we have been transformed by the study of the other, so that we are not simply judging by our old familiar standards. A favourable judgement made prematurely would be not only condescending but ethnocentric. It would praise the other for being like us.

Here is another severe problem with much of the politics of multiculturalism. The peremptory demand for favourable judgements of worth is paradoxically – perhaps tragically – homogenizing. For it implies that we already have the standards to make such judgements. The standards we have, however, are those of North Atlantic civilization. And so the judgements implicitly and unconsciously will cram the others into our categories. We will think of their "artists" as creating "works," which we then can include in our canon. By implicitly invoking our standards to judge all civilizations and cultures, the politics of difference can end up making everyone the same.[39]

In this form, the demand for equal recognition is unacceptable. But the story doesn't simply end there. The enemies of multiculturalism in the American academy have perceived this weakness, and have used it as an excuse to turn their backs on the problem. This won't do. A response like that attributed to Saul Bellow, to the effect that we will be glad to read the Zulu Tolstoy when he comes along, shows the depths of ethnocentricity. First, there is the implicit assumption that excellence has to take forms familiar to us: the Zulus should produce a *Tolstoy*. Second, we are assuming that their contribution is yet to be made (*when* the Zulus produce a Tolstoy). These two assumptions obviously go hand in hand. If the Zulus have to produce our kind of excellence, then obviously their only hope lies in the future. Roger Kimball puts it more crudely: "The multiculturalists notwithstanding, the choice facing us today is not between a 'repressive' Western culture and a multicultural paradise, but between culture and barbarism. Civilization is not a gift, it is an achievement – a fragile achievement that needs constantly to be shored up and defended from besiegers inside and out."[40]

There must be something midway between the inauthentic and homogenizing demand for recognition of equal worth, on the one hand, and the self-immurement within ethnocentric standards, on the other. There are other cultures, and we have to live together more and more, both on a world scale and commingled in each individual society.

What we have is the presumption of equal worth: a stance we take in embarking on the study of the other. Perhaps we don't need to ask whether it's something that others can demand from us as a right. We might simply ask whether this is the way we ought to approach others.

Well, is it? How can this presumption be grounded? One ground that has been proposed is religious. Herder, for instance, had a view of divine providence, according to which all this variety of culture was no mere accident but meant to bring about a greater harmony. I can't rule out such a view. But merely on the human level, one could argue that it's reasonable to suppose that cultures that have provided the horizon of meaning for large numbers of human beings, of diverse characters and temperaments, over a long period of time – that have, in other words, articulated their sense of the good, the holy, and the admirable – are almost certain to have something that deserves our admiration and respect, even if it goes along with much that we have to abhor and reject. Put another way: it would take supreme arrogance to discount this possibility a priori.

Perhaps there is a moral issue here after all. We only need a sense of our own limited part in the whole human story to accept the presumption. It is only arrogance, or some analogous moral failing, that can deprive us of this. But what the presumption requires is not peremptory and inauthentic judgements of equal value, but a willingness to be open to comparative cultural study of the kind that must displace our horizons in the resulting fusions. What it requires above all is an admission that we are very far away from that ultimate horizon where the relative worth of different cultures might be evident. This would mean breaking with an illusion that still holds many multiculturalists – as well as their most bitter opponents – in its grip.

Notes

1   "La nature de l'*honneur* est de demander des préférences et des distinctions" (Montesquieu, *De l'esprit des lois* bk. 3, ch. 7).

2   The significance of this move from "honour" to "dignity" is interestingly discussed by Peter Berger in his "On the Obsolescence of the Concept of

CHARLES TAYLOR

Honor," *Revisions: Changing Perspectives in Moral Philosophy*, ed. Stanley Hauerwas and Alasdair MacIntyre (Notre Dame, IN: U of Notre Dame P, 1983) 172–81.

3 Lionel Trilling, *Sincerity and Authenticity* (Cambridge, MA: Harvard UP, 1972).

4 I discuss the development of this doctrine at greater length, at first in the work of Francis Hutcheson, drawing on the writings of the Earl of Shaftesbury, and its adversarial relation to Locke's theory in my *Sources of the Self: The Making of the Modern Identity* (Cambridge, MA: Harvard UP, 1989) ch. 15.

5 "Le sentiment de l'existence dépouillé de toute autre affection est par lui-même un sentiment précieux de contentement et de paix qui suffiroit seul pour rendre cette existence chère et douce à qui sauroit écarter de soi toutes les impressions sensuelles et terrestres qui viennent sans cesse nous en distraire et en troubler ici bas la douceur. Mais la plupart des hommes agités de passions continuelles connoissent peu cet état et ne l'ayant goûté qu'imparfaitement durant peu d'instans n'en conservent qu'une idée obscure et confuse qui ne leur en fait pas sentir le charme" (Jean-Jacques Rousseau, "Cinquième promenade," *Les rêveries du promeneur solitaire*, in his *Oeuvres complètes*, vol. 1 [Paris: Gallimard, 1959] 1047).

6 "Jeder Mensch hat ein eignes Maas, gleichsam eine eigne Stimmung aller sinnlichen Gefühle zu einander" (Johann Gottfried Herder, *Ideen* bk. 8, sec. 1, in his *Sämtliche Werke*, ed. Bernhard Suphan, vol. 13 [Berlin: Weidmann, 1887] 291).

7 John Stuart Mill was influenced by this Romantic current of thought when he made something like the ideal of authenticity the basis for one of his most powerful arguments in *On Liberty*. See especially ch. 3, where he argues that we need something more than a capacity for "ape-like imitation": "A person whose desires and impulses are his own – are the expression of his own nature, as it has been developed and modified by his own culture – is said to have a character." "If a person possesses any tolerable amount of common sense and experience, his own mode of laying out his existence is the best, not because it is the best in itself, but because it is his own mode" (*Three Essays* [Oxford: Oxford UP, 1975] 73, 74, 83).

8 George H. Mead, *Mind, Self & Society: From the Standpoint of a Social Behaviorist* (Chicago: U of Chicago P, 1934).

9 This inner dialogicality was explored by Mikhail Bakhtin and those who have drawn on his work. See especially Bakhtin's *Problems of Dostoevsky's Poetics*, trans. Caryl Emerson (Minneapolis: U of Minnesota P, 1984). Also Katerina Clark and Michael Holquist, *Mikhail Bakhtin* (Cambridge, MA: Belknap, 1984); and James V. Wertsch, *Voices of the Mind: A Sociocultural Approach to Mediated Action* (Cambridge, MA: Harvard UP, 1991).

10 See Mikhail Bakhtin, "The Problem of the Text in Linguistics, Philology, and the Human Sciences: An Experiment in Philosophical Analysis," *Speech Genres and Other Late Essays*, trans. Vern W. McGee, ed. Caryl Emerson and Michael

Holquist (Austin: U of Texas P, 1986) 126, for this notion of a "superaddressee" beyond our existing interlocutors.

11 Rousseau is describing the first assemblies: "Chacun commença à regarder les autres et à vouloir être regardé soi-même, et l'estime publique eut un prix. Celui qui chantait ou dansait le mieux; le plus beau, le plus fort, le plus adroit ou le plus éloquent devint le plus considéré, et ce fut là le premier pas vers l'inégalité, et vers le vice en même temps" ("Discours sur l'origine et les fondements de l'inégalité parmi les hommes," *Discours sur les sciences et les arts. Discours sur l'origine de l'inégalité* [Paris: Garnier-Flammarion, 1971] 210).

12 See, for example, the passage in "Considérations sur le Gouvernement de Pologne" where he describes the ancient public festival in which all the people took part, *Du contrat social* (Paris: Garnier, 1962) 345-46; and the parallel passage in "Lettre à M. D'Alembert," *Du contrat social* 224-25. The crucial principle was that there should be no division between performers and spectators, but that all should be seen by all. "Mais quels seront enfin les objets de ces spectacles? qu'y montrera-t-on? Rien, si l'on veut. ... donnez les spectateurs en spectacle; rendez-les acteurs eux-mêmes; faites que chacun se voie et s'aime dans les autres, afin que tous en soient mieux unis" (225).

13 See G.W.F. Hegel, *Phenomenology of Spirit*, trans. A.V. Miller (Oxford: Clarendon, 1977) ch. 4.

14 There are a number of strands that have linked these two levels, but special prominence in recent years has been given to a psychoanalytically oriented feminism, which roots social inequalities in the early upbringing of men and women. See, for instance, Nancy J. Chodorow, *Feminism and Psychoanalytic Theory* (New Haven, CT: Yale UP, 1989); Jessica Benjamin, *The Bonds of Love: Psychoanalysis, Feminism, and the Problem of Domination* (New York: Pantheon, 1988). ·

15 A prime example of this charge from a feminist perspective is Carol Gilligan's critique of Lawrence Kohlberg's theory of moral development, for presenting a view of human development that privileges only one facet of moral reasoning, precisely the one that tends to predominate in boys rather than girls. See her *In a Different Voice: Psychological Theory and Women's Development* (Cambridge, MA: Harvard UP, 1982).

16 Will Kymlicka, in his very interesting and tightly argued book *Liberalism, Community, and Culture* (Oxford: Clarendon, 1989), argues for a kind of politics of difference, notably in relation to aboriginal rights in Canada, but from a basis that is firmly within a theory of liberal neutrality. He wants to argue on the basis of certain cultural needs – minimally, the need for an integral and undamaged cultural language with which one can define and pursue his or her own conception of the good life. In certain circumstances, with disadvantaged populations, the integrity of the culture may require that we accord them more resources or rights than others. The argument is parallel to that made in relation to socioeconomic inequalities. But where Kymlicka's argument fails to

recapture the actual demands made by the groups concerned – say Indian bands in Canada or French-speaking Canadians – is with respect to their goal of survival. Kymlicka's reasoning is valid (perhaps) for *existing* people who find themselves trapped within a culture under pressure, and can flourish either within it or not at all. But it doesn't justify measures designed to ensure survival in indefinite future generations. For the populations concerned, however, that's what is at stake. We need only think of the historical resonance of "la survivance" among French Canadians.

17 See Immanuel Kant, "Grundlegung zur Metaphysik der Sitten," in *Werke*, vol. 4 (Berlin: de Gruyter, 1968) 434; *Groundwork of the Metaphysic of Morals*, trans. H.J. Paton (New York: Harper & Row, 1964) 101–02.

18 I have no idea whether such a statement was actually made by Saul Bellow, or by anyone else. I report it only because it captures a widespread attitude, which is of course why the story had currency in the first place.

19 One hears both kinds of reproach today. In the context of some modes of feminism and multiculturalism, the claim is the strong one, that the hegemonic culture discriminates. In the former Soviet Union, however, alongside a similar reproach levelled at the hegemonic Great Russian culture, one also hears the complaint that Marxist-Leninist communism was an alien imposition on all equally, even on Russia itself. The communist mold, on this view, is truly nobody's. Solzhenitsyn made this claim, but it is voiced by Russians of a great many different persuasions today, and has something to do with the extraordinary phenomenon of an empire that has broken apart through the quasi-secession of its metropolitan society.

20 See John Rawls, *A Theory of Justice* (Cambridge, MA: Belknap, 1971); Ronald Dworkin, *Taking Rights Seriously* (Cambridge, MA: Harvard UP, 1977), and *A Matter of Principle* (Cambridge, MA: Harvard UP, 1985); Jürgen Habermas, *The Theory of Communicative Action*, trans. Thomas McCarthy, 2 vols. (Boston: Beacon, 1984-87).

21 Jean-Jacques Rousseau, *The Social Contract and Discourses*, trans. G.D.H. Cole (London: J.M. Dent, 1913) 3.

22 Jean-Jacques Rousseau, *Émile* (Paris: Garnier, 1964) 70.

23 Jean-Jacques Rousseau, "Considérations sur le Gouvernement de Pologne," *Du contrat social* 345; *The Government of Poland*, trans. Willmoore Kendall (Indianapolis: Bobbs-Merrill, 1972) 8.

24 Jean-Jacques Rousseau, "Lettre à M. D'Alembert," *Du contrat social* 225; "Letter to M. D'Alembert on the Theatre," *Politics and the Arts*, trans. Allan Bloom (Ithaca, NY: Cornell UP, 1968) 126.

25 A little later in the passage I quoted above from the essay on Poland, Rousseau describes gatherings in our depraved modern society as "des cohues licencieuses," where people go "pour s'y faire des liaisons secrètes, pour y chercher les plaisirs qui séparent, isolent le plus les hommes, et qui relâchent le plus les coeurs" (*Du contrat social* 346).

26 Jean-Jacques Rousseau, *Du contrat social* 244. I have benefitted in this area from discussions with Natalie Oman. See her "Forms of Common Space in the Work of Jean-Jacques Rousseau," Master's research paper, McGill U, 1991.

27 G.W.F. Hegel, *Phenomenology of Spirit* 110.

28 In justifying his famous (or infamous) slogan about the person coerced to obey the law as "forced to be free," Rousseau goes on: "car telle est la condition qui, donnant chaque citoyen à la patrie, le garantit de toute dépendance personnelle" (*Du contrat social* 246).

29 The Supreme Court of Canada did strike down one of these provisions, the one forbidding commercial signage in languages other than French. But in their judgement the justices agreed that it would have been quite reasonable to demand that all signs be in French, even though accompanied by another language. In other words, it was permissible in their view for Quebec to outlaw unilingual English signs. The need to protect and promote the French language in the Quebec context would have justified it. Presumably this would mean that legislative restrictions on the language of signs in another province might well be struck down for quite another reason. (Incidentally, the signage provisions are still in force in Quebec, because of a provision of the Charter that in certain cases allows legislatures to override judgements of the courts for a restricted period.)

30 For instance, the First Amendment, which forbids Congress to establish any religion, was not originally meant to separate church and state as such. It was enacted at a time when many states had established churches, and it was plainly meant to prevent the new federal government from interfering with or overruling these local arrangements. It was only later, after the Fourteenth Amendment, following the so-called incorporation doctrine, that these restrictions on the federal government were held to apply to all governments, at any level.

31 John Rawls, *A Theory of Justice*, and "Justice as Fairness: Political Not Metaphysical," *Philosophy and Public Affairs* 14 (1985): 223-51; Ronald Dworkin, *Taking Rights Seriously*, and "Liberalism," *Public and Private Morality*, ed. Stuart Hampshire (Cambridge, Eng.: Cambridge UP, 1978) 113-43; Bruce Ackerman, *Social Justice in the Liberal State* (New Haven, CT: Yale UP, 1980).

32 See, for instance, the arguments deployed by Laurence H. Tribe in *Abortion: The Clash of Absolutes* (New York: Norton, 1990).

33 Michael Sandel, "The Procedural Republic and the Unencumbered Self," *Political Theory* 12 (1984): 81-96.

34 See Guy Laforest, "L'esprit de 1982," *Le Québec et la restructuration du Canada 1980-1992: enjeux et perspectives*, ed. Louis Balthazar, Guy Laforest, and Vincent Lemieux (Sillery, PQ: Septentrion, 1991) 149-63.

35 The point is well argued in Larry Siedentop, "Liberalism: The Christian Connection," *Times Literary Supplement* 24-30 Mar. 1989: 308. See also my "The Rushdie Controversy," *Public Culture* 2.1 (1989) 118-22.

36 Hans-Georg Gadamer, *Wahrheit und Methode*, 2nd ed. (Tübingen, W. Ger.: Mohr, 1965) 289-90; *Truth and Method* (New York: Seabury, 1975) 273-74.

37 For fuller discussion of comparison, see my "Comparison, History, Truth," *Philosophical Arguments* (Cambridge, MA: Harvard UP, 1995) 146-64, 300; and my "Understanding and Ethnocentricity," *Philosophy and the Human Sciences* (Cambridge, Eng.: Cambridge UP, 1985) 116-33.

38 I discuss objectivity at somewhat greater length in Part I of my *Sources of the Self: The Making of the Modern Identity* (Cambridge, MA: Harvard UP, 1989).

39 The same homogenizing assumptions underlie the negative reaction that many people have to claims of superiority on behalf of western civilization, say in regard to natural science. But it is absurd to cavil at such claims in principle. If all cultures have made a contribution of worth, they can't be identical or even embody the same kind of worth. To expect this would be to vastly underestimate the differences. In the end, the presumption of worth imagines a universe in which different cultures complement one another with different kinds of contribution. This picture not only is compatible with but demands judgements of superiority-in-a-certain-respect.

40 Roger Kimball, "Tenured Radicals," *New Criterion* Jan. 1991: 13.

Beyond Disputation: Anglophone-Canadian Artists and the Free Trade Debate

Frank Davey

On the eve of the 1988 federal election two statements signed by various members of the Canadian arts community appeared as advertisements in the national edition of *The Globe and Mail*.[1] Both addressed the recently concluded tariff and trade-management agreement between Canada and the United States, popularly known as the "Free Trade Agreement," the implementation of which rested on the outcome of the election. One statement urged the reader "to vote for the party in your riding that will help to defeat this FREE TRADE DEAL," and was followed by thirty-nine names, among them, "Adrienne Clarkson," "Robertson Davies," "Don Harron," "Gordon Lightfoot," and "Sylvia Tyson." Nothing in the statement offered any identification of these names – the text implied they carried meanings well known to the reader. The second statement announced itself "in favour of the Canada-United States Free Trade Agreement" and was signed by sixty-two names, each identified by profession. Carrying in addition the heading "Artists and Writers for Free Trade," this advertisement suggested that the significance of its signatures – among them "Ken Danby, painter," "Mordecai Richler, writer," "Robert Fulford, journalist," and "Mira Godard, art dealer" – could be unknown to *Globe* readers.

The rather short statement of the thirty-nine argued "the Mulroney-Reagan Trade Deal is a hastily-concluded agreement that was made for political reasons, and not for the welfare of our country. It will irrevocably damage the Canada we care about." Its choice of "Mulroney-Reagan" rather than "Canada-United States" for the name of the agreement was a common rhetorical move during the election campaign to suggest that the agreement was an eccentric personal action of two unreliable men rather than one between two elected national governments; the use of "deal" rather than "agreement" was also a common move to imply "sleazy" and "corrupt" dimensions to the negotiations. This choice of language tended to affiliate the statement with other "popular" opposition to the agreement rather than to mark it as one from a specially authorized or interested constituency. Somewhat less commonplace was the statement's use of the word "political" in its claim that the agreement "was made for political reasons." This usage implied that "political" signifies "self-serving" and that the "political" is the realm only of corrupt party politics. It implies conversely that honest people are not "political," that the statement we are reading is not "political," and that the people who have signed it have not thereby performed a "political" action. Ultimately, it implies that "the" Canadian identity is undebatable, that it is an idealism outside of politics.

Although the statement offers no arguments against the trade agreement, it covertly signals two major objections. One of these concerns Canadians' construction of their country as a more caring society than the United States ("the Canada we care about") and as having more far-ranging social programs ("the welfare of our country"). The second, hidden in that seemingly innocent phrase "the Canada," is that Canada is a discrete, single, uniform entity, fully distinguishable from the United States, that stands in risk of adulteration by too much commerce with its neighbour – there is only one "Canada we care about." This monolithic notion of Canada is also reflected in the names of the signators. While the thirty-nine names include at least three from the West, and several of Maritime origin, almost all are associable with Ontario, and specifically with the Toronto region. The silences in the advertisement are large – a silence from Quebec, a silence (apart from Rudy Wiebe) from the Prairies, a silence (apart from Phyllis Webb) from British Columbia, a silence about its own political nature, a silence about which "the Canada" it defends.

The text offered by the sixty-two supporters of the trade agreement is quite a different piece of language. While the advertisement of the thirty-nine awarded the subject-position of its opening statement to the agreement ("The Mulroney-Reagan Trade Deal is a hastily-concluded agreement ..."), this advertisement gives it to its own signators. "*We* are not fragile" (implying that opponents of the agreement are both "fragile" and fearful of competition), the advertisement begins, even though its heading – "Artists and Writers for Free Trade" – has already indicated that the signators fear that their reputations may be indeed "fragile," perhaps non-existent, within their own country. "We, the undersigned artists and writers," it continues – here not only foregrounding its own signators in the subject-position and again reminding its readers of who this "we" is, but also adopting the authoritative rhetoric of public declamation. "We, the undersigned artists and writers, want the people of Canada to know we are in favour of the Canada-United States Free Trade Agreement." Rather than using the intimate "we-you" discourse of the thirty-nine opponents of the agreement, the sixty-two address Canadians in the more formal third person, "the people of Canada." Particularly revealing here, in terms of the explicit claims of both groups to endorse a participatory politics, is the fact that the artists who support the agreement choose not to address Canadians directly, while those who resist it do.

The statement continues:

There is no threat to our national identity anywhere in the

Agreement. Nor is there a threat to any form of Canadian cultural expression.

As artists and writers, we reject the suggestion that our ability to create depends upon the denial of economic opportunities to our fellow citizens.

What we make is to be seen and read by the whole world. The spirit of protectionism is the enemy of art and thought.

The first of these short paragraphs makes an assumption of the singleness of Canadian identity – "our national identity" – similar to that made by the statement of the thirty-nine, although it undercuts this with the ambiguity of "any form of Canadian cultural expression." The next tells the reader for the third time that the undersigned are "artists and writers" (they will later also be individually identified as "writer," "painter," "author," etc., after their signatures) and in the repetition of this insistence signals increasing anxiety about the stability of this identification. Reinstating the signators in the privileged subject-position, this paragraph has them "reject the suggestion" that their "ability to create" depends "upon the denial of economic opportunities to ... fellow citizens." This is a curious statement that on the one hand limits the activity of the artist to "creation" (excluding such things as dissemination and social intervention) while also implying a separation between "creation" and "economic opportunities." While appearing to affirm a romantic construction of the mystery and integrity of creativity, the statement is also, and rather more significantly, rejecting a materialist analysis of artistic activity. There is no relation, it implies, between art and economics. An artist's perceptions and choice of genres, as well as the time available to work, are unaffected by his or her economic experiences. An artist creates some materially disengaged and inevitable "creations" and leaves the business of publishing and distribution to those who have dedicated themselves to "economic opportunities." A reader may well wonder here whether this assumption of economic disengagement is perhaps behind the signators' uncertainty about how widely they are known by "the people of Canada."

The concluding paragraph suggests another explanation, however, for this uncertainty – the "creations" of the sixty-two were not specifically intended for "the people of Canada" but "to be seen and read by the whole world." Like the romantic notion of economically unbesmirched creativity, this is also a recognizable element in the Canadian text – the desire to be world-class, found elsewhere in Canadians' fascination with Lester Pearson and Ben Johnson, in John Metcalf's suspicion of the Canada Council, and in Morley Callaghan's pride that he boxed with Hemingway. As Robert Kroetsch mischievously quotes from a 1920s Mackenzie seed catalogue, "There is no place in the world where better cauliflowers can be grown than right here in the West" (1977: 29). But what if other parts of the world value different properties in a cauliflower? The "world-class" concept implicit in this advertisement is, like "the Canada" in the other, a monolithic and idealized construct. There is only one each of "art and thought," and these are to be found internationally, in texts written not for any one place but for "the whole world."

Such a notion of world-context is also that of multinational business: the world as a homogeneous market-place with uniform rules, practices, and economic forces. Since it is to help realize such a notion that the free trade agreement was conceived – to create for business the "level playing field" – it is not surprising that the sixty-two should support it. They too are arguing for a level playing field, "the whole world"; among the sixty-two signators are several – most prominently Metcalf – who have lamented Canadian arts grants and subsidies as distortions of the playing field. "We are not fragile," their advertisement began. Here too is evident the open competition theory which multinational capitalism and the sixty-two signators of the statement appear to share. "We are not fragile, we can survive international competition, we work to world standards and do not need protective legislation" is the subtext here – a subtext which not too subtly places artistic production on the same ground as that of any production which can thrive in an unregulated multinational economy. This message in the advertisement, that the signators represent a tough, internationally competitive Canadian art, an art which can compete economically like any other well-made product, appears, however, to contradict their other message that they represent a pure kind of creativity, unsullied by the market-place. But not quite: for the text also implies that these two are one and the same: the pure disinterested (and thus universal) artwork is also the tough internationally competitive (and thus universal) artwork. An illusion that the gap between these has been bridged is created in the advertisement by its silence on all issues of art distribution, and by the ambiguity it allows to hover around the word "fragile" – "fragile" artistically, perhaps like Ogden Nash or Mazo de la Roche, or "fragile" materially like Isabella Valancy Crawford?

This silence is joined by a silence within the names of its sixty-two signators similar to the silence within the names of the thirty-nine. Here again there are no Québécois (unless one so defines Irving Layton or Nick Auf Der Maur) and few identifiable Westerners. There are more names from the Maritimes, although none of these is a writer. There are thirteen women (there were also thirteen women among the thirty-nine opponents of free trade), with only three of these identified as "writers." This low representation of writers somewhat qualifies the advertisement's thrice-stated claim to be a statement by "artists and writers."

These two advertisements raise difficult questions about the relationship between politics and art, and between society and the artist. Both constitute attempts by artists to intervene in a nation's political debate either overtly or covertly on their authority as artists. The thirty-nine encode this authority in their assumption that their names possess public meaning; the sixty-two invoke it through their announcing three times in fifteen lines that they are "artists and writers." Yet both are uneasy about the political quality of the act they engage in; the thirty-nine speak disapprovingly of the "political," while the sixty-two take pains to insist that their "creativity" has not only nothing to do with national issues but also nothing to do with the "economic." The latter insistence is so strong that it leaves their statement without apparent motive except perhaps that of good citizenship. Both statements suggest that the activities of their supporters are in some way beyond politics. The thirty-nine do this through their attaching themselves to an idealized "Canada we care about," the sixty-two by attaching themselves to similarly idealized concepts of "creativity," "art," "thought," and "world." These strategies are, of course, and ironically so, *political* strategies. The idealization of one's own position – to offer it as archetypal, universal, or natural – is a pragmatic move to foreclose debate by attempting to raise one's position out of, "above," the ongoing contingent and continuingly contestable play of social interactions.

In the literary practices of Canada, as in those of most Western countries, readers, critics, and often writers have been diverted from awareness of the political dimensions of literature by the two ideologies apparent in the advertisements above: the aesthetic/humanist and the national. In the former the aesthetic is held to be a celebration of humanity, to be "above" politics in its enacting of a *homo* both *sapiens* and *fabrilis*. Northrop Frye writes in his conclusion to the *Literary History of Canada* of an "autonomous world of literature" (334), and in the *Anatomy of Criticism* of an "emancipated and humane community of culture" (347) and a "complete and classless civilization" (348). He urges "the ability to look at contemporary social values with the detachment of one who is able to compare them in some degree with the infinite vision of possibilities presented by culture" (348). Presumably this detachment would apply also to the seeking of "economic opportunities" by one's "fellow citizens." A.J.M. Smith similarly writes that the poet must be "true to the reality of nature and of human nature," as if such "reality" again were trans-cultural if not transcendent. Poetry "draws mankind together"; the poet returns "through language, rhythm, and the sound of verse – to humanity" (188–89). George Woodcock (engaged in 1988 by the ostensibly nationalist publisher ECW Press to write what its 1988 catalogue described as a series of "succinct monographs that offer fresh, lively readings of central Canadian works of fiction") writes of "the underlying universality of the personal and national experience" (23) and of "the transcending symphony of art" (75).

FRANK DAVEY

Nationalist ideology usually presents itself as contending against the aesthetic and humanist in arguing the particularity of human social forms within specific national boundaries. I say "usually presents itself as contending" because one often finds peculiar links between the two. One is the tendency, as in the two advertisements, to be similarly homogenizing. For the nationalist all literary production can be either recuperated as articulating some facet of the national archetype, whether this be the American Adam, the English garden, or the French struggle for the "fraternal" state, or dismissed as nationally irrelevant. A nation has, as D.G. Jones suggests in the preface to *Butterfly on Rock*, an "imaginative life," and criticism can "by isolating certain themes and images ... [attempt] to define more clearly some of the features that recur" in this "imaginative life" and reveal "something of the Canadian temper" (3-4). Canadian fiction, for John Moss, reflects a "geophysical imagination," "the progress of the Canadian imagination towards a positive identity" (7). As in the humanist "art" and "mind," the terms "temper," "identity," and "imagination" are offered as unitary constructs. The second link is an overt move in many nationalist readings to locate the unitary national text within the similarly unitary humanist one. The peculiarly "Canadian" imagination is thus validated by its participation in "themes common to western literature" (Jones 6), by its sharing "objectives of art" that are "universal" (Moss 8). Canadian writers are not only Canadian, but this Canadianness is of "world-rank": a Canadian construction such as "the hostile wilderness becomes not just a Canadian universe but the whole natural universe" (Jones 6). This move can allow a nationalist to deflect possible criticism from humanist ideological positions without having to develop a critique of humanism itself, and very likely accounts for the fact that it is possible to adopt both humanist and nationalist positions in Canada – to develop a national identity can also be, paradoxically, to acquire a place in universal culture.

My main concern in *Survival* was to distinguish Canlit from Britlit and Amlit. But to see the theme [victimization] as "universal" is to view it as a *constant* in human society – like saying "the poor you have always with you" – and therefore as an *unalterable* fact, like birth and death and the weather. It is to ignore the political and economic context of "victims." In fact, you have "victims" only where you have hierarchies.
– Margaret Atwood, "Mathews and Misrepresentation,"
Second Words (132-33)

It is significant that among nationalist theorists Margaret Atwood is one of the few to explicitly refuse humanist valorizations of the national. Although her critique here is fragmentary, it offers two key elements:

humanism mistakenly idealizes the "universal" as a "constant" in society, and correspondingly neglects the "political." All nationalist readings of Canadian literature are in a general sense "political." All attempt to construct links between the literary text and the cultural one, to show the literary as contributing in some way to the formation of the cultural. What has prevented nationalist literary theory in Canada from dealing more fully with the political than Atwood does above has been its tendency to construct the national text as unitary and thus as devoid of political contestation and debate. In Atwood's *Survival* politics enters her theory as conflict between the Canadian and the non-Canadian, between "Canlit" and "Britlit and Amlit," between those who view their victimization as changeable (her Position Three) and those possessed of what Marxists term a "false consciousness" in which they experience their own oppression from the point of view of the oppressor as either non-existent or "natural" (her Positions One and Two). Her text suggests little if any contestation within the "Canadian" position itself and tends overall to totalize this position through the "victim" metaphor. In a similar way Gaile McGregor's *The Wacousta Syndrome* subsumes the Canadian within one metaphor and portrays the political as a contestation between "American" and "Canadian" national ideologies. The analyses of Moss and Jones not only construct the Canadian cultural text as unproblematically first-person plural and conflict-free – as in Jones's "our own cultural house" (3) and Moss's "our emergence into national being" – but also, by aligning Canadian nationalism with Western humanism, suggest little conflict between Canadian and non-Canadian interests. For Moss, Canadian fiction "is continuous with world literature" (7); for Jones, literature is a means by which "man [can] discover his identity and community with the rest of nature" (8). All the nationalist critics, like the advertisement of the thirty-nine, are nervous about the term "political"; they tend to take shelter behind words like "culture" and "identity" and aestheticize literature by concealing its participation in the social and conflictual processes that produce culture.

The two "free trade" advertisements hint at a different story. The two construct very different groups of writers, each aligning itself with quite different arrays of fellow artists. They have conflicting interests, yet apparently each is Canadian and participating in a Canadian political debate. One group is confident it is known to *Globe* readers, while the other is nervous that it is not; one writes in the discourse of popular Canadian politics, the other in a more formal discourse of educated authority; one foregrounds the issues it addresses, the other foregrounds itself and its own significance; one addresses Canadians in the second person, the other indirectly in the third person; one is assured that it belongs to the community it addresses, the other uncertain; one idealizes the Canada it believes this

FRANK DAVEY

community to be named by, the other idealizes "creativity," "art," and "knowledge." Beyond the overt conflicts between the two groups suggested by the advertisements are further ones indicated by contradictions and silences. Why does one group of writers find allies in painters and art dealers, and the other in musicians? Why is the proportion of women higher in one than in the other? Why, among sixty-two supporters of free trade, are there only three women marked as writers, but fourteen men? Why, in the advertisement of the thirty-nine, is there no mention of a relationship between art and commerce? What are the positions on free trade of writers in other regions than Ontario?

Although a theory of the literary text which could take into account its roles within various political texts is probably not going to answer such specific questions, it might very well permit such interventions as the two advertisements to be made with less awkwardness and nervousness and possibly with more candour and effect. The misconceptions assumed or suggested by the refusal of the advertisement of the thirty-nine to construct itself as "political," and by that of the sixty-two to include "creativity" within the "economic," are fundamental misconceptions about textuality. Moreover, they are very similar to failures which appear to have prevented anglophone-Canadian literary works from participating as fully as they might in national argument, and have delayed the writing of a textually based and political accounting of this literature. Among these have been the failure to observe that gender, class, region, ethnicity, and economic structures can mark texts as decisively as can nation or "world culture," that the codes of literature are shared, and produced in concert, with the other written and unwritten texts of a society, that a writer's choice of codes, or positions in relation to these codes, can again be influenced by matters of gender, class, region, ethnicity, and economic practices, and that the usual relationship between codes, as between regions, classes, genders, ethnic affiliations, and economic practices, is one of contestation and/or dominance. This contestation is frequently more intense *within* a society than it is between it and other societies – in fact, such an intensity of internal conflict is probably the distinguishing feature of a separate society. A reluctance to acknowledge this contestation, or to recognize that people located at different positions within the complex of situations and codes that constitute any country have different and conflicting interests on most issues, can result not only in inarticulate debating of such critical issues as "free trade" but in misleadingly harmonious constructions of Canadian literature, politics, and culture. These, in turn, blur the edges of political conflict and suppress the positions of those who cannot be assimilated by metaphors of unity – whether "victim," "ellipse," "bush garden," "mainstream," "Wacousta," "Laurentian Shield," or "butterfly" – or who do not, unlike the sixty-two and thirty-nine, enjoy access to the Toronto media.

Basic to such a theorizing of the political role of the literary text in a society such as Canada's is Saussure's observation that the relationship between a signified and its signifier is arbitrary and rests on differentiations between phonemes rather than on fixed connections between signifier and signified – that is to say, language signifies by referring to itself. At an elementary level this observation allows a theorist to account for the signifying by single terms like "art" or "Canada" of different meanings to different speakers: terms receive their definitions within the differential system of linguistic signs specific to particular language communities. More important, however, Saussure's observation implies – as later writings by Sledd in grammar, Barthes in semiotics, Foucault in sociology, Hayden White in history, Lacan in psychoanalysis, Derrida in metaphysics, and Jane Gallop in feminism have explored – that all "experience" is linguistically mediated. We perceive not raw "things" but "things" placed within specific linguistic patterns of meaning.

The concept of the textuality of all experience is perhaps the most enabling one for any attempt to theorize the political functioning of literature, for it partly dissolves the difficult question for criticism of whether to remain "inside" the text and "faithful" to it, or to go "outside" a text into possibly spurious material. If all experience is social and textual, literary texts are produced as parts of this social text, from a great variety of positions within it, and constitute, in company with other sites of textual production, contributing parts of the overall social production of meaning. In terms of Canadian literature such a theory can propose literary texts as one of many producers of meaning through which a term such as "free trade" obtains significance. Literary texts can be seen as a sinuous and ultimately inextricable part of the general social text, both leaving their marks "outside" themselves and containing marks which refer "beyond" themselves. So invasive are their interweavings into the social text that they have, strictly speaking, neither an "outside" nor an "inside." Attempts to discuss how one might read a text thus struggle with and through metaphor. Although it is possible for a reader to bring gratuitously to a literary text materials and meanings neither signalled nor invited by it, it also becomes possible to theorize readings discouraged by formalist criticism. For example, whereas a formalism such as New Criticism was obliged to attempt to expel authorial biography from influencing its readings, a textual reading can read the author-name as one of the marks a literary text may carry, and can inquire into that name's ability to signify. The significance can vary with time and region. In 1965, on a new book entitled *But We Are Exiles*, the author-name "Robert Kroetsch" carried little signification beyond its not-female, not-Bob, not-ethnically British differentiations. In 1983 the same author-name on a new novel entitled *Alibi* carries numerous significations in Canada, upon which the paperback cover can rely in announcing the book to be "Kroetsch comedy ... in high gear." The range and number of these significations will be different, however, in countries other than Canada, and within Canada differ somewhat according to variously marked positions – by gender, region, class, etc. – of the perceiver.

The author-name, in the case of a well-known author, ceases to be merely a signifier and becomes itself a system of meaning, a system which for most readers the literary text will incorporate. Such a reference is "inter-textual," in the sense that Roland Barthes and Julia Kristeva elaborated in the early 1970s.[2] While a text announcing itself as a "novel" incorporates the socially circulating conventions of that genre, one announcing itself by an author known to a particular community incorporates not only that community's knowledge of her but its readings of her previous texts. Margaret Atwood's *The Handmaid's Tale*, for example, is marked by a reader's knowledge of her public life and her other books, as well as the codes of the novel and the dystopia; at its opening it adds to these the semiotic systems of the high school gymnasium, the concentration camp, and Protestant fundamentalism and returns to the latter two throughout. A reading which includes reflection on all these various elements is a textual reading – all of these are, in some reading contexts, available "parts" of the text.

Similarly useful for a nationalist criticism is the observation by numerous linguistic theorists (Foucault, Todorov, Marin) that speakers situated *within* such semiotic systems will often assemble sentences and strings of sentences in characteristic ways or "discourses."[3] The various elements of the discourses evident within a text can be seen to carry signification – of point of view, of specific patterns of meaning, of specific ways of constituting knowledge and value. In Margaret Laurence's *The Diviners*, when Morag learns to say "simply, *Please*, instead of *Oh yes thanks I'd love some*, or worse, *Okay that'd be fine*" (197), she is choosing between two discourses, each marked by class and, through class, by politics. The patterns of meaning which discourse signifies have been termed by many linguists (Macherey, Althusser, Pêcheux, Eagleton, Kristeva, Hirst) as *ideology*. Although this term has unfortunate connotations of the dogmatic in North American political discourse, in linguistic and critical discourse it is used to designate "a system of representations (images, myths, ideas, or concepts) endowed with specific historical context and functioning within a given society." "[I]t is usually taken for granted, considered as 'natural,' hence neither repressed ... nor intentionally propounded ..." (Roudiez 15).

Although much recent Marxist debate about ideology has focused on whether or not it is "material" and/or "autonomous," this question would appear to have arisen mostly from confusion over the persistence of ideological formations. Such patterns of meaning arise from specific material contexts, and reflect the circumstances and interests of the social group which generates them. The Prairie pattern of meaning in which Toronto signifies exploitive business practices has a material origin in the dependent economic relationship the agricultural economy of the Prairies has had with the financial and industrial sectors of Ontario. It is also, however, a pattern of meaning which is likely to persist and to influence meaning production long after this relationship has altered. Similarly, the Prairie pattern of meaning which perceives rural life as more rich and energetic than the urban (see my "A Young Boy's Eden: Some Notes on Prairie Poetry," in *Reading Canadian Reading*) flourishes despite the increasing urbanization and industrialization of Prairie society. The aesthetic is another area of ideology which shows extreme persistence. Notions of beauty or aesthetic value arise from the needs of particular sectors of society to valorize certain texts, textual practices, and positions. When these needs change, or the power of that sector to enforce its interests wanes, the particular aesthetic judgement may nevertheless persist, as if it were itself "material," and continue to influence new judgements. In the 1960s the "value" of F.P. Grove's novels rested largely on the needs of students and scholars of Canadian culture to have sufficient texts for a national literature; this value persisted through the 1970s, although that period's rapid production of new texts made the need less urgent. Only in the 1980s does the value of the Grove texts become problematical, and a new and partly mythological ground for this value begins to be articulated on the basis of the Felix Paul Greve story.

A re-situation of a culture's literary texts within its socio-political text, then, needs in no sense to be an impressionistic, evaluative, or (in the Canadian sense) "thematic" criticism. The various post-Saussurean theories of signification, discourse, and ideology offer a means of reading a text for political signification that, far from generalizing on plot patterns and overt declarations of theme, requires close attention to semiotic and discursive elements. These theories also allow the theorizing of a particular literature, characterized by such specific positions within its discourses as gender, region, class, or even nation, without arguing either its radical distinctness from other literatures or its subsumption within some "underlying universality" (Woodcock 23). Discourses are not compartments which contain or allude to one another, but systems which interact, overlap, and on occasion invoke each other's codes. Practitioners of specific discourses, whether writers or readers, do not occupy a single "emancipated and humane" position (Frye 1957: 347), but each a specific and irreproducible position within the global contention and interaction of discourses. A "Canadian" literature is theorizable as a literature produced at a large number of such positions within discourse. It is neither distinct and isolated from the contentions of global discourse nor identical with them; its marks are those of the specific contentions and nexuses of the sites of its production.

The two election-eve advertisements which began this analysis are, despite their conflicting political aims, both idealizing attempts to deny the heterogeneity of the Canadian discursive field. This is attempted by the thirty-nine through excluding the "political" from "the welfare of our country" – an exclusion which might prompt one to reply that it is by recognizing and participating in the political that one ensures that one *has* a country. The sixty-two place against heterogeneity "art," "thought," and writing and painting "to be seen and read by the whole world." In different ways both manoeuvres are counter-productive to a vigorous and "distinct" Canadian society. The latter, with its implicit "we are not fragile" aligning of its art with the non-fragile industrial production that seeks the homogenizing of economic rules which the free trade agreement moves towards, endorses one of the most homogenizing forces in the world today, multinational capitalism.[4] The former, by placing Canada beyond political disputation, risks depriving Canadians of the only means they have of defending themselves against multinational capitalism: participating in the arguments of a nation that is being continuously discursively produced and re-produced from political contestation.

Notes

1   *The Globe and Mail* [Toronto] 19 Nov. 1988: 14, 16.

2   The theory of intertextuality holds that just as individual phonemes acquire their ability to signify by differing from each other, and by occupying differential positions within a linguistic system, so too various *systems of textual organization* – literary genres, professional discourses, oral forms like gossip, cursing, whispering, a disk-jockey's "patter," social genres like wedding invitations, eulogies, birthday cards – and *particular patterns of meaning* (also known as "semiotic systems") – the English garden, the urban expressway, the nuclear family, the sailing ship – acquire meaning by occupying differential positions within the social text. Further, as parts of the social text, that is as parts of the general system of codes available for the communication of meaning in one's society, these are reader-activated rather than strictly writer-deployed.

3   Differing systems of textual organization have in recent linguistic theory become widely known as *discourses* or *discursive practices*. *Discourse* acquires its meaning in contemporary criticism from the French *discours*, speech, a much more widely used word than its English cognate, and which more readily signifies a general and characteristic pattern of organizing language. Determinants of discourse include not only characteristic items of vocabulary, recurrent syntactic structures, recurrent fields of image and metaphor, and recurrent rhetorical figures, but also particular ways of linking sentences together, or of structuring a text. Discourse can be described by genre (as in Todorov's *Les genres du discours*), by class (as in Foucault's *Les mots et les choses*), by semiotics (Barthes's *Mythologies*, McLuhan's *The Mechanical Bride*, Marin's *La critique du discours*), or through diction and sentence structure (Reiss, *The*

Discourse of Modernism).

4   Sociologist Andrée Michel has described the values of multinational capital-
    ism as "compétition, concurrence, culte de la croissance illimitée et du profit,
    asservissement de l'humain à la technique et à l'économisme, gigantisme des
    projets, valorisation de l'égoïsme de la nation et de la famille nucléaire, etc."
    (*Le féminisme* 122). She states, "les multinationales importent dans tous les pays
    grâce à la mondialisation du marché, un marché dans lequel le noyau central
    tout-puissant exploite et entretient la faiblesse de la périphérie" (122). The
    all-powerful exploit and maintain the weakness of the periphery: no wonder
    the sixty-two self-identified "artists and writers" are determined not to be
    "fragile." Although I would dispute the centre-periphery model Michel uses,
    I would also argue that her characterizations of "les multinationales" accord
    with many of the criteria most frequently invoked by free trade negotiators
    and supporters – a widening of the market-place, encouragement of compe-
    tition, rationalization of competitors, greater economic growth, larger and
    more powerful corporations. A homogenizing self-valorizing social forma-
    tion, whether it be one that idealizes "art and thought" or one that seeks
    unlimited expansion of economic power, is by its own epistemology
    unfriendly to difference. Difference is a departure from the ideal; it is lesser,
    if not parochial. Or difference is inefficient; its acknowledgement makes
    difficult the economic practices on which profit often rests – the co-opting
    of the unpaid labour of women, the production of uniform products, the
    making of minimal contributions to pension and health programs, the per-
    ceiving of commercial products, even entertainment and informational prod-
    ucts, as extra-political. Had there already been in Canada a recognition of the
    politics of difference, and of the ongoing working of that politics within and
    between its literary productions, as marking most of its best-received literary
    productions, the argument that the free trade agreement offered an exchange
    of difference for efficiency might have been made with force and precision.

Works Cited

Althusser, Louis. *For Marx.* 1965. Trans. Ben Brewster. New York: Pantheon, 1969.
Atwood, Margaret. *The Handmaid's Tale.* Toronto: McClelland and Stewart, 1985.
—. "Mathews and Misrepresentation." *Second Words: Selected Critical Prose.* Toronto:
    Anansi, 1982. 129-50.
—. *Survival: A Thematic Guide to Canadian Literature.* Toronto: Anansi, 1972.
Barthes, Roland. *Mythologies.* 1957. Trans. Annette Lavers. London: Cape, 1972.
Davey, Frank. "A Young Boy's Eden: Some Notes on Prairie Poetry." *Reading
    Canadian Reading.* Winnipeg: Turnstone, 1988. 213-29.
Derrida, Jacques. *Of Grammatology.* 1967. Trans. Gayatri Chakravorti Spivak.
    Baltimore: Johns Hopkins UP, 1976.
Eagleton, Terry. *Criticism and Ideology.* London: NLB, 1976.
Foucault, Michel. *Les mots et les choses: une archéologie des sciences humaines.* Paris:

Gallimard, 1966.

Frye, Northrop. *Anatomy of Criticism: Four Essays*. Princeton, NJ: Princeton UP, 1957.

—. Conclusion. *Literary History of Canada: Canadian Literature in English*. Gen. ed. Carl F. Klinck. Vol. 2. Toronto: U of Toronto P, 1976. 333-61.

Gallop, Jane. *Thinking through the Body*. New York: Columbia UP, 1988.

Hirst, Paul Q. *On Law and Ideology*. Atlantic Highlands, NJ: Humanities, 1979.

Jones, D.G. *Butterfly on Rock: A Study of Themes and Images in Canadian Literature*. Toronto: U of Toronto P, 1970.

Kristeva, Julia. *Desire in Language: A Semiotic Approach to Literature and Art*. 1977. Trans. Thomas Gora, Alice Jardine, and Leon S. Roudiez. Ed. Leon S. Roudiez. New York: Columbia UP, 1980.

Kroetsch, Robert. *Alibi*. Toronto: Stoddart, 1983.

—. *But We Are Exiles*. Toronto: Macmillan, 1965.

—. "Seed Catalogue." *Seed Catalogue*. Winnipeg: Turnstone, 1977. 11-47.

Lacan, Jacques. *Écrits*. Paris: Seuil, 1966.

Laurence, Margaret. *The Diviners*. Toronto: McClelland and Stewart, 1974.

Macherey, Pierre. *A Theory of Literary Production*. 1966. Trans. Geoffrey Wall. London: Routledge, 1978.

Marin, Louis. *La critique du discours: sur la "logique de port-royal" et les "pensées" de Pascal*. Paris: Minuit, 1975.

McGregor, Gaile. *The Wacousta Syndrome: Explorations in the Canadian Langscape*. Toronto: U of Toronto P, 1985.

McLuhan, Marshall. *The Mechanical Bride: Folklore of Industrial Man*. New York: Vanguard, 1951.

Michel, Andrée. *Le féminisme*. 2nd ed. Paris: Presses universitaires de France, 1980.

Moss, John. *Patterns of Isolation in English Canadian Fiction*. Toronto: McClelland and Stewart, 1974.

Pêcheux, Michel. *Language, Semantics and Ideology*. 1975. Trans. Harbans Nagpal. New York: St. Martin's, 1982.

Reiss, Timothy. *The Discourse of Modernism*. Ithaca, NY: Cornell UP, 1982.

Roudiez, Leon S. Introduction. *Desire in Language: A Semiotic Approach to Literature and Art*. 1977. By Julia Kristeva. Trans. Thomas Gora, Alice Jardine, and Leon S. Roudiez. Ed. Leon S. Roudiez. New York: Columbia UP, 1980. 1-20.

Saussure, Ferdinand de. *Course in General Linguistics*. 1916. Trans. Wade Baskin. Rev. ed. Glasgow: Fontana/Collins, 1974.

Sledd, James. *A Short Introduction to English Grammar*. Chicago: Scott, Foreman, 1959.

Smith, A.J.M. "Poet." *Towards a View of Canadian Letters: Selected Critical Essays, 1928-1971*. Vancouver: U of British Columbia P, 1973. 186-93.

Todorov, Tzvetan. *Les genres du discours*. Paris: Seuil, 1978.

White, Hayden. *Metahistory: The Historical Imagination in Nineteenth-Century Europe*. Baltimore: Johns Hopkins UP, 1973.

Woodcock, George. *Odysseus Ever Returning*. Toronto: McClelland and Stewart, 1970.

Anthologies and the Canon of Early Canadian Women Writers

Carole Gerson

One of our current cultural myths is that women writers enjoy remarkable prominence in English Canada. In a spirit of smugness, naïveté, or optimism, we eagerly embrace the view recently expressed by an editor of several anthologies that "Canada has produced an unusual, even a predominant, number of women writers" (Sullivan ix). Supporting evidence can be found without great difficulty. For example, there is *Books in Canada*'s recent readers' poll, in which seven of the top ten favourite authors were women: Alice Munro, Margaret Atwood, Margaret Laurence, Mavis Gallant, Janette Turner Hospital, Marian Engel, and Audrey Thomas outnumbered Timothy Findley, Robertson Davies, and Mordecai Richler (13). And there is Beryl Langer's study of the critical attention paid to Canadian and Australian women writers in selected academic periodicals of the late 1970s, which compares "the prominence of women writers in English Canada [with] their relative neglect in Australia" (133). Measuring the frequency of their appearance as the subjects of scholarly reviews and articles, Langer concludes that while "the critical attention accorded Canadian women is roughly proportional to their literary production, much of what Australian women write is simply not mentioned in critical journals" (170).[1]

Masked by these sanguine instances are other facets of the Canadian literary scene. Langer's Canadian figures are skewed by Atwood and Laurence, who enjoy a full 42 per cent of the total critical space given to female authors, leaving the remaining 58 per cent to be shared by another nineteen writers. This practice of conferring stardom on one or two representative women writers while neglecting the rest (see Nelson 99) will become significant when we examine the practices of Canadian anthologists. Moreover, recent research behind the scenes of the Canadian literary establishment suggests that a woman who completes a manuscript has

> a one-in-four chance of getting it published compared to any man and after that a one-in-four chance of seeing it reviewed in a magazine. [Her] chances of getting newspaper coverage are even lower (80 per cent of that space is allotted to reviews of books written by men), and should [she] decide to apply for a teaching position in a creative writing department or a writer-in-residency at a university to help

finance [her] next book, [she] is looking at a field that in 1980/81 hired women 20-29 per cent of the time (Crean 30).[2]

As an emblem of the marginalization of women writers in the Canadian literary canon, I would like to suggest one of the teaching anthologies from the early 1970s, *The Evolution of Canadian Literature in English: 1914-1945* (Parker). On the cover is a painting by Emily Carr, who won a Governor General's Award for *Klee Wyck* in 1941. Inside is the work of eighteen writers, three of them women, none of them Carr. (Mazo de la Roche, Dorothy Livesay, and Anne Marriott represent the period.)

"Literature," says Leslie Fiedler, "is effectively what we teach in departments of English; or conversely, what we teach in departments of English is literature" (73). What we teach in Canadian literature is largely determined by what appears in our anthologies, especially when we look at early writers who are otherwise out of print. For nearly two decades, feminist critics have been casting a scathing eye at the contents of general anthologies aimed at students in high school and first-year university. Tillie Olsen's finding that in the American literary institution of the 1970s the proportion of serious attention accorded women writers was one-twelfth of that given to men (209-16) concurs with Jean Mullen's 1972 analysis of American freshman English texts, which concludes that "the ratio of women writers to men [is] fairly constant: about 7% to 93%" (79). In Canada, Priscilla Galloway reported that during the 1970s the contents of Ontario high school English courses were 88 per cent male-authored and 86 per cent non-Canadian (10). These figures suggest that nascent editors of anthologies (and teachers who use them) have been unwittingly conditioned to regard literature as primarily a male preserve. Hence, the situation in the field of Canadian literature appears comparatively generous when a count of the contributors to thirty-five Canadian anthologies in common use from 1913 to 1980 concludes that a full 25 per cent are women (Dagg 31; Nelson 86).[3] As Margaret Atwood quipped, "Whether the glass is two-thirds empty or a third full depends upon how thirsty you are" (xxix).

Ostensibly the embodiment of a culture's objectively defined aesthetic achievement, a national literary canon is a malleable entity frequently reshaped by changes in taste and the appearance of new authors.[4] The values enshrined in a canon transcend aesthetic matters, reflecting the canon's identity as "a social construct" and "a means by which culture validates its social power" (Lauter 435, 452). In the literary world, less power is wielded by writers and readers than by what have been called "invisible colleges."[5] Comprised of publishers, the media, and the academy, they function as canonical "gatekeepers,"[6] conferring status by deciding what gets published and reviewed and who gets onto course lists and into anthologies, reprint series, textbooks, and reference sources.

How this structure has operated in English Canada is demonstrated by *Canadian Writers / Écrivains Canadiens: A Biographical Dictionary*, prepared by Guy Sylvestre, Brandon Conron, and Carl F. Klinck (1964, rev. 1966, rev. 1967, rpt. 1970). The editors' sole announced criterion for their selection of early and current authors is that those chosen "have for the most part produced a notable first or second book and have thereafter embarked upon a literary career with repeated publications of generally acknowledged merit" (1970: v). In English Canada, from the beginnings to 1950, women have represented 40 per cent of the authors of books of fiction and 37 per cent of the authors of books of poetry (Dagg 28). In *Canadian Writers*, women account for fewer than 19 per cent of the entries. Sociologists L.M. Grayson and J. Paul Grayson, who have used this book as the research base for their work on Canadian authors, choose their words wisely when they describe their subject as the Canadian "literary élite." Regarding the writers' occupations, they note that the English-Canadian male writer is most likely "to have found a home in the school or the university" (1978: 305). "Generally acknowledged merit," the overt qualification for canonization, thus involves an unacknowledged component based on education, occupation, academic connections,[7] and therefore by extension, gender.

Hence, among the included male writers are people like John O. Robins, professor of German at Victoria College and author of several books of humour; lawyer W.H. Blake, who translated *Maria Chapdelaine* and wrote fishing books; cabinet minister and essayist Martin Burrell; and academic authors like E.K. Brown, Douglas Bush, Claude Bissell, James Cappon, and Pelham Edgar. The excluded female writers include Kathleen Coburn, the noted Coleridge scholar; Charlotte Whitton, Canada's first woman mayor as well as the author of five monographs; novelist and journalist Madge Macbeth, who was the first woman and only three-time president of the Canadian Authors' Association; and the three formerly significant poets and women of letters, Ethelwyn Wetherald, Susan Frances Harrison, and Agnes Maule Machar, who top the list of lost women poets in Table 2. R.A.D. Ford, who won the Governor General's Award for poetry in 1956 and was also Canada's Ambassador to Russia, is included, but not Marjorie Wilkins Campbell, who won the award twice, in 1950 for non-fiction and in 1954 for juvenile writing. Children's literature, largely a female domain, is less canonical than sporting literature or humour. Fortunately, information about Campbell can be found in Norah Story's 1967 *Oxford Companion to Canadian History and Literature*, still the best reference source on earlier women authors. While the 1983 *Oxford Companion to Canadian Literature* adds eleven names to the roster of recognized female poets and fiction writers born before 1920, it drops another

CAROLE GERSON

eighteen, many of them popular authors active during the first four decades of the twentieth century.

The canonizing process, while invoking "merit," clearly involves a complex web of institutional factors. Americans studying their country's decanonization of its early women authors have focused on several particular elements, beginning with Nathaniel Hawthorne's 1854 attack on the "damn'd mob of scribbling women" who are his competitors. Investigating why in 1977 the canon of pre-1940 American writers included only one woman poet (Emily Dickinson) and no women novelists, Nia Baym concludes from her reading of the critics who shaped that canon that the woman writer "entered [American] literary history as the enemy" (130). Paul Lauter finds the tendency to define "American" literature as "masculine culture" (449) solidifying in the 1920s, with "the academic institutionalization of reading choices" (441). Under the control of a male professoriat, the activities of "choosing books to be remembered and read, building culture and taste" shifted from the woman-dominated family circle and local reading club to the male-dominated academy, which rejected female "gentility" (440-41).

The process by which women disappear from literary history, described as "the cycle of exclusion, the filtering out of women writers disproportionately to their numbers and the significance of their contributions," endures because "'minor' women writers are perceived as *more* minor than their male counterparts" (Rosenfelt 15, 16).[8] In Canada, this cycle has operated through reference books (like *Canadian Writers*) whose function is to "bestow not only accessibility but legitimacy" (Rosenfelt 13), in honorific organizations like the Royal Society of Canada, whose literary section acquired its first woman member in 1947 with the admission of Gabrielle Roy, and in anthologies of Canadian literature.

The literary periodicals of nineteenth-century Canada reflect a high level of activity among women writers. A page count of work by identified authors shows that in *The Literary Garland* (1838-51) women produced 55 per cent of the poetry and 70 per cent of the fiction; in *The Canadian Monthly and National Review* and its successor, *Rose-Belford's Canadian Monthly* (1872-82), 52 per cent of the poetry and 30 per cent of the fiction; and in *The Week* 1883-96) 29 per cent of both poetry and fiction. Moreover, their participation in the production of books indicates that the numerical presence of women on the English-Canadian literary scene has altered much less over the course of this century than our current myth of female literary dominance would lead us to expect. In 1984-85, a count of all books published in Canada and listed in *Quill & Quire* shows that 31 per cent of the authors were women; they comprised 57 per cent of the writers for children and young adults, 29 per cent of the poets, and 26 per cent of the novelists (Dagg 30). From Watters' *Checklist of*

Canadian Literature (which does not distinguish between adult and juvenile literature), a count of works published up to and including 1905 reveals that women represented about 30.5 per cent of the total number of authors of monographs of poetry and fiction, and produced about 31 per cent of the titles. There is a clear distinction by genre: women were 24 per cent of the poets and wrote 19 per cent of the poetry titles, but were 41 per cent of the fiction writers and produced 45 per cent of the titles of fiction books. This generic difference in itself has presumably had some bearing on the visibility of early women authors: until recently, poetry has been viewed as more respectable than fiction, and it has also been more frequently and easily anthologized and thus kept in print. Early Canadian women fiction writers were therefore at a triple disadvantage as a marginalized sex working in a marginalized genre in a marginalized colonial culture.

When we turn to current (post-1970) anthologies to find out who our early women authors were and what they wrote, we find that the entire period is represented by a handful of names (see Table 3). Male writers born in or before 1875 are represented by seventy-two names, thirty of which appear in four or more recent anthologies. Women writers from the same period are represented by fifteen names, eight of which appear in four or more recent anthologies. To discover how the "cycle of exclusion" has operated in Canada, I have examined the contents of some sixty literary anthologies which claim to be national in scope (the word "Canadian" appears in the title) and include early Canadian writing; most of these are represented in Table 1. Writing in French and translations, while included in some anthologies, have been eliminated from all calculations. For manageability, I have defined early writers as those born in or before 1875. This category includes authors who spill over both ends of the nineteenth century: Frances Brooke at the early end and Nellie McClung, L.M. Montgomery, and Emily Carr at the later. However, they are balanced by their male counterparts – the explorers at the beginning, Stephen Leacock, Robert Service, and Ralph Connor in the early twentieth century – thus giving us a framed picture of the situation.

Arranging these anthologies chronologically allows us to see how the practices of editors have altered and what effect these changes have had on the visibility of women writers. The first group, from Dewart's 1864 *Selections from Canadian Poets* to Carman and Pierce's 1935 *Our Canadian Literature*, is generally characterized by a principle of inclusiveness. Eager to demonstrate that there was indeed a Canadian literature, nineteenth- and early twentieth-century editors cast a broad net and drew in a proportion of women authors (30 per cent) that roughly corresponded with their degree of publishing activity. Yet even here there begins the tendency, which will become especially pernicious during the mid-twentieth century, of giving women less space than men. In thirteen cases out of seventeen, the figure in column C, the percentage of pages given to women, is less than the figure in column B, the percentage of authors who are women. The most notorious example in this regard is J.E. Wetherell's *Later Canadian Poems* (1893). Wetherell originally intended to limit his selection to seven male poets. However, under pressure from Pauline Johnson, he added the "Supplement" at the back of the book representing "within somewhat narrow limits the notable work produced in recent years by some of our women writers" (Preface n. pag.). The six women share 27 pages, compared with 159 pages for the seven men.[9]

Agreeing with Louise Berkinow that "most women writers have gotten lost," Lynne Spender insists that "in each case *someone has lost them*" (108). As can be seen in Table 2, nearly a dozen previously important Canadian women poets were mislaid by the anthologists of the mid-twentieth century (although Harrison has been revived as a fiction writer with one story that appears in two recent short story anthologies). In Canada during the 1940s and 1950s, the concept of the national survey anthology underwent a transition most clearly seen in the anthologies of Ralph Gustafson and A.J.M. Smith. The old preservative notion of defining a literature as the sum of its practitioners yielded to the evaluative principle of choosing only the "best," thus replacing an "accessible canon" with a "selective canon," in the terminology of Alastair Fowler (Golding 279-80[10]). As well, this period saw the birth of the pedagogical survey anthology intended for introductory university courses in Canadian literature. Together, the effect of the two trends was to limit the general representation of women writers and particularly narrow the canon of early female authors.[11]

In Gustafson's first major anthology, the 1942 Penguin/Pelican *Anthology of Canadian Poetry*, 23.5 per cent of the authors are women, six of whom (Isabella Valancy Crawford, Ethelwyn Wetherald, Helena Coleman, Isabel Ecclestone Mackay, Annie Charlotte Dalton, and Virna Sheard) were born in or before 1875. A seventh, Pauline Johnson, "was omitted because her publishers demanded too high a fee for her work" (Whiteman n. pag.). In this book's 1958 successor, *The Penguin Book of Canadian Verse*, the total representation of women authors has been reduced to 18 per cent, and the earlier period is represented by two: Crawford and Virna Sheard. At the same time, the number of male poets born in or before 1875 has increased, from fourteen to seventeen. The additions include Oliver Goldsmith, Charles Heavysege, Alexander McLachlan, Charles Sangster, Charles Mair, and John Frederic Herbin, who join such illustrious survivors from the first volume as George T. Lanigan, John McCrae, and Tom MacInnes (as well as the obligatory Confederation group). The net result is a nearly three-fold reduction in the proportional representation of early women writers. There are no changes to the selection of early writers in the 1967 and 1975 editions; in 1984, Pauline Johnson was finally added, along with Robert Service.

What occurred between 1942 and 1958 to cause a change of such magnitude was the publication of the three editions of A.J.M. Smith's *Book of Canadian Poetry* (1943, 1948, 1957) which culminated in his 1960 *Oxford Book of Canadian Verse*. In this series, the number of early women poets was reduced from seven (Susanna Moodie, Pamelia Vining Yule, Crawford, Harrison, Helena Coleman, Johnson, Annie Charlotte Dalton) to two (Moodie and Crawford), and their proportional representation from 16.5 per cent to 10 per cent. While winnowing out the early women, Smith gradually established the sequence of Jonathan Odell, Joseph Stansbury, Oliver Goldsmith, Standish O'Grady, Joseph Howe, Thomas D'Arcy McGee, Charles Heavysege, Alexander McLachlan, Charles Sangster, and Charles Mair that precedes the Confederation poets in Klinck and Watters' *Canadian Anthology* and to some degree structures most subsequent teaching surveys of Canadian literature. This Canadian decanonization of early women writers paralleled the practice of anthologists of American literature during the same period (Lauter 438-40, 450-51). In Canada, as in the United States, few women poets continued to appear in anthologies much past their date of death (Russ 66-68).

During the 1940-69 decades, there were several survivors of the earlier type of popular omnibus anthology. *Canadian Poetry in English* (1954), Lorne Pierce and V.B. Rhodenizer's revision of Carman and Pierce's *Our Canadian Literature* (1935), was the last resting place of many early poets, including all but one of the lost women listed in Table 2. The next omnibus survey anthology, Gordon Green and Guy Sylvestre's centennial volume, *A Century of Canadian Literature* (1967), recognizes only four early women writers: two poets (Crawford and Johnson) and two prose writers (Sara Jeannette Duncan and L.M. Montgomery). In the last of the sampler anthologies, John Robert Colombo's *The Poets of Canada* (1978), of twenty-nine early English-language poets only two are women, again Crawford and Johnson.

As the popular anthologies discarded the early women writers, there was scant effort on the part of the academy to recover them. And it is in the third period, 1970-86, that the full effects of the narrowing process can be seen. Gustafson and Smith, the most influential anthology editors of the middle decades of this century, performed as modernists purging Canadian literature of its residue of Victorian sentimentality and patriotism. As practising poets, they exercised their licence to edit literary history to suit their taste (and their network of literary acquaintances), re-inventing the past in the light of "a contemporary and cosmopolitan literary consciousness" in Smith's well-known phrase (1943: 3). Their landmark anthologies, intended to educate a public readership that had been raised on a diet of what Smith once called "maple fudge" (1942: 458), remapped the contours of early Canadian poetry.

Since the 1970s, however, the intended audience for survey texts has been largely composed of students dependent upon the wisdom and booklists of their professors for their picture and understanding of the past. When we examine the representation of early women writers in the anthologies of the 1970s, we can see that the process of decanonization has been absolute. Even in the anthologies dealing specifically with the nineteenth century, there has been almost no effort to reconstruct the period and recover its lost women authors. A case in point is Douglas Lochhead and Raymond Souster's *One Hundred Poems of Nineteenth Century Canada* (1974), which includes the work of thirty-four poets, twenty-nine of whom are men. Of the twelve poems by women, seven are by Crawford. There are two poems by Johnson, one by Moodie, one by Rosanna Leprohon, and one by Duncan. An annotated bibliography describes this book as "an excellent anthology" whose "chief value lies in its inclusion of several minor writers" (Moyles 34). So it is, if you define writers as male. David Arnason's *Nineteenth Century Canadian Stories* (1974), which revives Harriet Vining Cheney, gives us three women (all contributors to *The Literary Garland*), nine men (including Robert Barr), and three anonymous authors – not quite representative of the actual situation in the nineteenth century when women produced nearly half the fiction of English Canada.

As Table 3 makes clear, the recent academic anthologists have followed the practice of their immediate predecessors in limiting the canon of nineteenth-century women writers to six major figures from central Canada. Crawford functions as our Emily Dickinson, turning up in every possible anthology (with the surprising exception of Robert Weaver and William Toye's 1974 *Oxford Anthology of Canadian Literature*). Johnson may accompany her, especially when the editor is concerned about representing native peoples. Susanna Moodie and Catharine Parr Traill cover nonfictional prose, and selections from Duncan and Leprohon take care of fiction. Occasionally, Moodie, Duncan, and Leprohon have been seconded as poets and Crawford as a short story writer. Sheard survives only because of Gustafson's affection for her two humorous poems, "The Yak" and "Exile," which have remained in his Penguin anthologies. L.M. Montgomery and Nellie McClung, the most popular and successful Canadian women novelists of the early twentieth century, appear in the Canadian literature curriculum much less often than Ralph Connor, their male counterpart, who has been represented twice as frequently in post-1970 anthologies. Table 3 also shows that John McCrae and Oliver Goldsmith have each acquired canonical status on the strength of a single poem. Would the latter have done as well if his surname had not been Goldsmith and if his first name had been Olivia?

From the list of authors who now represent early Canadian literature, it is evident that importance has been granted on grounds other than aesthetic brilliance. Non-literary factors contribute substantially to the significance of the preserved male writer, whose cultural weight is enhanced by his historical public career as explorer, clergyman, educator, lawyer, newspaperman, or political figure, and by the personal connections fostered by his profession.[12] Feminist historians argue that to re-inscribe women's history into national history it is necessary to alter old concepts of significance and to accord social and domestic life the attention previously devoted to military and political events.[13]

To re-inscribe women into the literary history represented by our anthologies, we can begin by considering journalists and diarists along with the explorers, by including temperance and suffragist writers with the political writers, and by accepting social and domestic topics into the early poetic canon in poems like Rosanna Leprohon's "Given and Taken." As well as valorizing the literary spheres favoured by women, such as juvenile literature, we need to rediscover their work in the areas we think of as distinctly Canadian. For example, Crawford was not the only early woman author of interesting narrative poems; in 1892, Ethelwyn Wetherald was judged to stand "in the front rank of Canadian sonnet writers" (Campbell 177); Helen Mar Johnson's "The Watcher" (Dewart 153-55) conveys a fine Frygian sense of terror on a winter night. Tired of being "cheated of recognition" (Shields 18) by the literary establishment, the early Canadian woman poet has deviously begun to re-enter our literature in fictional form, in Carol Shields's Mary Swann (of Swann: A Mystery) and in Almeda Joynt Roth, heroine of Alice Munro's story "Meneseteung." These characters, elusive and intriguing, may have the effect of directing attention back to their quite "unobscure" historical counterparts like Wetherald, Machar, and Harrison, who all enjoyed long and prominent careers as poets, journalists, and vital members of their cultural community.

The self-replicating tendency of academic anthologies is a significant element in the process of canonization: "more people read these writers because their work is accessible in anthologies; these writers are included in anthologies because more people read them" (Nelson 86). Hence, a contributing factor is the availability of the writers' work in reprint series. Of the eight women who top Table 3, only Crawford, Moodie, and Pauline Johnson appeared consistently in Canadian anthologies over the past century, during which time Roughing It in the Bush and Johnson's books remained more or less in print. The poetry of Rosanna Leprohon and Sara Jeannette Duncan was included in several late nineteenth-century

CAROLE GERSON

anthologies but disappeared after 1900. Catharine Parr Traill's only early appearance is in one anthology from the 1920s. Frances Brooke, who makes her anthology debut in 1955 in the first edition of Klinck and Watters' *Canadian Anthology*, represents the pattern of recognition shared by the others. In the case of Brooke, Traill, Moodie, and Duncan, inclusion in the first or second edition of *Canadian Anthology* was soon followed by the reissue of a major prose work in the New Canadian Library (NCL) series, which was in turn followed by more anthology appearances. With Leprohon, recanonization was delayed until 1973, when Mary Jane Edwards included her in the first volume of *The Evolution of Canadian Literature* series and *Antoinette de Mirecourt* was added to the NCL list. Anna Jameson, whose *Winter Studies and Summer Rambles in Canada* was reissued by both Coles and NCL (originally in an abridged edition), is the only early woman writer whose reputation has not benefitted from reprinting in the latter series.

The current ascendancy of fiction as our major literary genre is another factor that has significantly affected the visibility of early women writers and perhaps diverted attention from the poets. The formerly anthologized poetry of Moodie, Duncan, Leprohon, and L.M. Montgomery has been almost completely overshadowed by their prose, and Crawford's oeuvre has been combed for fiction suitable for inclusion in short story anthologies. Harrison may now be re-entering the canon through the door of fiction, a route that could be followed by some of the other writers in Table 2, particularly Isabel Ecclestone Mackay and Florence Randal Livesay.

The relation between the sex of the editor and the inclusion of women writers is a topic that bears consideration. Until recently, the few appearances of a female editor had little effect on the representation of women authors. Going back to the first period presented in Table 1, we can see that Edmund Kemper Broadus, identified on the title page as "Professor of English in the University of Alberta," and Eleanor Hammond Broadus (unaffiliated) anticipated the pattern of the future in their restriction of women writers in their first book to four (Crawford, Pauline Johnson, Moodie, and Marjorie Pickthall) and in their second to seven (adding Dalton, Mazo de la Roche, and Audrey Alexandra Brown). Susan Frances Harrison's popular *Canadian Birthday Book* was just slightly more generous. On the other hand, in Donalda Dickie's *The Canadian Poetry Book* (1924), which I omitted from Table 1 because it is a school text which its editor claimed "[was] not, in any sense of the word an 'Anthology of Canadian Verse'" (5), women are 33 per cent of the contributors and occupy 40 per cent of the text.[14] In contrast, there were no women editors of major national survey anthologies during the next period, 1940-69, when many previously important women poets disappeared permanently from sight.

In my tabulation of the post-1970 period, the anthologies compiled by Brita Mickleburgh, Mary Jane Edwards, and Donna Bennett certainly help raise the proportional representation of early women writers. Disappointing, therefore, is Margaret Atwood's *New Oxford Book of Canadian Verse*. While Atwood justifies her inclusion of early poets on the grounds of historical significance, she has stopped short of extending her "excavationism" (xxx) to her own sex. "In the nineteenth century," she jests, "a woman Canadian poet was the equivalent, say, of a white Anglo-Saxon Protestant Inuit shaman" (xxix), and then proves her point by including only two (Crawford and Johnson) in her selection of nineteen early writers. Women fare better in her recently co-edited (with Robert Weaver) *Oxford Book of Canadian Short Stories in English* (1986), where Crawford and Harrison almost balance Roberts, Scott, and Leacock. Yet here too we can see the self-replicating process at work, for Atwood and Weaver's first two selections reproduce Rosemary Sullivan's Crawford and Harrison choices for *Stories by Canadian Women*, published two years earlier.

On the other hand, this duplication might be regarded as an example of what Elaine Showalter calls "mainstreaming" (19). One way to recover lost women authors is in anthologies devoted exclusively to women's work. These have not been plentiful in Canada. Rota Lister's substantial survey compilation of Canadian women's writing, which would help recover a broad range of fiction, non-fiction, and poetry, has been in search of a publisher for five years and now rests in the archives of the University of Waterloo. Rosemary Sullivan's historical anthology, *Poetry by Canadian Women*, was published by Oxford in 1989. Such books – when we have them – will be essential stages in the process of reconstructing the literary history of Canadian women, but they are only stages. Showalter cautions that unless this material can be integrated into a reconceived, broadened canon, all the archaeological work of feminist literary scholars may serve only to further marginalize women's writing. Using Harriet Beecher Stowe as her example, she describes the dilemma for American literature: "if we only teach Stowe in the women's courses, she remains ghettoized; if we simply squeeze in a lecture on Stowe, we have tokenism; if we drop *Moby-Dick* to make room for *Uncle Tom's Cabin*, the sacrifice will be unacceptable to many, including feminists" (20). Showalter's tentative resolution is to recognize that the 1980s are a period of canonical uncertainty and to look forward hopefully to "the emergence of bold new paradigms" that will lead to a complete reassessment of literary history and values (21).

In Canada, while we cannot condense the issue into an epigrammatic contest between Uncle Tom and Moby-Dick, we face the same problem of getting our early women writers into the canon and the curriculum.

Once we have acknowledged that "what is commonly called literary history is actually a record of choices" (Berkinow 3), we can start to exercise new options that would redesign the current picture of Canada's literary past. The task is large and multifaceted but not too daunting; women are accustomed to engaging in work that, in the words of the proverb, is "never done."

Notes

The research for this paper was assisted by a grant from the Social Sciences and Humanities Research Council of Canada's Women and Work strategic grants program.

1 The percentage of women authors reviewed in mainstream newspapers and magazines is less; see Dagg 35.

2 In 1983-84 women occupied 36 per cent of short-term and 33 per cent of long-term writers-in-residence positions, and received 30 per cent of the funding (Dagg 42). Crean's source is Nelson.

3 The count of Canadian poets in American anthologies from 1890 to 1960, in A.R. Rogers, "American Recognition of Canadian Authors," diss., U of Michigan, 1964, reveals that women were 23.5 per cent of the Canadian poets recognized in the United States, but received only 16 per cent of the space.

4 The major work on this subject is Jay B. Hubbell's *Who Are the Major American Writers?* (Durham, NC: Duke UP, 1972).

5 Nelson takes this term from Lewis A. Coser, Charles Kadushin, and Walter W. Powell, *Books: The Culture and Commerce of Publishing* (New York: Basic, 1982), who in turn borrow it from Diana Crane, *Invisible Colleges: Diffusion of Knowledge in Scientific Communities* (Chicago: U of Chicago P, 1972).

6 Nelson 70, 79; from Dale Spender 186 and Dorothy E. Smith 287.

7 For an assessment of the role of the university in contemporary Canadian literature, see Bruce W. Powe, "The University as the Hidden Ground of Canadian Literature," *Antigonish Review* 47 (1981): 11-15.

8 See, for example, Moyles' classification of Frances Brooke, Pauline Johnson, Rosanna Leprohon, and Catharine Parr Traill as "minor" and Charles W. Gordon and Ernest Thompson Seton as "major" (vii-viii).

9 See Carole Gerson, "Some Notes Concerning Pauline Johnson," *Canadian Notes & Queries* 34 (1985): 16-19.

10 Alastair Fowler, *Kinds of Literature: An Introduction to the Theory of Genres and Modes* (Cambridge, MA: Harvard UP, 1982) 213-16.

11 We can draw a rosier picture of the representation of women poets by looking only at anthologies whose focus is *current* authors. From *New Provinces* (1936), which contains no women, the situation could only improve. In Gustafson's *A Little Anthology of Canadian Poets* (1943) 13.5 per cent of the

poets are women, who occupy 7.7 per cent of the space. In A.J.M. Smith's *Modern Canadian Verse* (1967) 18 per cent of the poets are women; this figure rises to 35 per cent in Gary Geddes' and Phyllis Bruce's *Fifteen Canadian Poets Plus Five* (1978) and to 38 per cent in Dennis Lee's *The New Canadian Poets, 1970-1985* (1985).

12 For an example of this kind of male literary/political power network, see the guest list of the 1897 banquet of *Canadian Magazine*, which mixed poets and fiction writers with newspaper magnates, political figures, academics, and businessmen (*Canadian Magazine* 8 [1897]: 463-66).

13 See, for example, Veronica Strong-Boag, "Raising Clio's Consciousness: Women's History and Archives in Canada," *Archivaria* 6 (1978): 70-82; Gerda Lerner, "Placing Women in History: Definitions and Challenges," *Feminist Studies* 3 (1975): 5-14.

14 A higher representation of women appeared in anthologies of *current* poets, like the Toronto Women's Press Club's *Canadian Days* (1911), Ethel Hume Bennett's *New Harvesting: Contemporary Canadian Poetry, 1918-38* (1939), and Alan Creighton and Hilda Ridley, eds., *A New Canadian Anthology* (1938).

Works Cited

"Advice and Dissent." *Books in Canada* May 1987: 12-14.

Atwood, Margaret. Introduction. *The New Oxford Book of Canadian Verse in English*. Toronto: Oxford UP, 1982. xxvii-xxxix.

Baym, Nina. "Melodramas of Beset Manhood: How Theories of American Fiction Exclude Women Authors." *American Quarterly* 33 (1981): 123-39.

Berkinow, Louise. Introduction. *The World Split Open: Four Centuries of Women Poets in England and America, 1552-1950*. New York: Vintage, 1974. 3-47.

Campbell, Wilfred, et al. *At the Mermaid Inn*. Ed. Barrie Davies. Toronto: U of Toronto P, 1979.

Crean, Susan. "The Thirty Per Cent Solution." *This Magazine* Jan. 1984: 26-31, 38.

Dagg, Anne Innis. *The 50% Solution: Why Should Women Pay for Men's Culture?* Waterloo, ON: Otter, 1986.

Fiedler, Leslie A. "Literature as an Institution: The View from 1980." *English Literature: Opening Up the Canon*. Ed. Leslie A. Fiedler and Houston A. Baker, Jr. Baltimore: Johns Hopkins UP, 1981. 73-91.

Galloway, Priscilla. *What's Wrong with High School English?* Toronto: Ontario Institute for Studies in Education, 1980.

Golding, Alan C. "A History of American Poetry Anthologies." *Canons*. Ed. Robert von Hallberg. Chicago: U of Chicago P, 1984. 279-307.

Grayson, J. Paul, and L.M. Grayson. "Canadian Literary and Other Élites: The Historical and Institutional Basis of Shared Realities." *The Canadian Review of Sociology and Anthropology* 17 (1980): 338-56.

—. "The Canadian Literary Élite: A Socio-Historical Perspective." *The Canadian*

Journal of Sociology 3 (1980): 291-308.

Langer, Beryl Donaldson. "Women and Literary Production: Canada and Australia." *Australian-Canadian Studies* 2 (1984): 70-83. Rpt. as "Women and Literary Production" in *Australian/Canadian Literatures in English: Comparative Perspectives.* Ed. Russell McDougall and Gillian Whitlock. Melbourne: Methuen Australia, 1987. 133-50.

Lauter, Paul. "Race and Gender in the Shaping of the American Literary Canon: A Case Study from the Twenties." *Feminist Studies* 9 (1983): 435-63.

Moyles, R.G. *English-Canadian Literature to 1900: A Guide to Information Sources.* Detroit: Gale Research, 1976.

Mullen, Jean S. "Freshman Textbooks: Part I: Women Writers in Freshman Textbooks." *College English* 34 (1972-73): 79-84.

Munro, Alice. "Meneseteung." *The New Yorker* 11 Jan. 1988: 28-38.

Nelson, Sharon. "Bemused, Branded, and Belittled: Women and Writing in Canada." *Fireweed* 15 (1982): 65-102.

Olsen, Tillie. *Silences.* 1978. New York: Dell, 1983.

Rosenfelt, Deborah S. "The Politics of Bibliography: Women's Studies and the Literary Canon." *Women in Print I.* Ed. Joan E. Hartman and Ellen Messer-Davidow. New York: MLA, 1982. 11-35.

Russ, Joanna. *How To Suppress Women's Writing.* Austin: U of Texas P, 1983.

Shields, Carol. *Swann: A Mystery.* Toronto: Stoddart, 1987.

Showalter, Elaine. "Responsibilities and Realities: A Curriculum for the Eighties." *ADE Bulletin* 70 (1981): 17-21.

Smith, A.J.M. "Canadian Anthologies, New and Old." *University of Toronto Quarterly* 2 (1942): 457-74.

—. Introduction. *The Book of Canadian Poetry.* Chicago: U of Chicago P, 1943. 3-31.

Smith, Dorothy E. "A Peculiar Eclipsing: Women's Exclusion from Man's Culture." *Women's Studies International Quarterly* 1 (1978): 281-95.

Spender, Dale. "The Gatekeepers: A Feminist Critique of Academic Publishing." *Doing Feminist Research.* Ed. Helen Roberts. London: Routledge & Kegan Paul, 1981. 186-202.

Spender, Lynne. 1983. *Intruders on the Rights of Men: Women's Unpublished Heritage.* London: Pandora, 1983.

Story, Norah. *The Oxford Companion to Canadian History and Literature.* Toronto: Oxford UP, 1967.

Sylvestre, Guy, Brandon Conron, and Carl F. Klinck. *Canadian Writers / Écrivains Canadiens: A Biographical Dictionary.* Toronto: Ryerson, 1970.

Toye, William, ed. *The Oxford Companion to Canadian Literature.* Toronto: Oxford UP, 1983.

Watters, Reginald Eyre. *A Checklist of Canadian Literature and Background Materials, 1628-1960.* Toronto: U of Toronto P, 1972.

Whiteman, Bruce. *A Literary Friendship: The Correspondence of Ralph Gustafson and W.W.E. Ross.* Toronto: ECW, 1984.

Anthologies Consulted

Arnason, David, ed. *Nineteenth Century Canadian Stories.* Toronto: Macmillan, 1974.

Atwood, Margaret, ed. *The New Oxford Book of Canadian Verse in English.* Toronto: Oxford UP, 1982.

Atwood, Margaret, and Robert Weaver, eds. *The Oxford Book of Canadian Short Stories in English.* Toronto: Oxford UP, 1986.

Bennett, Ethel Hume, ed. *New Harvesting: Contemporary Canadian Poetry, 1918-1938.* Toronto: Macmillan, 1939.

Birney, Earle, ed. *Twentieth Century Canadian Poetry.* Toronto: Ryerson, 1953.

Broadus, Edmund Kemper, and Eleanor Hammond Broadus, eds. *A Book of Canadian Prose and Verse.* 1923. Rev. ed. Toronto: Macmillan, 1934.

Brown, Russell, and Donna Bennett, eds. *An Anthology of Canadian Literature in English.* 2 vols. Toronto: Oxford UP, 1982.

Burpee, Lawrence J., ed. *A Century of Canadian Sonnets.* Toronto: Musson, 1910.

—, ed. *Flowers from a Canadian Garden.* Toronto: Musson, [1909?].

Campbell, W.W., ed. *The Oxford Book of Canadian Verse.* Toronto: Oxford UP, 1913.

Carman, Bliss, and Lorne Pierce, eds. *Our Canadian Literature: Representative Verse, English and French.* Toronto: Ryerson, 1935.

Carman, Bliss, Lorne Pierce, and V.B. Rhodenizer, eds. *Canadian Poetry in English.* Toronto: Ryerson, 1954.

Colombo, John Robert, ed. *The Poets of Canada.* Edmonton, AB: Hurtig, 1978.

Creighton, Alan, and Hilda Ridley, eds. *A New Canadian Anthology.* Toronto: Crucible, 1935.

David, Jack, and Robert Lecker, eds. *Canadian Poetry.* 2 vols. Toronto: New, 1982.

Davis, N. Brian, ed. *The Poetry of the Canadian People, 1720-1920.* Toronto: NC, 1976.

Daymond, Douglas, and Leslie Monkman, eds. *Literature in Canada.* 2 vols. Toronto: Gage, 1978.

Dewart, Edward Hartley, ed. *Selections from Canadian Poets.* Montreal: Lovell, 1864.

Dickie, Donalda, ed. *The Canadian Poetry Book.* London and Toronto: Dent, 1924.

Dudek, Louis, and Irving Layton, eds. *Canadian Poems, 1850-1952.* 2nd ed. Toronto: Contact, 1953.

Edwards, Mary Jane, et al, eds. *The Evolution of Canadian Literature in English.* 4 vols. Toronto: Holt, Rinehart and Winston, 1973.

Garvin, John, ed. *Canadian Poets.* 1916. Rev. ed. Toronto: McClelland, 1926.

Gerson, Carole, and Kathy Mezei, eds. *The Prose of Life: Sketches from Victorian Canada.* Downsview, ON: ECW, 1981.

Grady, Wayne, ed. *The Penguin Book of Canadian Short Stories.* Harmondsworth, Eng.: Penguin, 1980.

Green, Gordon, and Guy Sylvestre, eds. *A Century of Canadian Literature / Un siècle de littérature canadienne.* Toronto: Ryerson; Montreal: HMH, 1967.

Gustafson, Ralph, ed. *Anthology of Canadian Poetry*. Harmondsworth, Eng.: Penguin, 1942.

—, ed. *The Penguin Book of Canadian Verse*. Harmondsworth, Eng.: Penguin, 1958; 2nd ed. 1967; 3rd ed. 1975; 4th ed. 1984.

Hardy, E.A., ed. *Selections from the Canadian Poets*. Toronto: Macmillan, 1920.

Harrison, Susan Frances, ed. *The Canadian Birthday Book*. Toronto: Blackett Robinson, 1887.

Klinck, Carl F., and R.E. Watters, eds. *Canadian Anthology*. Toronto: Gage, 1955; 2nd ed. 1966; 3rd ed. 1974.

Lighthall, W.D., ed. *Songs of the Great Dominion*. London: Walter Scott, 1889.

Lochhead, Douglas, and Raymond Souster, eds. *One Hundred Poems of Nineteenth Century Canada*. Toronto: Macmillan, 1974.

Lucas, Alec, ed. *Great Canadian Short Stories*. New York: Dell, 1971.

McLay, Catherine, ed. *Canadian Literature: The Beginnings to the 20th Century*. Toronto: McClelland and Stewart, 1974.

Mickleburgh, Brita, ed. *Canadian Literature: Two Centuries in Prose*. Toronto: McClelland and Stewart, 1973.

Pacey, Desmond, ed. *A Book of Canadian Stories*. 2nd ed. Toronto: Ryerson, 1950.

—, ed. *Selections from Major Canadian Writers: Poetry and Creative Prose in English*. Toronto: McGraw-Hill Ryerson, 1974.

Parker, George, ed. *The Evolution of Canadian Literature in English: 1914-1945*. Toronto: Holt, Rinehart, and Winston, 1973.

Rand, Theodore H., ed. *A Treasury of Canadian Verse*. Toronto: Briggs, 1900.

Robins, John D., ed. *A Pocketful of Canada*. Toronto: Collins, 1946.

Ross, George W., ed. *Patriotic Recitations and Arbour Day Exercises*. Toronto: Warwick, 1893.

Ross, Malcolm, et al, eds. *Poets of Canada*. New Canadian Library. 4 vols. Toronto: McClelland and Stewart, 1960-72.

Sinclair, David, ed. *Nineteenth-Century Narrative Poems*. Toronto: McClelland and Stewart, 1972.

Smith, A.J.M., ed. *The Book of Canadian Poetry*. Chicago: U of Chicago P, 1943; 2nd ed. 1948; 3rd ed. 1957.

—, ed. *The Book of Canadian Prose: Early Beginnings to Confederation*. Toronto: Gage, 1965.

—, ed. *The Canadian Century*. Toronto: Gage, 1973.

—, ed. *The Oxford Book of Canadian Verse*. Toronto: Oxford UP, 1960.

Stephen, A.M., ed. *The Golden Treasury of Canadian Verse*. Toronto: Dent, 1928.

—, ed. *The Voice of Canada: A Selection of Prose and Verse*. Toronto: Dent, 1926.

Sullivan, Rosemary, ed. *Stories by Canadian Women*. Toronto: Oxford UP, 1984.

Swayze, J.F., ed. *The Voice of Canada*. Toronto: Dent, 1946.

Watson, Albert Durrant, and Lorne Pierce, eds. *Our Canadian Literature: Representative Prose and Verse*. Toronto: Ryerson, 1923.

Weaver, Robert, and William Toye, eds. *The Oxford Anthology of Canadian Literature*. Toronto: Oxford UP, 1973.

Wetherell, James E., ed. *Later Canadian Poems*. Toronto: Copp Clark, 1893.

Table 1

Representation of Women in Canadian Survey Anthologies (English-language only)

Code
A: P = Poetry; M = Mixed Poetry and Prose; Pr = Prose
B: total authors, % women
C: total authors, % pages for women
D: authors born ≤ 1875, % women
E: authors born ≤1875, % pages for women
*: woman editor

Beginnings to 1935

A	Editor(s)	Pub. Date	B	C	D	E
				per cent		
P	Dewart, *Selections from Can. Poets*	1864	24	35.5	24	35.5
P	*Harrison, *Can. Birthday Bk.*	1887	21	16.5	21	16.5
P	Lighthall, *Songs of the Great Dominion*	1889	28	18.5	28	18.5
P	Wetherell, *Later Can. Poems*	1893	46	15.5	46	15.5
P	Rand, *Treasury of Can. Verse*	1900	22.5	22	22.5	22
P	Burpee, *Flowers from a Can. Garden*	1909?	50	33	50	33
P	Burpee, *Century of Can. Sonnets*	1910	16.5	18	16.5	18
P	Campbell, *Oxford Bk. of Can. Verse*	1913	21	18	21	17.5
P	Garvin, *Can. Poets*	1916	40.5	34	33	30.5
P	Hardy, *Selections from Can. Poets*	1920	29	32.5	29	32.5
M	Watson & Pierce, *Our Can. Lit.*	1923	22.5	25.5	24	25.5
M	*Broadus, *Bk. of Can. Prose & Verse*	1923	9.5	6	11	8
P	Garvin, *Can. Poets*	1926	38.5	34	33	30
M	Stephen, *Voice of Canada*	1926	30	26	27.5	20
P	Stephen, *Golden Tr. of Can. Verse*	1928	40	36	31	34
M	*Broadus, *Bk. of Can. Prose and Verse*	1934	15	7.5	15	8
P	Carman & Pierce, *Our Can. Lit.*	1935	38.5	29	31	23
	AVERAGE:		30	24	27.5	23

(Table 1 cont'd.)

1940-69

A	Editor(s)	Pub. Date	B	C	D	E
				per cent		
P	Gustafson, *Anth. of Can. Poetry*	1942	23.5	19.5	30	23.5
P	Smith, *Bk. of Can. Poetry*	1943	28.5	19.5	16.5	11
M	Swayze, *Voice of Canada*	1946	15	13	14.5	17
P	Smith, *Bk. of Can. Poetry*	1948	22.5	17.5	11.5	9
Pr	Pacey, *Bk. of Can. Stories*	1950	22	18.5	10	12
P	Dudek and Layton, *Can. Poems, 1850-1952*	1953	26	19	7	6
P	Carman, Pierce, Rhodenizer, *Can. Poetry*	1954	35	27	25	22
M	Klinck and Watters, *Can. Anth.*	1955	23	18.5	21	15.5
P	Smith, *Bk. of Can. Poetry*	1957	23.5	19.5	11.5	9.5
P	Gustafson, *Penguin Bk. of Can. Verse*	1958	18	16.5	10.5	10.5
P	Smith, *Oxford Bk. of Can. Verse*	1960	22	22	10	11.5
Pr	Smith, *Bk. of Can. Prose*	1965	13.5	15.5	13.5	15.5
M	Klinck and Watters, *Can. Anth.*	1966	17	15	15	16.5
M	Green and Sylvestre, *Cen. of Can. Lit.*	1967	25	21	28.5	31
P	Gustafson, *Penguin Bk. of Can. Verse*	1967	16.5	16.5	11	13
P	Ross, *Poets of Canada* (NCL; 4 vols.)	1960-72	20.5	17.5	0	0
	AVERAGE		20.5	18.5	14.5	14

(*Table 1 cont'd.*)

1970-86

A Editor(s)	Pub. Date	B	C	D	E
		per cent			
Pr Lucas, *Great Can. Short Stories*	1971	17	17	0	0
P Sinclair, *19th-C. Narrative Poems*	1972	17	17.5	17	17.5
Pr *Mickleburgh, *Can. Lit.*	1973	30	28	45.5	44
M *Edwards et al., *Evol. of Can. Lit. to 1970* (4 vols.)	1973	21.5	24.5	22	27.5
M Smith, *The Canadian Century*	1973	14.5	11.5	18	16
M *McLay, Can. Lit.	1974	17	20.5	17	20.5
P Lochhead and Souster, *100 Poems*	1974	14.5	20.5	14.5	20.5
Pr Arnason, *19th-C. Can. Stories*	1974	25	29	25	29
M Klinck and Watters, *Can. Anth.*	1974	22.5	20.5	20.5	20.5
M Weaver and Toye, *Oxford Anth.*	1974	26	24.5	23	23.5
M Pacey, *Selections from Can. Poets*	1974	21	20.5	0	0
P Gustafson, *Penguin Bk. of Can. Verse*	1975	17	17	10.5	13
M Daymond and Monkman, *Lit. in Can.* (2 vols.)	1978	23	26.5	21.5	27.5
P Colombo, *Poets of Canada*	1978	16.5	16.5	7	8
Pr Grady, *Penguin Bk. Can. Short Stories*	1980	29	33	33.5	36
P David and Lecker, *Can. Poetry* (2 vols.)	1982	24	22	14.5	15
M *Bennett and Brown, *Anth. of Can. Lit.* (2 vols.)	1982	30	26.5	21	32
P *Atwood, *New Oxford Bk. of Can. Verse*	1982	24.5	22	10.5	15.5
P Gustafson, *Penguin Bk. of Can. Verse*	1984	16.5	17	14	12.5
Pr *Atwood and Weaver, *Oxford Bk. of Can. Short Stories*	1986	41.5	39	40	41
AVERAGE:		22.4	22.5	18.5	21

Table 2: Lost Women Poets Born ≤ 1875

Code
No.: No. of appearances in "Anthologies Consulted"
Dates: Years spanned by anthology appearances

Name	Death	No.	Dates	Last Appearance
Ethelwyn Wetherald	1940	15	1887-1954	1935, 1942, 1954
Agnes Maule Machar	1927	14	1887-1954	1935, 1946, 1964
Susie Frances Harrison	1935	13	1887-1954	1935, 1943, 1954
Jean Blewett	1934	13	1900-1954	1935, 1946, 1954
Helena Coleman	1953	13	1909-1954	1942, 1943, 1954
Annie Charlotte Dalton	1938	11	1926-1954	1946, 1953, 1954
Isabel Ecclestone Mackay	1928	11	1913-1954	1942, 1946, 1954
Elizabeth Roberts MacDonald	1922	8	1889-1954	1923, 1935, 1954
Helen Merrill	1951	7	1900-1954	1926, 1935, 1954
Pamelia Vining Yule	1897?	7	1864-1943	1900, 1913, 1943
Florence Randal Livesay	1953	7	1916-1954	1935, 1939, 1954

Table 3: Women Authors Born before 1875 in Twenty Anthologies, published 1970– (listed in Table 1)

Code
No.: No. of appearances in twenty anthologies

Author	Dates	No.	Last Appearance
Isabella Valancy Crawford	1850-1887	14	1982(3), 1984, 1986
Susanna Moodie	1803-1885	9	1976, 1978, 1982, 1986
Pauline Johnson	1861-1913	8	1978(2), 1982, 1984
Sara Jeannette Duncan	1861-1922	7	1973(3), 1974(3), 1978
Frances Brooke	1723-1789	5	1974(2), 1978, 1982
Catharine Parr Traill	1802-1899	4	1978, 1982
Rosanna Leprohon	1829-1879	4	1973 1974, 1976, 1978
Emily Carr	1871-1945	4	1973(2), 1974, 1978
Virna Sheard	1865-1943	2	1975, 1984
Nellie McClung	1873-1951	2	1973, 1978
L.M. Montgomery	1874-1942	2	1973(2)
Harriet Vaughan Cheney	1796-1889	1	1973
Anna Jameson	1794-1860	1	1978
Susie Frances Harrison	1859-1937	1	1986*
Robina and Kathleen Lizars	d.1918; 1931	1	1973

* also in *Stories by Canadian Women* (1984)

(Table 3 cont'd.)

Male Authors Born before 1875 in Twenty Anthologies, published 1970-

No.	Author
19	Roberts
18	D.C. Scott
13	Carman, Lampman
12	Sangster
11	Campbell, Leacock
10	Goldsmith, Haliburton, McLachlan
9	Heavysege, Mair
7	Drummond
6	Cameron, Howe, Kirby, Service, Stansbury
5	"Ralph Connor," McCrae, McCulloch, McGee, Richardson, F. G. Scott, E. W. Thomson
4	Dewart, De Mille, Tom MacInnes, Parker, Odell
3	Alline, Robert Hayman, Hearne, O'Grady
2	Levi Adams, Jacob Bailey, Adam Hood Burwell, Norman Duncan, John Frederic Herbin, John Hunter-Duvar, G.T. Lanigan, Alexander Mackenzie, Goldwin Smith, David Thompson, Daniel Wilson
1	Adam Allan, Grant Allen, Isidore Ascher, Robert Barr, Samuel M. Baylis, Edward Blake, Sir Cavendish Boyle, John Burke, W.F. Butler, Edward John Chapman, Thomas Cary, John Gyles, Alexander Henry, Wilfrid Laurier, John Talon Lesperance, W.D. Lighthall, Evan MacColl, J. MacKay, Alexander Muir, John James Proctor, Theodore Harding Rand, Ernest Thompson Seton, George Vancouver, Arthur Weir, R. Stanley Weir

Total: 72 names for men (83%), 15 names for women (17%)

One More Woman Talking

Bronwen Wallace

I can't separate my personal poetics from the life I am leading or from the events that have brought me to this point in it. But since I can't work my whole life history into a statement of poetics, I'll go straight to one of the high points: a day in May, twenty-one years ago, at Queen's University. On that day, I left a provincial meeting of the Student Union for Peace Action with a number of other women (while the men grumbled that we were being "divisive") to meet and discuss what was then being called The Women's Movement. I think I probably left the room because it seemed to be Theoretically Correct to do so. I'd been in the peace movement / new left for about three years at this point; I'd started to read Marx; I was big on being TC. I had absolutely no idea, however, what we would talk about. And I certainly had no idea, theoretically or otherwise, how much this meeting was going to change my life.

What we talked about, in one way or another, for about four hours, were our lives. For me, that meeting represented the first time I had ever been in a room full of women talking *consciously* about their lives, trying to make sense of them, trying to see how the unique and private anecdotes became part of a story that gave each of our lives a public and collective meaning as well.

Since then, the majority of my time has been spent listening to women tell the story of their lives in one form or another. I have attended countless meetings to raise consciousness or disrupt beauty contests or plan antinuclear marches; I have listened to women tell about being beaten by husbands or boyfriends; I have held a woman's hand while I gave birth and another's as she lay dying. In being part of these events, I share what is common to many women *and* I also experience them uniquely, as myself. Like every other woman, I come to feminism from my own particular pain and strength and am changed by it as no one else will be ever, while at the same time I participate in events that change us all. The continuing dialectic between these two elements – the public and the private, the unique and the common – is what I enjoy most about living as I do in these particular times.

It is also the basis for my poems. I begin with what I have been given: women's stories, women's conversations. Since most of these stories come to me in pretty straightforward, conversational language, that's what I use in the poem. But as I begin to recreate that conversation on the page, I begin to listen to the voice that tells these stories, a voice that is angry sometimes, or frightened, or grieving, or ecstatic. And it becomes the voice I have heard in so many women's conversations, a voice that explores *both* the events in the story itself, *and* something else that lies within those events.

This something else is always a mystery for me, since I never know what the poem will discover (just as I never know, in my day-to-day conversations, what any particular woman will discover). For me that everyday language is a sort of safety net, a familiar place in which a deeper, often more dangerous exploration can take place. These stories, because they are women's stories, have never been heard before. For that reason, content, *what happens*, is extremely important in itself *and also* in what it conveys about a new way of looking at the world, of being in the world. What I hear in "ordinary conversation" is that movement that goes on among us when we feel safe enough or confident enough or loved enough to explore the power within us. This power is so often belittled or denied by the society around us (or by ourselves), but it remains the power by which, in our best moments, we manage to survive and to live, sometimes, with grace. This is what I hear in conversation and what I try to record in my poems. If this sounds like a statement of faith, as much as a statement of poetics, that's because it is.

The questions about language which my writing raises have to do primarily with voice, with how to convey this sense of inner discovery at the heart of the most prosaic anecdote. In that sense, my use of everyday language becomes a challenge for me in the poem, as it is in conversation, when we try to convey matters of life-and-death importance with the same words we also use to order a cheeseburger at Harvey's or teach our children how to swim. Sometimes I think the difference is not as great as we like to think, but mostly I just like the challenge.

Another challenge, obviously, lies in the fact that the language I am using has been used in the past primarily to tell men's stories or, more accurately, to tell everyone's stories from a patriarchal point of view. That point of view is embedded in the language itself and one of the questions raised by feminist theory is whether women can speak our piece using it. The following quotation from Xavière Gauthier is a typical representation of the issue:

Women are, in fact, caught in a real contradiction. Throughout the course of history, they have been mute, and it is doubtless by virtue of this mutism that men have been able to speak and write. As long as women remain silent, they will be outside the historical process.

But, if they begin to speak and write *as men do*, they will enter history subdued and alienated; it is a history that, logically speaking, their speech should disrupt.

While I definitely experience the problem of the male viewpoint being embedded in language in my own work, I have real difficulty with the way Gauthier (and others who share her view) pose the question and would like to address it in detail. Firstly, I am discouraged – almost offended – by Gauthier's use of "they" rather than "we" in talking about women. It seems to privilege a distant stance that implies theory is somehow separate from our lives.

Also a problem is the notion of women as mute. I just can't see it. I have no trouble seeing Mr. Historian in his study writing his official Report of the Battle, say, and I have no trouble seeing how the maid brings in his tea and takes it away without a word. In fact, I happen to know that her sister was raped by soldiers after that battle and that her sweetheart was killed in it, I can tell that Mr. H. doesn't even notice her swollen eyes and shaking hands, and I'm darn sure none of this will be part of his Account any more than her gossip with the cook will be. BUT I CANNOT, WILL NOT, BELIEVE THAT SHE WAS MUTE ABOUT IT.

Excluded, yes. Mute? Absolutely not!

For one thing, we have other records than those of Mr. H.'s: diaries, journals, letters, recipes, the liturgy of the Craft, lace, home-remedies, quilts, poems, essays, and novels, all of which feminist (and other) historians use all the time to develop other histories than the rather limited Patriarchal Record. Why are we judging women by the same standard that has oppressed us?

As to women, by their alleged silence, remaining outside the historical process... My Great Aunt Nettie, age ninety-four, is telling me a story. In it her father dies when she is three, leaving her mother alone on a farm with several children. That winter, she discovers she has breast cancer. Since she cannot leave the farmwork, she persuades her doctor to come out, chloroform her on the dining room table, and remove her breast while her oldest daughter holds the oil-lamp. A few days later, she is back in the barn. She goes on living for another ten years.

This story, out of all her stories, was the one my great aunt chose to give me at the end of her life. I put it in a poem once. I tell you now. So it becomes History.

But – and this is a Great Big But – regardless of what is recorded, the farm exists, the taxes were paid, the kids raised, the crops planted and harvested. My great grandmother can never be *outside* of these. She exists, she persists, she *moves events* as surely as her cells shape my hands, whether they write about her or no. What are we saying about ourselves, about millions of women like her, when we deny her that? Why are we *starting* from a view of history in which women are *always* the victims?

And then there is the issue of talking like a man. On the TV, Margaret Thatcher, a woman who "talks like a man" if I ever heard one. But when I say "talks like a man" I really mean "speaks the language of the patriarchy" (and by patriarchy I mean a structure originating in households where the father dominated which is reproduced in society in gender relations, language, ways of seeing, etc.). I'm certainly subdued by and alien to such language. I hear it as the language of *power over*, of estrangement, of a system which separates men from women, adults from children, people from other animals, people from nature, in a way that expresses difference as opposition, us versus them, life versus death, etc. It is a history which we must disrupt, I believe, both logically and passionately, because our survival, as a species, depends on it.

I have trouble when the issue is posed in a way which opposes men, *as a gender*, to women, *as a gender*, without any reference to the relationship between gender and power, say. It leaves me with the impression that anyone who uses the same syntax, vocabulary, etc. as persons of the male gender are on the side of the devil. Bad guys / good girls. Oppressor / victim. Same old story, just different sides. It's still, as far as I can hear, the patriarchy talking.

Such thinking includes the assumption that "men" and "language" are contained in each other. It's assumed that the patriarchy, that patriarchal language, is a monolith and that women are victimized, determined, totally, by the point of view embedded in it.

Such assumptions, if they remain unquestioned, create a situation in which our discussion of women and language becomes a discussion on men and language because it poses all the questions in the same old way, uses the same old methods of setting things up.

When I write of disrupting or changing history, I begin with the assumption that *people* can change, that we are not totally determined by, *bespoken* by the culture in which we live. I begin, always, with the power of the personal, the private, the unique in each of us, which resists, survives, and can change the power that our culture has over us. This is what I have learned from the women's movement and what I try to explore in my poems. I believe that when we speak and write of our lives in this way, we also change language, if only because we say things that have never been said before.

A woman who tells someone that her husband is beating her and she wants it to stop. A man who admits that he is violent and asks for help in changing. A poet who writes a poem that challenges conventional syntax and grammar. A feminist reading of *Jane Eyre*. A speech by Helen Caldicott. Two women sitting in a bar talking to each other.

For me, all of these change *language*. They change what can be said about women's lives because they disrupt the silence which has covered so much. They change what we think about each other in a culture which accepts things as they are and constantly erodes our power to change even ourselves. They challenge our assumption that how we speak or see or think is neutral, *not* culturally determined. They permit even feminists to have a sense of humour. They embrace passion and anger and even hysteria as appropriate responses to the present danger of the planet.

I personally believe that language will change – and does change – as women's lives change and not because one way of writing or speaking is theoretically correct. I don't think there is one way of writing and speaking that *is* theoretically correct. I'm excited by some of the language theory that forms the basis of Gauthier's statement. Some of it I just can't understand. Some of it simply doesn't correspond with my own experience, either of women or of language. That's generally how I respond to most theories.

What matters to me personally is *being here*, in another room, with another bunch of women, still talking.

I'd like to read a poem at the end of this:

Bones

for Barb

A story of yours got this one going,
so I'm sending it back now, changed of course,
just as each person I love
is a relocation, where I take up
a different place in the world.

The way you told it, it was after midnight,
you coming off the late shift, heading home
in a taxi, a woman driving,
and you ask her if she's ever scared
working these hours and she says, "No, I've got this
to protect me!" reaching under her seat
to pull up (you expected a crowbar,
a tire iron) this eight-inch, stainless steel
shank. "The pin from my mother's thigh,"
she tells you, "I got it when they put
one of those new plastic ones in."

Sometimes when I tell myself this story

I get caught up in logistics,
how the doctor must have delivered the thing
from layers of fat and muscle
into one of those shiny dishes
the nurse is always holding
and then she would have,
what? washed it off? wrapped it in towels?
carried it down to the waiting room, the daughter
sitting there, reading magazines, smoking cigarettes?
It's so improbable, like the foetus
pickled in a jar in the science lab in high school,
though other times it's just
there, natural as the light
that bounces off it,
somebody's mother's thigh bone,
for protection, like her face
in the hall light, rescuing you
from a nightmare.

You told me this
during my visit last year
when I'd just quit working
at the crisis centre, that job
that wrenched me round
until each morning stretched, a pale, dry skin,
over the real colour of the day,
ready to spring at me, like the child
whose hand had been held down
on a red-hot burner
reappearing in the face of a woman
met casually at a cocktail party.
Everywhere I went, my work experience
drew me through confessions I couldn't stop,
and I couldn't stop talking about them
so you had to listen
but, being you, in that way that listening
can be active, when the listener re-enters
the country of her own damage
from a new direction.

This can be like watching someone we love
return from the limits a body can be taken to
— a botched suicide, say, or an accident.

Years, it might be, before the eyes or the hands retrieve enough
to offer as a sign,
what doctors think they can detect
on a CAT scan, some pattern in the cells
to show them, once and for all,
how the mind, like the body, makes shape
of what's left, the terrible knowledge
it labours through, slowly regaining itself.

Though on an X-ray, even the bones show up
as light, a translucence that belies their strength
or renders it immeasurable,
like the distances we count on them to carry us,
right to the end of our lives and back again,
and again.

The Good Red Road: Journeys of Homecoming in Native Women's Writing

Beth Brant

There are those who think they pay me a compliment in saying that I am just like a white woman. My aim, my joy, my pride is to sing the glories of my own people. ... Ours [is] the race that taught the world that avarice veiled by any name is crime. Ours [is] the people of the blue air and the green woods, and ours the faith that taught men [and women] to live without greed and die without fear.[1]

These are the words of Emily Pauline Johnson, Mohawk writer and actor. Born of an English mother and Mohawk father, Pauline Johnson began a movement that has proved unstoppable in its momentum – the movement of First Nations women to write down our stories of history, of revolution, of sorrow, of love.

The Song My Paddle Sings

August is laughing across the sky,
Laughing while paddle, canoe and I,
Drift, drift,
Where the hills uplift
On either side of the current swift.[2]

This is the familiar poem of Pauline Johnson, the one that schoolchildren, white schoolchildren, were taught. Her love of land made her the poet she was. Yet, in reading Johnson, a non-Native might come away with the impression that she only wrote idyllic sonnets to the glory of nature, the "noble savage," or the "vanishing redman," themes that were popular at the turn of the century. It is time to take another look at Pauline Johnson.

The Cattle Thief

How have you paid us for our game? how paid us for our land?
By a *book*, to save our souls from the sins *you* brought in your other
    hand.
Go back with your new religion, we never have understood
Your robbing an Indian's *body*, and mocking his *soul* with food.

Go back with your new religion, and find – if find you can –
The *honest* man you have ever made from out a *starving* man.
You say your cattle are not ours, your meat is not our meat;
When *you* pay for the land you live in, *we'll* pay for the meat we
      eat.[3]

It is also time to recognize Johnson for the revolutionary she was. Publicized as the "Mohawk Princess" on her many tours as a recitalist, she despised the misconceptions non-Natives had about her people. Her anger and the courage to express that anger also made her the poet she was. She was determined to destroy stereotypes that categorized and diminished her people. Breaking out of the Victorian strictures of her day, she drew a map for all women to follow. She has political integrity and spiritual honesty, the true hallmarks of a revolutionary.

The key to understanding Native women's poetry and prose is that we love, unashamedly, our own. Pauline Johnson wrote down that love. Her short stories are filled with Native women who have dignity, pride, anger, strength, and spiritual empowerment.[4]

Pauline Johnson was a Nationalist. Canada may attempt to claim her as theirs, but Johnson belonged to only one Nation, the Mohawk Nation. She wrote at great length in her poems, stories, and articles about this kind of Nationalism. She had a great love for Canada, the Canada of oceans, mountains, pine trees, lakes, animals, and birds, not the Canada of politicians and racism that attempted to regulate her people's lives.

In 1892, she was writing articles on cultural appropriation, especially critiquing the portrayal of Native women in the fiction of the day. She tore apart popular white writers such as Charles Mair and Helen Hunt Jackson for their depictions of Native women as subservient, foolish-in-love, suicidal "squaws." Her anger is tempered with humour as she castigates these authors for their unimaginative use of language and for their insistence on naming the native heroines "Winona" or a derivative thereof.[5]

Pauline Johnson is a spiritual grandmother to those of us who are women writers of the First Nations. She has been ignored and dismissed by present-day critics and feminists, but this is just another chapter in the long novel of dismissal of Native women's writing.

Pauline Johnson's physical body died in 1913, but her spirit still communicates to us who are Native women writers. She walked the writing path clearing the brush for us to follow. And the road gets wider and clearer each time a Native woman picks up her pen and puts her mark on paper.

I look on Native women's writing as a gift, a give-away of the truest meaning. Our spirit, our sweat, our tears, our laughter, our love, our anger, our bodies are distilled into words that we bead together to make power. Not power *over* anything. Power. Power that speaks to hearts as well as to minds.

Land. Spirit. History, present, future. These are expressed in sensual language. We labour with the English language, so unlike our own. The result of that labour has produced a new kind of writing. I sometimes think that one of the reasons our work is not reviewed or incorporated into literature courses (besides the obvious racism) is that we go against what has been considered "literature." Our work is considered "too political" and we do not stay in our place – the place that white North America deems acceptable. It is no coincidence that most Native women's work that gets published is done so by the small presses: feminist, leftist, or alternative. These presses are moving outside the mainstream and dominant prescriptions of what constitutes good writing. The key word here is "moving." There is a movement going on that is challenging formerly-held beliefs of writing and *who* does that writing. And it is no coincidence that when our work is taught, it is being done so by Women's Studies instructors and/or those teachers who are movers and hold beliefs that challenge those of the dominant culture. This is not to say that *all* women's studies are as forward-thinking as we would like. At Women's Studies conferences, the topics of discussion usually centre on white, European precepts of theory and literature. I am tired of hearing Virginia Woolf and Emily Dickinson held up as the matriarchs of feminist and/or women's literature. Woolf was a racist, Dickinson was a woman of privilege who never left her house, nor had to deal with issues beyond which white dress to wear on a given day. Race and class have yet to be addressed; or if they are discussed, it is on *their* terms, not *ours*.

We are told by the mainstream presses that our work doesn't sell. To quote Chief Sealth – "Who can sell the sky or the wind? Who can sell the land or the Creator?" The few women of colour who have broken through this racist system are held up as *the* spokespeople for our races. It is implied that these women are the only ones *good* enough to "make it." These women are marketed as exotic oddities. (After all, we all know that women of colour can't write or read, eh?)

Pauline Johnson faced this racism constantly. The "Mohawk Princess" was considered an anomaly, and I can't say that things have changed all that much. I think of Pauline a lot, especially when I rise to read my stories. For like her, "My aim, my joy, my pride is to sing the glories of my own people."

Because of our long history of oral tradition, and our short history of literacy (in the European time frame) the amount of books and written material by Native people is relatively small. Yet, to us, these are precious treasures carefully nurtured by our communities. And the number of

Native women who are writing and publishing is growing. Like all growing things, there is a need and desire to ensure the flowering of this
growth. You see, these fruits feed our communities. These flowers give us
survival tools. I would say that Native women's writing is the Good
Medicine that can heal us as a human people. When we hold up the mirror to our lives, we are also reflecting what has been done to us by the
culture that lives outside that mirror. It is possible for all of us to learn the
way to healing and self-love.

It is so obvious to me that Native women's writing is a generous sharing of our history and our dreams for the future. That generosity is a collective experience. And perhaps this is the major difference between
Aboriginal writing and that of European-based "literature." We do not
write as individuals communing with a muse. We write as members of an
ancient, cultural consciousness. Our "muse" is *us*. Our "muse" is our ancestors. Our "muse" is our children, our grandchildren, our partners, our
lovers. Our "muse" is Earth and the stories She holds in the rocks, the
trees, the birds, the fish, the animals, the waters. Our words come from the
very place of all life, the spirits who swirl around us, teaching us, cajoling
us, chastising us, loving us.

The first known novel written by a Native woman was *Cogewea: The
Half-Blood*.[6] Written by Hum-Ishu-Ma, Okanagan Nation, in 1927, this
novel depicts the difficulties of being called half-breed. Hum-Ishu-Ma
concentrates on the relationship the female protagonist has with her
Indian grandmother, and how Cogewea does not turn her back on her
people, although she is courted and temporarily seduced by the white
world. Hum-Ishu-Ma worked as a migrant labourer, carrying her type-
writer everywhere with her, snatching moments to write. Again, I am
reminded of Pauline Johnson and her Indian women who remain stead-
fast in their Aboriginal beliefs and spiritual connections to their land and
people and the desire to make this truth known.

Fifty years later, Maria Campbell wrote her ground-breaking *Halfbreed*,[7]
taking up the theme of despair that comes as a result of the imbalance that
racism and poverty create in a people. Maria has a grandmother whose
words and strength give her nurturance and hope and a way back to the
Good Red Road. The Good Red Road is a way of life among Native
peoples that is one of balance and continuity. Again, this seems to be the
overwhelming message that Native women bring to writing. Creating a
balance in their protagonists' worlds, remembering what the Elders taught,
recovering from the effects of colonialism. This is not to say that Native
women's writing contains "happy" endings or resolutions. In fact, to wrap
things up in a tidy package is not following the Good Red Road – it's a
falsehood. Perhaps this is what irritates white critics – our work is said to
have no plots! If we won't conform, how can these conformist reviewers

write reviews?! Perhaps the questions should be: Why are critics so unimaginative in *their* writing? Why are they so ignorant of what is being written by my sisters? Why is a white-European standard still being held up as the criterion for all writing? Why is racism still so rampant in the arts?

Leslie Marmon Silko published her novel *Ceremony*[8] in 1977. In 1991, *Almanac of the Dead*,[9] by the same author, was published. Between those years and after, Paula Gunn Allen, Louise Erdrich, Jeannette C. Armstrong, Anna Lee Walters, Ella Cara Deloria, Beatrice Culleton, Ruby Slipperjack, Cyndy Baskin, Betty Louise Bell, Lee Maracle, Velma Wallis, and Linda Hogan also published novels.[10]

In the field of autobiographical works, the number of Native women's books is outstanding. Minnie Aodla Freeman, Maria Campbell, Ruby Slipperjack, Alice French, Ignatia Broker, Lee Maracle, Madeline Katt Theriault, Verna Patronella Johnston, Florence Davidson, Mary John, Gertrude Bonnin, and others[11] tell their stories for all to hear, and we become witness to the truth of Native lives. Throughout these writings, strong female images and personas are evident. The Cheyenne saying, "A Nation is not conquered until its women's hearts are on the ground," becomes a prophecy about Native women's writing. First Nations women's hearts are not on the ground. We soar with the birds and our writing soars with us because it contains the essence of our hearts.

Deep connections with our female Elders and ancestors is another truth that we witness. Grandmothers, mothers, aunties, all abound in our writing. This respect for a female wisdom is manifested in our lives; there-fore, in our writing.

Poetry seems to be the choice of telling for many Native women. In our capable hands, poetry is torn from the élitist enclave of intellectuals and white, male posturing, and returned to the lyrical singing of the drum, the turtle rattle, the continuation of the Good Red Road and the balance of Earth. We write poems of pain and power, of ancient beliefs, of sexual love, of broken treaties, of despoiled beauty. We write with our human souls and voices. We write songs that honour those who came before us and those in our present lives, and those who will carry on the work of our Nations. We write songs that honour the every-day, we write songs to food; we even incorporate recipes into our work. Chrystos, Mary TallMountain, Nora Marks Dauenhauer, Mary Moran[12] are just a few who have written about the joys of fry bread, salmon, corn soup, and whale blubber, then turn around and give instructions for preparing these treats! To me, this is so ineffably Indian. Mouths salivating with the descriptions of our basic foods, readers are then generously offered the gift of how to do this ourselves. No wonder the critics have so much trouble with us! How could food possibly be art? How can art remain for the élite if these

Native women are going to be writing recipes in poems? What will the world come to, when food is glorified in the same way as Titian glorified red hair?

There are numerous books of poetry written by Native women.[13] Our poems are being published in forward-thinking journals and magazines, although there are still the literary journals that wish to ghettoize our work into "special" issues, which, if you will notice, happen about every ten years or so. And their editors are usually white and educated in the mainstream constructs of European sensibility.

When I was asked in 1983 to edit a Native women's issue of the feminist journal *Sinister Wisdom*, I did not expect the earthquake that *A Gathering of Spirit* would cause. Eventually, this work became a book, published in 1984, then re-issued by Firebrand Books in 1988 and by Women's Press in 1989.[14] Perhaps there is a lesson here. When Natives have the opportunities to do *our own* editing and writing, a remarkable thing can happen. This thing is called *telling the truth for ourselves* – a novel idea to be sure and one that is essential to the nurturance of new voices in our communities. I conduct writing workshops with Native women throughout North America, and the overriding desire present in these workshops is to heal. Not just the individual, but the broken circles occurring in our Nations. So, writing does become the Good Medicine that is necessary to our continuation into wholeness. And when we are whole our voices sail into the lake of *all* human experience. The ripple-effect is inevitable, vast, and transcendent.

There are women who are writing bilingually. Salli Benedict, Lenore Keeshig-Tobias, Rita Joe, Beatrice Medicine, Anna Lee Walters, Luci Tapahonso, Mary TallMountain, Nia Francisco, Ofelia Zepeda, Donna Goodleaf[15] are just some of the Native women who are choosing to use their own Nation's languages when English won't suffice or convey the integrity of the meaning. I find this an exciting movement within our movement. And an exciting consequence would be the development of *our own* critics, and publishing houses that do bilingual work. Our languages are rich, full of metaphor, nuance, and life. Our languages are not dead or conquered – like women's hearts, they are soaring and spreading the culture to our youth and our unborn.

Pauline Johnson must be smiling. She was fluent in Mohawk, but unable to publish those poems that contained her language. There is a story that on one of her tours, she attempted to do a reading in Mohawk. She was booed off the stage. Keeping her dignity, she reminded members of the audience that she had to learn *their* language, wouldn't it be polite to hear hers? Needless to say, impoliteness won the day.

From Pauline Johnson to Margaret Sam-Cromarty,[16] Native women write about the land, the land, the land. This land that brought us into existence, this land that houses the bones of our ancestors, this land that was stolen, this land that withers without our love and care. This land that calls us in our dreams and visions, this land that bleeds and cries, this land that runs through our bodies.

From Pauline Johnson to Marie Baker, Native women write with humour. Even in our grief, we find laughter. Laughter at our human failings, laughter with our Tricksters, laughter at the stereotypes presented about us. In her play *Princess Pocahontas and the Blue Spots*,[17] Monique Mojica, Kuna/Rappahannock, lays bare the lies perpetrated against Native women. And she does it with laughter *and* anger – a potent combination in the hands of a Native woman. Marie Baker, Anishanabe, has written a play that takes place on the set of an Indian soap opera, "As the Bannock Burns." Baker's characters are few – the Native star of the soap, and the new co-star, a Native woman who gives shaman lessons to wannabes. In the course of the one-act play, the star shows the would-be shaman the error of her ways under the watchful eyes and chorus of a group of women of colour. Not only does Baker poke fun at the Greek chorus concept in theatre, she turns this European device to her own and *our* own amusement in a caustic but loving way, to bring the would-be shaman to a solid understanding of herself and her own tradition.

Sarah Winnemucca, Suzette La Flesch,[18] and Pauline Johnson also left them laughing as they took their work on the road. To tell a good story, one has to be a good actor. I remember my granddad telling me stories when I was little, punctuating the sentences with movement and grand gestures, changing his facial expressions and voice. I think we are likely to witness more Native women writing for the theatre. Marto Kane has ventured into that place with her play *Moon Lodge*. Vera Manuel has written *The Spirit in the Circle*, addressing the painful past of residential schools and the painful present of alcoholism and family dysfunction. But she also posits a vision for the future out of these violent truths. Spider Woman's Theatre has been writing, producing, and acting in their plays for a number of years. And Muriel Miguel, one of the Spiders, has done a one-woman show incorporating lesbian humour, Native tricksters, and female history. Native women are writing the scripts for their videos and directing and producing these films. How Pauline Johnson would have loved video!

As Native women writers, we have formed our own circles of support. At least once a week, I receive poems and stories in the mail, sent to me by First Nations women I know and some I have never met. It thrills me to read the words brought forth by my sisters. This is another form our writing takes – being responsible and supportive to our sisters who are struggling to begin the journey of writing truth. The WordCraft Circle, a mentoring program that matches up more experienced writers with our younger brothers and sisters, was born out of a Native writers' gathering held in 1992 in Oklahoma. I am currently working with a young, Native lesbian, and it moves my heart that it is now possible for lesbian Natives to give voice to *all* of who we are. Keeping ourselves secret, separating parts of ourselves in order to get heard and/or published has been detrimental to our communities and to our younger sisters and brothers who long for gay and lesbian role models. I am proud of the burgeoning Native lesbian writing that is expanding the idea of what constitutes Native women's writing.

There are my sisters who have internalized the homophobia so rampant in the dominant culture and that has found its way into our own territories and homes. These sisters are afraid and I understand that fear. Yet, I ask for a greater courage to overcome the fear. The courage to be who we are for the sake of our young and to honour those who have come before us. Courage of the kind that Connie Fife, Chrystos, Barbara Cameron, Sharon Day, Susan Beaver, Nicole Tanguay, Two Feathers, Donna Goodleaf, Janice Gould, Vickie Sears, Donna Marchand, Mary Moran, Elaine Hall, Lena ManyArrows, Shirley Brozzo, and many others have displayed.[19] Writing with our *whole* selves is an act that can re-vision our world.

The use of erotic imaging in Native lesbian work becomes a tool by which we heal ourselves. This tool is powerfully and deftly evident in the hands of these writers, especially the poems of Janice Gould and Chrystos. In my own work, I have explored such themes as self-lovemaking and the act of love between two women[20] as a way to mend the broken circles of my own life, and hopefully to give sustenance to other women who are searching for new maps for their lives. But Native lesbian writing is not only about sex and/or sexuality. There is a broader cultural definition of sexuality that is at work here. Strong bonds to Earth and Her inhabitants serve as a pivotal edge to our most sensual writing. Like our heterosexual sisters, Native lesbians who write are swift to call out the oppressions that are at work in our lives. Homophobia is the eldest son of racism; they work in concert with each other, whether externally or internally. Native lesbian writing *names* those twin evils that would cause destruction to us.

A major theme in the work of Vickie Sears, Cherokee Nation, is the power over children's bodies by the State.[21] Sexual abuse, physical abuse, emotional abuse are "normal" occurrences to the girl-children in Vickie's short stories. Herself a survivor of the foster-care system, Sears finds her solace and empowerment through the things of Earth and the love between women. Her short stories emphasize these possibilities of self-recovery. Indeed, one could say that much of Native lesbian writing celebrates Earth as woman, as lover, as companion. Woman, lover, companion celebrated as Earth. Two-Spirit writers are merging the selves that colonialism splits apart.

Recovery writing is another component in the movement of Native women writers. Recovery from substance abuse, as well as racism, sexism, and homophobia. Two Feathers, Cayuga Nation, is a wonderful example of this kind of recovery writing, as is Sharon Day of the Ojibway Nation.[22] Again, Chrystos, Menominee poet, excels in the naming of what it feels like to be hooked and in thrall to the substances that deaden the pain of being Native in the twentieth century. Highly charged with anger, this recovery-writing is, at the same time, gentle with the knowing of how difficult the path is toward the Good Red Road. There is empathy and compassion in the telling of our people's struggle to stay clean and sober. There is rage against the State that employed *and* employs addiction to attempt our cultural annihilation. Many of my short stories focus on that moment between staying sober and taking "just one" drink. The characters are caught in that timescape of traditional Native "seeing" and the unnatural landscape of colonization through addiction. In my stories, as in my life, Creator brings gifts of the natural to "speak" to these characters. It then becomes a choice to live on the Good Red Road, or to die the death of being out of balance − a kind of "virtual reality," as opposed to the real, the natural.

Pauline Johnson knew firsthand the effects of these attempts at annihilation. Her father, a Chief of the Mohawk Nation, was a political activist against the rum-runners who would have weakened his people. Severely beaten many times by these smugglers and murderers, his life was considerably shortened. Many of Pauline's stories are filled with righteous anger against the whiteman who wished to rape our land, using alcohol as a weapon to confuse and subjugate us. I think she would applaud the recovery-writing and name it for what it is − an Indian war cry against the assassination of our culture.

Oral tradition requires a telling and a listening that is intense, and intentional. Giving, receiving, giving − it makes a complete circle of Indigenous truth. First Nations writing utilizes the power and gift of story, like oral tradition, to convey history, lessons, culture, and spirit. And perhaps the overwhelming instinct in our spirit is to love. I would say that Native writing gives the gift of love. And love is a word that is abused and made empty by the dominant culture. In fact, the letters l-o-v-e have become just that, blank cyphers used frivolously to cover up deep places of the spirit.

I began writing when I turned forty. I imagine the spirits knew I wasn't ready to receive that gift until I was mature enough and open enough to understand the natural meaning of love. I believe that the writing being created by First Nations women is writing done with a community consciousness. Individuality is a concept and philosophy that has little meaning for us. Even while being torn from our spiritual places of home, having our ancestors' names stolen and used to sell sports teams, automobiles, or articles of clothing; having our languages beaten out of us through residential school systems even while having our spirits defiled and blasphemed, our families torn apart by institutionalized violence and genocide; even after this long war, we still remain connected to our own.

Our connections take many forms. I, as a Mohawk, feel deep spiritual bonds towards many who do not come from my Nation. These people, Carrier, Menominee, Cree, Cherokee, Lakota, Inuit, Abenaki, and many others, are like the threads of a weaving. This Mohawk and the people of many Nations are warp and woof to each other. While the colour and beauty of each thread is unique and important, together they make a communal material of strength and durability. Such is our writing, because such is our belief-system. Writing is an act that can take place in physical isolation, but the memory of history, of culture, of land, of Nation, is always present – like another being. That is how we create. Writing with all our senses, and with the ones that have not been named or colonized, we create.

Janice Gould, Maidu Nation, has written, "I would like to believe there are vast reserves of silences that can never be *forced* to speak, that remain sacred and safe from violation."[23] I feel that these sacred silences are the places *from* which we write. That place that has not been touched or stained by imperialism and hatred. That sacred place. That place.

Like Pauline Johnson, mixed-blood writers find those sacred places in the blood that courses through our bodies, whispering, "Come home, come home." Although we have never left that home, in a sense we have been pulled and pushed into accepting the lies told about our Indian selves. For those of us who do not conform to a stereotype of what Native people "look like," claiming our identities as Native people becomes an exercise in racism: "Gee, you don't look like an Indian." "Gee, I didn't know Indians had blue eyes." "My great-great-grandmother was a Cherokee princess, does that make me an Indian too?" After a while it almost becomes humorous, even as it's tiresome. Perhaps the feeling is that we're getting away with something, that we are tapping into unknown strengths, for which we are not entitled. And how the dominant culture loves to quantify suffering and pain! And how well it has worked to divide us from each other and from our self. Colourism is another face of racism. And we write about that, exposing our fears of abandonment by the people we love, the people whose opinion matters, the very people who, in our dreams, whisper, "Come home, come home." Yet, mixed-blood writing is also what I have been examining; for most of us are bloods of many mixes and nations. Linda Hogan, Chickasaw Nation, calls us "New People." New People are the survivors of five hundred years of colonial rule. Our grandmothers' bodies were appropriated by the conquerors, but the New People have not forgotten that grandmother, nor the legacy she carried in her womb.

In Mexico, a story is told of La Llarona. It is told that she wanders throughout the land, looking for her lost children. Her voice is the wind. She weeps and moans and calls to the children of her blood. She is the Indian, the mother of our blood, the grandmother of our hearts. She calls to us. "Come home, come home," she whispers, she cries, she calls to us. She comes into that sacred place we hold inviolate. She is birthing us in that sacred place. "Come home, come home," the voice of the umbilical, the whisper of the placenta. "Come home, come home." We listen. And we write.

Notes

1   E. Pauline Johnson as quoted in Betty Keller, *Pauline: A Biography of Pauline Johnson* (Vancouver: Douglas & McIntyre, 1981) 5.

2   E. Pauline Johnson, "The Song My Paddle Sings," *Flint and Feather* (1912; Toronto: Musson, 1917) 31.

3   E. Pauline Johnson, "The Cattle Thief," *Flint and Feather* 15.

4   E. Pauline Johnson, *The Moccasin Maker* (1913; Tucson: U of Arizona P, 1987).

5   E. Pauline Johnson, "A Strong Race Opinion on the Indian Girl in Modern Fiction," originally published in the *Toronto Sunday Globe* 22 May 1892; republished in Betty Keller, *Pauline: A Biography of Pauline Johnson* 116-21.

6   Hum-Ishu-Ma (Mourning Dove), *Cogewea: The Half-Blood* (1927; Lincoln: U of Nebraska P, 1981). Hum-Ishu-Ma's mentor was a white man. My reading of *Cogewea* is that much of it was influenced by his perceptions, not Hum-Ishu-Ma's.

7   Maria Campbell, *Halfbreed* (Toronto: McClelland and Stewart, 1973).

8   Leslie Marmon Silko, *Ceremony* (New York: Viking, 1977).

9   Leslie Marmon Silko, *Almanac of the Dead* (New York: Simon & Schuster, 1991).

10 Paula Gunn Allen, *The Woman Who Owned the Shadows* (San Francisco: Spinsters / Aunt Lute, 1983); Louise Erdrich, *Love Medicine* (New York: Holt, Rinehart and Winston, 1984); Jeannette C. Armstrong, *Slash*, rev. ed. (Penticton, BC: Theytus, 1988); Anna Lee Walters, *Ghost Singer* (Flagstaff, AZ: Northland, 1988); Ella Cara Deloria, *Waterlily* (Lincoln: U of Nebraska P, 1988); Beatrice Culleton, *In Search of April Raintree* (Winnipeg: Pemmican, 1983); Ruby Slipperjack, *Honour the Sun* (Winnipeg: Pemmican, 1987) and *Silent Words* (Saskatoon, SK: Fifth House, 1992); Cyndy Baskin, *The Invitation* (Toronto: Sister Vision, 1992); Betty Louise Bell, *Faces in the Moon* (Norman: U of Oklahoma P, 1994); Lee Maracle, *Ravensong* (Vancouver: Press Gang, 1993); Velma Wallis, *Two Old Women: An Alaska Legend of Betrayal, Courage and Survival* (Seattle, WA: Epicenter, 1993); Linda Hogan, *Mean Spirit* (New York:

Atheneum, 1990).

11   Minnie Aodla Freeman, *Life Among the Qallunaat* (Edmonton, AB: Hurtig, 1978); Maria Campbell, *Halfbreed*; Ruby Slipperjack, *Honour the Sun*; Alice French, *My Name Is Masak* (Winnipeg: Peguis, 1977) and *The Restless Nomad* (Winnipeg: Pemmican, 1991); Ignatia Broker, *Night Flying Woman: An Ojibway Narrative* (St. Paul: Minnesota Historical Society, 1983); Lee Maracle, *Bobbi Lee: Indian Rebel*, rev. ed. (1975; Toronto: Women's, 1990); Madeline Katt Theriault, *Moose to Moccasins: The Story of KaKita WaPa No Kwe* (Toronto: Natural Heritage / Natural History, 1992); R.M. Vanderburg, *I Am Nokomis, Too: The Biography of Verna Patronella Johnston* (Don Mills, ON: General, 1977); Janet Campbell Hale, *Bloodlines: Odyssey of a Native Daughter* (New York: Random House, 1993); Wilma Mankiller and Michael Wallis, *Mankiller: A Chief and Her People* (New York: St. Martin's, 1993); Bonita Wa Wa Calachaw Nuñez, *Spirit Woman: The Diaries and Paintings of Bonita Wa Wa Calachaw Nuñez*, ed. Stan Steiner (New York: Harper & Row, 1980); Ida S. Patterson, *Montana Memories: The Life of Emma Magee in the Rocky Mountain West, 1866-1950* (Pablo, MT: Salish Kootenai Community College, 1981); Helen Pease Wolf, *Reaching Both Ways* (Laramie, WY: Jelm Mountain, 1989); Zitkala-Ša, *American Indian Stories* (1921; Lincoln: U of Nebraska P, 1985).

12   Chrystos, "I Am Not Your Princess," *Not Vanishing* (Vancouver: Press Gang, 1988); Mary TallMountain, "Good Grease," *The Light on the Tent Wall: A Bridging* (Los Angeles: American Indian Studies Center, U of California, 1990); Nora Marks Dauenhauer, "How To Make Good Baked Salmon from the River," *The Droning Shaman* (Haines, AK: Black Current, 1988); Mary Moran, *Métisse Patchwork*, unpublished manuscript.

13   Poets include Beth Cuthand, Joy Harjo, Marie Baker (Annharte), Janice Gould, Wendy Rose, Diane Glancy, Marilou Awiakta, Elizabeth Woody, Joanne Arnott, Carol Lee Sanchez, Paula Gunn Allen.

14   Beth Brant, ed., *A Gathering of Spirit* (n.p.: Sinister Wisdom Books, 1984; Ithaca, NY: Firebrand, 1988; Toronto: Women's, [1989]).

15   Lenore Keeshig-Tobias, *Bineshiinh Dibaajmowin / Bird Talk* (Toronto: Sister Vision, 1991); Rita Joe, *Poems of Rita Joe* (Halifax: Abanaki, 1978); Beatrice (Bea) Medicine, "Ina, 1979," *A Gathering of Spirit*; Anna Lee Walters, *Talking Indian: Reflections on Survival and Writing* (Ithaca, NY: Firebrand, 1992); Luci Tapahonso, *Seasonal Woman* (Santa Fe, NM: Tooth of Time, 1982.); Mary TallMountain, *There Is No Word for Goodbye* (Marvin, SD: Blue Cloud Quarterly, 1981); Nia Francisco, *Blue Horses for Navajo Women* (Greenfield Center, NY: Greenfield Review, 1988); Ofelia Zepeda, unpublished manuscript; Donna Goodleaf, unpublished manuscript.

16   Margaret Sam-Cromarty, *James Bay Memoirs: A Cree Woman's Ode to Her Homeland* (Lakefield, ON: Waapoone, 1992).

17   Monique Mojica, *Princess Pocahontas and the Blue Spots* (Toronto: Women's, 1991).

18 Sarah Winnemucca and Suzette La Flesch (Bright Eyes) travelled and performed in the United States, talking about their people in poetry and story, within the same time frame as Pauline Johnson's career.

19 Makeda Silvera, ed., *Piece of My Heart: A Lesbian of Colour Anthology* (Toronto: Sister Vision, 1991); Will Roscoe, ed., *Living the Spirit: A Gay American Indian Anthology* (New York: St. Martin's, 1988); Connie Fife, ed., *The Colour of Resistance: A Contemporary Collection of Writing by Aboriginal Women* (Toronto: Sister Vision, 1993); Cherríe Moraga and Gloria Anzaldúa, eds., *This Bridge Called My Back: Writings by Radical Women of Color* (1981; Latham, NY: Kitchen Table / Women of Color, 1983) are just four of the collections containing Native lesbian work. See also Connie Fife, *Beneath the Naked Sun* (Toronto: Sister Vision, 1992); Chrystos, *Not Vanishing* (Vancouver: Press Gang, 1988), *Dream On* (Vancouver: Press Gang, 1991), and *In Her I Am* (Vancouver: Press Gang, 1993); Janice Gould, *Beneath My Heart* (Ithaca, NY: Firebrand, 1990).

20 Beth Brant, *Mohawk Trail* (Ithaca, NY: Firebrand, 1985; Toronto: Women's, 1990); Beth Brant, *Food & Spirits* (Ithaca, NY: Firebrand, 1991; Vancouver: Press Gang, 1991).

21 Vickie Sears, *Simple Songs* (Ithaca, NY: Firebrand, 1990).

22 Sharon Day and Two Feathers, unpublished manuscripts.

23 Janice Gould, "Disobedience in Language: Texts by Lesbian Natives," MLA Convention, New York, 1990.

Me voici, c'est moi, la femme qui pleure

François Paré

Qu'est-ce que l'exiguïté? Autant les *grandes* littératures se sont efforcées de créer les conditions, hautement sacralisées, de l'universalité, autant les *petites*, celles que la grandeur des unes excluait, se sont exténuées dans le morcellement et la diversité. Cette diversité, vécue comme un effritement de leur Être dans la Littérature, est d'ailleurs devenue très vite, au sein des discours du savoir, une de leurs conditions d'existence.

Les formes de l'altérité

Derrière la fragilité insoutenable et pourtant définitoire des *petites* littératures s'agitent les spectres de l'altérité. Les écrivains et leurs personnages y sont particulièrement susceptibles à la métamorphose et ultimement à la perte de l'identité formelle. Tout le discours du colonisé semble intérioriser les modes de comportement du colonisateur, semble épouser les rôles du dominant; ce discours devient ainsi le théâtre d'une aliénation, d'une présence en soi de l'altérité.

Au Québec, les rapports avec l'altérité sont complexes. Je ne suis pas le premier à le dire. Betty Bednarski, par exemple, en a montré le jeu obsédant chez Jacques Ferron. Et encore, il faut admettre que Ferron, écrivain, dépendait d'un contexte socio-politique où la définition de l'Autre était infiniment plus claire qu'elle ne l'est maintenant.[1]

Ce rapport avec l'altérité est encore plus débilitant, lorsqu'on considère le Canada français dans son ensemble. Car pour le Canadien français, ce personnage de l'Autre est d'une inexorable richesse, d'une inconcevable multiplicité, qui le rendent très difficile à saisir. Ainsi, pour l'écrivain franco-ontarien, tel qu'il s'est défini au tournant des années soixante-dix, les figures de l'altérité déclenchent de puissants désirs: désir d'intégration aux littératures métropolitaines de la France et de la Grande-Bretagne, désir de se fondre dans les paramètres du Canada anglais, désir de s'associer à un Québec contemporain devenu maintenant agent de domination, fascination pour l'américanité télévisuelle, désir d'être reconnu comme partie intégrante du multiculturalisme pancanadien, et désir enfin d'adopter la fausse innocence d'une certaine identité «francophile.» Face à cette panoplie de représentations collectives à la fois positives et négatives, il est facile de concevoir sa propre identité comme l'envers des désirs provoqués par l'Autre (je suis ce que les autres ne veulent pas que je sois).

C'est Lise Gauvin, au Québec, qui a le mieux décrit ces notions d'altérité culturelle, dans *Lettres d'une autre* d'abord, et dans d'autres textes un peu plus récents sur les diverses écritures de la francophonie.[2] En Belgique francophone, Marc Quaghebeur en a fait, dans la revue *Écriture*, une superbe analyse, surtout parce qu'elle fait entrer dans la notion d'altérité culturelle la présence des forces désirantes (vouloir être aimé de l'Autre à tout prix, à mort) qui se transforment toujours très rapidement en dénigrement: «l'envie dénégatrice ou le désir fusionnel.»[3] Je ne crois pas qu'il soit utile d'évoquer ici ce qu'il appelle «le lamento lyrique de la dépossession.» Mais il est clair que, dans toutes les cultures dominées, les rapports avec l'Autre déterminent l'identité, qu'ils ne peuvent être facilement distingués de la littérature, et qu'ils prennent, dans ce contexte de la littérature, la forme symbolisée de la dépossession et du désir intense de *mourir à l'Autre.*

La dépossession dont souffrent les cultures minoritaires peut signifier l'avènement d'une vision renouvelée du savoir. Ainsi s'agit-il, comme chez Patrice Desbiens ou Max Brathwaite d'une disponibilité plus grande, d'une capacité accrue d'adaptation à la genèse de tout savoir, d'une participation active, soutenue par le désir d'être Autre, aux luttes fragiles pour l'émergence du savoir. Et ce savoir-là ne serait nullement le produit de la belle arrogance dont l'histoire des discours culturels dominants est enrobée; il naîtrait plutôt de la disjonction, de la stupéfaction désirante où la conscience de l'Autre nous aura jetés.

C'est en cela, pure mise en disponibilité de l'esprit à l'égard du microscopique et de l'invisible, que je mets aujourd'hui toute ma confiance de chercheur en littérature.

Le théâtre

Qu'en est-il du théâtre? «Notre théâtre demeure le meilleur exemple du manque de maturité de notre littérature,» remarquait Jacques Poirier, il n'y a pas très longtemps, au sujet du théâtre franco-ontarien. «Nos "théâtreux" sont passés du théâtre engagé au théâtre enragé. Ils s'évertuent à nous convaincre qu'il existe un complot des "bourgeois de la culture" qui aurait, paraît-il, pour but de les faire taire à tout prix. [...] L'art n'est pas gratuit. Il est porteur de messages. [...] L'artiste incompris n'est qu'un impuissant.»[4] Ces remarques, très justes à plus d'un égard, doivent être nuancées. C'est qu'il y a, à mon sens, certains avantages heuristiques, en tant que culture, à jouer, à mettre en scène cette impuissance qu'illustre le théâtre.

Ce que ne voit pas Jacques Poirier, c'est que le théâtre, producteur du dédoublement et représentation de la complexité irréductible de l'altérité, est un outil puissant de savoir collectif. Dans le jeu théâtral, l'Autre peut être pensé ironiquement, non plus seulement comme agent de la dépossession (de cela le théâtre est aussi la représentation), mais également comme interlocuteur en lutte dialogique avec lui-même, avec nous-mêmes. Le jeu est violent, déterminant: les acteurs et actrices quittent la scène épuisés, exténués. Mais, en eux, de nos jours, la question de l'Autre est provisoirement réglée, c'est-à-dire que nous l'avons vue naître et mourir dans un cycle qui est celui de notre signification.

Critique littéraire et université

Dans la plupart des cultures à travers le monde, aussi surprenant que cela puisse paraître, il n'existe à proprement parler aucune critique formelle ou plus largement universitaire de la littérature. Les oeuvres sont simplement recensées et commentées au jour le jour dans la presse locale, si celle-ci existe et s'intéresse au domaine littéraire (ce qui n'est pas évident). Partout ailleurs que dans un petit groupe de cultures de très grande diffusion, il ne se fait aucune réflexion générale sur les théories de l'écriture, sur l'historiographie et ses méthodes, sur les besoins institutionnels d'une littérature, sur les langages narratifs, poétiques ou dramatiques. Rien de tout cela. Pire encore, si ces types de recherche existent, ils opèrent le plus souvent sur des corpus d'oeuvres étrangères appartenant aux grandes cultures d'enseignement. A cause de cette pauvreté chronique des moyens d'analyse et de formalisation, les oeuvres de moindre diffusion, soit par leur langue, soit par leur origine nationale, apparaissent et disparaissent au rythme des saisons, sans que les structures d'accueil ne permettent d'en évaluer, même provisoirement, la portée symbolique et le mérite.

Cette pauvreté de l'appareil critique est surtout aiguë dans les cultures minoritaires, celles qui ne disposent pas (la littérature frisonne aux Pays-Bas, ou coréenne au Japon, par exemple) d'établissements universitaires et de maisons d'édition, qui permettraient de détacher le commentaire des oeuvres du pur panégyrique. Il faut dire, cependant, que même dans les *petites* cultures où il existerait des universités et des éditeurs, ces derniers reproduisent très souvent les attitudes et les enseignements des collectivités dominantes, ne jetant qu'un coup d'oeil passager et parfois condescendant à une production littéraire qu'ils considèrent comme mineure par définition.[5]

Depuis que je me suis mis au travail de la littérature à l'intérieur d'une plus petite communauté culturelle, celle de l'Ontario français, analysant et commentant moi aussi les dernières parutions qui en émanent, je dois dire que mon statut d'enseignant et de critique s'est trouvé d'autant dévalorisé et marginalisé. Peut-être faut-il avoir vécu au sein d'une petite société minoritaire comme celle-ci, si représentative de toutes les autres, si incertaine de son avenir, si coupée des mécanismes de mémorialisation des oeuvres, si *seule* dans son travail collectif de l'écriture, pour apprécier plus justement la fragilité du travail critique et de l'histoire littéraire en général.

Dans les *petites* cultures, je regrette de le dire, la fonction critique de l'institution littéraire reste, pour beaucoup, une entreprise parasitaire et revancharde. Le critique littéraire est donc aux yeux des forces créatrices dans ces sociétés un être faible, sans entrailles, sans coeur au ventre, qui se nourrit des carcasses de ses compatriotes. Dans toutes les *petites* cultures que je connais, le travail critique est rejeté, soit parce qu'il représente une menace pour l'oeuvre au premier degré, si durement arrachée au silence, soit parce qu'il apparaît comme superflu, excédentaire dans une culture où l'essentiel existe à peine déjà. Voilà bien ce que disait Henri-Dominique Paratte, par exemple, dans sa critique d'*Écriture franco-ontarienne d'aujourd'hui*: «les confectionneurs de cet entrepain ontarois étant des amis (du moins jusqu'à ce qu'ils aient lu ce compte rendu-ci), poètes, universitaires, et bourrés de talent l'un comme l'autre, je risque d'être mal vu: la vocation du critique littéraire, en petit milieu, est en effet de s'extasier sur tout – faute de quoi le voilà inévitablement qualifié d'un manque de gratitude, sinon de discernement.»[6] Écrire dans les conditions de l'exiguïté est, on le rappelle souvent, un geste téméraire, complexe, scandaleux même, que tout commentaire critique semble réduire, appauvrir, destituer, détruire. Et cette rédemption de la communauté par l'écriture n'a, dit-on, nul besoin d'être commentée au second degré par un critique apocryphe: elle exigerait simplement d'être réitérée, confirmée et célébrée.

Pourquoi est-ce ainsi? Pourquoi les *petites* cultures ont-elles tendance à rejeter ce qui ultimement les ferait accéder à l'histoire? Car une culture qui n'est pas répertoriée et analysée formellement peut-elle se targuer d'être une culture? C'est que, dans les *petites* cultures, le commentaire critique porte les marques de l'Autre. La critique, c'est cet Autre, adoré et abhorré; cet Autre, dont on n'arrive jamais à endiguer l'ouvrage de destruction, dont on n'arrive jamais à se débarasser, car il est la part maudite de notre langage collectif. Nulle part, cette altérité de la critique n'est-elle aussi visible à mon sens que dans les cultures de la francophonie, dans la mesure où les composantes de l'appareil critique dont font usage les cultures périphériques sont issues de la France métropolitaine. «Pas question d'ironiser, d'innover ou de remettre en cause! On est proche de Paris. On en dépend. Quoi qu'il advienne, la France paraît en outre toujours l'ultime recours.»[7] Ce n'est pas que le discours critique est *en soi* un discours dominant, quoiqu'il le soit très souvent; mais il est simplement vécu dans les *petites* cultures comme une agression venant de l'extérieur, même lorsqu'il est le produit de développements internes.

Ainsi, je suis souvent tourmenté par le langage de ce texte; je voudrais arriver à l'empêcher de s'ériger, sans pourtant faire oeuvre de dépossession. Je vacille entre le dénigrement et le triomphe de l'Autre. Mêmes mots montrant leur endroit et leur envers. Plus l'institution culturelle est *petite* et tautologique, plus elle accuse son ambivalence, plus elle affiche l'angoisse de son étrangeté.

La vacance de l'image

Pour Roland Barthes, les discours s'*adjectivent* et tombent irrémédiablement dans la domination. Aussi Barthes dira-t-il de lui-même dans son autobiographie à la troisième personne: «Il supporte mal toute *image* de lui-même, souffre d'être nommé. Il considère que la perfection d'un rapport humain tient à cette vacance de l'image: abolir entre soi, de l'un à l'autre, les *adjectifs*; un rapport qui s'adjective est du côté de l'image, du côté de la domination, de la mort.»[8] C'est parce qu'il a un compte à régler avec une image de lui-même que Barthes rédige son *Barthes par lui-même* et veut ainsi, par cette curieuse autobiographie, faire lutte à l'hégémonie. Elle a beau être reportée dans une quelconque image de l'altérité, cette image est en fait «vacante» et la domination appartient pour Barthes au moi le plus intime, au moi désirant et désirable.

Or, ce qui m'importe ici, c'est que la domination habite toute la culture et est surtout identique à la fonction critique. Barthes reconnaît volontiers l'existence de deux lectures des textes, l'une *active*, mue par le plaisir, l'autre *réactive*, mue par l'indignation.[9] Mais il se trouve que cette lecture réactive, dont le *Barthes par lui-même* est tout de même un exemple, reste le produit du jugement classificateur, qu'elle est adjectivale dans ses assises les plus secrètes, qu'elle est en fin de compte une lecture critique du discours culturel.

Barthes, soupçonnant tous les discours critiques, craignait la multiplicité des formes que peut prendre la domination. «Une bonne part de notre travail intellectuel consiste à porter la suspicion sur n'importe quel énoncé en révélant l'échelonnement de ses degrés; cet échelonnement est infini et ce gouffre ouvert à chaque mot, cette folie du langage, nous l'appelons scientifiquement: énonciation.»[10] Mais, du même coup, le professeur du Collège de France n'arrive pas à se dissocier totalement de ces discours, car ce serait là remettre en question une image *pleine* de la Littérature, une certaine mémorialisation canonique des oeuvres de culture, triées, classées, hiérarchisées, mémorialisation dont le critique est après tout l'héritier et le célébrant. Barthes, privilégiant la multiplicité des approches critiques, ne soupçonne jamais l'unité fallacieuse du corpus des oeuvres sur lequel il travaille. C'est pourquoi, dans l'univers culturel de Barthes, la *littérature* correspond sans nul doute à l'unique «littérature française,» identifiée très rapidement à la Littérature, au sens dominant (Barthes semblant tout ignorer des autres littératures d'expression française et adhérant consciencieusement au corpus canonique de la *grande* littérature nationale française).

Barthes ne peut voir la pluralité, dont il dit faire l'apologie, que dans le confort du corpus littéraire de la France hégémonique. C'est là sa plus gênante limite.

Les littératures et l'enseignement

Il y a deux aspects à la question de l'enseignement des littératures.

D'abord, la plupart des littératures de notre monde actuel ne font jamais l'objet d'un enseignement. La littérature française est une exception. Elle donne lieu à des cours pré-universitaires et universitaires dans presque tous les coins de la planète, même là où la langue française jouit d'un rayonnement presque nul. Il en est ainsi des littératures de langue anglaise, espagnole, allemande et peut-être italienne. Pour les autres, le silence des pédagogues règne. Et ce ne sont pas que les très *petites* littératures nationales qui échappent à l'enseignement. Dans quels corpus universitaires trouve-t-on aujourd'hui les oeuvres de Dostoïevski, Langvist, Tagore, Petica, Multatuli, pour ne nommer que ces écrivains du tournant du siècle?

Je me souviens d'un cours monté dans ma propre université, voilà quelques années déjà, dont le titre était «La femme dans la littérature du monde entier» (Women and World Literatures). Sur les huit ou neuf oeuvres au programme de ce cours, que je dirais tout à fait typique à cet égard, aucune ne figurait qui n'ait été européenne ou nord-américaine. On aura beau vanter l'avènement du «village global,» reste que dans l'enseignement de la littérature cette expansion extraordinaire de la conscience planétaire ne s'est guère produite! N'en sommes-nous pas toujours restés au programme littéraire établi par la Renaissance européenne, issu de paramètres géographiques et culturels aujourd'hui largement dépassés?

Si les littératures du Japon ou de l'Inde, par exemple, ne jouissent pas des faveurs de nos facultés de lettres, on peut s'imaginer ce qui en est des littératures plus *petites*. En fait, on pourrait dire que, dans le sens particulier où j'entends le mot «petit,» ces grandes littératures ancestrales et modernes du Japon ou de l'Inde *sont* de *petites* littératures, ou en tout cas elles en ont plusieurs caractéristiques.

À ce titre, la littérature québécoise actuelle est un cas intéressant. Sauf dans les pays francophones, et en France notamment, elle est largement inconnue et subsumée par le plus grand ensemble, anglo-saxon, qu'est la littérature canadienne. Combien de fois ai-je vu, dans les pays d'Europe du Nord surtout, Gabrielle Roy (en traduction) intégrée au corpus «Canadian»? Ceci dit, la littérature québécoise a réussi à s'imposer à l'étranger, du moins dans plusieurs pays, comme une littérature digne d'enseignement universitaire et de recherche critique. Ce n'est certes pas le cas de la plupart des corpus littéraires de même envergure. En réalité, les littératures minoritaires échappent presque toujours à l'enseignement.

Mais, m'objectera-t-on, ne faut-il pas plutôt déplorer la dépendance de l'institution littéraire et de la littérature en général à l'égard de l'enseignement? Ne vaut-il pas mieux rêver d'oeuvres évoluant dans une pure instance créatrice, échappant à tout jugement critique, toute norme rhétorique, tout écho de lecture? Une oeuvre en soi et pour soi? Or ce désir d'autarcie de l'oeuvre littéraire est un leurre: un leurre bien vivace pourtant, puisque répété avec énergie et passion au cours de presque toutes les rencontres d'écrivains et tous les ateliers de création. Il n'y a pas de littérature vivante qui voudrait en fin de compte échapper au cycle de l'enseignement. Du moment qu'elle est publiée et mise en circulation, l'oeuvre littéraire entre dans un processus de diffusion, de lectures et de relectures, d'interprétation et de normalisation. En fait, ce ne sont pas les oeuvres, mais ces derniers et importants processus régulateurs qui manquent justement tragiquement aux *petites* cultures.

Je prends un exemple extrême. Je recevais récemment un exemplaire, que j'avais commandé (ne vous inquiétez pas!), de la revue *Cultura en movimento*, publiée dans la très petite république de Sao Tomé et Principe, au large de la côte ouest de l'Afrique. Voilà un petit pays, quelques auteurs, une minuscule institution littéraire distincte favorisée par l'idéologie socialiste des derniers gouvernements. Il y a, dans cette publication, très pauvre par rapport à nos instruments de diffusion littéraire (même en Ontario français!), une normalisation et une mémorialisation des oeuvres littéraires saotomiennes, conçues alors dans leur spécificité. Et, quand on songe qu'il existe une lusophonie, comme il existe une francophonie, on s'imagine déjà que cette production nationale minimale sera reprise en charge et véhiculée par l'institution élargie et l'enseignement des littératures de langue portugaise.

Pour moi, l'avenir de la Littérature, utilisation des langues humaines à des fins esthétiques, dépend du maintien et de la promotion de la diversité radicale. Il existe *des* littératures, et la question de leur inscription et de leur survie dans l'histoire est radicalement ouverte. Je ne crois pas, comme on le souhaite souvent dans les cultures minoritaires, qu'il faille abstraire ces littératures des mécanismes de l'enseignement et de la recherche. Au contraire, l'enseignement universitaire, s'il veut y comprendre quelque chose, doit accueillir et fouiller le microscopique, et dénoncer les stratégies de simplification et d'infériorisation qui réduisent et appauvrissent à outrance les *petites* littératures.

Les rituels de la dépossession

Lorsque des poètes minoritaires, comme Patrice Desbiens ou Xabier Bergaretxe, évoquent le silence et la dépossession, s'agit-il seulement d'une stratégie de l'écriture? Ces rituels de la dépossession sont-ils des stratégies rhétoriques pour mieux s'approprier un langage spécifique?

Traduire l'espace

Je le dis, parce que cela me semble crucial, les *petites* littératures tendent à glorifier l'espace. Or, si l'enseignement de la littérature s'attache traditionellement à définir les périodes et à situer les oeuvres dans le temps, c'est qu'il est le fruit d'une mentalité européenne tout à fait obsédée par la mort, par la quête de l'éternité. Cette obsession ne date pas d'hier. Elle remonte sans doute aux toutes premières histoires mémoriales des oeuvres au sortir du Moyen Age. Même les concepts linguistiques, qui ont servi à articuler notre compréhension de la littérature en Europe au cours du dernier demi-siècle, restaient des catégories du temps (syntagmatique ou paradigmatique) à travers lesquelles tout effort de traduire l'espace se trouvait réprimé.

D'autres diront que l'espace (territoire, région, pays) n'a jamais vraiment été évacué du littéraire, mais qu'il était considéré plutôt comme un acquis muet et évident. Je crois néanmoins qu'il y a eu meurtre de l'espace dans un certain nombre de *grandes* cultures; ce geste mémorial a permis et permet toujours rituellement d'inscrire ces cultures dans une pure problématique du temps et ainsi dans ce qu'on pourrait appeler un discours de l'éternité. Mais l'espace est prégnant de sens. Ce «pays du creux et des furieuses impuissances à être» n'est-il pas, comme le dit Jean-Marie Klinkenberg, une manière de renouveler la littérature, l'air de rien, «sur la pointe des pieds»?[11]

J'y crois, moi aussi en tout cas, très fermement.

L'anthologie

Les *petites* littératures souffrent très souvent d'une hypertrophie du discours anthologique. Les recueils d'auteurs divers, les répertoires d'écrivains, les albums, les collections annuelles et les revues de création littéraire occupent dans ces littératures une place démesurée. Je me rallie donc volontiers aux éclaircissements qu'apporte à ce sujet François Ricard dans son article de 1981 sur l'institution littéraire.[12] Ricard distingue deux sortes de répertoire anthologique: celui qui vise à refléter les acquis d'une littérature, et celui qui a plutôt pour objectif d'engendrer à partir de rien de tels acquis littéraires. Il existe alors, pour Ricard, des inventaires *produits* et des inventaires *producteurs*. Les *grandes* cultures, plus établies (mais pas nécessairement plus anciennes), tendent à engendrer du reflet (inventaires produits), tandis que les plus *petites* littératures, dans leur fragilité, se donnent l'illusion d'exister en accumulant les répertoires et les anthologies (inventaires producteurs). Ricard constate qu'ainsi les *petites* littératures en viennent à bénéficier du caractère fortement institutionnel de l'anthologie. En fait, par l'anthologie elles aspirent à se positionner dans l'institution littéraire dominante, en lui soutirant l'un de ses mécanismes institutionnels les plus prestigieux. Car ne suffit-il pas d'une anthologie pour confirmer l'existence d'une littérature nationale particulière?

Au cours des trente dernières années, le Québec a alimenté une véritable inflation anthologique, qui correspondait au désir de promouvoir cette littérature et d'en faciliter l'accession aux milieux de l'enseignement. Ces remarques sont à mon sens d'une grande importance. Car les anthologies constituent très souvent les seuls modes d'existence «publique» des *petites* littératures, surtout minoritaires. Cet état de fait se vérifie surtout dans le cas des littératures ne disposant pas des assises économiques suffisantes pour voir à la publication et à la diffusion des oeuvres individuelles.

En outre, dans l'anthologie, on dirait justement que l'écart entre le reflet critique et la création s'abolit merveilleusement; l'anthologiste dit presque toujours vouloir «donner la parole aux écrivains eux-mêmes,» sans interférence. Il veut se faire transparent. Le seul jugement (de taille, pourtant) qu'il dit émettre porte sur le processus de sélection des oeuvres représentées dans l'anthologie, mais ce dernier geste est souvent minimisé au profit du désir explicite de manifester une littérature jusque-là passée sous silence. Tout le projet anthologique, en réalité, sert à démontrer noir sur blanc l'existence, au niveau collectif, d'une production littéraire incapable d'assurer à chacun des écrivains une présence à l'écriture imprimée et une publicité adéquates. En fait, les *petites* institutions littéraires donnent parfois l'impression que les anthologies et répertoires «valent» plus que les oeuvres individuelles, puisqu'ils sont chargés des pouvoirs symboliques du rassemblement.

L'anthologie tend donc à briser temporairement l'étau de l'indifférence et de la solitude, d'une part, et à renforcer l'institution littéraire collective, d'autre part, dans la mesure où elle fait office de manuel scolaire. En Ontario français, par exemple, il s'est publié récemment de très nombreuses anthologies. Toutes ces anthologies s'attachaient à faire la preuve de l'existence d'une littérature franco-ontarienne distincte et vivante. Et elles y ont réussi dans une large mesure: la littérature franco-ontarienne *est devenue* le produit de ces anthologies. Mais, du même coup, cette littérature s'est trouvée réduite à une collection d'extraits coupés de leur contexte et éternellement embryonnaires.

Cela dit, l'anthologie possède des valeurs rédemptrices certaines: à preuve les nombreuses anthologies d'écrivaines, parues au moment même où à travers le monde on tentait de promouvoir, dans l'enseignement surtout, les oeuvres littéraires écrites par des femmes. Dans les cultures de

FRANÇOIS PARÉ

l'exiguïté, l'anthologie est la confirmation de l'implication *communautaire* de l'écrivain (voilà pourquoi certains écrivains refusent par principe de participer à tout projet anthologique!). Une anthologie de la littérature basque ou saotomienne, par exemple, n'indique pas seulement qu'il existe un nombre *suffisant* d'écrivains sanctionnés dans la communauté nationale basque ou saotomienne, mais aussi que ce nombre *suffisant* est le reflet compilatoire de la vitalité de ces cultures.

François Ricard reconnaît dans tout projet anthologique le désir de constituer une mémoire, d'inscrire l'espace spécifique dans un temps spécifique. C'est pourquoi l'anthologie est sacrale: elle consacre les écrivains qui y sont cités et sacralise le processus de formation d'une littérature autonome.

Les prix littéraires

Dans le même numéro de la revue *Liberté*, René Lapierre s'interroge sur l'impact des nombreux prix littéraires au Québec. Sa conclusion: au Québec, l'attribution de prix littéraires est «autoréférentielle,» de sorte qu'elle sert non pas vraiment à consacrer l'oeuvre d'un auteur en particulier, mais à confirmer l'existence et la vitalité de l'institution même qui attribue ces prix. «Ils parlent tout simplement d'eux-mêmes; ils ne cherchent pas alors à consacrer une oeuvre autant qu'à trouver dans cette oeuvre la consécration de leur propre existence en tant que prix, et partant, celle de l'ensemble de l'activité éditoriale du Québec [...] en tant que production littéraire.»[13] Cette analyse très fine permet d'entrevoir un mécanisme compensatoire de l'institution culturelle, qui n'est pas du tout spécifique à la culture québécoise, peu s'en faut, mais qui traverse un très grand nombre de réseaux culturels de moindre envergure et de moindre diffusion. Les micro-cultures, en effet, se dotent, quand elles le peuvent économiquement, des signes des grandes cultures, dont l'attribution de prix littéraires nombreux s'avère un exemple parmi d'autres. Ces signes institutionnels sont, dans les *petites* cultures, des indices plus ou moins vides, insensés, car leur portée est si réduite, l'impact sur un public lecteur très limité si dérisoire, leur existence même si autoréférentielle, qu'on en vient à n'y voir que de la matière idéologique.

Je prends un exemple ailleurs que chez nous. Depuis la fin du franquisme en Espagne, la Catalogne s'est dotée d'un gouvernement autonome fort efficace et d'une institution culturelle, et littéraire particulièrement, très animée. Cette institution a, dans le domaine de la littérature en langue catalane, multiplié les prix littéraires de toutes sortes. En littérature de jeunesse seulement, un domaine privilégié par le gouvernement autonome, il existe pas moins de vingt prix littéraires pour des oeuvres publiées en langue catalane. Cette hypertrophie a tendance à noyer le poisson, d'autant plus que le rayonnement de la langue catalane est très limité, même à l'intérieur de la Catalogne.

Certaines littératures de l'exiguïté disposent donc de tels moyens financiers et structurels pour se faire valoir, qu'elles en arrivent très souvent à des résultats disproportionnés, contraires au rayonnement réel de leur institution. Il suffit d'avoir fréquenté le circuit des colloques de littérature «canadienne» à travers le monde pour vite comprendre qu'il ne s'agit pas seulement de recherches spontanées et profondes sur une littérature fortement différenciée et reconnue comme telle, mais du «pauvre» spectacle d'une institution littéraire qui exporte sa prospérité économique.

Cependant, les *petites* cultures ne produisent pas de système cohérent de la littérature (cette cohérence découle essentiellement de l'enseignement); c'est alors qu'elles n'arrivent à engendrer que des simulacres de système, montrant alors ses failles criantes, sa grosse artificialité, sa plasticité beaucoup trop bavarde. Voilà qu'il faut pouvoir jouer aux grands, se mesurer à eux, même si les manches du costume sont visiblement trop longues. Les prix littéraires, comme la prolifération des anthologies, dans ces cultures exiguës, font partie du processus de simulation des cultures dominantes, auquel s'acharnent la plupart des *petites* institutions culturelles dans le monde.

Enfin, deux autres choses sur les prix littéraires. D'abord, le désir est toujours grand au Québec, au Canada français et dans toutes les cultures minoritaires, de chercher la consécration au sein de l'institution ou des institutions dominantes. C'est un réflexe naturel. Ce succès (en France, dans le cas du Québec; au Québec, dans le cas des littératures francophones hors Québec) ne signifie pas seulement la reconnaissance de l'institution littéraire marginale comme productrice (après tout) d'oeuvres de valeur, assez «bonnes» pour être lues par les lecteurs alertes des sociétés dominantes culturellement, mais cette reconnaissance est aussi un signe d'intelligibilité, d'accueil des oeuvres marginales dans le *sens*. Ainsi, lorsqu'Antonine Maillet se voit décerné le prix Goncourt en 1978, c'est évidemment un grand honneur pour l'auteure et pour toute la littérature acadienne dont elle ne se dissocie pas.[14] Mais, plus qu'un honneur, c'est tout à coup la marque de l'intelligible qui vient d'être attribuée à une oeuvre qui était jusque-là le produit d'une littérature échappant aux conditions normales de l'intelligibilité, même pour les lecteurs acadiens. Cette notion d'inintelligibilité est primordiale. En Catalogne, pour revenir encore à cet exemple instructif, l'abondance des prix littéraires peut être interprétée comme l'envers de l'inintelligibilité linguistique de la langue catalane, comprise par un nombre limité de lecteurs.

Enfin, les prix littéraires attirent l'attention, pour une fois, sur l'espace national et social où s'inscrit l'oeuvre primée. D'ailleurs, les prix ont tendance à se multiplier lorsque l'exercice de la littérature est encadré par un

État national, comme au Québec ou en Catalogne. Ainsi, plus le Québec des années soixante-dix aspire à définir son espace politique propre, plus il accumule les récompenses littéraires, souvent liées au projet nationaliste lui-même. Certains de ces prix binationaux (France-Québec, Wallonie-Québec) confirment le statut international de l'État québécois, de sorte que l'écrivain récipiendaire devient par là l'exemple vivant de la spatialité spécifique de sa propre écriture nationale. Dans le cas du Prix Wallonie-Québec, du reste, le phénomène de consécration opère dans les deux sens, chacune des institutions littéraires et chacun des gouvernements transcendant provisoirement les limites de leur pouvoir politique pour célébrer la consécration internationale de leur espace propre.

Moi, le Maître, je parle

Cette formule provient de l'Antiquité grecque, d'Héraclite plus précisément, qui l'avait empruntée d'Empédocle pour définir le *logos*, le lieu de la parole. A l'époque d'Héraclite, ce fameux *logos* n'avait pas encore été investi de valeurs sacrales, ce que fera plus tard le christianisme en l'associant à la divinité. Le *logos*, c'est donc ce qui parle. Mais c'est plus précisément encore ce qui parle en priorité: parole de celui qui est le premier à parler (j'utilise le masculin très consciemment). Héraclite suppose, en fait, qu'il y a aussi un auditoire à cette parole: «toi, l'élève, tu écoutes,» lit-on dans un des fragments exemplaires sur le *logos*. La prise de la parole fait partie d'un échange symbolique qui ressemble en tous points à celui qui unit maître et élève. Héraclite insiste sur la parole en écho chez l'élève, tout en assurant que jamais, dans ce processus, celui-ci ne pourra prendre la place du maître. L'on saura toujours qui possède le droit prioritaire de la parole.

Comment peut-on sauter, allègrement, de la Wallonie à l'Antiquité classique? C'est justement là *la* question, me semble-t-il. Sourcillera-t-on généralement à la lecture d'oeuvres théoriques, issues des cultures dominantes et se rapportant justement à l'Antiquité classique? En fait, les *grands* discours culturels occidentaux aiment se ressourcer dans la continuité d'une alliance avec le monde ancien (*un monde ancien, en particulier*), dans lequel ils découvrent un discours fondateur et une sorte de sacralisation à rebours.

Ainsi, le *logos*, dans le sens héraclitéen de la transmission de la vérité, a été accaparé par un nombre réduit de discours dominants. En supposant pour eux-mêmes un accès privilégié aux textes de l'Antiquité classique, ces discours dominants se sont empressés d'exclure les autres, multiples et tout à coup insaisissables, sur la base de cet accès. Et alors, en Wallonie, au Québec, en Afrique, en Océanie, partout où l'exclusion règne, se dresse la voix prioritaire de celui qui dit: «Moi, le premier, je parle.» Non pas au passé, mais dans le présent de l'éternité. Et à l'élève d'écouter et de confirmer les dires du maître!

Devant la puissance de ces affiliations culturelles où se fonde la domination, les discours dominés recherchent plutôt ce que Fernand Dorais appelle «la poïétique de l'impuissance,»[15] une transmutation par l'écriture du sentiment d'indignité en une affirmation iconoclaste de l'indignation. Cette quête tout à fait légitime doit passer par la remise en question des assises des discours dominants occidentaux dans l'héritage gréco-romain.

Un jour, je tenterai cette remise en question, sans doute à partir de la Renaissance et de ses curieuses fascinations pour une certaine Antiquité.

Vouloir pouvoir

Vouloir parler, vouloir parler en premier, c'est en fait une face du *vouloir pouvoir*. Dans les premiers textes de Paul Chamberland, dans *L'afficheur hurle* et les écrits connexes, émergent de superbes descriptions de cette exclusion du pouvoir que Chamberland voit comme la caractéristique de son écriture et de toute l'écriture québécoise. Le poète désire pouvoir et son désir établit déjà des hiérarchies dans le *logos*: «Je parle et tu me réponds. Je recueille tes silences et tu t'ouvres aux miens qui frémissent encore dans ta main levée vers moi; nos paroles sont brèves, fruits échus dans l'ordre sévère.»[16] Il n'y a pas d'oeuvres québécoises des années soixante qui expriment avec une telle clarté le désir acharné de la prise de la parole prioritaire et celui par celle-ci médiatisée du renversement du pouvoir. Le vouloir pouvoir habite le centre des *petites* cultures; il motive leur écriture, leur gestion du désir individuel et collectif, leur revendication du *logos*.

Me voici, c'est moi, la femme qui pleure

Dans ma mémoire, je revois encore la femme qui pleure sur la superbe page couverture du livre de Denise Desautels *Un livre de Kafka à la main*. C'est Kafka le minoritaire qui m'avait d'abord intéressé. Mais bientôt mon regard s'est épris des photographies de Jocelyne Alloucherie, celle surtout de la femme éplorée, accoudée à la balustrade comme une ancienne prêtresse de Rome. Et ce qui devient très tôt obsédant, c'est le rapport mystérieux entre la femme qui pleure et Kafka; l'on découvre vite que la vulnérabilité s'impose chez Denise Desautels comme un langage poétique distinct: «me voici, c'est moi, la femme qui pleure et qui raconte, pendant que ma main s'attaque à la blessure jusqu'à l'épuisement de sa trace; pendant que nous nous effleurons, inconsolables.»[17] Une sorte de clairvoyance persiste de cette rencontre douloureuse; elle émane de la fouille de l'histoire, notre histoire collective, mémoriale, contre laquelle la main, écrivant, veut, dans l'oeuvre de Denise Desautels, faire scandale.

Mais cette main de l'écriture lutte contre la disparition. «Une audace qui, violemment, divise et rapproche le désir. Je suis là à trop parler ou à me taire comme si l'outrance, seule, avait un sens. En somme, je ne disparais jamais complètement.»[18] Y a-t-il plus éloquente figuration de la minorisation que celle-là, juxtaposant la fragilité et l'outrance?

Notes

1   Betty Bednarski, *Autour de Ferron: littérature, traduction, altérité* (Toronto: GREF, 1989).

2   Lise Gauvin, *Lettres d'une autre* (Montréal: L'Hexagone, 1984).

3   Marc Quaghebeur, «Belgique: une littérature qui n'ose pas dire son nom,» *Écriture* 36 (1990): 19.

4   Jacques Poirier, «Réflexion sur la "littérature" franco-ontarienne,» *Atmosphères* 2 (1989): 63.

5   Voir à ce sujet un excellent livre sur la politique du développement culturel en Jamaïque: Rex M. Nettleford, *Caribbean Cultural Identity: The Case of Jamaica* (Kingston, Jamaica: Institute of Jamaica, 1978) 14 ff.

6   Henri-Dominique Paratte, «Émergence d'un espace littéraire distinct ou *fast-food* de la littérature,» *LittéRéalité* 4.1 (1992): 3.

7   Quaghebeur 19.

8   Roland Barthes, *Barthes par lui-même* (Paris: Seuil, 1975) 47.

9   Barthes 47.

10 Barthes 70.

11 Jean-Marie Klinkenberg, «Lettres belges: trop d'espaces pour une histoire,» *Écriture* 36 (1990): 54.

12 François Ricard, «L'inventaire: reflet et création,» *Liberté* 134 (1981): 33-34.

13 René Lapierre, «La politique des bas prix,» *Liberté* 134 (1981): 55.

14 Voir à ce sujet: James de Finney, «Antonine Maillet: un exemple de réception littéraire régionale,» *Revue d'histoire littéraire du Québec et du Canada français* 12 (1986): 17-33.

15 Fernand Dorais, *Entre Montreal ... et Sudbury: pré-textes pour une francophonie ontarienne* (Sudbury, ON: Prise de parole, 1984) 22.

16 Paul Chamberland, *L'afficheur hurle* (Montréal: Parti pris, 1964) 10.

17 Denise Desautels, *Un livre de Kafka à la main* (Saint-Lambert, PQ: Noroît, 1987) 23.

18 Desautels 44.

"Après Frye, rien"? Pas du tout!
From *Contexts* to *New Contexts*

Donna Palmateer Pennee

The subtitle of my essay signals this collection's relation to the 1971 collection of essays edited and introduced by Eli Mandel, *Contexts of Canadian Criticism*. Twenty-five years have passed since Mandel assembled those essays (with dates ranging from 1943 to 1969), written by philosophers, historians, literary critics, and creative writers E.K. Brown, W.L. Morton, H.A. Innis, William Kilbourn, F.H. Underhill, George Grant, Northrop Frye, Marshall McLuhan, Francis Sparshott, Milton Wilson, Paul West, Robert L. McDougall, Warren Tallman, Henry Kreisel, and Dorothy Livesay. Mandel divided his collection into three sections: The Social and Historical Context (six essays); The Theoretical Context (three essays); and Patterns of Criticism (seven essays). And he spoke of how

> it seems important to expand the notion of literary criticism in Canada to include the work of historians and philosophers.... Canadian literary criticism consistently seeks its organizing principles not only in theories of literature but in historical and social contexts. It may be that Canadian concern with historiography, social structure, and esthetics can be viewed best as an expression of an almost paranoiac self-consciousness or simply as part of an attempt to understand the importance of communication theories in a demanding physical setting. Whatever the explanation for this obsession with self-definition and theoretical configurations, this much is obvious: any collection of critical essays that aspires to represent Canadian critical writing fairly and accurately will obviously present selections concerned not only with traditional comments on patterns of literary development but with the history and form of Canadian society and with problems in poetic theory as well. And it is this threefold concern that the organization of this volume reflects. (Preface vii)

Should I be nervous about the fairness and accuracy of the present volume's representation of Canadian critical writing? For starters, we haven't divided our collection by three folds – but that in itself is, perhaps, a signal of one of innumerable new contexts, the reluctance to direct, shape, or otherwise potentially limit readers' engagement with the essays contained herein. This isn't to say that the choices we've made among the scores of essays that might have been included aren't in themselves profoundly delimiting, nor is it to say that the order of the essays is without design or intent. But conscious design and intent ranged from minimal for one of the editors (operating under the assumption that most readers don't read collections of essays in a linear fashion) to numerological for another of the editors (operating under the assumption that there is a logic and a magic in arrangement), to a medium ground for the other editor (operating with a preference for seeing some essays grouped closely together for the debate and dialogue that would ensue, should they be read in linear fashion, and happy to have other essays adrift in a calm sea of random association). The fact that I am in effect writing an introduction to the volume that appears roughly half way through the text is less the mark of some fanciful postmodern disruption of beginnings, middles, and ends than of a collaborative editorial will to agree to disagree. In other words, different voices and preferences among the editors of this volume in themselves represent, at a microcosmic level, debates about representation and form contained throughout the collection.

But to return to Mandel's remarks about "represent[ing] Canadian critical writing fairly and accurately" beyond the folds of the conscious imposition of (or opportunity for) direction by headings: the issue of representation itself and the possibility of fairness and accuracy are key to understanding one of many significant shifts in literary studies within and beyond the (most permeable) borders of Canada. Increasingly, the term "representation" in literary studies has less to do with mimesis, with representing an accurate reflection of Canada (or wherever), and more to do with the question of representing the different constituencies or voices that populate the country and its literature. The question of "where is here?" has been superseded by the question that Frye thought, at one point in his career, was less important, namely, "who am I?"[1] Or rather, the question of "where is here?" has turned out to be inseparable from the question "who am I?", for representation (the literary and the political, the literary as political) works from both the sites of individual subjectivity and place or context. Indeed, the dedication to the collection of essays from which M. Nourbese Philip's piece is reprinted here signals precisely this rearticulated notion of space and identity: "For Canada, in the effort of becoming a space of true true be/longing."

Geographical determinations of what constitutes a Canadian literature and a Canadian literary and cultural criticism have (always) been complicated by determinations of many sorts, those multiple and frequently conflicting constituents through which we construct and perceive our representations of where and who we are. These constituents have become what some disparagingly call the "litany" of literary studies of late: for example, class, race, gender, erotic preference, age, language, ethnicity, region, nation. The list of the myriad components of our engagements with ourselves, with each other, with the world, and with texts of all kinds, like one characteristic of litany, is unusually long, and so makes fairness and accuracy of representation a most complicated, even impossible, project. But let's not throw our hands in the air just yet, for a litany can more positively be thought of as a genre of call and response, and like any other genre, it is both constraining and enabling, capable of initiating new orthodoxies, yet capable of changing as it meets, shapes, and is traversed by histories, by "contexts," while at the same time functioning as a context through which we make sense of what we read.

A comparative glance at the tables of contents of *Contexts* and *New Contexts* goes some way to mapping the distance between the two volumes, the shifting contours of the critical terrain between 1971 and 1996, the foregrounding of different responses to different calls of identity and place. The subtitle of the volume of essays from which Arun Mukherjee's piece is reprinted here, "Readings from a Hyphenated Space," while it refers to a specific fracture in the armature of *the* Canadian identity, reminds us in brief that multiple answers have always been offered to the questions "where is here?" and "who am I?", but they haven't always been heard. Some of the reasons for that deafness are eloquently (some might say loudly) articulated in this collection by voices tuned out by one version of cultural patriotism, which was itself rather loud right around the time that *Contexts* was published and to which many of its essays speak: the nationalism of Canada's Centennial, the nationalism of the Massey Report, the nationalism of, say, George Grant, Harold Innis, and Margaret Atwood (in 1971 "a gifted young poet" who made it into *Contexts* by way of Susanna Moodie by way of Mandel's introduction [24], and who published a year later her critical guide to CanLit, *Survival*, itself a powerful engine of cultural nationalism, designed as it was for that handy ideological state apparatus, the education system). Cultural patriotism and political nationalism, like many other "isms," are not in themselves bad things: indeed, the nationalism in Grant's *Lament for a Nation* is timely reading again, in the face of the most recent round of US invasiveness known as Free Trade.[2] But, again, one of the new contexts of criticism is precisely the argument that there is no such thing as a thing in itself; there is no *per se* about the literary or the cultural or the national or the critical. Each is always in the face of, at the interface of, in relation to something else; each is context for and in turn is contextualized by other considerations.

But what is "context"? Here, I want to use our collection's title as an occasion for an exercise in keywords. But let's begin at the beginning of the title: What constitutes the "new" and why valorize the "new"? The attractiveness of the "new" is often a mark of an attitude to history (and

DONNA PALMATEER PENNEE

to capital) – as linear and as progressive, that is, "new" and "improved" – an attitude that is being questioned in recent contexts of cultural study. Yet one of the things that is most interesting and instructive about a comparison of *Contexts* and *New Contexts* is that some of what we might assume to be "old" in the original volume is actually a significant part of what's "new" here, but for some reason (or many reasons), it wasn't time for those positions and methods of reading to be taken up and disseminated in effective ways in the reading of cultural forms, including the literary. For example, what's the distance between H.A. Innis's material history of publishing in the excerpt from *The Strategy of Culture* (in *Contexts*) and Carole Gerson's material account (in this volume) of how a publishing history and editorial practices (among other things) produce a canonical literary history? Clearly, one writes as a professional historian, the other as a literary critic viewing literary history through the prism of gender, but their methods are, to me, very similar: namely, looking at the material circumstances and practices of publishing in Canada as a significant factor in what Innis called "the strategy of culture," and in what Gerson sees as the implicit strategy of gender traversing the strategy of culture. Likewise, what's the distance between Robert McDougall's analysis (in *Contexts*) of the relative absence of class issues in Canadian literature and criticism, and his call to examine the class recruitment of authors in Canada, and Gregory Baum's recommendation (in this volume) of a structural analysis of capitalism in Canada, both for the purposes of making us more aware of the uneven distribution of power? Obviously, the former speaks as a literary critic while the latter speaks as a radical theologian, but again their critical methods, their routes into reading culture, are very similar; both writers seek to prompt readers to locate those moments of contradiction in literature and in politics where class questions, apparently in the foreground, are occluded, managed through a narrative structure or a political and economic structure that writes or votes or legislates such questions into silence. And what's the distance between Frye's and Sparshott's insistence (in *Contexts*) that literature must be read as literature, as form, and Struthers' suggestion (in this volume) that in reading for politics, we hear only part of the creative and critical dialogue if we remain deaf to aesthetics? The former speak from what had become the normative mode for literary criticism, a product of a canonized (and hence decontextualized) late Romanticism, High Modernism, early Structuralism, and New Criticism, while the latter revisits and elaborates on that mode in the now normative recontextualizing of cultural practices represented in *New Contexts*. A careful consideration of other essays in the two volumes, without privileging the new or caricaturing the old, would illustrate further points of convergence between, say, Warren Tallman's and Robert

Kroetsch's essays, or Marshall McLuhan's essay and several essays in *New Contexts* that rework structuralist insights about form (or medium) in historicized ways.

Perhaps what distinguishes the cultural critical practices of 1971 and 1996 is the difference between what Mandel called the "extraordinarily oblique" (Introduction 3) relation of contexts and literature in his collection, and how the oblique has since moved into a more direct relation to studies of cultural forms. (It would be extremely difficult to separate the essays in this volume by the categories Mandel used to organize his collection, that is, social and historical context, theoretical context, and patterns of criticism.) Or, rather, perhaps the difference is that we have come to understand the oblique as not oblique at all, as part of a general shift in our understanding of the relations between cultural forms and their contexts. For as Mandel also noted of his collection,

> Our attention diverts itself from criticism to the field around it. Or it may be that we discover Canadian criticism is only its fields or contexts.... Present usage, of course, takes the word ["contexts"] to mean "framing devices" or "background." ... [A]s soon as we add the word *Canadian* to criticism, we move the object of our concern into a particular space and time, a geographical and historical context, where what might normally remain simply an element of the background – the sociology of literature – becomes the foreground. (Introduction 3)

Here, in his characteristic way, Mandel isolates what has always made the study of Canadian literature (or the study of any literature as a national literature) an apparently special case:

> It tries to find its boundaries outside itself, in some imperial world of literary tradition beyond nationality, and it seeks, both in its origins and in its development, for an authentic identity – something that expresses itself as a sort of conceptual space between its works of literature. ... At its worst, this sort of "composition by field" sounds more like heavy breathing than serious social, historical, or critical comment. At its best, it stands in relation to narrowly defined critical techniques as, say, the transistor to the vacuum tube: the latter throws some light, but the former allows for large-scale integration of materials of different characteristics. (Introduction 3-4)

I said above that this isolation of the relation between literary text and context makes the study of a national literature an apparently special case. I said "apparently" because shifts in our understanding of what constitutes context, and what constitutes its relation to literary forms, have illustrated that literary criticism, whether it is of a "major" (e.g., English) or a "minor" (e.g., Canadian) literature (or see Paré in this volume), is always already a sociology of literature (see, e.g., Baldick; Viswanathan; Itwaru): it's a question of whether or not you pretend otherwise. Thus, when Frye wrote his *Anatomy of Criticism* or his *Fearful Symmetry*, he was working with forms, myths, tropes, and authors whose status as "literary" and not something else (e.g., social, political, gendered, racialized, historical, English) was taken for granted, naturalized, mystified as something necessarily and properly beyond all those other modifiers. When Frye wrote his conclusion to the *Literary History of Canada* (1965) and most of his other essays on Canadian literature, he wrote a "sociology" of literature, in effect apologizing that what was produced in this country wasn't yet sufficiently "literary" to be spoken of outside of the very contexts that made it – and the literary critical consideration of it – obviously social, political, gendered, racialized, historical, Canadian, etc.:

> It is much easier to see what literature is trying to do when we are studying a literature that has not quite done it. If no Canadian author pulls us away from the Canadian context toward the centre of literary experience itself, then at every point we remain aware of his [sic] social and historical setting. The conception of what is literary has to be greatly broadened for such a literature. The literary, in Canada, is often only an incidental quality of writings which, like those of many of the early explorers, are as innocent of literary intention as a mating loon. Even when it is literature in its orthodox genres of poetry and fiction, it is more significantly studied as a part of Canadian life than as a part of an autonomous world of literature. (Frye, Conclusion 821-22)

Of course, Frye turned this not-yet, not-here status of Canadian literature into the occasion for some of the most interesting, stimulating, and influential criticism to be written in this country. And while it may have been an exercise in "heavy breathing," it facilitated the authorization and legitimation of Canadian literature as a field of its own, worthy of separate courses, separate specializations, within the curricular and post-graduate degree opportunities of literary study.[3]

Indeed, this is one of the most recent and important of new contexts since the 1971 collection: attention to precisely this legitimation of Canadian literature as a field worthy of institutional study, that is, attention to the "making" of CanLit as not only the poetry, fiction, and drama that gets written "here," but the whole ensemble of cultural practices by which that writing is produced, received, and disseminated.[4] But this exercise has not been a repetition of a would-be homogeneous cultural nationalism, for in the metacritical practice of narrativizing the making and institutionalization of Canadian culture (see, e.g., Gerson; New; Filewod; and Sugars in this volume), critics have wandered into the paradox of literary (or cultural) history as defined by David Perkins: "We must perceive a past age as relatively unified if we are to write literary [or cultural] history; we must perceive it as highly diverse if what we write is to represent it plausibly" (27).

The movement between the "relatively unified" and the "highly diverse" might be another way, then, to measure the distance from *Contexts* to *New Contexts*, as critics engage in what American poet and essayist Adrienne Rich, from a feminist point of view, recommended as a necessary reading strategy: "Re-vision – the act of looking back, of seeing with fresh eyes, of entering an old text from a new critical direction ..." (35). Still another way to measure the distance would be through the "incredulity toward metanarratives" (Lyotard xxiv), or master narratives, that has been identified with postmodernism (cf. Callinicos). This approach is explicitly addressed by Kroetsch, Hutcheon, Paterson, and Heble (in this volume); such incredulity implicitly underwrites most of the essays here, but also under names, motives, experiences, and forms other than postmodernism. Hearing the voices of the "highly diverse" necessarily complicates the past "relatively unified" story of Canadian literature. It leads to the unravelling of the threads of the national text or narrative and reweaves them, taking up the threads of contexts left dangling because if taken into account they would have made impossible – or certainly more difficult and provisional – the telling of a single or monologic story of Canadian culture and its criticism.

In other words, a significant contextual change between 1971 and 1996 is the telling, legitimation, and dissemination of different narratives (and in forms beyond the literary – Welsh writes about autobiographical filmmaking, Hutcheon about an ethnographic museum exhibition, Davey about newspaper advertisements, Johnston about native language, Mukherjee about teaching, Padolsky about the effects of the mainstream/ethnic binary, and so on). Different narratives of what constitutes "where is here?" and "who am I?" have emerged, often precisely in relation to past constructions that have precluded or occluded those different stories. Witness, for example, Beth Brant's essay "The Good Red Road," which introduces readers of Canadian literature not to the "Canadian" Pauline Johnson of "The Song My Paddle Sings," but to the Pauline Johnson, Mohawk nationalist, of "The Cattle Thief," thereby resituating Johnson as "a spiritual grandmother to those of us who are women writers of the First Nations" (7) (and for those of us who are not), and offering us from a lesbian pan-nationalist point of view a catalogue and a tradition of these women writers. This is a new context for Canadian criticism even

DONNA PALMATEER PENNEE

though Pauline Johnson was a late nineteenth-century writer. Christine Welsh similarly weaves an alternative narrative of Canadian history, reclaimed from women's oral history, to speak the silences that mark the place of eighteenth-century white politicians' "country wives" in the annals of official Canadian history. Carole Gerson examines a structurally similar silence around women writers who were well received in their own day but who have not survived the process of the legitimation of CanLit in the education system: the institutionalized study of Canadian literature has involved the operation of "'invisible colleges.' Comprised of publishers, the media, and the academy, they function as canonical 'gatekeepers,' conferring status by deciding what gets published and reviewed and who gets onto course lists and into anthologies, reprint series, textbooks, and reference sources" (57).

Part of a now vastly documented new context for literary studies, that is, critiques of the processes of canon formation (see, e.g., Guillory), Gerson's meticulous history of anthology publication for Canadian literature dispels any notion that what gets studied gets studied because it is inherently or intrinsically good, because it belongs to some timeless, universal realm of autonomous literary forms. Arun Mukherjee's essay likewise looks to the effects on students' reading practices of the critical apparatus within anthologies, precisely for the ways in which this apparatus – advocating a search for universal and timeless themes – actively discourages students from reading the racial, gendered, economic, political, social, and historical contexts so clearly inscribed in one of Margaret Laurence's African short stories. And Bronwen Wallace speaks of how one version and one language of feminist theory would seem to marginalize a different version and a different language that might help us to exit from the oppressor/victim binary we have inherited.

In terms of a "relatively unified" narrative of what constitutes Canadian literature and criticism, Wallace, Mukherjee, Gerson, Welsh, and Brant speak from various margins of class, race, gender, erotic preference, and nation, but as M. Nourbese Philip suggests,

> Margin ... has another meaning.... That meaning is "frontier." Surely this meaning is encapsulated in [Raymond] Williams' phrase "emergent energies and experiences which stubbornly resist" the dominant culture. The concept of frontier changes our perception of ourselves and the so-called mainstream. All of which is not to deny that there is a dominant culture, with a "central system of practices, meanings and values" (Williams). And this culture receives by far the lion's share of funding and government support. However, exploiting the other meaning of margin offers another perspective, one which challenges the old, lazy ways of thinking by which we have colluded in our own

management. To twist the aphorism somewhat – marginality is in the eye of the beholder. (41-42)

Nourbese Philip's essay speaks to how she writes out of two very different traditions, with "two archetypal figures symbolizing the two traditions that permeate [her] work": "John-from-Sussex," who "represents the white colonial tradition, the substance of any colonial education," and "Abiswa," who "represents the African-Caribbean context which, as typical of any colonial education, was ignored" (26). Her meditation on these inherited contexts leads her to speak of more immediate contexts, the audiences for her work and work like it from the African-Caribbean diaspora in Canada, the material circumstances of production, marketing, and reception of black Canadian poetry and First Nations drama, and how the choice of language of composition is complicated by the diversity of the audience by whom she might be received, or the granting agencies to which she might apply.

Indeed, in Nourbese Philip's essay we have another sort of shorthand for charting the distance between then and now. Her "archetypes" aren't Frye's, masquerading as timeless and universal; they are called up precisely because they are situated in race, gender, language, history, politics, nations, and institutions. Her Williams is not William Carlos Williams, the American Modernist poet taken up as postmodernist and influencing a significant generation of Canadian poets (especially George Bowering and Kroetsch; cf. DuPlessis). Rather, she refers to Raymond Williams, the Welsh Marxist humanist who was instrumental in moving literary studies into Cultural Studies (see, e.g., his *Culture and Society* and *Keywords*). And Nourbese Philip's "frontier" is an enabling cultural and formal space; it doesn't mask a belated longing for a Canadian equivalent to that American master narrative of the wild west which constituted a formative context and construct for American answers to the questions "where is here?" and "who am I?"

But I have wandered from the first term in this volume's title into the second, no doubt because "new" is a modifier for "contexts" – and so the two cannot be separated for convenience of discussion, nor can "new contexts" be viewed only as a metaphorical substitution for "contexts." This, too, signals a new context, the depriveleging (to some degree) of metaphor (and of lyric poetry as its pre-eminent genre) and the priveleging of metonymy (with its genre equivalent, fiction).[5] By metonymy I mean less that figurative device whereby a part stands for the whole and more the designation of figurative and material relations whereby the cultural artifact gets its meaning from its re-encoding of meanings and forms that circulate around and through it. That is, by metonymy I mean the relations of contiguity, of next-to-ness, that necessitate viewing cultural forms in

DONNA PALMATEER PENNEE

relation to their contexts and the related understanding of cultural forms and practices as interested and situated constructions, interested and situated fictions, which can be read for their effects (however unconscious) in producing and disseminating only parts that stand for the whole.

This shift from the metaphoric towards the metonymic pole of signification (or of making meaning), from late-Romantic, High-Modernist aesthetics (themselves reconstructed through interested literary critical practices) to Structuralist and Post-structuralist theories of the function and embeddedness of cultural practices and their meanings in social, historical, and political discourses, is perhaps the principal difference between Mandel's volume and this one (however adumbrated this shift was in some of the essays in the earlier volume, and however resisted this shift is by certain essays in this volume). The sources or contexts for this shift are multiple and often conflicting, but nevertheless might be identified (for literary theoretical and critical domains) in the following list:

- Saussurian linguistics, which argues that the relations between words, concepts, and things is not natural but arbitrary or convention-al, a product of historical, communal, and provisional agreements about meaning that thereby make meanings open to change (see, e.g., Saussure; Holdcroft; Rowe; Silverman);

- structuralist anthropology and semiotics, which argue that cultural forms are not static objects but constitute symbolic acts that organize the social, historical, and political in local, functional, and meaningful ways (see, e.g., Barthes; Clifford; Clifford and Marcus; Geertz; Lévi-Strauss);

- deconstruction, which, in part, takes one aspect of Saussurian linguistics, that words mean what they mean by virtue of their differences from each other, and argues that signification can only function, then, by suppression of the very differences on which it depends (see, e.g., Derrida; Johnson; Norris; Meese; Bonnycastle);

- feminisms, which argue that in the production and organization of knowledge, cultural forms, and social and political life, the part that stood for the whole was too frequently gendered masculine (as well as white and middle-class) and suppressed the feminine (and race and class) difference on which it depended (see, e.g., Godard, *Gynocritics*; Neuman and Kamboureli; Warhol and Price Herndl; Jardine and Smith; Silvera);

- metahistory, which argues that history is a fact but that history is only available to us in textual, and otherwise acculturated, forms, that history is re-made, re-presented in situated and rhetorical ways (see, e.g., White; Berger);[6]

- discourse theories, which argue that language isn't neutral and knowledge isn't objective, that the latter is power and the former the terrain of struggle and community (see, e.g., Foucault; Pêcheux; Voloshinov);

- other post-structuralisms, which, by reactivating and recontextualizing the suspicions of Marx, Hegel, Nietzsche, and Freud, advocate suspicion towards history-as-past, ethics-as-inherited, and the self-as-unified-and-rational (see, e.g., Sarup; Selden and Widdowson; Foucault; Coward and Ellis);

- and postcolonialisms, which argue that while some people might be incredulous towards master narratives, incredulity alone won't lead to de-colonization, and that we might need to be more selective about what we disbelieve about Enlightenment philosophy and politics (see Taylor in this volume) because others continue to be subjected to the lingering effects of those master narratives that made Empire and nationalisms possible in the first instance (see also King and Slemon in this volume; Findlay; Ahmad; Ashcroft, Griffiths, and Tiffin; Brydon; Tötösy de Zepetnek and Gunew).

These contexts, reductively summarized here, have rewritten critics' engagements with "Canadian" and with "criticism," the two remaining – and most vexing – keywords in this volume's title. They have encouraged critics to move away from an understanding of criticism as objective and value-free (see Heble's and Struthers' essays for two different meditations on "criticism," and remember Mandel's remark that the addition of the modifier "Canadian" to "criticism" moves what might have been background into the foreground). These contexts have also encouraged critics to move away from an understanding of "context" as static background, as historical or documentary fact that shows up mimetically as transparent content or theme and that uniformly produces transparent, indigenous, or appropriate "Canadian" forms and styles for the artifacts produced in Canadian space. Contexts are instead themselves practices that constitute in complicated and frequently opaque ways whatever the apparent object of criticism is as well as the assumptions and methods we bring to studying that object. But these contexts in turn are informed by, have helped to produce and disseminate (though how widely remains questionable), and thus also signal the most obvious difference between the 1971 volume and this one: that difference has to do with the political valence of the notion of representation, with what Taylor calls "the politics of recognition," whether it is representation and therefore recognition in literature, theatre, film, museums, etc., or representation and therefore recognition in the Canadian Constitution, or representation and therefore recognition in this volume of essays.[7]

Clearly, what constitutes "Canadian" and what constitutes "criticism" are in this volume differently representative of the different constituencies of this nation and its cultural practices than Mandel's volume was. Call and response have issued from many more sites than those represented by the predominantly white, male, anglophone, anglo-celtic, and professional class that produced *Contexts*. Yet even here, in *New Contexts*, selected parts must stand for a version of a whole whose contours can never be fully mapped, as further contexts, contiguities, will be brought into play and debate when readers and writers of this volume engage it anew from their differing constituencies, contingencies, and Canadas.

Notes

Thanks to Christine Bold, Susan Brown, Diana Brydon, Ann Wilson, Ajay Heble, and Tim Struthers for their advice in drafting this essay. Thanks also to Robert Pennee for editorial and other forms of assistance in working on this volume.

1   Frye's intervention in endless probings of the question of national identity inadvertently became a new orthodoxy, astutely recognized by, among others, Milton Wilson in Mandel's collection, when he remarked, "Some critic of critics ought to write an essay on 'The Geographical Fallacy'" (198).

2   See Emberley's very useful foreword to the 1995 edition of Grant's book.

3   For examples of critical work in this area, see Fee; Jasen; Lecker; and Murray.

4   See *Canadian Canons: Essays in Literary Value*, ed. Lecker, which goes a long way towards mapping in one place new contexts of Canadian criticism; see also Cameron; Godard, "Structuralism"; and Moss.

5   See Jakobson; see also Hutcheon's introduction to *The Canadian Postmodern*.

6   I have borrowed the phrase "après Frye, rien," for my essay's title, from A.B. McKillop's argument (in the essay reprinted in this volume) that Canadian cultural historians have been slow to take up metahistorical practices, such as those recommended by Dominick LaCapra. Such practices have been very influential in changing the contexts of literary criticism in the last twenty-five years.

7   The struggle for recognition is far from won. Witness, for example, the following remarks printed in *Books in Canada* May 1996. "One doesn't have to be a Joseph Campbell or a Claude Lévi-Strauss to realize that there is an element of truth in what Robert Graves said ...: 'There is one story and one

story only'" (Meyer 17). "Is Western civilization on the verge of committing cultural suicide? University students no longer have a passion for serious reading, and departments of literature are in the hand [sic] of professors who stand in the way of those who want to understand and appreciate the great books.... English departments [are] no longer the best places to develop a knowledge and appreciation of literature" (Phelan 23). "The Canadian enchantment with diversity, to say nothing of personal freedom and equality, often prevents us from wondering too much whether one way of life might not be better than all the rest" (Foster 27). "Canada's recent obsession with identity politics is not confined to the campuses. Diversity disciples have made substantial inroads into the business community.... The gurus of this movement build their case on a myopic reading of Canadian history. They hold that a world dominated by the unexamined mores of Christian, hetero-sexual, white males must be transformed to recognize the unique claims of a widening array of identity groups" (Loney 29). For a learned and cogent response to the backlash against new contexts and methods in the humanities, see Keefer.

Works Cited

Ahmad, Aijaz. *In Theory: Classes, Nations, Literatures*. London: Verso, 1992.

Ashcroft, Bill, Gareth Griffiths, and Helen Tiffin. *The Empire Writes Back: Theory and Practice in Post-Colonial Literatures*. New Accents. London: Routledge, 1989.

Atwood, Margaret. *Survival: A Thematic Guide to Canadian Literature*. Toronto: Anansi, 1972.

Baldick, Chris. *The Social Mission of English Criticism, 1848-1932*. Oxford: Clarendon, 1983.

Barthes, Roland. *Mythologies*. Trans. Annette Travers. New York: Hill and Wang, 1972.

Baum, Gregory. "The New Social Gospel in Canada." *Compassion and Solidarity: The Church for Others*. CBC Massey Lectures. Toronto: CBC, 1987. 51-77.

Berger, Carl. *The Writing of Canadian History: Aspects of English-Canadian Historical Writing since 1900*. 2nd ed. Toronto: U of Toronto P, 1986.

Bonnycastle, Stephen. *In Search of Authority: An Introductory Guide to Literary Theory*. 2nd ed. Peterborough, ON: Broadview, 1996.

Brant, Beth. "The Good Red Road: Journeys of Homecoming in Native Women's Writing." *Writing as Witness: Essay and Talk*. Toronto: Women's, 1994. 5-24.

Brydon, Diana, ed. *Testing the Limits: Postcolonial Theories and Canadian Literatures*. Spec. iss. of *Essays on Canadian Writing* 56 (1995).

Callinicos, Alex. *Against Postmodernism: A Marxist Critique*. Cambridge, Eng.: Polity, 1989.

Cameron, Barry. "English Critical Discourse in/on Canada." *Studies on Canadian Literature: Introductory and Critical Essays*. Ed. Arnold E. Davidson. New York:

MLA, 1990. 124-43.

Clifford, James. *The Predicament of Culture: Twentieth-Century Ethnography, Literature, and Art.* Cambridge, MA: Harvard UP, 1988.

Clifford, James, and George E. Marcus, eds. *Writing Culture: The Poetics and Politics of Ethnography.* Berkeley: U of California P, 1986.

Coward, Rosalind, and John Ellis. *Language and Materialism: Developments in Semiology and the Theory of the Subject.* London: Routledge and Kegan Paul, 1977.

Davey, Frank. "Beyond Disputation: Anglophone-Canadian Artists and the Free Trade Debate." *Post-National Arguments: The Politics of the Anglophone-Canadian Novel since 1967.* Theory/Culture. Toronto: U of Toronto P, 1993. 10-24.

Derrida, Jacques. "Différance." Trans. Alan Bass. *Margins of Philosophy.* Chicago: U of Chicago P, 1982. 1-27.

—. "Structure, Sign, and Play in the Discourse of the Human Sciences." Trans. Alan Bass. *Writing and Difference.* Chicago: U of Chicago P, 1978. 278-93.

DuPlessis, Rachel Blau. "*Pater*-Daughter: Male Modernists and Female Readers." *The Pink Guitar: Writing as Feminist Practice.* London: Routledge, 1990. 41-67.

Emberley, Peter C. Foreword to Grant 15-22.

Fee, Margery. "Canadian Literature and English Studies in the Canadian University." *Essays on Canadian Writing* 48 (1992-93): 20-40.

—. "English-Canadian Literary Criticism, 1890-1950: Defining and Establishing a National Literature." Diss. U of Toronto, 1981.

Filewod, Alan. "National Theatre / National Obsession." *Canadian Theatre Review* 62 (1990): 5-10.

Findlay, L.M. "Writing the Canadian Flag." *Alphabet City* 2 (1992): 46-47.

Foster, David. "Aristotle Meets Diversity." *Books in Canada* May 1996: 27-28.

Foucault, Michel. *The Foucault Reader.* Ed. Paul Rabinow. New York: Pantheon, 1984.

—. "The Order of Discourse." Trans. Ian McLeod. *Untying the Text: A Post-Structuralist Reader.* Ed. Robert Young. Boston: Routledge and Kegan Paul, 1981. 48-78.

Frye, Northrop. *Anatomy of Criticism: Four Essays.* Princeton: Princeton UP, 1957.

—. Conclusion. *Literary History of Canada: Canadian Literature in English.* Gen. ed. Carl F. Klinck. Toronto: U of Toronto P, 1965. 821-49.

—. *Fearful Symmetry: A Study of William Blake.* Princeton: Princeton UP, 1947.

—. "Preface to an Uncollected Anthology." Mandel, ed., *Contexts of Canadian Criticism* 181-97.

—. "The Road of Excess." Mandel, ed., *Contexts of Canadian Criticism* 125-39.

Geertz, Clifford. *The Interpretation of Cultures.* New York: Basic, 1973.

Gerson, Carole. "Anthologies and the Canon of Early Canadian Women Writers." *Re(Dis)covering Our Foremothers: Nineteenth-Century Canadian Women Writers.* Ed. Lorraine McMullen. Reappraisals: Canadian Writers 15. Papers presented at a conference, U of Ottawa, 29 Apr.-1 May 1988. Ottawa: U of Ottawa P,

1990. 55-76.

Godard, Barbara, ed. *Gynocritics: Feminist Approaches to Canadian and Quebec Women's Writing / Gynocritiques: Démarches féministes à l'écriture des Canadiennes et Québécoises.* Toronto: ECW, 1987.

—. "Structuralism/Post-Structuralism: Language, Reality and Canadian Literature." Moss 25-51.

Grant, George. *Lament for a Nation: The Defeat of Canadian Nationalism.* New ed. Carleton Library 50. Ottawa: Carleton UP, 1995.

Guillory, John. "Canon." Lentricchia and McLaughlin 233-49.

Holdcroft, David. *Saussure: Signs, System, and Arbitrariness.* Modern European Philosophy. Cambridge, Eng.: Cambridge UP, 1991.

Hutcheon, Linda. "The End(s) of Irony: The Politics of Appropriateness." *Irony's Edge: The Theory and Politics of Irony.* London: Routledge, 1995. 176-204.

—. Introduction. *The Canadian Postmodern: A Study of Contemporary English-Canadian Fiction.* Toronto: Oxford UP, 1988. 1-25.

Innis, H.A. "The Strategy of Culture." Mandel, ed., *Contexts of Canadian Criticism* 71-92.

Itwaru, Arnold Harrichand. *The Invention of Canada: Literary Text and the Immigrant Imaginary.* Toronto: TSAR, 1990.

Jakobson, Roman. "The Metaphoric and Metonymic Poles." *Fundamentals of Language.* Janua Linguarum, Series Minor, 1. The Hague: Mouton, 1956. 76-82.

Jardine, Alice, and Paul Smith, eds. *Men in Feminism.* London: Methuen, 1987.

Jasen, Pat. "The English-Canadian Liberal Arts Curriculum: An Intellectual History, 1800-1950." Diss. U of Manitoba, 1987.

Johnson, Barbara. "Writing." Lentricchia and McLaughlin 39-49.

Johnston, Basil H. "Is That All There Is? Tribal Literature." *Canadian Literature* 128 (1991): 54-62.

Keefer, Michael. *Lunar Perspectives: Field Notes from the Culture Wars.* Concord, ON: Anansi, 1996.

King, Thomas. "Godzilla vs. Post-Colonial." *World Literature Written in English* 30.2 (1990): 10-16.

Kroetsch, Robert. "Disunity as Unity: A Canadian Strategy." *The Lovely Treachery of Words: Essays Selected and New.* Toronto: Oxford UP, 1989. 21-33.

Lecker, Robert, ed. *Canadian Canons: Essays in Literary Value.* Toronto: U of Toronto P, 1991.

—. *Making It Real: The Canonization of English-Canadian Literature.* Concord, ON: Anansi, 1995.

Lentricchia, Frank, and Thomas McLaughlin, eds. *Critical Terms for Literary Study.* 2nd ed. Chicago: U of Chicago P, 1995.

Lévi-Strauss, Claude. *The Elementary Structure of Kinship.* Trans. James Harle Bell, John Richard von Sturmer, and Rodney Needham. Ed. Rodney Needham. Rev. ed. Boston: Beacon, 1969.

Loney, Martin. "Identity Politics as Management Fad." *Books in Canada* May 1996: 29.

Lyotard, Jean-François. *The Postmodern Condition: A Report on Knowledge.* Trans. Geoff Bennington and Brian Massumi. Theory and History of Literature 10. Minneapolis: U of Minnesota P, 1984.

Mandel, Eli, ed. *Contexts of Canadian Criticism: A Collection of Critical Essays.* Patterns of Literary Criticism 9. Chicago: U of Chicago P; Toronto: U of Toronto P, 1971.

—. Introduction. Mandel, ed., *Contexts of Canadian Criticism* 3-25.

—. Preface. Mandel, ed., *Contexts of Canadian Criticism* vii.

McKillop, A.B. "Culture, Intellect, and Context: Recent Writing on the Cultural and Intellectual History of Ontario." *Journal of Canadian Studies / Revue d'études canadiennes* 24.3 (1989): 7-31.

McLuhan, Marshall. "The Medium Is the Message." Mandel, ed., *Contexts of Canadian Criticism* 140-53.

Meese, Elizabeth A. "The Concept of 'Difference' and Feminist Literary Criticism." *Crossing the Double-Cross: The Practice of Feminist Criticism.* Chapel Hill: U of North Carolina P, 1986. 69-87.

Meyer, Bruce. "Folk Tales of Bicultural Anxiety." *Books in Canada* May 1996: 17.

Moss, John, ed. *Future Indicative: Literary Theory and Canadian Literature.* Reappraisals: Canadian Writers 13. Papers presented at U of Ottawa, 25-27 Apr. 1986. Ottawa: U of Ottawa P, 1990.

Mukherjee, Arun. "Ideology in the Classroom: A Case Study in the Teaching of English Literature in Canadian Universities." *Oppositional Aesthetics: Readings from a Hyphenated Space.* Toronto: TSAR, 1994. 30-38.

Murray, Heather. "Institutions of Reading: New Directions in English-Canadian Literary History." *Textual Studies in Canada* 3 (1993): 2-7.

—. "Reading for Contradiction in the Literature of Colonial Space." Moss 71-84.

—. "Resistance and Reception: Backgrounds to Theory in English-Canada." *Signature* 4 (1990): 49-67.

Neumann, Shirley, and Smaro Kamboureli, eds. *A Mazing Space: Writing Canadian Women Writing.* Edmonton, AB: Longspoon/NeWest, 1986.

New, W.H. "Back to the Future: The Short Story in Canada and the Writing of Literary History." *Australian-Canadian Studies* 4 (1986): 15-27.

Norris, Christopher. *Derrida.* Cambridge, MA: Harvard UP, 1987.

Padolsky, Enoch. "Cultural Diversity and Canadian Literature: A Pluralistic Approach to Majority and Minority Writing in Canada." *International Journal of Canadian Studies / Revue international d'études canadiennes* 3 (1991): 111-28.

Paré, François. *Les littératures de l'exiguïté.* Hearst, ON: Nordir, 1992.

Paterson, Janet M. "Le Postmodernisme québécois: tendances actuelles." *Études littéraires* 27.1 (1994): 77-88.

Pêcheux, Michel. *Language, Semantics, Ideology.* Trans. Harbans Nagpal. New York: St. Martin's, 1982.

Perkins, David. *Is Literary History Possible?* Baltimore: Johns Hopkins UP, 1992.

Phelan, Joseph. "How the West Has Been Taped." *Books in Canada* May 1996: 23-25.

Philip, M. Nourbese. "Who's Listening? Artists, Audiences and Language." *Frontiers: Selected Essays and Writings on Racism and Culture 1984-1992*. Stratford, ON: Mercury, 1992. 26-46.

Rich, Adrienne. "When We Dead Awaken: Writing as Re-Vision." *On Lies, Secrets, and Silence: Selected Prose 1966-1978*. New York: Norton, 1979. 34-49.

Rowe, John Carlos. "Structure." Lentricchia and McLaughlin 23-38.

Sarup, Madan. *An Introductory Guide to PostStructuralism and Postmodernism*. Athens: U of Georgia P, 1989.

Saussure, Ferdinand de. *Course in General Linguistics*. 1916. Trans. Wade Baskin. Rev. ed. Glasgow: Fontana/Collins, 1974.

Selden, Raman, and Peter Widdowson. *A Reader's Guide to Contemporary Literary Theory*. 3rd ed. Lexington: U of Kentucky P, 1993.

Silvera, Makeda, ed. *The Other Woman: Women of Colour in Contemporary Canadian Literature*. Toronto: Sister Vision, 1994.

Silverman, Kaja. *The Subject of Semiotics*. New York: Oxford UP, 1983.

Slemon, Stephen. "Unsettling the Empire: Resistance Theory for the Second World." *World Literature Written in English* 30.2 (1990): 30-41.

Sparshott, Francis. "Art and Criticism." Mandel, ed., *Contexts of Canadian Criticism* 154-77.

Sugars, Cynthia. "On the Rungs of the Double Helix: Theorizing the Canadian Literatures." *Essays on Canadian Writing* 50 (1993): 19-44.

Tallman, Warren. "Wolf in the Snow." Mandel, ed., *Contexts of Canadian Criticism* 232-53.

Taylor, Charles. "The Politics of Recognition." *Multiculturalism: Examining the Politics of Recognition*. Ed. Amy Gutmann. Princeton: Princeton UP, 1994. 25-73.

Tötösy de Zepetnek, Steven, and Sneja Gunew, eds. *Postcolonial Literatures: Theory and Practice / Les littératures post-coloniales: théories et réalisations*. Spec. iss. of *Canadian Review of Comparative Literature / Revue canadienne de littérature comparée* 22.3-4 (1995).

Viswanathan, Gauri. *Masks of Conquest: Literary Study and British Rule in India*. New York: Columbia UP, 1989.

Voloshinov, V.N. *Marxism and the Philosophy of Language*. Trans. Ladislav Matejka and I.R. Titunik. New York: Seminar, 1973.

Wallace, Bronwen. "One More Woman Talking." *Sudden Miracles: Eight Women Poets*. Ed. Rhea Tregebov. Toronto: Second Story, 1991. 237-43.

Warhol, Robyn R., and Diane Price Herndl, eds. *Feminisms: An Anthology of Literary Theory and Criticism*. New Brunswick, NJ: Rutgers UP, 1991.

Welsh, Christine. "*Women in the Shadows*: Reclaiming a Métis Heritage." *Descant* 24.3 (1993): 89-104.

White, Hayden. "The Fictions of Factual Representation." *Tropics of Discourse: Essays in Cultural Criticism*. Baltimore: Johns Hopkins UP, 1978. 121-34.

—. *Metahistory: The Historical Imagination in Nineteenth-Century Europe*. Baltimore: Johns Hopkins UP, 1973.

Williams, Raymond. *Culture and Society, 1780-1950*. London: Chatto and Windus, 1960.

—. *Keywords: A Vocabulary of Culture and Society*. Rev. ed. New York: Oxford UP, 1983.

Wilson, Milton. "Recent Canadian Verse." Mandel, ed., *Contexts of Canadian Criticism* 198-205.

Ideology in the Classroom: A Case Study in the Teaching of English Literature in Canadian Universities

Arun Mukherjee

This paper was written in order to articulate the sense of personal anguish and alienation that I feel as a teacher of literature whose sex, race, and birth in a newly independent Asian country set her constantly at odds with the consensus that appears to reign in the Departments of English across Canadian universities. The terms of this consensus, it seems to me, are not so very different from the ones prevailing in American universities as demonstrated, for example, by Richard Ohmann in his *English in America*.

Generally speaking, we, the Canadian university teachers of English, do not consider issues of the classroom worth critical scrutiny. Indeed, there is hardly any connection between our pedagogy and our scholarly research. A new teacher, looking for effective teaching strategies, will discover to her utter dismay that no amount of reading of scholarly publications will be of any help when she faces a class of undergraduates. In fact, the two discourses – those of pedagogy and scholarly research – are diametrically opposed and woe betide the novice who uses the language of current scholarly discourse in the classroom.

As an outsider, it has never ceased to amaze me that Canadian literary scholars do not seem perturbed by this doublespeak. Not having the same skills myself, I gape with open mouth at my colleagues who switch so easily from one to another. Perhaps, blessed with what Keats called "Negative Capability," they are able to hold two completely contradictory systems of thought in suspension.

Edward Said, in his essay in *The Politics of Interpretation*, says that the "mission of the humanities" in contemporary American society is "to represent *noninterference* in the affairs of the everyday world."[1] He charges the American practitioners of the humanities with concealing, atomizing, depoliticizing, and mystifying the "unhumanistic process" that informs the *laissez faire* society of what he calls "Reaganism." The classroom experience I narrate in this paper concretized for me the ahistorical realm in which American and, yes, Canadian, university teachers of literature ply their trade.

What I have recounted here is not unique at all and I continue to come across student papers that share the innocence about history I describe in this paper. However, this particular experience was a watershed in my personal history since it allowed me, for the first time, to articulate to myself the lineaments of my disagreement with the dominant academic discourses.

The case study presented here is taken from the period 1983-84, when I was teaching at the University of Regina, Saskatchewan. A large part of the teaching done at the Department of English of that university consists of English 100: Introduction to Literature. It is a compulsory course whereby the professors of English supposedly infuse first-year students with a love of literature. Since the aim of the course is to acquaint students with prominent literary genres, almost all teachers of the course use anthologies that contain short stories, poems, and, at times, plays and novels as well. Quite often, the anthologies are American.

The short fiction anthology I used for my introductory English 100 class – I deliberately chose a Canadian one – includes a short story by Margaret Laurence entitled "The Perfume Sea."[2] This story, as I interpret it, underlines the economic and cultural domination of the Third World. However, even though I presented this interpretation of the story to my students in some detail, they did not even consider it when they wrote their essays. While the story had obviously appealed to them – almost forty percent chose to write on it – they ignored the political meaning entirely.

I was thoroughly disappointed by my students' total disregard for local realities treated in the short story. Nevertheless, their papers did give me an understanding of how their education had allowed them to neutralize the subversive meanings implicit in a piece of good literature, such as the Laurence story.

The story, from my point of view, is quite forthright in its purpose. Its locale is Ghana on the eve of independence from British rule. The colonial administrators are leaving and this has caused financial difficulties for Mr. Archipelago and Doree who operate the only beauty parlour within a radius of one hundred miles around an unnamed small town. Though the equipment is antiquated, and the parlour operators not much to their liking, the ladies have put up with it for want of a better alternative.

With the white clientele gone, Mr. Archipelago and Doree have no customers left. The parlour lies empty for weeks until one day the crunch comes in the shape of their Ghanaian landlord, Mr. Tachie, demanding rent. Things, however, take an upturn when Mr. Archipelago learns that Mr. Tachie's daughter wants to look like a "city girl" and constantly pesters her father for money to buy shoes, clothes, and make-up. Mr. Archipelago, in a flash of inspiration, discovers that Mercy Tachie is the new consumer to whom he can sell his "product": "Mr. Tachie, you are a bringer of miracles! ... There it was, all the time, and we did not see it. We, even we, Doree, will make history – you will see" (221). The claim about making history is repeated twice in the story and is significantly linked to the history made by Columbus. For Mr. Archipelago is very proud of the fact that he was born in Genoa, Columbus's home town. The unpleasant aspect of this act of making history is unmistakably spelt out: "He [Columbus] was once in West Africa, you know, as a young seaman, at one of the old slave-castles not far from here. And he, also, came from Genoa" (217).

The symbolic significance of the parlour is made quite apparent from the detailed attention Laurence gives to its transformation. While the pre-independence sign had said:

ARCHIPELAGO
English-Style Barber
European Ladies' Hairdresser (211)

the new sign says:

ARCHIPELAGO & DOREE
Barbershop
All-Beauty Salon
African Ladies A Speciality (221)

With the help of a loan from Mr. Tachie, the proprietors install hair-straightening equipment and buy shades of make-up suitable for the African skin. However, though the African ladies show much interest from a distance, none of them enters the shop. Two weeks later, Mercy Tachie hesitantly walks into the salon "because if you are having no customers, he [Mr. Tachie] will never be getting his money from you" (222). Mercy undergoes a complete transformation in the salon and comes out looking like a "city girl," the kind she has seen in *Drum* magazine. Thus, Mr. Archipelago and Doree are "saved" by "an act of Mercy" (226). They have found a new role in the life of this newly independent country: to help the African bourgeoisie slavishly imitate the values of its former colonial masters.

These political overtones are reinforced by the overall poverty the story describes and the symbolic linking of the white salon operators with the only black merchant in town. The division between his daughter and other African women who go barefoot with babies on their backs further indicates the divisive nature of the European implant. Other indications of the writer's purpose are apparent from her caricature of Mr. Archipelago and Doree, a device which prevents emotional identification with them. The fact that both of them have no known national identities – both of them keep changing their stories – is also significant, for it seems to say that, like Kurtz in *Heart of Darkness*, they represent the whole white civilization. The story thus underplays the lives of individuals in order to emphasize these larger issues: the nature of colonialism as well as its aftermath when the native élite takes over without really changing the colonial institutions except for their names.

This, then, was the aspect of the story in which I was most interested, no doubt because I am myself from a former colony of the Raj. During class discussions, I asked the students about the symbolic significance of the hair straightening equipment, the change of names, the identification of Mr. Archipelago with Columbus, *Drum* magazine, and the characters of Mr. Tachie and Mercy Tachie.

However, the students based their essays not on these aspects, but on how "believable" or "likeable" the two major characters in the story were, and how they found happiness in the end by accepting change. That is to say, the two characters were freed entirely from the restraints of the context, i.e., the colonial situation, and evaluated solely on the basis of their emotional relationship with each other. The outer world of political turmoil, the scrupulously observed class system of the colonials, the contrasts between wealth and poverty, were nonexistent in their papers. As one student put it, the conclusion of the story was "The perfect couple walking off into the sunset, each happy that they had found what had eluded both of them all their lives, companionship and privacy all rolled into one relationship." For another, they symbolized "the anxiety and hope of humanity ... the common problem of facing or not facing reality."

I was astounded by my students' ability to close themselves off to the disturbing implications of my interpretation and devote their attention to expatiating upon "the anxiety and hope of humanity," and other such generalizations as change, people, values, reality, etc. I realized that these generalizations were ideological. They enabled my students to efface the differences between British bureaucrats and British traders, between colonizing whites and colonized blacks, and between rich blacks and poor blacks. They enabled them to believe that all human beings faced dilemmas similar to the ones faced by the two main characters in the story.

Though, thanks to Kenneth Burke, I knew the rhetorical subterfuges which generalizations like "humanity" imply, the papers of my students made me painfully aware of their ideological purposes. I saw that they help us to translate the world into our own idiom by erasing the ambiguities and the unpleasant truths that lie in the crevices. They make us oblivious to the fact that society is not a homogeneous grouping but an assortment of groups where we belong to one particular set called "us," as opposed to the other set or sets we distinguish as "them."

The most painful revelation came when I recognized the source of my students' vocabulary. Their analysis, I realized, was in the time-honoured tradition of that variety of criticism which presents literary works as "universal." The test of a great work of literature, according to this tradition, is that despite its particularity, it speaks to all times and all people. As Brent Harold notes, "It is a rare discussion of literature that does not depend heavily on the universal 'we' (meaning we human beings), on 'the human condition,' 'the plight of modern man,' 'absurd man,' and other convenient abstractions which obscure from their users the specific social basis of their own thought...."[3]

Thus, all conflict eliminated with the help of the universal "we," what do we have left but the "feelings" and "experiences" of individual characters? The questions in the anthologies reflect that. When they are not based on matters of technique – where one can short circuit such problems entirely – they ask students whether such and such a character deserves our sympathy, or whether such and such a character undergoes change, or, in other words, an initiation. As Richard Ohmann comments:

> The student focuses on a character, on the poet's attitude, on the individual's struggle towards understanding – but rarely, if ever, on the social forces that are revealed in every dramatic scene and almost every stretch of narration in fiction. Power, class, culture, social order and disorder – these staples of literature are quite excluded from consideration in the analytic tasks set for Advanced Placement candidates.[4]

Instead of facing up to the realities of "power, class, culture, social order and disorder," literary critics and editors of literature anthologies hide behind the universalist vocabulary that only mystifies the true nature of reality. For example, the editorial introduction to "The Perfume Sea" considers the story in terms of categories that are supposedly universal and eternal:

> Here is a crucial moment in human history seen from inside a beauty parlour and realized in terms of the "permanent wave." But while feminine vanity is presented as the only changeless element in a world of change, Mrs. Laurence, for all her lightness of touch, is not "making fun" of her Africans or Europeans. In reading the story, probe for the deeper layers of human anxiety and hope beneath the comic surfaces. (201)

Though the importance of "a crucial moment in history" is acknowledged here, it is only to point out the supposedly changeless: that highly elusive thing called "feminine vanity." The term performs the function of achieving the desired identification between all white women and all black women, regardless of the barriers of race and class. The command to probe "the deeper layers of human anxiety and hope" – a command that my students took more seriously than their teacher's alternative interpretation – works to effectively eliminate consideration of disturbing sociopolitical realities.

This process results in the promotion of what Ohmann calls the "prophylactic view of literature" (63). Even the most provocative literary work, when seen from such a perspective, is emptied of its subversive content. After such treatment, as Ohmann puts it, "It will not cause any trouble for the people who run schools or colleges, for the military-industrial complex, for anyone who holds power. It can only perpetuate the misery of those who don't" (61).

The editor-critic thus functions as the castrator. He makes sure that the young minds will not get any understanding of how our society actually functions and how literature plays a role in it. Instead of explaining these relationships, the editor-critic feeds students on a vocabulary that pretends that human beings and their institutions have not changed a bit during the course of history, that they all face the same problems as human beings. Thus, another anthology used by several of my colleagues divides its subject-matter into four groups called "Innocence and Experience," "Conformity and Rebellion," "Love and Hate," and "The Presence of Death." The preface justifies the classification thus: "The arrangement of the works in four thematic groups provides opportunities to explore diverse attitudes toward the same powerful human tendencies and experiences and to contrast formal treatments as well."[5]

The problem is that it is the editors' fiat that has decided what the "powerful human tendencies" are and how they should be treated. The introductions to the four sections talk about "the protagonist" and "tendencies" in a language that conveys to me that literature is about initiation and loss of innocence, about the lone rebel fighting against such authoritarian agencies as the state and society, about love and hate between men and women, and about the inevitability of death. Literature, according to this line of thinking, is obviously not about the problems of oppression and injustice, about how to create a just society, about how to understand one's situation in society and to do something about it. Literature does not speak about people as social beings, as members of political or social alliances that they have voluntarily chosen.

I would not like to act naïve and ask, like Barbara Bailey Kessel: "Why is it impossible for liberal critics to conceive of miserable, oppressed people freely choosing to struggle against their own oppression?"[6] The reason is that it is far more comfortable to hide behind a vocabulary which, on the one hand, overlooks one's own privileged position and, on the other, makes everyone look equally privileged. It creates, in the imagination of the user, a society "free, classless, and urbane," by lifting the work of art from "the bondage of history."[7] And if my students, who come mainly from the privileged section of an overall affluent society, perform the same sleight-of-hand, why should I feel unduly disturbed? After all, as Auden says, "Poetry makes nothing happen." The only remaining question, then, is what am I doing in that classroom?

Terry Eagleton says that "explanation and interpretation 'come to an end' ... when we arrive at a certain interpretative logjam or sticking-place and recognize that we shall not get any further until we transform the practical forms of life in which our interpretations are inscribed."[8] He makes me realize that I can't fight a quixotic battle in the classroom for historicity and politicization. In fact, I have at times been accused by some of my outraged students of "bringing politics into a literature class." In a similar vein, a very well-respected Canadian scholar in my field intimated to me that my research was "old-fashioned," i.e., "sociological," and that if I wanted to consolidate my precarious foothold in academia, I should think about doing some "fashionable" research, i.e., "semiotics," "decon-struction," "feminism," and so on. (I found it interesting that feminism to him was only another "fashion.")

My feeling is that the transformation of the practical forms of life which Eagleton speaks of is not around the corner in Canada. Those on the margin face an uphill task in terms of sheer physical and moral sur-vival in the system. Once accepted, they face the prospect of being type-cast as the "token black," or the "token ethnic," or the "token feminist." Their "diversion," then, becomes a nice variation in the vast edifice of cul-tural reproduction that goes on in departments of literature and literary journals.

Said talks about the need for "a fully articulated program of interfer-ence" (31). This paper is a partial attempt in that direction. I have hoped to generate a debate over issues that are very important to me as a teacher and a non-white woman from the Third World.

I am glad, let me add, that this paper has finally found an audience. It was submitted in an earlier version to the "Literature and Ideology" cate-gory of the annual conference of the Association of Canadian University Teachers of English (ACUTE) held at Guelph in 1984. While ACUTE may have turned down this submission for reasons other than ideological, what I found really disturbing was the total lack of attention to pedagogical issues in the conference program. After all, the bulk of our jobs are provided by first-year English courses and the communication strategies we adopt in our classrooms should therefore be an important part of our discussions when we meet for our annual conference, and it should be recognized that the responses of our students constitute an important mirror both of our performance and of our values. It does not behoove us as scholars to be oblivious to the social repercussions of our activities in the classroom.

If one looks at the 1984 ACUTE conference program, one gets the impression that the only officially sanctioned valid response to literary works is structuralist-formalist. The following topics are representative of the kind of fare conference participants were treated to: "Sedulous Aping?: Redefining Parody Today," "John Webster's Jacobean Experiments in Dramatic Mimesis," "What Does It Mean To Imitate an Action?," "Whalley on Mimesis and Tragedy," "Interruption in *The Tempest*," and so on. Even the "Literature and Ideology" category was appropriated for formalistic preoccupations: the two papers in this section were entitled "Christianity as Ideology in Rudy Wiebe's *The Scorched-Wood People*" and "Dickens' Good Women: An Analysis of the Influence of Social Ideology on Literary Form."

Surely, literature is more than form? What about the questions regarding the ideology and social class of a writer, the role and ideology of the patrons and disseminators of literature, the role of literature as a social institution, and, finally, the role of the teacher-critic as a transmitter of dominant social and cultural values? Have these questions no place in our professional deliberations?

Notes

1   Edward W. Said, "Opponents, Audiences, Constituencies, and Communities," *The Politics of Interpretation*, ed. W.J.T. Mitchell (Chicago: U of Chicago P, 1983) 28.

2   Margaret Laurence, "The Perfume Sea," *In Search of Ourselves*, ed. Malcolm Ross and John Stevens (Toronto: J.M. Dent, 1967) 201-27.

3   Brent Harold, "Beyond Student-Centered Teaching: The Dialectical Materialist Form of a Literature Course," *College English* 34 (1972-73): 201.

4   Richard Ohmann, *English in America: A Radical View of the Profession* (New York: Oxford UP, 1976) 59-60.

5   Richard Abcarian and Marvin Klotz, eds., *Literature: The Human Experience* (New York: St. Martin's, 1973) xiii.

6   Barbara Bailey Kessel, "Free, Classless, and Urbane?," *College English* 31 (1969-70): 539.

7   Northrop Frye, *Anatomy of Criticism: Four Essays* (Princeton, NJ: Princeton UP, 1957) 347.

8   Terry Eagleton, "Ineluctable Options," *The Politics of Interpretation*, ed. W.J.T. Mitchell (Chicago: U of Chicago P, 1983) 380.

Unsettling the Empire: Resistance Theory for the Second World

Stephen Slemon

My argument here comprises part of what I hope will become a larger meditation on the practice of "post-colonial criticism," and the problem it addresses is a phenomenon which twenty-five years ago would have seemed an embarrassment of riches. The sign of the "post-colonial" has become an especially valent one in academic life (there are even careers to be made out of it), and like feminist theory or women's studies programs a decade ago, the area is witnessing an enormous convergence within it of diverse critical practices and cultural forces. We are now undergoing an important process of sorting through those forces and tendencies, investigating where affiliations lie and where they cross, examining the political and pedagogical goals of the area, and re-negotiating basic issues such as where our primary "material" of study and of intervention lies. What I want to do in this paper is take a position within this process of questioning – but because this *is* a process, I want also to advance this position as provisional and temporary, a statement in search of that clarifying energy which emerges at the best of times out of friendly discussion and collegial exchange.

In specific terms, what I want to do in this paper is address two separate debates in critical theory, and then attempt to yoke them together into an argument for maintaining within a discourse of post-colonialism certain textual and critical practices which inhabit ex-colonial settler cultures and their literatures. The textual gestures I want to preserve for post-colonial theory and practice are various and dispersed, but the territory I want to reclaim for post-colonial pedagogy and research – and reclaim *not* as a unified and indivisible area but rather as a groundwork for certain modes of anti-colonial work – is that neither/nor territory of white settler-colonial writing which Alan Lawson has called the "Second World."

The first debate concerns the *field* of the "post-colonial." Is the "post-colonial" a synonym for what Wallersteinian world-systems theory calls the periphery in economic relations? Is it another way of naming what other discourses would call the Third and Fourth Worlds? Is it a name for a discursive and representational set of practices which are grounded in a politics of anti-colonialism? Or is the term post-colonial simply another name for the old Commonwealth of literary activity – a synonym for such unfortunate neologisms as "the new literatures in English," or what Joseph

Jones in a fleeting moment of unitary hopefulness wanted to call "Terranglia," or what the Modern Languages Association of America in its continuing moment of exclusionary and yet proprietorial backyardism still wants to call "English Literatures Other than British and American"?

The second debate I want to address concerns the nature of literary *resistance* itself. Is literary resistance something that simply issues forth, through narrative, against a clearly definable set of power relations? Is it something actually *there* in the text, or is it produced and reproduced in and through communities of readers and through the mediating structures of their own culturally specific histories? Do literary resistances escape the constitutive purchase of genre, and trope, and figure, and mode, which operate elsewhere as a contract between text and reader and thus a set of centralizing codes, or are literary resistances in fact necessarily *embedded* in the representational technologies of those literary and social "texts" whose structures and whose referential codes they seek to oppose?

These questions sound like definitional problems, but I think in fact they are crucial ones for a critical industry which at the moment seems to find these two central terms – "post-colonial" and "resistance" – positively shimmering as objects of desire and self-privilege, and so easily appropriated to competing, and in fact hostile, modes of critical and literary practice. Arun Mukherjee makes this point with great eloquence in "Whose Post-Colonialism and Whose Postmodernism?" – asking what specificity, what residual grounding, remains with the term "post-colonial" when it is applied indiscriminately to both Second- and Third-World literary texts. The term "resistance" recently found itself at the centre of a similar controversy, when it was discovered how very thoroughly a *failure* in resistance characterized some of the earlier political writing of the great theorist of *textual* resistance, Paul de Man. Both terms thus find themselves at the centre of a quarrel over the kinds of critical taxonomies that will be seen to perform legitimate work in articulating the relation between literary texts and the political world; and to say this is to recognize that critical taxonomies, like literary canons, issue forth from cultural institutions which continue to police what voices will be heard, which *kinds* of (textual) intervention will be made recognizable and/or classifiable, and what *authentic* forms of post-colonial textual resistance are going to look like. These debates are thus institutional: grounded in university curricula, and *about* pedagogical strategies. They are also about the question of authenticity itself: how a text emerges from a cultural grounding and speaks to a reading community, and how textual ambiguity or ambivalence proves pedagogically awkward when an apparatus called "English studies" recuperates various writing practices holistically as "literatures," and then deploys them wholesale towards a discourse of inclusivity and coverage.

The first debate – the question of the "post-colonial" – is grounded in the overlapping of three competing research or critical fields, each of which carries a specific cultural location and history. In the first of these fields, the term "post-colonial" is an outgrowth of what formerly were "Commonwealth" literary studies – a study which came into being *after* "English" studies had been liberalized to include "American" and then an immediate national or regional literature (Australian, Canadian, West Indian), and as a way of mobilizing the concept of national or geographical *difference* within what remains a unitary idea of "English." The second of these critical fields, in contrast, employs the term "post-colonial" in considering the valency of subjectivity specifically within Third- and Fourth-World cultures, and within black, and ethnic, and First-Nation constituencies dispersed within First-World terrain. The institutionalizing of these two critical fields has made possible the emergence of a third field of study, however, where nation-based examinations of a variable literary Commonwealth, or a variable literary Third World, give way to specific analyses of the discourse of colonialism (and neo-colonialism), and where studies in cultural representativeness and literary mimeticism give way to the project of identifying the kinds of anti-colonialist resistance that can take place in literary writing.

The past few years have therefore witnessed an extraordinary burgeoning of "post-colonial" criticism and theory, largely because the second and third of these pedagogical fields have at last gained hold within the First-World academy. "Post-colonial" studies in "English" now finds itself at a shifting moment, where three very different critical projects collide with one another on the space of a single signifier – and what will probably be a single course offering within an English studies programme. Not surprisingly, this situation has produced some remarkable confusions, and they underpin the present debate over the specificity of the "post-colonial" in the areas of literary and critical practice.

The confusion which concerns me here is the way in which the *project* of the third "post-colonial" critical field – that is, of identifying the scope and nature of anti-colonialist resistance in writing – has been mistaken for the project of the second critical field, which concerns itself with articulating the literary nature of Third- and Fourth-World cultural groups. For whereas the first and second of these post-colonial critical fields work with whole nations or cultures as their basic units, and tend to seek out the defining characteristics under which *all* writing in that field can be subsumed, the third critical field is concerned with identifying a social force, colonialism, and with the attempt to understand the resistances to that force, *wherever* they lie. Colonialism, obviously, is an enormously problematical category: it is by definition transhistorical and unspecific, and it is used in relation to very different kinds of cultural oppression and eco-

STEPHEN SLEMON

nomic control. But like the term "patriarchy," which shares similar problems in definition, the concept of colonialism, to this third critical field, remains crucial to a critique of past and present power relations in world affairs, and thus to a specifically *post*-colonial critical practice which attempts to understand the relation of literary writing to power and its contestations.

This mistaking of a pro-active, anti-colonialist critical project with nation-based studies in Third- and Fourth-World literary writing comes about for good reason – for it has been, and always will be, the case that the most important forms of resistance to any form of social power will be produced from within the communities that are most immediately and visibly subordinated by that power structure. But when the idea of anti-colonial resistance becomes *synonymous* with Third- and Fourth-World literary writing, two forms of displacement happen. First, *all* literary writing which emerges from these cultural locations will be understood as carrying a radical and contestatory content – and this gives away the rather important point that subjected peoples are sometimes capable of producing reactionary literary documents. And secondly, the idea will be discarded that important anti-colonialist literary writing can take place *outside* the ambit of Third- and Fourth-World literary writing – and this in effect excises the study of anti-colonialist Second-World literary activity from the larger study of anti-colonialist literary practice.

In practical terms, this excision springs in part from a desire to foreclose upon a *specific* form of "Commonwealth" literary criticism. For a small number of old-school "Commonwealth" critics, comparative studies across English literatures did indeed promise the renewal through "art" of that lost cross-cultural unity which a capricious twentieth-century history had somehow denied for Britain and the empire. And so this excision provides an effective way of figuring one important objective of post-colonial criticism: and that is the rejection of neo-colonialist, Eurocentrist, and late capitalist purchase in the practice of post-colonial literary analysis.

This excision also springs from a rather healthy recognition that – as Linda Hutcheon has recently put it – the experience of colonialism, and therefore of post-colonialism, is simply *not* the same in, say, Canada as it is in the West Indies or in Africa or in India. As Fourth-World literary writing continually insists, Second- and Third-World cultures do not inhabit the same political, discursive, and literary terrains in relation to colonialism. The excision of Second-World literary writing from the field of the "post-colonial" therefore figures the importance of cultural *difference* within post-colonial criticism and theory – even if that difference is conscripted to the service of what remains at heart an extended nation-based critical practice founded on a unitary model and on the assumption of equivalent (as opposed to, say, "shared") cultural and literary experience within a positivist and essentialist "post-colonial" sphere.

Nevertheless, I want to argue, this conflating of the projects of the second and third post-colonial critical fields, and the consequent jettisoning of Second-World literary writing from the domain of the post-colonial, remains – in the Bloomian sense – a "misreading," and one which seems to be setting in train a concept of the "post-colonial" which is remarkably purist and absolutist in tenor. Tim Brennan, one of the most interesting of the newly emerging US-based, First-World critics in the post-colonial field, has been an enormously forceful proponent for this conflation of the second and third post-colonial critical projects – for the refiguration of the post-colonial literary terrain as "the literature not of the 'colonies' but of the 'colonized'" (5) – and he puts the argument for this position as follows:

[Writers such as] Nadine Gordimer or John Coetzee of South Africa, along with others from the white Commonwealth countries, while clearly playing [a] mediating role [between colonizer and colonized], are probably better placed in some category of the European novel of Empire because of their compromised positions of segregated privilege within colonial settler states. They are too much like the fictional "us" of the so-called mainstream, on the inside looking out. (35-36)

Brennan's argument is actually more complex than this quotation suggests, for it hangs upon an extremely suggestive category called "the novel of Empire," which in another discussion would need to be unpacked. But for my purposes here, his argument is useful because it makes visible the fact that the foundational principle for this particular approach to the field of post-colonial criticism is at heart a simple binarism: the binarism of Europe and its Others, of colonizer and colonized, of the West and the Rest, of the vocal and the silent. It is also a centre/periphery model with roots in world-systems theory – and as so often happens with simple binary systems, this concept of the post-colonial has a marked tendency to blur when it tries to focus upon ambiguously placed or ambivalent material. In what seems to be emerging as the dominant focus of post-colonial literary criticism now – especially for literary criticism coming out of universities in the United States – this blurring is everywhere in evidence in relation to what world-systems theory calls the field of "semi-periphery," and what follows behind it is a radical foreclosing by post-colonial criticism on settler/colonial writing: the radical ambivalence of colonialism's middle ground.

This foreclosing most commonly takes the rather simple form of stark forgetfulness, of overlooking the Second World entirely as though its literature and its critical traditions didn't even exist. An example of this for-

STEPHEN SLEMON

getfulness is provided by Laura Donaldson in her otherwise scrupulously researched article in *Diacritics* entitled "The Miranda Complex." Here Donaldson argues that while the trope of Prospero and Caliban has been done to death in anti-colonialist criticism (and here she relies upon an article by Huston Baker published in *Critical Inquiry* as her authority), the trope of Miranda and Caliban – the trope of the Anglo-European daughter in the multiple interpellations of both colonialism and patriarchy – has been "virtually ignored" (68) by literary criticism. From a Second-World perspective, however, what *really* remains "virtually ignored" – in a gesture so common as to be symptomatic of much of the US-based, First-World "post-colonial" critical practice – is that body of critical work, published in Second-World critical journals by scholars such as Diana Brydon and Chantal Zabus, which discusses the Miranda-Caliban trope precisely in the terms Donaldson's article calls for. In cases like this, where *Diacritics* cites *Critical Inquiry*, Donaldson cites Baker, the academic star-system of First-World criticism inscribes itself wholesale into post-colonial studies, and a large and important body of astute anti-colonial literary critical work ends up simply getting lost in the move.

A more important form of this foreclosing process, however, is underscored by a much more substantive critical concern: and that is to preserve the concept of cultural *difference* in the critical articulation of literary post-colonialism. Arun Mukherjee's article, for example, advances in exemplary form the argument that "post-colonial" studies in literary resistance inherently totalize dissimilar cultures when they consider the resistances to colonialism of both imperialism's "white cousins" and its black, colonized subjects. Specifically, Mukherjee argues, this critical practice dangerously overlooks "realist" writing from the Third and Fourth Worlds, and ends up privileging the kind of post-colonial writing which takes resistance to colonialism as its primary objective. The argument for a post-colonial critical practice here, of course, has nothing to do with the kind of wilful forgetfulness which characterizes Donaldson's misreading; but it does promulgate a misreading of its own, I would argue, in mistaking the *project* of anti-colonialist criticism with the kind of nation-based descriptive criticism which characterizes the first post-colonial critical field I have been discussing. Here, I suspect, the conflation between the second and third post-colonial critical fields has become so naturalized that the *specific* project of the third post-colonial field seems no longer recognizable: the project of articulating the forms – and modes, and tropes, and figures – of anti-colonialist textual resistance, *wherever* they occur, and in *all* of their guises. A more damaging critique of the kind of critical practice Mukherjee objects to, I think, lies in the propensity of anti-colonialist critics (like myself) to overlook the range of anti-colonialist gestures which inhabit First-World, or imperial, writing itself.

At any rate, the new binaristic absolutism which seems to come in the wake of First-World accommodation to the fact of post-colonial literary and cultural criticism seems to be working in several ways to drive that trans-national region of ex-colonial settler cultures away from the field of post-colonial literary representation. The Second World of writing within the ambit of colonialism is in danger of disappearing: because it is not sufficiently pure in its anti-colonialism, because it does not offer up an experiential grounding in a common "Third-World" aesthetics, because its modalities of *post*-coloniality are too ambivalent, too occasional and uncommon, for inclusion within the field. This debate over the scope and nature of the "post-colonial," I now want to argue, has enormous investments in the second debate I want to discuss in this paper, for in fact the idea of both literary and political *resistance* to colonialist power is the hidden term, the foundational concept, upon which *all* these distinctions in the modality of the "post-colonial" actually rest.

The debate over literary resistance is in fact a very complicated one, and criticism offers a seemingly endless set of configurations for the kinds of reading and writing practices which a theory of resistance might possibly comprise. In order to simplify this debate, however, I want to suggest that in rudimentary form the idea of literary resistance collapses into two general movements or concepts, each of which contains important distinctions that I won't address here.

The first concept of resistance is most clearly put forward by Selwyn Cudjoe in his *Resistance and Caribbean Literature* and by Barbara Harlow in her *Resistance Literature*. For Cudjoe and Harlow, resistance is an act, or a set of acts, that is designed to rid a people of its oppressors, and it so thoroughly infuses the experience of living under oppression that it becomes an almost autonomous aesthetic principle. *Literary* resistance, under these conditions, can be seen as a form of contractual understanding between text and reader, one which is embedded in an experiential dimension and buttressed by a political and cultural aesthetic at work in the culture. And "resistance literature," in this definition, can thus be seen as that category of literary writing which emerges as an integral part of an organized struggle or resistance for national liberation.

This argument for literary "resistance" is an important one to hold on to – but it is also a strangely untheorized position, for it fails to address three major areas of critical concern. The first is a political concern: namely, that centre/periphery notions of resistance can actually work to *reinscribe* centre/periphery relations and can "serve an institutional function of securing the dominant narratives" (Sharpe 139). The second problem with this argument is that it assumes that literary resistance is simply somehow *there* in the literary text as a structure of intentionality, and *there*

STEPHEN SLEMON

in the social text as a communicative gesture of pure availability. Post-Lacanian and post-Althusserian theories of the *constructedness* of subjectivity, however, would contest such easy access to representational purity, and would argue instead that resistance is grounded in the *multiple* and *contradictory* structures of ideological interpellation or subject-formation – which would call down the notion that resistance can *ever* be "purely" intended or "purely" expressed in representational or communicative models. The third problem with this argument is that it has to set aside the very persuasive theory of power which Foucault puts forward in his *The Archaeology of Knowledge*: the theory that power *itself* inscribes its resistances and so, in the process, seeks to contain them. It is this third objection, especially, which has energized the post-structuralist project of theorizing literary resistance – and in order to clarify what is going on in that theatre of critical activity I want to focus especially on Jenny Sharpe's wonderful article in *Modern Fiction Studies* entitled "Figures of Colonial Resistance."

Sharpe's article involves a reconsideration of the work of theorists such as Gayatri Spivak, Homi Bhabha, Abdul JanMohamed, and Benita Parry, each of whom has worked to correct the critical "tendency to presume the transparency" of literary resistance in colonial and post-colonial writing (138), and who collectively have worked to examine the ways in which resistance in writing must go beyond the mere "questioning" of colonialist authority. There are important differences in how all of these theorists define literary resistance, but the two key points Sharpe draws out are, first, that you can never *easily* locate the sites of anti-colonial resistance – since resistance itself is always in some measure an "effect of the contradictory representation of colonial authority" (145) and never simply a "reversal" of power – and secondly, that resistance itself is therefore never *purely* resistance, never *simply* there in the text or the interpretive community, but is always *necessarily* complicit in the apparatus it seeks to transgress. As Sharpe puts it: "the colonial subject who can answer the colonizers back is the product of the same vast ideological machinery that silences the subaltern" (143); and what she is saying here, basically, is that a *theory* of literary resistance *must* recognize the inescapable partiality, the incompleteness, the untranscendable *ambiguity* of literary or indeed *any* contra/dictory or contestatory act which employs a First-World medium for the figuration of a Third-World resistance, and which predicates a semiotics of *refusal* on a gestural mechanism whose first act must always be an acknowledgement and a *recognition* of the reach of colonialist power.

Sharpe's argument, that is, underscores the way in which literary resistance is necessarily in a place of ambivalence: between systems, between discursive worlds, implicit and complicit in both of them. And from this recognition comes the very startling but inevitable claim – made most spectacularly by Tim Brennan in his book on *Salmon Rushdie and the Third World* – that the Third-World resistance writer, the Third-World resistance text, is necessarily self-produced as a doubly-emplaced and *mediated* figure – Brennan's term is "Third-World Cosmopolitan" – between the First and the Third World, and *within* the ambit of a First-World politics.

This brings me at last to the central thesis of my paper, which begins with the observation that there is a contradiction within the dominant trajectory of First-World post-colonial critical theory here – for that same theory which argues persuasively for the necessary *ambivalence* of post-colonial literary resistance, and which works to emplace that resistance squarely *between* First- and Third-World structures of representation, *also* wants to assign "Second-World" or ex-colonial settler literatures unproblematically to the category of the literature of empire, the literature of the First World, precisely *because* of its ambivalent position within the First-World/Third-World, colonizer/colonized binary. Logically, however, it would seem that the argument being made by Spivak, Bhabha, Sharpe, and others about the ambivalence of literary and other resistances – the argument that resistance texts are necessarily double, necessarily mediated, in their social location – is in fact nothing less than an argument *for* the emplacement of "Second-World" literary texts within the field of the "post-colonial": for if there *is* only a space for a *pure* Third- and Fourth-World resistance outside the First-World hegemony, then *either* you have to return to the baldly untheorized notion which informs the first position in the debate over literary resistance, *or* you have to admit that at least as far as writing is concerned, the "field" of the genuinely *post*-colonial can never *actually* exist.

It is for this reason, I think, and not because of some vestigial nostalgia for an empire upon which the sun will never set, that many critics and theorists have argued long and hard for the preservation of white Australian, New Zealander, southern African, and Canadian literatures within the field of comparative "post-colonial" literary studies. At bottom, the argument here is the one which Alan Lawson made at The Badlands Conference in Calgary in 1986: namely, that in order to avoid essentialism and to escape theoretical absolutism, we might profitably think of the category of the settler cultures of Australia, Canada, southern Africa, and New Zealand as inhabiting a "Second World" of discursive polemics – of inhabiting, that is, the space of dynamic *relation* between those "apparently antagonistic, static, aggressive, [and] disjunctive" (68) binaries which colonialism "settles" upon a landscape: binaries such as colonizer and colonized, foreign and native, settler and indigene, home and away. Lawson is careful to note that such a doubleness or ambivalence in emplacement is by no means an exclusive domain or prerogative for "Second-World" writing, and by no means an essentialist category governing *all* activity going on within the settler literatures. Rather, the "Second World" – like the third of the three "post-colonial" critical fields I have been discussing – is at root a *reading position*, and one which is and often has been taken up in settler and ex-colonial literature and criticism. The "Second World," that is, like "post-colonial criticism" itself, is a critical manoeuvre, a reading and writing action; and embedded within it is a theory of communicative action akin in some ways to Clifford Geertz's thesis about "intermediary knowledge," or Gadamer's theory of an interpretive "fusion of horizons." "The inherent awareness of both 'there' and 'here' and the cultural ambiguity of these terms," writes Lawson, "are not so much the boundaries of its cultural matrix, nor tensions to be resolved, but a space *within* which [the Second-World, post-colonial literary text] may move *while* speaking" (69). Lawson's definition of literary representation in the discursive "Second World" thus articulates a figure for what many First-World critical theorists would correctly define as the limits and the condition of *post-colonial* forms of literary resistance. The irony is that many of those same First-World critics would define that "post-colonial" as exclusively the domain of the Third and Fourth Worlds.

But what perhaps marks a *genuine* difference in the contestatory activity of Second- and Third-World post-colonial writing, I now want to argue, is that the *illusion* of a stable self/other, here/there binary division has *never* been available to Second-World writers, and that as a result the sites of figural contestation between oppressor and oppressed, colonizer and colonized, have been taken *inward* and *internalized* in Second-World post-colonial textual practice. By this I mean that the *ambivalence* of literary resistance itself is the "always already" condition of Second-World settler and post-colonial literary writing, for in the white literatures of Australia, or New Zealand, or Canada, or southern Africa, anti-colonialist resistance has *never* been directed at an object or a discursive structure which can be seen purely external to the self. The Second-World writer, the Second-World text, that is, has always been complicit in colonialism's territorial appropriation of land, and voice, and agency, and this has been their inescapable condition even at those moments when they have promulgated their most strident and most spectacular figures of post-colonial resistance. In the Second World, anti-colonialist resistances in literature must necessarily *cut across the individual subject*, and as they do so they also, necessarily, contribute towards that theoretically rigorous understanding of textual resistance which post-colonial *critical* theory is only now learning how to recognize. This ambivalence of emplacement is the *condition* of their possibility; it has been since the beginning; and it is therefore scarcely surprising that the ambivalent, the mediated, the conditional, and the radically *compromised* literatures of this undefinable Second World have an enormous amount yet to tell to "theory" about the nature of literary resistance.

This *internalization* of the object of resistance in Second-World literatures, this internalization of the self/other binary of colonialist relations, explains why it is that it has always been Second-World *literary* writing rather than Second-World *critical* writing which has occupied the vanguard of a Second-World post-colonial literary or critical *theory*. Literary writing is *about* internalized conflict, whereas critical writing – for most practitioners – is still grounded in the ideology of unitariness, and coherence, and specific argumentative drive. For this reason, Second-World *critical* writing – with some spectacularly transgressive exceptions – has tended to miss out on the rigours of what, I would argue, comprises a necessarily ambivalent, necessarily contra/dictory or incoherent, anticolonialist *theory* of resistance. In literary documents such as De Mille's *Strange Manuscript* or Furphy's *Such Is Life*, to name two nineteenth-century examples, or in the "re-historical" fictions of writers such as Fiona Kidman, Ian Wedde, Thea Astley, Peter Carey, Kate Grenville, Barbara Hanrahan, Daphne Marlatt, Susan Swan, and Rudy Wiebe – to name only a *few* from the contemporary period – this necessary *entanglement* of anticolonial resistances within the colonialist machineries they seek to displace has been consistently thematized, consistently worked *through*, in ways that the unitary and logical demands of critical argumentation, at least in its traditional genres, have simply not allowed.

A fully adequate version of the argument I am making here would attempt to show in detail how at least one of these Second-World fictional texts manages to articulate a post-colonial or anti-colonial reading for resistance. For the purposes of the larger debate I am attempting to address, however, it may prove more useful to close with two subsidiary arguments about post-colonial critical practice, and then to open the floor – if one can do that in writing – to the kinds of critical cross-questioning which the field of post-colonial research and teaching at present needs to engage with.

The first point concerns a loss that I think we sustain if we hold too nostalgically to an expanded but at heart nation-based model of post-colonial criticism – whether that model applies to a "Commonwealth" or to a "Third- and Fourth-World" constituency. If "post-colonial literature" becomes a term for designating an essential unitariness in the lived experience of different and dispersed peoples, all of the critical problems which accrue around nationalist models of critical definition – the hegemonic force of the concept of "nation," for example, and the necessary blindness that the concept settles upon the internally marginalized – will simply be carried forward into a new object of study, and we will be constrained to replay in our field all of the debates that have troubled each one of the positivist categories of period and place that comprise traditional English studies. Our object of attention will be differentiated from that of other areas by the usual categories, but our field, in essence, will remain an add-on discipline, a marker of the infinite ability of traditional English studies to accommodate national and historical difference within its inherently liberal embrace. We have a chance, however, to employ our field more radically: we can use it to raise questions about the kinds of work literary documents perform in culture, and we can use it to question the discourses of inclusivity and "coverage" which have so often been deployed within English studies to depoliticize literary writing and to obscure the struggle for power which takes place within textual representation.

The second and final point I want to make concerns the way in which our interest in multiple, racially mixed, gendered and engendered, national and trans-national post-colonial literatures not only carries us inescapably into the theatre of colonialist and neo-colonialist power relations, but also carries us into the figurative domains of other modes of power as they appear in and are contested through the field of literary writing. Post-colonial texts are *also* concerned with the problem of privilege through racism and patriarchy, also at work contesting the kinds of hierarchical exclusion which operate through homophobia, and nationalism, and adultism; and in part this means that the debate over the post-colonial field and over the question of anti-colonialist literary resistance will never tell us everything about the struggles for power that actually take place under colonialism's baleful gaze. Rather, this debate tells us that all of our negotiations for change – in literature and criticism, in pedagogy, in immediate political engagement – are marked by provisionality and partiality, and are bounded by an historical specificity that does not simply translate itself into other theatres of social contestation. But more encouragingly, it also hints to us of the presence of figural activity for agency and resistance going on in cultural places we have somehow been taught to ignore. We need to specify our resistances to power, but we need also to recognize the ubiquity of resistances and to understand their incompleteness, their strengths, their losses and their gains. "There is another world, but it is in this one," quotes Lawson. There is also a *second* world of post-colonial literary resistance, but it inhabits a place – a place of radical ambivalence – where too much post-colonial criticism in the First World has so far forgotten to look.

Works Cited

Brennan, Timothy. *Salman Rushdie and the Third World: Myths of the Nation.* London: Macmillan, 1989.

Brydon, Diana. "Re-writing *The Tempest.*" *World Literature Written in English* 23.1 (1984): 75–88.

Cudjoe, Selwyn R. *Resistance and Caribbean Literature.* Athens: Ohio UP, 1980.

Donaldson, Laura E. "The Miranda Complex: Colonialism and the Question of Feminist Reading." *Diacritics* 18.3 (1988): 65–77.

Foucault, Michel. *The Archaeology of Knowledge.* Trans. A.M. Sheridan Smith. New York: Pantheon, 1972.

Harlow, Barbara. *Resistance Literature.* New York and London: Methuen, 1987.

Hutcheon, Linda. "'Circling the Downspout of Empire': Post-Colonialism and Postmodernism." *Ariel* 20.4 (1989): 149–75.

Lawson, Alan. "A Cultural Paradigm for the Second World." The Badlands Conference on Canadian and Australian Literatures. U of Calgary. 29 Aug. 1986. *Australian-Canadian Studies* 9.1-2 (1991): 67–78.

Mukherjee, Arun. "Whose Post-Colonialism and Whose Postmodernism?" *World Literature Written in English* 30.2 (1990): 1–9.

Sharpe, Jenny. "Figures of Colonial Resistance." *Modern Fiction Studies* 35 (1989): 137–55.

Zabus, Chantal. "A Calibanic Tempest in Anglophone and Francophone New World Writing." *Canadian Literature* 104 (1985): 35–50.

Godzilla vs. Post-Colonial

Thomas King

I grew up in Northern California, and I grew up fast. I don't mean that I was raised in a tough part of town where you had to fight to survive. I was raised in a small town in the foothills, quite pastoral in fact. I mean I grew up all at once. By my first year of high school, I already had my full height, while most of my friends were just beginning to grow.

We had a basketball team at the high school and a basketball coach who considered himself somewhat of an authority on the subject of talent. He could spot it, he said. And he spotted me. He told me I had a talent for the game, and that I should come out for the team. With my size, he said, I would be a natural player. I was flattered.

I wish I could tell you that I excelled at basketball, that I was an all-star, that college coaches came to see me play. But the truth of the matter is, I wasn't even mediocre. Had I not been so very young and so very serious, I might have laughed at my attempts to run and bounce a ball at the same time. Certainly most everyone who saw me play did.

Now before you think that my embarrassment in basketball was the fault of an overzealous coach, you have to remember that we both made more or less the same assumption. The coach assumed that because I was tall, I would be a good player. And once the coach called my height to my attention and encouraged me, I assumed the same thing. We spent the rest of our time together trying to figure out why I was so bad.

Just before the first game of my second season, I tore my knee, mercifully ending my basketball career. My experience taught me little about basketball, but it did teach me a great deal about assumptions.

Assumptions are a dangerous thing. They are especially dangerous when we do not even see that the premise from which we start a discussion is not the hard fact that we thought it was, but one of the fancies we churn out of our imaginations to help us get from the beginning of an idea to the end.

Which brings me, albeit by a circuitous route, to post-colonial literature. I am not a theorist. It's not an apology, but it is a fact. So I can not talk to the internal structure of the theory itself, how it works, or what it tells us about the art of language and the art of literature. Nor can I participate to any great extent in what Linda Hutcheon calls "the de-doxifying project of postmodernism."

But having played basketball, I can talk about the assumptions that the term post-colonial makes. It is, first of all, part of a triumvirate. In order to get to "post," we have to wend our way through no small amount of literary history, acknowledging the existence of its antecedents, pre-colonial and colonial. In the case of Native literature, we can say that pre-colonial literature was that literature, oral in nature, that was in existence prior to European contact, a literature that existed exclusively within specific cultural communities.

Post-colonial literature, then, must be the literature produced by Native people sometime after colonization, a literature that arises in large part out of the experience that is colonization. These particular terms allow us to talk about Native literature as a literature that can be counterpoint to Canadian literature, a new voice, if you will, a different voice in the literary amphitheatre. I rather like the idea of post-colonial literature, because it promises to set me apart from the masses and suggests that what I have to offer is new and exciting. But then again, I rather liked the idea of playing basketball, too.

I said at the beginning that I was not a theorist and was not going to concern myself with how post-colonialism operates as a critical method. But I am concerned with what the term says about Natives and Native literature and the initial assumptions it makes about us and our cultures.

When I made that rather simplistic comparison between pre-colonial and post-colonial, I left out one of the players, rather like talking about pre-pubescence and post-pubescence without mentioning puberty. My apologies. It was a trick to make you think I was going to say something profound, when, in fact, I was going to make the rather simple observation that in the case of pre- and post-pubescence and pre- and post-colonial, the pivot around which we move is puberty and colonialism. But here, I'm lying again. Another trick, I'm afraid, for in puberty's case, the precedent, the root, and the antecedent are, at least, all part of a whole, whereas in the case of colonialism – within a discussion of Native literature – the term has little to do with the literature itself. It is both separate from and antithetical to what came before and what came after.

Pre-colonial literature, as we use the term in North America, has no relationship whatsoever to colonial literature. The two are neither part of a biological or natural cycle nor does the one anticipate the other, while the full complement of terms – pre-colonial, colonial, and post-colonial – reeks of unabashed ethnocentrism and well-meaning dismissal, and they point to a deep-seated assumption that is at the heart of most well-intentioned studies of Native literatures.

While post-colonialism purports to be a method by which we can begin to look at those literatures which are formed out of the struggle of the oppressed against the oppressor, the colonized and the colonizer, the term itself assumes that the starting point for that discussion is the advent of Europeans in North America. At the same time, the term organizes the literature progressively suggesting that there is both progress and improvement. No less distressing, it also assumes that the struggle between guardian and ward is the catalyst for contemporary Native literature, providing those of us who write with method and topic. And, worst of all, the idea of post-colonial writing effectively cuts us off from our traditions, traditions that were in place before colonialism ever became a question, traditions which have come down to us through our cultures in spite of colonization, and it supposes that contemporary Native writing is largely a construct of oppression. Ironically, while the term itself – post-colonial – strives to escape to find new centres, it remains, in the end, a hostage to nationalism.

As a contemporary Native writer, I am quite unwilling to make these assumptions, and I am quite unwilling to use these terms.

A friend of mine cautioned me about this stridency and pointed out that post-colonial is a perfectly good term to use for that literature which is, in fact, a reaction to the historical impositions of colonialization. She suggested I look at Maria Campbell's *Halfbreed* and Beatrice Culleton's *In Search of April Raintree* as examples of works for which the term is appropriate. She further suggested that post-colonial was not such a simple thing, that much of what I was concerned with – centres, difference, totalizing, hegemony, margins – was being addressed by post-colonial methodology. If this is true, then it is unfortunate that the method has such an albatross – as the term – hanging around its neck. But I must admit that I remain sceptical that such a term could describe a non-centred, non-nationalistic method.

If we are to use terms to describe the various stages or changes in Native literature as it has become written, while at the same time remaining oral, and as it has expanded from a specific language base to a multiple language base, we need to find descriptors which do not invoke the cant of progress and which are not joined at the hip with nationalism. Post-colonial might be an excellent term to use to describe Canadian literature, but it will not do to describe Native literature.

As a Native writer, I lean towards terms such as tribal, interfusional, polemical, and associational to describe the range of Native writing. I prefer these terms for a variety of reasons: they tend to be less centred and do not, within the terms themselves, privilege one culture over another; they avoid the sense of progress in which primitivism gives way to sophistication, suggesting as it does that such movement is both natural and desirable; they identify points on a cultural and literary continuum for Native literature which do not depend on anomalies such as the arrival of Europeans in North America or the advent of non-Native literature in this hemisphere, what Marie Baker likes to call "settler litter." At the same time, these terms are not "bags" into which we can collect and store the whole of Native literature. They are, more properly, vantage points from which we can see a particular literary landscape.

Two of these terms are self-apparent: tribal and polemical. Tribal refers to that literature which exists primarily within a tribe or a community, literature that is shared almost exclusively by members of that community, and literature that is presented and retained in a Native language. It is virtually invisible outside its community, partly because of the barrier of language and partly because it has little interest in making itself available to an outside audience. In some cases, tribes – the Hopi come to mind – take great pains in limiting access to parts of their literature only to members of their immediate community. Polemical refers to that literature either in a Native language or in English, French, etc. that concerns itself with the clash of Native and non-Native cultures or with the championing of Native values over non-Native values. Like Beatrice Culleton's *In Search of April Raintree*, Maria Campbell's *Halfbreed*, D'Arcy McNickle's *The Surrounded* and *Wind from an Enemy Sky*, and Howard Adams' *Prison of Grass*, polemical literature chronicles the imposition of non-Native expectations and insistences (political, social, scientific) on Native communities and the methods of resistance employed by Native people in order to maintain both their communities and cultures.

The terms interfusional and associational are not as readily apparent. I'm using interfusional to describe that part of Native literature which is a blending of oral literature and written literature. While there are contemporary examples that *suggest* the nature of interfusional literature – some of the translations of Dennis Tedlock and Dell Hymes work along with those of Howard Norman in *The Wishing Bone Cycle* – the only complete example we have of interfusional literature is Harry Robinson's *Write It on Your Heart*.

The stories in Robinson's collection are told in English and written in English, but the patterns, metaphors, structures as well as the themes and characters come primarily from oral literature. More than this, Robinson, within the confines of written language, is successful in creating an oral voice. He does this in a rather ingenious way. He develops what we might want to call an oral syntax that defeats readers' efforts to read the stories silently to themselves, a syntax that encourages readers to read the stories out loud.

The common complaint that we make of oral literature that has been translated into English is that we lose the voice of the storyteller, the gestures, the music, and the interaction between storyteller and audience. But by forcing the reader to read aloud, Robinson's prose, to a large extent, avoids this loss, re-creating at once the storyteller and the performance.

Yeah, I'll tell you "Cat With the Boots On."
Riding boots on.
That's the stories, the first stories.
There was a big ranch, not around here.
That's someplace in European.
Overseas.
That's a long time, shortly after the "imbellable" stories.
But this is part "imbellable" stories.
It's not Indian stories.
This is white people stories,
        because I learned this from the white people.
Not the white man.
The white man tell his son,
        that's Allison – John Fall Allison.
White man.
He is the one that tell the stories to his son.
His son, Bert Allison.
His son was a half Indian and a half white,
        because his mother was an Indian.
And his father was a white man.
So his father told him these stories.
But he told me – Bert Allison.
So he told me,
        "This is not Indian stories.
        White man stories."
You understand that?

This metamorphosis – written to oral, reader to speaker – is no mean trick, one that Robinson accomplishes with relative ease. More important, his prose has become a source of inspiration and influence for other Native writers such as Jeannette Armstrong and myself.

Associational literature is the body of literature that has been created, for the most part, by contemporary Native writers. While no one set of criteria will do to describe it fully, it possesses a series of attributes that help to give it form.

Associational literature, most often, describes a Native community. While it may also describe a non-Native community, it avoids centring the story on the non-Native community or on a conflict between the two cultures, concentrating instead on the daily activities and intricacies of Native life and organizing the elements of plot along a rather flat narrative line that ignores the ubiquitous climaxes and resolutions that are so valued in non-Native literature. In addition to this flat narrative line, associational literature leans towards the group rather than the single, isolated character, creating a fiction that de-values heroes and villains in favour of the members of a community, a fiction which eschews judgements and conclusions.

For the non-Native reader, this literature provides a limited and particular access to a Native world, allowing the reader to associate with that world without being encouraged to feel a part of it. It does not pander to non-Native expectations concerning the glamour and/or horror of Native life, and it especially avoids those media phantasms – glitzy ceremonies, yuppie shamanism, diet philosophies (literary tourism as one critic called them) – that writers such as Carlos Castenada and Lynn Andrews have conjured up for the current generation of gullible readers.

For the Native reader, associational literature helps to remind us of the continuing values of our cultures, and it reinforces the notion that, in addition to the usable past that the concurrence of oral literature and traditional history provides us with, we also have an active present marked by cultural tenacity and a viable future which may well organize itself around major revivals of language, philosophy, and spiritualism.

Two of the better examples of associational literature are Basil H. Johnston's *Indian School Days* and Ruby Slipperjack's *Honour the Sun*. Each creates an Indian community, Johnston at a Jesuit boarding school, Slipperjack in northern Ontario. The novels themselves describe daily activities and the interaction of the community itself, and, aside from the first-person narrator, no one character is given preference over another.

Because *Indian School Days* is about a boarding school, we might well expect to see a sustained attack on this particularly colonial institution, and, while Johnston does on occasion criticize the expectations that the Jesuits have for their Native wards, he defuses most of the conflicts by refusing to make easy judgements and by granting responsibility and choice to both the Jesuits and the Native boys. The boys are not portrayed as hapless victims, and the Jesuits are not cast as uncaring jailers. Particularly telling are the concerted efforts made by the clerics and the students to care for the very young students, "babies" as Johnston calls them, who "seldom laughed or smiled and often cried and whimpered during the day and at night." While the older boys tried to act "as guardians or as big brothers," the burden of care "fell on the young scholastics, who had a much more fatherly air than the senior boys in Grades 7 and 8."

Ruby Slipperjack concerns herself with an isolated Native community in northern Ontario. Written in the form of a diary, the book follows the everyday life of an extended family. The book has no pretense at plot nor is there a desire to glorify traditional Native life. The story is told in simple and unassuming prose that focuses on relationships:

THOMAS KING

There are seven of us in the family, four girls and three boys. My oldest brother got married and went away a long time ago. My other brother, Wess, spends most of his time at the cabin on our old trapline. The rest of us girls are all here. We live in a one-room cabin our father built before he died. Mom got someone to make a small addition at the back a couple of years ago. That's where she sleeps with our little brother, Brian. Brian was just a little baby when my father died and he's about six years old now. The rest of us sleep in the main room on two double beds and a bunk bed.

Three other kids live with us. Mom looks after them because their parents left their home. I guess three more doesn't make much difference aside from the fact the food and clothes have to stretch a little further. The father came to see them once. I heard Mom say that she has never gotten a penny for their keep. Their mother has never come. Actually, I am closer to them than to my own sisters, since mine are gone all winter. Maggie and Jane have become my regular sisters and Vera and Annie are my special sisters when they are home in the summer.

Within the novel, the narrator neither posits the superiority of Native culture over non-Native culture nor suggests that the ills that beset the community come from outside it. Her brother's tuberculosis, John Bull's violent rampages, and the mother's eventual alcoholism are mentioned and lamented, but they are presented in a non-judgemental fashion and do not provide an occasion for accusation and blame either of non-Native culture at large or the Native community itself.

Both books provide access to a Native world, but the access is not unlimited. It is, in fact, remarkably limited access. While Johnston hints at some of the reasons why Indian parents allow their children to be placed at St. Peter Claver's, he does not elaborate on the complex cultural dynamics that have helped to maintain these schools. Much of this is hidden, as are the Native communities outside the school from which the students come. While Slipperjack appears more forthright in her description of the family and the community, she refuses to share with us the reasons for the narrator's mother's alcoholism, the cause of John Bull's violent behaviour, and the reasons for the narrator's leaving the community. In the end, what is most apparent in these two books is not the information received but the silences that each writer maintains. Non-Natives may, as readers, come to an association with these communities, but they remain, always, outsiders.

Now it goes without saying that creating terms simply to replace other terms is, in most instances, a solipsistic exercise, and I do not offer these terms as replacements for the term post-colonial so much as to demonstrate the difficulties that the people and the literature for which the term was, in part, created have with the assumptions that the term embodies.

Unlike post-colonial, the terms tribal, interfusional, polemical, and associational do not establish a chronological order nor do they open and close literary frontiers. They avoid a nationalistic centre, and they do not depend on the arrival of Europeans for their *raison d'être*.

At the same time, for all the range they cover, they do not comfortably contain the work of such Native writers as Gerald Vizenor and Craig Kee Strete. Vizenor's postmodern novels *Darkness in St. Louis Bearheart* and *Griever: An American Monkey King in China* and Strete's short story collections of surreal and speculative fiction *The Bleeding Man* and *If All Else Fails* cross the lines that definitions – no matter how loose – create.

And it may be that these terms will not do in the end at all. Yet I cannot let post-colonial stand – particularly as a term – for, at its heart, it is an act of imagination and an act of imperialism that demands that I imagine myself as something I did not choose to be, as something I would not choose to become.

Back to the Future: The Short Story in Canada and the Writing of Literary History

W.H. New

My subject is threefold. I am concerned with the English-language short story in Canada, with the writing of literary history, and with the biases of time and critical expectation that have helped shape both story and history. I come to this topic from the work on which I have been recently engaged, trying to write literary history, and from my increasing awareness of the pressures of conformity and precedent that affect form, organization, judgement, and tone. I will focus ultimately on the writing of the most recent (1990) volume of the *Literary History of Canada*, but I will begin tangentially, referring to the first (1965) volume of this project and to the heritage of critical attitude on which it unconsciously draws. In particular I will look at attitudes to the short story, as a paradigm by which to estimate the processes of critical system.

I begin in retrospect in order to avoid the first pitfall of prospect: the temptation of predicting future practice in any art form. Existing volumes of literary history provide an illustration here. I can refer (as all commentators on Canadian short fiction now do) to a rash assertion Hugo McPherson made in 1965 in the "Fiction: 1940-1960" chapter of the first edition of the *Literary History of Canada*. He simply announced that the short story in Canada was dying out. He wrote: "Compared with *belles-lettres* and humour, the record of the short story is good, but its importance in Canadian expression is declining.... [T]he short story has lost much of its prestige; a generation ago it was the recognized proving-ground for aspiring novelists.... The short story ... [used to be] a major form, and a form particularly suited to the needs of writers who could not find time for the extended effort demanded of the novel" (720-21). But with the advent of television, "magazines recognized that they could not compete with the 'instant' short fiction of television drama, and turned almost exclusively to educational or documentary essays.... Special pleas for the short story would be futile at this date" (720-21). He went on to mention Wilson, Raddall, Garner, Gallant, Ross, Reaney, Spettigue, Ludwig, and Alice Munro, but said that Canadian writers had now to compete in international markets and concluded: "In this difficult, exacting, and now declining genre, Morley Callaghan is still the unacknowledged master" (720-21). When the second edition of the *Literary History of Canada* appeared in 1976, these generalizations were excised, and some account was taken of 1960s activities in the genre. Since 1976, far from declining, the form has burgeoned.

This statement does not mean that television drama has therefore declined; the point is not to see genres as mutually exclusive, binary alternatives, but as multiple options. There have been scores of books and individual stories to appear; also some short story theory by Canadians (notably Mary Louise Pratt), and also several anthologies which (following on those by Pacey and Weaver – I am thinking of collections edited by Metcalf, Bowering, Wiebe, Phillips, Nichol, Blaise, and Hancock) have provided some commentary on short fiction in their introductions and in apparatuses designed for student readers. My first concern here, however, is not – at least directly – with these recent developments. I am concerned more with the paucity of commentary before they came into existence and with the fact of statements like those of McPherson. What presumptions underlie them? How do such presumptions affect critical judgements? To what degree do they express critical expectations of literary history rather than constitute anything more than superficial observations of aesthetic practice? And why?

In order to approach these questions – I say "approach" deliberately, rather than "answer" – I want to review the comments on short fiction made by three writers prior to 1930, and then to consider some of the implications they have for an understanding both of the genre and of its history (real or received) in Canada. The three writers are Allan Douglas Brodie, for "Canadian Short-Story Writers," published in February 1895; Archibald MacMechan, for his 1924 history *Head-Waters of Canadian Literature*; and B.K. Sandwell, for his review of Raymond Knister's 1928 anthology *Canadian Short Stories*, in the August 25, 1928 issue of *Saturday Night*. In some ways, all three of them lie behind the generic assessments that structure the first edition of the *Literary History of Canada*.

Brodie's ten-page profile of current short story writers of the 1890s appeared in *The Canadian Magazine*; it appealed to a general readership. The influence of the American critic Brander Matthews suggests itself in the hyphen between "short" and "story" in Brodie's title (Matthews had employed the term "short-story" to describe a particular kind of magazine-length fiction, with such characteristics as brevity and ingenuity; unity and compression; action; logical structure; and, if possible, fantasy). But the hyphen disappears between Brodie's title and Brodie's text, so the influence may be illusory, an indication more of the copy editor's impulse than the critic's intention. Indeed, Brodie appears to be more concerned to celebrate a few national personalities (Macdonald Oxley, Marjory MacMurchy, Duncan Campbell Scott, Maud Ogilvy, Stuart Livingston, and a few others) than to reflect on the character of the art form.

His essay does open with a few justifications for the genre, but while these give lip service to verbal skill, they explain the art of the short story more fundamentally as a literary form that responds to laws of speed and demand. "In these days of excitement and confusion," Brodie writes, "caused by the general and all-absorbing pursuit of the elusive but ever mighty dollar, nothing plays so important a part in the delightful world of literature – even Canadian literature – as the 'short story.' The days of the three-volume novel are past and gone, it is earnestly hoped, never to return.... When [people now] wish to thoroughly enjoy themselves in a literary way, they crave, and must have, a terse, pithy, racy, and cleverly told short story, the writing of which is an art in itself" (334). Such comments then become his justification for whatever it is that Canadian magazine writers do. He continues: "It is a credit, rather than otherwise, to that little band of bright Canadian writers depicted in this article, that they have chosen, and have ably developed, this particular field of literature" (334). This assertion covertly declares a good deal about hierarchies in literary taste, hierarchies which themselves suggest that the criteria for judgement stem from outside the country. In Brodie's words, "Canadians are proud of the successes and triumphs of [those who have gone] abroad [meaning E.W. Thomson, Gilbert Parker, and Robert Barr]; but Canadians do not, or should not, forget that we still have some clever literary people among us" (334-35). For him there is, implicitly, a moral virtue in national enthusiasm, which "good" literature serves. The words of praise Brodie goes on to use begin after awhile to sound formulaic – D.C. Scott's works possess, he says, "both dramatic interest, and a certain poetic beauty all their own" (338); Livingston's are "possessed of power, brilliancy, and a certain poetic undercurrent" (343); MacMurchy and William McLennan are praised respectively for "a touch of pathos ... applied with a gentle and loving hand" (338), and for "dramatic interest" and "a pathos which is marvellously attractive" (340-41). It is never clear how these characteristics meet the demands for a clever, pithy, racy, terse literature. It suffices simply to name and praise; the nationality of the writers and the fact of their publishing magazine-length fiction constitute self-evident (and for Brodie interconnected) aesthetic values.

Some twenty-nine years later, Archibald MacMechan was less tolerant than Brodie of contemporary romance ("Parker," he wrote ironically, "has written many tales; and several are ostensibly Canadian in scene" [141]), but MacMechan was no less bound up than Brodie was in the unstated poetics of piety and received tradition. His title metaphor tells us something of his perspective: "Head-waters" is the term through which he conventionally implies a nation of source and flow, a single source and a linear flow, a notion of mainstream – like history itself (and the parallel is one which MacMechan's book argues). Indeed, MacMechan's main interest, in practice, is in history, for all his initial stated concerns about literature being the soul of a people. T.C. Haliburton, for example, is treated as a historian first and a satirist second, and such a set of priorities characterizes the drift of the book as a whole.

History for MacMechan is the fundament of culture rather than simply a context for it or a systematic rendering of it. History is deemed to be at once aesthetic and factual, a model for literary excellence. And then the idea of "factual" takes on a particular coloration. His primary criterion for assessing literature is its fidelity to empirical reality, an idea he narrows still further. Literary works are deemed to be Canadian insofar as they appear Canadian by setting. But while he tells us, as one manifestation of this criterion, that Sir Charles G.D. Roberts really found himself in his short stories of animal life and that journalism is important to literature in Canada, MacMechan does not pursue the ramifications of this belief. Instead, he constantly undermines it. For while he stresses the force of journalism and the relevance of the real to the subject and style of fiction – even referring to his own work as a "sketch," using that much-embraced nineteenth-century term of "objective" impressionism – he doesn't mention the sketch as an art form, nor treat journals as a place where a reader might look for "high" art.

Indeed, the relevance of MacMechan to short story history in Canada seems to lie in the degree to which he ignores the form. Poets were more important to him than short story writers. "In prose fiction ... Canadians had never shown the ability so manifest in their poetry" (135), he declares. But his treatment of poetry reflects indirectly on his expectations of fiction. He focuses on single lyric poems and full-length prose books, praising "unity" but defining "unity" in two different ways. He gives aesthetic and moral precedence to poetry and demands empirical fidelity of prose. Further, by ignoring *short* fiction, except as an aside, he consigns it to an aesthetic periphery, characterizing it inferentially as the apprentice work of writers who demonstrate their substance in other, longer prose forms – in history, for example, or in the novel: long works that by implication have book-length unity and embody the linear principles of historical discourse.

Within four years of MacMechan's *Head-Waters*, Raymond Knister had published his minor revolution in Canadian fictional aesthetics, his anthology *Canadian Short Stories*. It was, in some sense, the first real survey of short fiction in Canada. Knister included writers from the nineteenth century, writers from the generation before his own, and writers of his own generation such as William Murtha and Morley Callaghan. The immediate critical response to the book was favourable, but in B.K. Sandwell's review in *Saturday Night* it took a particularly interesting form, which focuses our attention once again back on the taste that was shaping

Canadian short fiction criticism. Sandwell located the anthology's strengths not in the moderns but in the work of Scott, Roberts, Thomson, and Parker, whom he called "those four princes of the last days of the century." The moderns, by contrast – Callaghan, for example – were "accomplished and earnest youngsters," whose "experiments" had "interest and value"; but of the extent of their value, Sandwell was uncertain. Would their subjects, he asked – their "types," their "lively interest in futility" – "be as durable" as the material that "fell to the hand of Roberts and Thomson and Parker"? Would an interest in futility "be permanent"? And would the "revolt against style, or against everything that passed for style in the good old days," work towards a "permanent good"? That is, how could they match up against the "dignity and formality" of "a language based on Addison and tempered by Scott," a language of people who regarded themselves as "literary men, with a tradition to uphold and a law to follow" (7)?

The main criterion operating in this review is unstated, but it is scarcely concealed. It involves a belief in the fixity of normative judgement, the existence of some codifiable universal standard, in which the Canadian romance/realists of the turn of the century participated, but which somehow could not be extended to Callaghan. This standard had an ethical core, but it could not deal with class or language or place or gender except insofar as it classified them through anglo- and andro-centric presumptions. Sandwell was simply resisting the kinds of change that by the 1920s were going on around him. Individual writers and the structures of society at large were challenging the presumptions on which his criticism rested in at least five ways: first of all by responding to shifts in ethnic and urban demography, and by attacking the existing structures of political power in the country; also by redefining the character of region and style, by resisting received notions of unity and logical sequence, and by using the idea of *parole* to combat the idea of dialect. In other words, the very indeterminacy of the short story form began to be both aesthetically and politically functional, reinforcing changes in social hierarchy and critical expectation.

We can take these three stances towards short fiction – the idea that it is an entertaining apprentice form, a peripheral form, and a normative vehicle of dignity and formality – and impose against them the several conventional theories, now currently in vogue, that attempt to explain what the short story in general, around the world, is and does. To do so is to begin to see how received notions of genre have shaped critical expectations and in turn, in Canada, shaped the design of literary tradition that people came, by the 1960s, to accept as their "natural" literary history. Canada was not alone, of course, in importing – or "receiving" – its conventions of critical estimation; I am using the Canadian experience as an example of a larger process, for which short fiction theory supplies a convenient paradigm.

Four standard ways of classifying the short story had come into existence by the 1920s; all of them to one degree or another were culturally biased. To generalize, British comment sought to find in short stories their link with other prose forms, and so to establish a tradition for the form: by seeing the story as a small history, moreover, such comment emphasized elements of narrative sequence and narrative consequence. American commentary, by contrast, considered the form to be both revolutionary and American, one that may have had some distant roots in other genres, but which was transformed by the power of the American speaking voice, which accorded "story" the legitimacy of cultural attitude. The practice of *conte* writers in France encouraged criticism there to pursue the patterns of folk culture. And from elsewhere – from Joyce in Ireland, Chekhov in Russia, Mansfield in New Zealand, for example – came the experiments in fragmentation which divided the new twentieth-century story from its nineteenth-century forebears. The new stories emphasized the passing moment, the flash of insight, the sudden epiphany, the character of absence: momentariness and interruption rather than eternals and continuity. Such categories – of sequence, orality, prototype, and fragmentation – inevitably fade into one another in literary practice, but in general terms these four critical concerns respectively suggest ways of justifying four forms of story: narrative history; anecdote; folktale and fable; and indirect narration. The trouble is, they have more characteristically been held to define the short story *in toto*, to describe the genre on the basis of one cultural practice and to claim it as a way of representing – or coding – "reality" as seen by all. Therein lies one of the main critical problems that colours analyses of the Canadian short story tradition. Up to 1965, English-Canadian critics, trained primarily to evaluate by means of British standards, were more receptive to versions of story as history than to versions of story as sketch or folk myth or fragment. Built into attitudes towards literary genres were particular cultural mindsets. And the systems of expectation determined declared value.

For example, any perception of the short story as merely a short version of a novel, or as an extended version of an illustrated parable, or as a simple written record of a vernacular entertainment, places it in an implied aesthetic hierarchy, codifies it as a "minor" form and establishes it "therefore" as a less-than-serious art. In parallel fashion, any identification of the "fragmentary" nature of the modern versions of the genre confirms to some critics that the short story lacks coherence or unity or "wholeness." By implication these criteria are themselves identifiable, their sacrosanct character not in question. The step from these underlying preconceptions to the critical history of the short story in Canada has interesting ramifications, which takes us back to Brodie, MacMechan, and Sandwell.

"Poetic charm" – that quality which Brodie found everywhere in Canadian magazine stories – is precisely what MacMechan would allow in poetry but reject in prose, insisting on historical argument instead; but, like Brodie, he identified the validity of a Canadian prose work by the documentary realism of its particular setting. The effect of the two impulses combined was to distort the way writers perceived landscape and society and the way they used language to artistic purpose. Subjects and settings carried more than their obvious resonance, feeding the hierarchical impulse. Consider, for example, stories of Quebec. To anglo-Canadian eyes, before 1930, the very word "Quebec" implied a whole set of attitudes, involving among other things Catholicism and provinciality. MacMechan, writing in *Head-Waters* a history of both English- and French-Canadian literature, nonetheless did so with a British-based historical bias. The folktales of Beaugrand and Fréchette go unremarked (except to note that some of Fréchette's prose presents such "oddities ... as are fostered by a restricted provincial existence" (78); moreover, what they represent goes unrecognized. These authors were not drawing on British patterns; they were attempting to adapt folk custom and local idiom to *conte* form and contemporary behaviour, sometimes with a political motive. But the ahistorical imagination of the surface narratives of their works apparently impedes for MacMechan any direct estimation of their fictional quality.

This pattern repeats itself even with MacMechan's treatment of the anglo-Canadian writer Duncan Campbell Scott, who from the 1890s to the 1920s was writing stories set in Quebec and poems about Indians. MacMechan acknowledges Scott for his biography of Governor Simcoe but mentions neither his fiction nor his verse. And while Brodie does acknowledge him, once again the version of Scott we get is one that has been skewed by expectation. Scott had attempted to use folktale form and sketch in order to probe the violence that lies beneath the more superficial realities of Quebec culture; but Brodie accepts these formal experiments as signs of poetic beauty and charm. Rather surprisingly, subsequent commentators have largely followed him, accepting Scott's stories as simple accounts of a quaint backwater. For the critics, a cultural stereotype about Quebec has become a fixed truth, governing the way they read. Though he ignored Scott, MacMechan still illustrates this attitude directly; his book goes so far as to give extended praise to the *patois* versifier William Henry Drummond – as poet and as national patriot. The fact that Drummond's voice was long accepted in English Canada as an authentic characterization of francophone speech and behaviour says a good deal about continuing presumptions concerning dialect and normative language, about cultural unfamiliarity and the misconceptions that stem from it. The case of D.C. Scott is the reverse side of Drummond's in stance: up to and including the treatment of Scott's books of short fiction, *In the Village of Viger* and *The Witching of Elspie*, in the 1965 version of the *Literary History of Canada*, to be quaint about Quebec was considered realistic, and to try to use the forms of Quebec in order to get past the stereotypes was regarded, in anglophone Canada, as mere "local colourism" – quaint, and perhaps even "escapist."

The animal stories of Roberts offer a parallel example of critical misreading. One of the things that characterizes these works is that they could be claimed equally by those who stood in demand of pathos and those who stood in need of real settings. As the opening of a sketch like "The Prisoners of the Pitcher-Plant" makes clear, the illusion of Roberts' objective realism inhered in his narrator's documentary stance and in the scientific terminology of the text. But the careful reader recognizes in a word like "prisoner" a whole tradition of romance conventions, and in the story's adjectival subtext, a subjective impressionism that no rigorously objective documentary could sustain. But the ambivalence was less debilitating than it was productive. The effect of the double claim upon Roberts – as the master of reality and as the master of romance – was to legitimize a romantic illusion of wilderness as the record of true Canadian reality. This was paradoxically an illusion perpetrated by an urban critical community – by Sandwell, among others – who applied their borrowed expectations of literature to the evaluation of local literary practice. They used the conventional image of Canada to claim Canada's literary distinctiveness and yet at the same time situated this native cultural tradition inside a so-called "universal" mainstream, one that depended on closed form, linear sequence, and received notions of literary language.

By the time of the *Literary History of Canada*, this conventional sense of what constituted the Canadian tradition in the short story had solidified. Closer analysis, however, shows that a number of questions were being begged. The tradition was selective in its recognition of form; its assertion of realism was suspect; it was bound by its identification of Canada with wilderness, hence limited by subject and setting; it was implicitly centralist; and it was naïve. These issues overlap. Some of them I have already noted at greater length: the centralist "mainstream" metaphors of MacMechan, for example; or the consignment of Haliburton's Atlantic Canada to a category called "history" (the "present" having somehow moved on and away); or the way Roberts was accepted as realistic and representative, although he was rural in subject, often impressionistic in language, hierarchical in stance, and immersed in a world of male norms. When such values are translated critically into the forms of the national tradition, something goes awry. There was in practice – among Canadian writers of short fiction before Callaghan – a substantial literary inventiveness that goes unnoticed if we accept as normative either Roberts's wilderness or Haliburton's satires.

There were other options being explored. There were options by place (there was a lively cultural activity in Victoria in the late nineteenth century, for example, and no-one has yet adequately recorded it). There were options by setting (there continues among anthologists a resistance to Canadian stories set outside Canada – Thomson wrote some lively Boston stories, for example, and Norman Duncan an instructive collection set in the Syrian quarter of New York: both of them urban as well as extraterritorial – but they seldom get read). There were options by race and culture, both of which had an impact on literary form (Quebec folktales and indigenous myth were both more sophisticated art forms than anglo-protestant rationalism was willing to admit). There were options by literary stance and design (there were mannered comedies as well as wilderness struggles, and to look closely at Haliburton is to discover a writer who deliberately experimented with literary genre, who worked with transformation tale as well as with history, with the conventions of sentimental romance as well as with those of the satiric dialogue). And there were options by gender. In all this discussion, where are the writers who were women? Brodie at least acknowledged their existence, though his terms of recognition are faintly patronizing: "In the realm of short story writing," he notes, "Canada has several clever lady writers whose work possesses a certain charm all its own" (337–38). Yet two of the most stylistically accomplished works of the later nineteenth and earlier twentieth centuries were Susan Frances Harrison's *Crowded Out! and Other Sketches* (1886) and Jessie Georgina Sime's *Sister Woman* (1919), neither book (and neither writer) recognized by Brodie or MacMechan. The problem was, neither book fit the critic's pattern. Harrison's sketches testily complained of British critical intransigence and wittily exposed the shallow mores of faddish urban American society; Sime's remarkable work adopted an interrupted narrative form in order to expose the inadequacies of a normative social pattern that consigned women to second-class status and abandoned them to penury, divorce, stillbirths, single parenthood, and domestic service.

The first point to make is that it is not subject alone but also the importance of the literary form to the subject that demands recognition, and that such recognition is the first step to re-evaluating the genre of short fiction in Canada and the tradition by which literary history has so far defined it. When Hugo McPherson in 1965 said that the short story was disappearing, he was in some sense right, if by what he said we understand a particular form of short story and a particular, closed notion of what the tradition was. New forms of story were on the way, resistant to then current narrative and social definitions. Such a need to redefine – and hence the need to re-evaluate individual works and their tradition – opens up the larger point to be made here. Any age, our own included, is subject to bias and preconception. What literary history valuably records is less a set of verifiable facts and universal principles than the perspective of the time and place in which it is written. To readers of literary history, such perspectives do not get in the way of knowledge; they are part of what is learned about literature. The "factuality" of data often changes. It is selective, and the very selectivity of design can shape both memory and expectations about the future. We have to remember that preconceptions, as well as the judgements to which they lead, illuminate for us the workings of a living culture.

*   *   *

I take these comments as a preface to the next stage of my remarks here. For it follows that if literary histories of the past reveal the expectations of the day, then literary histories of the present – for all the sophistication to which current methodologies lay claim – will not be free of bias either, and it is these reasons for judging more than our judgements themselves that may turn out to be of most interest to the future. The problem is that only some of the reasons are conscious and overt. The hidden ones, the unconscious ones, may be of more interest still. I want to specify how some of this process operates by looking at the work I have been involved in over the last ten years, the preparation of volume 4 of the *Literary History of Canada*, a volume which covers literary activity in the years between 1972 and 1984, and which is now complete. I should say "primarily" covers the years 1972-1984 because in fact the volume overlaps in certain sectors with volumes 1-3. That it does so, however, says something about the expectations and observations that the editors have of literature in these years, and about the deliberate designs of literary history.

Let me begin by referring to a short story that appeared first in *Impulse* in 1973 and was collected in 1978, right in the middle of the period covered by volume 4: Dave Godfrey's "A New Year's Morning on Bloor Street," from *Dark Must Yield*. I am not going to try to explicate the story here (partly because I find it a dense and complicated text) but rather to try to point to some of the features in it which would need to be taken into account in any reading. Some of the standard textbook features of short fiction are present: characters, setting, theme. There is little that could be called "plot," though there is a rough "eternal triangle" in the story which generates some of the events that take place. More is to be understood by tonal contrasts and allusive reverberations than by linear sequence. It is an aural story, as though written for radio. The "characters" include the narrator, his daughter, his wife (named Yseult), his male lover (named Christopher), and figures from Indian and Inuit myth (including, in particular, Sedna, the underwater woman). The "setting" is primarily the park beside the Royal Ontario Museum in Toronto, near St. George Street and Bloor – and the story takes place primarily at a time about 1975, when the free-form Rochdale College experiment was disintegrating under public and political pressure. The "theme" is not to be reduced to a single word, though it involves external presences in Canada (American ones especially), cultural nationalism, and the impact of past myths of inheritance upon present perceptions of self. In the narrator, a man of many voices, the worlds of Arthurian story (Yseult), Judaeo-Christian story (Christopher), and indigenous American story (Sedna, Coyote, Lumaaq, and so on) come together: the narrator is pressured into recognizing that his culture asks for the voices to act in concert but realizes simultaneously that his cultural history has asked him to choose among the forms of story or inheritance, to make a hierarchy out of them. His problem is to sort out what kind of freedom or what kind of solution he can hand on to the next generation.

The strategy of the story is to adopt a shifting form which itself refuses classification by any single category. As a play of voices, it mixes formal diction (of the sort Brodie would have found "poetic") with the most direct of vernacular earthiness; it mixes French and Inuktitut phrases in with English; it alters in intensity as the narrator at one moment adopts a stance of ironic detachment, at another invokes a passionate self-possession. Communicating by form, the story turns into a re-enactment of the Ojibway "Shaking Tent" ceremony, whereby the shaman takes on the voices of the spirits with the aim of resolving the problems of the group and reiterating for the group its sense of community. ("I will shake this tent, once I have freed myself from these rawhide knots" [131], the narrator specifies at the beginning.) Godfrey's narrator, that is, becomes a shaman for modern times, the agency through which the multiple voices of contemporary society can still constitute a community, reasserting the forces that give it substance and value – this is a "New Year's Morning" story, full of resolution – even while countervailing forces invite surrender and dissolution and despair. It is also a cry for freedom at a time when a desire for security seems the stronger social attraction.

It is a story like this one which volume 4 of the *Literary History of Canada* has to describe and account for. It is fragmented and aural; it is allusive and acutely conscious of its own artifice; it still has something to do with the empirical society. Reading it depends on reading the context: hearing the allusions to current sociological and economic and anthropological and scientific and critical disputes, and bringing them all to bear on language. The next question to be asked – what are the forces of substance and value? – takes me back to my main theme. When I became General Editor for volume 4 of the *Literary History* in 1977, I asked several people to help me as members of the Editorial Board: Henry Kreisel, Clara Thomas, Carl Berger, Douglas Lochhead, Francess G. Halpenny, Philip Stratford, and Alan Cairns. They have special expertise in such topics as comparative literature, biographical writing, historiography, political science, translation, the publishing industry, and women's studies. These interests shaped the book. Together we designed a volume to deal with literature happening in our own day, and we set out deliberately to try to resolve some of the problems we noted in earlier volumes – of which the history of the short story is but one example. To some degree we were involved in prediction. The Parti Québécois had been elected to power in 1976, and the 1980 Referendum on sovereignty-association had not yet taken place: would there be a Canada still to discuss in 1985? We were still in an age of economic expansion then: to what degree were we guided by expectations that existing trends (in encouragement for the arts, for example, or in cultural nationalism, or in technological change) would continue? To what degree were we governed by our collective sense of what mattered?

What impact, moreover, would the events of our own time have on the way we lived and thought? Before the Constitution Act of 1982, women had rights before the law, but not in law. In the midst of the oil boom, regions in Canada were flexing their economic muscles, and the politics of place had cultural implications. The Berger Commission Report in 1977 gave added force to native land claims. Even the language was altering: words like *Inuit* and *québécois* were coming into general parlance, with their implicit rejections of perceived marginality. The ethnic mix of the country was changing. So were philosophical allegiances: among the many statistics in the 1981 census is the information that the number of Pentecostals in Canada had increased by 54% over ten years, and the number of Buddhists by 223%.

Collectively, as critics and editors, I and the other Editorial Board members were interested in the texts of literature but not only as texts by themselves. We were uneasy about the way local literary texts were often read in relation to some received notion of universal aesthetic value, and uneasy with conventional definitions of the limits of literature. Hence we were interested in texts and also in contexts: in the ways in which writers wrote out of various frames of reference, or in reaction against them, or in recognition of the ideas of their time, or because the social institutions that affected them helped shape the way they thought or the kind of work they could publish. We were not unaware that such interests implied a disagreement with some other literary ideologies ("universalism," for one) – hence that the new volume would in some way be ideological itself. But how? Volume 4, therefore, tries to come to terms with its own time: with expanded reference to writing in the social sciences (with individual chapters, for example, on writing in psychology and anthropology) and with separate new chapters on short fiction, translation, and writing for radio, television, and film. In doing so, volume 4 not only extends the existing *Literary History of Canada*, it also enters into historical dialogue with it. It re-evaluates. Simply by recognizing subjects and genres that had not up to this time seemed to warrant extended attention, it alters their priority.

Among the recurrent themes in the new volume are the changes wrought by the literary politics of gender, region, and ethnicity, and from what I have already said, it will be apparent that these issues are present for at least two reasons: one, because they are there in the literature of the last decade, and two, because we were looking for them. All along I have been stressing the bias of selectivity, the illusion of objectivity, the implications of formal arrangement. Repeatedly, even the chapter writers cast their commentaries as "stories," conscious of the apparent determinacy of critical structure and at the same time of the indeterminacy of their subject. The chapter on critical theory and practice goes so far as to adopt a metatextual stance. The book is a book about discourse-in-process. Perhaps all contemporary histories are. But that, too, carries implications about the reach of judgement. And what we were possibly less prepared for was the recurrence of other motifs and the impact these have – as a "subtext," if you will, or (in the terms of feminist criticism) a "subversion" of the overt structure.

Assessing the subtexts at this proximity to the text is a problematic gesture, of course. It is affected by the same presumptions that designed the overt structure, hence is not free from attitudinal expectations. But, clearly, reading volume 4 of the *Literary History of Canada*, chapter by chapter, through to the end, turns up more interesting patterns than those that concern women, region, ethnicity, and Quebec. There is, for example, a whole series of approaches to the subject of absolute standards. Especially in a context so shaped by relativist assumptions, this fascination presumably also says something about the temper of the present and of the future that the present is helping prepare. There are repeated claims on the irrefragability of number, though the meaning of statistics is just as repeatedly in dispute. There is a fascination with system. And there are repeated binary distinctions, as though human and literary choices resolved themselves into "either-or" packages. What does this mean? Such motifs might call into consideration the implications of much current methodology. Is there a covert equation, we might ask, between "Not-us" or "Not-now" and "Not-good"? And have we been relying on it? Has the desire for status within a single discipline resulted in artificial linguistic barriers against communication? Does complexity of information and argument justify obscurity of lexicon and syntax? Is academic isolationism merely a retreat from the greater complexities of knowledge? Has the increase in the amount and availability of information led people to accept simplistic codes as answers or explanations because they have the merit of being graspable? Has the reluctance to accept the "élitism" of outmoded hierarchies led people to reject all distinctions of value for fear of discrimination? And is the willingness to accept all answers as valid preferable to the willingness to accept only one, or only the easy ones, or only the familiar ones, or only the institutionally approved ones? Safety-from-judgement is not the only option there is to safety-of-judgement. To accept it as though it were is to accept random change as the only alternative to stasis, to turn relativism into a new absolute, to deny both the subtlety and effect of choice and to reject even the possibility of a culture being a shared experience.

Overtly, volume 4 of the *Literary History of Canada* is not ideologically free. It is concerned very directly with some of the most effective forces of change in Canadian society during the 1970s and 1980s – the women's movement, native rights groups, economic and political regionalism, multiculturalism, Quebec Separatism – and with the impact of these forces not only on conventional normative attitudes but also on language and codes of connection. As with Godfrey's "New Year's Morning" story, these are arguments for a renewed perception of community. They thrive on possibility. But they are not wholly in control of all the directions in which they lead, and, without some reflective consideration, they can result in ends as static or chaotic as the systems they seek to redefine. Throughout volume 4 – and this was a subject we had not anticipated – there are (in addition to the calls for change) a series of accounts of attacks on fascism. Sometimes these are cast as memoirs and histories and poetic meditations, and it is possible to explain them as the experiential and retrospective view of a generation of the 1940s still alive. But that is not the limit to the way they function. There is a political point to be made. Sometimes (as most obviously in Hugh MacLennan's *Voices in Time*, Timothy Findley's *Not Wanted on the Voyage*, and Margaret Atwood's *The Handmaid's Tale*) they are cast as cautionary fantasies of tomorrow and yesterday, focusing finally on threats perceived today; they are narrative analyses of the binary structures of power that limit freedom (often in the name of security and sometimes in the name of objectivity) by delimiting the number of options people may have and the power of choice on which they may draw. That is a commentary on critical method as well as on social organization, and it is one that brings me to a close. It may well be that subsequent criticism will pay more attention to the subtext than to the text, will champion a principle of continuity over a principle of interruption, will seek meaning from shared humane values rather than passively accept whatever patterns that shifting norms of judgement create. But all of this is hypothetical. (It may well be that humane values and shifting patterns of judgement are not binary options.) Going back to Brodie, MacMechan, and Sandwell, we may discover we do not accept the priorities implied by their judgements, but disagreeing with them does not demand that we dismiss them, or to forget they, too, believed in value. Indeed, it might be more useful to remember that we generally resolve one set of problems only to set more in motion. Turning back to the future we envision for ourselves does not require us, yet, to turn our backs on the past.

Works Cited

Brodie, Allan Douglas. "Canadian Short-Story Writers." *The Canadian Magazine* 4 (1894-95): 334-44.

Duncan, Norman. *The Soul of the Street: Correlated Stories of the New York Syrian Quarter.* New York: McClure, Phillips, 1900.

Godfrey, Dave. "A New Year's Morning on Bloor Street." *Dark Must Yield.* Erin, ON: Porcépic, 1978. 131-42.

Harrison, Susan Frances. *Crowded Out! and Other Sketches.* Ottawa: Evening Journal, 1886.

Klinck, Carl F., gen. ed. *Literary History of Canada: Canadian Literature in English.* Toronto: U of Toronto P, 1965. 2nd ed. 3 vols. Toronto: U of Toronto P, 1976.

Knister, Raymond, ed. *Canadian Short Stories.* Toronto: Macmillan, 1928.

MacMechan, Archibald. *Head-Waters of Canadian Literature.* Toronto: McClelland, 1924. Rpt. as *Headwaters of Canadian Literature.* Introd. M.G. Parks. New Canadian Library 107. Toronto: McClelland & Stewart, 1974.

Matthews, Brander. *The Philosophy of the Short-Story.* New York: Longmans, Green, 1901.

McPherson, Hugo. "Fiction: 1940-1960." *Literary History of Canada: Canadian Literature in English.* Gen. ed. Carl F. Klinck. Toronto: U of Toronto P, 1965. 694-722.

New, W.H., gen. ed. *Literary History of Canada: Canadian Literature in English.* 2nd ed. Vol. 4. Toronto: U of Toronto P, 1990.

Pratt, Mary Louise. "The Short Story: The Long and the Short of It." *Poetics* 10 (1981): 175-94.

Roberts, Charles G.D. "The Prisoners of the Pitcher-Plant." *The Haunters of the Silences: A Book of Animal Life.* Boston: L.C. Page, 1907. 84-91.

Sandwell, B.K. "The Short Story in Canada." Rev. of *Canadian Short Stories,* ed. Raymond Knister. *Saturday Night* 25 Aug. 1928: 7.

Scott, Duncan Campbell. *In the Village of Viger.* Boston: Copeland and Day, 1896. Rpt. (expanded) as *In the Village of Viger and Other Stories.* Introd. Stan Dragland. New Canadian Library 92. Toronto: McClelland & Stewart, 1973.

—. *The Witching of Elspie: A Book of Stories.* New York: George H. Doran, 1923.

Sime, Jessie Georgina. *Sister Woman*. London: Grant Richards, 1919.

Thomson, Edward William. *Old Man Savarin Stories: Tales of Canada and Canadians*. Toronto: S.B. Gundy, 1917.

On the Rungs of the Double Helix:
Theorizing the Canadian Literatures

Cynthia Sugars

If, as Michael Coren states in a recent issue of *Books in Canada*, "Any study of literary criticism in Canada is in reality a study of Canada itself," then I suppose that is what this paper is about. I had suspected it all along in any case. And if literature plays an integral part in the construction of a country's cultural and political identity, then it is hardly a leap to shift one's discussion from the Canadian literary canon, to Canadian critics, to the construction of Canada itself. These connections are even more evident when one considers translated French-Canadian literature in Canada – the "English" French-Canadian canon – and its place within English-Canadian conceptions of Canadian literature generally.[1]

One's position as to whether the two literatures can indeed constitute part of a larger Canadian canon, one's notion whether they can even be compared as nationally distinct literary products, even the *names* that one gives to them – all betray an underlying conception of the political construction of Canada. Paramount is the definition of *nation* to which critics subscribe: whether they define a nation, to use Ramsay Cook's terms, as a predetermined cultural conglomerate or a self-determined political state (*Canada, Quebec* 186). This difference is frequently paralleled by translingual misunderstandings of the word: according to David Bell, anglophones use *nation* to imply "an entire state apparatus," while the francophone use of the term is largely informed by "a sense of tradition and identity" (3).

Although Ashcroft, Griffiths, and Tiffin contrast the dominance of thematic literary criticism in Canada with the Australian focus on "conflicting 'traditions'" (134), an emphasis on traditions, conflicting and otherwise, has formed the central element in critical configurations of French- and English-Canadian literatures. Common to all approaches is a hypostatization of difference between the two literatures, a reification that is seen to have timeless applicability, one that denies the specifics of individual texts and contexts. In Sylvia Söderlind's terms, this reification has taken the form of "an a priori valorization of a certain aesthetics and its subsequent translation/perversion into the realm of politics, a kind of ... wishful thinking which ... every generation insists on repeating" (229). This impulse, of course, can also operate in the opposite direction, in which a certain political configuration is translated into a timeless fact in the realm of aesthetics. Instead, both realms are textual constructs, coterminous and interdependent, and any adequate configuration of the Canadian literatures must allow for this fact. What I undertake here is a description, synthesis, and analysis of English-Canadian literary critics' approaches to the two literatures, followed by my own probings towards a new way of conceiving both. E.D. Blodgett's call for "taxonomy first, judgment second" ("Towards" 130) will roughly form the structuring principle of my discussion.

*   *   *

Blodgett is correct in saying that theorists of French- and English-Canadian literatures have typically ignored Philip Stratford's call "neither to unify nor to divide" (*Configuration* 19), for after some degree of inner turmoil, they generally do one or the other. Persisting with a binary formulation of the problem, English-Canadian critics have forced themselves to choose one of two poles: literary separatism or literary/national unity. This split position as to whether French-Canadian texts can be considered part of a larger Canadian literary canon parallels the "centralist" versus "separatist" positions outlined by Stratford in "Canada's Two Literatures: A Search for Emblems" (133). Yet even while many critics and anthologists articulate one or the other position, they often contradict themselves in practice, as if to satisfy a conception of an in-some-way–united Canada and, at the same time, express an awareness of Quebec as a distinct cultural nation.

The particularities of the Canadian political context render a cross-national comparative approach inadequate. On one level, and in conventional terms, comparative Canadian literature is necessarily an *intra*national endeavour (at least as long as Quebec remains a part of Canada). However, as Richard Cavell argues, a paradox arises because comparative Canadian literature attempts to transcend the concept of nationhood while locating difference within the Canadian nation, or, I might add, between Canadian nations. Hence, any discussion of the relationship between English- and French-Canadian literatures is necessarily a political one, for every position addressing the two literatures betrays an underlying position regarding the two cultures as constituting (or not) a politically and/or culturally unified Canada.

To apply a notion outlined by Robert Lecker in "A Country without a Canon?," each position is grounded in a desire for a canon as an ideal construct that transmits social values and cultural unity. Even those who ostensibly oppose or interrogate a canon do so under the assumption or desire that one exists to oppose. In the context of French- and English-Canadian literatures, this interpretation can be carried a step further: it is political unity as represented by a national Canadian canon that becomes the desired goal. This unity can take the form of an imagined community of French and English, a Canada that not only "comprend le Québec," but also one in which the literatures of the two groups have influenced one another or at least share common traits. Stratford notes the constructedness of such expressions of unity in describing his double helix model of the parallel and reciprocal nature of the two literatures: "it represents ... the comparative view, but not the reality itself" ("Emblems" 137). The desire for unity can also take the form of an equally constructed separation of the two societies, a move away from national unity, an assertion of distinctness between the two cultures and their literary products. In the latter case, national unity is a "reality" to be opposed; in the former, it is separation that is the threatening "reality."

In fact, every desire for political unity is counterbalanced by a desire for separation, for, theoretically, one is ultimately dependent on the other in an incessant cycle of self-definition and justification. Thus Stratford, who argues for a form of bicultural unity, is dependent on a notion of the separation of the two cultures (not to mention the everpresent threat of political separation), not only in order to make the distinctions that he does, but also to set himself up as a mediator between the two. Likewise, Blodgett, the Canadian critic to have most extensively theorized this complex issue, proposes an approach to "saving" Canada through an affirmation of its separate components, its multiple cultural and ethnic groups. Yet as he gropes towards a position vis-à-vis Canada's two literatures, he is dependent upon unifying positions such as Stratford's. He needs them as something against which to posit his theory in order to make it theoretically and politically efficacious.

As the preceding discussion indicates, to polarize the debate between a "separatist" and a "centralist" (or unifying) position is too reductive a way of conceiving the debate among English-Canadian critics. Throughout *All the Polarities*, Stratford's critical assessments of French- and English-Canadian literary texts are generally posed as binary ones, and his conception of the mutually exclusive separatist and centralist approaches to French- and English-Canadian literatures is no different. A closer consideration of the debate suggests that critics have expressed various ways of conceiving the relationship between the two literatures, approaches that are not in opposition but rather lie in a continuum. In general, one can identify four clusters along this continuum, overlapping positions based on critics' conceptions of Quebec's political and cultural relationship with the rest of Canada. Because most noncomparatists have not theorized their considerations of the two literatures, I identify three of the groups with the work of well-known Canadian comparatists – Ronald Sutherland, Stratford, and Blodgett.[2] I suggest this outline as a convenient means of discussing the debate in English Canada, of facilitating an understanding of the key arguments in the debate, not as a template or grid to be applied to every critical discussion of the two literatures. One could subdivide the categories to account for additional subtleties of distinction, just as one could combine positions to highlight connections among them.[3]

The first approach I roughly identify as the literary-separatist position (usually paralleled by political separatism). The argument is that Québécois and Canadian literatures are distinct: they share no common tradition or influences, have followed separate paths, and therefore should be considered only in mutual isolation. Significantly, the majority of literary separatists speak in terms of Quebec, not French Canada, using a territorial definition of nationhood that presupposes cultural and linguistic homogeneity within specific boundaries. Critics in this group thus support a form of "biological insiderism" (Sollers 275), arguing that only members of a particular cultural group can fully comprehend its literary productions. Furthermore, the literary separatist considers translation, from French to English, not only a form of diglossic cultural appropriation, but also an impossibility because the source text, it is assumed, cannot be rendered in a language and culture other than its own. Such "culturally prompted privileging acts ... define the source-text as an origin" (Blodgett, "Translation" 190), hence reaffirming the catchy but generalizing adage, "*traduttore, traditore.*" According to Sutherland, this view creates of Québécois literature "an exclusive preserve which would somehow be contaminated by the traditional comparative approach applied by scholars to all national literatures since the ancient Greek" (*New Hero* vii).

Chantal de Grandpré articulates such literary and cultural separatism in "La canadianisation de la littérature québécoise: le cas Aquin." She criticizes Russell Brown for his presumption in setting Hubert Aquin and Malcolm Lowry side by side, as if they could possibly have anything in common, and takes issue with Patricia Merivale for comparing Aquin and Brian Moore in terms of their distinct postcolonial heritages, which Grandpré sees as a means of erasing difference "pour mieux identifier ces deux auteurs comme Canadiens" (56). Grandpré's discussion represents a clear instance of a literary-separatist desire for unity. She charges all English-Canadian critics – without distinguishing between comparatists and noncomparatists, or bilingual and unilingual English Canadians – with an attempted assimilation of Québécois literature. Grandpré needs this monolithic body of literary appropriators against which to set her own position, so it is not in her interest to address the very different approaches to French- and English-Canadian literatures that such critics might advocate.

A mystifying conflation of all comparisons of the two literatures is characteristic of most literary-separatist arguments. To what extent this conflation is motivated by a need for a monolithic opponent, and to what extent it is due to a lack of awareness of the highly theorized level of debate surrounding the two literatures, I am not sure. Certainly there exist misconceptions of the latter in Canadian literary circles. For example, in his review of *Taking Stock*, Terry Goldie speaks of the "typical opinions" (96) of Canadian critics on the "bicultural problem" (95), linking them with Sutherland, one of "their leading supporters" (96). In truth, Sutherland is hardly representative – far from it – for many critics, comparatists and otherwise, are concerned to distance themselves from his global likenings of the two literatures.

Stratford's identification of a literary-separatist position places only French-Canadian and Québécois critics in the category. I include English Canadians in this group, though their arguments take a different tack. Many of these critics defend the separation of the two literatures on the grounds that they are not equipped to judge Québécois literature, that they are ignorant of French language and Québécois culture. Hence, their position is not rooted in an unrealistic sense of pan-Canadian bilingualism (though there have been critics to argue thus), but in its opposite. Critics such as W.J. Keith – who expressed embarrassment at the 1978 Calgary Conference on the Canadian Novel because no French-Canadian texts made it into the "top ten" and "top 100" lists of Canadian novels – fall into this category: "How on earth … can we – unless we are fully bilingual, and not many of us are – make a value judgement about Québécois fiction," said Keith in response to Malcolm Ross's presentation of the ballot results (Ross 146). In the introduction to his 1985 *Canadian Literature in English*, Keith is still advocating a separation of the two literatures (7). Terry Goldie argues a similar position, which he calls "cultural relativism" (94), in "Alas, Poor Beaver," claiming to be unqualified to comment on French-Canadian literature: "When will people learn that … we lack the knowledge or awareness to pronounce upon two cultures?" (96) – an ironic statement in view of his work on Native literatures. Numerous Canadian anthologists, editors, and literary historians – A.J.M. Smith, Desmond Pacey, Carl Klinck and Reginald Watters, and others – also fall into this category because they choose to consider French- and English-Canadian writings separately given the "artificial unity" that a combination of the two would produce (Pacey, *Book of Canadian Stories* vii).[4]

The second group gained predominance in the 1960s and '70s, though it had been taken for granted by many English-Canadian anthologists for some years before that. It could go by a variety of names: centralist, unifying, federalist, mainstream, or nationalist. Critics in this group generally think of the two literatures under the larger heading of Canadian literature, where the adjective *Canadian* is assumed to include French and English. They argue that there are clear links between French- and

English-Canadian literatures, more than there are differences, and that these likenesses should be highlighted. Often they attempt to prove that the two literatures have followed a single tradition. More overtly than any of the others, this position foregrounds a desire for national unity.

The comparatist most firmly in this camp is Sutherland, though non-comparatists in this group include Margaret Atwood, Catherine Rubinger, John Moss, Robin Mathews, and D.G. Jones.[5] Sutherland argues not just for similarities among literary texts, but more generally for likenesses between the two cultural groups, identifying a "common mystique" (*Second Image*) or "sphere of consciousness" (*New Hero*) shared by both. Atwood has her own twist on this. She defines Quebec as a microcosm of the rest of Canada, where particular Canadian themes, motifs, and fears are found in their purest form: "In many ways, Québec's situation – as reflected in its literature – epitomizes the situation of Canada as a whole ..." (230). Sutherland's concerns (like those of many critics in this group) are ultimately paraliterary: he finds links among the cultural and social realities of the two language groups, a shared history and psychological awareness, and a similar line of ideological development (*New Hero* viii, ix; "Twin Solitudes" 20) – he even argues that English and French Canadians have the same ancestral heritage (*Second Image* 31).

In his textual analyses, Sutherland focuses on the similarities between the literatures despite minor instances of cultural diversity. Above all, his conception of the "mainstream" of Canadian literature is a means by which to construct this French/English unity (*Second Image* 124-26; *New Hero* 84-97). This mainstream contains not, as one might expect, the most popular or canonical works of French- and English-Canadian literature, but those that express an author's ability to grasp the central issue of Canadian experience: an "awareness of and sensitivity to fundamental aspects of both major language groups in Canada, and of the interrelationships between these two groups" (*New Hero* 93-94). Ironically, in Sutherland's initial account of this Canadian mainstream in *Second Image*, he acknowledges that it includes few texts; Hugh MacLennan's *Two Solitudes* is his prime example (124). Later, in *The New Hero*, he includes such Quebec nationalist writers as Hubert Aquin and Jacques Godbout, assimilating them into the mainstream because of their "awareness" of Canada's two language groups: "Among French-language Quebec writers ... those who are the most nationalistic ... are generally the very ones who are right in the middle of the Canadian mainstream[,] ... exhibiting in their works an indisputable ... consciousness of the co-existence of two major ethnic groups in Canada" (95). These writers, of course, hardly conform to Sutherland's unifying aims despite his willed misreadings of problematic texts, a skill that he demonstrates in his optimistic interpretation of the conclusion to Godbout's *Le couteau sur la table* (*Second Image* 121-22).

The goal of the mainstream, Sutherland states, is to create "a *modus vivendi* between the nation's two major language groups" (*New Hero* 94), but in effect this is the goal of his construction of the concept. In his identification of the need for a grand Canadian myth to ensure national unity, he sets himself up as a prophet who will lift the veils of interlinguistic prejudice from all Canadians – literary critics, writers, and otherwise. His critical approach will bring the communication between the two language groups that necessarily precedes national unity (he overlooks the fact that communication among English Canadians, not to mention among the various linguistic, ethnic, and cultural groups that constitute "French" and "English" Canada, is an equally divisive problem).

The separatist and unifying positions cover the alternatives proposed by Stratford. Yet he sees himself as stationed somewhere between the two, advocating a liberal position that accepts the similarities and differences ("all the polarities") between the two cultures and literatures. This position of reconciliation forms the third main approach, and while Stratford is the comparatist most readily identified with it, like-minded critics include Milan Dimić, Louis Dudek, Richard Giguère, Archibald MacMechan, Clément Moisan, Lorne Pierce, Larry Shouldice, Sherry Simon, Antoine Sirois, and A.J.M. Smith. In Canadian political terms, one might call this the bicultural position, or "bifocal" as Stratford terms it in "Canada's Two Literatures" (136). It is based on the notion that English- and French-Canadian cultures have followed parallel but distinct paths, that they have experienced separate literary traditions that have nonetheless followed similar patterns or phases. Similarities occur in such areas as political development, geography, society, postcolonial status, and a sense of marginalization (Stratford, *Polarities* 2; Moisan 13). Critics in this group generally refer to the "Canadian literatures" or "Canadian literature in English and French," thereby identifying the two as composing the literature of one nation-state while also emphasizing their distinctness. The comparative enterprise is thus rendered relatively unproblematic: if French and English literatures, as distinct cultural products, form the literature of one Canada, then they can be likened or contrasted depending on the critic's focus.

Stratford's articulation of his approach occurs most plainly in his 1986 study *All the Polarities*, though he expresses it in numerous earlier publications. His goal is to compare the two literatures and elucidate their likenesses and differences, yet his affection lies unabashedly with the latter, in favour of polarities, often to the detriment of the integrity of individual texts. Despite a "98%" realm of similarity between the two literatures, he argues, the "burden for critics of Canadian literature" is to concentrate on the "small area of enormous vital difference between the two" ("Symposium" 6). Kathy Mezei notes this wary reluctance among

Canadian comparatists to document traces of interaction between the two literatures ("Bridge" 218). In fact, Stratford's definition of "comparative," in accordance with his approach, stresses difference over likeness: "[comparisons] are not really concerned with equating anything, for the second feature of a successful comparison ... consists ... in giving close attention to the definition of differences" (*Polarities* 96).

With this in mind, one cannot help but speculate on the potential biases informing Stratford's textual pairings. In "Canada's Two Literatures," he outlines a statistical survey – conducted with his Canadian literature students at the Université de Montréal – in which French- and English-Canadian novels were categorized according to specific thematic and stylistic elements (134). That these qualities were reproduced in the survey is not surprising given that the categories for comparison were devised beforehand. More telling, however, is the reproduction of these "expected differences" in *All the Polarities* (63). Nowhere in this publication does Stratford mention his earlier information-gathering experiment. Yet the differences that he "finds" here between his "successful pairings" (*Polarities* 96) of French- and English-Canadian novels mimic those noted in his earlier survey. Moreover, that he uses translations of French-Canadian works in *All the Polarities*, even when he analyzes the language and style of individual works, further confirms his dependence on preconceived differences in approaching the texts.

Like Sutherland, Stratford expresses little self-consciousness about his choice of texts to be paired. Just as Sutherland defuses Quebec nationalist novels by identifying in them an implicit impulse towards bicultural association (*Second Image* 112, 116), or by arguing that they provide a backhanded boost to Canadian national unity (*New Hero* 95-96), Stratford deradicalizes those English-Canadian novels that he wants to contrast with their more passionate, creative, and experimental French counterparts. His method is clear in his curious assessment of *The Diviners* as a form of documentary realism where memory acts as a reliable reconstruction of the past. His later comparison of Roch Carrier's *La Guerre, Yes Sir!* with Robert Kroetsch's *The Studhorse Man* leads one to wonder about his basis for comparing certain texts at all. At times his choices seem to be governed by a distinct dissimilarity between the novels, a setup that allows him to highlight the differences he has come to expect.

That Stratford's approach is grounded in a stereotyped conception of the two cultures is apparent by the time one is midway through *All the Polarities*. The chapters begin to reverberate with a predictable series of epithets, inciting one to chant the differences before they are uncovered: *The Diviners* is episodic, prosaic, rational, chronological, moralistic, documentary, historical, plodding, and flat; *Kamouraska* is intense, irrational, passionate, poetic, amoral, convoluted, obscure, and tragic (50-52).

French-Canadian fiction is poetic, fantastic, fatalistic; English-Canadian is factual, didactic, moralistic (107). "One might continue the list," Stratford reluctantly acknowledges, "but the further one moves from detailed analysis, the more one slides into vapid generalization" (108).

Many of those who advocate a bicultural position are committed to similar stereotypes in their assertion of cultural differences between the two groups, often forcing a distinction between textual practices where one may not exist, just as those who undertake a unifying approach may do the reverse. Sylvia Söderlind notes this blinkered tendency to identify "the preference in the literature of Quebec for myth and imagination as opposed to the realist bent of Canadian fiction" (209). "[V]apid generalization" is surely as much a danger with the bicultural approach as it is with Sutherland's unifying stance, though Moisan's more socio-historically informed study, *L'âge de la littérature canadienne*, escapes this pitfall. The cultural determinism that Stratford's position presupposes is equally objectionable, and here his approach overlaps with the separatist position described earlier. If Stratford is correct, one has little choice in the narrative approach one uses, for it has been determined long before by generations of cultural and perceptual conditioning – a sort of textual unconscious. He makes scant allowance for stylistic innovation or changing cultural and social awareness, especially where English-Canadian writers are concerned. Thus, in Stratford's view, Kroetsch's credulous use of historical detail/fact in *The Studhorse Man* is scarcely different from that in MacLennan's *Two Solitudes*. Likewise, one French-Canadian novel, Aquin's *Prochain épisode* for example, is hardly more or less radical, passionate, or immediate than another, such as Roy's *Bonheur d'occasion*.

Yet despite attempts to emphasize the distinctness of the two language groups, the bicultural approach as articulated by Stratford has been accused of being still too unifying, for it continues to conceive a vaguely homogeneous nation with two separable literatures. Blodgett has been at the forefront of this attack on the pernicious unifying or universalizing tendencies in critical approaches to the two literatures, but because he emphasizes this fact alone, he does not distinguish between the unifying and bicultural positions. Thus, when he insists that "Canadian and Québec Literatures" be distinguished from "Canadian literature" (*Configuration* 33) – primarily in a refusal to assimilate one literature to the other – he does not acknowledge Stratford's and others' articulations of a similar position.

Ironically, Blodgett, whom I will later identify with a distinct approach to the two literatures, began his theorizing of the subject in a manner close to Stratford's. In "The Canadian Literatures in a Comparative Perspective" (1979), Blodgett critiques the centralist model. He charges this unifying approach – which he sees as the only position articulated by Canadian critics vis-à-vis the two literatures – with obfuscating national difference, and calls for a history of the two that shows both parallel and divergent development, similar and different concerns, much as Stratford calls for in *All the Polarities*. Curiously, the critique of Stratford that one finds in Blodgett's *Configuration* is absent in this article. And this is where his desire for unity becomes clear. In all of his writings on French- and English-Canadian literatures, Blodgett is dependent upon a unifying approach as an antithesis to his own. Thus, in this early article, he posits a misguided unifying or federalist stance as the poison that has tainted discussions of the Canadian literatures. After Stratford articulated his double helix model later that year, however, Blodgett reformulated his position, an act that set him apart from other theorists of the subject and maintained his role as a trailblazer in the field. In *Configuration*, then, one finds Blodgett conflating the unifying and bicultural models by defining both much as I have described the unifying position alone. In opposition, he proposes his own formula, what I call a comparatist-separatist position.

Interestingly, to a separatist such as Chantal de Grandpré, all three paradigms become one unifying "Canadian" approach. This attitude is not surprising because they do all depend on some conception of Canadian unity. Yet her separatist position, like Blodgett's comparatist-separatist model, is dependent on all the others. This dependence suggests how intertwined these approaches are, and how willing individual theorists are to restrict their understanding of the opposition by conflating all to argue the same thing.

The fourth approach to English- and French-Canadian literatures might be called one of "sovereignty-association," a designation lightly applied by Blodgett himself in "How Do You Say 'Gabrielle Roy'?" (22). Blodgett is its most prominent advocate, though other critics who fall into this group are Mezei, Ben-Z. Shek, and Söderlind. This comparative position, however, has the fewest adherents, perhaps because it is the most theoretical and the only one not (yet) applicable to noncomparatists, who generally do not consider the two literatures as distinct national (as opposed to cultural) products that can be compared from an *inter*national perspective.

These critics posit a complete separation of the two literatures, based on the assumptions that there has been no influence between the two literary traditions and that there is essentially no common ground between them, admittedly an issue that Stratford frequently overlooks. Hence, advocates of this position oppose representations of both literatures in single anthologies, literary histories that link them to one Canadian literary tradition or context, thematic pairings that do not emphasize the different *uses* to which similar themes are put, and so on. What distinguishes this group from the separatist group is its vague notion of strategic association with English Canada, a form of "co-operative separatism" (Blodgett,

Configuration 34). However, unlike the literary separatists, this group allows for a comparative approach if it includes a recognition of both literatures as nationally distinct cultural products, and if a convincing case for comparison of individual texts can be made, namely, with a clear historical and ideological contextualization to accompany any aesthetic analysis. Likewise, it might condone a polysystemic approach to literary translation "that both relates the literatures of Canada and problematizes their relationship," one that privileges "acceptability in the polysystem of the target-language" over "adequacy with respect to the source-text" (Blodgett, "Towards a Model" 190-91).

Critics in this fourth group generally speak of the two literatures as "Canadian and Québécois/Quebec literatures," thereby avoiding any Canadian nationalist or unifying implications. This distinction, Blodgett writes, "corresponds to a reality, as well as to a refusal to assimilate" (*Configuration* 33). Yet to a certain extent, this model is as constructed as those that Blodgett counters, for the categories "Canadian" and "Québécois" are equally problematic. Even in Blodgett's text it is unclear how he means one to understand "Quebec." According to William Westfall, two different conceptions of region are involved in definitions of Quebec: formal regions are characterized by similarity of some kind, functional regions by functional relationships (7). In Westfall's analysis, "Quebec is a functional region based on the extent of the administrative and legal functions of a provincial government. It encompasses any number of formal regions. French Canada, however, is a formal region based on the criteria of ethnicity and culture" (9). The latter is not defined by strict geographical or provincial boundaries.

The uncertainty as to what constitutes "Québécois" literature has led to various contradictory uses of the term. For some it refers to francophone writers who live or have lived in Quebec; the writings of English and various ethno-Quebeckers thus have no identifying label. For others it extends to writings by francophones throughout Canada, despite the implied geographical restriction of the term. André Vachon emphasizes the political dimensions of an "écriture québécoise" by applying it to "les textes qui, depuis plus d'un siècle se nourrissent, et naissent, d'un doute réel quant à la possibilité d'une installation française en Amérique britannique du Nord" (194). While this position allows for political resistance on the level of content, Joseph Melançon stresses the need for a Quebec "writing of difference" (21) and sees "*québécité*" (Sarkonak 12) on the level of language only. In these terms, language is seen as "the mark of nationality in literature" (22), which, when applied to Canada, generally implies a static bicultural/bilingual vision of the country, a construction of two opposing homogeneous formal regions, resulting in the polarization of French and English that we still see today.

To Blodgett, it is not literary qualities but the "conception of 'Canadian'" that forms the basis of critical approaches to the two literatures (*Configuration* 27). It is this notion of "Canadian" or "Canada" that is debatable, he says: "despite the fact that Canada is at least two nations whose federal jurisdiction is still in the process of definition, literary critics continue to behave ... as if Canada were one country with literatures in two different languages" (17). In the course of his argument, however, his definition of nationhood changes. While at first he denies Canada's status as a politically unified nation-state, he later recoups it as a political entity whose task is to preserve cultural plurality (34).

Yet Blodgett rightly questions, as those who support a unifying position do not, "whether a shared place implies a shared time, a shared past, and a shared ideology" (*Configuration* 25). To answer yes, he argues, is to ignore the reality of difference not only between English and French but also among the various multicultural groups in Canada. Here Blodgett opposes the unifying concept of pan-Canadian cultural homogeneity, based, as it often is, on arguments supporting a form of geographical determinism. Yet the subdivision of Canada into geographically specific cultural and linguistic groups, as Cook notes, raises an additional problem: "namely that ethnic groups [are] inconveniently distributed geographically" (*Maple Leaf* xvi). In other words, it is a mistake to identify a province with a nation, just as one cannot always identify a nation with a state. That ethnic and cultural groups in Canada are not distributed in clearly definable areas – hence obviating the possibility of cultural and linguistic homogeneity necessary to the traditional constitution of nationhood – renders it difficult to establish national identities even within Canada, as, for example, with Quebec. It is in this sense that the figuration of place in the Canadian imagination, as Blodgett argues in "After Pierre Berton What?," is summarily ideological (66), though there remains a contradiction between his deconstruction of the geographical referentiality of "Canada" and his affirmation of "Quebec" as a distinct, national unit.

Cook's observation above is consistent with Blodgett's current refinement of these issues, namely, his suggestion that the identification of Canada as a "spatial referent" is a mistake propagated by Northrop Frye's famous question, "Where is here?" (Blodgett, "History"). In Blodgett's view, it is imperative that the frontiers of cultural distinction – and he does not mean these in the geographical sense, despite the metaphor – be maintained when approaching the two literatures: "The great temptation for the comparatist ... is to see oneself ... as other, to become so cosmopolitan as to obscure the metonymies of national literatures by the metaphor of universal forms" (*Configuration* 14). Stratford, making the move that Blodgett censures, transfers this desire to be "other" to a personal level, expressing wistful regret at his unicultural heritage: "Comparatists of

Canadian subjects are themselves condemned to maintain a paradoxical duality.... [They are] hamstrung by an inevitable ... affiliation to one of the two camps.... They must try to acquire the other culture while knowing full well that it will never become their true heritage" ("Emblems" 138). Such a universalizing impulse Blodgett attributes to Stratford, Sutherland, and Smith, those whom he believes conflate the two literatures (or overcome their dialectical relationship [14]) according to traditional power relations: English Canada subsuming or assimilating French.

✻   ✻   ✻

And so the debate meanders, little closer to uncovering a solution to the polarized opposition of French and English, still lacking a grand plan for relating the two literatures. Yet it is this grand-plan or template approach that restricts each of the four positions. One finds that each position, each theorist, constructs a generalizing, homogenizing, even universalizing pattern with which to approach the two literatures based on his or her conception of English and French cultural likeness or difference. Such plans demand that individual comparisons be conducted within the parameters of this larger configuration, and ultimately deny the context of any particular comparative undertaking. In each case, this restriction creates an all-or-none option. Searching for a foolproof and timeless fixative with which to preserve the two literatures, the critic backs into a corner with prescriptive generalizations, a fact most evident when they are applied to individual literary works.

The problem is that each approach continues to conceive of the possibilities in eenie-meenie terms, as an either/or hierarchical formulation: likeness versus difference, unity versus separation, English versus French. Blind to any alternative to this binary configuration, critics have not enunciated the possibility of different cultural nations or formal regions coexisting within a single polity, a single functional region. The only one to express an awareness of this dilemma is Blodgett, who claims to overcome the binary opposition with his multicultural approach to Canadian literature. Yet despite his affirmation of Canada's pluralist society, his reliance on dialectics keeps him trapped in an oppositional construction, what is initially an either/or quandary: unity versus separation, national versus cultural identity. Because the pluralist approach only extends the polarities into an infinite number of configurations, it creates, to use Frye's term, multiple garrisons (Conclusion 831), each of which remains divided between two poles: national unity and individual cultural identity, centre and margin. Even though Blodgett persists with the metaphor, the centre-versus-margin distinction, as it has been heretofore conceived, does not work in a Canadian context. In Westfall's analysis, these terms only confuse functional and formal regions, and in some cases imply the existence of two regions that actually function as one (9). And this is not only because each margin can be further subdivided into another centre-versus-margin. In Canada, to be at the margin *implies* identity; to be in the centre entails amorphousness, lack of identity, lack of community. To be in the centre is to locate oneself somewhere on the rungs of Stratford's double helix, dangling without a firm foothold, least of all a literary canon.

To speak in English (centre) versus French (margin) cultural terms implies a conception of English Canada as a distinct cultural entity (typically associated with a Scots, Calvinist heritage), which in reality does not exist. To be identified as a distinct – and unified – cultural or political group by virtue of language alone (as is also implied when speaking of "French-Canadian" or "Québécois" culture) is not sufficient, as any number of "English" Canadians could attest. Charles Taylor, speaking from Quebec, expresses the need for "a handy way of referring to the rest of the country as an entity, even if it lacks for the moment political expression" (184). Yet even Taylor finds fault with the "two nations" formula, which he sees as "an attempt by French Canadians to foist a symmetrical identity on their partners" (170). It is in this sense, as W.H. New notes, that "the language of perceived margins has the longstanding capacity to circumscribe ... the language of presumed centres of authority" (10). It is important to note the construction of English Canada as well as French within the French-English debate.

This persistent, polarizing method of conceiving not only the Canadian literatures, but the Canadian federation itself, has only led to an impasse. Invoking principles of exclusion and stereotype, Canadian literary critics are ultimately caught by their cultural determinism, producing static theories trapped within history. As long as one persists in perceiving national and cultural interrelationships in them-versus-us terms, one remains caught within the historical cycle of subjection, imperialism, and inequality. The solution to the impasse must involve a shift away from an exclusionary emphasis on history and ancestry. According to the West Indian novelist and critic Wilson Harris, cultures must be freed from the destructive dialectic of history: they must escape the "monolithic character of conquistadorial legacies of civilisation" (xv) and move "beyond polarised structures" (xviii). As is evident in the debate surrounding English- and French-Canadian literatures, critics are fixed on a past that stresses ancestry and values "the 'pure' over its threatening opposite, the 'composite'" (Ashcroft 36). Indeed, such backward gazing allows no other alternative than this binary opposition.

The error stems from an inability to conceive of unity and identity as distinct, but not mutually exclusive. This inability may be a flaw in the comparative enterprise generally, where the inscription of difference is overwritten by an impulse to universalize, and where language is often taken as the sole marker of nationality. The conflation of unity and identity is rooted in a nineteenth-century conception of nationalism that "insisted that legitimate nations were communities of people whose language and culture were homogeneous" (Cook, *Maple Leaf* xvi). Connected to this idea is the assumption, imported to Canada with the principles of Arnoldian humanism, "that national cultural greatness validates national sovereignty" (Fee 21). According to Frye, it has long been a mistake in Canada to promote Canadian unity and identity as though they could constitute one solid identity: "in Canada they are perhaps more different than they are anywhere else. Identity is local and regional, rooted in the imagination and in works of culture; unity is national in reference, international in perspective, and rooted in a political feeling" (*Bush Garden* ii). This view is expressed more pithily, perhaps, by Yvon Deschamps's famous joke about the apparent fickleness of the Québécois: "I don't know why the English think of us as inconsistent. All we want is an independent Quebec within a strong and united Canada" (qtd. in Newman 3). If by "national identity" a political federation is to be understood, surely by "cultural identity" a heterogeneous, multicultural, at times multiregional (in all the implied variations), and indeed multinational awareness is implicit. In other words, it is a mistake to think of Canada (or even "English Canada") in cultural terms alone, for this presupposes the nation as a formal region defined by cultural symmetry. Instead, Canada is a functional region composed of any number of formal regions – social, cultural, linguistic, ethnic, political – whose role is to protect the diversity and integrity of its constituents.

As Coral Ann Howells notes, "The Canadian problem of identity may not be the problem of having no identity but rather of having multiple identities, so that any single national self-image is reductive ..." (26). Can there in fact be a "Canadian" identity without multiple cultural and national identities? The Canadian historian J.M.S. Careless highlights this persistence of "'limited identities' of region, culture, and class" as the characteristic way in which Canadians interpret their nation-state as a whole (3). This consistent tension between unity and identity, says Frye, defines what it is to be Canadian, much like the "psychic unease" that results from a lack of union characteristic in postcolonial societies (Williams 19). So the split perception regarding the "English" French-Canadian canon that I identified among many English-Canadian anthologists and critics at the outset of this paper – an apparently conflicting desire for political unity and cultural diversity – is perhaps an accurate expression of Canadian experience after all.

In "Grounds for Translation," Jones highlights a corresponding tension. He argues that every act of communication includes a welcome element of mistranslation, comparable to the split between unity and identity that Frye notes. If, as I stated earlier, the desire for political unity underlying the critical approaches of Canadian literary theorists is counterbalanced by a desire for disunity, then it seems that both desires are consistently required to maintain the tension. All four positions, then, can be seen as balanced somewhere along a theoretical tightrope, quivering between unity and disunity, communication and babble.

The mistake, says Frye, has been the attempt to overcome this tension by assimilating one element to the other, an act that always yields contradictory polarities: "Assimilating identity to unity produces the empty gestures of cultural nationalism; assimilating unity to identity produces the kind of provincial isolation which is now called separatism" (*Bush Garden* iii). The former assimilation, of course, is clearly a problem in the unifying position (and perhaps the bicultural approach); the latter informs the separatist, bicultural, and comparatist-separatist models.

Frye's analysis can be used to counter Blodgett's account of critics' approaches to Canada's two literatures, particularly his polarization of metaphorical and metonymical conceptualizations in *Configuration*. Whereas Blodgett favours the metonymical, Frye's terms suggest that both impulses, when isolated, are flawed because each conflates unity and identity: assimilating identity to unity is certainly a metaphoric impulse; subsuming unity to identity is metonymic, reductive. By conceiving of unity and identity in dialectical terms, and stressing the need for a transmutation of the perceived standoff, Blodgett retains an oppositional construction.

Yet the conflation of unity and identity is an error committed by all the critics whom I have discussed, what New oxymoronically terms "unitary 'identity'" (6). Cultural validity (identity), says New, cannot be equated with "a set of particular cultural features that are taken to be distinguishing signs of nationality [unity]" (6). If conflation is the only way of conceiving unity and identity together, then the sole choice is between separation and unity, and it is this opposition that Canadian critics have been incapable of moving beyond. None of the four positions allows for a concept of unity and identity as coexistent.

Identity (or regionalism) without political unity always returns one to the historical impasse noted earlier: multiple nationalisms marked by sectarian and protective interests. Yet the political unity proposed by Frye is of a particular form. He clearly differentiates between unity and uniformity, a distinction unacknowledged by most theorists of French- and English-Canadian literatures: "a sense of unity is the opposite of a sense of uniformity. Uniformity, where everyone 'belongs,' uses the same clichés, thinks alike and behaves alike, produces a society which seems comfortable at first but is totally lacking in human dignity. Real unity tolerates dissent and rejoices in variety of outlook and tradition ..." (*Bush Garden* vi).

Frye's distinction corresponds to Cook's differentiation between nationalism and nationhood. Cook critiques the standard liberal conception of nationalism, which, based on cultural homogeneity, "led only to the tyranny of majority cultures over minorities. Nations were more properly seen as political rather than cultural entities that deserved the allegiance of citizens not through claims of cultural uniqueness, but rather because they protected cultural pluralism ..." (*Maple Leaf* xvii).

Sutherland, therefore, and others who advocate a unifying approach, clearly have a sense of uniformity (thematic or otherwise) when discussing the connections between the two literatures. Stratford, Blodgett, and others falling into any of the remaining positions conceive of uniformity (though they call it unity) as something to react against. Blodgett, for example, approves of the title of the Association for Canadian and Quebec Literatures as indicative of "a refusal to assimilate" (*Configuration* 33). "To do otherwise," he notes, "would be to commit the crime ... of '*symmetrization* ...'" (33). The alternatives posed here are explicit: maintain one's difference or cease to exist as a distinct entity. Cultural difference and political unity are seen as incompatible.

Missing from both Frye's and Cook's assessments of the political construction of Canada is an account of the "ways of belonging" experienced by different national communities within the federation (183), a distinction outlined by Taylor in *Reconciling the Solitudes*. In a sense, Frye and Cook impose their own brand of uniformity on Canadian multiculturalism through a symmetrical model of citizenship. As Margery Fee points out, such "master narratives of the nation" endorse a monolithic nationalism that overrides difference (33). Taylor offers a way out of this dilemma with a more coherent means of allowing for both unity and diversity within the Canadian polity. He outlines two levels of diversity in Canada. The first valorizes the multiethnic composition of the country, but sees each member as sharing a uniform sense of belonging to one multicultural mosaic that protects individual rights. "Second-level or 'deep' diversity" accounts for other ways of belonging in Canada, ways that would "'pass through' some other community" (183); examples here are First Nations peoples and Quebec. Only a combination of these levels of diversity, says Taylor, can provide a formula upon which a united, federated Canada can be built. This newly constructed Canada "would unquestionably be dual in one important respect. There would be two major societies, each defined by its own dominant language. But each of these societies within itself would be more and more diverse," constituted by ethnic, cultural, linguistic, and national variation (200). The key to political unity would involve coexistence through mutual recognition.

Earlier I noted that most critical approaches to French- and English-Canadian literatures have been informed by an underlying desire for political unity. Perhaps it would have been more accurate to speak of national uniformity in that context, for this is clearly how Canadian critics have understood the term. Blodgett's linking of attempts to unify the two cultures with impulses towards uniformity or universalization is thus based on an equivalence of the terms. By taking for granted that this is the implication of all conceptions of political unity, critics have been unable to carry the debate forward "into the distance of time, into futurity as dimension" (Harris xvi).

Apparently in Canada the "internal perception of a mosaic has not generated corresponding theories of literary hybridity to replace the nationalist approach" (Ashcroft 36). A reconception of political unity is required if Canadians are to escape the dialectic of history, combined with a parallel critical and creative refiguring of approaches to French- and English-Canadian literatures. And so, not to exempt myself after all, I too am constructing a means of having it both ways, by figuring the coexistence of political unity and cultural diversity, recognizing difference while allowing for historical and ideological contexts of similitude and interaction, and finally in suggesting the possibility of a "truly inclusive Canadian canon" (Söderlind 7). This reconception of the relationship between French- and English-Canadian literatures might provide one means of moving forward, of continuing the debate in nonpolarized terms. It might also allow us to refashion Stratford's double helix into a nonpolarized structure in which the two literatures do not compose the helical frame of the model, but are instead analogous to the genetic sequences themselves, constituting both the frame and the rungs of the molecule, and, most importantly, arranged along a single strand in contiguous or split intervals depending on where the critic chooses to slice it at any given time.

Notes

I would like to acknowledge the assistance of a SSHRCC Doctoral Fellowship in the research and preparation of this article.

1   I find the designations "English Canadian" and "French Canadian" (which refer to language alone and not to cultural or ethnic identification) the most useful for my purposes, primarily because I am not speaking solely of Québécois writing here, but of French-Canadian writing throughout Canada – writing of the "Québécois diaspora" (Sarkonak 10) – and also because the term "French Canadian" is appropriate to the discourse of many of the critics whom I will be discussing. To a certain extent, one can trace critics' perceptions of the position of French-Canadian literature within the general body of Canadian literature by their terminology: "Canadian literature" to encompass both; "the Canadian literatures" to recognize the separate exis-

tence of the two but still merge them within one national canon; "Canadian and Québécois literatures" to highlight them as distinct national literatures. Because critics tend to conceive the relationship between the two literatures in general political terms (Quebec vs. the rest of Canada), I will periodically speak of Québécois literature or culture when outlining the political configurations of the debate.

2   The discussion of the turbid relationship between the two literatures has, in English-Canadian literary circles, long been split between Canadian comparatists, who in the 1970s began to theorize their convoluted relationship, and noncomparatists, who have been concerned with the subject for much longer. The rift between the two is based largely on their lack of contact with one another (separate societies, separate publications, etc.), for both, in practice, undertake comparisons of the two literatures. In an age of increased interdisciplinary studies, when the separation of comparatists and noncomparatists is less valid, it is appropriate that these long-separate discussions be brought together, as I do in this paper. My use of the terms "comparatist" and "noncomparatist" is based on how the critic in question defines him- or herself.

3   This suggests that rarely is one critic firmly in one group at all times; rather, I have chosen generally representative critics for each group. Such is the case with John Moss, who articulates a bicultural stance in his introduction to *Patterns of Isolation in English Canadian Fiction* – "... English and French Canadian fiction participate in distinctly separable traditions which only occasionally converge" (10) – while his analyses elide the cultural and linguistic boundaries of the two literatures, leading him into discussions of similar thematic patterns in both. It is the case with many of these critics that their theoretical discussions of the Canadian literatures do not always coincide with their studies of specific texts.

4   I am distinguishing between Smith's separatist position as the anthologist of *The Book of Canadian Poetry* and his later critical discussions of the two literatures, particularly in his Oxford anthologies, which outline diverging, but at times parallel, traditions.

5   Of Jones's many critical writings, I am thinking primarily of his extended study *Butterfly on Rock*, and not his various writings on translation that might place him in the bicultural approach that I discuss later. Even though his focus in *Butterfly on Rock* is English-Canadian literature, he states that "a combined study would have been profitable" (9). Moreover, his inclusion of Gabrielle Roy, because of her Manitoba origins, in the "same imaginative world as that inhabited by the English-speaking writers" (10) is consistent with the unifying approach that posits geographical, rather than cultural, distinction as the key difference between the two language groups.

Works Cited

Ashcroft, Bill, Gareth Griffiths, and Helen Tiffin. *The Empire Writes Back: Theory and Practice in Post-Colonial Literatures.* New Accents. London: Routledge, 1989.

Atwood, Margaret. *Survival: A Thematic Guide to Canadian Literature.* Toronto: Anansi, 1972.

Bell, David V.J. *The Roots of Disunity: A Study of Canadian Political Culture.* Rev. ed. Toronto: Oxford UP, 1992.

Blodgett, E.D. "After Pierre Berton What? In Search of a Canadian Literature." *Essays on Canadian Writing* 30 (1985): 61-80.

—. "The Canadian Literatures in a Comparative Perspective." *Essays on Canadian Writing* 15 (1979): 5-24.

—. *Configuration: Essays in the Canadian Literatures.* Downsview, ON: ECW, 1982.

—. "How Do You Say 'Gabrielle Roy'?" *Translation in Canadian Literature, Symposium 1982.* Ed. Camille La Bossière. Reappraisals: Canadian Writers 9. Ottawa: U of Ottawa P, 1983. 13-14.

—. "Is a History of the Literatures of Canada Possible?" Paper presented at symposium, Aux Canadas: Reading, Writing, Translating Canadian Literatures, Colloque en l'honneur de Philip Stratford. Montreal, 18 Apr. 1993.

—. "Towards a Methodology of Comparative Canadian Studies: Canadian as Comparative Literature." *Comparative Canadian Literature.* Ed. Philip Stratford. Spec. iss. of *Canadian Review of Comparative Literature* 6 (1979): 127-30.

—. "Towards a Model of Literary Translation in Canada." *TTR: Traduction, Terminologie, Rédaction* 4.2 (1991): 189-206.

Careless, J.M.S. "'Limited Identities' in Canada." *Canadian Historical Review* 50.1 (1969): 1-10.

Cavell, Richard. "Querying the Canadian Literatures: Towards a Comparative Cultural Poetics." Paper presented at symposium, Aux Canadas: Reading, Writing, Translating Canadian Literatures, Colloque en l'honneur de Philip Stratford. Montreal, 18 Apr. 1993.

Cook, Ramsay. *Canada, Quebec, and the Uses of Nationalism.* Toronto: McClelland & Stewart, 1986.

—. *The Maple Leaf Forever: Essays on Nationalism and Politics in Canada.* 1977. Toronto: Copp Clark, 1986.

Coren, Michael. "Leggo Thy Ego." *Books in Canada* Feb. 1993: 55.

Dimić, Milan V. "Towards a Methodology of Comparative Canadian Studies: General Considerations." *Comparative Canadian Literature.* Ed. Philip Stratford. Spec. iss. of *Canadian Review of Comparative Literature* 6 (1979): 115-17.

Dudek, Louis. "The Mirror of Art: Relations between French and English Literature in Canada." *Selected Essays and Criticism.* Ottawa: Tecumseh, 1978. 290-96.

—. "The Two Traditions Literature and the Ferment in Quebec." *Selected Essays and Criticism.* Ottawa: Tecumseh, 1978. 157-65.

CYNTHIA SUGARS

Fee, Margery. "Canadian Literature and English Studies in the Canadian University." *Essays on Canadian Writing* 48 (1992-93): 20-40.

Frye, Northrop. *The Bush Garden: Essays on the Canadian Imagination*. Toronto: Anansi, 1971.

—. Conclusion. *Literary History of Canada: Canadian Literature in English*. Gen. ed. Carl F. Klinck. Toronto: U of Toronto P, 1965. 821-49.

Giguère, Richard. "Traduction littéraire et 'image' de la littérature au Canada et au Québec." *Translation in Canadian Literature, Symposium 1982*. Ed. Camille La Bossière. Reappraisals: Canadian Writers 9. Ottawa: U of Ottawa P, 1983. 47-60.

Goldie, Terry. "Alas, Poor Beaver." Rev. of *Taking Stock: The Calgary Conference on the Canadian Novel*, ed. Charles Steele. *Canadian Literature* 99 (1983): 93-97.

Grandpré, Chantal de. "La canadianisation de la littérature québécoise: le cas Aquin." *Liberté* 159 (1985): 50-59.

Harris, Wilson. *The Womb of Space: The Cross-Cultural Imagination*. Contributions in Afro-American and African Studies 73. Westport, CT: Greenwood, 1983.

Howells, Coral Ann. *Private and Fictional Worlds: Canadian Women Novelists of the 1970s and 1980s*. London: Methuen, 1987.

Jones, D.G. *Butterfly on Rock: A Study of Themes and Images in Canadian Literature*. Toronto: U of Toronto P, 1970.

—. "Grounds for Translation / Raisons d'être de la traduction." *Ellipse* 21 (1977): 58-91.

Keith, W.J. *Canadian Literature in English*. London: Longman, 1985.

Klinck, Carl F., and R.E. Watters, eds. *Canadian Anthology*. Toronto: Gage, 1955.

Lecker, Robert. "A Country without a Canon?: Canadian Literature and the Esthetics of Idealism." *Mosaic* 26.3 (1993): 1-19.

MacMechan, Archibald. *Headwaters of Canadian Literature*. 1924. Introd. M.G. Parks. New Canadian Library 107. Toronto: McClelland & Stewart, 1974.

Mathews, Robin. *Canadian Literature: Surrender or Revolution*. Toronto: Steel Rail, 1978.

Melançon, Joseph. "The Writing of Difference in Québec." *The Language of Difference: Writing in QUEBEC(ois)*. Ed. Ralph Sarkonak. Spec. iss. of *Yale French Studies* 65 (1983): 21-29.

Mezei, Kathy. "A Bridge of Sorts: The Translation of Quebec Literature into English." *Anglo-French Literary Relations*. Ed. C.J. Rawson. Spec. iss. of *Yearbook of English Studies* 15 (1985): 201-26.

—. "Speaking White: Literary Translation as a Vehicle of Assimilation in Quebec." *Canadian Literature* 117 (1988): 11-23.

Moisan, Clément. *L'âge de la littérature canadienne: essai*. Collection constantes 19. Montreal: HMH, 1969.

Moss, John. *Patterns of Isolation in English Canadian Fiction*. Toronto: McClelland & Stewart, 1974.

New, W.H. "The Very Idea." Editorial. *Canadian Literature* 135 (1992): 2-11.

Newman, Peter C. "Lévesque's Immaculate Conception: Quebec as Virgin, and a Mother Too." Editorial. *Maclean's* 13 Nov. 1978: 3.

Pacey, Desmond, ed. and introd. *A Book of Canadian Stories*. Rev. ed. Toronto: Ryerson, 1950.

—. *Creative Writing in Canada: A Short History of English-Canadian Literature*. Rev. ed. Toronto: Ryerson, 1961.

Pierce, Lorne. *An Outline of Canadian Literature (French and English)*. Toronto: Ryerson, 1927.

Ross, Malcolm. "The Ballot." *Taking Stock: The Calgary Conference on the Canadian Novel*. Ed. Charles Steele. Downsview, ON: ECW, 1982. 136-64.

Rubinger, Catherine. "Two Related Solitudes: Canadian Novels in French and English." *Journal of Commonwealth Literature* 3 (1967): 49-57.

Sarkonak, Ralph. "Accentuating the Differences." *The Language of Difference: Writing in QUEBEC(ois)*. Ed. Sarkonak. Spec. iss. of *Yale French Studies* 65 (1983): 3-20.

Shek, Ben-Z. "Diglossia and Ideology: Socio-Cultural Aspects of 'Translation' in Quebec." *TTR: Traduction, Terminologie, Rédaction* 1.1 (1988): 85-91.

—. *French-Canadian and Québécois Novels*. Perspectives on Canadian Culture. Toronto: Oxford UP, 1991.

—. "Quelques réflexions sur la traduction dans le contexte socio-culturel canado-québécois." *Ellipse* 21 (1977): 111-17.

Shouldice, Larry. "*Chacun son mishigos*: The Translator as Comparatist." *Essays on Canadian Writing* 15 (1979): 25-32.

—. "On the Politics of Literary Translation in Canada." *Translation in Canadian Literature, Symposium 1982*. Ed. Camille La Bossière. Reappraisals: Canadian Writers 9. Ottawa: U of Ottawa P, 1983. 73-82.

Simon, Sherry. "The True Quebec as Revealed to English Canada: Translated Novels, 1864-1950." *Canadian Literature* 117 (1988): 31-43.

Sirois, Antoine. "La périodisation dans les littératures du Canada." *Comparative Canadian Literature*. Ed. Philip Stratford. Spec. iss. of *Canadian Review of Comparative Literature* 6 (1979): 119-21.

Smith, A.J.M., ed. and introd. *The Book of Canadian Poetry*. Chicago: U of Chicago P, 1943. Rev. ed. Toronto: Gage, 1948.

—, ed. *Modern Canadian Verse in English and French*. Toronto: Oxford UP, 1967.

—, ed. and introd. *The Oxford Book of Canadian Verse in English and French*. Toronto: Oxford UP, 1960.

Söderlind, Sylvia. *Margin/Alias: Language and Colonization in Canadian and Québécois Fiction*. Toronto: U of Toronto P, 1991.

Sollers, Werner. "A Critique of Pure Pluralism." *Reconstructing American Literary History*. Ed. Sacvan Bercovitch. Cambridge, MA: Harvard UP, 1986. 250-79.

Stratford, Philip. *All the Polarities: Comparative Studies in Contemporary Canadian Novels in French and English*. Toronto: ECW, 1986.

—. "Canada's Two Literatures: A Search for Emblems." *Comparative Canadian*

Literature. Ed. Philip Stratford. Spec. iss. of *Canadian Review of Comparative Literature* 6 (1979): 131-38.

Sutherland, Ronald. *The New Hero: Essays in Comparative Quebec/Canadian Literature*. Toronto: Macmillan, 1977.

—. *Second Image: Comparative Studies in Québec/Canadian Literature*. Toronto: New, 1971.

—. "Twin Solitudes." *Canadian Literature* 31 (1967): 5-24.

"Symposium: Littérature Canadienne – Canadian Literature." *Comparative Literature in Canada Newsletter* 2.2 (1970): 5-8.

Taylor, Charles. *Reconciling the Solitudes: Essays on Canadian Federalism and Nationalism*. Ed. Guy Laforest. Montreal: McGill-Queen's UP, 1993.

Vachon, G.-André. "Naissance d'une écriture." *Études françaises* 9 (1973): 191-96.

Westfall, William. "On the Concept of Region in Canadian History and Literature." *Journal of Canadian Studies* 15.2 (1980): 3-15.

Williams, Denis. *Image and Idea in the Arts of Guyana*. Georgetown, Guyana: National History and Arts Council, 1969.

Culture, Intellect, and Context: Recent Writing on the Cultural and Intellectual History of Ontario

A.B. McKillop

The most obvious source for a historian to consult when reviewing the state of cultural and intellectual history in Canada is the category bearing that name in the "Recent Publications Related to Canada" section of *The Canadian Historical Review*. Other bibliographical guides exist to indicate what has been written on these subjects in the Ontario context,[1] but the *Canadian Historical Review*'s compilation presumably represents, explicitly or implicitly, the conceptual and thematic boundaries of sub-disciplinary units as they currently exist within the historical profession in English-speaking Canada. A historiographical essay that utilizes the *Canadian Historical Review*'s bibliography as its research base will also, therefore, be an implicit commentary on "cultural and intellectual history" as historiographical categories distinct from others, and possibly from each other.

What one discovers is that the section on "Cultural and Intellectual History" consists mainly of an eclectic mixture of historical categories left over among the index cards (or computer files) of whatever University of Toronto graduate student gets "the *CHR* job" in a given year. This, it must immediately be said, is not a criticism of that editorial assistant; in fact, the completed entry probably comprises an all too accurate reflection of the perceived nature of cultural and intellectual history in Canada – a conceptual residuum, a scholarly junkyard of all sorts of flotsam and jetsam.

This eclectic mixture, by itself, does not necessarily constitute a basis for criticism. One must ask rather if the corpus of material reflects, methodologically or philosophically, a serious desire to understand the nature of "culture" in a pluralistic society. Does the corpus deal with the relationships between sub-cultures in a country characterized for the past twenty years as one of "limited identities"? Unfortunately, with too few exceptions, neither is the case.

One should not be too negative. The hours of taking notes on Canadian cultural and intellectual history, searching for those that bear specifically on Ontario, were enjoyable ones. In fact, I was frankly relieved that I was not responsible for coming to grips with the larger significance of Glen Campbell's article "Dithyramb and Diatribe: The Polysemic Perception of the Métis in Louis Riel's Poetry."[2] A Blue Jays fan who barely survived the anxious summer of 1987, I was relieved that I would not be forced to recall those emotions by reading a book called *The Year*

the Expos Almost Won the Pennant (1980), published in Toronto.[3] I concluded – perhaps too quickly – that some topics transcended the culture
of Ontario. Thus, if the 1960s asked "What is the Canadian Identity?" and
the 1970s sought a location for it by pursuing the meaning of Northrop
Frye's enigmatic question "Where is here?", the 1980s provided a synthesis, of sorts, in the article "What Is a Canadian Chair?: Some Thoughts on
Documentation and Definition."[4]

Not that, in examining works on Ontario, I did not have my own
crosses to bear. I confess that I did not read D. Boc's M.A. thesis, "A
Musical Analysis of Folktunes in Deseronto, Ontario";[5] nor did I examine,
closely or otherwise, "Margaret Atwood's Hands," the title of the piece by
George Bowering in *Studies in Canadian Literature.*[6] My interest in the cul-
tural cross-currents of Hogtown – in spite of having lived two years in the
Annex – was not deep enough to look up David Rennie's "Survey of York
University 1976-78 Bachelor's Degree Graduates in Psychology Located in
Greater Toronto."[7] The words "custom" and "tradition" are reasonably central to cultural history in the age of Thompson and Hobsbawm, but I was
not fooled by one book's title, *Customs and Traditions of the Canadian Armed
Forces.*[8] I suspect that it belongs in a bibliography of cultural and intellectual history about as much as Shaw's play *Arms and the Man* does in a "further reading" supplement to *Soldier of Fortune* magazine.

It would be unfair, however, to conclude that among the hundreds of
items bearing on cultural subjects in the *Canadian Historical Review* bibliography there was little of consequence. Far from it. In fact, the record
demonstrated a fair amount of cultural observation and criticism – by
journalists, librarians, professors of English, professional critics, and others.
Many kinds of articles have been written on many kinds of subjects by
many kinds of people. One could find almost anything but items that were
specifically and consciously acts of cultural history produced by historians.

The distinction between cultural criticism (or observation) and cultural
history is not one that seems to exist to those who have organized the
Canadian Historical Review bibliography. For example, the relationship that
The Blue Notebook: Reports on Canadian Culture,[9] Doug Fetherling's per-
ceptive collection of essays, bears to cultural history is akin to that which
a collection of June Callwood's columns in *The Globe and Mail* are to
women's history. Both are insightful on a wide variety of topics; but both,
generally, lack sustained historical context. As a journalist, neither author
feels particularly obliged to provide it.[10] In any event, both examples may
be seen as the necessary yet "unseasoned" items that will eventually
become (if they are not so already) the primary sources from which actual
cultural history will one day be written. Such is also the case with insightful articles of literary criticism that threaten at times to overwhelm the
"cultural and intellectual history" section of the *Canadian Historical Review*

bibliography. "Faith and Fiction: The Novels of Callaghan and Hood" or "Dialectic, Morality, and the Deptford Trilogy" are articles of interest to Canadian cultural historians, for they illuminate themes of genuine historical significance.[11] But, like their journalistic counterparts, acts of scholarly "cultural history" they are not.

This lack of concern for broad historical context should not be surprising. Maria Tippett's 1986 review of "The Writing of English-Canadian Cultural History, 1970-85" for *The Canadian Historical Review* is remarkable for its lack of reference to professional historians — at least, to those who might likely be members of the "Cultural and Intellectual History" group of the Canadian Historical Association. Some familiar names appear in her footnotes — Ramsay Cook, Mary Vipond, Jack Bumsted, Douglas Cole, Tippett herself — but they just about exhaust the list of historians who, until 1986, had ventured to write about the visual arts, literature, drama, and music, those aspects of cultural history focused upon in the review. Understandably, Tippett concluded her article with the unhappy observation that "most scholars engaged in English-Canadian cultural studies have failed to fulfil the cultural historian's task."[12] Earlier in the essay, she had outlined that task:

> One must realize ... that the cultural artifact, like the historical "event," is shaped both by circumstance and the intention of its creator, and that it is received, interpreted, and made functional in a society at a given point in time in ways largely determined by the political, economic, social, and institutional framework of that society. It is with the disentangling of these various strands, and with the specifying of their relationship to one another, that the cultural historian must be primarily concerned.[13]

Tippett's main complaint was less with the quality of particular work undertaken than with its circumscribed nature. She lamented what she called its "limited dialogue with the end product," its seeming incapacity to "compare one cultural activity with another," its inclination to see individual cultural activities as discrete entities rather than to apply culture's horticultural etymon, as elements in the general endeavour of tending the natural growth of society in all its elements.[14] "The student of English-Canada's cultural history," she wrote,

> is ... left with the impression that avant-garde movements best represent the culture of any one epoch; that over time English-Canadian culture has grown "better" and become more "indigenous" without yet having come fully into its own; that the culture can best be defined and understood within the Canadian-American context; and,

finally, that cultural history consists of a series of specialized studies focused on particular fields of cultural activity, the development of which can be understood without the necessity of paying much attention to the process by which and the context within which the work in those fields came into being.[15]

This lack of historical context is understandable, since most of the cultural history with which Tippett was concerned had been done by scholars and others concerned with text, not context – with the internal significance of paintings, novels, or poems rather than with their social meaning as cultural artifacts. For their part, as Carl Berger pointed out in 1986, mainstream historians in university history departments seldom ventured into such élite aspects of the history of culture and have therefore contributed little. "The rise of social history," Berger noted, "expressed a distrust if not disdain for the activities and achievements of élites and a preference for attempting to understand the mentalities and popular beliefs of large groups of people. As a result historians of Canada seemed to possess a limited view of cultural history."[16]

Works varying in quality were produced across the spectrum of "culture studies" – whether in literary biography, literary criticism, architectural and art history, or the mass media of film, radio, and television. As in the past, much of the best recent "cultural history" has taken the form of biography. Biographies, some of them major two-volume efforts, appeared on public figures as diverse as Emma Albani, David Boyle, Isabella Valancy Crawford, Sara Jeannette Duncan, Sir Robert Falconer, E.J. Pratt, William Arthur Deacon, Vincent Massey, Frank Underhill, Marshall McLuhan, Neil Young, and others. In several, contextualization of the individual life has been so good that the biography has added, in major ways, to our understanding of the general cultural or intellectual history of the period.[17] Victorian architecture, especially in Toronto, has also been observed and studied.[18] And contextual studies have been done of major musical figures, most notably Frances James, Murray Adaskin, R. Murray Schafer, and Glenn Gould, thereby also adding significantly to the history of music in twentieth-century Canada.[19]

Likewise under scrutiny in the 1980s, but seldom by historians, was the mass media. The "early" and "inside" stories of radio and television have been told several times, usually by such journalist participants as Warner Troyer, Peter Trueman, Bill McNeil, Eric Koch, and Knowlton Nash.[20] The sub-title of Troyer's book, "An Anecdotal History of Canadian Broadcasting," captures their essential orientation. Thematic integration, when achieved, almost invariably hinged on the national question. Titles like Morris Wolfe's *You Are What You Watch: The TV Wasteland and the Canadian Oasis* (1985) and Herschel Hardin's *Closed Circuits: The Sellout of*

Canadian Television (1985) bear testimony to the nationalist passions of most authors; a notable exception is *The Patriot Game* (1986), a comprehensive criticism of the Canadian nationalist élite written by Peter Brimelow, a Canadian journalist working in Manhattan.[21]

One professional historian who has paid close attention to the historical origins and development of the mass media in Canada is Paul Rutherford. His *A Victorian Authority: The Daily Press in Late Nineteenth-Century Canada* (1982) and *The Making of the Canadian Media* (1978) are pioneering ventures in contemporary Canadian historical scholarship.[22]

That the intrusion of mass popular culture into Canada was consistently perceived by contemporary observers as "American Culture" is borne out in briefer studies. J.M. Bumsted examined "Canadian and American Culture in the 1950s," a time when English Canada was overwhelmed by the culture of a confident and expansive America. In "Science, Authority, and the American Empire," A.B. McKillop studied elements of the Ontario *intelligentsia* in the 1920s, when its largely European cultural values were under threat by the promise of technological "progress" associated with things American. John Herd Thompson examined the contours of culture – both élite and popular – of the inter-war period. His "The Conundrum of Culture" is one of the most innovative and illuminating chapters in his accomplished volume in the Canadian Centenary Series.[23]

Perhaps because most of those who have written what *The Canadian Historical Review* classifies as "cultural history" are not, in fact, historians, we should not be surprised at the virtual absence in their writings of much concern that there is a scholarly world beyond the Canadian borders – a world in which "culture" and its meanings have long been the subject of intense scrutiny. A decade of bibliographical entries in *The Canadian Historical Review* for all "regions" of Canadian cultural history does not yield a single article – by historian, librarian, English professor, art historian, or literary critic – that attempts in a serious way to theorize about the nature of culture or about its relationship to matters of ideology or social process.[24] One is tempted to conclude that the operating principle of the cultural historian has become "*après Frye, rien.*" Outside this northern rim nation the notion of what constitutes the contexts of culture is in a state of high ferment; within it, at least among historians, a benign calm seems to exist.[25] Elsewhere, the scholarly world is giving much attention to the legacy of cultural historian and critical theorist Raymond Williams; here, as Maria Tippett gently chided in 1986, his work scarcely appears on the academic conceptual landscape, even in footnotes. And if we, in our marginal border country, can blithely assume that this Welsh coal miner's son, this "soft Marxist" with a peculiarly charitable regard for the Tory Romanticism of Burke and Cobbett, this working-class scholar who made his way to Cambridge and mastered its heights, has nothing to say to us, then we are in trouble indeed.[26]

If the insights of a consequential figure like Williams are at present largely ignored by us, then it is reasonable to assume that many other scholars whose works on the matter of culture and its relation to ideology and social process are being debated elsewhere will receive even less attention. If we have not addressed Williams's analysis of culture, we appear not even to have heard of the generation-long debate it has aroused in the study of the relations of sub-cultures, cultures, and class; the feminist critique of sub-cultures; and the challenges posed to cultural definition and analysis by semiology, the philosophy of language, structuralism, and structural analysis of narratives. As cultural and intellectual historians, how can we address Linda Hutcheon's challenge to the conventional definitional boundaries of historiography in her book *The Canadian Postmodern: A Study of Contemporary English-Canadian Fiction* (1988)[27] when we have yet to examine the cultural matrix of the Canadian modern?

The point is not that Canadian historians should search for a conceptual guru – a Louis Hartz or Erik Erikson – for the 1990s. We scarcely need to repeat the fruitless 1960s search for a foreign paradigm to apply to the Canadian case – whether it be seen as "fragmentary theory" or "identity crisis." Required, instead, is simply an historical scholarship that is not parochial – one that recognizes that other national experiences can at times provide insights into the structures, dynamics, and contexts of culture that we may find of use in understanding our own cultural circumstance. This applies as well, it may be said, to the English-Canadian historian's historiographical relationship to the cultural history of Quebec – where the influence of Aquinas and Descartes still runs deep and strong in the structured currents of the francophone mind.

Is the culture of Canada – whether of Ontario, the Maritimes, or the prairie West – so unique in its historical development that we need not study French, English, American, and other nations' histories? Those interested in the co-existence of pre-industrial regional cultural forms and practices with avante-garde culture could well turn to Eugen Weber's study of post-Revolutionary France, *Peasants into Frenchmen: The Modernization of Rural France* (1976) or his *France, Fin de Siècle* (1986).[28] If the notion of "marginality" persistently intrudes upon our studies of Canadian ethnic, cultural, or regional circumstances, then perhaps we ought to examine the work of Anglo-French historian Richard Cobb.[29] In short, any foray into the scholarship of European "cultural history" is bound to provide some conceptual rigour, or at least comparative perspective, that would enhance our understanding of our own country's, or region's, history.

At this point in the development of Canadian historiography, the existence, legitimacy, and importance of regional culture is beyond dispute.

But the complexity of culture transcends region – see Warren I. Susman's *Culture as History: The Transformation of American Society in the Twentieth Century* (1984) or Richard Wightman Fox and T.J. Jackson Lears's *The Culture of Consumption: Critical Essays in American History 1880-1980* (1983) for object lessons[30] – without diminishing its significance. Accordingly, this essay has not been cast, as it might have been, to address directly Peter Oliver's 1975 challenge to discover "what it has meant and will mean 'to be an Ontarian.'"[31] In an age of rapidly-changing means of communication, words and images can be "faxed" virtually anywhere, and a single CD-I (Compact Disk Interactive) for a home computer in a Saskatchewan farm house, a cottage in the Gatineaus, or a condominium in Toronto can hold "a thousand video stills, a couple of thousand diagrams, six hours of high-quality sound, and ten thousand pages of text, along with a program to make it work as an organic whole, all intensely interactive with the user."[32] In the age of "E-mail" can we any longer afford to think that the foundation of cultural experience or identity, much less its transformation, lies primarily in the political province, or even within the domain of geography itself?

It is manifestly more important for historians to determine the structural and thematic relationships between forms of cultural communications and experience than to root them, abjectly, in varieties of cultural soil-sampling. Canadian scholars, no less than others, need to meet the challenge, as intellectual historian Dominick LaCapra puts it, of elaborating concepts for investigating "the complexity of 'culture,'" a complexity derived from the "vertical" sense of form and structure rather than the "horizontal" sense of region and place. In his essay "Is Everyone a *Mentalité* Case?: Transference and the 'Culture' Concept," LaCapra argues:

> one must at the very least distinguish among various aspects or levels of culture that require further differentiations within each category: high or élite culture, popular culture, and mass culture. What are these aspects or levels of culture? What are some important ways in which they interact, or fail to interact, at any given time and over time? What are some further differentiations within these aspects or levels? How do they – indeed do they – add up to a more or less unified conception of general or common culture?[33]

LaCapra puts forward a number of definitional and thematic means by which our own approach to cultural history might be enhanced, because made more systematic. We ignore such work, as well as that of others, such as Natalie Z. Davis, Peter Burke, and Tony Bennett, at the risk of a continuing conceptual poverty for which there is no longer (if there ever was) any excuse.[34]

A.B. McKILLOP

Intellectual history in the 1980s, as it related to Ontario, has grown from the handful of books and articles of the 1970s to a pluralistic and significant historiographical field. Almost always the product of academic historians, most recent works demonstrate their authors' awareness of the necessity for a broad contextual framework. Most, therefore, make serious attempts to examine intellectual history in relation to the cultural environment. None, as a result, exhibits the superficial glibness of trade books on Canadian culture. Indeed, they are generally characterized by a high seriousness worthy of most of their Victorian or Edwardian subjects. Several particularly meritorious books have recently been published – too recently in some cases to have appeared in the *Canadian Historical Review*'s "Cultural and Intellectual History" section. A consideration of some of the most recently-published works in areas such as political ideology, education, and religion will provide an estimate of the state of current historiography in the field at the end of the 1980s.

One area subjected to recent study is among the oldest in Canadian historiography: the political ideology of pre-Confederation Upper Canada. In a series of thoughtful articles, published mainly in the 1960s and early 1970s, S.F. Wise forced Canadian historians to take the thought of Upper Canadian political figures seriously. This was reinforced by the publication of Carl Berger's *The Sense of Power: Studies in the Ideas of Canadian Imperialism 1867-1914* (1970), which demonstrated not only that the earlier Loyalist ideology persisted in transmuted forms in the minds of late nineteenth-century Canadian imperialists, but also that the resulting loyalist-imperialist ideology was in fact a particular formulation of anglophone nationalism.[35] Recently, Jane Errington and David Mills have drawn attention once again to Upper Canadian thought. As might be expected of a student of George Rawlyk, Errington is concerned to remind readers that the developing ideology of articulate Upper Canadians must be understood as a product of American as well as British influences.[36] "The story of early Upper Canada and the development of a colonial ideology," she notes, "is the story of a community which consciously accepted its dual heritage." She concludes that, unfortunately, "only the few educated and articulate leaders of Upper Canada ... were both conscious of and concerned about the colony's social, political, and economic development and about its relationship to the world outside its boundaries." Moreover, even among this élite there was, in Errington's view, "no common understanding of either the United States or Great Britain or, in fact, of what type of society they hoped to build in Upper Canada."[37]

Errington's is largely a study of the opinions of political, social, and economic leaders usually as found in newspaper accounts. Having taken opinion to be belief, and the plethora of opinion to be a reflection of ideological diversity, she was bound to find "no common understanding." As a result, her conclusions are cautious and conventional, lacking analytical penetration into the possibility that Upper Canadian political discourse embodied elements of both pre- and post-revolutionary forms of consciousness, those of classical and romantic man. It is fully possible for these to exist in the language even of those who are scarcely capable of articulating them as formal ideological systems, and whose utterances as a result appear confused or at odds with each other. It is the job of the intellectual historian to establish the ways in which pre-modern and modern men utilized "the languages of thought" they inherited from literary tradition in order to interpret the social systems in which they found themselves.[38] Errington does not appear to be concerned with the deeper resonances of the language of her Upper Canadian political animals, and as a result her account scarcely differs from those of conventional textbooks.[39]

Concerned with the notion of "political culture," David Mills provides a more penetrating analysis than does Errington. Like Gordon T. Stewart, in his provocative and insightful book *The Origins of Canadian Politics: A Comparative Approach* (1986),[40] Mills is sensitive to the complexity of Upper Canadian political language as well as to the changing meanings of the concept of loyalty. Mills discerns two basic strands in loyalist ideology, one which came to be embodied in the language of political reform and the other in that of the conservative political tradition. The language of Upper Canadian conservatives was that of eighteenth-century English Toryism, the exclusivist ideology of Burke and Bolingbroke. But the language of constitutional reformers also drew upon an understanding of political inheritance, in the form of the assimilative language and assumptions of seventeenth-century Whig constitutionalism.[41] The result was not simply a rhetorical war over the meaning of responsible government; it concerned the meaning of English history itself. By 1850, Mills argues, the challenge of moderate reformers had produced a combination of beliefs and attitudes embracing elements of both strands of this political heritage and taking the form of a "broad conservative consensus which dominated Old Ontario." Tory exclusionism had been defeated by the capacity of the reform tradition to legitimate its agenda, to convince its constituency of the truth of its version of the past. This transformation "opened the political arena to groups which would hardly have acquiesced in their continued exclusion and which would otherwise have had to seek more radical justifications for their admission. It transformed the idea of loyalty from the aristocratic apologia of a narrow oligarchy into the basic assumption of a developing middle-class political system. It also enabled the idea of loyalty to encompass a provincial feeling, looking to the future rather than to the past, expressed in nationalist rather than Loyalist rhetoric. That provincial feeling, in turn, was called upon to support a desire for increased local autonomy, although the arguments for local autonomy were also

A.B. McKILLOP

legitimized by appeals to British constitutional principles."[42] The battle for responsible government had been won, in no little measure, by an appeal to a venerable political culture.

If the history of opinion, political or otherwise, can be viewed as intellectual history at its most ephemeral, the history of legal assumptions and structures, and with them constitutions, is one of the elements of its *longue durée*. The origins and meanings of nineteenth-century English-Canadian political ideology and discourse (as expressed largely in the Upper Canadian/Ontarian experience) have recently been the subject of intensive analysis by Canadian legal historians. David Howes, G. Blaine Baker, and Paul Romney, for example, have made controversial yet substantial contributions to an understanding of the life of the mind in pre-Confederation Canada. In Howes's long article "Property, God and Nature in the Thought of Sir John Beverley Robinson" and Baker's piece "'So Elegant a Web': Providential Order and the Rule of Secular Law in Early Nineteenth-Century Upper Canada," discussion of the thought of John Beverley Robinson moves significantly out of the realm of political labelling – whether or not he was a Burkean Tory[43] – to broader, more fundamental questions.[44] In the words of Paul Romney, Howes and Baker have sought nothing less than "to reconstruct the code of public and professional values of the legal-administrative élite of early nineteenth-century Ontario in order to appreciate élite thought and actions on their own terms, undistorted by the standards of a different time or place."[45] At stake is the nature of the historical origins and ideological underpinnings of the rule of law in English-speaking Canada.

Whether one emerges from a reading of this historiographical corpus of competing visions of the legal culture of nineteenth-century Ontario on one side or the other (for the scholarly debate has become an acrimonious historiographical battle), one can only admire and applaud the intellectual energy each author brings to a subject of profound importance. Moreover, a price of understanding the debate at all is that one must consider the possibility that the origins of the political realm of English-Canadian intellectual history significantly pre-date the Conquest or the American Revolution. Was the rule of law, in its Ontario manifestation, essentially a product of late nineteenth-century legal thought, or was it part of a stock of inherited seventeenth- and eighteenth-century legal assumptions brought, like other forms of baggage, into Canadian judicial and political life? In short, does the intellectual history of Ontario predate the existence of the province and, if so, by how many years, decades, or centuries?[46]

In *The Machiavellian Moment: Florentine Political Thought and the Atlantic Republican Tradition* (1975) historian J.G.A. Pocock has claimed "that certain enduring patterns in the temporal consciousness of medieval and early modern Europeans led to the presentation of the republic, and the citizen's participation in it, as constituting a problem in historical self-understanding." As such, he asserts, it forms "part of the journey of Western thought from the medieval Christian to the modern historical mode. To these continuing problems," Pocock concludes, "Machiavelli and his contemporaries ... left an important paradigmatic legacy: concepts of balanced government, dynamic *virtù*, and the role of arms and property in shaping the civic personality."[47] In Pocock's view, "the Machiavellian Moment," which was to result in a tradition of civic humanism that helped define the public meaning of citizenship, penetrates into the heart of seventeenth- and eighteenth-century England and America. Thus one reaches the post-Conquest period of English-Canadian thought, essentially the starting-point for Errington and Mills,[48] yet arguably a datum at which the history of Canadian political discourse was already several centuries old.

Whatever conclusions Canadian legal historians may reach about such matters as the origins of the rule of law or of the legal consequences of jurists' natural theology or political ideology, the "legal history" they write is almost bound to appropriate the concerns of the intellectual historian because they necessarily raise questions about the origins of juridical assumption and discourse. Such an orientation, in the view of historian Robert Gordon, would "treat legal forms as ideologies and rituals, whose 'effects' — effects that include people's ways of sorting out social experience, giving it meaning, grading it as natural, just, and necessary, or as contrived, unjust, and subject to alteration — are in the realm of consciousness."[49]

Other institutions in Ontario society have recently come under interpretative scrutiny in ways that bear on the life of the mind. The study of education — of both public schooling and universities — has resulted in recent books of high quality indeed. *Schooling and Scholars in Nineteenth-Century Ontario* (1988), by Susan E. Houston and Alison Prentice, sets a high standard for the history of public education in Canada. It is a work of substantial scholarship and mature judgement that makes very effective use of contemporary work on the history of women, children, the family, ethnicity, and the working class. A richly-textured book, it consciously rejects the notion that "schooling" is coequal with "schools." Instead, Houston and Prentice discuss learning in the context of family structures and needs, and organizations such as privately-run schools, Sunday schools, colleges, and academies. The thrust of their book is, therefore, not to demonstrate how public-schooling displaced ignorance, but rather how the public school system came to displace a "staggering variety of [educational] ideas and forms" so that by the end of the Ryerson era in the 1870s state-sponsored schooling had come largely to be seen as the process of education itself. Of particular interest to intellectual historians is the third and final section of the book, "Behind the Schoolroom Door," particularly Chapter Eight, "What One Might Teach and Another Learn," a fascinating excursion into the curricular history of an era in which educational standards were scarcely defined, much less set.[50]

Equally of interest to the historian of ideas is the historiographical reorientation the book embodies. Avoiding any substantial use of quantitative methods, and critical of the "social control" model that dominated historical writing on the subject in the late 1960s and 1970s, the book is also an unintentionally ironic commentary on the direct inspiration yet ambiguous legacy of social historian Michael B. Katz. The early published work of both authors was much indebted to the early work of Katz. Houston's first articles were strident in their application of the "social control" thesis.[51] Prentice's first book, *The School Promoters: Education and Social Class in Mid-Nineteenth Century Upper Canada* (1977), concluded categorically that "The response of school reformers in Upper Canada to the social dislocations of their times was, in sum, to promote an essentially inegalitarian view of society and an equally inegalitarian approach to schooling. Control of the uncivilized poor, on the one hand, and the promotion of middle class respectability and achievement on the other, were clearly their fundamental aims."[52] A decade and more later, *Schooling and Scholars* begins:

> In recent years, in analysing the nineteenth-century "origins" of public education in North America and elsewhere, various historians have generalized about the relationship of public schools to capitalism, proposing for schools a historically specific social function, particularly in disciplining a future wage-labour force. Such an approach has proved invaluable.... However, the limitations of too broadly conceived explanations are increasingly obvious. Virtually any social policy, after all, has diverse purposes that are rarely so coherent as to lend themselves to treatment as a single force. In the specific instance of public schooling, themes of social discipline and moral regulation, while of undoubted importance, form strands in a fabric tightly woven of multiple intentions and effects.[53]

One can scarcely conceive a juxtaposition of passages more apposite for illustrating the professional loss of innocence of those who in the 1960s and 1970s championed the "New Social History." The scholarship of the next decade produced fewer answers, historical and ideological, not more.

Schooling and Scholars is a work of synthesis; its richness of texture and tentativeness of tone testify to difficult lessons learned from the historiography of the 1970s and early 1980s. *Youth, University, and Canadian Society: Essays in the Social History of Higher Education* (1989), compiled under the firm editorial direction of historians Paul Axelrod and John G. Reid, is largely a manifesto for research that needs to be done in the 1990s. "By highlighting original research," they note, "the book hopes both to bring the historiography of higher education closer to the mainstream of Canadian social and intellectual history and to encourage more work in a dynamic and growing area." While Axelrod and Reid are able to discuss and (in an invaluable bibliography) produce a surprising volume of historical writing on higher education in Canada, they are nevertheless somewhat burdened by the legacy of an abjectly institutional approach that has characterized their field in the past. "Fawning, celebrationist biographies of great individuals and impressive buildings, written by ex-administrators instead of professional historians, long inhibited the growth and sophistication of the historiography. Those few researchers committed to serious scholarship were both compelled to work in isolation and frustrated by the minimal interest shown by their colleagues in the field as a whole."[54] A more detached observer of the scholarship confirmed the legitimacy of such a harsh judgement. Before the 1980s, writes Carl Berger in a model of understatement, "Historical writing on universities never quite managed to convey adequately the most essential elements in these institutions: the life of the mind, advances in knowledge, and changing perceptions of what was important to preserve and transmit."[55] The Axelrod and Reid collection, with articles by social historians such as Chad Gaffield, Judith Fingard, and James M. Pitsula, and by intellectual historians such as A.B. McKillop, Keith Walden, and Patricia Jasen, is a serious and sustained attempt to address these inadequacies by examining the experience of going to university as often as not from the perspective of students, the life of the mind, and socio-economic and geographical circumstance: hence, sections of the book draw the reader's attention to student life and culture, student movements and social change, and the intellectual and institutional environment in which they learn. Historical categories such as region, gender, and social class are also a major part of the analytical framework in which several of the authors set their individual contexts.

Youth, University, and Canadian Society is less a synthesis of previous scholarship than it is an invitation to ask new questions and to encourage more work. Since the middle of the nineteenth century university students have constituted a small segment of a generally ascriptive Canadian society; but they have been an element whose importance has been out of proportion to its size. As John Porter demonstrated in *The Vertical Mosaic: An Analysis of Social Class and Power in Canada* (1965),[56] the small Canadian clerisy of higher learning has largely been responsible for articulating, promoting, sustaining (but seldom challenging) the predominant values of the country's middle class. Studies of the structure and contents of higher education in the nineteenth and twentieth centuries would, therefore, also say much about the making of that middle class, so often the unexamined whipping-horse of labour and working class historians.[57] They would help demonstrate the way in which the university gradually became the agency primarily responsible for the intellectual formation of several generations of its *intelligentsia*, and would document, as well, the displacement (but not complete disappearance: witness Robertson Davies) of the "man of letters" genteel tradition from its halls.

Much needs to be done in the Ontario context on the intellectual history of academic disciplines, as well as on their broader place as units of epistemological and social significance within university "Faculties" such as "Arts," "Science," or "Public Administration."[58] Each discipline – Classics and English as well as Political Economy and History – carries its own ideological baggage, its own canon to construct or deconstruct, as the cultural and intellectual predispositions of an age dictate. As with other jurisdictions of scholarship, English and American studies are immensely valuable for contextual purposes. In *The Social Mission of English Criticism* (1983), for example, Chris Baldick establishes the English background essential for any understanding of literary criticism in English Canada before the 1960s. In *Literature Against Itself: Literary Ideas in Modern Society* (1979) and especially in his *Professing Literature: An Institutional History* (1987), Gerald Graff establishes the Anglo-American context in a brilliant fashion. *Youth, University, and Canadian Society* contains a bibliographic section of more than six pages on Canadian "Cultural, Intellectual, and Curriculum History," yet little of this work is integrative. The work of Patricia Jasen on the intellectual and cultural import of the liberal arts curriculum offers an outline of the kind of synthetic approach to curricular history that is needed to establish the Canadian context.[59]

The universities of Ontario, as elsewhere, grew out of a non-"intellectual" environment – that of evangelical Christian denominationalism. Beginning in the 1960s the history of religion, long marginalized if not simply ignored by professional historians in Canada because of its devotional origins, was transformed by historians – by wedding it first to nationalist sentiment,[60] then, in the era of "limited identities," to forms of cultural expression in a stridently pluralistic society. As a result, virtually all recent scholarship has addressed the broad and unresolved question of the relation of religion to secular modernity.

Ramsay Cook's Governor-General's Award-winning book, *The Regenerators: Social Criticism in Late Victorian English Canada* (1985), has become the interpretative fulcrum around which the question of religion's relationship to secular society has begun to hinge. Long interested in social criticism and reform, Cook inevitably faced the necessity of studying their relationship to religion. His conclusions hinged on one of the fundamental ironies of our time: that "the supreme irony of the regenerators was that the new birth to which they contributed was not, as they had hoped, the city of God on earth but rather the secular city."[61] Uniting sacred and secular realms by transforming orthodox Christianity into a search for social instead of personal salvation, Cook's social critics and reformers helped pave the way for the displacement of religious explanations of human behaviour by those of secular social science. Thus the sub-title that Cook originally gave to *The Regenerators*: "Or, The World that Made Mackenzie King."

Cook's book was informed in part by Richard Allen's pioneering study, *The Social Passion: Religion and Social Reform in Canada 1914-1928* (1971), and the two authors (both products of the United Church of Canada manse) do not fundamentally differ about the fact that social Christianity posed a serious challenge to orthodox religious tradition. But the conclusions of *The Regenerators* are very different. Whereas Allen viewed the Social Gospel as a fundamentally positive force responding to the evils of industrial capitalism, leaving an equally beneficial legacy for democratic socialist politics in Canada,[62] Cook's story is essentially one of unintentional subversion and betrayal: "the manner in which liberal Protestants responded to the socio-economic, scientific, and historical challenges of the nineteenth century resulted in Christianity becoming less rather than more relevant."[63]

Cook acknowledged that his own thinking was influenced by Owen Chadwick's *The Secularization of the European Mind in the Nineteenth Century* (1975), and he uses the term "secularization" more or less in the way that Chadwick had defined it, as "the relation ... in which modern European civilization and society stands to the Christian elements of its past and the continuing Christian elements of its present."[64] Yet there is more than a hint in *The Regenerators* of the language of emotion, the use of which Chadwick warned against, a tone almost of mockery as Cook's crackerbarrel philosophers of the post-Darwinian age "concocted" their "many recipes for a perfect Christian sociology."[65] There are hints, too, of what Chadwick characterizes as "*Decline and Fall* history; where the writer knows that he is setting out, for example, to describe a steady decline in civilization until he reaches the point which he thinks of as 'the triumph of barbarism and religion' ...";[66] or, in Cook's case, of social scientists and sociology. In this latter respect *The Regenerators* is not unlike McKillop's earlier study, *A Disciplined Intelligence: Critical Inquiry and Canadian Thought in the Victorian Era* (1979), which outlined in its concluding chapter the ways in which several influential liberal protestants early in the twentieth century appeared to be more interested in overtly sociological forms of understanding than in traditional Christian theology or forms of religious observance.[67]

Marguerite Van Die's recent study, *An Evangelical Mind: Nathanael*

Burwash and the Methodist Tradition in Canada, 1839-1918 (1989), seeks to challenge what appeared to be this essentially arithmetic interpretative thrust, in which an addition of secularization equals a subtraction of "religion." Concerned that intellectual historians such as Cook and McKillop have made judgements about the decline of religious faith while more knowledgeable of social criticism and philosophy than theology, Van Die sets out to examine the relationship between religious experience and individual belief by filling the theological vacuum. *An Evangelical Mind* centres on Nathanael Burwash, one of Canada's most influential Methodist educators and theologians in the second half of the nineteenth century; but its scholarly importance significantly transcends the knowledge it sheds on the life of Burwash. Combining a thematic and a chronological approach, Van Die seeks to answer two essential questions: first, the extent to which Wesley's evangelical doctrines retained a presence in late nineteenth-century Canadian Methodism; and second, "how social and intellectual changes affected religious faith during this period."[68] The result, using Burwash as a litmus test for the continuing presence of Wesleyan evangelical doctrines, is a study that includes discussions of the role of women and children in religious education, the relation of reason and revelation in Methodist higher education, the role of Baconian science and the Higher Criticism in the age of Darwinism, and the eventual end of Methodism as a separate denomination.

Van Die concludes that "contrary to what has generally been assumed, John Wesley's theology continued to be considered authoritative by both Burwash and the Methodist Church." Turn-of-the-century Canadian Methodism, in Van Die's interpretation, was simultaneously conservative doctrinally yet open to social change:

> for the spirit in which Wesley's thought was interpreted ... [generally] reflected the cultural optimism of the Victorian period. Convinced of the power of revivalism to transform culture and "make Christianity at home in the world," Burwash consistently sought to apply the old evangelical teachings to new institutions and scientific thought. This simultaneous affirmation of Wesley's thought and cultural change gave a dynamism to Canadian Methodism that, though fascinating, has also led to misinterpretation.

In short, for Van Die "an informed faith" persisted through the disruptive years of Darwin and the Higher Critics.[69]

Without question, the face of evangelicalism changed substantially during the course of the nineteenth century, yet continuity, not discontinuity, is the essential dynamic of *An Evangelical Mind*.[70] Methodism was, in the end, subverted by the rational working out of its own Wesleyan heritage by people of genuine faith, and by their sincerely-held belief that the power of their religious tradition would help them transform and Christianize culture. Van Die's book, like those of McKillop and Cook before it, points to the ironic conclusion

> that by the early decades of the twentieth century, evangelical Christianity had been undermined perhaps more by the compelling vision of men and women of faith than by the destructive seeds of religious doubt.... As evangelicals the world they envisaged was a world transformed in their own image. Ultimately that was not the world they bequeathed, but having examined their vision and its cultural expression, we may also question whether it was indeed, as some have suggested, the secular city.[71]

Even more ambitious in scope is William Westfall's *Two Worlds: The Protestant Culture of Nineteenth-Century Ontario* (1989). Like Van Die's work, it is a volume in the recently-launched "McGill-Queen's Studies in the History of Religion" series (George A. Rawlyk, Editor), a commendable editorial initiative that is an encouraging sign for the future of Canadian cultural and intellectual history. It is impossible to encapsulate briefly the complex nature of Westfall's historical argumentation, in part because his book is metahistorical in character. It is based on a comprehensive examination of a rich body of conventional published and unpublished historical documents, but its text is cast, for the most part, in the vocabulary of socio-historical theory and at a high level of abstraction. In essence, the author proclaims, the book is "a search for form rather than content." Concerned with elucidating "the structures of thought and perception that give meaning" to the historical record, the book is meant to operate at two levels: as a study of a nineteenth-century people who were "searching for a form that would give order and meaning to its collective existence," and as a representation of "the historian's search for a form that will give order and meaning to this historical quest. In both cases the form itself tells the real story."[72]

Beginning with those two icons of Upper Canadian religious history, John Strachan and Egerton Ryerson, Westfall uses them as vehicles for the construction of distinct patterns of religious expression: what he calls the culture of order and the culture of experience. The former, symbolized by the thought of Strachan the Anglican, offered a "highly rational and systematic representation of religion," and therefore "appealed to the values of order and reason"; the latter, expressed by Ryerson the Methodist, "appealed to the other side of early nineteenth-century psychology – the feelings – by reworking the Bible into a religion of intense personal experience." These two worlds of order and experience are, as Westfall is the first to admit, "composite pictures." Each is "an ideal type that sums up and integrates the ideas and beliefs of a religious culture...."[73] Placed in conjunction as a form of cultural dialogue in Upper Canada, however, these "cultures" take on a reified life of their own, and Westfall proceeds to use them as the basis for what may be one of the most sustained examples of historical dialectics in North American scholarship since the publication of Louis Hartz's *The Liberal Tradition in America* (1955).[74]

In his acknowledgements, Westfall notes that Canadian poet and York University colleague Eli Mandel explained to him "the trickery of doubles." Doubtless this is so, for Westfall seems to have taken to heart the line from Mandel's poem, "The Double," which serves as an epigraph for the book: "everything divides by two or is uneven." In Westfall's binary perspective, almost everything divides by two, for there are not many loose cultural ends left by the end of the book. By the middle of the nineteenth century, the dialogical exchange between proponents of the culture of order and that of experience has resulted in a major, if reluctant, synthesis: Methodists moderate their "excessive emotionalism" under the pressure of imminent middle-class respectability; Anglicans, abandoned by a secular State given over to forms of materialist expansion, discover the virtues of being a denomination just like the others. The result is the world of the evangelical protestant alliance of the second half of Ontario's first century.

In this process of cultural transformation, a new culture was formed, one with three major characteristics. First, it interpreted the world through "an almost limitless series of paired categories, all of which turned on the distinction between the secular and the sacred," but did so in a context in which they were rooted in "the immediate environment." Secondly, the new Protestant culture attempted to unite the secular and the sacred realms in common cause by articulating a view of history in which the institutions of the former would ultimately achieve the ends of the latter. Ontario Protestantism "divided everything into two worlds, which it then brought together; Ontario and indeed the whole earth would become the garden of the Lord." Thirdly, it was thought possible to achieve this because of the overwhelming belief in the transformative power of human agency: "strongly motivated individuals could convert the world to Christ, thereby reconciling the sacred and the secular." In this cause Protestant culture was aided by the power of nineteenth-century romanticism, whether in the form of the inspirational sermon, the inspiring cathedral, or the great historical event or literary epic.[75]

That, at least, was the aspiration. The power of the sacred was to redeem the world of the secular and, in so doing, transform it. Yet by articulating and entrenching the sacred–secular dualism within the Victorian mind, religionists helped distance their culture from the "real" (material) world while gaining no immunity from the forces of secularity. Westfall concludes:

> The Victorian accommodation gave the sacred a distinct and power-
> ful presence, but it also moved it away from the secular by placing it
> in discrete institutions or in specific places. In much the same way
> that Victorians took education out of life and put it into schools, so
> they took religion out of the world and put it safely away in church-
> es, temperance societies, and missionary organizations. In this guise
> the sacred might justify the canons of public morality, but it was much
> more difficult for it to sustain the spiritual quality of everyday life.
> Without a sense of integration and immediacy people could be
> reduced to worshipping a set of external forms, a hollow shell of pub-
> lic respectability.[76]

Thus, surprisingly, is reached a conclusion that differs little from that of
The Regenerators or *A Disciplined Intelligence*. Westfall's study uses historical
evidence in an imaginative and highly original way. Its appearance should
be applauded as the most sustained attempt in Canadian historical scholarship to set the world of ideas in the context of culture. Yet in spite of its
metahistorical plane, its relentless dialecticalism, its socio-cultural theorizing, and its structuralist preoccupation, the book, however brilliant, alters
the fundamental interpretive thrust of older accounts less than it does their
vocabulary.

This rather discursive treatment of the works of Cook, Van Die, and
Westfall is meant to suggest the relative richness of current scholarship in
the field. The recent appearance of John Webster Grant's *A Profusion of
Spires: Religion in Nineteenth- Century Ontario* (1988) demonstrates how
perilous it is for anyone interested in the social, cultural, or intellectual history of Ontario to ignore its religious dimension. The work of an historical master craftsman, *A Profusion of Spires* is a synthesis of older accounts
and new scholarship, and provides a general overview of the religious history of nineteenth-century Ontario that is as helpful as it is unpretentious.
Sensitive to the current debate over secularization, for example, Grant
warns against interpreting "signs of confusion or doubt as evidence of
decline" in religious faith. Grant finds little evidence of any "overall falling
off in religious commitment," and concludes that "The shift from organic
to mass societies [which accompanied industrialization and urbanization],
replacing coherent communities with combinations of atomistic individuals, was probably, in the long run, more corrosive of religious commitment
than any of the specific questions with which the churches had to wres-
tle in the late nineteenth century."[77]

Other notable recent works should be mentioned. Philosopher J.D.
Rabb has edited a useful collection of primary sources, *Religion and Science*

in *Early Canada* (1988), including lectures or articles by John Watson, George Paxton Young, George Blewett, Daniel Wilson, J.W. Dawson, and W.D. LeSueur. Carl Berger's 1982 Joanne Goodman Lectures, published as *Science, God, and Nature in Victorian Canada* (1983), provide a brief discussion of the Darwinian debate in Canada, set in the helpful context of the "grass-roots" Victorian preoccupation with natural history. Suzanne Zeller's brilliant and comprehensive *Inventing Canada: Early Victorian Science and the Idea of a Transcontinental Nation* (1987) elaborates upon the Victorian Canadian fascination with making inventories of the natural world, demonstrating also the way in which the various forms of "inventory science" (geology, terrestrial magnetism and meteorology, and botany) helped shape nationalist aspiration.[78]

The years after the Great War have received significantly less detailed treatment from intellectual historians. Nevertheless, the terrain is beginning to be mapped. Thomas P. Socknat's fine study, *Witness Against War: Pacifism in Canada 1900-1945* (1987), examines the pre-nuclear peace movement as it arose out of the anabaptist and social gospel traditions, and leaves the reader waiting for a sequel that will not only examine the Canadian peace movement itself but also evoke the post-Hiroshima *mentalité*.[79] Michiel Horn and R. Douglas Francis have substantially added to our knowledge of social democratic thought in the inter-war period in their books on the intellectual origins of the League for Social Reconstruction and on the life and thought of historian Frank H. Underhill, respectively.[80] Doug Owram's comprehensive study, *The Government Generation: Canadian Intellectuals and the State 1900-1945* (1986), combines the history of bureaucratic administration and policy formation with that of the growth of secular social science and its emergence from a protestant social reform ethos. Like the work of Marlene Shore on the growth of social research at McGill University, *The Government Generation* enriches our understanding of the legacy of the nineteenth-century crisis of epistemic and social authority, although neither work places its subject matter in its broadest context: that of what historians of science have begun to call "the probabilistic revolution."[81] Canadian historians have yet systematically to treat the role of intellectuals as a category of social analysis, but they will be encouraged by the work of political scientists Stephen Brooks and Alain G. Gagnon. Their *Social Scientists and Politics in Canada* (1988),[82] which focuses on the period from 1944 to 1986, is brief but analytically penetrating and will likely inspire further historical research. It says much, in the comparative context of English- and French-Canadian social science, about the elder-statesmen and the heirs of Owram's "government generation."

No Canadian historian has recently written at length about the thought, lives, and work of those Ontarians of international intellectual significance in the years after 1945, much less attempted an intellectual history or cultural synthesis of the period. The *Canadian Historical Review* bibliography contains many articles and books by and about Harold Innis, George P. Grant, Marshall McLuhan, and Northrop Frye, but Grant has largely become the preserve of political scientists, Frye of literary critics. As for Innis and McLuhan, one might simply note two recent works in which they are treated collectively. James W. Carey, in *Communications as Culture: Essays on Media and Society* (1989), takes Innis and to a lesser extent McLuhan as the founding fathers of the North American cultural approach to communication. Hence, his chapter "Space, Time, and Communications: A Tribute to Harold Innis."[83] Inspired by Carey, Daniel J. Czitrom has written his own book, *Media and the American Mind: From Morse to McLuhan* (1982). Its sub-title hints of themes to come, particularly in the chapter "Metahistory, Mythology, and the Media: The American Thought of Harold Innis and Marshall McLuhan."[84] The vast empire south of the 49th parallel has appropriated central figures of Canadian thought as its own, but Canadian intellectual and cultural historians – at least those working within academic settings – have largely been silent on these voices of their own past, as on others. Until Canadian scholarship becomes "conscious of what it is doing" by studying the processes of cultural and intellectual continuity and change already scrutinized elsewhere, until histories of Canadian minds and of Canadian culture become histories of "meaning" in the broadest sense,[85] such insights into the nation's cultural and intellectual life will continue to be the property of others. To reiterate a favourite theme of Frank Underhill: where is the successor to André Siegfried, the Tocqueville of Canada?[86]

Notes

1   See Olga B. Bishop, *Bibliography of Ontario History 1867-1976 Cultural, Economic, Political, Social*, 2nd ed., 2 vols. (Toronto: U of Toronto P, 1980), published for the Ontario Historical Studies Series. "Cultural and Intellectual History" is treated in vol. 2, pp. 959-1042. See also the *Annual Bibliography of Ontario History*, published by the Ontario Historical Society since 1980.

2   Glen Campbell, "Dithyramb and Diatribe: The Polysemic Perception of the Métis in Louis Riel's Poetry," *Canadian Ethnic Studies* 17.2 (1985): 31-43.

3   Brodie Snyder, *The Year the Expos Almost Won the Pennant* (Toronto: Virgo, 1980).

4   John McIntyre, "What Is a Canadian Chair?: Some Thoughts on Documentation and Definition," *Canadian Collector* 15.2 (1980): 54-55.

5   D. Boc, "A Musical Analysis of Folktunes in Deseronto, Ontario," M.A. thesis, Memorial U of Newfoundland, 1984[?]. For unknown reasons, the "Guide to Recent Publications" does not provide any date for theses listed.

6   George Bowering, "Margaret Atwood's Hands," *Studies in Canadian Literature* 6 (1981): 39-52.

7   David L. Rennie, "Survey of York University 1976-78 Bachelor's Degree Graduates in Psychology Located in Greater Toronto," *The Canadian Journal of Higher Education* 11.1 (1981): 45-57.

8   G.C. Russell, *Customs and Traditions of the Canadian Armed Forces* (Ottawa: Deneau and Greenberg, 1980).

9   Doug Fetherling, *The Blue Notebook: Reports on Canadian Culture* (Oakville, ON: Mosaic, 1985).

10 As Fetherling notes of his book: "Its claim is only that it sets out one observer's impressions of recent Canadian culture, defining culture broadly enough to include such matters as feature films and political cartoons" (9).

11 Barbara Helen Pell, "Faith and Fiction: The Novels of Callaghan and Hood," *Journal of Canadian Studies* 18.2 (1983): 5-17; Marco P. Loverso, "Dialectic, Morality, and the Deptford Trilogy," *Studies in Canadian Literature* 12 (1987): 69-89.

12 Maria Tippett, "The Writing of English-Canadian Cultural History, 1970-85," *The Canadian Historical Review* 67 (1986): 549. A notable exception to Tippett's claim of failure is the work of Tippett herself, especially *Art at the Service of War: Canada, Art, and the Great War* (Toronto: U of Toronto P, 1984).

13 Tippett, "English-Canadian Cultural History" 556.

14 Tippett, "English-Canadian Cultural History" 556-57; Raymond Williams, *Culture and Society* (Harmondsworth, Eng.: Penguin, 1963) 16.

15 Tippett, "English-Canadian Cultural History" 557.

16 Carl Berger, *The Writing of Canadian History*, 2nd ed. (Toronto: U of Toronto P, 1986) 297.

17 Cheryl MacDonald, *Emma Albani: Victorian Diva* (Toronto: Dundurn, 1984); Gerald Killan, *David Boyle: From Artisan to Archaeologist* (Toronto: U of Toronto P, 1983); Dorothy Farmiloe, *Isabella Valancy Crawford: The Life and Legends* (Ottawa: Tecumseh, 1983); Marian Fowler, *Redney: A Life of Sara Jeannette Duncan* (Toronto: Anansi, 1983); James G. Greenlee, *Sir Robert Falconer: A Biography* (Toronto: U of Toronto P, 1988); David G. Pitt, *E.J. Pratt: The Truant Years, 1882-1927* (Toronto: U of Toronto P, 1984); David G. Pitt, *E.J. Pratt: The Master Years, 1927-1964* (Toronto: U of Toronto P, 1987); Clara Thomas and John Lennox, *William Arthur Deacon: A Canadian Literary Life* (Toronto: U of Toronto P, 1982); Claude Bissell, *The Young Vincent Massey* (Toronto: U of Toronto P, 1981); Claude Bissell, *The Imperial Canadian* (Toronto: U of Toronto P, 1986); R. Douglas Francis, *Frank H. Underhill: Intellectual Provocateur* (Toronto: U of Toronto P, 1986); Philip Marchand, *Marshall McLuhan: The Medium and the Messenger* (Toronto: Random House, 1989); Scott Young, *Neil and Me* (Toronto: McClelland and Stewart, 1984). Despite their physical location in Montreal for much of their lives, Hugh MacLennan and F.R. Scott are as much part of the cultural experience of

Ontarians as those listed above. See, therefore: Elspeth Cameron, *Hugh MacLennan: A Writer's Life* (Toronto: U of Toronto P, 1981); Sandra Djwa, *The Politics of the Imagination: A Life of F.R. Scott* (Toronto: McClelland and Stewart, 1987).

18   Margaret McKelvey and Merilyn McKelvey, *Toronto Carved in Stone: The Sculpture and Decorative Stonework in Toronto Architecture* (Markham, ON: Fitzhenry & Whiteside, 1984); William Dendy and William Kilbourn, *Toronto Observed: Its Architecture, Its Patrons, and History* (Toronto: Oxford UP, 1986); Nancy Tausky and Lynne Destefano, *Victorian Architecture in London and Southwestern Ontario: Symbols of Aspiration* (Toronto: U of Toronto P, 1986); Kelly Crossman, *Architecture in Transition: From Art to Practice, 1885-1906* (Kingston, ON: McGill-Queen's UP, 1987).

19   Gordana Lazarevitch, *The Musical World of Frances James and Murray Adaskin* (Toronto: U of Toronto P, 1987); Stephen Adams, *R. Murray Schafer* (Toronto: U of Toronto P, 1983); Otto Friedrich, *Glenn Gould: A Life and Variations* (Toronto: Lester & Orpen Dennys, 1989).

20   Warner Troyer, *The Sound & the Fury: An Anecdotal History of Canadian Broadcasting* (Rexdale, ON: John Wiley & Sons, 1980); Peter Trueman, *Smoke and Mirrors: The Inside Story of Television News in Canada* (Toronto: McClelland and Stewart, 1980); Bill McNeil and Morris Wolfe, *Signing On: The Birth of Radio in Canada* (Toronto: Doubleday, 1982); Eric Koch, *Inside Seven Days: The Show That Shook the Nation* (Scarborough, ON: Prentice-Hall, 1986); Knowlton Nash, *Prime Time at Ten: Behind-the-Camera Battles of Canadian TV Journalism* (Toronto: McClelland and Stewart, 1987). See also Mary Jane Miller, *Turn Up the Contrast: Thirty Years of CBC English Television Drama* (Vancouver: U of British Columbia P, 1987).

21   Morris Wolfe, *Jolts: The TV Wasteland and the Canadian Oasis* (Toronto: James Lorimer, 1985); Herschel Hardin, *Closed Circuits: The Sellout of Canadian Television* (Vancouver: Douglas & McIntyre, 1985); Peter Brimelow, *The Patriot Game: National Dreams & Political Realities* (Toronto: Key Porter, 1986).

22   Paul Rutherford, *A Victorian Authority: The Daily Press in Late Nineteenth-Century Canada* (Toronto: U of Toronto P, 1982); Rutherford, *The Making of the Canadian Media* (Toronto: McGraw-Hill Ryerson, 1978). See also his "Researching Television History: Prime-Time Canada, 1952-1967," *Archivaria* 20 (1985): 79-93.

23   J.M. Bumsted, "Canada and American Culture in the 1950s," in Bumsted, ed., *Interpreting Canada's Past*, vol. 2 (Toronto: Oxford UP, 1986) 398-411; A.B. McKillop, "Science, Authority, and the American Empire," in McKillop, *Contours of Canadian Thought* (Toronto: U of Toronto P, 1987) 111-28,148-54; John Herd Thompson, with Allen Seager, *Canada, 1922-1939: Decades of Discord* (Toronto: McClelland and Stewart, 1985). It must be noted, however, that this chapter is weak on evidence drawn from the 1930s.

24   Yet see Peter Narváez and Martin Laba, eds., *Media Sense: The Folklore-Popular*

Culture Continuum (Bowling Green, OH: Bowling Green State University Popular Press, 1983), which examines primarily the folklore and popular culture of Newfoundland; William H. Melody, Liora Salter, Paul Heyer, eds., *Culture, Communication, and Dependency: The Tradition of H.A. Innis* (Norwood, NJ: Ablex, 1981). It may be that the combination of technological innovation in the field of communications and the implications of the Canada-U.S.A. Free Trade Agreement will necessitate such theorizing. Certain very recent publications point in this direction. See Rowland Lorimer and Donald Wilson, eds., *Communication Canada: Issues in Broadcasting and New Technologies* (Toronto: Kagan and Woo, 1988); Ian Parker, John Hutcheson, and Pat Crawley, eds., *The Strategy of Canadian Culture in the 21st Century* (Toronto: TopCat Communications, 1988).

25   A notable exception is scholarship on ethnohistory, which transcends disciplinary boundaries. See, for example, Bruce G. Trigger, "The Historians' Indian: Native Americans in Canadian Historical Writing from Charlevoix to the Present," *The Canadian Historical Review* 67 (1986): 315-42; Trigger, "Ethnohistory and Archaeology," *Ontario Archaeology* 30 (1978): 17-24; Trigger, "Alfred G. Bailey – Ethnohistorian," *Acadiensis* 18.2 (1989): 3-21; Berger, *The Writing of Canadian History*, 2nd ed., 298-301; Ramsay Cook, "The White Man Cometh," in Cook, *Canada, Quebec, and the Uses of Nationalism* (Toronto: McClelland and Stewart, 1986) 19-47. Ethnohistorical scholarship is not placed in the "Cultural and Intellectual History" section of the *Canadian Historical Review* bibliography.

26   Raymond Williams, *Culture and Society* (London: Chatto and Windus, 1958); Williams, *The Long Revolution* (London: Chatto and Windus, 1961); Williams, *Marxism and Literature* (Oxford: Oxford UP, 1977); Williams, *Problems in Materialism and Culture* (London: New Left, 1980); Williams, *Culture* (London: Fontana, 1981).

27   Linda Hutcheon, *The Canadian Postmodern: A Study of Contemporary English-Canadian Fiction* (Toronto: Oxford UP, 1988). See especially "Historiographic Metafiction" 61-77 and "The Postmodern Challenge to Boundaries" 78-106.

28   Eugen Weber, *Peasants into Frenchmen: The Modernization of Rural France* (Stanford, CA: Stanford UP, 1976); Weber, *France: Fin de Siècle* (Cambridge, MA: Belknap, 1986).

29   See, for example, Richard Cobb, *A Second Identity: Essays on France and French History* (London: Oxford UP, 1969); Cobb, *The Police and the People: French Popular Protest 1789-1820* (London: Oxford UP, 1970); Cobb, *Paris and Its Provinces 1792-1802* (London: Oxford UP, 1975); Cobb, *Death in Paris* (Oxford: Oxford UP, 1978). See also Martyn Lyons, "Cobb and the Historians," in Gwynne Lewis and Colin Lucas, eds., *Beyond the Terror: Essays in French Regional and Social History, 1794-1815* (Cambridge, Eng.: Cambridge UP, 1983) 1-20; Robert Darnton, "The History of *Mentalités*: Recent Writings on Revolution, Criminality, and Death in France," in Richard Harvey Brown

and Stanford M. Lyman, eds., *Structure, Consciousness, and History* (Cambridge, Eng.: Cambridge UP, 1978) 106-36.

30   Warren I. Susman, *Culture as History: The Transformation of American Society in the Twentieth Century* (New York: Pantheon, 1984); Richard Wightman Fox and T.J. Jackson Lears, eds., *The Culture of Consumption: Critical Essays in American History 1880-1980* (New York: Pantheon, 1983). See also T.J. Jackson Lears, *No Place of Grace: Antimodernism and the Transformation of American Culture 1880-1920* (New York: Pantheon, 1981); Roland Marchand, *Advertising the American Dream: Making Way for Modernity, 1920-1940* (Berkeley: U of California P, 1985); Larry May, ed., *Recasting America: Culture and Politics in the Age of Cold War* (Chicago: U of Chicago P, 1989).

31   Peter Oliver, *Public & Private Persons: The Ontario Political Culture 1914-1934* (Toronto: Clarke, Irwin, 1975) 14. The reader will note, therefore, that, as Yvan Lamonde has reminded me, there is "a recurrent *va et vient* in [this] paper between Ontario and Canada." Quite so, but not because of a belief in "Empire Ontario" (deep and abiding Manitoba roots prevent this). The point is that to bind discussions of cultural and intellectual history to romantic forms of geographical determinism is effectively to preclude serious discussion of the transnational (much less regional) nature of modern cultural and intellectual production and transformation. This essay is, therefore, specifically cast in the form of an objection to the very notion of organizing a panel discussion on cultural and intellectual history based solely on regional instead of conceptual or thematic boundaries.

32   Stewart Brand, *The Media Lab: Inventing the Future at M.I.T.* (Harmondsworth, Eng.: Penguin, 1988) 22-23.

33   Dominick LaCapra, "Is Everyone a *Mentalité* Case? Transference and the 'Culture' Concept," in LaCapra, *History & Criticism* (Ithaca, NY: Cornell UP, 1985) 73.

34   See Natalie Z. Davis, *Society and Culture in Early Modern France* (Stanford, CA: Stanford UP, 1975); Peter Burke, *Popular Culture in Early Modern Europe* (London: Temple Smith, 1984); Tony Bennett, ed., *Culture, Ideology and Social Process: A Reader* (London: B.T. Batsford, 1987); Bennett, ed., *Popular Culture: Past and Present* (London: Croom Helm, 1982). See also Steven L. Kaplan, ed., *Understanding Popular Culture: Europe from the Middle Ages to the Nineteenth Century* (Berlin: Mouton, 1984).

35   See A.B. McKillop, "Nationalism, Identity, and Canadian Intellectual History," in McKillop, *Contours of Canadian Thought* (Toronto: U of Toronto P, 1987) 8-12 for a brief review of these works. See also Joseph Levitt, *A Vision Beyond Reach: A Century of Images of Canadian Destiny* (Ottawa: Deneau, 1982) for an examination of the nationalist preoccupation of English-Canadian intellectuals, particularly historians.

36   Thus, much attention is given to Thomas Jefferson and James Madison but no mention is made of William Blackstone or Edmund Burke.

37 Jane Errington, *The Lion, the Eagle, and Upper Canada: A Developing Colonial Ideology* (Kingston, ON: McGill-Queen's UP, 1987), 5-6.

38 See J.G.A. Pocock, "On the Non-Revolutionary Character of Paradigms: A Self-Criticism and Afterpiece," in Pocock, *Politics, Language and Time: Essays on Political Thought and History* (1971; Chicago: U of Chicago P, 1989) 273-76.

39 Errington, *The Lion, the Eagle, and Upper Canada* 186-92. For example: "Yet underlying the political controversy of the 1820s, and present, indeed, since Simcoe had first arrived in Upper Canada, was the colony's attempt to find a unique and special identity. The United States and Great Britain provided the colonists with constant points of reference in their search" (192).

40 Gordon T. Stewart, *The Origins of Canadian Politics: A Comparative Approach* (Vancouver: U of British Columbia P, 1986).

41 David Mills, *The Idea of Loyalty in Upper Canada 1784-1850* (Kingston, ON: McGill-Queen's UP, 1988) 17-19.

42 Mills, *The Idea of Loyalty* 3-11, 132-36.

43 Terry Cook, "John Beverley Robinson and the Conservative Blueprint for the Upper Canadian Community," in J.K. Johnson, ed., *Historical Essays on Upper Canada* (Toronto: McClelland and Stewart, 1975) 338-60.

44 David Howes, "Property, God and Nature in the Thought of Sir John Beverley Robinson," *McGill Law Journal* 30 (1984-85): 365-414; G. Blaine Baker, "'So Elegant a Web': Providential Order and the Rule of Secular Law in Early Nineteenth-Century Upper Canada," *University of Toronto Law Journal* 38 (1988): 184-205. See also G. Blaine Baker, "The Reconstitution of Upper Canadian Legal Thought in the Late-Victorian Empire," *Law and History Review* 3 (1985): 219-92; David Howes, "Dialogical Jurisprudence," in W. Wesley Pue and Barry Wright, eds., *Canadian Perspectives on Law & Society: Issues in Legal History* (Ottawa: Carleton UP, 1988) 71-90.

45 Paul Romney, "Very Late Loyalist Fantasies: Nostalgic Tory 'History' and the Rule of Law in Upper Canada," in Pue and Wright, eds., *Canadian Perspectives on Law & Society* 119. See also Romney's "Re-inventing Upper Canada: American Immigrants, Upper Canadian History, English Law, and the Alien Question," in Roger Hall, William Westfall, and Laurel Sefton MacDowell, eds., *Patterns of the Past: Interpreting Ontario's History* (Toronto: Dundurn, 1988) 78-107.

46 Romney, "Very Late Loyalist Fantasies" 121. For other articles that bear witness to this "longer view" of Canadian legal history, see Greg Marquis, "Doing Justice to 'British Justice': Law, Ideology and Canadian Historiography," in Pue and Wright, eds., *Canadian Perspectives on Law & Society* 43-69; Mark Francis, "The Contemplation of Colonial Constitutions as Political Philosophy," *Political Science* 40.1 (1988): 142-59.

47 J.G.A. Pocock, *The Machiavellian Moment: Florentine Political Thought and the Atlantic Republican Tradition* (Princeton, NJ: Princeton UP, 1975) vii-viii. See also "Languages and Their Implications: The Transformation of the Study of

Political Thought," "Civic Humanism and Its Role in Anglo-American Thought," and "Machiavelli, Harrington and English Political Ideologies in the Eighteenth Century" in Pocock, *Politics, Language and Time* 3-41, 80-103, 104-47.

48   Pocock's *Machiavellian Moment* is noted in Errington's bibliography, but not in Mills's. His work is not used directly by either author.

49   Gordon as quoted in Marquis, "Doing Justice to 'British Justice,'" in Pue and Wright, eds., *Canadian Perspectives on Law & Society* 45. For indications of the degree to which current research and writing in legal history has come to approximate intellectual history, see Barry Wright, "An Introduction to Canadian Law in History" and W. Wesley Pue, "Theory and Method in the History of Law," in Pue and Wright, eds., *Canadian Perspectives on Law & Society* 7-19, 23-28.

50   Susan E. Houston and Alison Prentice, *Schooling and Scholars in Nineteenth-Century Ontario* (Toronto: U of Toronto P, 1988) 338, 235-72.

51   Susan E. Houston, "Politics, Schools, and Social Change in Upper Canada," *The Canadian Historical Review* 53 (1972): 249-71; Houston, "Victorian Origins of Juvenile Delinquency: A Canadian Experience," *History of Education Quarterly* 12 (1972): 254-80. See Michael B. Katz, *The Irony of Early School Reform* (Cambridge, MA: Harvard UP, 1968).

52   Alison Prentice, *The School Promoters: Education and Social Class in Mid-Nineteenth Century Upper Canada* (Toronto: McClelland and Stewart, 1977) 184.

53   Houston and Prentice, *Schooling and Scholars* xi. When discussing the notion of "social control" or of relations of the educational system to the state, Houston and Prentice consistently defer to the work of historical sociologist Bruce Curtis. See Bruce Curtis, "The Speller Expelled: Disciplining the Common Reader in Canada West," *The Canadian Review of Sociology and Anthropology* 22 (1985): 346-68; Curtis, "Preconditions of the Canadian State: Educational Reform and the Construction of a Public in Upper Canada, 1837-1846," *Studies in Political Economy* 10 (1983): 99-121; Curtis, *Building the Canadian State: Canada West, 1836-1871* (London, ON: Falmer/Althouse, 1988).

54   Paul Axelrod and John G. Reid, eds., *Youth, University, and Canadian Society: Essays in the Social History of Higher Education* (Kingston, ON: McGill-Queen's UP, 1989) xiii, xi.

55   Berger, *The Writing of Canadian History*, 2nd ed., 294-95.

56   John Porter, *The Vertical Mosaic: An Analysis of Social Class and Power in Canada* (Toronto: U of Toronto P, 1965) 491-511.

57   See Paul Axelrod, "Higher Education, Utilitarianism, and the Acquisitive Society: Canada, 1930-1980," in Michael S. Cross and Gregory S. Kealey, eds., *Modern Canada: 1930-1980s* (Toronto: McClelland and Stewart, 1984) 179-205; Keith Walden, "Respectable Hooligans: Male Toronto College Students Celebrate Hallowe'en, 1884-1910," *The Canadian Historical Review* 68 (1987):

1-34; Paul Axelrod, "Moulding the Middle Class: Student Life at Dalhousie University in the 1930s," *Acadiensis* 15.1 (1985): 84-122; C.M. Johnston and J.C. Weaver, *Student Days: An Illustrated History of Student Life at McMaster University from the 1890s to the 1980s* (Hamilton, ON: McMaster University Alumni Association, 1986). For the North American context, see also Paula Fass, *The Damned and the Beautiful: American Youth in the 1920s* (New York: Oxford UP, 1977); Helen Lefkowitz Horowitz, *Campus Life: Undergraduate Cultures from the End of the Eighteenth Century to the Present* (Chicago: U of Chicago P, 1987).

58   Some good studies of individual academic departments have been done. See, for example, Ian Drummond, *Political Economy at Toronto: A History of the Department, 1888-1982* (Toronto: University of Toronto Governing Council, 1983); Barry Ferguson, "Political Economists and *Queen's Quarterly*, 1893-1939," *Queen's Quarterly* 90 (1983): 623-43; and Ferguson, "The New Political Economy and Canadian Liberal Democratic Thought: Queen's University 1900-1925," diss., York U, 1982. Likewise, Philip C. Enros has investigated scientific research in Toronto: "The University of Toronto and Industrial Research in the Early Twentieth Century," in Richard A. Jarrell and Arnold E. Roos, eds., *Critical Issues in the History of Canadian Science, Technology and Medicine* (Thornhill, ON: HSTC, 1983) 155-66. For North American context, see Hugh Hawkins, "University Identity: The Teaching and Research Functions," in Alexandra Oleson and John Voss, eds., *The Organization of Knowledge in Modern America, 1860-1920* (Baltimore: Johns Hopkins UP, 1979) 285-312; Roger L. Geiger, *To Advance Knowledge: The Growth of American Research Universities, 1900-1940* (New York: Oxford UP, 1986); David O. Levine, *The American College and the Culture of Aspiration 1915-1940* (Ithaca, NY: Cornell UP, 1986).

59   Chris Baldick, *The Social Mission of English Criticism* (Oxford: Clarendon, 1983); Gerald Graff, *Literature Against Itself: Literary Ideas in Modern Society* (Chicago: U of Chicago P, 1979); Graff, *Professing Literature: An Institutional History* (Chicago: U of Chicago P, 1987); Patricia Jasen, "Arnoldian Humanism, English Studies, and the Canadian University," *Queen's Quarterly* 95 (1988): 550-66; Patricia Jasen, "'In Pursuit of Human Values (or Laugh When You Say That)': The Student Critique of the Arts Curriculum in the 1960s," in Axelrod and Reid, eds., *Youth, University, and Canadian Society* 247-71; Patricia Jasen, "The English-Canadian Liberal Arts Curriculum: An Intellectual History, 1800-1950," diss., U of Manitoba, 1987. See also Grant Webster, *The Republic of Letters: A History of Post-War American Literary Opinion* (Baltimore: Johns Hopkins UP, 1979); Margerie Fee, "English-Canadian Literary Criticism, 1890-1927: Defining and Establishing a National Literature," diss., U of Toronto, 1981.

60   See, for example, Neil Gregor Smith, "Nationalism in the Canadian Churches," *Canadian Journal of Theology* 9 (1963): 112-25; John S. Moir, "The

Canadianization of the Protestant Churches," *Canadian Historical Association Report* (1966): 56-69.

61 Ramsay Cook, *The Regenerators: Social Criticism in Late Victorian English Canada* (Toronto: U of Toronto P, 1985) 4.

62 Richard Allen, *The Social Passion: Religion and Social Reform in Canada 1914-1928* (Toronto: U of Toronto P, 1971) 3-4.

63 Cook, *The Regenerators* 6.

64 Owen Chadwick, *The Secularization of the European Mind in the Nineteenth Century* (Cambridge, Eng.: Cambridge UP, 1975) 264.

65 Cook, *The Regenerators* 228.

66 Chadwick, *The Secularization of the European Mind* 3.

67 A.B. McKillop, *A Disciplined Intelligence: Critical Inquiry and Canadian Thought in the Victorian Era* (Montreal: McGill-Queen's UP, 1979) 205-32. The book did not, it appears, adequately convey the author's view that, in an anthropological sense, Salem Bland or S.D. Chown were as "religious" as their more orthodox forebears. (Hence the stress in *A Disciplined Intelligence* on the essential continuity of a "moral imperative" derived from the power and vision of evangelical protestantism.) See A.B. McKillop, "Moralists and Moderns," *Journal of Canadian Studies* 14.4 (1979-80): 144-50.

68 Marguerite Van Die, *An Evangelical Mind: Nathanael Burwash and the Methodist Tradition in Canada, 1839-1918* (Kingston, ON: McGill-Queen's UP, 1989) 7-13.

69 Van Die, *An Evangelical Mind* 12.

70 This persistence of evangelical spirituality has been the subject of other recent studies. See Phyllis Airhart, "The Eclipse of Revivalist Spirituality: The Transformation of Canadian Methodist Piety 1884-1925," diss., U of Chicago, 1985; Michael Gauvreau, "The Taming of History: Reflections on the Canadian Methodist Encounter with Biblical Criticism, 1830-1900," *The Canadian Historical Review* 65 (1984): 315-46.

71 Van Die, *An Evangelical Mind* 13, 196.

72 William Westfall, *Two Worlds: The Protestant Culture of Nineteenth-Century Ontario* (Kingston, ON: McGill-Queen's UP, 1989) 18.

73 Westfall, *Two Worlds* 30, 45.

74 Louis Hartz, *The Liberal Tradition in America* (New York: Harcourt, Brace & World, 1955).

75 Westfall, *Two Worlds* 194-95.

76 Westfall, *Two Worlds* 206.

77 John Webster Grant, *A Profusion of Spires: Religion in Nineteenth-Century Ontario* (Toronto: U of Toronto P, 1988) 229. The book is a volume in the Ontario Historical Studies Series.

78 J.D. Rabb, ed., *Religion and Science in Early Canada* (Kingston, ON: Ronald P. Frye, 1988); Carl Berger, *Science, God, and Nature in Victorian Canada* (Toronto: U of Toronto P, 1983); Suzanne Zeller, *Inventing Canada: Early Victorian Science*

and the Idea of a Transcontinental Nation (Toronto: U of Toronto P, 1987).

79   Thomas P. Socknat, *Witness Against War: Pacifism in Canada 1900-1945* (Toronto: U of Toronto P, 1987). See Spencer R. Weart, *Nuclear Fear: A History of Images* (Cambridge, MA: Harvard UP, 1988) for a fascinating study of the "nuclear" frame of mind.

80   Michiel Horn, *The League for Social Reconstruction: Intellectual Origins of the Democratic Left in Canada, 1930-1942* (Toronto: U of Toronto P, 1980); R. Douglas Francis, *Frank H. Underhill: Intellectual Provocateur* (Toronto: U of Toronto P, 1986).

81   Like the study of legal structures and assumptions, the "probabilistic revolution" constitutes an element of intellectual history's "*longue durée*," and no serious historian of the origins of the social sciences in any national context can afford to ignore its implications. See Lorraine Daston, *Classical Probability in the Enlightenment* (Princeton, NJ: Princeton UP, 1988). Daston relates her subject to changing legal ideas and forms (such as the notion of "risk") and, in a general way, to emergent forms of social knowledge such as "moral science" and political economy. See especially her Chapter Two, "Expectation and the Reasonable Man" 49-111, but note her caveat not to "identify the Enlightenment moral sciences narrowly with their twentieth-century descendants" (110). See also Ian Hacking, *The Emergence of Probability: A Philosophical Study of Early Ideas about Probability, Induction and Statistical Inference* (Cambridge, Eng.: Cambridge UP, 1975) for the seventeenth- and eighteenth-century philosophical context.

See Lorraine J. Daston, "The Domestication of Risk: Mathematical Probability and Insurance 1650-1830" 237-60 and her "Rational Individuals versus Laws of Society: From Probability to Statistics" 295-304, in Lorenz Krüger, Lorraine J. Daston, and Michael Heidelberger, eds., *The Probabilistic Revolution. Volume 1: Ideas in History* (Cambridge, MA: MIT, 1987). Several other articles in this volume deal directly with the relationship between "the probabilistic revolution" and the social sciences, but see especially Stephen M. Stigler, "The Measurement of Uncertainty in Nineteenth-Century Social Science" 287-92 and M. Norton Wise, "How Do Sums Count? On the Cultural Origins of Statistical Causality" 395-425. In Lorenz Krüger, Gerd Gigerenzer, and Mary S. Morgan, eds., *The Probabilistic Revolution. Volume 2: Ideas in the Sciences* (Cambridge, MA: MIT, 1987), see Anthony Oberschall, "The Two Empirical Roots of Social Theory and the Probability Revolution" 103-37.

82   Stephen Brooks and Alain G. Gagnon, *Social Scientists and Politics in Canada: Between Clerisy and Vanguard* (Kingston, ON: McGill-Queen's UP, 1988). See also Alain G. Gagnon, ed., *Intellectuals in Liberal Democracies: Political Influence and Social Involvement* (New York: Praeger, 1987).

83   James W. Carey, *Communication as Culture: Essays on Media and Society* (Boston: Unwin Hyman, 1989) 143-72.

84 Daniel J. Czitrom, *Media and the American Mind: From Morse to McLuhan* (Chapel Hill: U of North Carolina P, 1982) 147–82.

85 William J. Bouwsma, "Intellectual History in the 1980s: From History of Ideas to History of Meaning," *The Journal of Interdisciplinary History* 12 (1981–82): 279–91.

86 See Frank H. Underhill, "Introduction to the Carleton Library Edition," in André Siegfried, *The Race Question in Canada* (Toronto: McClelland and Stewart, 1968) 1.

A.B. McKILLOP

Once More to the Lake:
Towards a Poetics of Receptivity

J. R. (Tim) Struthers

> when you see the land naked, look again
> (burn your maps, that is not what I mean),
> I mean the moment when it seems most plain
> is the moment when you must begin again
>   — Gwendolyn MacEwen, "The Discovery"

"To this day I like to believe that one must be older to begin," Robert Kroetsch confides in "The Moment of the Discovery of America Continues" (11). Whether I imagine myself at age five, or forty-five, or eighty-five, I too feel that I am only beginning. The most I can hope for is that the beginning I essay here will provide a hint of possibility, an opening, permission, for someone else. Maybe for the lanky young woman hunched over a notebook in the back row of one of my classes, writing most feverishly (a new idea? a new poem?) when my voice fades from her hearing, when she is enveloped by a different sort of communication.

Northrop Frye notes in "Criticism as Education" that possibly the oldest idea of education involves "the dramatic transformation of the mind, the sudden entry into a new plane of reality" (151). For this purpose, as John Newlove states in "The Pride,"

> one line only
> will be enough,
> a single line
> and then the sunlit brilliant image suddenly floods us
> with understanding.... (91)

All that we know about this phenomenon, however, as Frye says, is that it never occurs to "those who are totally unprepared for it" (151). But in what ways can we prepare to receive its visitations? How are we to begin? Or, as Clark Blaise emphasizes in "To Begin, To Begin" (161), as Eli Mandel reiterates in "Strange Loops" (25), and as Gwendolyn MacEwen urges in "The Discovery" (30), how are we to begin again?

By chance as I began to imagine the shape this essay might take — though can we say that anything imaginative happens by chance? — I rediscovered novelist, short story writer, and critic Keath Fraser's "Notes toward a Supreme Fiction," an essay that borrows its title from a poem of the same name by Wallace Stevens. Fraser describes Stevens' poem as "the distillation of a lifetime's thought about the nature of poetry" (223) and calls attention to how Stevens structured the poem by means of three statements: "It Must Be Abstract," "It Must Change," "It Must Give Pleasure." I considered the three statements Fraser invented when he sought to distill into a single essay the thought of half his lifetime about the nature of fiction: "It Must Be Autobiographical," "It Must Subvert," "It Must Be Wonderful."

Then I began to wonder what statements paralleling Stevens' and Fraser's I might invent to assist me in defining my views about the nature, the possibilities, of criticism — what statements I might invent to assist me in answering a question raised by Eli Mandel in "The Poet as Critic": "What happens ... when we begin to think of a work of criticism as a work of art?" (12)

I. It Must Be Personal

Jack Hodgins, in *A Passion for Narrative*, offers the following observations about creativity and creation:

> I think of my writer's reservoir — all memory and imagination and hoarded experience — as a kind of private aquarium whose thick waters teem with a wondrous population of unusual creatures, all constantly in motion.... Swimming past, circling, and swimming past again, they contemplate my presence like malevolent sharks, or cheerful porpoises, or comical blowfish, while they anticipate the moment they will swim to the surface and throw themselves into my world. When they do, as often as not it will be for the purpose of nudging a story into life. Anything might do it; a story can begin with anything, however small, so long as it fascinates or worries or puzzles me enough:
>
> - a person, a group of people
> - an event
> - an idea
> - a place
> - a voice heard, remembered, or imagined
> - a metaphor. (30-31)

Here in Hodgins' remarks lies the seed of a possibility that we might begin to think of criticism in a new way. What if teachers and essayists sought to discover, to explore, in their own minds and in the imaginations of their

J.R. (TIM) STRUTHERS

listeners, the resources – the reservoir, to echo Hodgins – on which poetry or fiction or drama depends?

Seeking a beginning to her essay "One More Woman Talking," Bronwen Wallace comments: "I can't separate my personal poetics from the life I am leading or from the events that have brought me to this point in it" (237). Wallace explains how for more than twenty years "the majority of my time has been spent listening to women tell the story of their lives in one form or another. ... In being part of these events, I share what is common to many women *and* I also experience them uniquely, as myself" (237-38). Wallace's aims as a woman and as a writer are indivisible. She concludes: "I begin, always, with the power of the personal, the private, the unique in each of us, which resists, survives, and can change the power that our culture has over us. This is what I have learned from the women's movement and what I try to explore in my poems" (242).

The conversation of a lifetime, a continuing conversation: this is an idea put forward, a metaphor shared, by Bronwen Wallace and many other writers. Thus John Metcalf remarks in *What Is A Canadian Literature?* that "Every day of my life is lived with other writers. Their shapes and forms, a use of language peculiar to them, this one's tone, that loved one's flash and filigree – all this informs my work. ... My converse is with ... the living *and* the dead" (41). And is it not possible to imagine criticism as being receptive to, as being committed to, the same means and ends as art? Hence Robert Kroetsch, in the acknowledgements for *The Lovely Treachery of Words*, recognizes: "I see now that these essays are very much the consequence of extended conversation" (ix), that together they represent "the narrative of an individual voice in conversation with the announced world" (x).

Such a conversation is recorded, recreated, in the five-paragraph opening sequence of Alice Munro's "Walker Brothers Cowboy," where the young girl who tells the story takes a walk with her father down to Lake Huron. The sequence begins: "After supper my father says, 'Want to go down and see if the Lake's still there?' We leave my mother sewing under the dining-room light, making clothes for me against the opening of school" (1). Then at the climax of the sequence the father relates to his daughter a Southwestern Ontario version of a creation myth: "He tells me how the Great Lakes came to be. All where Lake Huron is now, he says, used to be flat land, a wide flat plain. Then came the ice, creeping down from the north, pushing deep into the low places. ... And then the ice went back, shrank back towards the North Pole where it came from, and left its fingers of ice in the deep places it had gouged, and ice turned to lakes and there they were today" (3).

The father's story, like the story by Munro that surrounds it, is a genesis story in different senses. His story supplies an account of the geographical origins of the region, contributes to his daughter's awareness of place and therefore to her individual growth, and suggests an entire mythology on which Southwestern Ontario writers might base their artistic genesis. Here for father and daughter, for teller and listener, for artist and critic, are the constituents of a personal mythology, what Northrop Frye in *Fearful Symmetry: A Study of William Blake* calls "an iconography of the imagination" (420) – a notion that James Reaney sought to emphasize in founding his magazine *Alphabet: A Semiannual Devoted to the Iconography of the Imagination.*

For those writers who were born and raised in the place James Reaney, repeating a word invented by painter Greg Curnoe, calls "Souwesto" – that is, for writers such as Sara Jeannette Duncan, Raymond Knister, George Elliott, James Reaney, Alice Munro, Douglas Glover, William Butt, Christopher Dewdney, Daniel David Moses, Tracy Shepherd, and me – this personal mythology is a Southwestern Ontario mythology. It involves what Robert Kroetsch in "The Moment of the Discovery of America Continues" terms, with a nod to William Carlos Williams' long poem *Paterson*, "a local pride" (6). This local pride, Kroetsch argues, "does not exclude the rest of the world, or other experiences; rather, it makes them possible. It creates an organizing centre" (6). The point is elaborated by William Butt in "Canada's Mental Travellers Abroad" – "However expressed, when a traveller can put two worlds together in this way, then something else new and very important occurs: as that foreign land grows no longer quite so foreign, ... the home land in consequence grows the clearer" (298-99). Moreover, Butt adds, in "looking back and round from abroad, not just your own country but your own *self* swings into view" (299).

The title of William Butt's essay alludes to Blake's "The Mental Traveller," and what we see in Blake, Frye argues in *Fearful Symmetry*, is "a drama of creation, struggle, redemption and restoration in the fallen life of a divine Man" (340). It is a drama that transforms the individual "from a centre to a circumference of perception" (349), that allows individuality to be developed to a point where it can be relinquished, where it effaces itself, where it emerges into a vision of community. This community, for Blake and Frye, constitutes, in Frye's words, "the real Church, the total vision which is the city of God" (344-45). The cultivation of a personal mythology, then, permits a revelation of the divine vision, which Frye describes as "something infinitely greater than any individual imagination can achieve" (405). In an interview by Gregory Baum, Frye explains that this is a "vision of the community of man which we may or may not be fortunate enough to get in our lives" (40); but it is something, Frye insists, that we must continue working towards.

Frye notes in *Fearful Symmetry* that "The Romantic tradition has one thing in it of great value: it encourages the poet to find his [or her] symbols in his [or her] own way, and does not impose *a priori* patterns on his [or her] imagination" (423). So, too, for the critic, argues Harold Bloom in "Criticism, Canon-Formation, and Prophecy: The Sorrows of Facticity" – "The quest of contemporary criticism is for method, and the quest is vain. *There is no method other than yourself.* All those who seek for a method that is not themselves will find not a method, but someone else, whom they will ape and involuntarily mock. Poetry and fiction share with criticism the mystery that post-Structural speculation seeks to deny: the spark we call personality or the idiosyncratic, which in metaphysics and theology once was called presence" (413-14). The nature of this mental and spiritual activity is characterized by Frye in "The Search for Acceptable Words": "Every creative person has an interconnected body of images and ideas underneath his [or her] consciousness which it is his [or her] creative work to fish up in bits and pieces. Sometimes a phrase or a word comes to him [or her] as a kind of hook or bait with which to catch something that he [or she] knows is down there" (11). This is the method that the critic as artist – to echo the title of a brilliantly prophetic essay from Oscar Wilde's 1891 collection *Intentions* – must pursue, must have the liberty to pursue.

In *Fearful Symmetry* Frye cautions us that "To dissolve art back into the artist's experience is like scraping the paint off a canvas in order to see what the 'real' canvas looked like before it assumed its painted disguise" (326). Autobiography, however, is a way of transforming the materials of a personal mythology into an individual and communal vision; as Wilde points out in the preface to his novel *The Picture of Dorian Gray*, "The highest as the lowest form of criticism is a mode of autobiography" (235). In an interview by Justin Kaplan, Frye notes the difficulty he has explaining, whenever anybody urges him to write his autobiography, that "everything I write *I* consider autobiography, although nobody else would" (211). Criticism of this sort – *Fearful Symmetry* for instance, which Frye wrote and rewrote, as John Ayre relates, from 1934 to 1945, under the shadow of the Second World War – conveys nothing less than all that we dream of being, nothing less than what Maggie Kyle, the heroine of Jack Hodgins' epic novel *The Invention of the World*, imagines as "all that she was capable of being" (380). According to Keath Fraser, the creative writer's mandate (and I would add the critic's and the teacher's) "isn't to change the world but to show that within the imagination, capable of evoking both the sublime and darkness together, exists a metaphor for God" (229). This God, this imagination, this supreme fiction, says Fraser, envelops, transforms, directs us because "there is no getting through or around the authority of its vision and the intuitive logic of its means" (229). Consequently, as William Butt remarks about Hodgins' fiction, about reading it actively, "The artists and the audience of art join as workers at the hallowed job of constructing a civilization – invention of our world, which is also the coming-in of God. So long as we remain at the task, our world is revived – resurrected – at each moment" (63).

For Northrop Frye and for William Butt and for me, William Blake provides a persistently courageous and fascinating model, perhaps most notably during the last twenty years of his life when, as Frye explains, "Blake's chief interest in writing passes from creation to criticism, and from poetry to prose" (414). Having completed his own major poems and having illustrated them, Blake turned to illustrating, to commenting on, to recreating other poets' visions – as seen in his illustrations to the Bible. "Finally," notes Frye, "comes the *Vision of the Book of Job*, where comment is made entirely by quotation" and where illustration becomes "an independent art-form" (415). Of Blake's late illustrations Frye concludes: "Here he found a formula for uniting the work of the creator with that of the teacher, of combining mythopoeic art with instruction in how to read it" (415). Exactly the same can be said of the deeply personal, profoundly imaginative, and liberating criticism of Wilde, Frye, Bloom, Mandel, Reaney, and other prophetic artists like them: criticism in which personal contexts, traditions, influences, experiences, metaphors, landscape, vision, and belief – all the elements of a personal mythology – can unite and resonate.

II. It Must Be Imaginative

In "Blake's Reading of the Book of Job," Frye concludes that "Blake's vision of the Book of Job was certainly a work of the creative imagination, but what made it possible was a powerful critical analysis of the book, of the whole Bible of which it forms a microcosm, and of the human life which, according to Matthew Arnold, is the theatre in which creation and criticism have become the same thing" (244). The unity of creation and criticism exemplified for Frye by Blake is strongly evident in the criticism written by authors as different from one another as Keath Fraser, Bronwen Wallace, Robert Kroetsch, M. Nourbese Philip, John Metcalf, Jack Hodgins, George Bowering, Hugh Hood, James Reaney, D.G. Jones, Eli Mandel, and Frye himself. Thus in "Northrop Frye and the Canadian Literary Tradition" Mandel argues that Frye's criticism must be "retrieved as poetry" (284) – a phrase echoed in the title of Margery Fee's "Retrieving the Canadian Critical Tradition as Poetry: Eli Mandel and Northrop Frye." Fee, like Smaro Kamboureli, considers Mandel's response to Frye in terms of Harold Bloom's theories of literary influence, of how writers must struggle with particular precursors, of how writers need to produce strong creative misreadings of their precursors. Certainly Frye's criticism represented a crucially formative body of thought for Mandel, which he remained in dialogue with, sometimes in debate with, for a quarter-century, from "Toward a Theory of Cultural Revolution: The Criticism of Northrop Frye," published in 1959, onward. But to the recipients of Frye's and Mandel's joint legacy, it is not the points of divergence but rather the points of convergence between the two critics – their continuous cultivation of the life-sustaining power of one's imagination, one's metaphors, one's mythology – that will undoubtedly prove to be most important.

Juxtaposition of passages from Frye's essays "Literature as Context: Milton's *Lycidas*" and "Criticism, Visible and Invisible" with passages from Mandel's essays "Banff: The Magic Mountain" and "Northrop Frye and the Canadian Literary Tradition" will serve to demonstrate the profundity of their interrelations. In "Literature as Context: Milton's *Lycidas*," Frye states that "It is literature as an order of words, therefore, which forms the primary context of any given work of literary art. All other contexts – the place of *Lycidas* in Milton's development; its place in the history of English poetry; its place in seventeenth-century thought or history – are secondary and derivative contexts. Within the total literary order certain structural and generic principles, certain configurations of narrative and imagery, certain conventions and devices and *topoi*, occur over and over again. In every new work of literature some of these principles are reshaped" (127). Frye develops this argument in "Criticism, Visible and Invisible," where he re-emphasizes that "The central activity of criticism, which is the understanding of literature, is essentially one of establishing a context for the works of literature being studied ... in the total structure of literature itself, or what I call the order of words" (88). Yet beyond this central activity, Frye continues, is "a further context" with "a lower and an upper limit": "On the lower limit is criticism militant, a therapeutic activity of evaluation, or separating the good from the bad, in which good and bad are not two kinds of literature, but, respectively, the active and the passive approaches to verbal experience. ... On the higher limit is criticism triumphant, the inner possession of literature as an imaginative force to which all study of literature leads, and which is criticism at once glorified and invisible" (88).

Compare Mandel, who, in "Banff: The Magic Mountain," states that "Even the most radical argument about the arts must finally recognize something in art that goes beyond politics. I know how grudging the politicized writer is about this, but nonetheless, I cite Orwell...: 'Every piece of writing has its propaganda aspect, and yet in any book, or play, or poem, or what not that is to endure there has to be a residuum of something that simply is not affected by its moral or meaning – a residuum of something we call art'" (158). And in "Northrop Frye and the Canadian Literary Tradition" Mandel remarks: "Northrop Frye's criticism, then, in its formal and literary aspect, appears to provide a fusing link between poet and critic (criticism and creativity – idea and image) and – to use James Reaney's phrase – 'an electrifying organizing effect with regard to the imagination'" (291). Mandel cites a passage from Frye's reviews of Canadian poetry during the 1950s, a passage in which Frye conveys "his sense of the literary tradition in Canada, its development from impressionism to myth-making poetry" (290) – a view which Mandel in his introduction to *Contexts of Canadian Criticism* regards as providing "a central clue to a genuine cultural history" (19). In "Northrop Frye and the Canadian Literary Tradition," Mandel affirms the continuing importance of this view, while noting that in "Haunted by Lack of Ghosts: Some Patterns in the Imagery of Canadian Poetry," an essay published after *The Bush Garden*, Frye shifts from seeing tradition as something linear to seeing it as something kaleidoscopic (an image that brings to mind P.K. Page's poem "Kaleidoscope"). Frye's understanding of tradition, Mandel states, "shows no tendency to become dated or obsolete but rings a contemporary note, as the line from Frye to Reaney to bp Nichol suggests" (291). "But," Mandel observes, "the effort to hold the discussion of Canadian writing at the formal or literary level produces an oddly strained effect" (291). For Mandel, even Frye's seminal essay "Preface to an Uncollected Anthology" "loses some focus in trying to sort out the literary question from the social and historical ones with which the critic must 'settle uneasily'" (290).

Here Eli Mandel isolates the area of concern which, increasingly, has come to preoccupy, to inspire, much of the criticism written in the quarter-century and more since he edited and introduced *Contexts of Canadian Criticism*. Later in the same essay, however, Mandel points out how Frye sought to resolve this issue. Citing Frye's preface to *The Bush Garden* against older statements by Frye collected in the same volume, Mandel explains how Frye "restructures his earlier argument about Canadian writing by shifting the question of identification (the central literary question of his work) from its Canadian context" (293). Frye states in his preface that "the question of Canadian identity, so far as it affects the creative imagination, is not a 'Canadian' question at all, but a regional question" (xxii). "But that," Mandel explains, "shifts the political terminology too. Identity is not a political term, but a cultural one. The political question of Canada is a question of unity" (293-94). As a result, Frye concludes in his preface that "Identity is local and regional, rooted in the imagination, and in works of culture; unity is national in reference, international in perspective, and rooted in political feeling.... The tension between this political sense of unity and the imaginative sense of locality is the essence of whatever the word 'Canadian' means" (xxii-xxiii). Though sometimes challenging Frye's arguments, and sometimes restructuring them, Mandel ends by emphasizing the understanding he and Frye share.

For both Frye and Mandel, criticism must be retrieved, must be redeemed, as poetry. Yet how may the poetic act be described? Bronwen Wallace, in "One More Woman Talking," suggests: "I begin with what I have been given: women's stories, women's conversations. Since most of these stories come to me in pretty straightforward conversational language, that's what I use in the poem. But as I begin to recreate that conversation on the page, I begin to listen to the voice that tells these stories, a voice that is angry sometimes, or frightened, or grieving, or ecstatic. And it becomes the voice I have heard in so many women's conversations, a voice that explores *both* the events in the story itself, *and* something else that lies within those events" (238-39). "This something else is always a mystery for me," she continues; yet it is here, at the heart of this mystery, that "a deeper, often more dangerous exploration can take place" (239). Wallace concludes: "What I hear in 'ordinary conversation' is that movement that goes on among us when we feel safe or confident enough or loved enough to explore the power within us. This power is so often belittled or denied by the society around us (or by ourselves), but it remains the power by which, in our best moments, we manage to survive and to live, sometimes, with grace. This is what I hear in conversation and what I try to record in my poems. If this sounds like a statement of faith, as much as a statement of poetics, that's because it is" (239).

What Wallace offers us in her poems is something seemingly recorded but, as she knows, actually transfigured. In "Why I Don't (Always) Write Short Stories," Wallace elaborates on her views about the poetic act: "For me, writing a poem is a journey.... And for me, the narrative elements of the poem, the stories, 'what happened,' are part of an extended metaphor for that journey. But the poem as a whole is the voice, discovering" (176-77). Writing a poem, Wallace argues, gets us closer to a mystery to which poetry alone provides a "sense of immediate testimony, of prayer" (178). She quotes a passage from John Berger's essay "The Storyteller": "'Poems are nearer to prayer than to stories, but in poetry there is no one behind the language being prayed to. It is the language itself which has to hear and acknowledge'" (177). Furthermore – as Wallace suggests in the poem "Into the Midst of It" included in her essay "Lilacs in May: A Tribute to Al Purdy," and as Al Purdy's poem "The Country North of Belleville," which she mentions there, suggests as well – writing a poem may be an act of rediscovery, a possibly sustaining, possibly bewildering, inevitably haunting rediscovery.

As for the poet, so for the critic: an essay is a voice, discovering and rediscovering. And if the critic is Northrop Frye, the impact on subsequent readers may be that described by Robert Kroetsch in "Learning the Hero from Northrop Frye." Kroetsch talks about going to the United States to do his Ph.D. and about giving a seminar report using Frye's *Anatomy of*

Criticism as his starting point the year the book was published, 1957. When asked by his teacher to explain who this critic might be, Kroetsch tells us, "I began, in answering that request, to talk about the hero, the nature of the hero, in literature, in the modern world, in my Canadian world" (154). And, many years later, Kroetsch explains, "I'm still giving the report, though now Northrop Frye himself has become the hero under discussion, a peculiarly Canadian hero, in a modern world that has assigned to critics and theorists a hero's many tasks" (154).

Kroetsch concludes of Frye's achievement: "It is difficult, almost impossible, to imagine a nation without its epic poem. Northrop Frye's work is an extended commentary on the great Canadian epic poem, a poem whose text we do not have, but whose intention and design and accomplishment he makes everywhere present in his elaborate response. ... Northrop Frye becomes, by that inscription, by that revealing of prophetic presence in absence, by that locating of the denied or at least concealed story in his own commentary, the voice of the epic we do not have. In his collected criticism, he locates the poetry of our unlocatable poem. In talking about that poem, he becomes our epic poet" (161). So, too, I would argue, do Eli Mandel in his collected criticism, Robert Kroetsch in *The Lovely Treachery of Words* and *A Likely Story: The Writing Life*, Bronwen Wallace in *Arguments with the World*, and M. Nourbese Philip in *Frontiers*. So, too, I would argue, do any number of other prophetic critics like them.

Eli Mandel extends, restructures, or contextualizes Frye's arguments in a way that allows us to see Frye, Mandel, and, say, Nourbese Philip together, at the place that Mandel identifies, in "Banff: The Magic Mountain," as theoreticians', critics', artists' "deepest point of creative activity" (159). Thus Nourbese Philip, in "Who's Listening?: Artists, Audiences & Language," acknowledges that "writing about one's anger and pain without appearing to descend into rhetoric, polemic, and cant is difficult" (35), and she urges pursuit of "the less tangible, less certain rewards of 'growth' or 'practising one's art seriously'" (36). Of course we must not obscure the differences and the points of contestation between individuals. We must not ignore the possibilities these differences allow. Moreover, it is precisely the differences and the points of contestation between, say, Frye and Nourbese Philip that mark the distance between *Contexts of Canadian Criticism* and *New Contexts of Canadian Criticism*. Yet what interests me most is how the criticism of Frye, Mandel, and Nourbese Philip begins to bridge these differences.

What Mandel refers to as aestheticians' "deepest point of creative activity" is, for me, a place where individuals as different as Frye, Mandel, and Nourbese Philip come together. As Mandel observes in "Banff: The Magic Mountain," "At one extreme we find writing we call radical, at the other formalist. Obviously, there is room for all sorts of shading in between. For 'radical' you can read: marxist, leftist, engaged, or whatever; for 'formalist' you can read: aesthetic, metaphysical, fantastic – or whatever. I've recently heard the distinction put as between an aesthetic of space and an aesthetic of time" (155). Mandel explains: "Radical approaches insist on grounding writing in history, in time, within specific historical, political, economic, and social *causes*: material reality. In Canada, this calls for a recognition of Americanization as a political, economic, and cultural fact, and decolonization as a programme. Formalist approaches find their cause, or the cause of writing, in literary forms. Northrop Frye provides the influential and instructive theory: poems imitate poems, forms derive from forms" (155-56). It is Borges' essay "The Argentine Writer and Tradition," Mandel suggests, that "points to the real meaning of formalism: literary forms are forms of fantasy, and fantasy tells us that the world is only our dream in which we ourselves are dreamt or dreaming" (156).

Mandel elaborates on the differences between "radical" and "formalist" approaches as follows: "Radical aesthetics tends to regard 'culture' as a superstructure. Its real cause is material and specific. Formal aesthetics tends to regard society, or material reality, as a formal element of literature: no more than any other necessity in a story, and no realer than a spell cast on the liberating creative power the work celebrates" (156). In the end for Mandel, "The problem or puzzle in Frye's work, and in radical critiques, is not, I think, confusion. Anything but. It has to do with the distinction between the *nature* of forms and their *source*, or more accurately, their *location*. Examine their nature and you move into the world of fantasy or the realm of the ideal. Look at their location and you see them in an historical context, in a given place and time. The first is a formalist approach; the second the radical. In either case, the unremitting tension between the two possibilities remains" (158).

An awareness of this tension, and of the importance of handling it judiciously, is evident in Nourbese Philip's "Who's Listening?: Artists, Audiences & Language." In this essay she describes two figures: "Male, white, and Oxford-educated, he stands over my right shoulder; she is old, Black, and wise and stands over my left shoulder – two archetypal figures symbolizing the two traditions that permeate my work. He – we shall call him John-from-Sussex – represents the white colonial tradition, the substance of any colonial education. Abiswa, as we shall call the other figure, represents the African-Caribbean context which, as typical of any colonial education, was ignored. She is also representative of a certain collective race memory of the African" (26-27). "Neither of these archetypes," Nourbese Philip explains, "individually represents what I would call my ideal listener or audience" (27). And admittedly for Nourbese Philip, "Bridging the split that these two archetypes represent is a difficult process: each represents what the other is not – each is, so to speak, the other's Other" (27). Yet, for her and for ourselves, "A dialogue between the two is essential" (27).

Through the criticism of Eli Mandel we are led to recognize both the differences and the similarities (or, to echo Nourbese Philip, the dialogue) between the various aesthetic, formalist, romantic, and nationalist positions presented in *Contexts of Canadian Criticism* and the various political, radical, postmodern, and postcolonial positions of *New Contexts of Canadian Criticism*. In his introduction to the earlier anthology, Mandel remarks how "one looks for the sort of argument which will resolve the form-content dichotomy that comes into being when the material of art – the 'Canadian' content – calls for special attention for either political or social purposes. But then 'content' is not so simply disposed of" (15). And in "Banff: The Magic Mountain," while Mandel stresses that "much of this essay has been directed to style as well as ideology, and particularly to the question as to whether a radical politics and literature could ever afford to ignore style," he proceeds to emphasize what is shared by aesthetic and political approaches: "In my terms, both the radical and formalist aesthetics converge at their deepest point of creative activity. Anything less, on either side, is brutal and exploitative" (159).

III. It Must Give Permission

Much in the way that for Coleridge, in *Biographia Literaria*, the poetic imagination "reveals itself in the balance or reconciliation of opposite and discordant qualities" (2: 12), the writing of critics such as Frye, Mandel, and Nourbese Philip bridges numerous differences, lifts the imaginations of their readers into what Frye, in "Criticism as Education," terms "a new plane of reality" (151) – and, indeed, a new community. Similarly, Bronwen Wallace begins her essay "Lilacs in May: A Tribute to Al Purdy" by discussing two views of tradition, how both of these views need to be brought into focus, how they need to be bridged: "a literary tradition involves the building of a space in which there is room, safety, *permission*, if you will, to say what you need to say. It's an understanding of tradition that sometimes gets forgotten, since younger writers often tend to think of what has been done before only as a limitation, something we have to escape from, break with, whatever. Both meanings exist, of course, but what I want to talk about here is what it has meant to me, as a writer in this country, to have had Al Purdy as part of my tradition. I want to talk about what I have been allowed to do that I don't believe I could have done without him" (163). The view Wallace chooses to discuss represents a way of writing that closely resembles what John Metcalf says about tradition in *What Is A Canadian Literature?*: "A tradition is alive, various, densely populated, intricate. It is interconnected. It is like a river which accommodates within its general flow different currents and eddies and whirlpools and backwaters. A tradition teaches and trains. It is like a family which is constantly expanding yet managing somehow to contain and sustain contradictory personalities and disparate aims and ambitions" (40-41). I'd like to help foster a tradition of literature, of criticism, of education, that is accommodating, lively, and sustaining.

I'm a small-press publisher, an editor, a university teacher, a literary critic, an interviewer, a writer of autobiography, a literary historian, a bibliographer, a collector. I want to bring everything these identities involve into each part of my work. When I first began this essay, I imagined calling it "Collecting" since, for me, collecting is as indispensable to the art of criticism as it is, according to John Metcalf in an interview I did with him (36-37), to the art of fiction. Later, I imagined calling my essay "Where the Myth Touches Us" after the title of an important story in Hugh Hood's first story collection, *Flying a Red Kite* – a collection whose title story had already given me the name of my own publishing company, Red Kite Press. (If publishing in this country isn't an act of faith, represented in Hugh Hood by flying a red kite, what is it?) Then, half-jokingly, I imagined using "In Search of the Big Metaphor." Yet as I continued working on this essay, I recalled some advice given by Jack Hodgins in *A Passion for Narrative*: "Revising requires re-seeing. ... most 'breakthroughs' I've observed ... have come about after the writer has worked through draft after draft ... then steps back, abandons the 'almost wonderful' story, and begins afresh. That is, after staring at the existing story until she knows it intimately, she sits down at the desk and begins a brand-new 'first draft' from scratch" (237). And I decided to begin again – including searching for a different title.

I thought of a remark made about an early draft of my essay by my friend William Butt, a playwright and historian and critic living in Woodstock, Ontario and, like me, a former student of James Reaney: Bill said it seemed I was trying to rewrite Alice Munro's story "Walker Brothers Cowboy." Subsequently, out of the imaginative reservoir of my memories arose the title of E.B. White's enormously moving memoir-essay "Once More to the Lake." I talked about possible titles for my essay with my friend Doug Daymond – now recently retired from the University of Guelph and, like me, a former student of the general editor of the first three volumes of the *Literary History of Canada*, Carl F. Klinck. I reflected on the name of the two-volume anthology of Canadian criticism that Doug Daymond and Les Monkman produced at the University of Guelph just before I came to teach here, called *Towards a Canadian Literature: Essays, Editorials & Manifestos*, a companion to their earlier two-volume anthology, *Literature in Canada*. And I happened upon a word, "receptivity," in Frye's essay "Criticism as Education," where we are told:

"The sense of relaxing the mind and the body, of making time for receptivity, seems to me to have a most important role to play in education from earliest childhood. ... Reading whatever is worth reading cannot be hurried, because what we have to do is to take possession of it, absorb its power, and that will take time" (148-49).

Perhaps most importantly, I rediscovered Keath Fraser's "Notes toward a Supreme Fiction." I noted that Harold Bloom, in "Coda: The Criticism of Our Climate, A Self-Review," had rewritten Wallace Stevens' comment "It Must Give Pleasure" as "It Must Give Power" (428). Then I remembered the word "permission" that Bronwen Wallace used in "Lilacs in May: A Tribute to Al Purdy." And I wrote: It Must Be Personal, It Must Be Imaginative, It Must Give Permission. Once again I recalled Frye's "Criticism as Education." And I began to think more deeply about criticism as autobiography, about criticism as poetry and poetics, about criticism, finally, as education, as discovery.

All these phrases and more are meant to resound throughout this essay: in its title and sub-title, its section titles, its "progress," to use a musical term discussed by Ray Smith in his essay "A Refusal To Mourn the Death, by Bullshit, of Literature in the Eighties" (24). The analogy to music reminds me of remarks made by James Reaney in "Some Critics Are Music Teachers," a tribute to Northrop Frye. The better the music is taught, Reaney explains, the better it will be played and the better our lives will be. The analogy to music reminds me, too, of remarks made by composer, critic, and educator R. Murray Schafer in "A Statement on Music Education":

> Every teacher ought to be allowed to teach idiosyncratically, or at least to infuse his teaching with his own personality. I am going to speak to you today about some personal ideas. From your own experiences you may be able to amplify, correct or change them.
>
> My work in music education has been concentrated mostly in three fields.
>
> 1) To try to discover whatever creative potential children may have for making music of their own.
>
> 2) To introduce students of all ages to the sounds of the environment; to treat the world soundscape as a musical composition of which man is the principal composer, and to make critical judgments which would lead to its improvement.
>
> 3) To discover a nexus or gathering-place where all the arts may meet and develop harmoniously. (243)

To this I would only add: every student ought to be allowed to study idiosyncratically, or at least to infuse her studying with her own personality.

In "Lilacs in May: A Tribute to Al Purdy," Bronwen Wallace describes how her university education wounded her. She remarks: "I didn't discover Al Purdy until the early 1970s. One of the main reasons for this was that I was studying English at a university where Canadian Literature had not yet been heard of, let alone been considered fit to scoff at. In fact, I didn't read a Purdy poem until I dropped out of my Ph.D. program. I now believe that the one act was a necessary pre-requisite to the other – and to my becoming a writer period" (163). Wallace explains: "my university education was daily taking me further and further away from my parents, who had worked like hell for me to get it. Not only was it allowing me opportunities they never had, it was teaching me contempt for their lives and for my own class background, my own cultural context. What this meant for me as a writer, I see now, was that I was taught to deny and reject the very stuff, the only stuff, that could give my work as a writer authenticity. I was being robbed of my language and I almost didn't know it. What I felt at the time was that I didn't belong in university. I 'wasn't good enough'" (163-64). Wallace goes on to explain this another way: "I was being taught that what I had to say – the only thing I had to say – wasn't 'worth saying.' That attitude was all around me. In the literature I read, in the classrooms where I studied, people spoke, literally, with the accents of another culture, another class. They made fun of people who said 'eh,' and who used the flat, everyday speech of rural and working-class southern Ontario. People like my parents, in other words, and my grandparents and my great-grandparents and ..." (164). She concludes: "To put it simply, I gained a great deal from my education, yes. But I lost, too. I lost my family, my history, my language – as well as the smells and shapes and colours of my life. Without those, I could not be the writer I wanted to be" (164-65).

Wallace talks about quitting university, travelling around Canada, starting to write poems, and discovering Al Purdy's *The Cariboo Horses*, including his poem "The Country North of Belleville." I imagine her reading these lines in Purdy's poem:

> This is the country of our defeat and
>   yet
> during the fall plowing a man
> might stop and stand in a brown valley of the furrows
>   and shade his eyes to watch for the same
>   red patch mixed with gold
>   that appears on the same
>   spot in the hills
>   year after year
>   and grow old

plowing and plowing a ten acre field until
the convolutions run parallel with his own brain. (76)

I think of other poems by Purdy that are important to me. Lines from
"Roblin's Mills (2)" about forefathers and foremothers and their legacies:

The black millpond
                    holds them
movings and reachings and fragments
the gear and tackle of living
under the water eye
all things laid aside
                    discarded
                              forgotten
but they had their being once
and left a place to stand on. (66)

Lines from "The Freezing Music" – the first published version of the
poem, not the later versions. Lines about immanence, about receptivity,
about redemption:

I have maneuvered myself near them
my face close to the little tubular crystals
kneeling uncomfortably
on this rocky shoreline near Ameliasburg
temperature 32 degrees Fahrenheit
shining my flashlight on them
trying to observe the exact instant
water becomes ice
intently observing metamorphosis
but unable to escape myself
Running into the house to escape cold
clapping both hands on my breast grandiloquently
"I have heard the music of the spheres"
But yes I have
yes I have. (319)

And I go back to Bronwen Wallace's essay on Al Purdy, where she
explains how Purdy's poetry gave her confidence to create: "His work gave
me permission to write about the people I knew, and the landscape I saw,
and – most importantly – in the voice I'd heard in my head all my life.
The voice of the men and women in my family. A voice that tells its stories in the same meandering and magical way that highways move through

southeastern Ontario, until you understand that what happens in the story, like the landscape around you, is a metaphor for an inner journey, a journey that takes you to the centre of the speaker's life, to his or her discoveries about that life and to the mystery that lies there, always. I've taken that voice and that journey and made it my own, of course, but I needed Al Purdy" (165-66). Considering this passage, I understand why Bronwen Wallace, years earlier, felt compelled to write an essay in acknowledgement of Alice Munro – and I understand why I keep returning to and talking about Alice Munro.

Voice, form, permission. I remember Hugh Hood's comment to me, in an interview, that "Coleridge, as poet and critic at once, is the great model in English literature for the union of intellect and the poetic gift" (62-63). I remember Hood explaining to me how he had modelled his conversation, his university teaching, and the structure of successive novels in his twelve-volume epic, beginning with *The Swing in the Garden*, on Coleridge's pattern of thought: "the very wide range of reference without apparent connection on the surface which nonetheless will yield connections and networks and links and unities if you wait and allow them to appear" (63). And I return to two lines from Al Purdy's "The Country North of Belleville": "plowing and plowing a ten acre field until / the convolutions run parallel with his own brain" (76). How am I to catch that in my own writing? Not according to the conventions in which I have been trained – as Carol Shields realized of her training in her essay "Arriving Late, Starting Over," a discovery that offered her "permission" (251) to write the delightfully original stories in *Various Miracles*. I suspect I just can't think in straight lines. Would, I wonder, some sort of curve suffice?

I imagine myself standing on the beach near St. Joseph, Ontario – Alice Munro country – in the summertime. I imagine myself as a child of five with my parents, as a man of forty-five with my wife and two daughters, then perhaps alone as a man of eighty-five, looking down the shoreline of Lake Huron, following the trajectory of the sandy beach and the clay cliffs as they curve gradually past Grand Bend seven or eight miles away. I remember a discussion by Ray Smith in his essay "Dinosaur" of how he came to write his story "Peril": "I began with a cluster of images, moods, words, people that took the shape of a line starting out in front of my eyes ... but curving gracefully ... and disappearing in the hazy distance. A very relaxing vision. Obviously the curve took shape as the beach in Part 3, but I hadn't thought of the beach when I began to write" (83).

The curve I am imagining extends gradually, gracefully, as if along a dotted line, around Lake Huron, containing it like some mighty reservoir. The curve follows the entire shore and comes around behind me, down from Goderich to Bayfield to where I stand at St. Joseph – a favoured retreat, in his youth, of Brother André, my parents told me. And I remember the opening lines of Alice Munro's "Walker Brothers Cowboy": "After supper my father says, 'Want to go down and see if the Lake's still there?' We leave my mother sewing under the dining-room light, making clothes for me against the opening of school" (1). I remember the phrase "the real material" that Munro once used in conversation with me (23). I remember Jack Hodgins' statement that "I think of my writer's reservoir – all memory and imagination and hoarded experience – as a kind of private aquarium whose thick waters teem with a wondrous population of unusual creatures, all constantly in motion" (30). I remember Northrop Frye's remarks that "Every creative person has an interconnected body of images and ideas underneath his [or her] consciousness which it is his [or her] creative work to fish up in bits and pieces. Sometimes a phrase or a word comes to him [or her] as a kind of hook or bait with which to catch something that he [or she] knows is down there" (11).

Then I think of lines from Eli Mandel's "Houdini": "I suspect he knew that trunks are metaphors, / could distinguish between the finest rhythms / unrolled on rope or singing in a chain / and knew the metrics of the deepest pools" (45). I think of lines from Anne Michaels' "Miner's Pond": "Memory is cumulative selection. / It's an undersea cable connecting one continent / to another, / electric in the black brine of distance" (9). I think of lines from Raymond Knister's "Lake Harvest": "In the sun, / The men are sawing the frosted crystal. / ... / And diamonds and pieces of a hundred rainbows are strown around" (7). I think of Chris Banks's "The Drowning of Raymond K.," of F.R. Scott's "Lakeshore," of Al Purdy in "The Freezing Music": "kneeling uncomfortably / on this rocky shoreline near Ameliasburg / ... / intently observing metamorphosis" (319). I think of Daphne Marlatt, in "Litter, wreckage, salvage," observing: "she keeps her walls intact, her tidal pool the small things of her concern still swim alive alive – oh" (15). And I think of how A.M. Klein effaced himself, how he placed himself, in the final lines of "Portrait of the Poet as Landscape": "and lives alone, and in his secret shines / like phosphorus. At the bottom of the sea" (56). And I wonder how much is down there, in that imaginative reservoir of mine, and how best I can retrieve it.

After discovering certain memorable passages by nineteenth-century writer Isabella Valancy Crawford, James Reaney tells us in his introduction to a reissue of Crawford's *Collected Poems* that he found himself contemplating "the beginning of a long poem (*not* lyrical) she should have, could have written, but never quite did" (xx). He suggests that "Readers who get to like her voice will probably construct this hidden sub-poem best by themselves" (xx). Then after quoting the lines beginning "From his far wigwam sprang the strong North Wind" from Crawford's "Malcolm's

J.R. (TIM) STRUTHERS

Katie" (214), Reaney states: "If you now ask why the book within the book, the sub-poem I have hitherto spoken of, never fully rose to the surface, my answer is that we never asked her to use her talents that way. Where was the audience? Where the critics?" (xxxiv). Now, however, "Whether they know it or not, Crawford has followers who are raising the beneath, the submerged architecture of icons and identities, to visible articulation" (xxxiv). And Reaney urges readers to summon up all the energy they can "to assist ... in the description above, so typical of Isabella Crawford's best work, of a wind at work" (xxxiv).

I am amazed to find this introduction. I am amazed by all it imagines.

I think of Nourbese Philip's poem "She Tries Her Tongue; Her Silence Softly Breaks." I think of the power in her line "i came upon a future biblical with anticipation" (84).

One line only will be enough.

Breathlessly, I decide to begin again.

Acknowledgements

I'd like to thank Doug Daymond, William Butt, Michael Carbert, Marianne Micros, and many others for their encouragement and inspiration at various points in the writing of this essay. I'd also like to give special thanks to Ajay Heble and Donna Palmateer Pennee for their insight and co-operation.

Works Consulted

Ayre, John. *Northrop Frye: A Biography*. Toronto: Random House of Canada, 1989.

Banks, Chris. "The Drowning of Raymond K." *Carousel* [U of Guelph] 9 (1993): 74.

Baum, Gregory. "The Voice in the Crowd." *A World in a Grain of Sand: Twenty-Two Interviews with Northrop Frye*. Ed. Robert D. Denham. New York: Peter Lang, 1991. 23-40.

Berger, John. "The Storyteller." *The Sense of Sight: Writings by John Berger*. Ed. Lloyd Spencer. New York: Pantheon, 1985. 13-18.

Blaise, Clark. "To Begin, To Begin." *How Stories Mean*. Ed. John Metcalf and J.R. (Tim) Struthers. Critical Directions 3. Erin, ON: Porcupine's Quill, 1993. 158-62.

Blake, William. *Blake's Job: William Blake's Illustrations to the Book of Job*. Ed. S. Foster Damon. Providence, RI: Brown UP, 1966.

—. "The Mental Traveller." *The Complete Poetry and Prose of William Blake*. Ed. David V. Erdman. Commentary by Harold Bloom. Newly rev. ed. Garden City, NY: Anchor/Doubleday, 1982. 483-86.

Bloom, Harold. "Coda: The Criticism of Our Climate, A Self-Review." *Poetics of Influence: New and Selected Criticism*. Ed. John Hollander. New Haven, CT: Henry R. Schwab, 1988. 425-30.

—. "*The Covering Cherub* or Poetic Influence." *Poetics of Influence: New and Selected Criticism*. Ed. John Hollander. New Haven, CT: Henry R. Schwab, 1988. 77-99.

—. "Criticism, Canon-Formation, and Prophecy: The Sorrows of Facticity." *Poetics of Influence: New and Selected Criticism*. Ed. John Hollander. New Haven, CT: Henry R. Schwab, 1988. 405-24.

Borges, Jorge Luis. "The Argentine Writer and Tradition." *Labyrinths: Selected Stories & Other Writings*. Ed. Donald A. Yates and James E. Irby. Pref. André Maurois. New York: New Directions, 1964. 177-85.

Bowering, George. *Craft Slices*. Ottawa: Oberon, 1985.

Butt, William. "Canada's Mental Travellers Abroad." *World Literature Written in English* 28 (1988): 287-307.

—. "Contexts of *Fuseli Poems*." *The Politics of Art: Eli Mandel's Poetry and Criticism*. Ed. Ed Jewinski and Andrew Stubbs. Cross/Cultures: Readings in the Post/Colonial Literatures in English 8. Amsterdam, Neth.: Rodopi, 1992. 71-81, 151-56.

—. "Jack Hodgins and the Resurrection of the World." *On Coasts of Eternity: Jack Hodgins' Fictional Universe*. Ed. J.R. (Tim) Struthers. Lantzville, BC: Oolichan, 1996. 49-65.

—. "Robert Gourlay's Millennial Vision: A Reader's Guide." *Journal of Canadian Studies* 24.1 (1989): 66-80.

Coleridge, Samuel Taylor. *Biographia Literaria*. Ed. J. Shawcross. 2 vols. London: Oxford UP, 1907.

Cooper, Elizabeth. "sonnet ii." *Carousel* [U of Guelph] 4 (1987-88): 82.

Crawford, Isabella Valancy. "Malcolm's Katie: A Love Story." *The Collected Poems of Isabella Valancy Crawford*. Ed. J.W. Garvin. Toronto: William Briggs, 1905. Introd. James Reaney. Literature of Canada: Poetry and Prose in Reprint. Toronto: U of Toronto P, 1972. 193-236. Rpt. (revised) as *Malcolm's Katie: A Love Story*. Ed. D.M.R. Bentley. London, ON: Canadian Poetry, 1987.

Curnoe, Greg. *Deeds / Abstracts: The History of a London Lot*. Ed. Frank Davey. London, ON: Brick, 1995.

—. *Deeds / Nations*. Ed. Frank Davey and Neal Ferris. Occasional Publications of the London Chapter, Ontario Archaeological Society 4. London, ON: London Chapter, Ontario Archaeological Society, 1996.

Daymond, Douglas M., and Leslie G. Monkman, eds. *Literature in Canada*. 2 vols. Toronto: Gage, 1978.

—, eds. *Towards a Canadian Literature: Essays, Editorials & Manifestos*. 2 vols. Ottawa: Tecumseh, 1984-85.

Denham, Robert D. *Northrop Frye: An Annotated Bibliography of Primary and Secondary Sources*. Toronto: U of Toronto P, 1987.

Dewdney, Christopher. "Bibliography of Creatures." *Spring Trances in the Control Emerald Night: Book One of A Natural History of Southwestern Ontario*. Berkeley, CA: The Figures, 1978. [42-45]. Rpt. in *Spring Trances in the Control Emerald Night & The Cenozoic Asylum: A Natural History of Southwestern Ontario Books I*

& II. Berkeley, CA: The Figures, 1982. [42-45]. Rpt. (revised) in *Predators of the Adoration: Selected Poems 1972-82.* Toronto: McClelland & Stewart, 1983. 71-72.

—. "Grid Erectile." *Spring Trances in the Control Emerald Night & The Cenozoic Asylum: A Natural History of Southwestern Ontario Books I & II.* Berkeley, CA: The Figures, 1982. 51-54. Rpt. (revised) in *The Cenozoic Asylum: A Natural History of Southwestern Ontario Book II.* Liverpool, Eng.: Délires, 1983. 1-3. Rpt. in *Predators of the Adoration: Selected Poems 1972-82.* Toronto: McClelland & Stewart, 1983. 128-31.

Dragland, Stan. "Afterword: Reaney's Relevance." *James Reaney Issue.* Guest ed. Stan Dragland. *Essays on Canadian Writing* 24-25 (1982-83): 211-35. Rpt. in *Approaches to the Work of James Reaney.* Ed. Stan Dragland. Downsview, ON: ECW, 1983. 211-35. Rpt. (revised) in *The Bees of the Invisible: Essays in Contemporary English Canadian Writing.* By Stan Dragland. Toronto: Coach House, 1991. 47-65.

Duffy, Dennis. "'More dear, both for themselves and for thy sake!': Hugh Hood's *The New Age.*" *The Montreal Story Tellers: Memoirs, Photographs, Critical Essays.* Ed. J.R. (Tim) Struthers. Montreal: Véhicule, 1985. 169-75.

—. "Present at the Creation: John Richardson and Souwesto." *Journal of Canadian Studies* 28.3 (1993): 75-91.

Duncan, Sara Jeannette. "From *Saunterings.*" *Literature in Canada.* Ed. Douglas Daymond and Leslie Monkman. 2 vols. Toronto: Gage, 1978. 1: 350-55.

—. *The Imperialist.* 1904. Ed. Thomas E. Tausky. Ottawa: Tecumseh, 1988.

—. *Selected Journalism.* Ed. Thomas E. Tausky. Ottawa: Tecumseh, 1978.

Elliott, George. *The bittersweet man.* Guelph, ON: Red Kite, 1994.

—. *Crazy Water Boys.* Guelph, ON: Red Kite, 1995.

—. *God's Big Acre: Life in 401 Country.* Photography by John Reeves. Toronto: Methuen, 1986.

—. *The Kissing Man.* Toronto: Macmillan of Canada, 1962.

Fee, Margery. "An Interview with Eli Mandel." *Essays on Canadian Writing* 1 (1974): 2-13.

—. "Retrieving the Canadian Critical Tradition as Poetry: Eli Mandel and Northrop Frye." *Eli Mandel Issue.* Guest ed. Julie Beddoes. *Essays on Canadian Writing* 45-46 (1991-92): 235-53.

Fraser, Keath. *Foreign Affairs.* Toronto: Stoddart, 1985.

—. "Notes toward a Supreme Fiction." *Canadian Literature* 100 (1984): 109-17. Rpt. in *How Stories Mean.* Ed. John Metcalf and J.R. (Tim) Struthers. Critical Directions 3. Erin, ON: Porcupine's Quill, 1993. 220-29.

—. *Popular Anatomy.* Erin, ON: Porcupine's Quill, 1995.

—. *Taking Cover.* Ottawa: Oberon, 1982.

—. *Telling My Love Lies.* Erin, ON: Porcupine's Quill, 1996.

Frye, Northrop. *Anatomy of Criticism: Four Essays.* Princeton, NJ: Princeton UP, 1957.

—. "Blake's Biblical Illustrations." *The Eternal Act of Creation: Essays, 1979-1990.* Ed.

Robert D. Denham. Bloomington: Indiana UP, 1993. 62-78.

—. "Blake's Reading of the Book of Job." *Spiritus Mundi: Essays on Literature, Myth, and Society.* Bloomington: Indiana UP, 1976. 228-44.

—. "Criticism as Education." *On Education.* Markham, ON: Fitzhenry & Whiteside, 1988. 138-52.

—. "Criticism, Visible and Invisible." *The Stubborn Structure: Essays on Criticism and Society.* London: Methuen, 1970. 74-89.

—. *Fearful Symmetry: A Study of William Blake.* 1947. Pref. Northrop Frye. Princeton, NJ: Princeton UP, 1969.

—. "Haunted by Lack of Ghosts: Some Patterns in the Imagery of Canadian Poetry." *The Canadian Imagination: Dimensions of a Literary Culture.* Ed. David Staines. Cambridge, MA: Harvard UP, 1977. 22-45. Rpt. in *Reflections on the Canadian Literary Imagination.* By Northrop Frye. Ed. Branko Gorjup. Afterword by Agostino Lombardo. Studi e Recherche 39. Rome: Bulzoni Editore, 1991. 117-37.

—. "Literature as Context: Milton's *Lycidas.*" *Fables of Identity: Studies in Poetic Mythology.* New York: Harcourt, Brace & World, 1963. 119-29.

—. Preface. *The Bush Garden: Essays on the Canadian Imagination.* Toronto: House of Anansi, 1971. i-x. Rpt. as "Author's Preface." *The Bush Garden: Essays on the Canadian Imagination.* Introd. Linda Hutcheon. Concord, ON: House of Anansi, 1995. xxi-xxx.

—. "Preface to an Uncollected Anthology." *Contexts of Canadian Criticism.* Ed. Eli Mandel. Patterns of Literary Criticism 9. Chicago: U of Chicago P; Toronto: U of Toronto P, 1971. 181-97. Rpt. in *The Bush Garden: Essays on the Canadian Imagination.* By Northrop Frye. 1971. Introd. Linda Hutcheon. Concord, ON: House of Anansi, 1995. 165-82.

—. "The Search for Acceptable Words." *Spiritus Mundi: Essays on Literature, Myth, and Society.* Bloomington: Indiana UP, 1976. 3-26.

Glover, Douglas. *A Guide to Animal Behaviour.* Fredericton, NB: Goose Lane, 1991.

—. *The Life and Times of Captain N.* Toronto: McClelland & Stewart, 1993.

Hodgins, Jack. *The Invention of the World.* 1977. Afterword by George McWhirter. The New Canadian Library. Toronto: McClelland & Stewart, 1994.

—. *A Passion for Narrative: A Guide for Writing Fiction.* Toronto: McClelland & Stewart, 1993.

Hood, Hugh. "Afterword: What Is Going On." *Trusting the Tale.* Downsview, ON: ECW, 1983. 131-40.

—. "Fallings from Us, Vanishings." *Flying a Red Kite.* 1962. *The Collected Stories: I.* Introd. Hugh Hood. Erin, ON: Porcupine's Quill, 1987. 27-41.

—. "Flying a Red Kite." *Flying a Red Kite.* 1962. *The Collected Stories: I.* Introd. Hugh Hood. Erin, ON: Porcupine's Quill, 1987. 185-96.

—. "The Governor's Bridge Is Closed." *The Governor's Bridge Is Closed: Twelve Essays on the Canadian Scene.* Ottawa: Oberon, 1973. 8-20.

—. "The Intuition of Being: Morley, Marshall and Me." *Unsupported Assertions.*

Concord, ON: House of Anansi, 1991. 112-21.

—. *The Swing in the Garden.* 1975. New Press Canadian Classics. Toronto: General, 1984.

—. "Where the Myth Touches Us." *Flying a Red Kite.* 1962. *The Collected Stories: I.* Introd. Hugh Hood. Erin, ON: Porcupine's Quill, 1987. 197-221.

Jones, D.G. *Butterfly on Rock: A Study of Themes and Images in Canadian Literature.* Toronto: U of Toronto P, 1970.

Kamboureli, Smaro. "The Critic as Poet: Eli Mandel's *The Family Romance.*" *The Politics of Art: Eli Mandel's Poetry and Criticism.* Ed. Ed Jewinski and Andrew Stubbs. Cross/Cultures: Readings in the Post/Colonial Literatures in English 8. Amsterdam, Neth.: Rodopi, 1992. 105-20, 151-56.

Kaplan, Justin. "'The Emphasis is on the Individual, the Handful of Shepherds, the Pairs of Lovers ...'." *Harvard Magazine* July-Aug. 1975: 52-56. Rpt. (revised) in *On Education.* By Northrop Frye. Markham, ON: Fitzhenry & Whiteside, 1988. 206-11.

Klein, A. M. "Portrait of the Poet as Landscape." *The Rocking Chair and Other Poems.* Toronto: Ryerson, 1948. 50-56. Rpt. (revised) in *The Collected Poems of A.M. Klein.* Ed. Miriam Waddington. Toronto: McGraw-Hill Ryerson, 1974. 330-35. Rpt. (revised) in *Complete Poems: Part 2.* Ed. Zailig Pollock. Collected Works of A.M. Klein. Toronto: U of Toronto P, 1990. 634-39.

Klinck, Carl F. *Giving Canada a Literary History: A Memoir.* Ed. Sandra Djwa. Ottawa: Carleton UP, 1991.

—, gen. ed. *Literary History of Canada: Canadian Literature in English.* Toronto: U of Toronto P, 1965.

—, gen. ed. *Literary History of Canada: Canadian Literature in English.* 2nd ed. 3 vols. Toronto: U of Toronto P, 1976.

Knister, Raymond. *The First Day of Spring: Stories and Other Prose.* Ed. Peter Stevens. Literature of Canada: Poetry and Prose in Reprint. Toronto: U of Toronto P, 1976.

—. "Lake Harvest." *Collected Poems of Raymond Knister.* Ed. Dorothy Livesay. Toronto: Ryerson, 1949. 7. Rpt. (revised) in *Windfalls for Cider ... The Poems of Raymond Knister.* Ed. Joy Kuropatwa. Pref. James Reaney. Afterword by Imogen Knister Givens. Windsor, ON: Black Moss, 1983. 17.

—. *White Narcissus.* 1929. Introd. Philip Child. New Canadian Library 32. Toronto: McClelland & Stewart, 1962. Afterword by Morley Callaghan. The New Canadian Library. Toronto: McClelland & Stewart, 1990.

Kroetsch, Robert. Acknowledgements. *The Lovely Treachery of Words: Essays Selected and New.* Toronto: Oxford UP, 1989. ix-x.

—. "Learning the Hero from Northrop Frye." *The Lovely Treachery of Words: Essays Selected and New.* Toronto: Oxford UP, 1989. 151-62.

—. *A Likely Story: The Writing Life.* Red Deer, AB: Red Deer College, 1995.

—. "The Moment of the Discovery of America Continues." *The Lovely Treachery of Words: Essays Selected and New.* Toronto: Oxford UP, 1989. 1-20.

Layton, Irving. "The Cold Green Element." *The Improved Binoculars*. 1956. Sherbrooke Street. Pref. William Carlos Williams. Afterword by Michael Gnarowski. Erin, ON: Porcupine's Quill, 1991. 110-11.

—. "In the Midst of My Fever." *The Improved Binoculars*. 1956. Sherbrooke Street. Pref. William Carlos Williams. Afterword by Michael Gnarowski. Erin, ON: Porcupine's Quill, 1991. 118-19.

Lee, Monika. "Shelley's *A Defence of Poetry* and Frye: A Theory of Synchronicity." *The Legacy of Northrop Frye*. Ed. Alvin A. Lee and Robert D. Denham. Toronto: U of Toronto P, 1994. 190-200.

MacEwen, Gwendolyn. "The Discovery." *The Shadow-Maker*. Toronto: Macmillan of Canada, 1969. 30. Rpt. in *The Poetry of Gwendolyn MacEwen: Volume One: The Early Years*. Ed. Margaret Atwood and Barry Callaghan. Introd. Margaret Atwood. Toronto: Exile Editions, 1993. 153.

Mandel, Eli. "Banff: The Magic Mountain." *Another Time*. Erin, ON: Porcépic, 1977. 151-60.

—. *Criticism: The Silent-Speaking Words*. Toronto: Canadian Broadcasting Corporation, 1966.

—. "Houdini." *An Idiot Joy*. Edmonton, AB: M.G. Hurtig, 1967. 31. Rpt. in *Crusoe: Poems Selected and New*. Toronto: House of Anansi, 1973. 70. Rpt. in *Dreaming Backwards: The Selected Poetry of Eli Mandel 1954-1981*. Pref. Robert Kroetsch. Don Mills, ON: General, 1981. 45.

—. Introduction. *Contexts of Canadian Criticism*. Ed. Eli Mandel. Patterns of Literary Criticism 9. Chicago: U of Chicago P; Toronto: U of Toronto P, 1971. 3-25.

—. Introduction. *A Passion for Identity: An Introduction to Canadian Studies*. Ed. Eli Mandel and David Taras. Toronto: Methuen, 1987. 218-21.

—. "The Limits of Dialogue." *A World in a Grain of Sand: Twenty-Two Interviews with Northrop Frye*. Ed. Robert D. Denham. New York: Peter Lang, 1991. 5-22.

—. "Northrop Frye and the Canadian Literary Tradition." *Centre and Labyrinth: Essays in Honour of Northrop Frye*. Ed. Eleanor Cook, Chaviva Hošek, Jay Macpherson, Patricia Parker, and Julian Patrick. Toronto: U of Toronto P, 1983. 284-97.

—. "The Poet as Critic." *Another Time*. Erin, ON: Porcépic, 1977. 11-14.

—. Preface. *The Family Romance*. Winnipeg: Turnstone, 1986. ix-xii.

—. "Strange Loops." *The Family Romance*. Winnipeg: Turnstone, 1986. 11-27.

—. "Toward a Theory of Cultural Revolution: The Criticism of Northrop Frye." *Canadian Literature* 1 (1959): 58-67.

Marlatt, Daphne. "Litter, wreckage, salvage." *Salvage*. Red Deer, AB: Red Deer College, 1991. 15-23.

Metcalf, John. *Freedom from Culture: Selected Essays 1982-92*. Toronto: ECW, 1994.

—. *Kicking Against the Pricks*. Downsview, ON: ECW, 1982. 2nd ed. Guelph, ON: Red Kite, 1986.

—. *What Is A Canadian Literature?* Guelph, ON: Red Kite, 1988.

Michaels, Anne. "Miner's Pond." *Miner's Pond*. Toronto: McClelland & Stewart, 1991.

J.R. (TIM) STRUTHERS

3-9.

Micros, Marianne. "The Poem Becomes: A Journey for a Song." *A Sacred Mosaic: Spiritual Poetry in Canada*. Ed. Robert Sward and Penny Kemp. *CV/II* 6.1-2 (1982): 14-19.

Moses, Daniel David. "Grandmother of the Glacier." *The White Line*. Saskatoon, SK: Fifth House, 1990. [64-65].

Munro, Alice. "Walker Brothers Cowboy." *Dance of the Happy Shades*. Toronto: Ryerson, 1968. 1-18. Rpt. in *Selected Stories*. Toronto: McClelland & Stewart, 1996. 3-15.

Newlove, John. "The Pride." *The Tamarack Review* 36 (1965): 37-44. Rpt. (revised) in *Black Night Window*. Toronto: McClelland & Stewart, 1968. 105-11. Rpt. (revised) in *The Fat Man: Selected Poems 1962-1972*. Toronto: McClelland & Stewart, 1977. 67-74. Rpt. in *Apology for Absence: Selected Poems 1962-1992*. Erin, ON: Porcupine's Quill, 1993. 86-93.

Nourbese Philip, Marlene. *Looking for Livingstone: An Odyssey of Silence*. Stratford, ON: Mercury, 1991.

—. "She Tries Her Tongue; Her Silence Softly Breaks." *She Tries Her Tongue, Her Silence Softly Breaks*. Charlottetown: Ragweed, 1989. 84-99.

—. "Who's Listening?: Artists, Audiences & Language." *Frontiers: Selected Essays and Writings on Racism and Culture 1984-1992*. Stratford, ON: Mercury, 1992. 26-46.

O'Brien, Kevin. *Oscar Wilde in Canada: An Apostle for the Arts*. Toronto: Personal Library, 1982.

Orange, John. "Ernest Buckler: Memory and Reflections." *New Directions from Old*. Ed. J.R. (Tim) Struthers. Canadian Storytellers 1. Guelph, ON: Red Kite, 1991. 44-55.

Page, P.K. "Kaleidoscope." *The Glass Air: Poems Selected and New*. Toronto: Oxford UP, 1991. 180-82.

Purdy, Al. "The Country North of Belleville." *The Cariboo Horses*. Toronto: McClelland & Stewart, 1965. 74-76. Rpt. (revised) in *The Collected Poems of Al Purdy*. Ed. Russell Brown. Toronto: McClelland & Stewart, 1986. 61-62.

—. "The Freezing Music." *The Second Macmillan Anthology*. Ed. John Metcalf and Leon Rooke. Toronto: Macmillan of Canada, 1989. 319. Rpt. (revised) as "The Woman on the Shore." *The Woman on the Shore*. By Al Purdy. Toronto: McClelland & Stewart, 1990. 81-82. Rpt. (revised) as "The Freezing Music." *Naked with Summer in Your Mouth*. By Al Purdy. Toronto: McClelland & Stewart, 1994. 43-44.

—. "Roblin Mills." *Wild Grape Wine*. Toronto: McClelland & Stewart, 1968. 46-47. Rpt. (revised) as "Roblin's Mills [II]" in *The Collected Poems of Al Purdy*. Ed. Russell Brown. Toronto: McClelland & Stewart, 1986. 132-33. Rpt. (revised) as "Roblin's Mills (2)" in *Rooms for Rent in the Outer Planets: Selected Poems 1962-1996*. Ed. Al Purdy and Sam Solecki. Madeira Park, BC: Harbour, 1996. 65-66.

Reaney, James. "An ABC to Ontario Literature and Culture." *Black Moss: A Semi-Annual of Ontario Literature and Culture* 2nd ser. 3 (1977): 2-6.

—, ed. *Alphabet: A Semiannual Devoted to the Iconography of the Imagination* 1–18/19 (1960–71).

—. *The Box Social and Other Stories.* Erin, ON: Porcupine's Quill, 1996.

—. *The Dance of Death at London, Ontario.* Drawings by Jack Chambers. London, ON: Alphabet, 1963. Rpt. in *Poems.* Ed. Germaine Warkentin. Toronto: New, 1972. 231–50. Rpt. in *Selected Longer Poems.* Ed. Germaine Warkentin. Erin, ON: Porcépic, 1976. 59–76.

—. *The Donnellys.* Afterword by James Noonan. Victoria: Porcépic, 1983.

—. Introduction. *Collected Poems.* By Isabella Valancy Crawford. 1905. Literature of Canada: Poetry and Prose in Reprint. Toronto: U of Toronto P, 1972. vii–xxxiv.

—. "Some Critics Are Music Teachers." *Centre and Labyrinth: Essays in Honour of Northrop Frye.* Ed. Eleanor Cook, Chaviva Hošek, Jay Macpherson, Patricia Parker, and Julian Patrick. Toronto: U of Toronto P, 1983. 298–308.

—. "Souwesto." *Performance Poems.* Goderich, ON: Moonstone, 1990. 36–37.

Schafer, R. Murray. "A Statement on Music Education." *The Thinking Ear: Complete Writings on Music Education.* Toronto: Arcana Editions, 1986. 243–50.

Schell, Winston G. "James Reaney." *Parts of People in These Parts.* London, ON: Schellter, 1985. [42–57].

Scott, F.R. "Lakeshore." *Events and Signals.* Toronto: Ryerson, 1954. 2–3. Rpt. (revised) in *Selected Poems.* Toronto: Oxford UP, 1966. 12–13. Rpt. in *The Collected Poems of F.R. Scott.* Toronto: McClelland & Stewart, 1981. 50–51.

Shepherd, Tracy. "Permission." *Room of One's Own* 18.3 (1995): 21.

Shepherd, Tracy, and J.R. (Tim) Struthers. "The Home Place: An Investigation into the Archival and Imaginative Potential of Scotland, Ontario." Outline for 37-6691 Interdisciplinary Studies Reading Course, M.A. Programme, Department of English, U of Guelph, 1995.

Shields, Carol. "Arriving Late: Starting Over." *How Stories Mean.* Ed. John Metcalf and J.R. (Tim) Struthers. Critical Directions 3. Erin, ON: Porcupine's Quill, 1993. 244–51.

—. *Various Miracles.* 1985. Toronto: Vintage / Random House of Canada, 1995.

Smith, Ray. "Dinosaur." *How Stories Mean.* Ed. John Metcalf and J.R. (Tim) Struthers. Critical Directions 3. Erin, ON: Porcupine's Quill, 1993. 76–83.

—. "Peril." *Cape Breton Is the Thought-Control Centre of Canada.* 1969. Introd. Ray Smith. Illus. Ken Tolmie. Sherbrooke Street. Erin, ON: Porcupine's Quill, 1989. 87–95, 97–104.

—. "A Refusal To Mourn the Death, by Bullshit, of Literature in the Eighties." *Carry On Bumping.* Ed. John Metcalf. Toronto: ECW, 1988.

Solecki, Sam, John Metcalf, and W.J. Keith. *Volleys.* Critical Directions 1. Erin, ON: Porcupine's Quill, 1990.

Stelter, Gilbert A. "John Galt: The Writer as Town Booster and Builder." *John Galt: Reappraisals.* Ed. Elizabeth Waterston. Guelph, ON: U of Guelph, 1985. 17–43.

Stevens, Wallace. "Imagination as Value." *The Necessary Angel: Essays on Reality and the Imagination.* New York: Alfred A. Knopf, 1951. 131–56.

—. "Notes toward a Supreme Fiction." *The Collected Poems of Wallace Stevens*. New York: Alfred A. Knopf, 1967. 380-408.

—. "Of Modern Poetry." *The Collected Poems of Wallace Stevens*. New York: Alfred A. Knopf, 1967. 239-40.

Struthers, J.R. (Tim). "Confluences: An Interview with John Metcalf." *Carousel* [U of Guelph] 8 (1992): 35-52.

—. "An Interview with Hugh Hood." *Hugh Hood's Work in Progress*. Guest ed. J.R. (Tim) Struthers. *Essays on Canadian Writing* 13-14 (1978-79): 21-93. Rpt. in *Before the Flood: Our Exagmination round His Factification for Incamination of Hugh Hood's Work in Progress*. Downsview, ON: ECW, 1979. 21-93.

—. "The Real Material: An Interview with Alice Munro." *Probable Fictions: Alice Munro's Narrative Acts*. Ed. Louis K. MacKendrick. Downsview, ON: ECW, 1983. 5-36.

Stubbs, Andrew. *Myth, Origins, Magic: A Study of Form in Eli Mandel's Writing*. Winnipeg: Turnstone, 1993.

Wallace, Bronwen. "Into the Midst of It." *Common Magic*. Ottawa: Oberon, 1985. 20-22. Rpt. in "Lilacs in May: A Tribute to Al Purdy." *Arguments with the World: Essays by Bronwen Wallace*. Ed. Joanne Page. Kingston, ON: Quarry, 1992. 166-69.

—. "Lilacs in May: A Tribute to Al Purdy." *Arguments with the World: Essays by Bronwen Wallace*. Ed. Joanne Page. Kingston, ON: Quarry, 1992. 162-69. Rpt. in *Al Purdy Issue*. Guest ed. Louis K. MacKendrick. *Essays on Canadian Writing* 49 (1993): 86-92.

—. "One More Woman Talking." *Two Women Talking: Correspondence 1985-87*. By Erin Mouré and Bronwen Wallace. Ed. Susan McMaster. Living Archives. Toronto: The Feminist Caucus of the League of Canadian Poets, 1993. 74-80. Rpt. (revised) in *Sudden Miracles: Eight Women Poets*. Ed. Rhea Tregebov. Toronto: Second Story, 1991. 237-43.

—. "Why I Don't (Always) Write Short Stories." *Arguments with the World: Essays by Bronwen Wallace*. Ed. Joanne Page. Kingston, ON: Quarry, 1992. 169-79.

—. "Women's Lives: Alice Munro." *The Human Elements: Critical Essays*. Ed. David Helwig. Ottawa: Oberon, 1978. 52-67.

White, E.B. "Once More to the Lake." *Essays of E.B. White*. New York: Harper & Row, 1977. 197-202.

Wilde, Oscar. *Intentions*. 1891. *The Artist as Critic: Critical Writings of Oscar Wilde*. Ed. Richard Ellmann. 1969. Chicago: U of Chicago P, 1982. 290-432.

—. "Preface to *The Picture of Dorian Gray*." 1891. *The Artist as Critic: Critical Writings of Oscar Wilde*. Ed. Richard Ellmann. 1969. Chicago: U of Chicago P, 1982. 235-36.

Williams, William Carlos. *Paterson*. New York: New Directions, 1963.

Wilson, Milton. "Klein's Drowned Poet: Canadian Variations on an Old Theme." *Canadian Literature* 6 (1960): 5-17.

Is That All There Is? Tribal Literature

Basil H. Johnston

In the early '60s Kahn-Tineta Horn, a young Mohawk model, got the attention of the Canadian press (media) not only by her beauty but by her articulation of Indian grievances and her demands for justice. Soon after Red Power was organized threatening to use force. Academics and scholars, anxious and curious to know what provoked the Indians, organized a series of conferences and teach-ins to explore the issues. Even children wanted to know. So for their enlightenment experts wrote dozens of books. Universities and colleges began Native Studies courses. Ministries of Education, advised by a battery of consultants, adjusted their Curriculum Guidelines to allow units of study on the Native Peoples of this continent. And school projects were conducted for the benefit of children between ten and thirteen years of age.

One such project at the Churchill Avenue Public School in North York, Ontario lasted six weeks and the staff and students who had taken part mounted a display as a grand finale to their studies. And a fine display it was in the school's library.

In front of a canvas tent that looked like a teepee stood a grim chief, face painted in war-like colours and arms folded. On his head he wore a headdress made of construction paper. A label pinned to his vest bore the name Blackfoot. I made straight for the chief.

"How!" I greeted the chief, holding up my hand at the same time as a gesture of friendship.

Instead of returning the greeting, the chief looked at me quizzically.

"How come you look so unhappy?" I asked him.

"Sir! I'm bored," the chief replied.

"How so, chief?"

"Sir, don't tell anybody, but I'm bored. I'm tired of Indians. That's all we've studied for six weeks. I thought they'd be interesting when we started, because I always thought that Indians were neat. At the start of the course we had to choose to do a special project from food preparation, transportation, dwellings, social organization, clothing, and hunting and fishing. I chose dwellings," and here the chief exhaled in exasperation, "and that's all me and my team studied for six weeks: teepees, wigwams, long-houses, igloos. We read books, encyclopedias, went to the library to do research, looked at pictures, drew pictures. Then we had to make one. Sir, I'm bored."

"Didn't you learn anything else about Indians, chief?"

"No sir, there was nothing else.... Sir? ... Is that all there is to Indians?"

Little has changed since that evening in 1973. Books still present Native Peoples in terms of their physical existence as if Indians were incapable of meditating upon or grasping the abstract. Courses of study in the public school system, without other sources of information, had to adhere to the format, pattern, and content set down in books. Students studied Kawlijas, wooden Indians, who were incapable of love or laughter; or Tontos, if you will, whose sole skill was to make fires and to perform other servile duties for the Lone Ranger; an inarticulate Tonto, his speech limited to "Ugh!," "Kimo Sabi," and "How."

Despite all the research and the field work conducted by anthropologists, ethnologists, and linguists, Indians remain "The Unknown People" as Professor George E. Tait of the University of Toronto so aptly titled his book written in 1973.

Not even Indian Affairs of Canada, with its more than two centuries of experience with Natives, with its array of experts and consultants, with its unlimited funds, seems to have learned anything about its constituents, if we are to assess their latest publication titled *The Canadian Indian*. One would think that the Honourable William McKnight, then Minister of Indian Affairs and Northern Development, under whose authority the book was published in 1986, should know by now the Indians who often come to Ottawa do not arrive on horseback, do not slay one of the RCMP mounts and cook it on the steps of the Parliament Buildings. Moreover, most Indians he has seen and met were not dressed in loincloths, nor did they sleep in teepees. Yet he authorized the publication of a book bereft of any originality or imagination, a book that perpetuated the notion and the image that the Indians had not advanced one step since contact, but are still living as they had one hundred and fifty, even three hundred, years ago. There was not a word about Native thought, literature, institutions, contributions in music, art, theatre. But that's to be expected of Indian Affairs: to know next to nothing of their constituents.

Where did the author or authors of this latest publication by Indian Affairs get their information? The selected readings listed at the back of the book provide a clue: Frances Densmore, Harold Driver, Philip Drucker, Frederick W. Hodge, Diamond Jenness, Reginald and Gladys Laubin, Frank G. Speck, Bruce G. Trigger, George Woodcock, Harold A. Innis, Calvin Martin, E. Palmer Patterson, eminent scholars, none of whom spoke or attempted to learn the language of any of the Indian nations about whom they were writing. Modern scholars, because they are not required by their universities to learn, are no more proficient in a Native language than were their predecessors.

Herein, I submit, is the nub and the rub. Without the benefit of knowing the language of the Indian nation that they are investigating, scholars can never get into their mind, the heart and soul and the spirit, and understand the Native's perceptions and interpretations. The scholar must confine his research and studies to the material, physical culture, subsistence patterns, and family relationships.

Without knowing the spiritual and the intellectual, aesthetic side of Indian culture, the scholar cannot furnish what the little grade five youngster and others like him wanted to know about Indians.

Admitting his boredom was that grade five youngster's way of expressing his disappointment with the substance of the course that he and his colleagues had been made to endure. In another sense, it was a plea for other knowledge that would quench his curiosity and challenge his intellect.

Students such as he, as well as adults, are interested in the character, intellect, soul, spirit, heart of people of other races and cultures. They want to know what other people believe in, what they understand, what they expect and hope for in this life and in the next, how they keep law and order and harmony within the family and community, how and why they celebrated ceremonies, what made them proud, ashamed, what made them happy, what sad. Whether the young understand what they want to know and learn does not matter much; they still want to know in order to enrich their own insights and broaden their outlooks.

But unless scholars and writers know the literature of the peoples that they are studying or writing about they cannot provide what their students and readers are seeking and deserving of.

There is, fortunately, enough literature, both oral and written, available for scholarly study, but it has for the most part been neglected. Myths, legends, and songs have not been regenerated and set in modern terms to earn immortalization in poetry, dramatization in plays, or romanticization in novels.

What has prevented the acceptance of Indian literature as a serious and legitimate expression of Native thought and experience has been indifferent and inferior translation, a lack of understanding and interest in the culture, and a notion that it has little of importance to offer to the larger white culture.

In offering you a brief sketch, no more than a glimpse, as it were, of my tribe's culture, I am doing no more than what any one of you would do were you to be asked, "What is your culture? Would you explain it?" I would expect you to reply, "Read my literature, and you will get to know something of my thoughts, my convictions, my aspirations, my feelings, sentiments, expectations, whatever I cherish or abominate."

First, let me offer you an observation about my language for the sim-

BASIL H. JOHNSTON

ple reason that language and literature are inseparable, though they are too often taught as separate entities. They belong together.

In my tribal language, all words have three levels of meaning. There is the surface meaning that everyone instantly understands. Beneath this meaning is a more fundamental meaning derived from the prefixes and their combinations with other terms. Underlying both is the philosophical meaning.

Take the word "Anishinaubae." That is what the members of the nation, now known as Chippewa in the United States or Ojibway in Canada, called themselves. It referred to a member of the tribe. It was given to the question "What are you?" But it was more than just a term of identification. It meant "I am a person of good intent, a person of worth," and it reflected what the people thought of themselves, and of human nature: that all humans are essentially, fundamentally good. Let's separate that one word into its two terms. The first, "Onishishih," meaning good, fine, beautiful, excellent; and the second, "naubae," meaning being, male, human species. Even together they do not yield the meaning "good intention." It is only by examining the stories of Nanabush, the tribe's central and principal mythical figure who represents all men and all women, that the term "Anishinaubae" begins to make sense. Nanabush was always full of good intentions, ergo the people of the tribe. The Anishinaubaeg perceived themselves as people who intended good and therefore were of merit and worth. From this perception they drew a strong sense of pride as well as a firm sense of place in the community. This influenced their notion of independence.

Let's take another word, the word for "truth." When we say "w'daebawae," we mean he or she is telling the truth, is correct, is right. But the expression is not merely an affirmation of a speaker's veracity. It is as well a philosophical proposition that is saying a speaker casts his words and his voice as far as his perception and his vocabulary will enable him or her; it is a denial that there is such a thing as absolute truth; it is saying that the best and most the speaker can achieve and a listener expect is the highest degree of accuracy. Somehow that one expression, "w'daeb-awae," sets the limits to a single statement as well as setting limits to truth and the scope and exercise of speech.

One other word, "to know." We say "w'kikaendaun" to convey the idea that he or she "knows." Without going into the etymological derivations, suffice it to say that when the speaker assures someone that he knows it, that person is saying that the notion, image, idea, fact that that person has in mind corresponds and is similar to what he or she has already seen, heard, touched, tasted, or smelled. That person's knowledge may not be exact, but is similar to that which has been instilled and impressed in his or her mind and recalled from memory.

The stories that make up our tribal literature are no different from the words in our language. Both have many meanings and applications, as well as bearing tribal perceptions, values, and outlooks.

Let us begin at the beginning with the tribe's story of creation which precedes all other stories in the natural order. Creation stories provide insights into what races and nations understand of human nature; ours is no different in this respect.

This is our creation story. Kitchi-manitou beheld a vision. From this vision The Great Mystery, for that is the essential and fundamental meaning of Kitchi-manitou and not spirit as is often understood, created the sun and the stars, the land and the waters, and all the creatures and beings, seen and unseen, that inhabit the earth, the seas, and the skies. The creation was desolated by a flood. Only the manitous, creatures and beings who dwelt in the waters, were spared. All others perished.

In the heavens dwelt a manitou, Geezhigo-quae (Sky-woman). During the cataclysm upon the earth, Geezhigo-quae became pregnant. The creatures adrift upon the seas prevailed upon the giant turtle to offer his back as a haven for Geezhigo-quae. They then invited her to come down.

Resting on the giant turtle's back, Geezhigo-quae asked for soil.

One after another water creatures dove into the depths to retrieve a morsel of soil. Not one returned with a particle of soil. They all offered an excuse: too deep, too dark, too cold, there are evil manitous keeping watch. Last to descend was the muskrat. He returned with a small knot of earth.

With the particle of mud retrieved by the muskrat, Geezhigo-quae recreated an island and the world as we know it. On the island she created over the giant turtle's shell, Geezhigo-quae gave birth to twins who begot the tribe called the Anishinaubaeg.

Millenia later the tribe dreamed Nanabush into being. Nanabush represented themselves and what they understood of human nature. One day his world too was flooded. Like Geezhigo-quae, Nanabush recreated his world from a morsel of soil retrieved from the depths of the sea.

As a factual account of the origin of the world and of being, the story has no more basis than the biblical story of creation and the flood. But the story represents a belief in God, the creator, a Kitchi-manitou, The Great Mystery. It also represents a belief that Kitchi-manitou sought within himself, his own being, a vision. Or perhaps it came from within his being and that Kitchi-manitou created what was beheld and set it into motion. Even the lesser manitous, such as Geezhigo-quae and Nanabush, must seek a morsel of soil with which to create and recreate their world, their spheres. So men and women must seek within themselves the talent or the potential and afterwards create their own worlds and their own spheres and a purpose to give meaning to their lives.

BASIL H. JOHNSTON

The people begotten by Geezhigo-quae on that mythological island called themselves Anishinaubaeg, the good beings who meant well and were human beings, therefore were fundamentally good. But they also knew that men and women were often deflected from fulfilling their good intentions and prevented from living up to their dreams and visions, not out of any inherent evil, but rather from something outside of themselves. Nanabush also represented this aspect of human nature. Many times Nanabush or the Anishinaubaeg fail to carry out a noble purpose. Despite this, he is not rendered evil or wicked but remains fundamentally and essentially good.

Men and women intend what is good, but they forget. The story called "The Man, The Snake, and The Fox" exemplifies this aspect of human nature.

In its abbreviated form the story is as follows. The hunter leaves his lodge and his family at daybreak to go in search of game to feed his wife and his children. As he proceeds through the forest, the hunter sees deer, but each time they are out of range of his weapon.

Late in the afternoon, discouraged and weary, he hears faint cries in the distance. Forgetting his low spirits and fatigue, he sets out with renewed optimism and vigour in the direction of the cries. Yet the nearer he draws to the source of the cries, the more daunted is the hunter by the dreadful screams. Only the thought of his family's needs drove him forward; otherwise he might have turned away.

At last he came to a glade. The screams came from a thicket on the opposite side. The hunter, bow and arrow drawn and ready, made his way forward cautiously.

To his horror, the hunter saw an immense serpent tangled fast in a thicket as a fish is caught in the webbing of a net. The monster writhed and roared and twisted. He struggled to break free.

The man recoiled in horror. Before he could back away, the snake saw him.

"Friend!" the snake addressed the man.

The man fell in a heap on the ground the moment that the snake spoke. When he came to much later, the snake pleaded with the man to set him free. For some time the man refused but eventually he relented. He was persuaded by the monster's plea that he too, though a serpent, had no less right to life than did the man. And the serpent promised not to injure the man on his release. The hunter was convinced.

The snake sprang on his deliverer the moment the last vine was cut away.

It was like thunder as the man and the snake struggled. Nearby a little fox heard the uproar. Never having seen such a spectacle, the fox settled down to watch. Immediately he realized that the man was about to be killed.

Why were the snake and the man locked in mortal struggle? The little fox shouted for an explanation. The man and the snake stopped.

The hunter gasped out his story, then the snake gave his version. Pretending not to understand the snake's explanation, the fox beguiled the aggressor into returning to the thicket to act out his side of the story.

The snake entangled himself once more.

Realizing that he had been delivered from the edge of death by the fox, the man was greatly moved. He felt bound to show his gratitude in some tangible way. The fox assured him that no requital was required. Nevertheless the hunter persisted. How might he, the hunter, perform some favour on behalf of the fox?

Not only was there no need, the fox explained, there was nothing that the man could do for the fox; there was not a thing that the fox needed or desired of human beings. However, if it would make the man happier, the fox suggested that the man might feed him should he ever have need.

Nothing would please the man more than to perform some good for his deliverer; it was the least that he could do for a friend who had done so much.

Some years later the hunter shot a little fox who had been helping himself to the family storage. As the man drew his knife to finish off the thief, the little fox gasped, "Don't you remember?"

That no snakes as monstrous as the one in the story are to be found on this continent makes no difference to the youngsters' sense of outrage over the treachery of the snake and the forgetfulness of the man; nor does the exercise of speech which enables the snake and the fox to communicate with the hunter and each other prevent the young from being moved to compassion for the fox. Their sense of justice and fairness bears them over the anomalies in the story.

Before the last words "Don't you remember?" have echoed away, the young begin to ask questions. "Why? Why did the man not recognize the fox? Why did he forget? How did the man feel afterwards? Why did the snake attack the man? Why did the snake break his promise? Why didn't the man leave the snake where he was? Do animals really have as much right to live as human beings do?"

Indians cared, loved, as passionately as other people.

The story called "The Weeping Pine" raises the same questions about love and marriage and the span of either that have been asked by philosophers, poets, and lovers of every race and generation. It does not pretend to give answers to these age-old questions beyond suggesting that love may bloom even in circumstances where it is least expected to flower and endure. But owing to shoddy translation, the story has been presented as

BASIL H. JOHNSTON

an explanation for the origin of pine trees.

According to the story, the elders of a village came to a certain young woman's home where she lived with her parents, brothers, and sisters. They had come to let her family know that they had chosen her to be the new wife of an old man. This particular man had been without a friend since the death of his first wife some years before. The old man was described as good-natured and kind. As one who had done much to benefit the tribe in his youth, the old man deserved something in return from his neighbours. In the opinion of the elders the most fitting reward the old man could have was a wife. In their judgement the young woman they had chosen would be a suitable companion for the old man.

They assured her that the tribe would see to it that they never had need.

Because this sort of marriage was a matter that the young woman had not considered, it was unexpected. The delegation understood this. They did not demand an immediate answer but allowed the young woman a few days in which to make up her mind.

The young woman cried when the delegation left. She didn't want to marry that man. That old man whose days were all but over and who could never look after her. She had hoped, like every young girl her age, to marry someone young, full of promise, someone she would love and who would love her in return. Besides, it was too soon. How could she, not yet eighteen, be a companion to an old man of seventy or more? The disparity was too great.

At first her parents too were aggrieved. But soon after they prevailed upon her to defer to the wishes of the elders, and her father delivered word of their daughter's consent to the elders.

But neither the disparity in age nor the disposition of the young girl towards entering into a loveless marriage was too great; in the years that followed she came to love this old man. And they had many children.

Thirty years later the old man died.

On the final day of the four-day watch, the mourners went home but the widow made no move to rise. She continued to keen and rock back and forth in great sorrow.

"Come mother, let us go home," her children urged, offering to assist her to her feet and to support her on their way home.

"No! No! Leave me. Go," she said.

"Mother! Please. Come home with us," her children pleaded. Nothing they said could persuade their mother to leave.

"No. You go home. This is where I belong. Leave me."

Her children prayed she would relent; give in to the cold and hunger. They went home, but they did not leave their mother alone. During the next few days a son or daughter was always at her side, watching with her and entreating her to come home. They tried to comfort her with their own love and care, assuring her that her wound would pass and heal. They even brought her food and drink to sustain her. She refused everything.

As their mother grew weaker with each passing day, the children besought the elders to intercede on their behalf. Perhaps the elders could prevail on their mother.

But the elders shook their heads and said, "If that is what she wants, there is nothing that you can do to change her mind. Leave her be. She wants to be with him. Leave her. It's better that way."

And so the family ceased to press their mother to come home, though they still kept watch with her. They watched until she too died by the graveside of her husband, their father.

Using the term "grandchild" that all elders used in referring to the young, the elder who presided over the woman's wake said, "Our grand-daughter's love did not cease with death, but continues into the next life."

The next spring a small plant grew out of the grave of the woman. Many years later, as the sons, daughters, and grandchildren gathered at the graveside of their parents, they felt a mist fall upon their faces and their arms. "It is mother shedding tears of love for dad," cried her daughter.

And it is so. On certain days, spruces and pines shed a mist of tears of love.

By remaining at her husband's graveside until she too died, the woman fulfilled the implied promise "whither thou goest, there too will I go" contained in the term "weedjeewaugun," companion in life, our word for "spouse."

As she wept for her love, she must have wept for the love of her children. Their love threatened to break that bond that held her to her husband. No! She would not let even death part her from the man to whom she had given her heart, her soul, her spirit forever.

It is unlikely that the woman ever uttered more than "K'zaugin" (I love you) during her marriage. In this respect she was no different from most other women, or men for that matter, who are not endowed with the poetic gift, though they feel and love with equal passion and depth. "K'zaugin" said everything. I love you, today, tomorrow, forever. It expressed everything that the finest poets ever wrote and everything that the unpoetic ever thought and felt but could not put into rhyme or rhythm.

In sentiment the story compares to Elizabeth Barrett Browning's immortal poem "How do I love thee?" which ends with the words "and, if God choose, I shall but love thee better after death."

Disunity as Unity: A Canadian Strategy

Robert Kroetsch

The organizers of this conference,[1] by a narrative strategy that fills me with admiration, juxtapose the completion of the CPR tracks across Canada with the hanging of Louis Riel, in 1885. Two narratives, here, come into violent discord. In 1885 the completion of the railway seemed the dominant narrative, an expression of, as the journalists would have it, the national dream. The story of the Métis leader, Louis Riel, with his rebellion or uprising or resistance – the troubles in the northwest – seemed at best a sub-plot. In the Canadian imagination one hundred years later, the story of the railway has turned into a nasty economic scrap in the name of something called The Crow Rates, while the Riel story has become the stuff of our imaginative life, with fifty-some plays, for example, making use of Louis Riel's uncertain career.

My concern here is with narrative itself. The shared story – what I prefer to call the assumed story – has traditionally been basic to nationhood. As a writer I'm interested in these assumed stories – what I call metanarratives. It may be that the writing of particular narratives, within a culture, is dependent on these metanarratives.

An obvious example is the persistence of The American Dream, with its assumptions about individual freedom, the importance of the frontier, the immigrant experience, as it functions in the literature of the United States. Even the cowboy story and the American version of the detective story are dependent on that metanarrative.

To make a long story disunited, let me assert here that I'm suggesting that Canadians cannot agree on what their metanarrative is. I am also suggesting that, in some perverse way, this very falling-apart of our story is what holds our story together.

In the 1970s the Conseil des Universités of the Government of Quebec invited the French critic Jean-François Lyotard to write a report on the state of universities in the western world. Lyotard's reflections were published in English in 1984 under the title *The Postmodern Condition: A Report on Knowledge*. In that report Lyotard writes: "Simplifying to the extreme, I define *postmodern* as incredulity toward metanarratives. ... To the obsolescence of the metanarrative apparatus of legitimation corresponds, most notably, the crisis of metaphysical philosophy and of the university institution which in the past relied on it. The narrative function is losing its functors, its great hero, its great dangers, its great voyages, its great goal. It is being dispersed in clouds of narrative language elements...."[2]

I am suggesting that by Lyotard's definition, Canada is a postmodern country.

The high modern period is a period that ended at some time during or shortly after the Second World War. T.S. Eliot, living in London in the 1940s, was writing his great modernist text *Four Quartets* at the same time that William Carlos Williams, in New Jersey, was writing his great postmodernist text *Paterson*. In Eliot I hear still a longing for the unity of story or narrative. In Williams I hear an acceptance of, even a celebration of, multiplicity. The stories that gave centre and circumference to the modern world were losing their centripetal power. As Yeats observed, the centre does not hold.

It was this very decentring that gave a new energy to countries like Canada. Canada is supremely a country of margins, beginning from the literal way in which almost every city borders on a wilderness. The centredness of the high modern period – the first half of the twentieth century – made us almost irrelevant to history. I remember the shock, after the Second World War, of reading a popular history of that war and finding Canada mentioned only once – and that in connection with the Dieppe raid. Yet as a high-school student during the war years I, with my community, was obsessively concerned with the war. In a high modern world, with its privileged stories, Canada was invisible.

Lyotard attributes the decentring to developments in science. I feel that the movement away from the European-centred empires to the current domination by America and the USSR has had an equal impact. In fact, I suspect that those two empires, in attempting to assert or reassert their metanarratives, turn all other societies into postmodern societies.

Timothy Findley in his novel *The Wars* gives an account of the particularly Canadian experience. His protagonist, Robert Ross, in the course of being destroyed by and in a marginal way surviving the First World War, acts out for the colonial society the destruction and the loss of its European centres, cultural, political, economic. For Findley, form and content speak each other's plight in *The Wars* as the traditional authority of the novel itself begins to falter. He resorts to an archival approach, using letters, photographs, interviews, family history, to recover the story, allowing the reader in turn to wonder how the fictional narrative centre relates to the writer writing. A doubt about our ability to know invades the narrative. What we witness is the collapse, for North American eyes, of the metanarrative that once went by the name Europe. Europa. Findley's more recent novels, *Famous Last Words* and *Not Wanted on the Voyage*, in their titles and in their stories remind us of Lyotard's observation that in postmodern writing there appears a scepticism or hesitation about the metanarrative's great voyages, its great goal.

ROBERT KROETSCH

The centre does not hold. The margin, the periphery, the edge, now, is the exciting and dangerous boundary where silence and sound meet. It is where the action is. In our darker moments we feel we must resist the blind and consuming power of the new places with their new or old ideas that now want to become centres. In our happier moments we delight in the energy of the local, in the abundance that is diversity and difference, in the variety and life that exist on any coastline of the human experience.

This willingness to refuse privilege to a restricted or restrictive cluster of metanarratives becomes a Canadian strategy for survival. We must, in Mikhail Bakhtin's terms, remain polyphonic, and the great Russian theorist was in his carnivalesque way a great master of survival. We are under pressure from many versions of the metanarrative, ranging from *Star Wars* to programs like *Dynasty* and *Dallas* – and again we hear the shorthand of the metanarrative in the naming. The trick is, I suppose, to resist the metanarrative and still to avoid Riel's fate. Or did he, rather, by his very strategies, trick the privileged centre into allowing and even applauding his survival? *Sir* John A. Macdonald becomes a failure, even as villain. Louis Riel, the outcast, the halfbreed, the man from the periphery, becomes, as villain or hero, the stuff of myth.

Rudy Wiebe, in his novels *The Temptations of Big Bear* and *The Scorched-Wood People*, explores the process by which we reject the metanarrative and assert the validity of our own stories. Rudy, as a Mennonite, the first Canadian-born child of exiles from Russia, living on a bush farm in Saskatchewan, then in a small town in southern Alberta, experienced the margin and its silence and its compulsion to speak its own validity. But what I want to do now is to look at some of the implications operating behind his and similar texts.

In this postmodern world, we trust a version of archaeology over the traditional versions of history. History, in its traditional forms, insisted too strongly on a coherent narrative. Timothy Findley speaks for many Canadians when he uses an archival method in *The Wars*, trusting to fragments of story, letting them speak their incompleteness. There is resistance to this mode, of course. A great Canadian architect like Arthur Erickson is at heart a modernist. A great Canadian critic like Northrop Frye is at heart a modernist, trying to assert the oneness, the unity, of all narrative. But the writers of stories and poems nowadays, in Canada, are not terribly sympathetic to Frye and his unifying sense of what a mythic vision is. Against this *over*riding view, we posit an archaeological sense that every unearthing is problematic, tentative, subject to a story-making act that is itself subject to further change as the "dig" goes on.

One of the functions of art, traditionally, is the location and elaboration of the metanarratives. Canadian writing is obsessively about the artist who can't make art. That model is securely established by Sinclair Ross and Ernest Buckler.

Ross, in his novel of the Saskatchewan prairies during the Depression, *As For Me and My House*, has a minister's wife tell the story in the form of her diary. Her husband is a minister who doubts his ministry and who wants both to paint and to write and who succeeds at neither. The book is in effect a powerful novel about the inability to make art – it is a novel as a set of diary entries about an unwritten novel. The metanarratives – religious, artistic, social, economic – do not hold. Even the great European metanarrative about "nature" does not hold here, as nature turns into wind and moving dust and an unreachable horizon.

Ernest Buckler sets his novel *The Mountain and the Valley* in Nova Scotia. His protagonist, David Canaan, is a young man who wants to write great stories and who dies with his ambition unrealized. The metanarratives of art, of family, of love, don't hold. The narrative itself turns into brilliant and static passages of description, speculation, repetition. The story quite simply cannot *move*.

Both these novels are set on geographical margins – the prairies, a rural area in Nova Scotia on the Bay of Fundy. Both deal with lives that the people themselves see as marginal – in both novels the ambition is obsessively to move into a bigger city. David Canaan gets into a car that will take him there, then gets out when he sees it's actually going to happen. Mrs. Bentley in Ross's novel – and we never know her first name or her family name – believes she and her husband are going to succeed by opening a secondhand bookstore in a city – and again, I hear Ross mocking this metaphoric (or is it metonymic?) representation of the metanarratives.

In both it is a kind of archaeological act that succeeds, against the traditional narrative. Mrs. Bentley does keep a journal, and in that journal, without recognizing it, she makes her art. In *The Mountain and the Valley* it is David Canaan's grandmother, hooking a rug out of the scraps of clothing that represent traces of family history, who is the successful artist.

In this model of narrative, the generalizations are tentative. In traditional narrative, a new detail fits into the story. Here, a single new detail can alter the possible story – as when, at the end of *As For Me and My House* – a question of paternity shakes our very sense of whatever narrative it is we've been reading. Instead of answers we have questions. Instead of resolution we have doubt. The endings of both novels are hotly and endlessly debated. While not outlining the debate, I want to suggest that the debates themselves – is Mrs. Bentley a good woman or a wicked woman? – is David Canaan an idealist or a self-deceiving failure? – are what create "unity." We come to a Bakhtinian version of the dialogic, in which the possibility of a single or privileged voice announcing the *right* version of the narrative is talked away. The unity is created by the very debate that seems to threaten the unity.

Do the provinces or does the federal government deserve the revenue from oil? Was Riel the hero, or was it really Gabriel Dumont? Why is the expression "the CPR" a curse in western Canada?

Given the failure of ends, of goals – and it's interesting to look at the hesitancy built into the ends of Canadian novels – process becomes more important than end. The novel that acts out this concern for process with greatest effect might well be Margaret Laurence's *The Diviners*.

Again, the protagonist of the novel is a writer, Morag Gunn. Morag is an orphan. She lives on geographical margins – she is born in a small town in Manitoba and when we see her writing she is in a cottage on a river in rural Ontario. She is aware of other margins – through her Celtic background she is reminded of threatened mythologies and of a language that she has in fact lost. She is a writer obsessively concerned to locate the meta-narratives of her own life and of Canada – and what she finds, over and over, is a set of contradictions, sets of variations. As an archaeologist of her own stories, she finds traces, lies, misreadings, concealments, fragments.

There is a moment in *The Diviners* that has become a touchstone passage in Canadian writing. Morag Gunn, living in London, meets a Scottish painter, Daniel McRaith. Morag had gone to London expecting to find a centre. Instead, she finds her closest friend (and lover) in an artist who is as uncertain as she about the centre. And, like her, he does his best work by remaining decentred. But Morag goes on believing she might still find a centre if she goes to Scotland, to what she believes must be her true "home." McRaith takes her there:

> McRaith points across the firth, to the north.
> "Away over there is Sutherland, Morag Dhu, where your people came from. When do you want to drive there?"
> Morag considers.
> "I thought I would have to go. But I guess I don't, after all."
> "Why would that be?"
> "I don't know that I can explain. It has to do with Christie. The myths are my reality. Something like that. And also, I don't need to go there because I know now what it was I had to learn here."
> "What is that?"
> "It's a deep land here, all right," Morag says. "But it's not mine, except a long long way back. I always thought it was the land of my ancestors, but it is not."
> "What is, then?"
> "Christie's real country. Where I was born."

McRaith holds her hand inside his greatcoat pocket. Around them the children sprint and whirl.[3]

One of the important elements in metanarratives is the story of the place and moment of origin. In the American story we hear of the apparently infinite crowd that was aboard the *Mayflower*, we hear of the moment in July 1776 when there seems to have been no opposition at all to the impulse toward revolution and, regrettably, little toleration for peoples who want to emulate that moment. In Canada we cannot for the world decide when we became a nation or what to call the day or days or, for that matter, years that might have been the originary moments. If we can't be united, we can't be disunited. Our genealogy is postmodern. Each move of a generation back into time doubles the number of ancestors instead of refining itself toward a sacred moment. (I remember vividly, as a student, hitting on Lord Raglan's *The Hero*, and for the first time being made aware of the mathematics of genealogy.) Morag Gunn is there but she isn't there; she isn't there but she's there. Margaret Laurence attempts some counting of ancestral sources – and her heroine gets stories from the official histories, from the mouths of the veterans who actually fought in the trenches, from the survivors of the trek from the Scottish villages, from her Métis lover in Manitoba, from the professor of English to whom she is married for a while, from her own daughter who has songs of her own to sing. The abundance, the disunity, is her saving unity. Christie Logan is indeed of and in the "real country" of Canadian art and story. He is a garbage man who "reads" what he finds in the nuisance grounds, and as such he is the ultimate archaeologist of that old new place called Canada.

The attempt at allowing versions of narrative might explain the extreme intertexuality of Canadian culture. Where the impulse in the US is usually to define oneself as American, the Canadian, like a work of postmodern architecture, is always quoting his many sources. Our sense of region resists our national sense. I hear myself saying, I'm from *western* Canada. Or, even beyond that – because I was born in Alberta and now live in Manitoba – people ask me, seriously, if I think of myself as an Albertan or a Manitoban. We maintain ethnic customs long after they've disappeared in the country of origin. We define ourselves, often, as the cliché has it, by explaining to Americans that we aren't British, to the British that we aren't Americans. It may be that we survive by being skilful shape-changers. But more to the point, we survive by working with a low level of self-definition and national definition. We insist on staying multiple, and by that strategy we accommodate to our climate, our economic situation, and our neighbours.

Morag Gunn works this experience through by encountering the many versions of herself as artist, ranging from shaman and prophet to fool and clown. In Canadian writing there is little sense of a privileged self at the centre. Contrast Morag Gunn in *The Diviners* with Jay Gatsby in F. Scott Fitzgerald's *The Great Gatsby*. Fitzgerald's hero, we are told, springs from the Platonic concept of himself. Morag Gunn springs from a multiplicity of stories.

At the centre of any metanarrative is a traditional hero. Canadians, uncertain of their metanarratives, are more than uncertain of their heroes. We have no "dearly loved" leaders. The Fathers of Confederation tend to be an anonymous bunch. When Canadian TV producers tried to find an equivalent of America's frontier hero Daniel Boone, they came up with Radisson and Groseilliers. How they thought they would make a single hero out of that pair of look-alike fur thieves I don't know.

The struggle with the concept of hero illuminates much about the faltering metanarrative in Canadian life. The western story, in Canada as in the US, seems to offer the best possibility for a fresh and genuine story. In the American west, the "free" or the "criminal" figure becomes heroic – the cowboy or the outlaw. In the Canadian west, the figure of authority is often the fictional protagonist. A remarkable number of school teachers ride into town – in the fiction not only of a comic writer like W.O. Mitchell but also in the near-tragic writings of Gabrielle Roy or in a novel like Martha Ostenso's *Wild Geese*. In this kind of fiction the authority figure as good guy ends up being treated parodically. The best example is Sinclair Ross's *As For Me and My House*. In that novel the "stranger" who "violates" the order of the town is the new minister, Philip Bentley. We first see him when he is unpacking. Or rather, when he is sleeping instead of unpacking. It is obvious from the first page of the story that his wife has the faster gun-hand. "He hasn't the hands for it," Mrs. Bentley says. "I could use the pliers and hammer twice as well myself...."[4]

Philip is white-faced and tight-lipped, quick, mostly, at drawing shut the door – of his study or of the bedroom. In this truly magnificent novel, the potential hero, Philip, has his role usurped by his nameless wife, the endlessly fascinating woman who, by quietly keeping a diary, creates the work of art that her artist-minister-husband cannot create. Perhaps the TV producers were right in looking for a doubled hero in the Canadian psyche. They might have fared better, however, had they turned to Louis Riel and Gabriel Dumont, those paired leaders who in their division of action and meditation, gun and book, act out the disunity that becomes our dance of unity.

Rudy Wiebe tried to find a single hero in the great Plains Cree leader of the nineteenth century, Big Bear, and in a way he succeeds profoundly. Big Bear refused to be baptized and he refused to settle his people on a reserve. In his refusals, in his resistance to the temptations, he resisted a whole new set of metanarratives. In a sense he became the archetypal

Canadian by refusing to become a Canadian. The divisions within him became the mark of his unified "Canadianness." Wiebe makes of Big Bear a powerful and attractive figure who in his defeat asserts his values – and the stories that carry those values. Again, here, it is the authority figures – the Queen's representatives, the agents of the eastern Canadian government – who ride in from the east and begin to parody what they claim to stand for. In this new world, the old stories break down. The systems of law, being used to take the land away from the Indians, become a parody of law. The systems of writing, up against the elaborate oral codes and traditions of the Indians, become a parody. Justice itself becomes a parody of justice. And yet the parodic forms, in their single-mindedness and in their greed, triumph; in the final inversion the forces of "civilization" destroy a prospering civilization that was based on a buffalo economy and the complex inter-relatedness of tribal life and geography. The railway, in Wiebe's book – the iron horse of 1885 – announces the arrival of a new story – of immigration, of dustbowl economics, of life and death on the reservation – and in this new story, by that ambiguous process we call art, the defeated Big Bear is transformed into an emblem of what the new story claims to cherish. In this near-hopeless separation of hero from communal behavior, the Canadian psyche, once again, both survives and flourishes.

One of the most fascinating studies of the hero in recent Canadian writing is that in Michel Tremblay's novel *The Fat Woman Next Door Is Pregnant*. The nameless woman at the centre of this story is the mother pregnant with the author who is writing the book. She is largely silent. She is almost immobile. To go back to Lyotard's definition, she is a kind of vast inversion of the traditional hero who goes out on a quest and who explores the implications of that quest, encounters great dangers and incredible trials. Tremblay is one of the most effective writers we have in the telling of our urban story.

A great deal of Canadian writing centres on the small town or the isolated community – and I suspect this is revealing in the ways it announces the hesitation we feel about our metanarrative. In Sheila Watson's *The Double Hook*, the young man who murders his mother in an isolated community in the interior of BC manages to escape from that community to a town where he might catch a train. Again, the ubiquitous train. Again, the train that might offer freedom, but does not. Young James Potter gets back onto his horse and rides back to his community. He, like David Canaan in Buckler's novel, cannot or will not break out of the circle, into a larger story.

Michel Tremblay confronts us with the same predicaments and the same impulses, in the urban setting of Montreal. The resemblance between his urban story, written in French, and that of the English-language writers is unnerving. Tremblay's characters, too, resist the metanarratives – of war, of religion, of the consumer society represented by the downtown Eaton's store in Montreal – and in that resistance they are kept apart and brought together. Tremblay, like Sinclair Ross, uses the house as the place of this diabolic and heavenly exchange. Ross has two people, man and wife, in a small house in a small prairie town, next to the church which they never seem quite to enter. Tremblay packs his house with generations, with the past and the present, with the natural and the supernatural. Yet in both novels there is, at the centre, not the traditional hero, but rather the unborn child. That child is at once an enormous potential and a terrible, obsession-making absence. At the centre of the story is zero. The story is decentred. All the reality of the story, the speech against the silence, is on the circumference. The margin. We live a life of shifting edges, around an unspoken or unspeakable question. Or, at best, in asking who we are, we are who we are.

It is no accident that the hero of the Canadian story, often, is the artist. David Canaan, writing or not writing. Mrs. Bentley, writing about her husband's not writing or painting. Margaret Laurence's Morag Gunn, growing old, still learning. Michel Tremblay's writer, waiting to be born. In a rock-bottom situation like ours, in which the very shape of story itself falters, the artist in the act of creating art becomes the focus.

The nameless woman in Margaret Atwood's *Surfacing* is an artist, an illustrator of children's books who can't make her illustrations match the folk-tales she's trying to illustrate. A second character in *Surfacing*, David, back in the fifties wanted to be a minister and tried selling Bibles door-to-door to put himself through the theological seminary. Now he's trying to make a film, with his friend Joe. At the end of the story, the nameless heroine exposes their film and drops it into a lake. By the end of the story, she has mated with Joe, who is on the way to becoming a bear-like creature, and she *might* be pregnant. The story becomes that minimal for Atwood. In making that minimal statement, she has become for many the quintessential *Canadian*, not just the Canadian artist. She locates our story by not finding it. The missing father is the central metaphor in *Surfacing*, the central metaphor in a failed and successful quest that is full of cryptic messages and languages that yield up their meaning by not speaking. Again, all is periphery and margin, against the hole in the middle. We are held together by that absence. There is no centre. This disunity is our unity.

I can suggest other novels that deal with the same paradox or strategy. Michael Ondaatje's *Coming through Slaughter*, the story of a black American jazz musician, Buddy Bolden, who left behind no record of his music. Alice Munro's *Lives of Girls and Women*, the growing-up into artist of Del

Jordan, a girl in a small town in Ontario, born into the silence of a small town, learning the fragments of story that make her life cohere. The *künstlerroman* is basic to the Canadian search for and rejection of metanarrative. Audrey Thomas's *Latakia*, the search of a woman writer that takes her back to the place where the alphabet is supposed to have developed, only to discover the chaos of unreadable maps, languages she can't understand, an archaeological site that yields up only a bewildering multitude of fragments.

Let me end, however, by glancing at one metanarrative that has asserted itself persistently in the New World context – and that is the myth of the new world, the garden story. The dream of Eden.

That dream, and the falling into fragments of the dream, haunts Canadian writers from nineteenth-century figures like Thomas C. Haliburton, berating his fellow Nova Scotians for their failures, from Susanna Moodie, arriving from England into Quebec and Ontario, to Stephen Leacock, making his comic readings of life in a small town, to contemporary writers like myself. It haunted the politicians like Sir John A., building his railway in the name of a slogan (from sea to sea); like Louis Riel, proclaiming his Métis nation; like Tommy Douglas, again in the west, announcing the formation of a socialist party; to John Diefenbaker of Saskatchewan, dreaming his further dream of the Canadian north.

Perhaps it is the novelist Frederick Philip Grove who most tellingly explores that Eden dream. He was a German novelist, Paul Greve, who faked his suicide and managed his own rebirth as a Canadian writer, as a teacher, living on the prairies of Louis Riel. In his novel *Settlers of the Marsh*, he takes his characters from Sweden and Germany and England, from the United States and Ontario, to the promised new world of Manitoba. Grove, in that setting, shows that life in the new world meant mind-numbing and body-breaking work. And, more than that, he shows, before our eyes, the collapse of the stories the settlers of the marsh brought with them. In the opening of the story, two Swedish immigrants are walking through a blizzard, lost. The narrator tells us: "Both would have liked to talk, to tell and to listen to stories of danger, of being lost, of hairbreadth escapes: the influence of the prairie snowstorm made itself felt. But whenever one of them spoke, the wind snatched his word from his lips and threw it aloft."[5]

Perhaps the literal word is being dispersed, as Lyotard would have it, "in clouds of narrative language elements...."

In this silence the two men are unhooked from their old stories, and from the unified world-view (whatever its virtues and vices) that those stories allowed. There, on the old hunting-grounds of Louis Riel's Métis, delivered to this place by railway, the two immigrants enter into the

Canadian story. And the hero is, again, two, as if the disunity is so radical that it physically splits the hero. And yet, out of that division comes the discovery of unity.

The unnaming allows the naming. The local pride speaks. The oral tradition speaks its tentative nature, its freedom from the authorized text.

Notes

1   Tenth Annual Conference of the British Association for Canadian Studies, Edinburgh, 9-12 Apr. 1985.

2   Jean-François Lyotard, *The Postmodern Condition: A Report on Knowledge*, trans. Geoff Bennington and Brian Massumi (Minneapolis: U of Minnesota P, 1984) xxiv.

3   Margaret Laurence, *The Diviners* (Toronto: McClelland and Stewart, 1974) 318-19.

4   Sinclair Ross, *As For Me and My House* (1941; Toronto: McClelland and Stewart, 1957) 3.

5   Frederick Philip Grove, *Settlers of the Marsh* (1925; Toronto: McClelland and Stewart, 1966) 16.

The End(s) of Irony: The Politics of Appropriateness

Linda Hutcheon

> Irony is the rhetorical necessity of the age, the critical accessory no
> one should leave home without. It has also replaced patriotism as the
> last refuge of scoundrels, for it means never having to say you really
> meant it.
> – Brenda Austin-Smith "Into the Heart of Irony" (51)

The suspicion voiced in these remarks is perhaps a good place to start to
review that edgy "problematic of affect" accompanying irony's "problematic of meaning" (Hebdige 223). Some of you may recall the outcry when
Randy Newman released his record "Short People Got No Reason To
Live," thinking that by ironizing a benign object of prejudice he could sat-
irize all prejudice. His good intentions turned out to be irrelevant to those
who were angered by the song: "Some simply declared that he had lied.
Others invoked the familiar distinction between intention and utterance:
he may have intended no slur on short people, but his words say otherwise. Still others turned to psychology and explained that while Newman
perhaps *thought* he was free of prejudice, his song displayed his true feelings" (Fish 175). Irony's edge cuts many ways.

The example that I have chosen to study here is another one in which
the risks of irony were made manifest, not only through the proliferation
of public as well as academic discourse on the topic but also through real
material consequences for the participants. My "text" is a cultural text: a
museum exhibition that can be read as a "text" because it is very much
the "product of social interaction, contingent upon social process" (Stewart
14). From 16 November 1989 to 6 August 1990, the Royal Ontario
Museum in Toronto presented an exhibition entitled "Into the Heart of
Africa." This was the first complete (and thus long-awaited) showing of
the African collection of the museum, but what began with good intentions ended with picketing by members of the African Canadian community, court injunctions against them by the museum, encounters between
demonstrators and police that led to criminal charges being laid, and the
later decision of Jeanne Cannizzo, the curator (a white anthropologist and
expert on African art), to leave her part-time university classroom for a
complex set of reasons, including continuing harassment by former
demonstrators who accused the show of racism. (For details of the events,
see Young and, especially, Butler.) Throughout this essay, I will refer to

Cannizzo as "the curator" in order to put the emphasis on her institutional role and, implicitly, to remind you that curators do not work alone but in conjunction with both museum administration and technical, design, and educational workers in the institution. I do not wish to downplay her personal role (or the consequences of the controversy for her). I do want to contextualize it all. This is also one of the reasons for the existence of explanatory notes in this essay: a desire to give you as much context as possible for the complex and contentious issues raised.

What was so surprising about the controversy and the degree of emotional furor unleashed was that this was an exhibition that *attempted* to be the opposite of the kind of thing one might find in an institution like the Royal Museum of Central Africa near Brussels, where a statue of Leopold II dominates a room "celebrating the triumphs of colonialism with the guns and flags of expeditions and the chests carried by native bearers, the plumed hats of the conquerors, models of their railway lines and the honoured names of those who laid down their lives controlling the natives" (Horne 222). Those guns and flags and plumed hats were present in the (similarly named) Royal Ontario Museum too, but the stated intention of this exhibition was to expose the imperial ideology of the people – Canadian soldiers and missionaries – who had borne them and who had brought back to Canada many African objects which, over time, found their way into the museum. My own engagement with this controversy dates from the weeks in the summer of 1990 – at the height of the public confrontations taking place in front of the museum – when I was teaching a seminar on the politics of irony right across the road: police sirens and chanting demonstrators provided choral commentary on the political perils of irony.

"Into the Heart of Africa" provides a pointed case study of the transideological complexities of irony – with a particular focus on the question of when and whether irony is deemed appropriate and even ethical (see Swearingen vii) as a discursive strategy. The degree of anger – from, as you will see, all possible sides of the issue – was ample testimony to the affective charge of irony's edge. There were serious disagreements over the identifying and evaluating of the functioning of the irony. Was it élitist or inclusive? Was it evasive or cautiously indirect? The said and the unsaid were held in a semantic suspension so unstable that irony did not always happen for everyone, and, when it did, disagreement about interpretation was rife. Ironic meaning here was relational in several senses: it came into being in the interactions between the said and the unsaid, most obviously, but also between intention and interpretation, as well as between verbal and visual sign systems. The ironies in "Into the Heart of Africa" could not be explained by any simple antiphrastic semantic model or any theory of meaning substitution: operating more inclusively and differentially, irony's indirect meanings were born of the rubbing of the edge of the said against the plural edges of the unsaid – in such a way that sparks were certainly created for some viewers. In addition to these semantic and affective complications, the complexity of possible discursive communities involved in the presentation and viewing of an exhibit in a public institution is staggering. Do curators and the "general public" share enough assumptions to make irony safe? Given the nature of this particular show about the role of the British Empire (here represented by colonial Canadians) in Africa, the usual community categories to be taken into account (such as age, education, language, gender, and so on) were greatly expanded. Race and nationality, of course, were primary community-defining factors, but so was timing of viewing and background knowledge: it mattered whether you attended in the first few months, before the controversy erupted, or after; it mattered how much you knew about the conflict and where you had got your information about it. The discursive communities to which viewers belonged determined how they might construct ironic meaning from the exhibition's objects and texts.

The experience of visiting a museum is, as one commentator explains, the result of variable effects of "the original makers' intentions in making the displayed object, the curator's and designer's intentions in displaying it in a certain way, and the observer's own interests and assumptions about all these matters and the museum itself" (Jones 917). The curator's intentions – which I will address in detail shortly – in deploying irony in the displaying of objects were not necessarily either interpreted as such or appreciated when they were. The intentional acts of a wide variety of interpreters/viewers – those for whom the ironies did happen, those for whom they did not, and those for whom irony was felt to be utterly inappropriate – illustrate the difficulties of relying on intentional theories in discussing irony's politics. Were imperial racist attitudes simply repeated – though in quotation marks – or were they ironized by those very marks? Does any repetition in a different context necessarily change meaning (Mizzau 43)? Or are only some echoes going to be real examples of ironic echoic mention that involve the implication of a judgemental attitude (Sperber and Wilson 303)? Who is to decide? What markers are needed to insure that irony happens? Are quotation marks around certain words on explanatory panels sufficient signals of irony's possible presence – especially when they were used in varying ways throughout the exhibition?

On top of all this, the contexts that framed "Into the Heart of Africa" for viewers were complex and multiple, so difficulties in signalling were bound to increase. For some – anthropologists, museum workers – the exhibit might have been viewed as an example of the "new" museology, revealing the changes in the discipline of ethnography over the last decades. For others, the frame of viewing might have been the challenges

LINDA HUTCHEON

to the cultural authority of museums as institutions of "modernity." For still others, it was the current postcolonial interest in the material and cultural consequences of Empire that might have been the focus of attention. The general debates over multiculturalism in Canada and the more specific ones over the relations of the Metropolitan Toronto Police and the black community provided still other contexts for Canadians and Torontonians. In addition, the positioning of this exhibition within the museum and the display conventions of the rest of the institution were important framing elements for most viewers. All of these now familiar theoretical points of reference – affect, semantics, discursive communities, intention, markers and contexts – will be discussed in much more detail in what follows, but this brief overview might already give you a sense of why "Into the Heart of Africa" seemed to me to be such a fitting test case for theorizing irony and its politics.

Few would disagree that, here, irony turned out to be tendentious, and part of the reason was that, as always, irony took interpreters "out of the text and into codes, contexts, and situations" (Scholes 76). In order to set the scene for the conflict, I would like to fill in some of those situations and contexts, beginning with the most general ones that came into play. For me, the broadest context was the relation of museums to what has been generalized and usually demonized into this thing called "modernity." Put in the admittedly reductive (but perhaps heuristically useful) terms of "cultural shorthand": in most accounts these days, the movement from Renaissance humanism to the beginning of the "modern project," to use Jürgen Habermas's term, starts with the Cartesian and Enlightenment shift to what has been described as "a higher, stratospheric plane, in which nature and ethics conform to abstract, timeless, general, and universal theories" (Toulmin 35). On this plane – or so goes the simplified version of the story – connections between knowledge and objects of knowledge (nature, the self, history, society) are said to be objectively determined, providing a foundation which permits a systematization that works toward what is seen as an inherently progressive grasp of "truth." Knowledge thus accrued is said to be not only culture-neutral, but value-free. Doubt and contingency, however, are just as much a part of this modern heritage, and of course, the debates over the politics of the ordering, legitimizing, system-building power of reason and method are part of the very history of modernity; they are also ongoing, however, with Habermas arguing that the "project of modernity" has not yet been completed, that its moral imperative to free humanity from injustice and to extend equality to the oppressed through rational communal grounds of consensus has not yet been achieved. Yet, what Habermas sees as liberatory consensus, others have seen as inhibiting conformism, as an "obsessively legislating, defining, structuring, segregating, classifying, recording and universalizing state [which] reflected the splendour of universal and absolute standards of truth" (Baumann xiv).

As an academic, I know that I work within one of the major cultural institutions of modernity and, whatever my individual evaluation of the modern project and, whatever my personal position (consensual support or oppositional resistance), I participate in what has been called the "exercise of social control through the meting out of learning, mediated and identified with the achievement of worth" (Hooper-Greenhill 224). But these words were, in fact, written to describe the ideological and historical assumptions of curators of ethnographic museums, not literature teachers like me. Nevertheless, both the museum and the academy in Europe and North America have traditionally shared an institutionalized faith in reason and method, not to mention an unavoidable intersection with governmental agencies; together (and when added to the often imposing architecture of such institutions), these connections have contributed to the "authority effect" (Hooper-Greenhill 225) they each create. Not surprisingly, both institutions have come under considerable scrutiny from various branches of contemporary theory, intent on deconstructing that effect and its ideological consequences. Both institutions could be said to work toward the acquisition of knowledge (Jordanova 22) through collecting, ordering, preserving, and displaying – in their different ways – the "objects" of human civilization in all its varieties. If it is the ideology of these processes of constructing meaning and significance that has provoked the recent theoretical critique, it is the nature of those very "objects" that has initially brought the *postcolonial* into the current academic debates – in literary criticism and anthropology especially – and, increasingly, into the discourse of museums, especially ethnographic ones.

An important context for many viewers of "Into the Heart of Africa" was the fact that, over the last few decades, museums have begun to see themselves as cultural texts and have become increasingly self-reflexive about their premises, identity, and mission. Among the questions being asked anew are: Do objects speak for themselves? If so, how? What objects have been collected, and why? What constitutes the so-called authenticity of an object? (See Crew and Sims.) The history and economics of collecting have received much attention lately from many quarters, as have the current legal, ethical and financial constraints on acquisition, custody and disposal of "cultural property" (see Palmer). But the history of most European and North American ethnographic museum collections is one that cannot be separated from the specific history of imperialism (Ames 3; Thomas; see, for a bibliography, Arnoldi 454-55n2). Not only were the objects collected often the spoils of colonial conquest – seen at the time as "discovery" and "exploration" – but their acquisition and retention have been legitimated by the institutionalization of an ideal (and an ideology)

LINDA HUTCHEON

of apolitical, detached objectivity and a positivist commitment to science (Durrans 155).

This connection between historical imperialism and what some see as intellectual imperialism (C.S. Smith 17) might best be understood within the context of the common denominator of what I too have here been calling "modernity." However much they might be called into question in *theory*, the assumptions of neutrality and objectivity and of the value of rationality, empiricism, and technology are modern assumptions that form the *practical* foundations of the post-Enlightenment public museum (MacCannell 84), even to this day. If museums are still structured on "rigid taxonomies and classification, whereby it was believed that artefacts could be laid out in a consistent, unitary and linear way" (C.S. Smith 19), it is because they are still in some ways the physical embodiments of what (in those shorthand terms, once again) can be called modernity's desire to make order and therefore meaning. What some see as the universalization inherent in the Enlightenment project (Fisher 95) works to smooth over gaps and unite fragments into a systematized cultural totality. One of the manifestations of this process is the display of diverse, culturally specific objects in highly aestheticized (C.S. Smith 17), (architecturally) late modernist galleries that effectively wipe out particularity of context or history. Of course, the very act of technically preserving objects from the ravages of time and decay (not to mention that of "restoring" them to their "original" state) could be seen as universalizing in its denial of change over time. This stewardship model of the museum as the guardian of the human heritage entails a going beyond this conservation function to include a scholarly and educational mandate, both for experts and for the general public.

In the last twenty years or so, however, experts working in the field of ethnography have articulated in a museum context the view of culture as "text," reminding all that texts are interpreted and contextualized by ethnographers themselves. To borrow from the title of one of Clifford Geertz's influential books, the aim of "interpretive anthropology" is "local knowledge" (Geertz 1983; see also Geertz 1973; Crapanzano). What has been called a "conceptual shift, 'tectonic' in its implications" (Clifford, "Introduction" 2), in ethnography is, in fact, a response to modernity that has major postcolonial implications. Gone are the days when anthropology (conceived of as apolitical and neutral) could speak "with automatic authority for others defined as unable to speak for themselves" (Clifford, "Introduction" 10). The acknowledgement – at last – of the "unequal power encounter" (Asad 16) that marks both the discipline of anthropology and, in a different way, colonialism itself has brought the politics of representation to the fore. The universalizing urge of modernity then begins to give way to the cultural politics of difference, described as the drive to trash the monolithic and homogeneous in the name of diversity, multiplicity and heterogeneity; to reject the abstract, general and universal in light of the concrete, specific and particular; and to historicize, contextualize and pluralize by highlighting the contingent, provisional, variable, tentative, shifting and changing. (West 19)

What has been referred to (if not generally accepted) as the "new museology" works in this contentious territory, asking what the different purpose of the museum would be if it gave up its modern claims of neutrality and objectivity, and what the role of the spectator could be in the now acknowledged act of the interpretation of objects, objects which do not independently transmit meaning. Instead, they are open to many possible constructions of meaning, depending on things like the design of the display, the context in the institution, the visual semiotics engaged, the historical background presented. However, not only objects change meaning over time; so too does the museum itself as institution, for it too is a constantly evolving social artifact (Weil xiv) that exists in a constantly changing social world. The current discourse of museums now includes a discourse of community access and involvement, of two-way interactive communication models, and of empowerment through knowledge (see Gurian). There is talk of a desire to find ways to engage with living cultures rather than only with objects of the past, of a desire not only to inform but to provoke thought.

These are the most general contexts, then, for the particular focus of this essay: one museum exhibition that certainly did engage with its immediate community and that definitely provoked thought, not to say controversy; as I mentioned at the start, it was an exhibition that intended to put into play irony and reflexivity in order to attempt to deconstruct the ideology of Empire that had determined its particular collection of African objects. It thus ran counter to the more customary (unavoidable, but usually discreet) indirect mention of imperial provenance that could be read as an attempt to "close its history at the end of the colonial era itself" (Durrans 150).

The intention – according to museum authorities – was to offer a (postcolonial) "critical examination of the Canadian missionary and military experience in turn-of-the-century Africa";[1] the mode of presentation was what museologists might have recognized as consciously "new" in its foregrounding of how objects changed meaning over time and in different contexts. But the self-evident difficulty of effectively deconstructing a museum *from the inside* became acute when that institution was viewed by at least some members of the African Canadian community as part of European modernity's "attempt to measure, categorize and hierarchize the world with the white male at the top. And all at the expense of the

African, Asian and aboriginal peoples."² In a city like Toronto (and in a country like Canada),³ where the multicultural and multiracial mix is perhaps as great as anywhere in the world today, what cannot be ignored is the inevitable change in what the social meaning of a museum might entail. If a museum is a means by which a society represents its relationship to its own history and to that of other cultures (Lumley 2), then changes in that society should also be reflected in the institution, whose meaning – like that of the objects within it – is a constructed and negotiated one.

A bit of context for non-Canadians: Canadian society has changed radically since World War II. Outside Québec, its once British majority has sometimes found itself, in large urban centres in particular, in a minority position. Such is the case in Toronto, where the influx of immigrants from southern Europe, South Asia, Africa, the West Indies, and the Middle and Far East has made the city multiracial as well as multiethnic. Since many of the new arrivals have come from other Commonwealth countries, there has been an inevitable new awareness of both similarity and difference in the experience of Empire. If colonialism can be defined as a broad form of structural domination (Stam and Spence 4), there are going to be many varieties of it: "to be one of the colonized is potentially to be a great many different, but inferior, things, in many different places, at many different times" (Said 1989: 207; see also Said 1993). Many working in the field of postcolonial studies today stress the distinctions even within communities, based on gender, class, race (see Spivak; Donaldson). Others have pointed to what are, in this particular case, important differences between kinds of colonies – for example, between so-called settler colonies⁴ like Canada and subjugated ones like the many in Africa (see Tiffin; Brydon; Ashcroft, Griffiths, and Tiffin). Both may indeed partake of that "specifically anti-colonial counter-discursive energy" (Slemon 3) that some see as postcolonial, but there are important differences⁵ that are crucial to the responses to "Into the Heart of Africa," differences that obviously involve the "unbridgeable [racial] chasm" (Mishra and Hodge 408) between white and non-white colonies, as well as the related cultural and historical chasms between settler and subjugated colonies. In the latter, cultural imposition took place on "the body and space" of Empire's "Others" (Slemon 30; see also Tiffin 31) through military and bureaucratic power.

While I do not in any way want to underestimate either the multiplicity of past and present responses to Britain and Empire from Canadians of other nationalities or the very real trauma of settler colonies like Canada, which have had to deal with the psychic and cultural (as well as economic) dependency of colonization and have struggled to articulate autonomy through constitutional or cultural means,⁶ I cannot help thinking that the problems at the Royal Ontario Museum a few years ago stemmed in part,

at least, from the difference between Canada's relation to Empire (as a settler colony)[7] and that of Africa's nations, invaded by European (and in this
case, Canadian) powers and subjugated to them by military might or missionary evangelism. While Canada may well want to position itself today
oppositionally, as either anti- or post-colonial, in order to make a "space-
clearing gesture" (Appiah 348) for its New World self-definition, this particular exhibition – with its focus on the Canadian role in the colonizing
of Africa – forced an awareness of English Canada's official historical position *within* Empire. Not everyone liked this new self-image: to borrow
Albert Memmi's strong but not inappropriate terms, Canada was suddenly
"disfigured into an oppressor, a partial, ... treacherous being, worrying only
about ... privileges and their defense" (89). Canadians (or more specifically
white English Canadians) were shown that their own history was not separable from the colonizer's struggle to reconcile "the notions of political
freedom cherished by [the] home country with the actual political suppression and disfranchisement of the colonized people" (JanMohamed 4-
5).[8] Black Canadians, as you will see, were positioned rather differently.
But, as a nation, Canada was represented as having an uncomfortable dual
historical identity, as both colony and colonizing force.

What particularly interests me here about this exhibition and about the
explosive affective responses to it is that its ironic and allusive nature was
identified early on as part of the problem. Yet the postcolonial and the
feminist enterprises, among others, have often turned to irony as a
"counter-discourse," as the rhetorical figure of the dialogic whose "function is to project an alternative through which any element of the here-
and-now may be shown as contingent, and thereby subject the whole
configuration of power within which it took its adversative meaning to
the erosive, dialectical power of alterity" (Terdiman 76-77). As the "linguistic repository of difference," irony, when seen as an oppositional strategy, can work to problematize authority, including those modern
assumptions about museums' structures and forms of historical authority.
But, to recall irony's transideological politics, irony can work in many
other ways too.

An important and, here, relevant theme of much writing on the "new
museology" is a call to institutions to make themselves and their publics
aware of the history of their collections and of the values embodied
therein (see C.S. Smith 20; Jordanova 40; Wright 1367; Weil 52). Against the
view that it is high time to abandon the concepts of irony and reflexivity
(Jameson 64), it has been argued that reflexivity about historical role and
museum context can have the potential to raise important political, epistemological and aesthetic issues: the idea is that the "metatext" would
make visible to the public the ways to read and make sense of a display as
"text," as well as offer the history of the choices leading to it (Lumley 13).

It seems to be assumed that such internal self-awareness would lead to a liberation from the constraints of modernity's concepts of apolitical scientificity and authority (Greenhalgh 95), and thus free museums to take on what previously might have been considered risky or controversial subjects, because the public would now be made more aware and less complacent about what they expect to find in a museum. If combined with "wider historical experiences such as explorations of colonial relations" (Durrans 162), it has been argued, new questions might be provoked. "Into the Heart of Africa" certainly provoked many questions – about colonialism and the relationship between the politics of culture and the politics of meaning and representation (Seidel 230) – but it was reflexivity itself, like irony, that came under fire. (For a full analysis of this see Butler 67-73.)

Actually, almost everything about this exhibition came under fire, from its focus to its subject matter – indeed, even its title. Depending on how you interpret Conrad's *Heart of Darkness*, the echoing of the novel's title in "Into the Heart of Africa" is going to suggest either an adventurist/imperialist perspective or a critique thereof (see Torgovnick). From the start, then, this ideologically freighted doubleness encodes in microcosm the terms of the ensuing conflict over the show's interpretation and evaluation of imperialism. According to the curator, writing *after* the fact, the title was intended to signal that the exhibition would deal "with the past, with journeys, interaction and the disjunction between Canadian images and African realities" (Cannizzo 1991: 151-52). The museum later asserted that its intent was "to explore attitudes of the past but not, for a moment, to suggest that the ROM endorsed the biases of those times."[9] That there was considerable confusion about the realization of this intention was evident within a few months of the opening, however.

Prior to this occasion, the museum's small and fragmentary collection of 375 objects from Central and West Africa had remained in its basement for most of the century, available (as a whole) only to researchers, though parts of it had been displayed in some of the ethnographic galleries. It was fragmentary because it lacked, in the curator's words, "chronological depth, geographical concentration or ethnographic focus" (Cannizzo 1991: 150) and the reasons for this lay in the history of its acquisition. It had come into being largely through bequests from the families of Canadian missionaries and soldiers in the British African colonies at the end of the last century and the beginning of this one. This is where the problems with the collection's unrepresentative nature also began: military men often collected weapons (and I suppose it is not hard to imagine how at least some of them might have been obtained) and missionaries tended to bring home things like hair pins or combs or musical instruments that they could display when fund-raising. In other words, this was not a full collection of a range of African objects; there could be little pretence that it would represent the cultural diversity, social complexity, or artistic achievement of the multiple peoples of Central Africa.[10]

For this reason, the decision was made to foreground in the exhibition both the material limitations of the collection and the history and politics of its coming into being in this one, specifically Canadian, cultural institution. The openly articulated intent was a familiar one in current anthropological theory: to focus on the imperial ideology of those who collected the objects (for which rich archival materials did exist), on how those objects came to enter this museum, and thus on the more general cultural assumptions of museums and of the disciplines of museology, anthropology, and history. In short, the focus was not to be on Africa itself. In addition, given this meta-museological conception, it would seem that the primary intended audience was more academic than general – an impression that was borne out by the catalogue. In accord with that "new museology" being articulated during those very years, it emphasized what the curator later called the "transformational power of context" – the importance to the meaning and significance of objects of the circumstances in which they appear and are understood (Cannizzo 1991: 151). The catalogue constantly called the reader's attention to the history of objects, tracing the cultural transformations of each as its context changed (through what have been called "unanticipated appropriations" [Fisher 96]) from that of use in African society to being collected by Canadian missionaries or soldiers to being exhibited in the Royal Ontario Museum (known as the ROM). But, as I mentioned, there was yet another transformation to come after the exhibition opened: from museum specimen to political symbol. There are times when the failure of discursive communities to overlap can be particularly risky, and this was one of them.

A few months after the opening, an umbrella group known as the "Coalition for the Truth about Africa" began picketing the museum, handing out leaflets which called the show "a clear and concise attempt to mislead the public and to further tarnish the image of Africa and African people." These handouts also stated that "Into the Heart of Africa," "according to the ROM, is a portrayal of African history." And indeed, despite the catalogue and despite later statements of intent, the museum's advertising brochure describing the exhibition does invite you "on an historical journey through the world of sub-Saharan Africa.... The rich cultural heritage of African religious, social and economic life is celebrated through objects brought back by Canadian missionaries and military men over 100 years ago." But this description misrepresented not so much the *material* as the *focalization* of the exhibition: the focus was never intended to be entirely on Africa itself, but on the material remains of the ideology of Empire in Africa. That "historical journey" was a Canadian one.

Why, then, would the brochure appear to mislead? One reason might be that this was the second one printed. At the cost of over $20,000, the first was scrapped when consultations with members of the African Canadian community led to complaints against what was called its "tired, stereotypical language" about Africa, language which "subtly recalled the glory of the Imperial Age" (da Breo 33). But the fact remained that the second brochure, however closer it might have been to representing what the community would have liked the exhibit to be, actually proved seriously misleading with respect to the reality. In this way, the initial decision as to the focalization of the show became a primary point of contention for those in certain discursive communities. The first printed message at the entry to the exhibition openly stated that *Canadians* (implicitly, white British Canadians) were to be the focus, that their "experience of Africa, as seen in this exhibition, was very different from the way Africans perceived themselves, their own cultures, and these events." The objects presented, it continued, "remind us of a little-remembered era of Canada's past." Now, first-person plural pronouns always function to "hail" a discursive community; here, however, that "us" was problematic, not only in its implicit exclusions (perhaps some African Canadians did indeed remember that past[11]), but also because not all of those white Canadians so "hailed" wanted to be reminded of such a past.

Certainly, the initial, almost empty (and, for me, imperial) blue rooms labelled "For Crown & Empire" set up the historical relation of Canada to the British Empire in Africa in the last century (see Figure 1). A few objects (both African and imperial) were presented here in a traditional museum fashion, isolated in their beauty in glass cases, abstracted from their context and function. Although everyone connected to the museum[12] insisted that the irony and reflexivity of the show were meant to signal the detachment of the institution from the imperial perspective being presented, the textual markers of that intention were less than clear and self-evident from the start. In these first rooms, for instance, I could find no semiotic signal to separate the African from the imperial, despite the later claims that the intent was to show the beauty of the African objects as a way of refuting "the 19th century [sic] Canadian supposition of barbarism" (Cannizzo 1991: 152). But was one also to admire the shining, ribboned British-Canadian officer's helmet similarly placed in a locked glass case? The curator may have intended a kind of reflexive, ironic "ethnographizing" effect (Cannizzo 1991: 153), but the context of the museum as a whole (where such glass cases are un-ironized commonplaces) inevitably worked against such a result for some viewers. The beauty of the objects and the emptiness of the room made this feel like a kind of holy place where Empire was being revered, or at the very least, admired.[13]

What jolted the viewer out of this mood, however, was the fact that,

Figure 1: "For Crown & Empire." Installation from "Into the Heart of Africa" exhibition, 1989-90, Royal Ontario Museum, Toronto, Canada. Photo courtesy of the Royal Ontario Museum.

visible from the entrance, was an enormous, wall-sized enlargement of an image of a mounted British soldier thrusting his sword into the breast of an African warrior (see Figure 2). This was labelled (none too readably) "Lord Beresford's Encounter with a Zulu," and it wouldn't be hard to imagine viewers engaging differently with the named aristocratic soldier than with the generic Zulu victim. The text posted nearby identified this as the cover of *The Illustrated London News* of 6 September 1879. As you can imagine, the impact of this kind of image is going to be different on a small catalogue page, where it is also reproduced, than it is on a large wall. As many commentators subsequently noted, the violence of this representation worked not to produce a response against jingoistic Victorian imperialism (as was intended[14]), but to turn the tables against the exhibition itself for perpetuating precisely such representations. In today's culture, where visual images may indeed make more of an impression than printed text, and in an institution visited by schoolchildren of all ages and races who just might not stop to read the contextualizing accompanying texts, the placing and size of this image were, at the very least, signs of semiotic inattention or inexperience. While the relationship of text to image is a general problem for all museum exhibits, here it proved critical because many African Canadian visitors could not bring themselves to go beyond this violent representation of their race's history.

After the contentious "Military Hall" section over which this image loomed, a relatively small area called "The Life History of Objects" constituted the only explicitly meta-museological part of the exhibition itself, though this was a major focus of the catalogue. The reconstituted front hallway of a Canadian house revealed the movement of African objects (such as spears and shields) from being spoils of war to becoming pure (if exotic) decoration – before being donated to the museum. This section indirectly raised questions about appropriation and exploitation, but did not offer any answers or even any extended commentary (Schildkrout 19). The ambiguities made possible by the general rhetorical strategy of indirection here even allowed one visitor to suggest that, for her, this home setting was a kind of humanizing of the experience of imperialism (Crean 26).

The next section took the form of a large, bright, white, cross-shaped room, labelled "Civilization, Commerce, and Christianity," and in it were presented the artifacts collected by missionaries (who thought they were bearing "light" to the "dark continent," as accompanying texts explained). There were also photographs of these evangelical Christians with their African converts. The last and largest area of the exhibition was introduced by a reconstruction of an Ovimbundu village compound from Angola, wherein some of the objects seen in cabinets elsewhere were inserted into a simulated context of use. At the entrance of the final large room, con-

Figure 2: "Lord Beresford's Encounter with a Zulu." Cover of *The Illustrated London News*, No. 2099, Vol. LXXV, Saturday, 6 September 1879. Photo courtesy of the Royal Ontario Museum.

LINDA HUTCHEON

taining drums, masks, textiles, head-dresses, weapons, and musical instruments (with headphones to listen to African music), was a reflexive message attesting to the "impossibility actually to reconstruct another cultural reality in a museum. The artifacts you see here are displayed according to their 'function' or 'form' in a way that would be quite familiar to late nineteenth-century museum-goers, but not the people who made them. The things are theirs, the arrangement is not." Such a sign was intended to mark the change in interpretive emphasis at this point in the exhibition, as the theme changed from the history of the collection to the objects themselves which were said to "speak of the varied economies, political or cosmological complexities, and artistry of their African creators" (Cannizzo 1991: 156). Yet the problem with calling attention to the fictional or artificial arrangement of the objects in this particular space became evident when you considered it in the context of the *rest* of this museum, where such traditional arrangements are still the norm for even the twentieth-century museum-goer. Given that, in Western culture, priority is usually signalled by position, there was yet another potential conflict between the intention – to show that "African cultural life and historical experience were not being reduced to a codicil of imperial history" (Cannizzo 1991: 152) – and the fact that this section did come *after* the one that focused on imperial acquisition.

The corridor leading out of the exhibition housed a scattered and miscellaneous collection of small photographs of Africans today, perhaps in an attempt to give a sense that, although the collection may be historical, the realities of urbanization and industrialization have brought many changes to African society. Just outside the doorway was a special African museum-store "boutique" which eased the visitor (who could now become a "collector" too) back into Canadian consumer society, thereby coming full circle, since the initial (conventional) sign thanking corporate sponsors set up (for me, as for others) an unintended ironic frame: if anyone should have been acknowledged as being those without whom this show would not have been possible, it was the Africans who made the objects displayed.

Even my brief description (itself hardly innocent of interpretation) might offer some clues as to why "Into the Heart of Africa" managed to engage so much strong emotion in so many very different people. As one critic remarked:

> What was most amazing was that the exhibition offended audiences
> from all parts of the political spectrum: missionaries whose colleagues were depicted in the exhibition, the descendants of colonial
> officers whose collections were shown…, and most strongly, Africans
> and people of African descent who saw the exhibition as racist and

insulting. The exhibition was also offensive to some within another, somewhat less vocal group, that is, historians of Africa, art historians, and anthropologists working in universities and museums. (Schildkrout 17)

One might add to that list even liberal, white Canadians who thought of themselves as multiculturally tolerant and even postcolonially oppositional. But what specifically enraged and offended people? From all accounts (see, for a summary, Fulford 24), the anger of many was provoked as much by the visual representation of verbal texts as by any actual objects or pictures. Here it was again irony's edge that cut, but in ways different from those I have explored so far. From the start, explanatory signs presented certain words framed in quotation marks. An interpretive conflict was set up at once: were these citations (and thus historically authenticated and validated) or were they echoic mentions to be read ironically? Words like "the unknown continent," "barbarous," and "primitive" were placed in these quotation marks, but the problem was that so too were metaphors, titles, and some object descriptions. In other words, the proliferation of quotation marks made the visitor wonder whether those placed around words like "Dark Continent" and "primitive" could or should be read as markers intended both to signal ironic distance (see Chung 7) and also to act as accurate citations – in other words, to represent the colonial perspective that the *post*colonial exhibition wanted to show it did not share (Nazareth 11). In the museum's own initial news release, there was arguably some awareness that people might not know exactly how to interpret such quotation marks, for it added "*what was then called by some the 'unknown continent'*" (emphasis added). The curator, in a later article, likewise wrote of "the *alleged* barbarity of 'savage customs'" (Cannizzo 1991: 154; emphasis added). Of course, inverted commas or quotation marks are a commonplace rhetorical technique (used to disclaim and to distance, while still echoing) in "new" museological theorizing (and even, obviously, in this essay). But when the context is not academic or museological (and depending on your discursive community), the interpretation of these ironizing quotation marks may differ. For some visitors to "Into the Heart of Africa," they were simply disapproving disclaimers;[15] for others they were a form of devious "sugarcoating."[16] For many, irony was also simply an inappropriate strategy to use. One viewer, whose great-uncle was featured as one of the Canadian military, found that they created too subtle an irony, one "lost on those who can't (or don't) read the explanatory texts." She added: "it is also a pretty limp way to examine a subject as grave as racially motivated genocide" (Crean 25). The Curriculum Adviser on Race Relations and Multiculturalism for the Toronto Board of Education went even further, stating: "In dealing with issues as sensitive as cultural imperialism and racism, the use of irony is a highly inappropriate luxury."[17] And yet, as explored earlier, postcolonial theorists have argued that irony is one of the most effective ways of dealing with precisely such difficult issues – at least when used oppositionally from within. But there was the transideological rub: this irony was perceived as coming from a colonial source, even if a self-deconstructing one, and even if the irony was largely at the expense of imperialists not Africans.

One instance of ironic citational signalling was mentioned in almost every public response to this exhibition:[18] it was the relation between a missionary photograph of a (named and standing) white woman watching a number of (unnamed and crouching) black women doing washing and its caption – "Taken in Nigeria about 1910, this photograph shows missionary Mrs. Thomas Titcombe giving African women 'a lesson in how to wash clothes.' African labour was the mainstay of mission economies." To the interpretation offered in the Coalition's handout – "Did Africans not know how to wash before the arrival of Europeans?" – one white Canadian reviewer replied: "An observant reader will note that the words 'a lesson in how to wash clothes' are in quotation marks. The description is offered as evidence, not of the actual activity, but of Mrs. Titcombe's intentions and sense of superiority."[19] But I hasten to add the obvious: the comprehension of irony has never been quite that simple. The curator might have intended the labels in this "Civilization, Commerce, and Christianity" section to show "the sense of cultural superiority" inherent in the missionary goals (Cannizzo 1991: 155), but if colonial discourse contains both colonizer and colonized, caught in a problematics of indeterminacy and ambivalence (Bhabha 1984), then does this sort of irony re-enact (even as it critiques) "an ambivalent mode of knowledge and power" (Bhabha 1990: 71)? Does this particular irony embody Manichean dualisms or subvert them? Or, does it depend on who is doing the interpreting? And, on a more pragmatic level, what about visitor expectations about the conventions of museum labelling? In an institution where the norm is that visual messages and verbal texts convey the *same* meaning, the risks taken through ironic disjunction here are great. And, of course, what if people do not read the labels at all?[20]

Another related and equally problematic part of the exhibition was a small white room where visitors could sit to watch a slide show and listen to a male voice give a seven-minute recreation (from missionary archives) of a magic-lantern illustrated lecture called "In Livingstone's Footsteps." This was presented as what a missionary might have said, in 1919, to his Ontario protestant congregation when fund-raising for his African mission. The fictional context was asserted orally at the outset and again at the end. In addition, outside the room was a notice that read:

The sense of cultural superiority and paternalism that you will hear in this fictional narrative was characteristic of the missionary world-view at the time. So was the genuine spirit of adventure and the sincere belief that missionaries were bringing "light" to the "dark continent."

But what if you did not read the sign? What if you missed the beginning or end of the long seven-minute tape? Well, you certainly heard the "cultural superiority and paternalism," but without the ironizing, contextualizing frame. And, even more unfortunately, the paternalistic voice could be heard as you walked through this part of the exhibition, aurally framing your viewing, driving one exasperated visitor to exclaim that the "unctuous voice delivering highly derogatory commentary could have been that of the ROM's director on his intercom for all I knew" (Crean 25).

However didactic or heavy-handed[21] some people might have found the ironies in the exhibition, it was not by any means a matter of their being paradoxically too subtle for the protesters; nor do I think the negative response was the result of wilful misreading.[22] One commentator (Schildkrout 21) felt that the ROM acknowledged the failure of the ironies but implied that it was the fault of an unsophisticated audience. The Coalition for the Truth about Africa argued that the subtleties of irony could not compete with the power of images of subjugation;[23] yet some of the demonstrators themselves used irony in their protests to claim a position. This too was an example of irony that was interpreted in a different way than was intended. For still others, the show's ironies were both scholarly and subtle and therefore élitist (Mackey 46-47). Irony has always been risky, but in this context the stakes were particularly high for this institution: this was its first major African exhibit; the city was facing racial tensions over police shootings of black youths. Even if irony were deemed appropriate here, the desirability of framing it less ambiguously became increasingly evident.

Framing helps to delimit response, of course; nevertheless, response also depends on the particular audience doing the responding. The very indirection of the ironies here might well presuppose an audience (liberal, white, European Canadian) that can – or is willing to – read between the lines: that is, an audience that positions itself as anticolonial or postcolonial and multicultural, and not as colonial and racist. Is there not a danger, however, that even this audience might be lulled into thinking that the irony has done its critical work for it, and that it need *only* bother to question those words set apart in quotation marks?[24] After all, there are no ironic quotation marks around the description of David Livingstone as a hero – though many Africans (were their point of view offered) might insist upon their appropriateness (Crean 25). Do the intended ironies

implicitly rely too much on an audience that can be affectively and politically detached from the pain represented in the exhibition's visual images
(Austin-Smith 52)?

The issues of the so-called "misreading" of irony and of the appropriateness of its very use on this occasion are issues which engage in complex ways the exclusionary potential of irony – and therefore of the anger
it can cause. But the affective charge of anger can also extend to the tar-
get of the ironies, of course. And, indeed, many did protest the stereotyped
portrayal of the Canadian missionaries in the exhibit, arguing the case for
their more complex and frequently oppositional relationship with colonial
authorities.[25] But this was a muted protest compared to the Coalition's,
which argued that African Canadian children came away from "Into the
Heart of Africa" with a negative impression of black history, with the idea
that Africans did not know how to wash their clothes or comb their hair
before the whites arrived.[26] No one, to my knowledge, however, argued
that white, British Canadian children came away embarrassed or trauma-
tized to learn that their families had been guilty of everything from paternalism and exploitation to extermination. Yet columnists did note that, if
the exhibition was hard on any group, "it was the white missionaries and
soldiers; their prejudices and ignorance are documented in some detail";[27]
one black reviewer even suggested that the exhibit promoted racism
against whites who were made to look ignorant and dangerous.[28] As
another viewer summed it up: "old-time Christian missionaries are now
almost beyond the range of human sympathy" (Fulford 19).

Irony is a discursive strategy that depends on context and on the identity and position of both the ironist and the audience. So, a feminist critic,
writing in a book about women and comedy, can begin an article entitled
"Jane Austen: Irony and Authority" with: "It is a truth universally
acknowledged, right now, that language is involved in giving and taking
both power and pleasure" (Brownstein 57), and expect that her readers
(themselves self-selected and having at least read her title) will understand
both the allusion to the opening of *Pride and Prejudice* and the irony. If it
is true that jokes do not travel well because of the need for shared knowledge (Chiaro 10-12), then this is even more the case with irony. Discursive
communities do not come into being as the result of sharing irony
together; they are what make irony possible in the first place. The many
discursive communities to which we each belong in our different ways
can, of course, be based on things like language, race, gender, class, and
nationality – but they might also encompass all the other elements that
constitute (or are made to constitute) our identities. The infinite variations
and combinations possible are what make irony both relatively rare and in
need of markers or signals. It is almost a miracle that irony is ever understood as an ironist might intend it to be: all ironies, in fact, are probably

unstable ironies.

Those intentionally deployed in "Into the Heart of Africa" were received very differently by different discursive communities, as was the show as a whole. To a black lawyer and activist, the effect of seeing Africa through the eyes of those who colonized and killed was chilling;[29] to a self-described "white Canadian liberal," the exhibit was "a recognizable piece of British-Canadian history" – not a show about Africa and not about the present.[30] Research on the complexity of how people experience an exhibit suggests that responses might be idiosyncratic, but that the general public (whatever that might be) is very likely going to respond differently from what professional critics and curators might expect (Durrans 163). One of the reasons is that they usually belong to different discursive communities: "visitors bring a multiplicity of different attitudes and expectations and experiences to the reading of an artefact, so that their comprehension of it is individualized" (C.S. Smith 19; see also Wright 133–34). So too is their affective response to it. Where certain white Canadians might find the exhibit a self-searching, ironic examination[31] of historical intolerance, some black Canadians saw the "painful detritus of savage exploitation and attempted genocide" and a perpetuation of racist attitudes of white superiority.[32] Even the use of irony was read by some as belonging to a white culture's model of discourse,[33] and its use (and alleged incomprehension) seen as a replication of the missionaries' attitudes (Austin-Smith 52). In other words, this kind of objection goes well beyond the issue of whether, in this particular case, irony was used *well* to question its very appropriateness as a discursive strategy.

As a white Canadian visitor of European (though Italian, not British) background, I certainly felt that I was being "hailed" by the references to "Canadians" in the show, in the press releases, and also in the brochure, where the late nineteenth century in Africa was described as a "turbulent but little-known period in history." The point was made well by the visitor who pointed out: "For whom ... was this period merely turbulent, and to whom is the period so little-known?" (Crean 25). The answer is: white Canadians ... perhaps. The answer is likely *not*: the black protester who said, "All my life I've been looking for my roots, I come here looking for them – and you've shown me nothing" (Fulford 23).

The exhibition's configuration of the "imagined community" (Anderson) called Canada was a limited one, to be sure. But race was not the only issue involved in this complex "lack of fit" of discursive communities. If position in "social space" determines the point of view of each individual agent (Bourdieu 1990: 130), then your perspective on "Into the Heart of Africa" was not going to be separable from things like class and education. If economic power is mobilized through symbolic power – which comes from having and accumulating "cultural capital" (Bourdieu

LINDA HUTCHEON

1984) – then the very question of who it is who regularly goes to a museum becomes a relevant issue. Surveys in North America and Europe suggest that the most frequent adult museum visitors are well educated, middle-class,[34] and relatively affluent. They may visit as tourists, volunteers, teachers (with student groups), self-educators, or researchers. The question is whether, despite this relative homogeneity, you should ever assume that visitors will necessarily share the "values, the assumptions and the intellectual preoccupations that have guided not only the choice and presentation of exhibitions, but also, more fundamentally, the selection and acquisition of objects" (Hooper-Greenhill 215). When the audience includes African Canadians, from whose ancestors' cultures came the objects displayed in "Into the Heart of Africa," such a question is not a politically neutral one. Many commentators noted that the show seemed to be designed for and aimed at white, educated, liberal-minded people with an interest in museums and anthropology;[35] to assume any broader consensus on an exhibition of African objects was, perhaps, not to take sufficiently into account the growing black population of Toronto and the different discursive communities to which people might well belong[36] (and along with those, the different expectations, different assumptions, different associations with museums in general).

In an explanatory article written after the closing of the exhibition, the curator herself defined museums as social institutions which "cannot be divorced from the historical context in which they developed, and their collections occasionally reflect the violence and disruptive social forces characterizing the European colonization of Africa" (Cannizzo 1991: 154). While that violence was made more than clear in some of the visual images within the exhibition, what was missing from "Into the Heart of Africa" was this very kind of overt statement of judgement. The indirection and obliqueness of its irony worked to render the exhibition's position ambiguous. The use of irony might well have been intended as a way of subverting the ideology of colonialism from within – and thereby also avoiding openly offending the missionary and military families (and their descendents) who had loaned and donated so much to the museum.[37] Yet, the very depiction of racism (in the past) was interpreted by some as – not only Eurocentric – but racist (in the present).[38] The problem of embodying that which one is trying to analyse and the difference between endorsing and examining are pragmatic issues of crucial importance in postcolonial theory today. In this exhibition, Africans tended to be represented as passive, as victims, as physically smaller and positioned lower in pictures: this was because such indeed was the view of the colonizers. But the difficulty was that it was also the *only* view offered in the exhibition; so too was the colonizers' the only authenticated voice. Presumably, the assumption was that the visitors would be able to distinguish between the voice represented on the labels (some in quotation marks) and the voice of the museum. There was much evidence of a certain confusion over this, however. And, after all, why should visitors assume, knowing all that these colonial collectors had given to the museum, that the institution was necessarily (or even likely) going to be ironic about or critical of them?

The ideology of collecting itself has become a major interest of "new" museology, it is true. Theorists have studied issues such as the gendered and historically specific way in which the passion to collect, preserve and display has been articulated, the role of collections in the processes of western identity formation (Clifford 1990: 144), and the representativeness and presentation of collections. There has been a certain amount of demystification of what I earlier referred to as the "modern" – and unacknowledged – institutional practices that, in the language of the "new" ethnology, might be expressed in such terms as: "The collector discovers, acquires, salvages objects. The objective world is given, not produced, and thus the historical relations of power in the work of acquisition are occulted. The *making* of meaning in museum classifications and display is mystified as adequate *representation*" (Clifford 1990: 144). It was in order to contest precisely this ideological position of modernity that the catalogue of "Into the Heart of Africa" argued:

> A museum collection may be thought of as a cultural text, one that can be read to understand the underlying cultural and ideological assumptions that have influenced its creation, selection, and display. Within such a collection, objects act as an expression not only of the worldviews of those who chose to make and use them, but also of those who chose to collect and exhibit them. (Cannizzo 1989: 62)

The catalogue directly addressed issues such as the museum as cultural "charnel house" (80), full of the remains of dead civilizations; the decontextualized museum display as "cultural vandalism" (84) and aestheticism (88); and the danger of partial collections promoting stereotypes (86). This was a theoretically aware document in that it did indeed work to show how the "relations of power whereby one portion of humanity can select, value, and collect the pure products of others need to be criticized and transformed" (Clifford 1988: 213).

As I understand the term to be invoked today, to be unequivocally *postcolonial*, however, the exhibition would have had to present and then make a judgement about the effects of colonization, not simply outline its intentions and then imply an indirect, oblique evaluative attitude. Let me give you an example of what I see as emblematic of the rhetorical strategy of the show as a whole. This is the curator's later description of the Europeanization of African social structures, dress, and habitation: "These changes would transform the women from producers of baskets, garden foods and pottery into consumers of soaps, spoons, forks, while tying them tightly to the developing mission economy" (Cannizzo 1991: 155). Whether you read this as ironic would depend upon your valuing of soaps, spoons, and forks (as well as "consuming"). Likewise, the subsequent statement that such practices "weakened alliances between lineages, discouraged the intergenerational and polygynous family, emphasized the loyalty of the couple to each other at the expense of kindred, and created a different concept of privacy" would not necessarily be read as critical at all within certain discursive communities. Indeed, it would not be hard to read it as a (modern) authoritative-sounding assertion of anthropological or historical "fact." A black writer responded to this strategy by saying that the exhibit "used the propaganda of the period without proper explanation or preamble. [The curator] did not want to manipulate the material, but she ended up implanting racist images because the critique of 'intellectual arrogance' did not come through. People missed it" (Ayanna Black, cited in Crean 27). Sometimes, they might have "missed" an intended, critical irony because it was not adequately marked, because it thus remained ambiguous in its silence about the effect of such "arrogance" upon the Africans. Because the only perspective offered was that of the colonizers, you were indeed told that the missionary involved in the social transformations described above never understood the effect his changes of custom had on kinship alliances, for example (Cannizzo 1989: 35), but you were not told what those effects actually were. As one anthropologist reviewing the exhibit remarked, it went to great lengths to remind you of the process by which objects arrived in the museum as the result of Canadians' participation in an act of conquest, but:

> What about this conquest? Was it brutal, violent and shameful? Or should we, when passing the soldiers' suits and the prizes the soldiers stole from sovereign African kingdoms, swell with pride and admiration for men who braved great distances and terrible dangers to subdue fierce natives? The exhibition is strangely silent here, as if there were no moral or political issues involved. (Freedman 40)

For a museum to choose not to take an unequivocal stand might be interpreted as a refusal of any single, modern, "master narrative" of Truth; but from a postcolonial perspective – given the position of authority of the institution – the possible reading was more problematic. What might be read as irony or ambiguity becomes, from a postcolonial perspective, potential evasion.[39] To go one step further, for those, like the Coalition, seeking the "Truth about Africa," ambiguity within an institution associated with cultural and educational authority itself makes a kind of truth-claim. In the face of the Coalition's tactical desire for what might (awkwardly, if aptly) be called an emancipatory metanarrative articulated from a position of strategic essentialism,[40] the institution (in press releases) fell back on very "modern" assertions of historical accuracy and curatorial expertise, thereby arguably undermining even the exhibition's reflexive and ironic deconstructive intentions.

However, it must also be said that, for *this* visitor, those intentions were not always consistently realized in the exhibition itself. The curator may indeed have believed that museums are fictional in nature, that "the meaning of their collection is generated in the interaction between the curator, the object, and the visitor" (Cannizzo 1991: 151). But both within the structure of the exhibit and in the response to the protests, this particular museum did not live up to its definition as a "negotiated" reality. There was none of the dialogic museum mode that theorists (such as Tchen) have argued should replace the impersonal, objective, distanced observer-model of modernity: there was no answering African voice in "Into the Heart of Africa." While implicitly acknowledging that, in theory, "culture" is indeed relational, "an inscription of communicative processes that exist, historically, *between* subjects in relations of power" (Clifford, "On Ethnographic Allegory" 15), the exhibit none the less never let the other side be heard. One did hear the interaction between the museum officials of 1989 and the collectors of a century before,[41] but none at all with the Africans whose objects are presented. This was ethnography ("in which European metropolitan subjects present to themselves their others" [usually their conquered others]) and not "autoethnography" ("in which people undertake to describe themselves in ways that engage with representations others have made of them") (Pratt 35; see also hooks 150-52).

Given the complex public stands taken by both sides on this issue of voice, more communication took place, on this occasion, through the press than face to face. Both the Coalition and the museum implicitly acknowledged, in different ways, that communication always involves political interaction and thus power differences.[42] It is this realization that has led museological theory to advocate more community consultation and dialogue in the mounting of exhibitions.[43] But the specificities of context are relevant and important here, for in 1989 Canadian public institutions were still trying to deal with the implications of the controversy over the boycott by the Lubicon Lake First Nations of the Native art exhibition "The Spirit Sings" at the Glenbow Gallery during the 1988 Calgary Olympics.[44] There have been generally recognized examples of more successful dialogue, however (see Vogel). For instance, a small gallery, the Valentine Museum in Richmond, Virginia, did consult with its community to discover what people felt they needed to learn about their past. One result,

LINDA HUTCHEON

in the same year as "Into the Heart of Africa," was "Jim Crow: Racism and Reaction in the New South." Unlike the ironic Canadian exhibition, this one was frequently confrontational, judgemental, and even unpleasant in its openly anticolonial dealings with racist attitudes.[45]

Museums are finding still other reflexive ways to deal with the post-colonial implications of collecting and exhibiting. Having been given 100 pieces of African art from a private collection, the University of British Columbia Museum of Anthropology in 1991 mounted a show entitled "Fragments," the premise of which was that it is "neither possible nor ethical, in the 1990s, to exhibit Africa; what we can and do exhibit in 'Fragments' are historic African objects valued by a Canadian museum and a Canadian collector" (Halpin 2). In a challenge to the "modern" anonymous, expert narrative voice of labels and text, this exhibit offered instead a plurality of voices and perspectives on the care, handling, and collecting of African objects, as well as on Africa itself. In a more confrontational postcolonial vein, African American artist Fred Wilson mounted, in "The Other Museum," an overt and bold critique of colonialism, stereotyping, and racial misrepresentation. Visitors were given a brochure upon entering the gallery that explained this intention to expose prejudices and even announced how irony would be used to label objects and parody the presentation of a natural history museum. In addition, the brochure's style was a parody of a *National Geographic* magazine, and, at the entrance to the displays, an upside-down map of the world signalled the entry into the realm of ironic inversion. This may indeed be heavy-handed – Dan and Ibo masks were blind-folded and gagged with imperial flags – but there was little chance of mistaking the artist's intent (Schildkrout 22). It is also the case, however, that this exhibit was considered as *art* and viewed in an art gallery, not *ethnography* presented in a museum: visitors' expectations about politicized art exhibitions are not the same as those about anthropological or historical ones. By mounting this particular show in an art gallery, Wilson also reversed the usual associations with that location: works displayed in galleries are traditionally provided with no cultural background information (as is normal in ethnographic museums), as if "great art" is recognizable by some universal standards (Clifford 1988: 200). Context is crucial for all interpretation, of course, but especially so for risky ironic interpretation. It is not as if television and film have not represented images of imperialist conquest of Africans for years and in ways much more offensive than "Into the Heart of Africa," with its reflexivity and indirection. But part of the heritage of modernity is that museums are places of special authority and respect, and therefore have special cultural responsibilities that come with their institutional positions of cultural and educational power within the communities in which they exist. No single exhibit is going to change this situation overnight, no matter how powerful its critique and deconstruction. However, if museums really are "historical-cultural theaters of memory" (Clifford 1990: 164), more than institutional memory will have to be dramatized on their stages. In deciding not to focus the Royal Ontario Museum exhibit on Africa itself, but on the emissaries of Empire who journeyed "into the heart of Africa," the curator, one might argue, was actually being careful to avoid appropriation and to stay within the boundaries of her unavoidably white Canadian point of view. Yet, in some eyes, she managed to perpetuate the very situation she sought to critique, offering yet another example of the controlling colonizing gaze. Yet, silence about the collection's imperial origins was likely not the answer either. It seems to have been this choice of one single focalization (and its consequences) that provoked much of the controversy. An American African Studies professor, Molefi Asante, is said to have compared the choice here to presenting the Holocaust from the viewpont of the Nazis.[46] There is no doubt that many felt that those once subjected to the gaze of Empire should have been given a voice. An important line of argument in the "new" museology – one of particular interest to the understanding of irony's workings – is that "Exhibitors cannot *represent* cultures. Exhibitors can be tactful but stimulating impresarios, but exhibition is a social occasion involving at least three active terms" – makers of objects, exhibitors of those objects, and interpreting viewers (Baxandall 41).

The "Epilogue" to the exhibition catalogue makes for sad reading in the aftermath of the initial decision about single focalization:

> By studying the museum as an artifact, reading collections as cultural texts, and discovering the life histories of objects, it has become possible to understand something of the complexities of cross-cultural encounters. In the same process, the intricacies of different cultural configurations are revealed in objects through which various African peoples have expressed not only their individual artistry but also their deepest communal concerns. Finally, by placing in context the relationships, however brief, problematic, and painful, that developed as Canadian soldiers and missionaries travelled into the heart of Africa, it has become clear that the past is part of the present. (Cannizzo 1989: 92)

When a Canadian reviewer began her analysis with the words, "We consider ourselves a former colony, not a colonizing power,"[47] she put her finger on how difficult it was for some members of the white, English Canadian community to see that past as "part of the present." According to the Coalition, black Canadians had no trouble at all seeing the continuity; nor might Irish, Scots, Native, or some other Canadians. The cura-

LINDA HUTCHEON

tor intended (white) Canadians to be "horrified by the Canadian participation in this history. Remember that until fairly recently, Canada was a
part of the British Empire and participated fully in all aspects of it, including negative ones" (Cannizzo and da Breo 37). The exhibit certainly did
place British Canadians and Torontonians right in the middle of Empire,
citing James Morris's *Pax Britannica* about Canada at the end of the nineteenth century: "Hundreds of thousands of British Canadians regarded the
imperial saga as part of their own national heritage. The excitement of the
New Imperialism was almost as intense in Toronto as it was in London"
(repeated in Cannizzo 1989: 14; see Figure 3).

To turn that around, today, the excitement of the new *postcolonial* critique is equally intense in Toronto (or in Canada as a whole) as elsewhere
in the once colonized world, and perhaps for that very reason, there are
times when a reflexive, ironic challenge is either not appropriate or simply not strong enough, no matter how demystificatory it might be of
modernity's assumptions and even if there had not been those unfortunate
internal inconsistencies and difficulties.[48] The question of irony's appropriateness in this situation was one raised often: "Given the difficulty of using
irony, the ROM would have been well advised to consider whether there
really was a need to couch a critique of colonialism in ironic terms"
(Schildkrout 21). But it is a question that has haunted the history of irony
too (see McKee 91) and one that consistently points to the transideological nature of irony's politics. The many-voiced play of said and unsaid can
be used to ironize the single-voicing of authoritative discourse – no matter what the politics of that discourse. And not only those on the receiving end are perhaps going to find this inappropriate. But, are there times
when indirection is wise? Or is irony's evasiveness always suspect? To what
end can irony work – both in intentions and in attributions? What are the
dangers, in the extreme, "of putting the whole world in quotation marks"
(Clifford, "Introduction" 25)? What is at stake when irony happens – and
when it does not?

These are among the questions that have interested me in this essay.
Irony's transideological politics complicate the theorizing of irony might-
ily, and part of the reason is irony's edge. The affective responses provoked
by "Into the Heart of Africa" show that viewers (like readers and listeners)
are not passive receivers; they are interpreting agents, with the emphasis on
agency and, thus, on action. Because of this there were real, material consequences for the intending ironist. I raise this issue of the risks of irony
most forcefully here at the end of this essay primarily because it is too easy
to forget the dangers in the face of the valorization of irony's subversive
potential by much feminist, gay and lesbian, postcolonial, and poststruc-
turalist[49] theory and practice. While it is likely the case that "Every act of
saying is a momentary intersection of the 'said' and the 'unsaid'" (Tyler

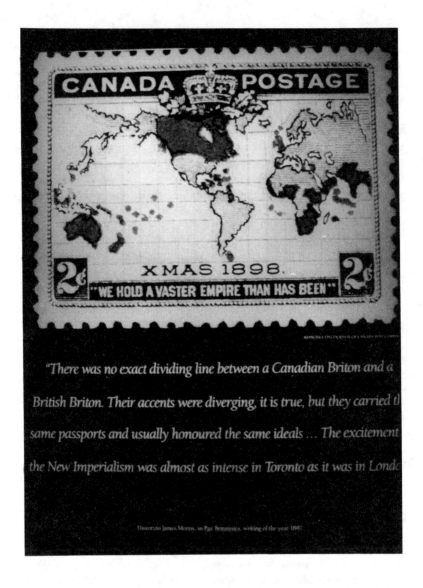

Figure 3: Canadian stamp and explanatory panel from "Into the Heart of Africa" exhibition, 1989-90, Royal Ontario Museum, Toronto, Canada. Photo courtesy of the Royal Ontario Museum.

　　　　　　　　　　　　　　LINDA HUTCHEON

459), the particular intersection – in the communicative space set up by both meaning and affect – that makes irony happen is a highly unstable one, sometimes even a dangerous one. Whether it will become too dangerous, too risky is for the future to decide. Will there ever be another – safe – "age of irony"? Did one ever really exist?

Notes

1 John McNeill, cited by Isabel Vincent in *The Globe and Mail* [Toronto], 21 Sept. 1990: C9. See also Young 178.

2 Marlene Nourbese Philip, *The Toronto Star* 14 Jan. 1991: A13.

3 Since 1971, Canada has had an official government policy of what is called "multiculturalism"; in 1988 the "Act for the Preservation and Enhancement of Multiculturalism in Canada" was passed. The term has always been accepted as a description of the demographic realities of Canada, but the policy and law have been seen in different ways. Some view it still as a federal government ploy to divert attention from Québec separatist energies; others accuse it of assimilationist aims. The word and policy certainly gained currency when Canada's unofficial self-image as a northern nation was being challenged from within by the immigration of people from southern European and non-white nations, largely those of the British Commonwealth. The law has been called custodial, paternalistic, anachronistic, reductive, retentive; it has been said to create an enforced inclusiveness and a kind of ethnicity industry. But its defenders argue that, as an ideal of civic tolerance, it has liberal and liberating possibilities. It makes room for diversity and specificity as the defining characteristics of a nation that seems to feel it is in need of self-definition.

4 To generalize, settler colonies are those in which new arrivals (in Canada's case, from Europe) could be motivated by any number of reasons – from enforced exile to adventure; they often marginalized or exterminated the indigenous populations, rather than merging with them; they transplanted and internalized (while deracinating) Old World culture and traditions, including language, of course.

5 Among these is the relation settler colonies have with their aboriginal peoples, of course. In addition, each settler colony, like each forcibly colonized nation, has its own history that cannot be ignored. As the example of the USA and Canada reveals, it matters whether a nation has fought for political independence or has evolved a form of government out of imperial institutions: breaks and ruptures force an articulation of difference and enable the creation of a discourse of identity. This may explain why Canada perpetually lives out its identity crisis.

6 One way to think of the difference here is as between being considered (or considering yourself) "inferior" by metropolitan standards because your

"official" culture is generally seen as continuous with and derivative of Empire's, and doing so because your indigenous culture is radically different from that of the imperial power (and thus suppressed). My thanks to Shirley Neuman for this concise and cogent articulation of the distinction.

7 I am bracketing here Canada's problematic and likely neo-colonial relationship with the United States, a nation whose cultural, political, and economic hegemony and whose relation to multinational capitalism have rendered it one of the new imperial nations of the world. See Jara and Spadaccini 10; Hitchens.

8 See too Homi Bhabha's discussion of the double role of the colonizer, "'in double duty bound,' at once civilizing mission and a violent subjugating force" (1990: 71).

9 From a public letter of apology for the offence "felt by some," written over six months after the close of the exhibition (issued on 1 March 1991).

10 As Cannizzo explained to the The Toronto Star 5 June 1990: A17.

11 In the context of the Canadian debates over "appropriation of voice," Cannizzo rightly noted that at least the exhibit did not appropriate the black voice (1991: 152). That it also silenced that voice is not discussed, however.

12 Though the acting director of the museum and, especially, the curator took most of the pressure, it is worth yet another reminder that there was a team involved in creating this (like any other) show: in addition to the curator, there was a graphic designer, an architect, an artist, and an interpretive planner. Since, as you will see shortly, display involves design as much as conceptual framing, many of the problems could not be directly attributed only to the curator.

13 See Jordanova 32 on how trophies from colonial expansion in museums usually express "victory, ownership, control and dominion" which trigger "fantasies and memories" and elicit admiration.

14 Cannizzo notes that the intention was to expose "a rather brutal historical reality" and make "clear that the imperial advance was not some sort of adventure story but resulted in death and destruction" (1991: 157).

15 Robertson 4; Charles Roach, The Toronto Star 5 June 1990: A17.

16 The word is that of one of the demonstrators, as cited in The Toronto Star 13 May 1990: A3.

17 Cited in "Analyzing Racism at ROM" in The Varsity [Toronto] June 1990: 4.

18 Individual visitors saw other ironies which the evidence of the curator's comments and the catalogue would suggest were not actually intentional ones. For instance, see Schildkrout 21: "In both text and image, the exhibition attempted to use irony in order to present its condemnation of the colonial point of view. In addition to the unfortunate quotations and pseudo-quotations, the exhibition contained section titles that were meant to be read as ironic cues. For example, the ROM assumed (wrongly) that the audience would understand the irony intended in the use of the word 'Commerce' as

a title for an exhibit case devoted to artifacts of the slave trade."

19 Christopher Hume, *The Toronto Star* 19 May 1990: H6.

20 See Vergo 53 on the persistent museological belief that elucidation can only take the form of words.

21 This term was used quite often in the press: see, for example, the editorial in *The Globe and Mail* [Toronto] 19 Oct. 1990: A16; Bronwyn Drainie's article in the same newspaper, 24 Mar. 1990: C1.

22 Cf. David Cayley, *The Globe and Mail* [Toronto] 10 Aug. 1990: A13.

23 Oji Adisa and Ras Rico, cited by Isabel Vincent in *The Globe and Mail* [Toronto] 14 July 1990: D1-D2.

24 This question was raised by Zhao Meichang in 1990 in a thought-provoking graduate course paper (Department of English, University of Toronto) entitled "ROM's 'Into the Heart of Africa': A Commentary."

25 See the letter to the editor by A.W. Frank Banfield, the son of one of those missionaries, in *The Toronto Star* 26 May 1990: D3; Isabel Vincent, *The Globe and Mail* [Toronto] 28 July 1990: C12 on William Samarin's defense in *Christian Week*; cf. Colan Mitchell, letter to the editor, *The Toronto Star* 5 June 1990: A16. On the nineteenth-century missionary conjunction of the construction of white English ethnicity in relation to "otherness" and the moral power of speaking "God's Word," see Hall.

26 See Isabel Vincent, *The Globe and Mail* [Toronto] 20 June 1990: C6.

27 Christopher Hume, *The Toronto Star* 29 Sept. 1990: F3.

28 Hazel A. da Breo, cited in Nazareth 11; see too Doug Robinson, *Now* [Toronto] 5-11 Apr. 1990.

29 Charles Roach, *Now* [Toronto] 22 Mar.-4 Apr. 1990; Charles Roach, *The Toronto Star* 5 June 1990: A17.

30 Michael Valpy, *The Globe and Mail* [Toronto], 6 June 1990: A8.

31 Austin-Smith felt only white audiences could have "access to the luxury of ironic detachment" (52).

32 See Bronwyn Drainie, *The Globe and Mail* [Toronto] 24 Mar. 1990: C1 and 6 Apr. 1991: C3. Part of the reason for such a response, as Marlene Nourbese Philip pointed out, is that, for Africans, museums have been seen as "a significant site of their racial oppression" (*The Toronto Star* 14 Jan. 1991: A13).

33 The powerful use of irony by black artists such as Robert Colescott or, working within the museum setting, Fred Wilson would suggest that this view is not shared by all.

34 Indeed Merriman suggests that people who are better off in the present and who visit museums "because of their cultured connotations, as a way of legitimating their higher status with an appropriate leisure activity," are more likely to have a negative view of the past, "seeing it as something we have progressed from, as a way of legitimating their present status" (170).

35 Eva Mackey has described herself as the "perfect" viewer of the exhibit: a student of anthropology, with a grounding in reflexive anthropological and fem-

inist theory, and therefore interested in how "meaning about 'others' is constructed," she had also done research on the white colonial presence in Africa and was part of the white, anglophone majority of Canada (7).

36   Unlike the situation in the USA, there was historically no large black former slave population in Canada. In Toronto, there are a variety of black communities from various Caribbean islands and African nations, most recently Somalia.

37   See Gaunt 32: an ironist "can pander to the tastes and requirements of one section of his public whilst ridiculing its trite and commonplace ideas and use of language for another section of his audience."

38   Cf. Donna Laframboise, *The Toronto Star* 22 Oct. 1990: A23.

39   See Crean 24: the organizers were "awfully quiet and oblique in their disapproval, never directly condemning or examining its legacy."

40   See Mackey 61 (via Lyotard) and Fuss 105–07 especially. See also Clifford 1988: 12: "If authenticity is relational, there can be no essence except as a political, cultural invention, a local tactic." For a detailed discussion of the Coalition and its strategies, see Butler 90–132.

41   Cannizzo notes that "period quotations and historical photographs were used to suggest interaction, the process of collection and the presence of individuals behind the objects" (1991: 156).

42   See B.H. Smith 102: "Communication is ... a political interaction, not only in that its dynamics may operate through differences of power between the agents but also in that the interaction may put those differences at stake, threatening or promising (again it must cut both ways) either to confirm and maintain them or to subvert or otherwise change them." See too Haraway 163 on the "informatics of domination."

43   In this case, the difficulties with consultation began with the multiple and fragmented African communities in the city of Toronto – of West Indian, African, and American/Canadian origins. The museum did have its promotional, publicity, and educational material screened for possible problems by paid experts from the black community; it introduced the show five months before its opening at a reception for that community and, subsequent to a negative response at this stage, set up focus groups and made changes to some of the promotional material – though not, I believe, to the show itself. An expert in African anthropology vetted the catalogue. Lectures and other events were set up by a black African historian, Dr. Kasozi, in conjunction with the exhibition. Some of these were later cancelled because of lack of attendance (after the demonstrations began). See Young and Butler.

44   As a possible example of how it might indeed be possible to live "openly with differences in a dialogic community" (Stimpson 408), this led to a "Task Force on Museums and First Peoples" whose 1992 report was introduced by a letter from Ovide Mercredi, National Chief of the Assembly of First Nations: "Out of controversy can come understanding and an opening for construc-

tive dialogue. The Assembly of First Nations is pleased to have been involved in the Task Force on Museums and First Peoples. The many cultures of the peoples of Canada have so much to share with each other. Out of this sharing can only come a renewed pride in their respective cultures." What the actual result of the task force's recommendations for museum practice will be remains to be seen, of course.

45 Not every anticolonial or postcolonial exhibit has been well received, of course. The Smithsonian's 1991 "West as America" showed how some nineteenth-century artists glorified the European conquest of the Americas, downplaying exploitation, genocide, cultural displacement, and greed, while representing the indigenous peoples as fierce, brutal, and thus worthy of suppression. The museums planning to host the show after the Washington opening backed out in the face of negative response from the American public. This was also the fate of "Into the Heart of Africa": the four American and Canadian museums which had agreed to present the show cancelled after the Toronto protests.

46 Cited by Ahmed Elamin, *Share* [Toronto] 4 Apr. 1991: 1.

47 Adele Freedman, *The Globe and Mail* [Toronto] 17 Nov. 1989: C11.

48 With the notoriously fine vision of hindsight and admittedly *not* taking into account the difficulties of timing and of institutional constraints, it is (perhaps too) easy to suggest a number of design and framing changes that might have been made to the exhibition even after it opened: reducing the size of certain violent visual images; being more clear and consistent about the function of quotation marks; perhaps choosing to rely less on ironic indirection; reducing the necessity of having to read texts to get meaning; being more aware of the power and semiotic coding of visual images; removing the African "boutique" and its white staff; even inverting the order of the exhibition – introducing the objects in their African context first, then tracing how they came to enter the museum's collection.

49 On Derrida's work as operating under the sign of catachresis, "the *ironic* trope par excellence," see White 281, and also Ulmer on Derrida's ironizing of the conventions of criticism. On Foucault's viewing the human sciences in the twentieth century as "projections of the trope of irony," see White 255. Foucault himself defined his archaeological project in what I see as structurally ironic terms as erecting "the primacy of a contradiction that has its model in the simultaneous affirmation and negation of a single proposition" (155).

Works Cited

Ames, Michael M. *Cannibal Tours and Glass Boxes: The Anthropology of Museums.* Vancouver: U of British Columbia P, 1992.

Anderson, Benedict. *Imagined Communities: Reflections on the Origin and Spread of*

Nationalism. London: Verso, 1983.

Appiah, Kwame Anthony. "Is the Post- in Postmodernism the Post- in Postcolonial?" *Critical Inquiry* 17 (1990-91): 336-57.

Arnoldi, Mary Jo. "A Distorted Mirror: The Exhibition of the Herbert Ward Collection of Africana." *Museums and Communities: The Politics of Public Culture*. Ed. Ivan Karp, Christine Mullen Kreamer, and Steven D. Lavine. Washington, DC: Smithsonian Institution, 1992. 428-57.

Asad, Talal. Introduction. *Anthropology & the Colonial Encounter*. Ed. Talal Asad. Atlantic Highlands, NJ: Humanities, 1973. 9-19.

Ashcroft, Bill, Gareth Griffiths, and Helen Tiffin. *The Empire Writes Back: Theory and Practice in Post-Colonial Literatures*. London: Routledge, 1989.

Austin-Smith, Brenda. "Into the Heart of Irony." *Canadian Dimension* Oct. 1990: 51-52.

Bauman, Zygmunt. *Intimations of Postmodernity*. London: Routledge, 1992.

Baxandall, Michael. "Exhibiting Intention: Some Preconditions of the Visual Display of Culturally Purposeful Objects." *Exhibiting Cultures: The Poetics and Politics of Museum Display*. Ed. Ivan Karp and Steven D. Lavine. Washington, DC: Smithsonian Institution, 1991. 33-41.

Bhabha, Homi K. "Of Mimicry and Man: The Ambivalence of Colonial Discourse." *October* 28 (1984): 125-33.

—. "The Other Question: Difference, Discrimination and the Discourse of Colonialism." *Out There: Marginalization and Contemporary Cultures*. Ed. Russell Ferguson, Martha Gever, Trinh T. Minh-ha, and Cornel West. New York: New Museum of Contemporary Art; Cambridge, MA: MIT, 1990. 71-87.

Bourdieu, Pierre. *Distinction: A Social Critique of the Judgement of Taste*. Trans. Richard Nice. London: Routledge & Kegan Paul, 1984.

—. *In Other Words: Essays Towards a Reflexive Sociology*. Trans. Matthew Adamson. Cambridge, Eng.: Polity, 1990.

Brownstein, Rachel M. "Jane Austen: Irony and Authority." *Last Laughs: Perspectives on Women and Comedy*. Ed. Regina Barreca. New York: Gordon and Breach, 1988. 57-70.

Brydon, Diana. "The Myths That Write Us: Decolonising the Mind." *Commonwealth* 10.1 (1987): 1-14.

Butler, Shelley Ruth. "Contested Representations: Revisiting 'Into the Heart of Africa.'" MA Thesis York U, 1993.

Cannizzo, Jeanne. "Exhibiting Cultures: 'Into the Heart of Africa.'" *Visual Anthropology Review* 7.1 (1991): 150-60.

—. *Into the Heart of Africa*. Toronto: Royal Ontario Museum, 1989.

Cannizzo, Jeanne, and Hazel A. da Breo. Interview. *Fuse* 13 (1989-90): 36-37.

Chiaro, Delia. *The Language of Jokes: Analysing Verbal Play*. London: Routledge, 1992.

Chung, Simon. "Into the Heart of the ROM's Racism." *Lexicon* 10 Oct. 1990: 7.

Clifford, James. "Introduction: Partial Truths." *Writing Culture: The Poetics and*

Politics of Ethnography. Ed. James Clifford and George E. Marcus. Berkeley: U of California P, 1986. 1-26.

—. "On Collecting Art and Culture." *Out There: Marginalization and Contemporary Cultures*. Ed. Russell Ferguson, Martha Gever, Trinh T. Minh-ha, and Cornel West. New York: New Museum of Contemporary Art; Cambridge, MA: MIT, 1990. 141-69.

—. "On Ethnographic Allegory." *Writing Culture: The Poetics and Politics of Ethnography*. Ed. James Clifford and George E. Marcus. Berkeley: U of California P, 1986. 98-121.

—. *The Predicament of Culture: Twentieth-Century Ethnography, Literature and Art*. Cambridge, MA: Harvard UP, 1988.

Crapanzano, Vincent. *Hermes' Dilemma and Hamlet's Desire: On the Epistemology of Interpretation*. Cambridge, MA: Harvard UP, 1992.

Crean, Susan. "Taking the Missionary Position." *This Magazine* Feb. 1991: 23-28.

Crew, Spencer R., and James E. Sims. "Locating Authenticity: Fragments of a Dialogue." *Exhibiting Cultures: The Poetics and Politics of Museum Display*. Ed. Ivan Karp and Steven D. Lavine. Washington, DC: Smithsonian Institution, 1991. 159-75.

da Breo, Hazel A. "Royal Spoils: The Museum Confronts Its Colonial Past." *Fuse* 13 (1989-90): 28-36.

Donaldson, Laura E. *Decolonizing Feminisms: Race, Gender, and Empire-Building*. Chapel Hill: U of North Carolina P, 1992.

Durrans, Brian. "The Future of the Other: Changing Cultures on Display in Ethnographic Museums." *The Museum Time-Machine: Putting Cultures on Display*. Ed. Robert Lumley. London: Routledge, 1988. 144-69.

Fish, Stanley. "Short People Got No Reason To Live: Reading Irony." *Daedalus* 112.1 (1983): 175-91.

Fisher, Philip. *Making and Effacing Art: Modern American Art in a Culture of Museums*. New York: Oxford UP, 1991.

Foucault, Michel. *The Archaeology of Knowledge and the Discourse on Language*. Trans. A.M. Sheridan Smith. New York: Pantheon, 1972.

Freedman, Jim. "Bringing It All Back Home: A Commentary on 'Into the Heart of Africa.'" *Museum Quarterly* 18.1 (1990): 39-43.

Fulford, Robert. "Into the Heart of the Matter." *Rotunda* Sept. 1991: 19-28.

Fuss, Diana. *Essentially Speaking: Feminism, Nature, and Difference*. London: Routledge, 1989.

Gaunt, Simon. *Troubadors and Irony*. New York: Cambridge UP, 1989.

Geertz, Clifford. *The Interpretation of Cultures*. New York: Basic, 1973.

—. *Local Knowledge: Further Essays in Interpretive Anthropology*. New York: Basic, 1983.

Greenhalgh, Paul. "Education, Entertainment and Politics: Lessons from the Great International Exhibitions." *The New Museology*. Ed. Peter Vergo. London: Reaktion, 1989. 74-98, 210-11.

Gurian, Elaine Heumann. "Noodling Around with Exhibition Opportunities." *Exhibiting Cultures: The Poetics and Politics of Museum Display*. Ed. Ivan Karp and Steven D. Lavine. Washington, DC: Smithsonian Institution, 1991. 176-90.

Habermas, Jürgen. "Modernity: An Incomplete Project." *The Anti-Aesthetic: Essays on Postmodern Culture*. Ed. Hal Foster. Port Townsend, WA: Bay, 1983. 3-15.

Hall, Catherine. "Missionary Stories: Gender and Ethnicity in England in the 1830s and 1840s." *Cultural Studies*. Ed. Lawrence Grossberg, Cary Nelson, and Paula A. Treichler. London: Routledge, 1992. 240-70.

Halpin, Marjorie. *Fragments: Reflections on Collecting*. Museum Note 31. Vancouver: University of British Columbia Museum of Anthropology, 1991.

Haraway, Donna. *Simians, Cyborgs, and Women: The Reinvention of Nature*. London: Routledge, 1991.

Hebdige, Dick. *Hiding in the Light: On Images and Things*. London: Routledge, 1988.

Hitchens, Christopher. *Blood, Class, and Nostalgia: Anglo-American Ironies*. London: Chatto & Windus, 1990.

hooks, bell. *Yearning: Race, Gender and Cultural Politics*. Boston: South End, 1990.

Hooper-Greenhill, Eilean. "Counting Visitors or Visitors Who Count?" *The Museum Time-Machine: Putting Cultures on Display*. Ed. Robert Lumley. London: Routledge, 1988. 213-32.

Horne, Donald. *The Great Museum: The Re-presentation of History*. London: Pluto, 1984.

Jameson, Fredric. *Modernism and Imperialism*. Pamphlet 14. Derry: Field Day Theatre Company, 1988.

JanMohamed, Abdul R. *Manichean Aesthetics: The Politics of Literature in Colonial Africa*. Amherst: U of Massachusetts P, 1983.

Jara, René, and Nicholas Spadaccini. "Introduction: Allegorizing the New World." *1492-1992: Re/Discovering Colonial Writing*. Ed. René Jara and Nicholas Spadaccini. Minneapolis: U of Minnesota P, 1989. 9-50.

Jones, Peter. "Museums and the Meanings of Their Contents." *New Literary History* 23 (1992): 911-21.

Jordanova, Ludmilla. "Objects of Knowledge: A Historical Perspective on Museums." *The New Museology*. Ed. Peter Vergo. London: Reaktion, 1989. 22-40, 207-09.

Lumley, Robert. Introduction. *The Museum Time-Machine: Putting Cultures on Display*. Ed. Robert Lumley. London: Routledge, 1988. 1-23.

Lyotard, Jean-François. *The Postmodern Condition: A Report on Knowledge*. Trans. Geoff Bennington and Brian Massumi. Minneapolis: U of Minnesota P, 1984.

MacCannell, Dean. *The Tourist: A New Theory of the Leisure Class*. New York: Schocken, 1976.

Mackey, Eva. "The Politics of Race and Representation in Toronto, Canada: Events and Discourses around the Royal Ontario Museum's 'Into the Heart of Africa' Exhibit." MA Thesis U of Sussex, 1991.

McKee, John B. *Literary Irony and the Literary Audience: Studies in the Victimization of the Reader in Augustan Fiction.* Amsterdam, Neth.: Rodopi, 1974.

Memmi, Albert. *The Colonizer and the Colonized.* 1957. Trans. Howard Greenfeld. New York: Orion, 1965.

Merriman, Nick. "Museum Visiting as a Cultural Phenomenon." *The New Museology.* Ed. Peter Vergo. London: Reaktion, 1989. 149-71, 217-19.

Mishra, Vijay, and Bob Hodge. "What Is Post(-)Colonialism?" *Textual Practice* 5 (1991): 399-414.

Mizzau, Marina. *L'ironia: la contraddizione consentita.* Milan, IT: Feltrinelli, 1984.

Nazareth, Errol. "Royal Ontario Museum Showcase Showdown." *Now* 29 Mar.-4 Apr. 1990: 10-12.

Palmer, Norman. "Museums and Cultural Property." *The New Museology.* Ed. Peter Vergo. London: Reaktion, 1989. 172-204, 219-21.

Pratt, Mary Louise. "Arts of the Contact Zone." *Profession 91* [MLA] (1991): 33-40.

Robertson, Heather. "Out of Africa, into the Soup." *The Canadian Forum* Sept. 1990: 4.

Said, Edward W. *Culture and Imperialism.* New York: Knopf, 1993.

—. "Representing the Colonized: Anthropology's Interlocutors." *Critical Inquiry* 15 (1988-89): 205-25.

Schildkrout, Enid. "Ambiguous Messages and Ironic Twists: 'Into the Heart of Africa' and 'The Other Museum.'" *Museum Anthropology* 15.2 (1991): 16-23.

Scholes, Robert. *Semiotics and Interpretation.* New Haven, CT: Yale UP, 1982.

Seidel, Gill. "'We Condemn Apartheid, BUT ...': A Discursive Analysis of the European Parliamentary Debate on Sanctions (July 1986)." *Social Anthropology and the Politics of Language.* Ed. Ralph Grillo. London: Routledge, 1989. 222-49.

Slemon, Stephen. "Modernism's Last Post." *Past the Last Post: Theorizing Post-Colonialism and Post-Modernism.* Ed. Ian Adam and Helen Tiffin. Calgary: U of Calgary P, 1990. 1-11.

Smith, Barbara Herrnstein. *Contingencies of Value: Alternative Perspectives for Critical Theory.* Cambridge, MA: Harvard UP, 1988.

Smith, Charles Saumarez. "Museums, Artefacts, and Meanings." *The New Museology.* Ed. Peter Vergo. London: Reaktion, 1989. 6-21, 205-07.

Sperber, Dan, and Deirdre Wilson. "Irony and the Use–Mention Distinction." *Radical Pragmatics.* Ed. Peter Cole. New York: Academic, 1981. 295-318.

Spivak, Gayatri Chakravorty. *The Postcolonial Critic: Interviews, Strategies, Dialogues.* Ed. Sarah Harasym. London: Routledge, 1990.

Stam, Robert, and Louise Spence. "Colonialism, Racism and Representation." *Screen* 24.2 (1983): 2-20.

Stewart, Susan. *Nonsense: Aspects of Intertextuality in Folklore and Literature.* Baltimore: Johns Hopkins UP, 1979.

Stimpson, Catharine R. "Presidential Address 1990: On Differences." *PMLA* 106 (1991): 402-11.

Swearingen, C. Jan. *Rhetoric and Irony: Western Literacy and Western Lies.* New York:

Oxford UP, 1991.

Tchen, John Kuo Wei. "Creating a Dialogic Museum: The Chinatown History Museum Experiment." *Museums and Communities: The Politics of Public Culture.* Ed. Ivan Karp, Christine Mullen Kreamer, and Steven D. Lavine. Washington, DC: Smithsonian Institution, 1992. 428-57.

Terdiman, Richard. *Discourse/Counter-Discourse: The Theory and Practice of Symbolic Resistance in Nineteenth-Century France.* Ithaca, NY: Cornell UP, 1985.

Thomas, Nicholas. *Entangled Objects: Exchange, Material Culture and Colonialism in the Pacific.* Cambridge, MA: Harvard UP, 1991.

Tiffin, Helen. "Commonwealth Literature: Comparison and Judgement." *The History and Historiography of Commonwealth Literature.* Ed. Dieter Riemenschneider. Tübingen, W. Ger.: Gunter Narr, 1983. 19-35.

Torgovnick, Marianna. "Traveling with Conrad." *Gone Primitive: Savage Intellects, Modern Lives.* Chicago: U of Chicago P, 1990. 141-58, 270-75.

Toulmin, Stephen. *Cosmopolis: The Hidden Agenda of Modernity.* New York: Free, 1990.

Tyler, Stephen A. *The Said and the Unsaid: Mind, Meaning, and Culture.* New York: Academic, 1978.

Ulmer, Gregory L. "Of a Parodic Tone Recently Adopted in Criticism." *New Literary History* 13 (1981-82): 543-60.

Vergo, Peter. "The Reticent Object." *The New Museology.* Ed. Peter Vergo. London: Reaktion, 1989. 41-59, 209-10.

Vogel, Susan. "Always True to the Object, in Our Fashion." *Exhibiting Cultures: The Poetics and Politics of Museum Display.* Ed. Ivan Karp and Steven D. Lavine. Washington, DC: Smithsonian Institution, 1991. 191-204.

Weil, Stephen E. *Rethinking the Museum and Other Meditations.* Washington, DC: Smithsonian Institution, 1990.

West, Cornel. "The New Cultural Politics of Difference." *Out There: Marginalization and Contemporary Cultures.* Ed. Russell Ferguson, Martha Gever, Trinh T. Minh-ha, and Cornel West. New York: New Museum of Contemporary Art; Cambridge, MA: MIT, 1990. 19-36.

White, Hayden. *Tropics of Discourse: Essays in Cultural Criticism.* Baltimore: Johns Hopkins UP, 1978.

Wright, Philip. "The Quality of Visitors' Experiences in Art Museums." *The New Museology.* Ed. Peter Vergo. London: Reaktion, 1989. 119-48, 213-17.

Young, T. Cuyler, Jr. "'Into the Heart of Africa': The Director's Perspective." *Curator* 36 (1993): 174-88.

Acknowledgements

Baum, Gregory. "The New Social Gospel in Canada." *Compassion and Solidarity: The Church for Others* (1987). Reprinted with permission.

Brant, Beth. "The Good Red Road: Journeys of Homecoming in Native Women's Writing." *Writing as Witness: Essay and Talk* (1994). Reprinted by permission of Women's Press, 517 College Street, Suite 233, Toronto, Ontario, M6G 4A2.

Davey, Frank. "Beyond Disputation: Anglophone-Canadian Artists and the Free Trade Debate." *Post-National Arguments: The Politics of the Anglophone-Canadian Novel since 1967* (1993). Reprinted by permission of University of Toronto Press Incorporated, 10 St. Mary Street, Suite 700, Toronto, Ontario, M4Y 2W8.

Filewod, Alan. "National Theatre / National Obsession." *Canadian Theatre Review* 62 (1990). Reprinted by permission of the author.

Gerson, Carole. "Anthologies and the Canon of Early Canadian Women Writers." *Re(Dis)covering Our Foremothers: Nineteenth-Century Canadian Women Writers* (1990). Reproduced with University of Ottawa Press's authorization.

Heble, Ajay. "New Contexts of Canadian Criticism: Democracy, Counterpoint, Responsibility." First published in this volume.

Hutcheon, Linda. "The End(s) of Irony: The Politics of Appropriateness." *Irony's Edge: The Theory and Politics of Irony* (1995). Reprinted by permission of the author.

Johnston, Basil H. "Is That All There Is? Tribal Literature." *Canadian Literature* 128 (1991). Reprinted with permission of *Canadian Literature*.

King, Thomas. "Godzilla vs. Post-Colonial." *World Literature Written in English* 30.2 (1990). Reprinted by permission of the author.

Kroetsch, Robert. "Disunity as Unity: A Canadian Strategy." *The Lovely Treachery of Words: Essays Selected and New* (1989). Reprinted by permission of Westwood Creative Artists, 94 Harbord Street, Toronto, Ontario M5S 1G6.

McKillop, A.B. "Culture, Intellect, and Context: Recent Writing on the Cultural and Intellectual History of Ontario." *Journal of Canadian Studies* 24.3 (1989). Reprinted with permission of *Journal of Canadian Studies*, Trent University, Peterborough, Ontario K9J 7B8.

Mukherjee, Arun. "Ideology in the Classroom: A Case Study in the Teaching of English Literature in Canadian Universities." *Oppositional Aesthetics: Readings from a Hyphenated Space* (1994). Reprinted with permission.

New, W.H. "Back to the Future: The Short Story in Canada and the Writing of Literary History." *Australian-Canadian Studies* 4 (1986). Reprinted with permission.

Padolsky, Enoch. "Cultural Diversity and Canadian Literature: A Pluralistic Approach to Majority and Minority Writing in Canada." *International Journal of Canadian Studies* 3 (1991). Reprinted by permission of the author.

Paré, François. Excerpt from *Les littératures de l'exiguïté* (1992). Reprinted with permission of Les Éditions du Nordir, C.P. 580, Hearst, Ontario, P0L 1N0.

Paterson, Janet M. "Le Postmodernisme québécois: tendances actuelles." *Études littéraires* 27.1 (1994). Reprinted with permission.

Pennee, Donna Palmateer. "'Après Frye, rien'? Pas du tout! From *Contexts* to *New Contexts*." First published in this volume.

Philip, M. Nourbese. "Who's Listening? Artists, Audiences & Language." *Frontiers: Selected Essays and Writings on Racism and Culture 1984-1992* (1992). Reprinted by permission of the author.

Slemon, Stephen. "Unsettling the Empire: Resistance Theory for the Second World." *World Literature Written in English* 30.2 (1990). Reprinted by permission of the author.

Struthers, J.R. (Tim). "Once More to the Lake: Towards a Poetics of Receptivity." First published in this volume.

Sugars, Cynthia. "On the Rungs of the Double Helix: Theorizing the Canadian Literatures." *Essays on Canadian Writing* 50 (1993). Reprinted with permission.

Taylor, Charles. "The Politics of Recognition." *Philosophical Arguments* (1995). Reprinted with permission.

Wallace, Bronwen. "One More Woman Talking." *Sudden Miracles: Eight Women Poets* (1991). Reprinted by permission of the estate of Bronwen Wallace.

Wallace, Bronwen. "Bones." *The Stubborn Particulars of Grace* (1987). Reprinted by permission of McClelland & Stewart, Inc., *The Canadian Publishers*, 481 University Avenue, Suite 900, Toronto, Ontario, Canada M5G 2E9.

Welsh, Christine. "*Women in the Shadows*: Reclaiming a Métis Heritage." *Descant* 24.3 (1993). Reprinted by permission of the author.

The publisher has made every effort to locate all copyright holders of the texts published in this collection and would be pleased to hear from any party not duly acknowledged.